"A bracing challenge—just what the Christian church needs to hear in the new millennium. A very powerful book."—**The Honorable Jack Kemp**

"How Now Shall We Live?" is truly inspiring for those who want to restore to our culture the values that made America great. It reminds us that we must not only defend what we believe, but also inspire others to give witness to the truth alongside us."—**The Honorable Tom DeLay,** Majority Whip, United States House of Representatives

"The singular pleasure that comes from it is its absolute—learned—refusal to give any quarter to the dogged materialists who deny any possibility that there was a creator around the corner. This is a substantial book, but the reader never tires, as one might from a catechistic marathon. The arguments are cogently and readably presented."—**William F. Buckley** in *National Review*

"The newest—and certainly the most important—of Charles Colson's books . . . the essence of this book is that the Christian faith is not just a theory, not just a system, not just a framework. It is an all-consuming way of life, robustly applicable to every minute of every day of the rest of your life."—*World*

"There is something wrong with the historical development of the evangelical mind, . . . a lopsidedness, a prodigious development of one divine gift coupled with the atrophy of another. . . . We know a great deal about saving grace, but next to nothing—though it is one of our doctrines—about common grace. The ambition of Charles Colson and Nancy Pearcey is to do something about this lopsidedness, to strike a blow against the scandal of the evangelical mind. . . . A highly intelligent book, it is not ashamed to speak to ordinary folk."—*First Things*

"How Now Shall We Live?" is brilliantly lit by its in-depth and succinct diagnosis of the modern mentality . . . an intelligent and thoroughgoing critique from a Scriptural perspective, of the American/Western culture. . . . The book is a veritable mosaic of precious intellectual gems, artistically designed by Charles Colson and Nancy Pearcey. . . . This book is a virtual 'must' for the thinking Orthodox reader."—*DOXA,* a quarterly review serving the Orthodox Church

"A magnum opus in the best Schaefferian tradition. It is clearly intended to be . . . a handbook for today's Christian. . . . The authors presuppose that Christianity is more than just a religion of personal salvation: it involves a total world-and-life view."—*Christianity Today*

"A very good and much needed book. . . . Colson argues that Christianity isn't a private faith but a public worldview that, for believers, permeates politics, the arts, education, science and culture."—*Insight*

An "elegantly written tutorial on adopting a biblical worldview and the discipline of thinking Christianly."—*Good News*

"I'd like to recommend a book. It's *How Now Shall We Live?* by Charles Colson, the Watergate guy who got religion while in prison. . . . Now I don't agree with everything Colson says, but the importance of the book is that it raises a question every American ought to face and then answer to his or her own satisfaction: What is your world view?" —**Charley Reese,** nationally syndicated columnist.

One of "Ten Books Every Preacher Should Read This Year."—*Preaching*

"Deeply troubled by the lack of biblical literacy within the American Church, this is Colson's heroic effort to enable believers to accept the importance of having a biblical worldview and devoting themselves to adopting such a life perspective. . . . This book provides a wealth of insight into how we may effectively challenge the post-Christian, post-modern culture in which we live."—*The Barna Report*

"Colson and Pearcey aren't talking about influencing business, politics and culture—they want it transformed through a coherent Christian world view. Their book will challenge every Christian leader to make an honest assessment about his or her commitment to use leadership gifts in the new millennium to the cause of Christ."—*Christian Management Report*

"Colson and Pearcey challenge the church to stay on the front lines. Believing that America is on the verge of a great spiritual breakthrough, the authors want to equip readers to show the world that Christianity is a life system that *works* in every area—family relationships, education, science, and popular culture."—*Virtue*

"A radical challenge to all Christians to understand biblical faith as an entire world view, a perspective on all of life. Through inspiring teaching and true stories, Colson discusses how to expose the false views and values of modern culture, how to live more fulfilling and satisfying lives in line with the way God created us to live—and more."—*Youthworker*

(In developing and implementing an organizational learning strategy and integrating it with their organizational practices) "When it came to selecting materials, your *How Now Shall We Live?* was at the top of the list. To our minds this is now the best introduction to a Christian worldview and Christian cultural engagement available in English. At least in our organization, *How Now Shall We Live?* should become an indispensable resource."—*Christian Labour Association of Canada*

1999 Books of the Year—Award of Merit—*Christianity Today*

HOW NOW SHALL WE LIVE?

CHARLES COLSON

AND NANCY PEARCEY

Tyndale House Publishers, Inc.
WHEATON, ILLINOIS

Library of Congress Cataloging-in-Publication Data

Colson, Charles W.
  How now shall we live? / Charles Colson.
    p. cm.
  ISBN 0-8423-1808-9 (hardcover : alk. paper)—0-8423-5588-X (softcover)
    1. Christianity and culture. 2. Christianity—20th century. 3. Christian life. I. Title.
BR115.C8C554 1999
261—dc21   99-22149

Printed in the United States of America

10 09 08 07 06 05 04
7   6   5   4   3   2   1

We dedicate this book to the memory of
Francis A. Schaeffer, whose ministry at L'Abri
was instrumental in Nancy's conversion
and whose works have had a profound influence
on my own understanding of Christianity
as a total worldview.

CONTENTS

INTRODUCTION—HOW NOW SHALL WE LIVE?

Without a biblical worldview, all the great teaching goes in one ear and out the other. There are no intellectual pegs . . . in the mind of the individual to hang these truths on. So they just pass through. They don't stick. They don't make a difference.

GEORGE BARNA

Centuries ago, when the Jews were in exile and in despair, they cried out to God, "How should we then live?"[1] The same question rings down through the ages. How shall *we* live today?

The year 2000 marks the beginning of the new millennium—an extraordinary moment for the Christian church. After two thousand years, the birth of the Son of God still remains the defining moment of history. Jesus founded a church that could not be destroyed—not by the deaths of his followers in the Colosseum, not by barbarian hordes or mighty Turkish emperors, not by modern tyrants or the power of sophisticated ideologies. After two thousand years, we can affirm that Jesus Christ is indeed the same yesterday, today, and forever. This alone should make the opening decade of the millennium a cause for jubilation, a time when Christians boldly and confidently recommit to engaging contemporary culture with a fresh vision of hope.

Yet my sense is that most Christians are anything but jubilant. And for good reason. We are experiencing some of the same sense of exile that the Jews did in the time of Ezekiel. We live in a culture that is at best morally indifferent. A culture in which Judeo-Christian values are mocked and where immorality in high places is not only ignored but even rewarded in the voting booth. A culture in which violence, banality, meanness, and disintegrating personal behavior are destroying civility and endangering the very life of our communities. A culture in which the most profound moral dilemmas are addressed by the cold logic of utilitarianism.

What's more, when Christians do make good-faith efforts to halt this slide into barbarism, we are maligned as intolerant or bigoted. Small wonder that many people have concluded that the "culture war" is over—and that we have lost. Battle weary, we are tempted to withdraw into the safety of our sanctuaries, to keep busy by plugging into every program offered by our megachurches, hoping to keep ourselves and our children safe from the coming desolation.

Right after signing the contract for this book, and while still plagued by writer's remorse (was I really convinced that this book needed to be written?), my wife, Patty, and I visited old friends for a weekend and attended their local evangelical church, which is well known for its biblical preaching. I found the message solidly scriptural and well delivered. That is, until the pastor outlined for the congregation his definition of the church's mission: to prepare for Jesus' return through prayer, Bible study, worship, fellowship, and witnessing. In that instant, all lingering doubts about whether I should write this book evaporated.

Don't get me wrong. We need prayer, Bible study, worship, fellowship, and witnessing. But if we focus exclusively on these disciplines—and if in the process we ignore our responsibility to redeem the surrounding culture—our Christianity will remain privatized and marginalized.

Turning our backs on the culture is a betrayal of our biblical mandate and our own heritage because it denies God's sovereignty over all of life. Nothing could be deadlier for the church—or more ill-timed. To abandon the battlefield now is to desert the cause just when we are seeing the first signs that historic Christianity may be on the verge of a great breakthrough. The process of secularization begun in the Enlightenment is grinding to a halt, and many people believe that the new millennium will mark "the desecularization of world history."[2]

Do we sound delusional? Or like Pollyannas wearing rose-colored glasses? If you think so, consider just a few signs of the times.

First, several cultural indicators are at long last reversing, which suggests that some of the most destructive pathologies are beginning to decline. The divorce rate is down 19 percent since 1981; the birth rate among unmarried teens is down 7.5 percent since 1994; abortion is down 15.3 percent since 1990; and there has been an astonishing 37 percent decrease in people on welfare since 1993. Even crime is down, despite a surge in the teen population, the age-group that commits the most crime.[3]

Second, moral discourse is reviving. Just a few years ago, it was all but impossible to discuss serious moral issues in public forums. In 1997, for example, I was invited to a popular week-in-review program where Washington talking heads dispense inside-the-beltway wisdom to the masses. In the course of the discussion, I suggested that the breakdown of the inner cities has a moral component—only to be greeted with incredulous stares. After an awkward pause, the host quickly changed the subject. But only a year later, as a result of the Monica Lewinsky–White House scandals, I was asked to appear on most major news shows in the country to discuss, of all things, the nature of repentance. For the first time in years, many people are actually willing to admit that private immorality has public consequences.

Why are cultural trends shifting? Because modernity has played out its destructive logical consequences. All the ideologies, all the utopian promises that have marked this century have proven utterly bankrupt. Americans have achieved what modernism presented as life's great shining purpose: individual autonomy, the right to do what one chooses. Yet this has not produced the promised freedom; instead, it has led to the loss of community and civility, to kids shooting kids in schoolyards, to citizens huddling in gated communities for protection. We have discovered that we cannot live with the chaos that inevitably results from choice divorced from morality.

As a result, Americans are groping for something that will restore the shattered bonds of family and community, something that will make sense of life. If the church turns inward now, if we focus only on our own needs, we will miss the opportunity to provide answers at a time when people are sensing a deep longing for meaning and order. It is not enough to focus exclusively on the spiritual, on Bible studies and evangelistic campaigns, while turning a blind eye to the distinctive tensions of contemporary life. We must show the world that Christianity is more than a private belief, more than personal salvation. We must show that it is a comprehensive life system that answers all of humanity's age-old questions: Where did I come from? Why am I here? Where am I going? Does life have any meaning and purpose?

As we will argue in these pages, Christianity offers the only viable, rationally defensible answers to these questions. Only Christianity offers a way to understand both the physical and the moral order. Only Christianity offers a comprehensive worldview that covers all areas of life and thought, every aspect of creation. Only Christianity offers a way to live in line with the real world.

But if Christians are going to carry this life-giving message to the world, we must first understand it and live it ourselves. We must understand that God's revelation is the source of *all truth,* a comprehensive framework for all of reality. Abraham Kuyper, the great nineteenth-century theologian who served as prime minister of Holland, said that the dominating principle of Christian truth is not soteriological (i.e., justification by faith) but rather cosmological (i.e., the sovereignty of the triune God over the whole cosmos, in all its spheres and kingdoms, visible and invisible).[4] The entire cosmos can be understood only in relation to God.

The church's singular failure in recent decades has been the failure to see Christianity as a life system, or worldview, that governs every area of existence. This failure has been crippling in many ways. For one thing, we cannot answer the questions our children bring home from school, so we are incapable of preparing them to answer the challenges they face. For ourselves, we cannot explain to our friends and neighbors why we believe, and we often cannot defend our faith. And we do not know how to organize our lives correctly, allowing our choices to be shaped by the world around us. What's more, by failing to see Christian truth in every aspect of life, we miss great depths of beauty and meaning: the thrill of seeing God's splendor in the intricacies of nature or hearing his voice in the performance of a great symphony or detecting his character in the harmony of a well-ordered community.

Most of all, our failure to see Christianity as a comprehensive framework of truth has crippled our efforts to have a redemptive effect on the surrounding culture. At its most fundamental level, the so-called culture war is a clash of belief systems. It is, as Kuyper put it, a clash of principle against principle, of worldview against worldview. Only when we see this can we effectively evangelize a post-Christian culture, bringing God's righteousness to bear in the world around us.

Evangelism and cultural renewal are both divinely ordained duties. God exercises his sovereignty in two ways: through *saving grace* and *common grace.* We are all familiar with saving grace; it is the means by which God's power calls people who are dead in their trespasses and sins to new life in Christ. As God's servants, we may at times be agents of his saving grace, evangelizing and bringing people to Christ. But few of us really understand common grace, which is the means by which God's power sustains creation, holding back the sin and evil that result from the Fall and that would otherwise overwhelm his creation like a great flood. As agents of God's common grace, we are called to help sustain and renew his creation, to uphold the created institutions of family and society, to pursue science and scholarship, to create works of art and beauty, and to heal and help those suffering from the results of the Fall.

Because we wanted to communicate a fuller sense of how we cooperate with God's common grace, Nancy Pearcey and I felt compelled to write this book. Our goal is to equip believers to present Christianity as a total worldview and life system, and to seize the opportunity of the new millennium to be nothing less than God's agents in building a new Christian culture.

To that end, we have divided our discussion into five parts. In part 1, we explain what we mean by the term *worldview,* why it is important, and how to develop the skills to "think christianly" about all of life. In parts 2, 3, and 4, we take you through the contours of a Christian worldview: first, the *creation* of both the universe and human life; second, the *fall* into sin and how it marred God's good creation; and third, how God has provided a means of *redemption.*

These categories provide the means to compare and contrast the various ideas and philosophies competing for allegiance in today's world, for they cover the central questions that any worldview must answer:

1. Creation—Where did we come from, and who are we?
2. Fall—What has gone wrong with the world?
3. Redemption—What can we do to fix it?

This method of analysis is indispensable, for it will enable each of us to discern and defend the truth of what we believe. For Christianity is, after all, a reasonable faith, solidly grounded in human experience. It provides a worldview that fits the structure of reality and enables us to live in harmony with that structure.

On a personal note, I can't help mentioning that preparing the section on redemption has been one of the most rewarding and exciting experiences of my writing career. The process of contrasting the various false claims of salvation that clamor for our attention turned out to be profoundly faith-affirming. And what became unmistakably clear as we studied and wrote is that only Christianity provides credible, defensible answers to life's most crucial questions, and only Christianity offers a reasonable strategy for how we are to live in the real world.

The final section of the book, part 5, applies the basic worldview principles—creation, fall, redemption—to the restoration of culture. It illustrates how we can use these principles as tools not only to critique the false worldviews holding sway today but also to build a new culture. Examining everything from politics to education to the arts, we give examples of the way the Christian worldview provides a more coherent and rational way of living in the world—examples that provide a rough blueprint for living out a biblical worldview and renewing the culture in whichever arena of life God has placed us.

While this book contains serious and sometimes weighty material, we have written it for laypeople in a style we hope is accessible. For this reason, we have included stories throughout the book to illustrate the principles in action. If you are interested in a more scholarly, in-depth approach to worldview questions, you will find a good selection of recommended reading at the end of the book.

We will be delighted if you are inspired to read the works on which we have relied most heavily. Our controlling source, of course, is Scripture. Beyond that, we are indebted to many who have gone before us and upon whose shoulders we stand, especially John Calvin, Abraham Kuyper, C. S. Lewis, and Francis Schaeffer.[5] (For a more complete list, please see the recommended reading section at the back of the book: Or, if you are interested in deepening your understanding of this book by doing individual or group study, you may want to use the companion study guide published for that purpose.) We have seen our task not as a trailblazing effort to produce new theological revelations or to uncover hidden philosophical insights, but rather as an attempt to renew timeless and enduring truths. C. S. Lewis once wrote that though he was often celebrated for offering innovative thoughts, his only purpose was to present ancient truth in a form that the contemporary generation could understand. That has been our modest aim as well.

Is there yet time in this epic moment, at the dawn of the third millennium, to revive the church's sense of hope and to bear witness to the immutable truth of biblical revelation? Can a culture be rebuilt so that all the world can see in its splendor and glory the contours of God's kingdom? Emphatically yes. Pope John Paul II has urged Christians everywhere to work to make the new millennium a "springtime" of Christianity. We can indeed make the year 2000 the beginning of a new season for the faith.

For that to happen, however, we must first listen to the answer God gave his people when they cried out, "How should we then live?" Through the prophet Ezekiel, God admonished his people to repent—turn *from* their evil ways and turn *toward* him—and to show their neighbors that their hope was in his justice and righteousness.

God's word to us today is precisely the same. And to unfold what obedience to that word means, we begin our journey in an unlikely place, among unlikely people, where you will first descend into hell and later catch a glimpse of heaven. Our opening story reveals the pattern by which we must redeem the world around us.

Soli Deo Gloria
Charles W. Colson
Nancy R. Pearcey
      April 1999
      Washington, D.C.

WORLDVIEW:
WHY IT MATTERS

CHAPTER 1

A NEW CREATION

In Ecuador, the peaks of the Andes jut more than two miles into thinning air. Within their cratered throat, the green incisor-shaped mountains hold the old colonial center of Quito, its ornate Spanish architecture surrounded by poured-concrete high-rises. Puffy clouds drawn through high mountain passes drift low over the city. Beneath them, banks of pink and white houses scatter like petals over the base of the mountains.

From the air, Quito is an exotic jungle orchid, appearing suddenly amid the foliage. But in its center is a place where the two forces vying for allegiance in the human heart become dramatically visible in an allegory of good and evil, heaven and hell.

In December 1995, I traveled to Quito with a group of Prison Fellowship friends to visit the deteriorating García Moreno Prison, one wing of which had been turned over to Prison Fellowship. We were met at the airport by one of the most remarkable men I've ever known: Dr. Jorge Crespo de Toral, the chairman of Prison Fellowship Ecuador.[1]

Though now seventy-five, Crespo remains an imposing figure, tall and patrician, with silvery hair and ruggedly handsome features. Born into aristocracy and educated in the law, he seemed destined for a life of affluence and power. Instead, Jorge Crespo became a labor lawyer and took up the cause of the poor, battling the monopolies that enslaved the workers and filled the pockets of the ruling elite. He became so well known as the champion of the poor that during one case an owner shouted at him, "So, Dr. Crespo, you are our guardian angel?" Indeed he was, although the industrialists were unwilling to admit it.

During Ecuador's tumultuous transition from military rule to democracy, Jorge Crespo was twice arrested and imprisoned. But the democratic forces ultimately prevailed, and in the 1960s, he was selected to help draft Ecuador's constitution. He was also a candidate in the nation's first presidential election, finishing a strong third. In the midst of all this, Crespo found time to write and publish poetry as well as literary criticism, winning a well-deserved reputation as a writer and a statesman.

But it was not his literary or political accomplishments that drew me to Ecuador. By the time I met him, Jorge Crespo had forsaken a personal career in politics and was engaged in what he considered the most important task of his life: reforming Ecuador's criminal justice system and its prisons.

■   ■   ■

I WILL NEVER forget the moment we arrived at García Moreno Prison in the center of Quito. The sights and smells are seared indelibly in my memory.

The prison's white baroque bell tower hovers like an evil eye, while its heavy dome seems to be collapsing into the sprawling old building. Jorge Crespo elbowed his way through the ragged crowds clustered outside—families waiting in hope of a brief visit—and led us to the front entrance, a small doorway at the top of a few steps. On each side of the steps were huge mounds of garbage, decaying in the heat, and the putrid odor was nearly overpowering. The uneven steps were slippery in places, the top step splattered with fresh blood.

"Someone was beaten and then dragged over the threshold," said Crespo, shaking his head. Such things were routine at García Moreno, he added.

We passed from the sun-drenched street into the dim, narrow passageways in the first section of the prison, known as the Detainees Pavilion, where Crespo pointed out several black, cell-like holes in the concrete walls. These were the notorious torture chambers. They were no longer in use—thanks to his work—but still they gaped there, grotesque evidence of their bloody history. Knowing that Crespo himself had twice been cast into this prison, I watched him, wondering what horrors this sight must bring to his mind. At one point his self-control slipped when he told us about a torture cell that was actually a water tank; prisoners had been kept there until their flesh began decaying and sloughing off the bone—a means of extracting confessions.

As we moved along, we seemed to be descending into darkness, our eyes straining to make out the contours of the narrow passageways, until we came to a series of cells that were still in use. They were eerily illuminated by narrow shafts of light penetrating downward from tiny orifices high on the mold-covered limestone walls. From the walls of each cell hung four bunks, which were nothing more than iron slabs. Twelve inmates shared each cell, so the men had to sleep in shifts or stretch out on the floor, thick with grime and spilled sewage. There was no plumbing, and the air was fetid. Water was brought into the cells in buckets; when empty, these same buckets were filled with waste and hauled back out.

I was stunned. I've been in more than six hundred prisons in forty countries, yet these were some of the worst conditions I had ever seen. Worse than Perm Camp 35, one of the most notorious in the Soviet Gulag. Worse than prisons in the remotest reaches of India, Sri Lanka, and Zambia. Even more startling, the prisoners here had not been convicted of any crimes. The cells in the Detainees Pavilion were for men awaiting trial. In Ecuador, as in much of Latin America, there is no presumption of innocence nor any right to a speedy trial. A detainee can wait four to five years just to come to trial—and sometimes even longer if no one outside is agitating for his rights, knocking almost daily on some prosecutor's door, or paying off some official. There are palms to be greased at every level. In such a system, the poor are powerless, cast into dungeons and easily forgotten.

The guards urged us onward from the cells to a courtyard, where we could see inmates milling about in the open air. The yard was bounded by high-walled cellblocks and monitored by armed guards patrolling the parapets. As we gazed into the courtyard through a barred iron gate, the image was so surreal that I felt I had been transported to a scene of human desperation out of a Dickens novel. The men shuffled around the yard, many dressed in rags and wearing a vacant look of hopelessness on their pale, drawn faces.

A group of garishly made-up women huddling together against one of the walls caught my attention. "What are the women doing in there?" I asked Crespo.

"There are no women in García Moreno," he replied. "When we first started working here, the fathers sometimes brought their children in with them, even little girls, because there was no one else to take care of them. But now we have a home for the children."

Puzzled by his answer, I nodded toward the wall. "Over there. Those women."

"Oh," said Crespo. "Those are transvestites and male prostitutes. They usually stay together for protection from the other inmates."

My heart sank. Truly this was a kingdom of evil. Hell on earth.

Crespo began talking with the official standing at the gate, and he appeared to be arguing with him. Finally Crespo turned to me, shrugged his shoulders and said, "I'm sorry. The guard says it's impossible to enter the compound. Much too dangerous."

"Tell him we insist, Jorge. Tell him the minister of justice promised us access."

No doubt there was a bit of bravado mixed in with my adamant persistence, but I was certain that God had brought us here for a purpose. Crespo resumed his animated conversation with the guard until finally the man, shaking his head in disgust, unlocked the gate.

In the New Testament, Jesus described the gate into heaven as narrow, but this gate into hell was narrow as well. We could pass through only one at a time. Crespo stepped briskly into the yard before I could even collect my thoughts. My heart racing, I moved in behind him.

As we walked to the center of the compound, conversation ceased, and the inmates turned to watch us. I prayed a silent prayer for grace and started speaking. As I did, the men began shuffling toward us. Several were limping; a man who had only one leg had to be helped along by another prisoner. Directly in front of me was a man with an empty eye socket and open sores spotting his face. Several men had scarves covering most of their faces, perhaps to cover sores or to filter the vile smells.

Suddenly, despite the wretched scene before me, I felt the same freedom I've known thousands of times in the past years, whether in palaces, universities, or television studios—but especially in prisons. It is that special anointing God gives us to communicate his boundless love to even the most pitiful souls. I will never know who responded to the invitation to receive him that day, but afterward, scores of men reached out to us, many smiling. Yet no one broke the sacred canopy of silence, the sense of God's presence, that seemed to settle over the courtyard.

As I shook hands or just reached out to touch the shoulders of the men clustered around us, I kept thinking of the time John the Baptist asked whether Jesus was the Messiah. "Tell him," Jesus replied, that "the blind see, the lame walk, . . . and the Good News is being preached to the poor" (Matt. 11:4-5, NLT).

■　　■　　■

THE HOLY SILENCE held as the guards led us out of the yard and through heavy iron gates into another darkened corridor. Crespo told us that we were approaching the prison area that had been turned over to Prison Fellowship. We walked through a wide door and were ushered into a huge, triple-tiered cellblock.

All at once, we stepped out of the darkness and into a radiant burst of light.

"This is Pavilion C," Crespo said proudly with a wide smile.

At the far end of the corridor was what looked like an altar, with a huge cross silhouetted against a brightly painted concrete wall. Gathered in an open area before the altar were more than two hundred inmates, who rose up out of their seats, singing and applauding. Some were playing guitars. All were glowing with joy and enthusiasm. Within seconds, we were surrounded, and the prisoners began embracing us like long-separated brothers.

In Pavilion C, Prison Fellowship volunteers and inmate leaders provided rigorous instruction in Christian faith and character development to inmates who were brought out of the other pavilions, including the Detainees Pavilion. Regular worship services were led by a variety of priests and ministers. This was a holy community, a church like none I had ever seen.

Yet Jorge Crespo was quick to point out that Pavilion C was only a stop on the way, a place of preparation. The ultimate destination was Casa de San Pablo (St. Paul's House), so named because of Paul's imprisonment in the Philippian jail (see Acts 16:22-34). This was a prison wing for those who had been received into full Christian fellowship and who ministered to the rest of the prisoners. Crespo hustled us on to see it.

Like Pavilion C, Casa de San Pablo was spotlessly clean, with the added beauty of tiled floors and separate dormitories, furnished with wooden bunks made by inmates. Beneath a flight of stairs, the inmates had partitioned off a small prayer closet containing only a bench with a cross on it. Because of the low ceiling, the men had to stoop down upon entering the room, then remain on their knees inside. The prayer closet was in use all day.

Pictures of Christ and other religious symbols were everywhere, and I momentarily forgot that we were in a prison. In fact, it wasn't called a prison, but "the Home," and it was populated not by prisoners but by "residents."

The means by which the Home came into being is nothing less than miraculous. When Crespo first approached authorities about taking over a wing of the prison, these facilities were considered unfit even by García Moreno standards. The bright and airy main room where we now stood,

Crespo told us, was once scarcely more than a cave, dark and unlit, shrouded with spiderwebs. Once he got the go-ahead, however, Christian inmates and an army of volunteers from local churches went to work with shovels and tools. Tradesmen volunteered their services, as did local contractors. Many churches raised money. And overseeing it all was the tall, imposing figure of Jorge Crespo himself, the visionary who could see what others could not—a church inside a prison. It took several years of sweat and sacrificial labor—and no end of Crespo's cajoling the officials—but eventually the vision became a reality.

That afternoon, as we assembled with residents in the meeting room, I noticed that the windows were barred on only one side: the side facing the main prison compound. The windows facing out to the street were open—a powerful symbol of trust and hope.

The meeting room was dominated by a huge mural, painted across the main wall by the prisoners themselves, depicting the emerging freedom of life in Christ. On the left, a ragged figure huddled in a blue shadow of despair. The next figure turned to the rising sun, and the next traveled toward it. Finally, a figure lifted his hands to heaven in praise of his Creator. The men in this room knew exactly what those symbols meant, for once they had been just like the men in the Detainees Pavilion, without hope and left to rot like garbage. But now they were new creatures in Christ.

As we worshiped together, several men gave stirring testimonies. "Coming to this prison is the best thing that ever happened to me," said one man, who had been a high-ranking operator in a drug cartel. "I found Jesus here. I don't care if I ever leave. I just want others to know that this place is not the end. There is hope. God can change us even here—*especially* here."

The inmates included both Protestants and Catholics, but they drew no distinctions. Bible studies were led by Protestant ministers and by Father Tim, the resident Catholic chaplain. They loved the same Lord, studied the same Word. It was the kind of fellowship one longs for (but seldom finds) in our comfortable North American churches. Perhaps only those who have plumbed the depths of despair and depravity can fully appreciate the futility of life without Christ and can thus learn to love one another in the way Jesus commanded.

Father Tim summed it up best, speaking in his charming Irish lilt. "I never learned about God in seminary," he said, embracing Jorge Crespo. "I learned about God through this man."

We, too, had learned about God from this man and the transformation he had helped work in this place. From the time we entered García Moreno, we had not traveled far in physical terms—mere yards. But in spiritual terms we had made a great journey: from the hell of the Detainees Pavilion to Pavilion C, an analogy of the church here on earth with its struggles, and then to the Home, a foretaste of heaven. A world transformed within a single building. It was nothing short of miraculous.

·   ·   ·

HOW WAS SUCH a miraculous transformation possible? It all began several years earlier as Jorge Crespo was leaving his career in politics. One Sunday at church, his wife, Laura, was moved by something the priest said in his homily.

"What if we really lived by what we say we believe?" she whispered to her husband.

Crespo smiled, for of late he had been pondering similar questions. And for the first time it struck him full force that his faith was not just a personal matter but a framework for all of life. Everything he did—his literary work, his political work, and his work on behalf of the poor—had to be motivated by God's truth.

An opportunity to put his convictions into action came in 1984 when Javier Bustamante, the Prison Fellowship regional director, visited Quito and urged Crespo to begin a ministry bringing Christ to prisoners and reforming Ecuador's criminal justice system. One walk through the Detainees Pavilion at García Moreno convinced Crespo. He was appalled by the filthy, inhumane conditions, by the darkness, hopelessness, and despair. Against the cautions of the authorities, he demanded entrance to some of the punishment cells, where the men quickly recognized him and surrounded him with pleas for help. Most had been there many months, some for years.

When he and Bustamante stepped out into the sunlit street, he said, "All right. I'll lead the effort."

Jorge Crespo's great work had begun. He was sixty-one years old.

Crespo began by campaigning within the national legislature for criminal justice reform. In Ecuador the saying was "The wheels of justice grind slowly, and sometimes they need to be lubricated," meaning most detainees had to bribe the judges just to see their cases come to trial. The judges reasoned that because they were underpaid, they deserved such rewards. But the legislature, noting the corruption, refused to vote the judiciary better salaries. Thus, those arrested found themselves in a catch-22, and those unable to pay the bribes simply languished in jail for years.

Crespo argued that the right to a speedy trial constitutes one of the hallmarks of democracy, and his persistent advocacy finally paid off when legislation was passed to guarantee every detainee a trial within three years. (This law has yet to be consistently observed, but its passage gave prisoners throughout Ecuador a significant legal victory.) Yet his crowning accomplishment, as we have seen, was the creation of a prison based on Christian principles.

Pavilion C was a "spiritual boot camp," preparing its residents for life in Casa de San Pablo, or the Home. And there were no guards within the Home; security was maintained exclusively by internal and external councils. Prisoners were allowed to leave the facility on temporary furlough passes for medical appointments or other urgent business; they also helped carry on the work in Pavilion C and among the prison's general population. Crespo believed that the transforming power of Christ could so change former criminals that they would even accept responsibility for their own imprisonment.

But Crespo's experiment was not without its opponents. Many of Ecuador's "experts" in rehabilitation, the bureaucrats who ran the prison system, bridled at the unflattering comparisons now evident between Prison Fellowship's work and their own. Furthermore, the guards who ran García Moreno's black markets rebelled at having their day-to-day activities exposed to the Christian volunteers who constantly trekked into the place. How long would it be before their lucrative enterprises were exposed to something more than inadvertent scrutiny? As a result, the guards began harassing volunteers and confiscating supplies.

Trouble of this sort had been brewing since Crespo's first efforts in the prison. But with the opening of the Home, the campaign to sabotage the work became far more aggressive.

In early 1995, guards greeted two residents of the Home, a Canadian and an Israeli, returning from a morning's furlough granted for medical appointments, and marched them to the warden's office. There, they were told that the Home had been closed and that they were being returned to the regular prison.

The two men were horrified. The warden suggested that they take the easy way out and simply leave. The men refused, demanding to see Crespo, but the warden grimly began filling out a form.

"I'm filing the report of your escape," he said and had the two residents thrown out of the prison. The men had no option but to "escape."

Within a short time a manhunt was underway. The Canadian and Israeli embassies were drawn into the matter, guaranteeing this would be no minor incident. But the warden's real intent became clear when the police report named Crespo as an accessory to the escape, charging him with negligence for allowing the prisoners to leave. Hostile authorities took advantage of the opportunity to suspend the in-prison ministry, threatening that the residents would be cast back into the Detainees Pavilion.

The warden had done his work well, and all the official reports lined up. It seemed to be an open-and-shut case.

Providentially, the testimony of a released inmate, a man who had been led to Christ by Crespo, created the first break in the solid phalanx of officials who were determined to scuttle the project and put Crespo behind bars. The inmate, it turned out, was a friend of a high government official, and word soon spread that Crespo was not implicated after all. Negotiations began with the police chief, the minister of government, and the prosecutors.

It was during those negotiations that I made the visit to García Moreno described earlier in this chapter. At that time Crespo told me that he fully expected to be sent to prison; yet not for a moment did he consider backing down, either in his human rights campaign or his ministry in the prison.

"I know why Jesus Christ lives among the poor," he told the residents at the Home during those tension-filled days. "I know why he became poor in order to serve humankind. Only the poor are rich in mercy. Only the poor possess nothing—nothing but gratitude.

"Whatever happens, whether I am imprisoned once again, whether I am separated from my family as you have been, whether the work is damaged and we are separated from each other, we shall never be separated from the love of Christ. Neither height nor depth, nor any human power, can separate us from that love!"

■   ■   ■

IN THE END, the conspiracy to destroy Crespo's work and put him behind bars was exposed, and in May 1997, all charges against him were dropped. And in the years since our visit, García Moreno Prison has become an even more striking parable of God's kingdom at work in the midst of a fallen world. Although guards and government officials continue to harass Crespo (the work was even suspended for a second time), enormous progress continues to be made.

By nurturing the flower of justice in what was once the most evil of gardens, by living out the reality of being a new creation in Christ, Jorge Crespo has helped to create a whole new world for others. And the forces of hell are being conquered by the power of heaven.

CHAPTER 2

CHRISTIANITY IS A WORLDVIEW

When [Christ's] cosmic battle came to an end, the heavens shook . . . stones were split open, and the world might well have perished. . . . And then, when He ascended, His divine spirit gave life and strength to the tottering world, and the whole universe became stable once more, as if the stretching out, the agony of the Cross, had in some way gotten into everything.

ST. HIPPOLYTUS

The way we see the world can change the world. Jorge Crespo and his work at Garcia Moreno are living proof. The sharp contrast between the hellish darkness of the Detainees Pavilion and the whitewashed brilliance of the Home is a stark reminder of the way our own moral and spiritual choices are realized in the world. In every action we take, we are doing one of two things: we are either helping to create a hell on earth or helping to bring down a foretaste of heaven. We are either contributing to the broken condition of the world or participating with God in transforming the world to reflect his righteousness. We are either advancing the rule of Satan or establishing the reign of God.

The evil forces that created the hell of the Detainees Pavilion are the same forces that ravage families, cities, and whole cultures around the globe. Conversely, the divine force that brought new life to dejected inmates is the same divine force that can renew people anywhere. How does this happen? Renewal can occur when Christians are committed to living out their faith, seeing the world as God sees it, viewing reality through the lens of divine revelation. Jorge Crespo saw the battered inmates of Garcia Moreno as potential citizens of the kingdom of God, and he helped create a corner of that kingdom even in a dark prison.

Our choices are shaped by what we believe is real and true, right and wrong, good and beautiful. Our choices are shaped by our worldview.

The term *worldview* may sound abstract or philosophical, a topic discussed by pipe-smoking, tweed-jacketed professors in academic settings. But actually a person's worldview is intensely practical. It is simply the sum total of our beliefs about the world, the "big picture" that directs our daily decisions and actions. And understanding worldviews is extremely important.

Our major task in life is to discover what is true and to live in step with that truth. As we saw earlier, every worldview can be analyzed by the way it answers three basic questions: Where did we come from, and who are we *(creation)*? What has gone wrong with the world *(fall)*? And what can we do to fix it *(redemption)*? These three questions form a grid that we can use to break down the inner logic of every belief system or philosophy that we encounter, from the textbooks in our classrooms to the unspoken philosophy that shapes the message we hear on *Oprah*. In this book, we will show you how to apply the three-part grid to critique nonbiblical worldviews, while at the same time framing a biblical worldview on any subject, from family life to education, from politics to science, from art to popular culture.

The basis for the Christian worldview, of course, is God's revelation in Scripture. Yet sadly, many believers fail to understand that Scripture is intended to be the basis for all of life. In the past centuries, the secular world asserted a dichotomy between science and religion, between fact and value, between objective knowledge and subjective feeling. As a result, Christians often think in terms of the same false dichotomy, allowing our belief system to be reduced to little more than private feelings and experience, completely divorced from objective facts.

Evangelicals have been particularly vulnerable to this narrow view because of our emphasis on personal commitment. On one hand, this has been the movement's greatest strength, bringing millions to a relationship with Christ. Somewhere in most of our spiritual journeys is a sawdust trail, as there certainly is in mine. I remember as vividly as if it were yesterday that sultry summer night in 1973, in the midst of the Watergate scandal, when I, a former marine captain—often called the "toughest of the Nixon tough guys," the "White House hatchet man,"—broke down in tears and called out to God.[1] Apart from that encounter with Christ and assurances of his forgiveness, I would have suffocated in the stench of my own sin. My soul would never have found rest.

But this emphasis on a personal relationship can also be evangelicalism's greatest weakness because it may prevent us from seeing God's plan for us beyond personal salvation. Genuine Christianity is more than a relationship with Jesus, as expressed in personal piety, church attendance, Bible study, and works of charity. It is more than discipleship, more than believing a system of doctrines about God. Genuine Christianity is a way of seeing and comprehending *all* reality. It is a worldview.

The scriptural basis for this understanding is the creation account, where we are told that God spoke everything into being out of nothing (see Gen. 1 and John 1:1-14). Everything that exists came into being at his command and is therefore subject to him, finding its purpose and meaning in him. The implication is that in every topic we investigate, from ethics to economics to ecology, the truth is found only in relationship to God and his revelation. God created the natural world and natural laws. God created our bodies and the moral laws that keep us healthy. God created our minds and the laws of logic and imagination. God created us as social beings and gave us the principles for social and political institutions. God created a world of beauty and the principles of aesthetics and artistic creation. In every area of life, genuine knowledge means discerning the laws and ordinances by which God has structured creation, and then allowing those laws to shape the way we should live.

As the church fathers used to say, all truth is God's truth.

What's more, that comprehensive truth is embodied in Christ, who is our Savior and yet also much more. In the first chapter of John, Christ is called the *logos* (John 1:1). In the Greek, *logos* literally means the idea, the word, the rational pattern of creation, the order of the universe. The apostle Paul expands on this: "For by him all things were created: things in heaven and on earth, visible and invisible . . . ; all things were created by him and for him. He is before all things, and in him all things hold together" (Col. 1:16-17). Jesus himself is the word that God spoke to create the world.

Perhaps the most astonishing claim Jesus makes is, "I am the way and the truth and the life" (John 14:6). Jesus is the origin and end of all things, the Alpha and the Omega. Nothing has meaning apart from him. Nothing exists apart from him. He is the agent of creation, author of all that is and ever will be. Christ is Lord over all of creation, from the human soul to the vast reaches of the cosmos (see Pss. 2; 8; 110; Phil. 2:5-11).

When we truly grasp this, we are compelled to see that the Christian faith cannot be reduced to John 3:16 or simple formulas. Christianity cannot be limited to only one component of our lives, a mere religious practice or observance, or even a salvation experience. We are compelled to see Christianity as the all-encompassing truth, the root of everything else. It is ultimate reality.

NOT SPITTING INTO THE WIND

Understanding Christianity as a total life system is absolutely essential, for two reasons. First, it enables us to make sense of the world we live in and thus order our lives more rationally. Second, it enables us to understand forces hostile to our faith, equipping us to evangelize and to defend Christian truth as God's instruments for transforming culture.

Because the world was created by an intelligent being rather than by chance, it has an intelligible order. As Abraham Kuyper wrote, "All created life necessarily bears in itself a law for its existence, instituted by God Himself."[2] The only way to live a rational and healthy life is to ascertain the nature of these divine laws and ordinances and then to use them as the basis for how we should live. We tend to understand this principle very well when it comes to the physical order. We know that certain laws exist in the physical world and that if we defy those laws, we pay a steep price. Ignoring the law of gravity can have very unpleasant consequences if we happen to be walking off the edge of a cliff. To live in defiance of known physical laws is the height of folly.

But it is no different with the moral laws prescribing human behavior. Just as certain physical actions produce predictable reactions, so certain moral behavior produces predictable consequences. Adultery may be portrayed as glamorous by Hollywood, but it invariably produces anger, jealousy, broken relationships, even violence. Defiance of moral laws may even lead to death, whether it is the speeding drunk who kills a mother on her way to the store or the drug addict who contracts and spreads AIDS. No transgression of moral law is without painful consequences.

If we want to live healthy, well-balanced lives, we had better know the laws and ordinances by which God has structured creation. And because these are the laws of our own inner nature, Kuyper notes, we will experience them not as oppressive external constraints but as "a guide through the desert," guaranteeing our safety.[3]

This understanding of life's laws is what Scripture calls wisdom. "Wisdom in Scripture is, broadly speaking, the knowledge of God's world and the knack of fitting oneself into it," says Calvin College professor Cornelius Plantinga. A wise person is one who knows the boundaries and limits, the laws and rhythms and seasons of the created order, both in the physical and the social world. "To be wise is to know reality and then accommodate yourself to it." By contrast, those who refuse to accommodate to the laws of life are not only immoral but also foolish, no matter how well educated they may be. They fail to recognize the structure of creation and are constantly at odds with reality: "Folly is a stubborn swimming against the stream of the universe . . . spitting into the wind . . . coloring outside the lines."[4]

Precisely. To deny God is to blind ourselves to reality, and the inevitable consequence is that we will bump up against reality in painful ways, just as a blindfolded driver will crash into other drivers or run off the road. We make the bold claim that serious Christians actually live happier, more fulfilled, more productive lives by almost every measure. (Studies are beginning to bear this out, as we will see in later chapters.) This simply makes sense. Someone who accepts the contours and limits of the physical and moral order doesn't engage in folly—whether stepping off a cliff or committing adultery or driving drunk.

THE REAL CULTURE WAR

Our calling is not only to order our own lives by divine principles but also to engage the world, as Crespo did. We are to fulfill both the great commission and the cultural commission. We are commanded both to preach the Good News and to bring all things into submission to God's order, by defending and living out God's truth in the unique historical and cultural conditions of our age.

To engage the world, however, requires that we understand the great ideas that compete for people's minds and hearts. Philosopher Richard Weaver has it right in the title of his well-known book: Ideas have consequences.[5] It is the great ideas that inform the mind, fire the imagination, move the heart, and shape a culture. History is little more than the recording of the rise and fall of the great ideas—the worldviews—that form our values and move us to act.

A debilitating weakness in modern evangelicalism is that we've been fighting cultural skirmishes on all sides without knowing what the war itself is about. We have not identified the worldviews that lie at the root of cultural conflict—and this ignorance dooms our best efforts.

The culture war is not just about abortion, homosexual rights, or the decline of public education. These are only the skirmishes. The real war is a cosmic struggle between worldviews—between the Christian worldview and the various secular and spiritual worldviews arrayed against it. This is what we must understand if we are going to be effective both in evangelizing our world today and in transforming it to reflect the wisdom of the Creator.

CHAPTER 3

WORLDVIEWS IN CONFLICT

From barbarism to civilization requires a century; from civilization to barbarism needs but a day.

WILL DURANT

The world is divided not so much by geographic boundaries as by religious and cultural traditions, by people's most deeply held beliefs—by worldviews. So argued the distinguished Harvard scholar Samuel Huntington in a celebrated article a few years ago.[1] And Christians would agree. Because we are religious creatures, our lives are defined by our ultimate beliefs more sharply than by any other factor. The drama of history is played out along the frontiers of great belief systems as they ebb and flow.

But if this is so, what does it tell us about the divisions in the world today? Where is the clash of civilizations most bitter?

Huntington predicted a clash between the worldviews of three major traditional civilizations: the Western world, the Islamic world, and the Confucian East. But one of his former students, political scientist James Kurth, took issue with him, contending that the most significant clash would be within Western civilization itself—between those who adhere to a Judeo-Christian framework and those who favor postmodernism and multiculturalism.[2]

I believe Kurth is right. And the reason this conflict within Western culture is so significant is that Western culture may soon dominate the globe. Information technology is rapidly crossing traditional barriers of geography and national boundaries. The fall of the Iron Curtain has opened a large area of the world to Western ideas. Asian and Islamic societies find they cannot insulate themselves from the influx of Western books, movies, and television programs. In Singapore, I met with a Christian cabinet minister who lamented that because Asians associate the West with Christianity, the flood of smut from the West is making his Christian witness difficult. Across the globe, people are complaining about what one French politician described as a "U.S. cultural invasion."[3]

As a result, people around the world are wrestling with the same questions that we face in the States. In Africa, one of the continent's most respected Christian leaders asked for permission to reprint transcripts of my radio program, *BreakPoint*. Though the program is targeted at an American audience, he found that the subjects are the same as those he is dealing with in Africa. Another African Christian leader told me that Western notions of multiculturalism are being used to justify tribalism, and the local church is baffled over how to counter the divisive force. As people in Pakistan get on-line with people in Pennsylvania, America's culture war is increasingly spilling over into other nations.

The sobering conclusion is that our own effectiveness in defending and contending for truth has repercussions across the entire globe. American Christians had better get serious about understanding biblical faith as a comprehensive worldview and showing how it stands up to the challenges of our age.

CHRISTIANITY VS. NATURALISM

What is the major challenge today? In the broadest categories, the conflict of our day is theism versus naturalism. *Theism* is the belief that there is a transcendent God who created the universe; *naturalism* is the belief that natural causes alone are sufficient to explain everything that exists. The most fundamental questions reflect these categories: Is ultimate reality God or the cosmos? Is there a supernatural realm, or is nature all that exists? Has God spoken and revealed his truth to us, or is truth something we have to find, even invent, for ourselves? Is there a purpose to our lives, or are we cosmic accidents emerging from the slime?

These two major systems are utterly opposed, and if we are going to defend the truth effectively, we must grasp their full implications. Naturalism is the idea that nature is all that exists, that life arose from a chance collision of atoms, evolving eventually into human life as we know it today. In its broadest sense, naturalism can even include certain forms of religion—those in which the spiritual is conceived as completely inherent within nature, such as neo-pagan and New Age religions. By contrast, Christianity teaches that there is a transcendent God who existed before the world existed and who is the ultimate origin of everything else. The universe is dependent at every moment on his providential governance and care.

Moral relativism. In morality, naturalism results in relativism. If nature is all there is, then there is no transcendent source of moral truth, and we are left to construct morality on our own. Every principle is reduced to a personal preference. By contrast, the Christian believes in a God who has spoken, who has revealed an absolute and unchanging standard of right and wrong, based ultimately on his own holy character.

Multiculturalism. As a consequence of relativism, the naturalist treats all cultures as morally equivalent, each merely reflecting its own history and experience. Contemporary trends like postmodernism and multiculturalism are rooted firmly in naturalism, for if there is no transcendent source of truth or morality, then we find our identity only in our race, gender, or ethnic group. But Christians can never equate truth with the limited perspective of any group. Truth is God's perspective, as revealed in Scripture. Hence, while we appreciate the cultural diversity, we insist on the propriety of judging particular cultural practices as morally right or wrong. Furthermore, Christians regard the Western tradition and heritage as worth defending; that is, to the degree that historically it has been shaped by a biblical worldview.

Pragmatism. Since naturalists deny any transcendent moral standards, they tend to take a pragmatic approach to life. Pragmatism says: Whatever works best is right. Actions and policies are judged on utilitarian grounds alone. By contrast, the Christian is an idealist, judging actions not by what works but by what ought to be, based on objective standards.

Utopianism. Naturalists generally embrace the Enlightenment notion that human nature is essentially good, which leads to utopianism. Utopianism says: If only we create the right social and economic structures, we can usher in an age of harmony and prosperity. But Christians can never give their allegiance to utopian projects. We know that sin is real, that it has deeply twisted human nature, and that none of our efforts can create heaven on earth. Heaven is an eschatological hope that will be fulfilled only by divine intervention at the end of human history. In the meantime, the human propensity to evil and disorder must be hemmed in by law and tradition.

This-world perspective. Naturalists consider only what happens in this world, this age, this life. But Christians see things from an eternal perspective. Everything we do now has eternal significance, because one day there will be a judgment, and then it will become evident that our choices in this life have consequences that last into eternity.

CHRISTIANITY IN A POST-CHRISTIAN ERA

If we are going to make a difference in our world, we must grasp these profoundly contrary views of reality, for they are the root of our cultural crisis.
The dominant worldview today is naturalism, which has created a culture
that is both post-Christian and postmodernist. By post-Christian, we do not
mean Americans no longer profess to be Christians or no longer attend
church. As a matter of fact, most Americans do both. Rather, by
post-Christian we mean that Americans, along with most other Western cultures, no longer rely on Judeo-Christian truths as the basis of their public
philosophy or their moral consensus.

This is a significant cultural shift. At the birth of our nation, no
one—not even deists and skeptics—doubted that basic biblical truths undergirded American institutions and informed the nation's values. Though the
Founding Fathers drew heavily from Enlightenment philosophy as well as
from Christian tradition, few at the time saw any contradiction between the
two. And for most of our nation's history, these basic truths remained the
foundation of the social consensus.

Today that is no longer true. To see how rapidly the shift occurred, one
need look only at Supreme Court decisions. As recently as 1952, Justice William O. Douglas wrote: "We are a religious people whose institutions presuppose a Supreme Being."[4] The Court's language caused no stir: It reflected
what most Americans believed.

But in 1996, little more than a generation later, Court watchers were
scandalized when Justice Antonin Scalia announced in a speech that as a
Christian he believed in miracles and in the resurrection of Jesus.[5] Cartoon-
ist Herbloc depicted the Supreme Court justices all holding law books—except Scalia, who was holding a Bible. *Washington Post* columnist Richard
Cohen suggested that Scalia had disqualified himself from handling further
church-state questions. (Does Cohen believe only atheists are qualified to
make such decisions?) The talking heads on TV savaged Scalia for his "bias."

Similar attitudes have filtered through all levels of society. In 1997, a
Boy Scout troop was denied the use of a public facility at the National Zoo,
which is owned by the Smithsonian. Why? Because the Smithsonian ruled
that the Boy Scouts organization is "biased" when it requires that its members believe in God.[6] Religious expressions in public places are increasingly
discouraged, if not by court order, then by social pressure. One major city has
renamed the Christmas holiday "sparkle season"; and many others forbid the
singing of Christmas carols, at least those that mention the Christ child, in

public places. One school district even changed "Easter eggs" to "spring ovals."

CHRISTIANITY IN A POSTMODERNIST WORLD

But antireligious pressure is not the worst of it. As we said, today's culture not only is post-Christian but also is rapidly becoming postmodernist, which means it is resistant not only to Christian truth claims but to *any* truth claims. *Postmodernism* rejects any notion of a universal, overarching truth and reduces all ideas to social constructions shaped by class, gender, and ethnicity.

Once again, the shift to this new philosophy has been breathtakingly rapid. In the 1960s the percentage of young people going to college suddenly surged, and attitudes once held only by the intellectual elite suddenly became common coinage. The philosophy of *existentialism*, a precursor of postmodernism, swept the campuses, proclaiming that life is absurd, meaningless, and that the individual self must create his own meaning by his own choices. Choice was elevated to the ultimate value, the only justification for any action. America became what one theologian aptly describes as the "imperial republic of the autonomous Self."[7]

It was a small step from existentialism to postmodernism, in which even the self is dissolved into the interplay of the forces of race, class, and gender. Multiculturalism is not about appreciating folk cultures; it's about the dissolution of the individual into the tribal group. In postmodernism, there is no objective, universal truth; there is only the perspective of the group, whatever the group may be: African-Americans, women, gays, Hispanics, and the list goes on. In postmodernism, all viewpoints, all lifestyles, all beliefs and behaviors are regarded as equally valid. Institutions of higher learning have embraced this philosophy so aggressively that they have adopted campus codes enforcing political correctness. Tolerance has become so important that no exception is tolerated.

But if all ideas are equally valid, as postmodernism insists, then no idea is really worth our allegiance; nothing is worth living or dying for—or even arguing about. And this climate of apathy can actually make it harder than ever to witness to the truth of Christianity. In the past, Christians proclaiming their faith might expect to encounter a vigorous debate over the rational grounds for belief, but today the same message is likely to be met with bored indifference.

This is exactly the attitude I witnessed when I spoke at Yale Law

School in 1996. A few fearless Christian students had organized a forum to address the provocative question of how Yale had contributed to undermining the rule of law. (It was at Yale that Critical Legal Studies was born, a deconstructionist movement to strip the law of any objective meaning.) When the students invited me to speak, I wondered if the meeting might erupt into a riot—or, at least, an unpleasant confrontation.

Before my lecture, I dined with Professor Stephen Carter, the brilliant Yale legal scholar, committed Christian, and author of several best-sellers, including *The Culture of Disbelief* and *Integrity*. Over a plate of enchiladas in a small campus hangout, I voiced my apprehensions.

"Don't worry about a riot," he chuckled. "They'll listen quietly and walk away without saying a word."

"But I'm going to tell them that there can be no basis for law without a Christian consensus, or at least a recognition of natural law," I said.

Carter smiled patiently. "When these kids come to Yale, they are taught that the law has nothing to do with morality. And they accept that. So you can have your opinions, and they'll find those interesting, but they won't even bother to argue."

When I arrived at Levensen Auditorium, shortly before eight o'clock, the hall was full. Down in front were perhaps two hundred townspeople, most of them Christians, I supposed, and then row on row of students. As I spoke, I searched the students' eyes, hoping for some sign of engagement. Nothing. As I progressed into my material, I became more provocative, but they remained impassive.

During the question-and-answer period, no one challenged a single premise I had advanced. Most of the queries came from the Christians in the front rows. Carter had sized up his students well. They listened politely, took a few notes, then packed up their papers and quietly slipped out of the auditorium.

Debate can be unpleasant at times, but at least it presupposes that there are truths worth defending, ideas worth fighting for. In our postmodernist age, however, your truths are yours, my truths are mine, and none are significant enough to get passionate about. And if there is no truth, then we cannot persuade one another by rational arguments. All that's left is sheer power—which opens the door to a new form of fascism.

Stanley Fish, a leading postmodernist scholar at Duke University, author of the article "There's No Such Thing As Free Speech: and It's a Good Thing, Too," argues that all statements of principle are really just expressions of personal preferences, and therefore, an appeal to principle is no more than a power play, an attempt to impose one's own private preferences on others in the guise of "objective truths." And if the game is about power, the only thing you worry about is coming out on top. "Someone is always going to be restricted next," Fish writes, "and it is your job to make sure that the someone is not you."[8]

The demise of truth is not confined to the academic halls of Yale Law School or Duke University. Across the country, a generation of college graduates have marched off, degrees in their hands and a postmodernist ideology in their heads, to work in executive suites, political centers, and the editorial rooms of newspapers, magazines, and television studios. The result has been the emergence of a new and influential group of professionals who work primarily with words and ideas—what some sociologists call the New Class or the knowledge class or, more derogatorily, the chattering class. And because they control the means of public discourse, their philosophy has become dominant. No longer is the majority view the outlook of morally conservative, religious, patriotic middle America—the group Richard Nixon in 1970 called the "silent majority," or what Jerry Falwell a few years later labeled the "moral majority." The worldview framed on campuses from the 1960s on has now entered the mainstream of American life.

American Demographics magazine, summarizing a demographic study done in 1997, noted that there has been "a comprehensive shift in values, worldviews, and ways of life" that so far affects about one-fourth of American adults; this is the New Class, or what the article called the "Cultural Creatives."[9] They embrace a new "trans-modernist" set of values, including "environmentalism, feminism, global issues, and spiritual searching." They often have a background in movements for social justice, civil rights, feminism, and New Age spirituality. Thoroughly postmodernist, they are skeptical, if not resentful, of moral absolutes. They "see nature as sacred" and emphasize self-actualization and spiritual growth. They tend to be antihierarchical and embrace a public philosophy that is decentralized, democratic, and egalitarian.

This new worldview is emerging against the backdrop of two already existing worldviews, the study noted. The first is "Traditionalism," held by 29 percent of adults, labeled "Heartlanders." They are often "country folks," holding to "a nostalgic image of small towns and strong churches."

The other existing worldview is "Modernism," held by 47 percent of adults. They value technological progress and material success, and they tend to be politicians, military leaders, scientists, and businesspeople. They are pragmatic, comfortable with the economic establishment, and less concerned with ideology and social issues.

Most significant, however, are the demographic projections. According to the study, the number of Traditionalists and Modernists is in decline. The average age of Traditionalists, for example, is fifty-three, and they are dying faster than they are being replaced. By contrast, individuals in the fast-growing Cultural Creatives group tend to be young, well educated, affluent, and assertive. (Interestingly, six out of ten are women.) They are on the cutting edge of social change, and if they are not already the dominant influence, they soon will be.

•   •   •

THE UPSHOT IS that the most significant clash of worldviews is not between traditional religions or cultures; it is between classic Christian theism and naturalism—in both its modernist and its rapidly growing postmodernist forms. The task for the Christian church appears daunting. But this should not discourage us, for our faith tells us that the truth will ultimately prevail. And as we will see in later chapters, even postmodernists are beginning to realize the inadequacy of their beliefs as they come face-to-face with the social chaos that naturalism breeds.

Christians must understand the clash of worldviews that is changing the face of American society. And we must stand ready to respond as people grow disillusioned with false beliefs and values and as they begin to seek real answers. We must know not only what our worldview is and why we believe it but also how to defend it. We must also have some understanding of the opposing worldviews and why people believe them. Only then can we present the gospel in language that can be understood. Only then can we defend truth in a way that is winsome and persuasive.

It can be done—as I discovered in the fall of 1996 during a trip to Sofia, Bulgaria, one of Europe's most impoverished countries, both materially and spiritually.

CHAPTER 4

CHRISTIAN TRUTH IN AN AGE OF UNBELIEF

False ideas are the greatest obstacles to the reception of the gospel. We may preach with all the fervor of a reformer and yet succeed only in winning a straggler here or there, if we permit the whole collective thought of a nation or of the world to be controlled by ideas which by the resistless force of logic, prevent Christianity from being regarded as anything more than a harmless delusion.

J. GRESHAM MACHEN

When I visited Bulgaria in 1996, not only was the country extremely poor, but it was also the last major Eastern European nation still in the grip of a Marxist regime. Though the Iron Curtain had fallen in 1989, communist officials in Bulgaria simply took new party labels, ran in the first free elections, and won. Most never even changed offices.

But while the government didn't change, the church did. A young Orthodox priest from Bulgaria, Father Nikolai, traveled to Poland to attend a Prison Fellowship training session and was gripped by a vision to work in prisons. After his return home, Father Nikolai built a thriving ministry with the help of 150 volunteers, all of whom worked and sacrificed to restore the chapel and to refurbish the antiquated hospital in the century-old prison in Sofia.

The purpose of my visit was to dedicate the hospital, and the event attracted an unexpectedly high level of interest. Government officials arrived in black limousines, joined by more than a hundred reporters, along with a crowd of local Prison Fellowship volunteers. Among the dignitaries was Bulgaria's minister of justice, who had remained an uncompromising communist.

In his official comments, the minister of justice praised Prison Fellowship profusely for supplying new cots, medicines, and operating-room equipment. But later, during the dedication ceremony, as Father Nikolai explained that the work was motivated by faith in God, the official drew furiously on his cigarette and was noticeably ill at ease. A dark, brooding young man, he kept shifting his position and staring into the distance, broadcasting to everyone that he, at least, had nothing to do with Father Nikolai, who was leading us in prayer in front of the brightly painted icons placed on the hospital steps. The official's disdain was so evident that even newspaper reports the next day mentioned it.

At a press conference following the dedication, I spoke on the theme that crime is ultimately a moral problem and that the solution, therefore, is moral reformation. The hospital we were dedicating that day would heal the body, I said, but the chapel would heal the soul. The minister of justice watched me intently as I spoke, and afterward he invited me to his office the next day.

So the next morning, accompanied by Father Nikolai and my associates, I arrived at the office of the minister of justice. He led us into a bare-walled conference room painted in characteristic communist drab green. But in a move uncharacteristic of officials of the Communist Party, who are always followed by nodding minions, he was alone. And what ensued was a remarkable conversation.

The official seated himself at the head of a long conference table, cigarette in hand, and immediately started firing questions in a brisk, businesslike voice, speaking flawless English. "Mr. Colson, yesterday you said crime is a moral problem. What do you mean by that? Do you say that in a sociological sense?"

"No," I said. "Crime is a matter of people choosing to do wrong. It is the individual's moral failure."

He demurred politely. "It seems to me that crime is caused by social and economic forces, that people respond to environmental conditions."

My turn to demur politely. "The moral dimension transcends social forces. People are genuine moral agents, and they make real moral choices." I cited several studies, including one showing that crime decreased during the great American religious revivals and one concluding that crimes are the result of "wrong moral choices."[1]

As our conversation continued, the outlines of the minister's own worldview became clear, and I could see why he was having trouble understanding me. Educated in a communist school system, he had been steeped in Marxist philosophy. In Marxism, human beings are merely a complex form of matter, and their identity lies in the way they relate to other forms of matter—that is, how they shape and make material things, or the means of production. Economics is the foundation, while everything else—culture, art, morality, religion—is mere superstructure, reflecting the dominant class's economic interests. Because of this, the minister couldn't even grasp what I meant by individuals making moral choices. "What I don't understand," he said, "is why some people know the law of the land but blatantly disregard it."

He set his cigarette pack on the table, using it to symbolize the barrier that the law sets up against certain behavior; then his hand jumped over the pack to illustrate a criminal ignoring the law. "It seems that only fear will stop people from committing crimes." And he alluded to Talleyrand, the nineteenth-century French foreign minister who hung corpses in the street every night to deter the restless masses from fomenting revolution.

"No, sir," I responded. "Fear does not stop people. If it did, no one would smoke." The official juggled his cigarette pack nervously, and we both smiled.

"Only love changes human behavior," I said. "If I love another person, I want to please him or her; if I love God, I want to please him and do what he wants. Only love can overcome our sinful self-centeredness."

I soon realized, however, that before I could even begin to explain biblical concepts to this man, I would have to engage in what the late Francis Schaeffer called "pre-evangelism." In other words, I would have to address the huge gap between his worldview and mine, the gap that kept him from grasping concepts such as sin and guilt, responsibility and forgiveness. For the next hour, I challenged the official's basic presuppositions.

I led off with Plato, a philosopher who would be familiar to him and who taught that there is a spiritual aspect to human nature. "At the core," I said, "people are spiritual beings, not pawns of economic forces." He arched his eyebrows at me as I challenged his most basic belief.

Then I explained the reality of the Fall and sin, so tragically evident in the horrors of the twentieth century, which, in naked evil, surpasses all previous centuries. Sin begins in the heart, I said, where it battles for control of our very being. And when the darker side of our nature prevails, we do wrong things. This is the source of crime.

At each point, trying to remain sensitive to his feelings, I gently rebutted the basic Marxist assumptions, showing how they fail to conform to the reality of human experience. I saw understanding slowing dawning in his eyes. It was as if a new world gradually opened to him, a new way to see human nature.

Finally he asked about my own life, and I shared the gospel, telling the story of how I met Jesus Christ in the darkest days of Watergate. Then I saw his face light up, as if a dark cloud had lifted, and for the first time he could see clearly. We even prayed together at the end of the meeting.[2]

PRE-EVANGELISM

My experience with the Bulgarian minister of justice illustrates the great gaps dividing worldviews and how we have to work to bridge them. Here was a man steeped in a view that rejects sin and promises utopia through social and economic revolution. So who needs salvation? Besides, the notion of God has been disproved by science, which explains life by purely natural causes. Religion is a fiction, an opiate for the masses. To get through to the young man, I had to challenge these presuppositions.

The church faces a similar task. For in many ways the church today must function like the first-century church, which crafted different approaches to Jews and Greeks. The Jews were steeped in the Old Testament Scriptures. They knew there was one God and that he was the Creator; they understood sin and guilt and sacrifice; they looked forward to the coming Messiah. The apostles were able to approach them by beginning with the message that Christ was, in fact, the awaited Messiah.

By contrast, the Greeks had no knowledge of Scripture, and the concepts of sin and redemption were not familiar to them. Their concept of "god" was a pantheon of deities who operated from human passions, merely on a grander scale. As a result, the apostles had to find a different starting point. The classic example is the apostle Paul's speech on Mars Hill in Athens, where he began by referring to one of the city's religious sites, an altar that bore the inscription "TO AN UNKNOWN GOD" (see Acts 17). Later he quoted Greek poetry: "As some of your own poets have said, 'We are his offspring'" (Acts 17:28). In other words, Paul appealed to his audience's own experience and literature to find a foothold in their understanding for the biblical message.

Even then, Paul didn't begin with salvation. He first laid a foundation with the doctrine of creation: "The God who made the world and everything in it is the Lord of heaven and earth" (Acts 17:24). He then argued that his listeners ought to understand for themselves that this God could not be like a gold or silver idol. For if he created them, then he must be a personal being, someone to whom they owed a personal allegiance—and someone to whom they were personally accountable. Only after establishing who God is and why we are morally responsible to him did Paul talk about repentance and Christ's resurrection.

Western culture once resembled the first-century Jewish culture: Most people knew the Scriptures, even if they weren't always obedient to its commands. Likewise, most Americans had some sort of church affiliation and knew the basic tenets of Christianity, even if they went to church only on Easter. But that is no longer the case. Today, many people are completely unfamiliar with even basic biblical teaching, and we must find ways to engage those who think more like Greeks than Jews. We must follow the New Testament pattern for addressing a pagan culture.

"Why not rely on the simple gospel?" some may ask. The answer is that God calls us to love people enough to go where they are—not only physically but also conceptually. We are to listen to their questions and frame answers they can understand. God is sovereign, of course, and can penetrate even the hardest heart with his Word. But we, as his instruments, are called to love people enough to reach out to them in their own language. This is, of course, what foreign missionaries do; and today, more than ever, we are aliens in our own land, worldview missionaries to our own post-Christian, postmodernist culture.

APOLOGETICS

Grasping Christianity as a worldview is important not only for pre-evangelism but also for apologetics. The apostle Peter tells us, "Always be prepared to give an answer to everyone who asks you to give the reason for the hope that you have" (1 Pet. 3:15). The word *answer* comes from the Greek word *apologia*, from which we get our word *apologetics*, meaning a defense or vindication of what we believe.

The late Henri Nouwen, when he was a professor at Harvard, asked me why I devoted half of a presentation at the Harvard Divinity School to apologetics—to evidence supporting the existence of God. "Christianity is like marriage," he said in his gentle way. "You can explain that you love Jesus the same way you love your wife."

"Yes, Henri, but they can *see* my wife," I replied. "They don't need me to convince them that she exists. But they do need reasons to believe that God exists."

The world can accept that we love Jesus—they can even acknowledge the social benefits of religion—and yet they can still think that he is merely a human or mythical figure. That's why we need to offer reasons for belief. While it is true that no one comes to God apart from faith, Christian faith is not an irrational leap. Examined objectively, the claims of the Bible are rational propositions well supported by reason and evidence. In fact, as we will argue throughout this book, all other explanations of reality are irrational. J. Gresham Machen, one of the great fundamentalist theologians in the early part of this century, said that the purpose of apologetics is to "mold the thought of the world in such a way as to make the acceptance of Christianity something more than a logical absurdity."[3]

But, you might ask, in a culture so hostile and hardened, can we really persuade others of the truth of Christianity? Yes, indeed, for we have a strong case to make, and people will listen if we cast it in terms of the questions they have.

Consider the common charge hurled against Christians—that they want to impose their views on others, restrict the liberty of others. My response whenever I hear this is to list the great martyrs who brought down the Soviet Union, pointing out the "odd coincidence" that the overwhelming majority were members of the clergy. The truth is that Christians vigorously defend the persecuted because they believe human rights are God-given.

The responsibility for apologetics is not limited to Christian pastors or intellectuals. When I challenge people to learn how to defend their faith and "think christianly," they often respond, "Oh, I'm not up to this," or "It's too deep for me." But God has created each of us with a mind, with the capacity to study, think, and ask questions. No one is an expert in every area, but each of us can master the subjects in which we have some experience.

If our culture is to be transformed, it will happen from the bottom up—from ordinary believers practicing apologetics over the backyard fence or around the barbecue grill. To be sure, it's important for Christian scholars to conduct research and hold academic symposia, but the real leverage for cultural change comes from transforming the habits and dispositions of ordinary people.

And let us always bear in mind the final words of Peter's admonition—that when we give reasons for our hope, we do so "with gentleness and respect" (1 Pet. 3:15). A living example of the right attitude is Ron Greer, an ex-offender who once hated all white people but then was gloriously converted and is now a Prison Fellowship instructor and pastor of an evangelical church in Madison, Wisconsin. Greer was dismissed from his regular job at a fire department for passing out Christian tracts describing homosexuality as a sin. Madison's homosexual activists were enraged and stormed into Greer's church, disrupting the service, throwing condoms at the altar, and shouting obscenities. Ron Greer responded by graciously inviting them to join in the worship service.

Later, when the press asked how he had kept his cool, he smiled and said, "I have no more reason to be angry with them than I would with a blind man who stepped on my foot." Precisely. Most of those who object to Christianity are simply spiritually blind, and our job is lovingly to help bring them into the light.

THE CULTURAL COMMISSION

Understanding Christianity as a worldview is important not only for fulfilling the great commission but also for fulfilling the cultural commission—the call to create a culture under the lordship of Christ. God cares not only about redeeming souls but also about restoring his creation. He calls us to be agents not only of his saving grace but also of his common grace. Our job is not only to build up the church but also to build a society to the glory of God.

Though we live in a pluralistic society, we serve a God who is sovereign over all, and all aspects of personal and social life are at their best when they reflect his character. All citizens live better in a world that more closely conforms to reality, to the order God created. Making such prudential arguments is a much more effective way to reform or rebuild a culture than mounting political campaigns. Changing laws to conform to biblical standards of righteousness is a crucial task, of course, but the law alone cannot reform the heart or change behavior. How people live is determined more by their shared values, and this in turn is changed by patient persuasion and example.

When advancing the biblical perspective in public debate, we ought to interpret biblical truth in ways that appeal to the common good. So although we believe that Scripture is God's inerrant revelation, we do not have to derive all arguments directly from Scripture.

For example, when I argue in state legislatures that criminals should be required to pay restitution to their victims, I do not say, "Do this because the Bible says so." Rather, I present it as sound public policy. It makes sense to give back what you have taken, to restore what you have destroyed. (Almost always, someone will ask me where the idea came from, and then I say, "Go home and check your Bible. Read Exodus 22 or the New Testament story of Zacchaeus.")

Yet whenever I write about the need to use reasoned arguments in the public square, I can count on a barrage of letters from shocked readers, asking, "Isn't the Bible adequate for salvation? Doesn't the Bible tell us that the Word will not return void?" The answer is that of course God's Word is sufficient for salvation—for *saving grace*. But here we are talking about *common grace*—that is, carrying out God's work of maintaining creation by promoting righteousness and restraining evil. To do this, we must translate God's revelation into the language of the world. We must be able to speak to the scientist in the language of science, to the artist in the language of art, to the politician in the language of politics.[6]

DISCIPLESHIP OF THE MIND

The Christian calling is not only to save souls but also to save minds. In the words of Harry Blamires, a student of C. S. Lewis, "There is no room in Christendom for a culture of the spirit which neglects the mind."[4] That notion might sound alien to many people, but it is surely biblical. The greatest commandment, Jesus says, is to "love the Lord your God with all your heart and with all your soul and with all your *mind*" (Matt. 22:37, emphasis added). Loving the Lord with your *mind* means understanding God's ordinances for all of creation, for the natural world, for societies, for businesses, for schools, for the government, for science, for the arts. The apostle Paul tells us to take "every thought captive to the obedience of Christ" (2 Cor. 10:5, NASB). Offer your bodies as "a living and holy sacrifice," he also says, and then explains that this means we must not "be conformed to this world, but be transformed by the renewing of [our] mind" (Rom. 12:1-2, NASB).

Sadly, many Christians have been misled into believing there is a dichotomy between faith and reason, and as a result they have actually shunned intellectual pursuits. In *The Christian Mind,* Blamires stated the problem succinctly in his opening sentence: "There is no longer a Christian mind."[5] What he meant was that evangelicals have not developed a distinctively Christian perspective on all of life. Recently, Wheaton College historian Mark Noll made a similar point in *The Scandal of the Evangelical Mind.*

Today we must break down this false dichotomy between the spiritual and the intellectual and recover the calling to save minds—especially in our highly educated society. Unlike a generation ago, churches today are filled with college graduates; in fact, polls show that evangelicals are better educated than the general populace, a striking change from forty years ago. Pastors must begin to redefine their task to include intellectual evangelism, for if they do not preach to issues of the mind, they will find themselves increasingly alienated from their own flock.[6]

This is not a burdensome task—one more thing to whip ourselves into doing. I have found that developing a Christian mind is a rewarding and enriching act of discipleship. Back when I was in college, I was a moderately

good student, at least in subjects I enjoyed, like history and political philosophy. But studying was work for me, even drudgery at times, particularly
when it conflicted with fraternity parties. In law school, I was at the top of
my class, but rarely because of genuine intellectual curiosity; I simply wanted
to be the best at my profession. But after my conversion to Christianity, I felt
a keen desire to learn about God's work throughout history. Dr. Richard
Lovelace, a professor from Gordon-Conwell Seminary, began tutoring me
in church history, and I found it enthralling. It was like having my mind
born again, along with my spirit. History and literature and science all took
on new meaning because I began to see these disciplines as explorations of
God's truth. I found it exciting to be able to see through all the pretensions
of the philosophies I had studied in college. It was as if a searchlight were
shone into a cave, exposing the dark holes and crevices.

My intellectual curiosity has not abated. When I read about the history
of modern liberalism, for example, or Renaissance art or ancient understand-
ings of law, I am not merely absorbing knowledge for its own sake. I am understanding God's creative handiwork. I am witnessing God's great morality
drama that we call human history. And I am learning new ways to defend
God's truth.

It is especially crucial to cultivate the mind in order to avoid the snares
and expose the false values of modern culture. Every day we face attempts to
seduce us into worshiping the idols of modern life, sometimes cleverly disguised. For example, two years ago, one television network produced a
Christmas movie advertised as pure family entertainment. A huge picture of
Julie Harris, costumed as a nun, adorned the cover of the newspaper's TV
section, with rave reviews inside. "A warm holiday drama," gushed one reviewer, "calculated to tap comforting memories."

Assuming that a story about a nun would carry some Christian message and wanting to "tap comforting memories," I gathered the Colson clan
to watch *Christmas Tree*. But the story that unfolded was more about nature
worship than about Christianity. The plot involved an abandoned, psychologically disturbed child who was drawn almost mystically to a particular
pine tree. Eventually she entered a religious order because she wanted to
spend her life caring for the tree. When the disturbed child, now miraculously transformed, was asked what turned her life around, she said, "It was
the tree."

I do not recall a single reference to Jesus or even to God in the entire
wearisome two hours. The film was blatant naturalism: Nature will "save" us
and give our lives meaning; the tree is the naturalistic messiah.

Often the message is much more subtle. For example, you may

remember Saab's "Find your own road" campaign in the mid-nineties. "You are having lunch with a large man who just happens to be your boss," said one ad. The boss makes a statement you know to be in error. "What do you do?" The voice-over offered two options: a polite, respectful response or "Come on, J. B., blow it out your ear." Four out of five Saab owners, the ad confided, would choose the latter. In other words, tell the stuffy old establishment to chuck it, and "find your own road," do your own thing. Along with selling cars, Saab was selling a philosophy of autonomy and rebellion against authority. (The sequel to this story shows that Christians can make a difference. After I broadcast a *BreakPoint* program criticizing the ad, I received a call from Saab's U.S. president, who happened to be a serious Christian, telling me the ads were being withdrawn.)

.   ▪   ▪

J. GRESHAM MACHEN challenged his Princeton seminary students in a charge every Christian today should take to heart: "You can avoid the debate [over contested issues of the faith] if you choose. You need only drift with the current. Preach every Sunday during your seminary course, study as you studied in college—and these questions will probably never trouble you. The great questions may be easily avoided. Many preachers are avoiding them. And many preachers are preaching to the air." Then Machen added: "The church is waiting for men of another type."[7]

As we begin the new millennium, the mission for Christians is nothing less than becoming men and women of "another type." We must be men and women who will dare to wrest Christianity free from its fortress mentality, its sanctuary stronghold, and establish it once again as the great life system and cultural force that acknowledges the Creator as sovereign over all. We must be men and women who understand that the task is much more than launching spasmodic crusades to fight one battle or another—be it gay rights or abortion. We must be men and women who see, as Kuyper did, that the struggle is one of first principles. "If the battle is to be fought with honor and with a hope of victory, then principle must be arrayed against principle." We must understand opposing views as total life systems and then "take our stand in a life system of equally comprehensive and far-reaching power."[8]

The contours of a Christian life system will become clear in the four sections that follow: *creation*—God spoke the universe into existence and created humanity in his image; *fall*—the human condition is marred by sin; *redemption*—God in his grace provided a way to be reconciled to himself; and *restoration*—we are called to bring these principles into every area of life and create a new culture. Equipped with this understanding, we can show not only that the Christian worldview gives the best answers—answers that accord with common sense and the most advanced science—but also that Christians can take up spiritual arms in the great cosmic struggle between conflicting worldviews.

Dare we believe that Christianity can yet prevail? We must believe it. As we stated at the outset, this is an historic moment of opportunity, and when the church is faithful to its calling, it always leads to a reformation of culture. When the church is truly the church, a community living in biblical obedience and contending for faith in every area of life, it will surely revive the surrounding culture or create a new one.[9]

Religion is not a reflection or product of culture, but quite the reverse. As the great twentieth-century historian Christopher Dawson argued, cult is at the root of culture (taking "cult" in its most basic meaning as a system of religious worship). The late political philosopher Russell Kirk agreed: "It's from association in a cult, a body of worshipers, that human community grows."[10]

The oyster offers a good analogy. Oysters make their own shells, so if the shell is badly formed, the problem is not in the shell but in the oyster. Likewise, when a culture deforms and decays, don't ask what went wrong with the culture; ask what went wrong with the cult—the religious core. "When belief in the cult has been wretchedly enfeebled, the culture will decay swiftly," Kirk wrote. "The material order rests on the spiritual order."[11]

The hope for today's world is a renewed and vibrant spiritual order, a culture-creating cult, men and women of another type, arrayed for the great battle of principle against principle. A battle that begins, "In the beginning. . . ."

CREATION: WHERE DID WE COME FROM, AND WHO ARE WE?

DAVE AND KATY'S METAPHYSICAL ADVENTURE

By day four, the last day of their once-in-a-lifetime trip together, Dave Mulholland and his fifteen-year-old daughter, Katy, had memorized the turnoffs along Disney World Drive: Pleasure Island, River Country, Discovery Island, Disney MGM Studios, and the Magic Kingdom itself. Today they were pressing on to Epcot Center to have "a look at the future," as the brochure advertised.[1]

Disney World Drive itself was as broad as Interstate 4, Dave marveled, with its own castle-marked, fireworks-bursting signs. It was like entering a foreign but familiar country. The idea behind the trip had been for Dave to draw closer to his daughter, to get behind the emotional walls she had thrown up over the past year. And in their wanderings through this Luxembourg of the fantastic, he had felt he was reconnecting with her. Until today. It was Sunday, and Dave had irritated Katy by insisting that they attend church. Now his daughter's stiff silence made him hyperaware of the rental car's four-cylinder, sewing-machine whine.

Suddenly Katy broke her silence. "You think we really saw as much of Disney World as we wanted?" she asked, with just a hint of petulance. "The lines might not be as long today for The Haunted House."

"I want to see Epcot Center," Dave said. "I've heard you have to spend most of the day there to do it justice."

"Dad, *I* told you that this morning." She sighed extravagantly, crossed her arms, and wedged herself back against the door. David knew she was making a show of pouting. And he knew why.

"Look, Katy, the worship service took only an hour. We're still going to be there when the gates open."

She looked pointedly out the window. "Most people just skip church on vacation, Dad. I wanted to sleep in."

Their resort had offered an ecumenical service, and listening to the sentimental, candy-cane sermon, Dave had grimaced inwardly, even feeling a bit guilty for having dragged his daughter out of bed for *this*. But he had reminded himself that at least he was making a testimony about putting first things first. They had gone to church! Now he realized that his great idea had only reinjected much of the tension they had come here to smooth away.

He turned into the exit for Epcot Center and headed for the parking lot.

"Okay," Katy said, picking up her line of argument, "but if this stinks, can we bail? We can just take the monorail over and—"

"If it stinks, we'll be sure to stay until nightfall," Dave teased. "Because personally, you know, I'm down here to have as *bad* a time as possible. I'm really hoping this Epcot thing is *excruciating*."

"Oh, Dad," she groaned. But he sensed some of her anger dissipating.

He paid for their parking ticket and turned back to her. "You know, hon, this is probably the last spring break you'll have time for your male parental unit. I'm glad you wanted to come. Let's have a good day, okay?"

Before he had finished parking, he heard her seat belt unlatch. She leaned across the console and kissed his cheek. "It's been the best," she said.

Kids' moods turn on a dime, Dave thought. *Thank you, Lord.*

"Let's go, then," he said.

The great globe of AT&T's "Spaceship Earth," Epcot's symbol, loomed ahead, but the waiting lines were already filled with people. Dave and Katy had learned to hit second-choice rides or exhibits first; at the start of the day, most visitors were determined to check the big ones off their lists. So the two of them made their way to "The Living Seas."

The exhibit was housed in a building whose curvilinear design evoked waves upon a shore. Inside a blue-green room with low lighting were exhibits of antiquated diving gear and photos of early submarines and diving pools. Dave and Katy hurried through the display, urged forward by an omnipresent recorded voice inviting them to enter a theater where they would witness the birth of the seas.

In the semicircular theater they took their seats, and as they waited for the program to begin, Dave glanced proudly at his daughter. Her pretty, girlish face was acquiring new touches of a more dramatic, womanly beauty, but underneath, he knew, was still a confused mixture of fear and bravado.

Dave and his wife, Claudia, had sensed that Katy was in trouble. It wasn't only the marijuana they had found in her purse, though that in itself had sent them reeling. Worse, they felt they were losing her to a secular world smugly satisfied with itself and deeply hostile to their own. And what stabbed most deeply was that Katy herself was becoming more and more antagonistic to their religious beliefs, to the point where she resisted any involvement in the church's high school group and the Sunday worship services. This from a girl who at age nine had responded to an altar call and given her life to Jesus with free-flowing tears of joy.

The theater darkened, and Dave's attention was drawn to a man with a handheld mike. "Ocean exploration has come a long way," the man intoned. "But how did the ocean form? When did it form? The answers to those and many other questions are about to surface in a dramatic film simply titled, 'The Sea.'"

With a wave of sound, screens lit up all around, and the audience was surrounded by vivid images. First, the dark eeriness of outer space, suddenly punctuated by countless white spots of brilliance, while a voice invited the audience to imagine a place "somewhere in the endless reaches of the universe, on the other edge of the galaxy of a hundred-thousand-million suns." In this tiny corner of the universe, the mesmerizing voice went on, "deep within the cluster of slowly forming planets," is "a small sphere of just the right size," a sphere "just the right distance from its mother star."

The right size and the right distance for what? Dave was caught up by the spectacular sights unfolding before his eyes, but something pricked his attention in those words. *Just right for life, I suppose,* he thought. Though of course Earth didn't just *happen* to have the right conditions for life; God made it that way, as his faith had taught him. He wondered whether Disney would give even a token nod to the Creator behind it all.

But Dave had little time for reflection. Action was erupting on the huge screen again, where the molten Earth was being shown as a young planet, slowly cooling. It spawned thousands of volcanoes, spewing out gases and steam until the planet was swathed in clouds. The roar of the great eruptions shook the entire room.

Finally, the recorded voice broke in again: "And then the clouds of gas and steam condense and rain upon the planet." Dave heard a sudden, loud rush of rain, so realistic he thought it was pelting the roof of the theater. "Rain and rain and rain," the voice continued, more intensely now. "A deluge!" Torrents of water washed down bare slopes of the lifeless planet.

Finally, the seas themselves were born, green waters foaming and churning; and here, the voice said, began the greatest mystery of the universe: life itself. From the play of chemicals in the primeval ocean arose "tiny, single-celled plants that captured the energy of the sun," producing the oxygen required for the more advanced organisms to evolve.

Once again Dave was strangely uneasy. Like the science programs he had watched on television, this one made it sound as if God had nothing to do with any of this, that nature by itself had the power to create the universe and the wonders of life on Earth.

Dave hazarded a sidelong glance at Katy to see if she was at all troubled. But her eyes were fastened to the screen, her uplifted face entranced. And suddenly it struck him that she had no reason to be troubled because she had been hearing the message of evolution all her life from textbooks, teachers, and TV science programs.

When the film ended, they were ushered into "hydrolators," escalator-type contraptions that plunged down to another set of exhibits. There, Katy was delighted with the gigantic aquarium, where divers were training dolphins to communicate with humans. But Dave remained haunted by the image of blue-green seas generating primeval forms of life. Maybe this was one reason for the barrier that had grown up between him and Katy. Was she so inundated with images of a universe without any need for God that she was questioning her faith? Was her rebellion against him and her mother coming from deeper doubts about whether the Bible was true?

When they emerged from "The Living Seas" exhibit, Dave resorted to humor to break through his obsessive thoughts. He looped Katy's arm through his and strutted like Rex Harrison playing Doctor Dolittle as he sang "If I Could Talk to the Animals."

"*Doctor Dolittle* wasn't a Disney film, Dad," Katy said.

"I don't care. Sing with me."

She was game, and they staged their own little parade, zigzagging down the asphalt, singing under their breath at first and then louder as several passersby offered mock applause.

As they broke apart and stood for a moment laughing, Dave thought of Katy's childhood, when he had called her Miss Disney. During grammar school she had sported Goofy sweatshirts and carried her Minnie Mouse lunch box, even when her friends had moved on to the Ninja Turtles. All of which had led to this moment, for Katy had always longed to come to Disney World, and that almost forgotten wish had resurfaced in Dave's and Claudia's minds as they groped for a way to make her feel special.

Shaking off these memories, Dave steered her toward "The Universe of

Energy," with its towering topiary in the shape of a dinosaur. They settled quickly into seats in a large movie theater, where Bill-Nye-the-Science-Guy was soon taking them on an imaginary tour of the history of energy. He started at the ultimate beginning—pointing to a spot where the universe was about to come into existence through the big bang. A spot of light expanded into a thunderous crashing flood as stars exploded and galaxies formed.

Once again, niggling questions began whispering in Dave's mind: What was there *before* the big bang? And how were all the millions of people who trooped through Epcot every year affected when they saw the history of the universe retold in completely natural terms, as if God were irrelevant and unnecessary? More important, what impact was it having on his own daughter?

Just then Katy gasped as the theater seats began to move under them, transforming sections of seating into a thrill-ride minitrain. Bill Nye had transported them to the age of the dinosaurs, explaining that fossil fuels had come from this era millions of years ago in Earth's history. Then a giant comet crashed into the earth, raising a global dust cloud, and the age of the dinosaurs was over.

The moveable seats carried them along to another era, featuring a mock celestial media station with reporters describing a "major upset," the victory of mammals over the dinosaurs in the survival of the fittest. Suddenly another reporter broke in with a news update about the Ice Age, explaining the need for creatures to evolve thick skins and heavy wool coats. That was followed in quick succession by another reporter, who had scooped a story about the glaciers of the Ice Age retreating to the polar circles, making conditions favorable for the emergence of a "whole new kind of creature."

What kind of creature? "Our early ancestors," Bill Nye announced—a creature that screamed like an ape as it kindled a fire.

Dave winced. There it was again—the notion that human beings emerged from a long line of evolutionary forebears through survival of the fittest. No place for the God of the Bible. Just creatures emerging from the slime by chance, as if natural selection were our creator.

The rest of the exhibit covered the various types of energy resources—solar, wind, nuclear, coal, and petroleum—until finally, the trainlike auditorium seats reassembled themselves into a theater.

Relieved that it was over, Dave said, "Let's get lunch."

As he and Katy sat at an outdoor table and munched on their sandwiches, Dave resorted to commenting on the weather. "Sure seems hotter today." But that wasn't what he really wanted to say. Time was running out for the heart-to-heart talk he had planned to have with Katy on this trip, yet he didn't know how to launch it. The heat seemed to sizzle into his emotions. He knew the only way was to force himself simply to plunge in.

"I told you I wanted to have at least one serious talk before we go back. Remember?" He paused briefly. "How about now?"

Katy looked wary. "Are you and Mom still worried about the purse thing?"

"That wasn't good."

"Come on, Dad. You didn't have to bring me down here to convince me not to do marijuana. I only tried it once."

Dave fiddled with his diet Coke. "I worry about *why* you did it," he said finally.

"You and Mom don't trust me. You act as if I'm ten years old. You have no idea. . . . You should see how some of my friends act."

"Oh, I have some idea. I won't bore you with tales of my years in high school, but I do remember what it was like."

"Could we just get back to being on vacation here? It's almost over." Katy tilted her head back and pursed her lips.

"I don't know how to explain exactly why I'm worried, Katy. You *are* a good kid. But I am worried."

"That's your job as a parent, isn't it? And I mean, you are very, *very* good at it. But it's okay, Dad." She grinned at him. She could win him in an instant.

Suddenly, Dave lost all sense of where he wanted this conversation to go. He had to admit that he had seen none of the typical symptoms of drug use in Katy. No, it wasn't the marijuana episode he was really concerned about. It was something else that had been worrying him, and it had been brought into focus at Epcot. He was concerned most of all about the state of Katy's spiritual life.

After they left the restaurant, they circled around a lagoon and came to the Norway exhibit, which included a tall, medieval-looking wooden structure shingled in elaborate layers and appearing strangely out of place in this Land of the Future. Dave grabbed Katy's hand and headed inside. There they were greeted by recorded music, not the usual blare but gentle strains of hymns. The interior was tiny and dark, the light drifting in from openings high up in the steeply sloped ceiling. A placard indicated that the building was a *stave kirke,* a reproduction of Norway's famous twelfth-century wooden churches. Photos of genuine stave churches lined the walls. In one glass case lay an elaborately worked gold crucifix with Christ robed in blue.

The exhibit was intended as a historical artifact, a museum piece of ancient history. But Dave lingered, suddenly aware of an ethereal quality permeating the dim light, a subtle memory of the days when Christian faith was robust, even heroic.

Katy began fidgeting. "Come on, let's go," she whispered. "There's nothing here."

"Nothing?" Dave asked, without turning around.

"No rides or anything. Let's go."

"In a minute."

Katy snorted and stalked outside. Dave murmured a quick prayer and followed her. But his serious mood was hard to break. As he stopped at a vendor and bought some ice cream and then headed for a nearby bench, he could tell that Katy sensed the change in his mood and knew she could no longer put off "the big talk."

"So why don't you want to go to church with us anymore?" he said, deciding to jump in with both feet. "What have you got against Christianity?"

Katy turned her head aside. "I don't have anything against it."

"You act as if you're going to die every time we get near anything that has to do with it. You did in there just now."

"Dad, do we have to talk about this? I thought we were just supposed to be here—"

"No," he interrupted, "we aren't *just* supposed to be here on vacation. Your mom and I planned this so that you and I could have some time to talk. That's the hidden agenda. So let's have that talk before we get off this park bench."

Katy attacked her ice cream, her eyes fixed on the dish.

"Look, Katy, your whole attitude toward spiritual things has changed. I want to know what you're thinking."

She took a long breath, then said, "It's just that I don't want to be so different. And I don't have to be," she added in a rush. "I can be a good person without believing the things you believe."

"Different from what?"

"Different from *everybody.*" She waved her hands as if to take in everyone at Disney World. "Hardly anybody believes what you and Mom believe. I have lots of friends who are good people, and they aren't religious."

Katy's words were like barbs piercing his heart, but at least she was talking, at least she was finally opening up to him.

"I don't think it's a question of what anyone *believes*," Dave said after a painful pause. "Not even what Mom and I believe. It's a question of what's *true.*"

"How does anyone know what's really true?"

"A lot of people think *they* know what's true. We just spent the day going to exhibits where a whole bunch of ideas were presented as true."

"That's science, Dad," Katy said patiently, as if teaching a child. "Science is things that are proved."

"Most of it was more like philosophy, Katy."

"No, it wasn't."

"Yes, it was. Most of the exhibits here share one version of the truth, even when they're talking about different things. It's a story more than anything, and it goes like this: By chance the universe came into existence, by chance Earth was just right for life to exist, by chance life developed into birds and bees and butterflies, by chance human beings came along, and by chance human beings turned out to be so smart that all the world's problems will someday succumb to our technological prowess. End of story. Hallelujah, amen."

"But scientists can prove all that, Dad. No one can know for sure about God."

"Come on, how can anyone 'prove' that the universe came about by chance? Everything I know about the universe, including my incredibly beautiful daughter, indicates to me that Somebody designed it. Created it." All the questions that had been eating at Dave's mind from the time they entered "The Living Seas" were finally taking shape.

"My biology teacher says . . . he says that's our ego talking. People want to believe they're important, so they invent religion. They invent the idea of a God who created them so they'll feel better."

"You really think life came about by chance?"

"It's chemicals. It's *all* chemicals. We *saw* how it happened in 'The Living Seas' exhibit. Volcanoes erupting, then the ocean, then chemicals coming together. Scientists have done it in a test tube. I read about it in my science book. I even saw a photo of this thing with glass tubes and electrical sparks and then, you know, molecules came out."

Katy flopped back against the bench, and Dave put his head in his hands. So that was it. She had been so indoctrinated with a secular view of the world, a view backed by the prestige of "science," that Christianity no longer made sense to her. He saw it now. But what could he say to make her change her mind?

"I just can't believe this beautiful world came about by chance." He said it again, more out of desperation than out of any hope that it would make a difference.

"If what you believe is true, Dad, then how come no one else believes it? Listen, last semester in English class we saw a movie called *Inherit the*

Wind, and you could see that all the scientists are on the side of Darwin. Christians just close their minds to the facts of science."

Dave sucked in his breath. He felt as if he had been hit in the chest. It made him angry. "Come on, Katy. You know we didn't come from the monkeys." It was a pretty weak response, but it was the best he could muster on the spur of the moment.

Katy looked away without answering.

In despair, Dave realized that he didn't even know how to begin tackling this subject with his daughter. He knew very little about Darwin or evolution. All he really knew—what he felt instinctively—was that if you dismissed God as the Creator, then the whole foundation of faith dissolved. He decided to take a different tack.

"When you went forward in church and became a Christian, Katy . . . doesn't that mean anything to you anymore?" he asked.

Katy bit her knuckle. "I've thought about that—a lot. But how can you trust how you feel in those situations? I mean, I get emotional when I'm watching a movie, and *that's* not real."

"Katy, the two are hardly the same. Giving your life to Christ and . . . and watching a movie."

"All I know is, you and Mom expect me to believe what you believe. If I go to church and pretend to be happy about it, we'll get along. If I don't, you get all serious and make everyone miserable. Just like this trip. It's as if you're blackmailing me."

"Katy, I . . ."

"Do you really love *me,* Dad? The Katy you're talking to right now? Because this is the real me. I'm not the little girl you have in your head."

"Wait a minute. Don't I have a right to disagree with your ideas without you accusing me of not loving you? Who's doing the blackmailing here?"

"They're not just *my* ideas, Dad. They're what I learned in school. They're what everyone believes—even what we saw in the exhibits today. And you can't argue with that."

On that point, she was right, Dave thought grimly. He couldn't argue with *that,* because he didn't know how to begin to counter what she was saying. His daughter seemed to be throwing away her faith, and he had no idea how to stop her. But what he said next came out of a place much deeper than his own frustration and helplessness.

"I'll find out."

"What?"

"I'll find out how to argue with it. I'll find out why the story we heard here today is wrong."

She rolled her eyes scornfully. "Oh come—"

"Or I'll give up my faith, too," he concluded.

She started, as if he had slapped her. Then suddenly she dropped her mock sophistication. "Oh Dad, I don't want . . . you know, *everything* to change."

"But *everything* is at stake here, Katy. That's what you've got to realize. Everything is at stake. Look, if Christianity is true, then it's not my belief or your mother's belief. It's the truth about *reality,* about what is ultimately real. And somehow I am going to find the facts that will show you it's true."

CHAPTER 6

SHATTERING THE GRID

The chief aim of all investigations of the external world should be to discover the rational order and harmony which has been imposed on it by God.
                                                                JOHANNES KEPLER

What hit Dave Mulholland hard in the days that followed his vacation with Katy was the realization that his daughter had soaked up a way of thinking that was totally contrary to all he and Claudia had taught her. And he had discovered this at Disney World, of all places, where each year more than forty million people visit, waiting in line to be thrilled, dazzled, and educated. Many families scrimp all year so they can afford to take their kids to this Magic Kingdom, this great American icon.

And for what? Dave asked himself grimly. To experience this paean to secularism, this altar to the power of human ingenuity and technology?

But at least he now understood what had happened to his daughter. She had absorbed the idea that science is the source of truth, while religion is merely subjective opinion, something we tolerate for those weak enough to need that kind of comfort. And for the first time, he realized that he had been foolishly overconfident. He had allowed his daughter to be exposed to these ideas in school, on television, and in her books without ever bothering to teach her how to respond.

Perhaps this was not surprising. Dave's own generation had not had to weather such pervasive challenges to Christian faith. For them, religion had been respected, part of the establishment. Dave had never experienced the anguish of doubt. He had always been satisfied with just going to church and holding a set of beliefs that made sense of life.

But now everything had changed. Now he needed to defend what he believed. For his daughter's sake, if not for his own.

"These are not just *my* ideas, Dad," Katy had argued that day at Disney World. "They're what I learned in school. They're what everyone believes."

IS NATURE OUR CREATOR?

Katy was right. The dominant view in our culture today is radically one-dimensional: that this life is all there is, and nature is all we need to explain everything that exists. This is, at heart, the philosophy of naturalism, and not only has it permeated the classroom curriculum, but it has also been expressed widely in popular culture, from Disney World to television nature shows to children's books.

Every worldview has to begin somewhere, has to begin with a theory of how the universe began. Naturalism begins with the fundamental assumption that the forces of nature alone are adequate to explain everything that exists. Whereas the Bible says, "In the beginning God created the heavens and the earth" (Gen. 1:1), naturalists say that in the beginning were the particles, along with blind, purposeless natural laws. That nature created the universe out of nothing, through a quantum fluctuation. That nature formed our planet, with its unique ability to support life. That nature drew together the chemicals that formed the first living cell. And naturalism says that nature acted through Darwinian mechanisms to evolve complex life-forms and, finally, human beings, with the marvels of consciousness and intelligence.

Naturalistic scientists try to give the impression that they are fair-minded and objective, implying that religious people are subjective and biased in favor of their personal beliefs. But this is a ruse, for naturalism is as much a philosophy, a worldview, a personal belief system as any religion is.

Naturalism begins with premises that cannot be tested empirically, such as the assumption that nature is "all that is or ever was or ever will be," to use a line from the late Carl Sagan's popular science program *Cosmos*. This is not a scientific statement, for there is no conceivable way it could be tested. It is a philosophy. And as we will see throughout the rest of this section, it is the philosophy that supports the entire evolutionary enterprise, from its assertions about the beginning of the universe to the beginning of life to the appearance of complex life-forms.

As much as anyone else, it was Sagan who popularized the naturalistic worldview and entrenched it firmly in the mind of the average American.

The dark hair swept to one side, the Colgate smile, the telegenic personality—it all added up to a powerful influence on the millions of viewers who tuned in to his PBS program *Cosmos*. Week after week, he brought stunning images of exploding stars and sprawling nebulae into homes and classrooms across the nation.

But that's not all Sagan brought. With his engaging manner, he was a televangelist for naturalism, a philosophy he held with religious fervor. And logically so, for whatever you take as the starting point of your worldview does function, in effect, as your religion.[1]

Take Sagan's trademark phrase, "The Cosmos is all that is or ever was or ever will be" (the opening line in *Cosmos,* his book based on the television series).[2] Here, Sagan is capitalizing on liturgical forms. Ever since the early church, Christians have sung the Gloria Patri: "Glory be to the Father, and to the Son, and to the Holy Ghost; As it was in the beginning, is now, and ever shall be, world without end." Sagan is clearly offering a substitute liturgy, a cadence to the cosmos. The sheer fact that he capitalizes the word *Cosmos,* just as religious believers capitalize the word *God,* is a dead giveaway that he is gripped by religious fervor.

In Sagan's television program and books, he makes it clear that he has no use for the transcendent Creator revealed in the Bible. The cosmos is his deity. In one of his many best-selling books, Sagan mockingly describes the Christian God as "an outsized, light-skinned male with a long white beard, sitting on a throne somewhere up there in the sky, busily tallying the fall of every sparrow."[3] Sagan regards the cosmos as the only self-existing, eternal being: "A universe that is infinitely old requires no Creator."[4]

On point after point, Sagan offers a naturalistic substitute for traditional religion. While Christianity teaches that we are children of God, Sagan says that "we are, in the most profound sense, children of the Cosmos," for it is the cosmos that gave us birth and daily sustains us.[5] In a passage that is almost certainly autobiographical, Sagan hints that the astronomer's urge to explore the cosmos is motivated by a mystical recognition that the chemicals in our bodies were originally forged in space—that outer space is our origin and our true home: "Some part of our being knows this is from where we came. We long to return."[6] And the astronomer's "awe" is nothing less than religious worship. "Our ancestors worshiped the Sun, and they were far from foolish." For if we must worship something, "does it not make sense to revere the Sun and the stars?"[7]

Like any religion, Sagan's worship of the cosmos prescribes certain moral duties for its adherents. The cosmos has created human life in its own image—"Our matter, our form, and much of our character is determined by the deep connection between life and the Cosmos"—and in return, we have a moral duty to the cosmos.[8] What is that duty? It is an "obligation to survive," an obligation we owe "to that Cosmos, ancient and vast, from which we spring."[9]

Sagan's worship of the cosmos even tells us how to be saved. Threats to human survival—pollution, war, food shortages—have nothing to do with moral failings. Instead, they result from technological incompetence, Sagan writes, which is hardly surprising since he believes that humanity is still in its evolutionary childhood.[10] As a result, the solutions may well come from more advanced civilizations somewhere out there, descending to Earth to save us. For this reason Sagan was an avid supporter of efforts to scan the far reaches of space for radio messages.[11] "The receipt of a single message from space would show that it is possible to live through such technological adolescence," he writes breathlessly, for it would prove that an advanced extraterrestrial race has survived the same stage and gone on to maturity.[12]

If this isn't a vision of salvation, what is? The cosmos will speak to us. It is there, and it is not silent.

In every human being is a deep, ongoing search for meaning and transcendence—part of the image of God in our very nature. Even if we flee God, the religious imprint remains. Everyone worships some kind of god. Everyone believes in some kind of deity—even if that deity is an impersonal substance such as matter, energy, or nature. That's why the Bible preaches against idolatry, not atheism. Naturalism may parade as science, marshaling facts and figures, but it is a religion.

This religion is being taught everywhere in the public square today—even in the books your child reads in school or checks out of the public library. Not long ago, Nancy picked up a Berenstain Bears book for her young son. In the book, the Bear family invites the young reader to join them for a nature walk. We start out on a sunny morning, and after running into a few spiderwebs, we read in capital letters sprawled across a sunrise, glazed with light rays, those familiar words: Nature is "all that IS, or WAS, or EVER WILL BE!"[13]

Sound familiar? Of course. It is Sagan's famous opening line, now framed in cute images of little bears and bugs and birds—the philosophy of naturalism peddled for toddlers. And to drive the point home, the authors have drawn a bear pointing directly at the reader—your impressionable young child—and saying, "Nature is you! Nature is me!"[14] Human beings, too, are nothing more than parts of nature.

Is there any more poignant example of why Christians need to learn how to argue persuasively against naturalism? It is pressed on our children's imaginations long before they can think rationally and critically. It is presented everywhere as the only worldview supported by science. And it is diametrically opposed to Christianity.

The Christian must be ready to separate genuine science from philosophy. Evolution, as it is typically presented in textbooks and museums, confuses the two, presenting as "science" what is actually naturalistic philosophy. Indeed, many secular scientists insist that only naturalistic explanations qualify as science.

But why should we let secularists make the definitions? Let's be clear on the distinction between empirical science and philosophy, and then let's answer science with science and philosophy with philosophy.

This becomes all the more imperative when we realize what we're up against. The moment a Christian questions evolution, he or she is labeled a backwoods Bible-thumper, an ignorant reactionary who is trying to halt the progress of science. Like Katy, most schoolchildren today have seen the movie *Inherit the Wind* (or its counterpart on television), and their imaginations are peopled with blustery, ignorant Christians going toe-to-toe with intelligent, educated, urbane defenders of Darwin. When we question Darwinism in public, we are viewed through the grid portrayed in these media pieces.

Our first task, then, before we can even expect to be heard, is to shatter that grid, to break that stereotype. We must convince people that the debate is not about the Bible versus science. The debate is about pursuing an unbiased examination of the scientific facts and following those facts wherever they may lead. We must challenge the assumption that science by definition means naturalistic philosophy.

The real battle is worldview against worldview, religion against religion. On one side is the naturalistic worldview, claiming that the universe is the product of blind, purposeless forces. On the other side stands the Christian worldview, telling us we were created by a transcendent God who loves us and has a purpose for us. Nature itself is covered with his "fingerprints," marks of purpose in every area of scientific investigation. Our case is fully defensible, if only we learn how to make it.

The Christian worldview begins with the Creation, with a deliberate act by a personal Being who existed from all eternity. This personal dimension is crucial for understanding Creation. Before bringing the world into existence, the Creator made a choice, a decision: He set out a plan, an intelligent design.

According to the apostle Paul's writings, this design, which gives the world its form and structure, is evident to all. "What may be known about

God is plain to them," Paul writes, "because God has made it plain to them" (Rom. 1:19). How? In the form and complexity of the world he made: "For since the creation of the world God's invisible qualities—his eternal power and divine nature—have been clearly seen, being understood from what has been made" (Rom. 1:20). Even unbelievers know somewhere deep within that God must exist. Therefore, "they are without excuse" (Rom. 1:20, NASB). In other words, Paul teaches that those who look honestly at the world around them should be able to conclude that it was created by an intelligent Being.

In the chapters that follow, we will look over Dave Mulholland's shoulder in his search for answers to his daughter's questions. Was Sagan right, or was the apostle right in teaching that the evidence for creation can be clearly seen by all? Did the universe create itself? Did life arise from a sea of chemicals? Can you get the intricate complexity of plants and animals without an intelligence to guide the process?

What we will discover may be as startling to you as it was to Dave.

CHAPTER 7

LET'S START AT THE VERY BEGINNING

[Design] is the most empirical of the arguments for God [based on]
observational premises about the kind of order we discover in nature.
FREDERICK FERRÉ

The first question any worldview must answer is how it all started. How did the universe begin? Dave Mulholland was about to discover one of the most exciting breakthroughs in recent scientific research, for in the past few decades, science has completely reversed itself on the question of the origin of the universe. After maintaining for centuries that the physical universe is eternal and therefore needs no creator, science today has uncovered dramatic new evidence that the universe did have an ultimate origin, that it began at a finite time in the past—just as the Bible teaches.

To grasp just how revolutionary this is, we must understand that most ancient cultures believed that the universe is eternal—or, more precisely, that it was formed from some kind of primordial material that is eternal. The ancient Greeks even argued that the idea of an ultimate beginning was rationally inconceivable. Their arguments were revived during the late Middle Ages and Renaissance, when classical literature was rediscovered. Then, in the eighteenth century, scientists formulated the law of conservation of matter (that matter can be neither created nor destroyed), and it became a potent weapon in the hands of ardent materialists, who argued that science itself now ruled out any ultimate creation. "Today the indestructibility or permanence of matter is a scientific fact," wrote a nineteenth-century proponent of materialism. "Those who talk about an independent or supernatural creative force" that created the universe out of nothing "are in antagonism with the first and simplest axiom of a philosophical view of nature."[1]

And there things stood. The idea that the universe had a beginning was reduced to a bare article of religious faith, standing in lonely opposition to firmly established science.

Then, in the early twentieth century, several lines of evidence began a curious convergence: the implication from general relativity theory that the universe is expanding; the finding that the stars exhibit a "red shift," implying that they are moving outward; and finally, the realization that the two laws of thermodynamics actually make it imperative to believe in a beginning to the universe.

The second law of thermodynamics, the law of decay, implies that the universe is in a process of gradual disintegration—implacably moving toward final darkness and decay. In other words, the universe is running down, like a wound-up clock. And if it is running down, then there must have been a time when it was wound up. In the eloquent words of Lincoln Barnett in *The Universe and Dr. Einstein,* "the inescapable inference is that everything had a *beginning:* somehow and sometime the cosmic processes were started, the stellar fires ignited, and the whole vast pageant of the universe brought into being."[2]

What's more, the first law of thermodynamics (the conservation of matter) implies that matter cannot just pop into existence or create itself. And therefore, if the universe had a beginning, then something *external* to the universe must have caused it to come into existence—something, or Someone, transcendent to the natural world. As a result, the idea of creation is no longer merely a matter of religious faith; it is a conclusion based on the most straightforward reading of the scientific evidence. British physicist Paul Davies, though not a professing Christian, says the big bang is "the one place in the universe where there is room, even for the most hard-nosed materialist, to admit God."[3]

WAS THERE AN ULTIMATE BEGINNING?

These various lines of evidence coalesced in the 1960s and led to the formulation of big bang theory, which asserts that the universe began with a cosmic explosion. The new theory hit the scientific world like a thunderclap. It meant that the idea of an ultimate beginning was no longer merely religious dogma. Science itself now indicated that the universe burst into existence at a particular time in the remote past.

Big bang theory delivers a near fatal blow to naturalistic philosophy, for the naturalistic credo regards reality as an unbroken sequence of cause and effect that can be traced back endlessly. But the big bang represents a sudden discontinuity in the chain of cause and effect. It means science can trace events back in time only to a certain point; at the moment of the big bang explosion, science reaches an abrupt break, an absolute barrier. In fact, when the theory was first proposed, a large number of scientists resisted it for that very reason. The great physicist Arthur Eddington summed up the feelings of many of his colleagues when he stated that the idea of a beginning is philosophically "repugnant."[4] Albert Einstein fiddled with his equations in the vain hope of avoiding the conclusion that the universe had a beginning. Astronomer Robert Jastrow, an agnostic who nevertheless delights in tweaking the noses of his naturalistically minded colleagues, maintains that science has reached its limit, that it will never be able to discover whether the agent of creation was "the personal God of the Old Testament or one of the familiar forces of physics."[5]

Yet many secularists are still squirming to avoid the clear implications of the theory. Some argue that the big bang actually advances naturalistic philosophy—that it has extended naturalistic explanations back to the moment of the origin of the universe itself. That means that if God exists, he has been pushed back to a shadowy first cause who merely started things off, with no role to play after that. But this is sheer bluster. Far from supporting naturalism, big bang theory shows the *limits* of all naturalistic accounts of reality by revealing that nature itself—time, space, and matter—came into existence a finite period of time ago.

Perhaps the most common strategy among scientists and educators today is simply to ignore the startling implications of the big bang, labeling them "philosophy" or "religion" and shunting them aside. We deal only with science, they say. Discussion of the ultimate cause *behind* the big bang is dismissed as philosophy and is given no place in the science classroom. As a result, schoolchildren never dream what fascinating vistas are veiled from their sight, what interesting questions they are essentially forbidden to ask. This is the approach Dave Mulholland witnessed at Disney World, when Bill-Nye-the-Science-Guy, with theatrical flourish, directed the audience's attention to an artistic rendering of the big bang. A thundering wave of light swept over the screen, but not a word was uttered about what came before the primeval explosion or what caused it.

Still other scientists try to get around the big bang by tweaking the theory in ways that allow them to insist that matter is eternal after all. For example, Carl Sagan proposed that the explosion that started our universe was only one of a series—that the universe is expanding today, but at some point the process will reverse itself and begin to contract, until it is once again a tiny point, which will then explode once again, starting the entire process over. This oscillation will go on forever in endless repetition, like an accordion opening and closing.[6] But Sagan's speculation runs up against the basic laws of physics: Even an oscillating universe would use up the available energy in each cycle, and it would eventually run down. The second law of thermodynamics, the law of decay, shoots down any notion of an eternal universe.[7]

Other scientists face the facts of an ultimate beginning, but in an effort to avoid the idea of a creator, they craft notions that are, frankly, illogical. Some speak of the self-generation of the universe, overlooking the obvious logical contradiction in such a notion (if the universe doesn't exist yet, there is no "self" to do the generating.) Others, like Stephen Hawking of Cambridge University, probably the best-known theoretical physicist today, propose that the early universe existed in "imaginary time," an idea that is for all purposes little more than fantasy. Still others have proposed that the universe simply popped into existence—completely uncaused—out of nothing. For example, philosophy professor Quentin Smith proposes that the universe "came from nothing, by nothing, for nothing."[8] But this is to leave the domain of science for sheer magic. One of the most established laws of experience is that something cannot come out of nothing.

Naturalists simply have no way to avoid the challenge posed by the big bang without twisting themselves into impossible logical contortions. The facts clearly indicate that the universe is not eternal, and it cannot originate itself. The implication is that the universe began at a definite moment in time, in a flash of light and energy. Science has begun to sound eerily like Genesis 1: "And God said, 'Let there be light'" (1:3).

These are arguments we can make when we encounter people hostile to Christian faith. One day my wife, Patty, came home from a Bible study and told me how outraged the entire group was over an episode at the local school. One of the women in the group had a thirteen-year-old son who had received a low grade for giving a wrong answer on his weekly quiz for his earth science class. To the question "Where did Earth come from?" Tim had written, "God created it." His test came back with a big red check and twenty points marked off his grade. The "correct" answer, according to the teacher, was that Earth is the product of the big bang.

The women in Patty's Bible study urged Tim's mother to march into the classroom and show the teacher what the Bible says. "It's right there in Genesis 1," they said. *"God created the heavens and the earth."*

But as soon as Patty told me the story, I reached for the phone to call Tim's mother. "Don't go to the teacher with Bible in hand," I said.

She was taken aback. "But the Bible shows that the teacher was wrong."

"As believers, we know that Scripture is inspired and authoritative," I explained, "but Tim's teacher will dismiss it out of hand. She'll say, 'That's religion. I teach science.'"

What we need to avoid in such situations is giving the mistaken idea that Christianity is opposed to science. If we are too quick to quote the Bible, we will never break out of the stereotype spread by *Inherit the Wind*. We should not oppose science with religion; we should oppose *bad* science with *better* science.

We ought to raise questions such as What came before the big bang? What caused it? If the big bang was the origin of the universe itself, then its cause must be something *outside* the universe. The truth is that big bang theory gives dramatic support to the biblical teaching that the universe had an ultimate beginning—that space, matter, and time itself are finite. Far from being a challenge to Christian faith, as Tim's teacher seemed to think, the theory actually gives startling evidence *for* the faith.

And the case for creation is even stronger if we look at the *nature* of our universe. It is a universe that speaks at every turn of design and purpose.

ARE WE COSMIC ACCIDENTS?

In the days and weeks after coming home from his vacation with Katy at Disney World, Dave Mulholland could hear the phrases from various exhibits reverberating over and over again in his memory, like a CD on replay, each time hammering in a sense of helplessness as he realized he had no good answers. He mimicked the message from "The Living Seas" with grim irony: A small sphere, the planet Earth, "just happened" to be the right size and "just happened" to be the right distance from the sun so that life "just happened" to arise. And through a process of random mutations and natural selection, we humans "just happened" to appear on the scene.

What a message for kids to hear, Dave groaned. *It tells them they're nothing more than a cosmic accident. Small wonder that, over time, language about a loving God who created them and loves them sounds more and more like a fairy tale.*

But are all these coincidences really just . . . coincidences? Or did Someone design the universe this way? This was the second question Dave was determined to tackle. He set about studying just as he had in college—by collecting books and articles on the subject. And what he discovered, to his surprise, is another dramatic shift in recent scientific thought. Not only are scientists acknowledging an ultimate beginning, but they are also recognizing that the physical structure of the universe gives striking evidence of purpose and design. They have proposed what is known as the *anthropic principle*, which states that the physical structure of the universe is exactly what it must be in order to support life.

After the first spacecraft landed on the moon, one stunning photograph quickly became familiar to all Americans: a view of the cloud-wrapped Earth, seen just above the horizon of the black and cratered surface of the moon. The contrast was striking. Our beautiful blue-and-white planet, so hospitable to life, seen against the stark, barren, lifeless lunar landscape.

Yet even the moon is a friendly place compared to Venus, where a rain of sulfuric acid falls toward a surface as hot as boiling lead. And even Venus is hospitable compared to the icy crystals that make up Jupiter, with frozen clouds of gas stretching across its surface, giving the planet its striped look. And even Jupiter might be considered approachable compared to the million-degree temperature inside the stars or compared to the immense reaches of hard vacuum between them.

From the perspective of the space age, it has become clearer than ever that Earth is unique. It boasts a wealth of characteristics that make it capable of supporting life—a nearly endless list of preconditions that have been exquisitely met only, as far as we know, on our planet.

How does Earth happen to be so special? Is it just coincidence? Luck? Or was it designed by a loving Creator who had us in mind from the outset?

Consider, for example, Earth's orbit. "The Living Seas" exhibit is quite right in describing Earth as "a small sphere of just the right size [that] lies just the right distance from its mother star." If Earth were even slightly closer to the sun, all its water would boil away, and life would be impossible. On the other hand, if Earth were only slightly farther away from the sun, all its water would freeze, and the terrestrial landscape would be nothing but barren deserts.

And it's not only the landscape that is affected by the position of our planet. The processes inside our bodies also rely on these hospitable conditions. The chemical reactions necessary for life to function occur within a narrow temperature range, and Earth is exactly the right distance from the sun to fall within that range. What's more, for all this to happen, Earth must remain about the same distance from the sun in its orbit; that is, its orbit must be nearly circular—which it is, in contrast to the elliptical orbits of most other planets in our solar system.

Are these finely calibrated distances a product of mere happenstance? Or were they *designed* to support life?

For another example, consider the existence of water, that common substance we take for granted. Water has a host of unique properties absolutely indispensable for life. For example, it is the only known substance whose solid phase (ice) is less dense than its liquid phase. This is why ice forms on the top of oceans and lakes instead of on the bottom, allowing fish and other marine life to survive the winter. On the microscopic level, water molecules exhibit something called the hydrophobic effect, which gives water the unique ability to shape proteins and nucleic acids in DNA. From a molecular standpoint, "the various properties of water are nothing short of miraculous," writes Michael Corey in *God and the New Cosmology;* "no other compound even comes close to duplicating its many life-supporting properties."[9]

But Earth could not support life unless the cosmos itself had the right physical properties. The anthropic principle draws together a staggering number of "cosmic coincidences" that make life possible. For example, the big bang had to have exploded with just the right degree of vigor for our present universe to have formed. If it had occurred with too *little* velocity, the universe would have collapsed back in on itself shortly after the big bang because of gravitational forces; if it had occurred with too *much* velocity, the matter would have streaked away so fast that it would have been impossible for galaxies and solar systems to subsequently form. To state it another way, the force of gravity must be fine-tuned to allow the universe to expand at precisely the right rate (accurate to within 1 part in 10^{60}). The fact that the force of gravity just happens to be the right number with "such stunning accuracy," writes physicist Paul Davies, "is surely one of the great mysteries of cosmology."[10]

Take another example: the structure of the atom. Everything in the universe is made of atoms, from the stars in the farthest heavens to the cells in the human body—and the atom itself is a bundle of fortuitous "coincidences." Within the atom, the neutron is just slightly more massive than the proton, which means that free neutrons (those not trapped within an atom) can decay and turn into protons. If things were reversed—if it were the proton that was larger and had a tendency to decay—the very structure of the universe would be impossible.

Why? Because a free proton is simply a hydrogen atom, and if free protons had a tendency to decay, then everything made of hydrogen would decay. The sun, which is made of hydrogen, would melt away. Water, a liquid oxide of hydrogen (H_2O) would be impossible. In fact, the universe itself would decay, since about 74 percent of the observed universe consists of hydrogen.

And why is the neutron larger than the proton? No one knows. There is no physical cause to explain why the neutron is larger. It is simply a fact. So apparently the only "reason" for the difference in size is that it allows the universe to exist and to support life.

Not only do atomic particles have a size, but they also have an electrical charge. What child hasn't delighted in rubbing his feet on the carpet and giving people a shock by touching them? This annoying practice works because rubbing the carpet knocks off some of the electrons and gives the child a negative charge.

Within the atom, electrons have a negative charge, and protons have a positive charge. Yet, aside from carpet-rubbing pranksters or socks that stick together in the dryer, most of the objects we encounter in daily life have no electrical charge. Why not? Because the charge of the proton exactly balances that of the electron.

And it's a good thing it does. If the electron carried more charge than the proton, all atoms would be negatively charged. In that case—since identical charges repel—all the atoms composing all the objects in the universe would fly apart in a catastrophic explosion. On the other hand, if the proton carried more charge than the electron, all atoms would be positively charged—with the same disastrous consequences.

There is no known physical reason, no natural explanation, for the precise balance in the electrical charges of the proton and the electron—especially when you consider that the two particles differ from one another in all other respects: in size, weight, magnetic properties, and so on. And since there is no natural explanation, no natural law to account for this extraordinarily precise adjustment, is it not reasonable to conclude that this intricate arrangement is the product of a choice, a plan, a design?

The list of "coincidences" goes on and on. It turns out that the slightest tinkering with the values of the fundamental forces of physics—gravity, electromagnetism, the strong and weak nuclear forces—would have resulted in a universe where life was utterly impossible. The anthropic principle states that in our own universe, all these seemingly arbitrary and unrelated values in physics have one strange thing in common: They are precisely the values needed to get a universe capable of supporting life.

The term *anthropic principle* comes from the Greek word *anthropos*, which means human being, and it begins to appear that the laws of physics were exquisitely calibrated from the outset for the creation of human life. Of course, many scientists shy away from this conclusion because it presupposes a creator, and they have been trained to believe that such a concept has no place in science. So what do they do about these obvious marks of design and purpose in the universe? They scramble to explain them away, searching for ways to account for design in the universe without having to acknowledge a designer. Yet, ironically, all these attempts to explain away the design turn out to be far *less* scientific than a straightforward acknowledgment of a creator.

One of the widely held versions of the anthropic principle is the "many worlds" hypothesis. According to this theory, an infinite number of universes exist, all with different laws and different values for fundamental numbers. Most of these universes are dark, lifeless places. But by sheer probability, some will have just the right structure to support life. The "fit" universes survive, while the "unfit" are weeded out. Our own, of course, happens to be a universe "fit" for life.

But how do we know whether these numberless other universes really exist? The answer is, we *cannot* know. The idea is purely a product of scientific imagination. Even if alternative universes did exist, they would be inherently impossible for science to detect. Candid scientists admit that the whole idea is motivated by a desire to avoid the theological implications of the anthropic principle. Physicist Heinz Pagels says that if the universe appears to be tailor-made for life, the most straightforward conclusion is that it *was* tailor-made, created by a transcendent God; it is only because many scientists find that conclusion "unattractive" that they adopt the theory of multiple universes, Pagels explains. And he adds wryly, "It is the closest that some atheists can get to God." In other words, atheists are squirming every which way to avoid the obvious.[11]

Another version is the *participatory anthropic principle.* Drawing a wild extrapolation from quantum mechanics, this version says that the universe did not fully exist until human beings emerged to observe it. And so, in order to become fully real, the universe decided to evolve human consciousness. In the words of Nobel prize–winning biologist George Wald, "The universe wants to be known."[12]

This is indeed a strange picture of the universe—as if it had a heart, longing to be known, and a mind, deciding to evolve human beings. Yet it seems to be a picture shared by physicist Freeman Dyson, who says, "I find that the universe in some sense must have known that we were coming."[13] And astronomer George Greenstein echoes a similar refrain: "If this is the best way to make a universe, how did the universe find that out?"[14]

Here we have a concept of the universe as a quasi-intelligent being that can know and be known, that can plot and plan. It is astonishing that scientists will dismiss the idea of a Creator as unscientific, yet turn around and embrace the bizarre, almost mystical concept of a conscious universe.

Scientists are not being forced to these speculative forms of the anthropic principle by the facts; instead, they are driven by a religious motive—or rather, by an *anti*religious motive. So strong is their desire to avoid the conclusion of divine creation that they will resort to irrational notions, such as the existence of millions of unknowable universes or a pantheistic universe that "knew" we were coming. In the words of Patrick Glynn of George Washington University, the fact that so many scientists are willing to accept "wild speculations about unseen universes for which not a shred of observational evidence exists suggests something about both the power of the modern atheistic ideology and the cultural agenda of many in the scientific profession." Then Glynn delivers this searing indictment: "The mainstream scientific community has in effect shown its attachment to the atheistic ideology of the random universe to be in some respects more powerful than its commitment to the scientific method itself."[15]

Precisely.

The anthropic principle acknowledges that we can identify and recognize the products of design, and that many of the features of the physical universe bear the marks of design. In many ways, the scientific method is merely the codification of common sense, and the detection of design is no exception. I remember as a child visiting the "Old Man in the Mountains," a tourist attraction in New Hampshire's White Mountains. At an overlook station, our family would join other eager tourists to see if we could detect, in the outline of the rocks, what looked like the profile of an old man. Of course, we knew it wasn't really a carving of a man; it was like many other places that are billed as natural wonders—places where, over the ages, the wind and rain have carved out shapes that resemble a face or a bridge or some other familiar object.

By contrast, imagine you are driving through South Dakota and suddenly come upon a mountain bearing the unmistakable likenesses of four American presidents, looking just as you remember them from your history books. Instantly you recognize Lincoln's jutting chin and Washington's high forehead. Would you—would anyone?—conclude that these shapes were the product of wind or rain or glacial erosion? Of course not. Immediately you realize that artists with chisels and drills have painstakingly carved these four famous faces out of the stone.

We intuitively recognize the products of design versus the products of natural forces. And in his exciting new book *The Design Inference*, mathematician William Dembski has offered an "explanatory filter" to give logical form to this intuition. When we try to explain any natural phenomenon, there are three possibilities: chance, law, or design. If the natural phenomenon is irregular, erratic, and unspecified, we conclude that it is a random event. If it is regular, repeatable, and predictable, we conclude that it is the result of natural forces. But if it is unpredictable and yet highly specified, we conclude that it is designed. The four presidents' faces on Mt. Rushmore are irregular (not something we see happening generally as the result of erosion), yet specified (they fit a particular, preselected pattern). Applying the explanatory filter, the evidence clearly points to design.[16]

According to the anthropic principle, evidence for design is found throughout the physical universe. If we apply Dembski's explanatory filter, we find that many of the major features of the physical universe are irregular (there is no natural law accounting for them) and highly specified (they appear preselected to support life). In short, they bear the unmistakable characteristics of design.

And if the universe exhibits design, it is logical to conclude that there is a designer. The most obvious inference is that the universe *appears* to be designed because it *is* designed—powerful evidence for the biblical worldview that a loving God created the world.

That answers the question about the ultimate origin of the universe. But what happened after that? Where did living things come from? Did life evolve from the merging of molecules in a primordial sea?

Dave knew his search for answers had only begun.

CHAPTER 8

LIFE IN A TEST TUBE?

A little science estranges a man from God. A lot of science brings him back.
FRANCIS BACON

You don't have to drive to Disney World to indoctrinate your kids in the Gospel according to Evolution. Whose toddler these days doesn't know *The Land Before Time* video series? There's no debating that the little dinosaurs are endearing, but along with the story, each video offers an excursion into evolution. Children sit wide-eyed, watching primal one-celled organisms arise out of the blue-green churning seas—organisms that "change again and again," until they finally evolve into cute little dinos.[1] It is a delightful, fairy-tale introduction to naturalistic evolution. And once a child's imagination is populated with these bright images, it is nearly impossible for a parent to dislodge them. When the imagination is later bolstered with classroom teaching, Christian parents like Dave face an uphill battle.

So let's peel back the colorful images to look for the cold, sober truth about the origin of life. Have scientists created life in a test tube? Have they proven that life arose from a primordial soup?

The way scientists try to prove that life arose in the primitive seas is to re-create the same conditions in the laboratory and see what happens. One of the best-known experiments occurred in 1953. Newspapers across the country carried photos of Stanley Miller of the University of Chicago, wearing a white laboratory coat and heavy square-rimmed glasses, reporting his sensational claim that he had accomplished the first step toward creating life in a test tube.

Miller had mixed simple chemicals and gases in a glass tube, then zapped them with an electrical charge to induce chemical reactions. The idea was to simulate conditions on the early earth and show that simple chemicals could indeed have reacted to create the building blocks of life. To everyone's surprise, what emerged at the other end of the laboratory apparatus were amino acids, the building blocks of protein, an important constituent of living things. The news was electrifying. Few people had dared dream that the elements of a living cell could be produced under conditions allegedly existing on the early earth. Miller's success seemed to provide dramatic evidence for a naturalistic account of life's origin.

It also set off a domino series of similar experiments, some using heat as an energy source instead of Miller's electrical charge, others using ultraviolet light to simulate light from the sun. Most of these experiments have succeeded in producing amino acids, and the amino acids have even linked up in chains resembling proteins. The results have been reported in one breathless headline after another.

The problem with all this frenetic activity is that no one is asking critical questions about what the experiments really prove. The conventional wisdom is that they support the theory that life evolved spontaneously from simple chemicals in a primeval pond about four billion years ago. But do they?[2]

Let's start with the amino acids that came out of Miller's test tube. The truth is that these differ in critical ways from those found in living things. Amino acids come in two forms, what scientists call left-handed and right-handed. Living things are highly selective: They use only the left-handed form. But when Miller and his colleagues mixed chemicals in the laboratory, they got both kinds—an even fifty-fifty mix of left-handed and right-handed. In fact, this is what happens every time anyone mixes the chemicals randomly in the laboratory. There is no natural process that produces only left-handed amino acids, the kind required by living things. All of this means that the amino acids formed in the test tube are useless for life.

And that's only the first problem. The next step to "creating life" is to get amino acids to link up and form proteins. In 1958 Sidney Fox, a chemist at the University of Miami, started with already existing amino acids and boiled them in water to induce them to react with one another. The result was proteinlike chains of amino acids, and, like Miller, Fox was promptly inducted into the Modern Hall of Scientific Heroes.

But serious problems are hidden beneath the hype, because once again, life is much more selective than anything we get from a test tube. The proteins in living things are comprised of amino acids hooked together in a very particular chemical bond called a peptide bond. But amino acids are like Tinkertoy pieces: They're capable of hooking together in all sorts of different ways, forming several different chemical bonds. And in the test tube, that's exactly what they do. They hook up in a variety of ways, never producing a genuine protein capable of functioning in a living cell.

In addition, for a protein to be functional, the amino acids must link up in a particular sequence, just like the sequence of letters in a sentence. If you scramble the letters in a sentence, you get nonsense; if you scramble the amino acids in a protein, you get a nonfunctional protein. Yet in laboratory experiments, all we get are scrambled, random sequences. There's no natural force capable of selecting the right amino acids and lining them up in the right order. As a result, the proteinlike chains that appear in the test tube are useless for life.

The fact is, the much-touted experiments tell us very little about where real, functional proteins came from. Yet this inconvenient fact is rarely mentioned when headlines blare out the news that scientists have succeeded in creating the building blocks of life.

WHEN SCIENTISTS "CHEAT"

And there's more. If scientists really wanted to duplicate what might have happened in a primordial soup billions of years ago, they would simply mix up some chemicals in a vat, expose them to an energy source (heat or light), and see what happens. Yet no one ever does this. Why not? Because it is impossible to get any important chemical compounds that way. Instead, to get even useless, nonfunctional amino acids and proteins, researchers have to control the experiment in various ways.

For example, in nature, chemicals are almost never found in a pure state. As a result, one cannot predict with confidence which reactions will take place. Substances A and B might react effectively in the laboratory, where isolated and purified forms are used. But out in nature, there are almost always other chemicals—C and D—lying about, which means substance A might react with C instead of with B, yielding a completely different result from what the scientist expected. In other words, out in nature there are all kinds of competing reactions.

So how do scientists avoid the problem of competing reactions? They uncap their bottles and pour out only pure isolated ingredients. And when the experiment involves more than one step, such as going from amino acids to proteins, researchers start over each step with fresh ingredients.

Obviously, this rigs the experiment. Nature doesn't have flasks of pure ingredients to pour out at each step of the way.

Or consider another typical experiment, one that uses ultraviolet light instead of electricity to get the chemicals to react. The idea is to simulate sunlight beaming down on a primeval pond on the early earth. There's just one little problem: The longer wavelengths of ultraviolet light are very destructive and would destroy the very amino acids that scientists are hoping to get. So what do they do? They screen out the longer wavelengths and use only shorter wavelengths.

But once again, success is bought at the price of rigging the experiment. A real primeval pond would have no screens to protect the fragile amino acids from destructive wavelengths of sunlight. As a result, these experiments don't tell us what could realistically have happened on the early earth; they tell us only what happens when researchers carefully control the conditions.

Another device that every origin-of-life experiment resorts to is the use of a trap to protect the end products after they have formed. Amino acids are delicate, and they easily break down into the elements of which they are composed. When electricity or heat is used as an energy source to induce the chemicals to link up and form amino acids, that same energy can also break them back down. Hence the researcher has to find some way to protect the delicate chemical compounds.

The solution is to build a trap that removes the amino acids from the reaction site as soon as they form, to protect them from disintegrating. Miller's apparatus was a square of glass tubing with a bulb on top, bristling with electrodes to create sparks, and a U-shaped bulge on the bottom, filled with water to trap the amino acids. Miller would drain the trap to remove the amino acids from the reaction area so they would not break down again.

To understand why this is so important, imagine you are a child eating a bowl of alphabet soup. When you stir the soup, you are an energy source. Stirring slowly, you might cause a few letters to line up and form short words, such as "T-O" or "A-N-D." But as you keep stirring, your spoon will quickly cause the letters to scatter again—unless you scoop the words out with your spoon and put them carefully on your plate. That's what the trap does: It takes amino acids out of harm's way and preserves them.

The trouble is that, once again, nature doesn't come equipped with handy traps to protect the delicate building blocks of life. Any amino acids that might form spontaneously in nature would disintegrate just as quickly. A trap is absolutely necessary for a successful experiment, but it just as surely makes the experiment completely irrelevant to confirming any naturalistic theory of life's origin.

At every turn, the experiments that have ignited so much excitement turn out to be artificial. As a result, even the most successful origin-of-life experiments tell us next to nothing about what could have happened under natural conditions. They tell us only what happens when a brilliant scientist manipulates the conditions, "coaxing" the materials down the chemical pathways necessary to produce the building blocks of life.

So what do these experiments really prove? That *life can be created only by an intelligent agent directing, controlling, and manipulating the process.* The latest scientific findings do not discredit biblical faith; rather, they provide positive evidence that the origin of life requires an intelligent agent, a creator.

NOT A CHANCE

If we need additional confirmation, it comes from a surprising place: from the use of computers in biology. Long before the information age, the living cell was thought to be quite simple, and it was easy enough to think life arose by chance. Darwin himself thought the cell was a simple blob of protoplasm, and he conjectured that it evolved in a "warm little pond." But as science began uncovering the marvelous complexity of the cell, it became harder and harder to hold on to chance theories.

Biologists typically took refuge in the idea of nearly endless time. Given enough time, they argued, anything can happen. Over millions of years, the unlikely becomes likely, the improbable is transformed into the inevitable. And for a while, biologists got away with this argument—only because the number of millennia invoked were so immense that no one was capable of conceptualizing what that kind of time scale really meant.

But the computer revolution put an end to any chance theory of life's origin. Beginning in the 1960s, mathematicians began writing computer programs to simulate every process under the sun, and they cast their calculating eyes on evolution itself. Hunched over their high-speed computers, they simulated the trial-and-error processes of neo-Darwinian evolution over the equivalent of billions of years. The outcome was jolting: The computers showed that the probability of evolution by chance processes is essentially zero, no matter how long the time scale.[3]

In 1966, at a landmark symposium at the Wistar Institute in Philadelphia, a group of computer specialists presented their findings to the nation's biologists. The charge was led by Murray Eden of MIT and Marcel Schutzenberger of the University of Paris. At first, the biologists were angry at the upstart computer whizzes for invading their territory. But the numbers could not be denied. And after the symposium, chance theories began to be quietly buried.

As a result, today it is common to hear prominent scientists scoff at the idea that life arose by chance. The famous astronomer Sir Fred Hoyle compares it to lining up 10^{50} (ten with fifty zeros after it) blind people, giving each one a scrambled Rubik's Cube, and finding that they all solve the cube at the same moment.[4]

What has been put in the place of chance? For the naturalist who assumes life evolved spontaneously, there is only one other logical possibility: If life did not arise by random processes, then it must have arisen under the compulsion of forces in matter itself. Hence biologists working in the field today are searching for some force within matter that directed the process—some impulse that caused life to emerge. The assumption is that life will arise inevitably whenever conditions are right. A widely used college textbook sums up the approach in its title: *Biochemical Predestination*.[5]

Yet there is no agreement on *which* forces in matter are up to the job. Dean Kenyon of San Francisco State University, one of the original exponents of this doctrine and coauthor of *Biochemical Predestination*, has since repudiated his own theory. If you look at the experiments, Kenyon explained in an interview, "one thing that stands out is that you do not get ordered sequences of amino acids. . . . If we thought we were going to see a lot of spontaneous ordering, something must have been wrong with our theory."[6] Kenyon has since accepted the idea of an intelligent Designer as the answer to the origin of life.

Sadly, too few scientists have this kind of courage. Yet it is becoming ever clearer that the experiments fail to support any naturalistic theory of life's origin. What they *do* support is the idea of intelligent design. The experiments give positive evidence that life arises only when the raw materials are carefully selected, arranged, controlled, and organized by an intelligent cause.

The advance of science is not casting up new challenges to Christian faith, as we are so often told. Instead, it is uncovering ever more powerful evidence that what Christians believe is true on all levels, including the natural world. And that is becoming even clearer today as scientists learn more about what is inside the cell—and especially the structure of DNA.

THE LANGUAGE OF LIFE

We've all heard the term *DNA,* thanks to its use in controversial court cases like the O. J. Simpson trial, but few of us really understand what it is. Simply put, DNA is like a language in the heart of the cell, a molecular message, a set of instructions telling the cell how to construct proteins—much like the software needed to run a computer. Moreover, the amount of information DNA includes is staggering: A single cell of the human body contains as much information as the *Encyclopedia Britannica*—all thirty volumes—three or four times over. As a result, the question of the origin of life must now be redefined as the question of the origin of biological information. Can information arise by natural forces alone? Or does it require an intelligent agent?

Scientists committed to naturalism must try to construct an explanation of life based solely on physical-chemical laws. They must explain the information in DNA as a product of natural processes at work in the chemicals that comprise living things. Recall Katy's words to her father at Epcot: "It's chemicals. It's all chemicals."

It's true that DNA is composed of ordinary chemicals (bases, sugars, phosphates) that react according to ordinary laws. But what makes DNA function as a message is not the chemicals themselves but rather their *sequence,* their pattern. The chemicals in DNA are grouped into molecules (called nucleotides) that act like letters in a message, and they must be in a particular order if the message is going to be intelligible. If the letters are scrambled, the result is nonsense. So the crucial question comes down to whether the sequence of chemical "letters" arose by natural causes or whether it required an intelligent source. Is it the product of law or design?

More than two hundred years ago, the English clergyman William Paley framed the classic argument for design by comparing a living organism to a watch. Upon finding a watch lying on the beach, no one would say, "Oh, look what the wind and the waves have produced." Instead, we instantly recognize that a watch has a structure that can be produced only by an intelligent agent. Likewise, Paley argued, living things have a type of structure that can be produced only by an intelligent cause.[7]

The naturalistic scientist insists that the idea of an intelligent cause has no place in science. But the truth is that several branches of science already use the concept of intelligence and have even devised tests for detecting the work of an intelligent agent. Consider forensic science. When police find a body, their first question is, Was this death the result of natural causes or foul play (an intentional act by an intelligent being)? Pathologists perform a battery of fairly straightforward tests to get an answer.

Likewise, when archaeologists uncover an unusually shaped rock, they ask whether the shape is a result of weathering or whether the rock is a primitive tool, deliberately chipped by some ancient hunter. Again, certain tests are used to detect whether it is a product of intelligent activity.

When cryptographers are given a page of scrambled letters, how do they determine whether it is just a random sequence or a secret code? When radio signals are detected in outer space, how do astronomers know whether it is a message from another civilization? There are rules that can be applied to determine whether the letters or the signals fit the structure of a language.

For example, in 1967 astronomers were startled to discover radio pulses coming from outer space. "Our first thought," they said, was that "this was another intelligent race" trying to communicate with us, and they labeled the signals "LGM" (Little Green Men). However, further analysis showed that the pulses formed the wrong kind of pattern for a language. Instead of a new life-form, what they had discovered was a pulsar, a rotating star that mimics a radio beacon.[8]

In everyday life, we weigh natural versus intelligent causes all the time without thinking much about it. If we see ripples on a sandy beach, we assume they were formed by natural processes. But if we see words written in the sand—"John loves Mary"—immediately we recognize a different kind of order, and we know that a couple of lovers recently lingered there. Or consider the children's game of finding shapes in the clouds. As adults, we know the shapes are just the result of wind and temperature acting on the water molecules. But what if we see "clouds" that spell out a message? In the film *Reunion in France,* set in Nazi-occupied Paris in the 1940s, a plucky pilot flies over the city every day and uses skywriting to spell out the single word "COURAGE."[9] Had you and I been there, we would never have mistaken the skywriting for an ordinary cloud; even though the words were white and fluffy, we would have been certain that natural forces did not create the message.

In the same way, when scientists probed the nucleus of the cell, they came across something analogous to "John loves Mary" or "COURAGE"—the only difference being that DNA contains vastly more information. What this means is that we can now revive the design argument using a much closer analogy than Paley's analogy between living things and watches. The new analogy is between DNA and written messages. Are there natural forces capable of writing a book or programming a computer disk or writing a symphony? Clearly not. The discovery of DNA provides powerful new evidence that life is the product of intelligent design. It's an argument that is simple, easy to explain, and based solidly on experience.

THE MESSAGE IN THE MOLECULE

Since DNA contains information, the case can be stated even more strongly in terms of *information theory*, a field of research that investigates the ways information is transmitted. As we said earlier, the naturalistic scientist has only two possible ways to explain the origin of life—either chance or natural law. But information theory gives us a powerful tool for discounting both these explanations, for both chance and law lead to structures with low information content, whereas DNA has a very high information content.[10]

A structure or message is said to have high or low information content depending on the minimum number of instructions needed to tell you how to construct it. To illustrate, a random sequence of letters has low information content because it requires only two instructions: (1) select a letter of the English alphabet and write it down, and (2) do it again (select another letter and write it down). By the same token, a regular, repetitive pattern of letters has low information content as well. Using your computer to create Christmas wrapping paper requires only a few instructions: (1) type in "M-e-r-r-y C-h-r-i-s-t-m-a-s," and (2) do it again. By contrast, if you want your computer to print out the poem "The Night before Christmas," you must specify every letter, one by one. Because the process of writing down the poem requires a large number of instructions, it is said to have high information content.

Similarly, in nature, both random patterns and regular patterns (like ripples on a beach) have low information content. By contrast, DNA has a very high information content. It would be impossible to produce a simple set of instructions telling a chemist how to synthesize the DNA of even the simplest bacterium. You would have to specify every chemical "letter," one by one—and there are literally millions. So DNA has a completely different structure from the products of either chance or natural law, and information theory gives us the conceptual tools to debunk any such attempts to explain the origin of life.

As we noted earlier, most scientists today are looking for some kind of self-organizing force in matter itself to explain life's origin, and yet there are currently no real candidates. As a result, most treatments of the subject resort to analogies, pointing to spontaneous ordering in *non*living structures, such as crystals. Browse through the library, and you'll find many books that use the analogy of crystal formation to explain how life might have started.

But does this analogy work? Not at all, and information theory cuts through the fog surrounding this subject. Whether they are ordinary (like salt and sugar) or exquisite (like rubies and diamonds), all crystals are examples of repetitive order. The unique structure of any crystal is the result of what we might think of as the "shape" of its atoms (or ions), which causes them to slot into a particular position and to layer themselves in a fixed, orderly pattern. In salt, the atoms always form a six-sided box, whereas sugar atoms always come together in a rectangular crystal slanted on both ends. "If we could shrink ourselves to the atomic scale," writes zoologist Richard Dawkins in *The Blind Watchmaker,* "we would see almost endless rows of atoms stretching to the horizon in straight lines—galleries of geometric repetition."[11]

This "geometric repetition" is precisely the problem, for it means crystals carry very little information. It's as if someone said, "pick a shape" and "do it again." If the DNA molecule were really analogous to a crystal, it would consist of a single pattern repeating again and again, like Christmas wrapping paper, so crystal formation gives us no clue whatsoever to the origin of DNA.

Another attempt to find a naturalistic answer to the origin of life comes from the new field of *complexity theory.* On their computer screens, researchers "grow" marvelous shapes that resemble ferns and forests and snowflakes. This is being touted as the answer to the spontaneous origin of order.

Is this new field of research finally going to uncover a law that can account for the spontaneous origin of life itself? The verdict is already in, and it is no. The truth is that the ferns and swirls constructed by complexity theorists on their computer screens represent the same kind of order as crystals. In the words of Stuart Kauffman of the Santa Fe Institute, the patterns are constructed by the repeated application of only a few "astonishingly simple rules."[12] In other words, like crystals, these structures can be specified with just a few instructions, followed by "do it again."[13]

The conclusion is that there are no known physical laws capable of creating a structure like DNA with high information content. Based on both the latest scientific knowledge and on ordinary experience, we know only one cause that is up to the task: an intelligent agent. Only an intelligent person can type out "The Night before Christmas" or devise a computer program or compose a musical score. And only an intelligent cause could create the information contained in the DNA molecule.

■   ■   ■

MANY CHRISTIANS ARE nervous about invoking God to answer any scientific question, even the origin of life. We're afraid of being accused of resorting to the "God of the gaps" argument—of using God to cover over our ignorance—only to have a natural explanation turn up later and embarrass us. This fear is understandable, given the fact that Christians often have been cast into the same category as primitives who attribute thunder to the raging of their gods. But there are times when Christians ought to turn the tables on the critics. There are times when it is more rational to accept a supernatural explanation and when it is actually irrational to hold out for a natural explanation.

We know from science itself that there are some things nature cannot do. We know that we will never fulfill the alchemists' dream of chemically transmuting lead into gold. We know that a parent of one species will never give birth to offspring of another species. To persist in seeking natural laws in such cases is as irrational as any primitive myth of the thunder gods. Science reveals consistent patterns that allow us to make negative statements about what natural forces cannot do.

Empirical evidence makes it clear that natural forces do not produce structures with high information content. This is not a statement about our *ignorance*—a "gap" in knowledge that will be filled in later by a natural explanation. Rather, it is a statement about what we *know*—about our consistent experience of the character of natural processes. Today, holding on to the hope that some natural process will be found to explain DNA is supremely irrational. The elusive process that naturalists hope to find would have to be completely unprecedented, different in kind from any we currently know. Surely *this* is an argument from ignorance.

When it comes to the origin of life, science is squarely on the side of creation by an intelligent agent. We have nothing to fear from the progress of science. And parents like Dave have solid answers to give their questioning teens.

CHAPTER 9

DARWIN IN THE DOCK

*As long as Darwinists control the definitions of key terms [such as science],
their system is unbeatable, regardless of the evidence.*

PHILLIP JOHNSON

Since coming home from Disney World, Dave Mulholland had been conscientious in his search for answers. With the help of his pastor and several friends, he had found a handful of books that focused on the issues. He could now tell Katy what the big bang really means—how, instead of disproving that God created the world, the big bang theory actually gives scientific evidence for an ultimate beginning to the universe and points toward a transcendent source. He could put into words, without too much trouble, how the anthropic principle draws together overwhelming evidence for design running through the physical universe at every level. He could even field most of Katy's questions about where life came from—how laboratory experiments often "cheat" to get even the flimsiest results, and how the discovery of DNA gives positive evidence for a creator.

"Look, Katy," he had said to her. "Just think of your own experience. Have you ever seen a message written in the sky or on a rock by some kind of natural force?"

"Hmmm," she replied noncommittally.

Dave grabbed a book at random off his cluttered desk and flipped it open to a page of densely printed text. "Anyone who says some natural force in the chemicals 'wrote' the DNA code—well, that's like saying the chemicals in the paper and ink wrote the words on this page."

He was gaining confidence, and at times Katy dropped her defensive attitude and seemed genuinely interested in what he was learning. But today she was back to her old combative mode.

She tossed her head. "Oh, I don't have any problem with God being at the start of it all," she said airily. "Maybe he did kick everything off, you know, back at the very beginning."

Dave smiled inwardly. He knew this admission represented progress, even though Katy refused to show it.

"But everyone knows that once life was here, it evolved just as Darwin said it did. I saw it in my textbook at school."

It was her turn to grab a book. She rustled through her backpack and pulled out a heavy biology textbook, opening it to a full spread of colorful, eye-catching photos showing several breeds of dogs and horses as well as a vast variety of orchids and roses. Here, the caption proclaimed, is "evolution in action." Evolution happening before our very eyes.

Dave took the book from her hands and felt his stomach tighten. He hadn't covered these issues yet. And those colorful photos certainly were impressive.

Katy gazed at him triumphantly. "It's right in the book, Dad."

Dave didn't answer. His eyes had moved down to the text to find out exactly what his daughter was learning. Katy waited a few moments, then walked out of the room, leaving him sitting with the textbook still open on his lap. Dave clenched his hands. *God,* he prayed, *no wonder she keeps fighting me—fighting you. Everything she gets at school is saying that nature can do it on its own, that you are irrelevant.*

■   ■   ■

THE TACTIC USED in textbooks like Katy's is rarely a direct attack on religion. Instead, God is quietly but surely nudged into a position of irrelevance, where there's simply nothing left for him to do. Consider this typical example from the widely used college textbook *Evolutionary Biology:* "By coupling undirected, purposeless variation to the blind, uncaring process of natural selection, Darwin made theological or spiritual explanations of the life processes superfluous."[1]

The same message is aimed at high school students as well. In a 1995 statement, the National Association of Biology Teachers (NABT) asserted that all life is the outcome of "an unsupervised, impersonal, unpredictable, and natural process."[2] The words "unsupervised" and "impersonal" mean that God is not to be tolerated even in the role of directing and guiding the evolutionary process. Life is declared to be the outcome of material processes acting blindly by chance.

Clearly, Katy's father is not the only one in a bind. All Christians need to know how to respond to the challenge posed by Darwinian naturalism. Fortunately, a few basic concepts will help us cut through the rhetoric and enable us to think more clearly. The best argument against Darwinism has been known for centuries by farmers and breeders, and it can be stated in a simple principle: Natural change in living things is limited. Or, stated positively: Organisms stay true to type.

Take the pictures in Katy's textbook. They tout the variation in dogs and horses and roses as "evolution in action." The Darwinist seems to overlook the obvious fact that the dogs are all still dogs, the horses still horses, the roses still roses. None of the changes has created a novel kind of organism. Dog breeding has given rise to varieties ranging from the lumbering Great Dane to the tiny Chihuahua, but no variety shows any tendency to leave the canine family.

The magnificent Tyler Municipal Rose Garden in Tyler, Texas, showcases some five hundred varieties of roses of nearly every shade and hue. But despite intensive breeding, they are all still roses. None of the examples cited in biology textbooks are evolving to a new level of complexity; they all simply illustrate variation around a mean.

Darwinism cannot deny that all observed change is limited; what the theory suggests is that over time, these minor variations add up to create major changes—the vast changes necessary to go from a primeval one-celled organism to bees and butterflies and little boys.[3] This is the core of Darwinian theory—and yet, ironically, it is also the easiest part of the theory to discredit. Even Charles Darwin's own work breeding pigeons demonstrates the limits of biological change.

In Victorian England, pigeon breeding was extremely popular, and when Darwin returned from his famous sea voyage to the Galapagos Islands, he took up pigeon breeding. In the skillful hands of a breeder, the pigeon can be transformed into a fantail, with feathers like a Chinese fan; it can become a pouter, with a huge crop bulging under its beak; it can become a Jacobin, with a "hood" of feathers on the back and sides of its head resembling the hoods worn by Jacobin monks. Yet despite this range of diversity, all pigeons are descendants of the common rock pigeon, the ordinary gray birds that flock to our city parks. And despite the spectacular variation in tails and feathers, all the pigeons Darwin observed remained pigeons. They represent cyclical change in gene frequencies but no new genetic information.

How did Darwin devise a theory of unlimited change from such examples of limited change? He took the changes he had *observed* and extrapolated them back into the distant past—which, of course, he had *not* observed. If the common rock pigeon can be so greatly transformed within a few years at the hand of a breeder, he asked, what might happen to the same pigeon in nature over thousands, even millions, of years? Given enough time, change would be virtually unlimited, and the pigeon might even be transformed into a completely different kind of bird.[4]

It was a bold speculation, but no one should be misled into thinking it was more than that. Neither Darwin nor anyone else has ever actually witnessed evolution occurring. It is a conjecture, an extrapolation going far beyond any observed facts. Now, there's nothing wrong with extrapolation per se, as long as we keep in mind that it is only that, not observable fact. And to make a reasonable extrapolation, we must have good grounds for believing that the process being extrapolated will continue at a steady rate.

And therein lies the fatal flaw in Darwin's theory. Centuries of experiments show that the change produced by breeding does *not* continue at a steady rate from generation to generation. Instead, change is rapid at first, then levels off, and eventually reaches a limit that breeders cannot cross.

Consider one historical example. Beginning in 1800, plant breeders started trying to increase the sugar content of the sugar beet, with excellent success. Over seventy-five years of selective breeding, they increased the sugar content of beets from 6 percent to 17 percent. But then they could go no further. Although the same intensive breeding was continued for another half century, the sugar content never rose above 17 percent. At some point, biological variation always levels off and stops.

Why does progress halt? Because once all the genes for a particular trait have been selected, breeding can go no further. Breeding shuffles and selects among existing genes in the gene pool, combining and recombining them, much as you might shuffle and deal cards from a deck. But breeding does not create new genes, any more than shuffling cards creates new cards. A bird cannot be bred to grow fur. A mouse cannot be bred to grow feathers. A pig cannot grow wings.

What's more, as breeders keep up the selection pressure, the organism grows weaker until it finally becomes sterile and dies out. This is the bane of modern farming: Our highly bred cows and chickens produce more milk and eggs, but they are also much more prone to disease and sterility. There is a natural barrier that no amount of breeding is able to cross.

Moreover, when an organism is no longer subject to selective pressure, it tends to revert to its original type. Left to themselves, the offspring of the fancy pigeons that so charmed Darwin will revert to the wild rock pigeon.

So Darwin was simply mistaken in his extrapolation. Whether in the breeding pen or out in nature, the minor change produced by shuffling genes is not an engine for the unlimited change required by evolution. The natural tendency in living things is not to continue changing indefinitely but to stay close to the original type.

WHAT DID DARWIN REALLY PROVE?

Since breeding does nothing more than shuffle existing genes, the only way to drive evolution to new levels of complexity is to introduce new genetic material. And the only natural source of new genetic material in nature is mutations. In today's neo-Darwinism, the central mechanism for evolution is random mutation and natural selection.

The concept of mutations was popularized for the younger set a few years ago by the Teenage Mutant Ninja Turtles, and today virtually every sci-fi movie features mutants. But what exactly is a mutation? Since a gene is like a coded set of instructions, a mutation is akin to a typing error—a changed letter here, an altered punctuation mark there, a phrase dropped, or a word misspelled. These typing errors are the only source of novelty in the genetic code.

But already there is an obvious problem. If you introduce a typing error into a report you are writing, it is not likely to improve the report. An error is more likely to make nonsense than to make better sense. And the same is true of errors in the genetic code. Most mutations are harmful, often lethal, to the organism, so that if mutations were to accumulate, the result would more likely be *de*volution than evolution.

In order to make this theory work, neo-Darwinists must hope that some mutations, somewhere, somehow, will be beneficial. And since the evolution of a single new organ or structure may require many thousands of mutations, neo-Darwinists must hope that vast numbers of these rare beneficial mutations will occur in a single organism. The improbabilities are staggering.

If we take neo-Darwinism into the laboratory and test it experimentally, the difficulties only multiply. The handiest way to study mutations in the laboratory is with the help of the ordinary fruit fly—the kind you see hovering around overripe bananas in the kitchen. Since this tiny fly reaches sexual maturity in only five days, the effects of mutations can be observed over several generations. Using chemicals or radiation to induce mutations, scientists have produced flies with purple eyes or white eyes; flies with oversized wings or shriveled wings or even no wings; fly larvae with patchy bristles on their backs or larvae with so many bristles that they resemble hedgehogs.[5]

But all this experimentation has not advanced evolutionary theory in the slightest. For nothing has ever emerged except odd forms of fruit flies. The experiments have never produced a new type of insect. Mutations alter the details in *existing* structures—like eye color or wing size—but they do not lead to the creation of *new* structures. The fruit flies have remained fruit flies. Like breeding, genetic mutations produce only minor, limited change.

Furthermore, the minor changes observed do not accumulate to create major changes—the principle at the heart of Darwinism. Hence, mutations are not the source of the endless, limitless change required by evolutionary theory. Whether we look at breeding experiments or laboratory experiments, the outcome is the same: Change in living things remains strictly limited to variations on the theme. We do not see the emergence of new and more complex structures.

The same pattern holds throughout the past, as we see in the fossil record. The overwhelming pattern is that organisms appear fully formed, with variations clustered around a mean, and without transitional stages leading up to them. The fossil record as a whole gives persuasive evidence against Darwinism.[6]

Mastering these basic facts gives us the tools to think critically about the examples typically used to support evolution. Take Darwin's famous finches, whose variation in beak size helped inspire his initial theory. A recent study designed to support Darwinism found that the finches' beaks grow larger in dry seasons, when the seeds they eat are tough and hard, but grow smaller again after a rainy season, when tiny seeds become available once more. This is evolution happening "before [our] very eyes," the author of the study concluded. But in fact, it is precisely the opposite. The change in finch beaks is a cyclical fluctuation that allows the finches to adapt and survive, points out Phillip Johnson in *Reason in the Balance*. In other words, it's a minor adjustment that allows finches to . . . stay finches. It does not demonstrate that finches are evolving into a new kind of organism or that they originally evolved from another organism.[7]

The same holds for all the frequently cited "confirmations" of evolution, such as organisms that develop a resistance to antibiotics and insects that develop resistance to insecticide. Even more disturbing, some of the most famous examples have been exposed as hoaxes—most recently, the black-and-white peppered moths in England. Standard textbooks assert that during the Industrial Revolution, when the tree trunks were darkened by soot, a light-colored variety of the moth became easier for birds to see and were eaten up, while a darker moth flourished. This is touted as a classic illustration of natural selection, the theory that nature preserves those forms that function better than their rivals in the struggle for existence. But recently it was discovered that photographs showing the light moths against the darkened tree trunks were faked. Peppered moths fly about in the upper branches of trees and don't perch on the trunks at all. Even more recently, biologist Theodore Sargent of the University of Massachusetts admitted that he glued dead samples of the moths onto the tree trunks for a *NOVA* documentary. The respected journal *Nature* says the moth example, once the "prize horse in our stable" to illustrate evolution by natural selection, must now be thrown out.[8]

No scientific finding has contradicted the basic principle that change in living things is limited. Luther Burbank, regarded as the greatest breeder of all time, said the tendency for organisms to stay true to type is so constant that it can be considered a natural law—what he called the law of the Reversion to the Average. It's a law, he said, that "keeps all living things within some more or less fixed limitations."[9]

Despite what the textbooks say, Darwin did not prove that nature is capable of crossing those "fixed limitations." He suggested only that it was theoretically possible—that minor changes might have accumulated over thousands of years until a fish became an amphibian, an amphibian became a reptile, and a reptile became a mammal. But after more than 150 years, it has become clear that Darwin's speculation flies in the face of all the results of breeding and laboratory experimentation, as well as the pattern in the fossil record.

The simple words from the first chapter of Genesis still stand firm: And God made every living thing to reproduce "after their kind" (see Gen. 1:11-12, 21, 24-25, NASB).

IRREDUCIBLE COMPLEXITY

The late Christian evangelist Francis Schaeffer used to offer an argument against evolution that was simple, easy to grasp, and devastating: Suppose a fish evolves lungs. What happens then? Does it move up to the next evolutionary stage?

Of course not. It drowns.

Living things cannot simply change piecemeal—a new organ here, a new limb there. An organism is an integrated system, and any isolated change in the system is more likely to be harmful than helpful. If a fish's gills were to begin mutating into a set of lungs, it would be a disaster, not an advantage. The only way to turn a fish into a land-dwelling animal is to transform it all at once, with a host of interrelated changes happening at the same time—not only lungs but also coadapted changes in the skeleton, the circulatory system, and so on.

The term to describe this kind of interdependent system is *irreducible complexity*. And the fact that organisms are irreducibly complex is yet another argument that they could not have evolved piecemeal, one step at a time, as Darwin proposed. Darwinian theory states that all living structures evolved in small, gradual steps from simpler structures—feathers from scales, wings from forelegs, blossoms from leaves, and so on. But anything that is irreducibly complex cannot evolve in gradual steps, and thus its very existence refutes Darwin's theory.

The concept of irreducible complexity was developed by Michael Behe, a Lehigh University professor of biochemistry, in his 1993 book *Darwin's Black Box*. Behe's homey example of irreducible complexity is the mousetrap. A mousetrap cannot be assembled gradually, he points out. You cannot start with a wooden platform and catch a few mice, add a spring and catch a few more mice, add a hammer, and so on, each addition making the mousetrap function better. No, to even *start* catching mice, all the parts must be assembled from the outset. The mousetrap doesn't work until all its parts are present and working together.[10]

Many living structures are like the mousetrap. They involve an entire system of interacting parts all working together. If one part were to evolve in isolation, the entire system of interacting parts would stop functioning; and since, according to Darwinism, natural selection preserves the forms that function better than their rivals, the nonfunctioning system would be eliminated by natural selection—like the fish with lungs. Therefore, there is no possible Darwinian explanation of how irreducibly complex structures and systems came into existence.

Interestingly, Darwin himself grasped the problem and even admitted that it could falsify his theory. "If it could be demonstrated that any complex organ existed which could not possibly have been formed by numerous, successive, slight modifications," he wrote, "my theory would absolutely break down."[11] Today we can confidently say that his theory *has* broken down, for we now know that nature is full of examples of complex organs that could not possibly have been formed by numerous, slight modifications—that is, organs that are irreducibly complex.

Take the example of the bat. Evolutionists propose that the bat evolved from a small, mouselike creature whose forelimbs (the "front toes") developed into wings by gradual steps. But picture the steps: As the "front toes" grow longer and the skin begins to grow between them, the animal can no longer run without stumbling over them; and yet the forelimbs are not long enough to function as wings. And so, during most of its hypothetical transitional stages, the poor creature would have limbs too long for running and too short for flying. It would flop along helplessly and soon become extinct.

There is no conceivable pathway for bat wings to be formed in gradual stages. And this conclusion is confirmed by the fossil record, where we find no transitional fossils leading up to bats. The first time bats appear in the fossil record, they are already fully formed and virtually identical to modern bats.

A classic example of irreducible complexity is the human eye. An eye is no use at all unless all its parts are fully formed and working together. Even a slight alteration from its current form destroys its function. How, then, could the eye evolve by slight alterations? Even in Darwin's day the complexity of the eye was offered as evidence against his theory, and Darwin said the mere thought of trying to explain the eye gave him "a cold shudder."

Darwin would have shuddered even harder had he known the structure of cells *inside* the eye. Contemporary Darwinists such as Richard Dawkins have tried to solve the problem by tracing a pathway to the evolution of the eye, starting with a light-sensitive spot, moving to a group of cells cupped to focus light better, and so on through a graded series of small improvements to produce a true lens. But as Behe points out, even the first step—the light-sensitive spot—is irreducibly complex, requiring a chain reaction of chemical reactions, starting when a photon interacts with a molecule called 11-*cis*-retinal, which changes to *trans*-retinal, which forces a change in the shape of a protein called rhodopsin, which sticks to another protein called transducin, which binds to another molecule . . . and so on. And where do those cupped cells that Dawkins talks about come from? There are dozens of complex proteins involved in maintaining cell shape, and dozens more that control groups of cells. Each of Dawkins's steps is itself a complex system, and adding them together doesn't answer where these complex systems came from in the first place. It's as if we asked how a stereo system is made, and someone answered, "By plugging a set of speakers into an amplifier and adding a CD player and a tape deck." Right. The real question is how to make those speakers and amplifiers in the first place.[12]

The most advanced, automated modern factory, with its computers and robots all coordinated on a precisely timed schedule, is less complex than the inner workings of a single cell. No such system could arise in a blind, step-by-step Darwinian process. The most rational explanation of irreducibly complex structures in nature is that they are products of the creative mind of an intelligent being.

■   ■   ■

ON ALL FRONTS, scientists are being forced to face up to the evidence for an intelligent cause. Ever since big bang theory was proposed, cosmologists have had to wrestle with the implications that the universe had an absolute beginning—and therefore a transcendent creator. The discovery of the information content in DNA is forcing biologists to recognize an intelligent cause for the origin of life. So, too, the fact of irreducible complexity is raising the question of design in living things.

Science cannot tell us everything we might wish to know about this intelligent cause, of course. It cannot reveal the details of God's character, and it cannot explain his plan of salvation. These are tasks for theology. But a study of the design and purpose in nature does clearly support the existence of a transcendent creator—so clearly that, as the apostle Paul writes in the New Testament, we stand before him without excuse (see Rom. 1:20).

Since the scientific evidence is so persuasive, why does the scientific establishment cling so tenaciously to Darwinian evolution? Why is Darwinism still the official creed in our public schools? Because the real issue is not what we see through the microscope or the telescope; it's what we adhere to in our hearts and minds. Darwinism functions as the cornerstone propping up a naturalistic worldview, and therefore the scientist who is committed to naturalism before he or she even walks into the laboratory is primed to accept even the flimsiest evidence supporting the theory. The most trivial change in living things is accepted as confirmation of the most far-flung claims of evolution, so that minor variation in finch beaks or insecticide resistance is touted as evidence that finches and flies both evolved ultimately from the slime by blind, unguided natural processes.

The core of the controversy is not science; it is a titanic struggle between opposing worldviews—between naturalism and theism. Is the universe governed by blind material forces or by a loving personal being? Only when Christians understand this—only when we clear away the smoke screens and get to the core issue—will we stop losing debates. Only then will we be able to help our kids, like Katy, face the continual challenges to their faith.

DARWIN'S DANGEROUS IDEA

Consider the situation of Christian parents, not necessarily fundamentalists,
who suspect that the term evolution *drips with atheistic implications. The*
whole point of [the more consistent Darwinists] is that the parents are dead
right about the implications and the science educators who deny this are either
misinformed or lying.

PHILLIP JOHNSON

Do evolution and religion really conflict? For public relations purposes
many Darwinists veil their antagonism toward religion. For example, Harvard
paleontologist Stephen J. Gould, though a prominent critic of design theory,
insists he is not irreligious. Science and religion cannot conflict, he says,
because they deal with different things: Science is about facts, while "religion
struggles with human morality."[1]

Even many Christians have fallen for this tactic, with the result that we
are often unprepared for the intellectual battles we face in a secular culture.
For though Darwinism is a scientific theory and must be answered with scientific evidence, it is more fundamentally a worldview—or, more precisely, a
crucial plank in the worldview of naturalism. And unless we engage it on that
level, we will remain ineffective in answering its challenges.

One evolutionist who is boldly up-front about this underlying
worldview is biologist William Provine of Cornell University. He declares
forthrightly that Darwinism is not just about mutations and fossils; it is a
comprehensive philosophy stating that all life can be explained by natural
causes acting randomly—which implies that there is no need for the Creator. And if God did not create the world, he notes, then the entire body of
Christian belief collapses.

Provine preaches his message on college campuses across the country,
often flashing the following list on an overhead projector to hammer home

what consistent Darwinism means: "No life after death; no ultimate foundation for ethics; no ultimate meaning for life; no free will."[2] The only reason
anyone still believes in such things, Provine says, is that people have not yet
grasped the full implications of Darwinism.

His ideas may sound radical, but Provine is being brutally honest. He
recognizes that the biblical teaching of creation is not just a theological doctrine; it is the very foundation of everything Christians believe.

On the other side of the debate, Berkeley law professor Phillip Johnson
travels around the country arguing *against* Darwinism, yet he agrees whole-
heartedly with Provine on the far-reaching implications of the theory. These
implications often emerge when Johnson speaks before secular audiences.
As he writes, "I have found that any discussion with modernists about the
weaknesses of the theory of evolution quickly turns into a discussion of politics, particularly sexual politics." Why? Because modernists "typically fear
that any discrediting of naturalistic evolution will end in women being sent
to the kitchen, gays to the closet, and abortionists to jail."[3]

In other words, most people sense instinctively that there is much more
at stake here than a scientific theory—that a link exists between the material
order and the moral order. Though the fears Johnson encounters are certainly exaggerated, this basic intuition is right. Our origin determines our
destiny. It tells us who we are, why we are here, and how we should order our
lives together in society. Our view of origins shapes our understanding of
ethics, law, education—and yes, even sexuality. Whether we start with the
assumption that we are creatures of a personal God or that we are products of
a mindless process, a whole network of consequences follows, and these consequences diverge dramatically.

Take ethics. If a transcendent God created us for a purpose, then the
most rational approach is to ask, What is that purpose, and how must we live
in order to fulfill it? The answer is found in divine revelation; its moral commands tell us how we can become the people God created us to be. So Christian morality is not subjective, based on our personal feelings; it is objective,
based on the way God created human nature. Skeptics often dismiss Christianity as "irrational," but if we were indeed created, then the truly irrational
course is to ignore the Creator's moral rules.

By contrast, naturalism claims that God did not create us; rather, it is
we who created the idea of God. He "exists" only in the minds of those who
believe in him. If this claim is true, then the most rational course is to dismiss
religion as wishful thinking and to base morality squarely on what is
real—on scientific knowledge. And science tells us that humans are products
of evolutionary forces, that morality is nothing more than an idea that

appears in our minds when we have evolved to a certain level. Consequently, there is no ultimate objective basis for morality; humans create their own standards. Since the only objective reality that exists is the natural world, and it is in constant evolutionary flux, our ideas about right and wrong are constantly changing as well. The result is radical ethical relativism.

Or consider the subject of law. Traditionally, a nation's laws were understood to be based on a transcendent moral order (based in turn on divine law). The belief was that "men do not make laws. They do but discover them. Laws . . . must rest on the eternal foundation of righteousness." These words may sound as if they came from the pen of a sixteenth-century divine, but they were written in the early twentieth century by our thirtieth president, Calvin Coolidge.[4]

Yet if Darwinism is true, there is no divine law or transcendent moral order, and there is no final, authoritative basis for law. The influential legal theorist Oliver Wendell Holmes, an avowed Darwinian, taught that laws are merely a codification of political policies judged to be socially and economically advantageous. Law is reduced to a managerial skill used in the service of social engineering—the dominant view in the legal profession today.

In education, Darwinism has molded not only the content but also the methodology of teaching. The key figure is John Dewey, who sought to work out what Darwinism means for the learning process. If human beings are part of nature and nothing more, he reasoned, then the mind is simply an organ that has evolved from lower forms in the struggle for existence—just as wings or claws have evolved—and its value depends on whether it works, whether it enables the organism to survive. Dewey rejected the traditional belief that an idea is an insight into an objective reality, to be judged by whether it is true or false. Instead, he argued that ideas are merely hypotheses about what will get the results we want, and their validity depends on whether they work. Dewey's pragmatic philosophy is the source of much of the relativism that has gutted both academic and moral education today.

Darwinism is even a key source of postmodernism, which dismisses the idea of universal truth as a tool of oppression wielded by "Dead White Males." Because Darwinism eliminates the transcendent, postmodernism draws the inevitable conclusion that there is no transcendent truth. Each of us is locked in the limited perspective of our race, gender, and ethnic group. The "search for truth" that supposedly motivates education is a sham; there is only the black perspective, the feminist perspective, the Hispanic perspective, and so on. Any claim to universal truth is considered an attempt to impose the perspective of one group on all the others.

Despite its flamboyant skepticism toward objective truth, ironically, postmodernism rests on an assumption that *something* is objectively true—namely, Darwinism.

If tying Darwinism to postmodernism seems a bit of a stretch, listen to the personal odyssey of the influential postmodernist guru Richard Rorty, now at Stanford University. In an autobiographical essay, Rorty reveals that he was once attracted to Christianity. But finding himself "incapable" of "the humility that Christianity demanded," he turned away from God—only to discover that a world without God is a world without any basis for universal truth or justice.[5] Rorty then determined to work out a philosophy consistent with Darwinism. Like Dewey, he accepted the Darwinist notion that ideas are problem-solving tools that evolve as means of adapting to the environment. "Keeping faith with Darwin," Rorty writes, means understanding that the human species is not oriented "toward Truth," but only "toward its own increased prosperity."[6] Truth claims are just tools that "help us get what we want."[7] (Which means, of course, that Rorty's own ideas are just tools for getting what *he* wants—including the idea of postmodernism. Thus, postmodernism refutes itself.)

Darwinism thus forms the linchpin to the fundamental debate between Christianity and naturalism in virtually every subject area. Since modern culture has given science authority to define the way the world "really is," Darwinism provides the scientific justification for a naturalistic approach in every field. As British biologist Richard Dawkins puts it, Darwin "made it possible to be an intellectually fulfilled atheist."[8]

Many Christians shrink from drawing such a stark contrast between theism and Darwinism. They hope to combine Darwin's biological theory with belief in God—suggesting that God may have used evolution as his method of creating. Yet Darwin himself insisted that the two are mutually exclusive.[9] For natural selection acts as a sieve, sifting out harmful variations in living things and preserving helpful variations. But if God were guiding evolution, he would ensure that each variation was beneficial from the start. Natural selection would be, in Darwin's own words, "superfluous."[10] The whole point of his theory was to identify a natural process that would mimic intelligent design, thus making *design* superfluous.

Darwin is typically portrayed as a man forced to the theory of natural selection by the weight of the facts. But today historians recognize that he was first committed to the philosophy of naturalism and then sought a theory to justify it scientifically. Early in his career, he had already turned against the idea of creation and developed a settled conviction that, as he put it, "Everything in nature is the result of fixed laws."[11] In other words, the deck was already stacked in favor of a naturalistic account of life before he actually uncovered any convincing facts.

Indeed, nature became virtually a substitute deity for Darwin. "As regards his respect for the laws of Nature," wrote his son William, "it might be called reverence if not a religious feeling. No man could feel more intensely the vastness and the inviolability of the laws of nature."[12] With his attitude akin to religious worship, it is not surprising that Charles Darwin eventually attributed godlike creative powers to natural selection.

Modern Darwinists insist that evolution is so obviously supported by the facts that anyone who dissents must be ignorant or dishonest. But Darwin was more candid. He knew quite well he had not proved his theory of natural selection. He described it as an inference, grounded chiefly on analogy. It can be judged only by how useful it is, he wrote, how well "it groups and explains phenomena."[13]

Likewise, many of Darwin's earliest and most ardent supporters were quick to spot the scientific weaknesses in his theory, yet they chose to champion it because they saw it as a useful means of promoting naturalistic philosophy. Herbert Spencer, the first person to extend evolution into every discipline, from ethics to psychology, explained frankly that he felt an enormous internal pressure to find a naturalistic alternative to the idea of creation. "The Special Creation belief had dropped out of my mind many years before," he wrote, "and I could not remain in a suspended state: acceptance of the only conceivable alternative was peremptory." Moreover, Spencer admitted, once you accept the philosophy of naturalism, some form of naturalistic evolution is an "inevitable corollary"—regardless of the strength of the scientific evidence. [14]

Thomas Huxley christened himself "Darwin's bulldog" and fought fiercely for the cause, and yet by his own admission, he never thought Darwin's theory amounted to much scientifically. He, too, rallied to the cause for philosophical reasons. Long before his encounter with Darwin, Huxley had rejected the biblical teaching of creation and was actively looking for an alternative. Huxley declared that Darwin "did the immense service of freeing us forever from the dilemma—Refuse to accept the creation hypothesis, and what have you to propose that can be accepted by any cautious reasoner?"[15] Apparently Huxley was willing to champion *any* naturalistic theory, even one he found scientifically flawed, as long as it provided an alternative to creation.

The historical data makes it clear that the contest over evolution in the nineteenth century was philosophically "rigged." Darwinism won not so much because it fit the evidence but because it provided a scientific rationale for naturalism. If the world is governed by uniformly operating laws, as Huxley said, then the successive populations of beings "must have proceeded from one another in the way of progressive modification."[16] The operative word here is "must." Once you accept philosophical naturalism, then something very much like Darwinism *must* be true—regardless of the facts.

Darwin's early opponents likewise understood what was at stake. In 1874, Princeton theologian Charles Hodge published an essay asking "What Is Darwinism?" And he answered bluntly that it is tantamount to atheism. "Natural selection is selection made by natural laws, working without intention and design," Hodge wrote. And "the denial of design in nature is virtually the denial of God."[17]

In our own day, one of the most explicit statements of the philosophical motivation behind Darwinism comes, surprisingly enough, from Harvard geneticist Richard Lewontin. In an article arguing for the superiority of science over religion (which he groups with things like UFOs and channeling), Lewontin freely admits that science has its own problems. It has created many of our social problems (like ecological disasters), and many scientific theories are no more than "unsubstantiated just-so stories." Nevertheless, "in the struggle between science and the supernatural," we "take the side of science." Why? "Because we have a prior commitment to materialism."[18]

Note carefully those last few words. Lewontin is admitting that the hostility to religion that is fashionable in the scientific establishment is not driven by the facts but by materialistic philosophy.

And there is more, for Lewontin says even the methods of science are driven by materialistic philosophy. The rules that define what qualifies as science in the first place have been crafted by materialists in such a way as to ensure they get only materialistic theories. Or, as Lewontin puts it, "we are forced by our *a priori* adherence to material causes to create an apparatus of investigation and a set of concepts that produce material explanations."[19]

This is a stunning admission. The authority of science rests primarily on its public image—on the impression that its theories rest firmly on a foundation of empirical facts. But Lewontin has pulled back the curtains in Oz to reveal the wizard's strings and levers. The truth is that much of Darwinism is not science but naturalistic philosophy masquerading as science. So an honest debate between Darwinism and Christianity is not fact versus faith but philosophy versus philosophy, worldview versus worldview.

We must be clear about what is at stake here. As long as Darwinism reigns in our schools and elite culture, the Christian worldview will be considered the madwoman in the attic—irrational and unbelievable. That's why we can no longer allow naturalists to treat science as a sanctuary where their personal philosophy reigns free from challenge.

WHO IS "THIS GUY"?

In William Steig's *Yellow & Pink,* a delightfully whimsical picture book for children, two wooden figures wake up to find themselves lying on an old newspaper in the hot sun. One figure is painted yellow, the other pink.

Suddenly, Yellow sits up and asks, "Do you know what we're doing here?"

"No," replies Pink. "I don't even remember getting here."

So begins a debate between the two marionettes over the origin of their existence.

Pink surveys their well-formed features and concludes, "Someone must have made us."

Yellow disagrees. "I say we're an accident," and he outlines a hypothetical scenario of how it might have happened. A branch might have broken off a tree and fallen on a sharp rock, splitting one end of the branch into two legs. Then the wind might have sent it tumbling down a hill until it was chipped and shaped. Perhaps a flash of lightning struck in such a way as to splinter the wood into arms and fingers. Eyes might have been formed by woodpeckers boring in the wood.

"With enough time, a thousand, a million, maybe two and a half million years, lots of unusual things could happen," says Yellow. "Why not us?"

The two figures argue back and forth.

In the end, the discussion is cut off by the appearance of a man coming out of a nearby house. He strolls over to the marionettes, picks them up, and checks their paint. "Nice and dry," he comments, and tucking them under his arm, he heads back toward the house.

Peering out from under the man's arm, Yellow whispers in Pink's ear, "Who is this guy?"[20]

●   ■   ●

THAT IS PRECISELY the question each one of us must answer, and it's no storybook fantasy. It is deadly serious. Beyond the public debates and rhetoric, beyond the placard waving and politicizing, at the heart of every worldview are the intensely personal questions: Who made me, and why am I here?

Every worldview has to begin somewhere—God or matter, take your choice. Everything else flows from that initial choice. This is why the question of creation has become such a fierce battleground today. It is the foundation of the entire Christian worldview. For if God created all of finite reality, then every aspect of that reality must be subject to him and his truth. Everything finds its meaning and interpretation in relation to God. No part of life can be autonomous or neutral, no part can be sliced off and made independent from Christian truth. Because creation includes the whole scope of finite reality, the Christian worldview must be equally comprehensive, covering every aspect of our lives, our thinking, our choices. Both friends and foes of Christianity realize that everything stands or falls on the doctrine of creation.

Christians often seek to evangelize others by starting with salvation—John 3:16 and the gospel message. And for an earlier generation, that approach worked. Most people had some kind of church experience in their background, even if they did not have strong personal beliefs. But in today's post-Christian world, many people no longer even understand the meaning of crucial biblical terms. For example, the basic term *sin* makes no sense to people if they have no concept of a holy God who created us and who therefore has a right to require certain things of us. And if people don't understand sin, they certainly don't comprehend the need for salvation.

Consequently, in today's world, beginning evangelism with the message of salvation is like starting a book at the middle—you don't know the characters, and you can't make sense of the plot. Instead, we must begin with Genesis, where the main character, God, establishes himself as the Creator, and the "plot" of human history unfolds its first crucial episodes. And the scientific evidence supporting these opening episodes is powerful, as Dave Mulholland discovered in his personal odyssey.

First, cosmology has discovered the shattering truth that matter is not eternal after all, as naturalistic scientists once confidently assumed. The universe began at a finite period of time—which in turn implies that something *outside* the universe must have set it going.

Second, there are the staggering "coincidences" that make the universe fit for life. From the molecular properties of water to the balance of electrical charges in the proton and electron, the entire structure of the physical universe is exquisitely designed to support life on Earth.

Third, laboratory experiments touted as proof that life can arise spontaneously by random natural forces turn out to prove nothing of the sort. Instead, they provide positive evidence that life can be created only by an intelligent agent controlling, directing, and manipulating the process. The discovery of DNA gives explosive new force to the argument for design. If we rely on experience—and, after all, science is *supposed* to be based on experience—the only known source of information is an intelligent cause.

Fourth, Darwin did not succeed in demonstrating that life developed by means of mindless, undirected natural forces. Experiments with breeding and mutations have shown that his fundamental assumption—that living things can vary endlessly—is fatally flawed. Today, the most advanced investigations into the heart of the cell confirm that the irreducible complexity of living things can be explained only by intelligent design.

The continued dominance of Darwinism has less to do with its scientific validity than with a commitment to naturalism. Naturalism, in turn, has spread like a toxic oil spill into fields as diverse as ethics, law, education, postmodernism—to name just a few. As a result, Darwinism has become the cornerstone for a comprehensive philosophy that stands in stark opposition to Christianity.

ROAD MAP TO REALITY

Every worldview is a proposed map of reality, a guide to navigating in the world. One effective test of any truth claim, therefore, is to ask whether we can live by it. If you follow a map but still find yourself splashing into rivers or crashing off cliffs, you can be quite sure something is wrong with the map. By the same token, if you live according to a certain worldview but keep bumping up against reality in painful ways, you can be sure something is wrong with the worldview. It fails to reflect reality accurately.

Let's apply this test to the naturalistic worldview of the well-known science popularizer Carl Sagan, whom we have referred to several times in this section. Sagan literally canonized the cosmos, openly plugging his personal philosophy on his popular television program. And far from repudiating this transformation of science into religion, the scientific establishment richly rewarded him, even awarding him the National Academy of Science's Public Welfare Medal in 1994.

One consequence of Sagan's religion of the cosmos was that he was actively committed to the cause of animal rights. And quite logically so. For if humans evolved from the beasts, there can be no intrinsic difference between them. It would be just as cruel and immoral to kill a cow as to murder a person. "In my writings," Sagan said in a *Parade* magazine article, "I have tried to show how closely related we are to other animals, how cruel it is to gratuitously inflict pain on them."[21] As a result, he was adamantly opposed to using animals for medical research. For if animals have the same value as humans, how can we justify expending their lives to save humans?

But on this issue, Sagan bumped up against reality in a very painful way. In 1994, he discovered that he had myelodysplasia, a rare blood disease. With possibly just months to live, he was told that his only chance for survival was an experimental bone-marrow transplant. But there was one catch: The procedure that might save his life had been developed by research on animals—the kind of research Sagan passionately opposed.

Sagan faced an excruciating dilemma: Should he remain true to his naturalistic philosophy and reject the marrow graft as something acquired by immoral means? Or should he agree to undergo the medical treatment in hope of saving his life, though it meant acting in contradiction to his moral convictions?

Sagan didn't take long to reach a decision: He underwent three bone-marrow treatments, which did extend his life for a time (though he ultimately succumbed to the disease and died in 1996). At the time Sagan wrote the *Parade* article, he was still, in his words, "very conflicted" over the choice he had made. He recognized clearly that his decision to accept the treatment was a practical denial of his naturalistic worldview. But when he came up against reality, he abandoned his naturalistic road map and, whether he admitted it or not, implicitly shifted to the biblical road map, which says that humans do have a value transcending that of plants and animals.

Christianity is not merely a religion, defined narrowly as personal piety and corporate worship. It is also an objective perspective on all reality, a complete worldview. Only Christianity consistently stands up to the test of practical living. Only Christianity gives us an accurate road map. Only Christianity matches the way we must act if we are to live humanely and rationally in the real world.

Creation is the first element of the Christian worldview, the foundation on which everything else is built. It is the basis of human dignity, for our origin tells us who we are, why we are here, and how we should treat one another. The questions of human life have become the most pressing issues of our day, as two men discovered in a very personal way on a battlefield on the other side of the globe.

CHAPTER 11

A MATTER OF LIFE

Vietnam, 1968

From their hovering position fifteen hundred feet above the ground, the men in Colonel Yarborough's Command & Control (C&C) helicopter kept watch at the end of an anxious day. For the past two weeks, their Ghostrider division had been shuttling in troops and supplies for a big push in the central highlands at Plei Merong. The atmosphere was tense, the territory unsecured. During reconnaissance, as Yarborough's crew had hovered over the area for the first time, they had spotted a stockpile of empty rocket crates not more than three hundred yards from the present landing zone. The enemy could be anywhere.

As the C&C copter circled slowly over the jungle, the crew watched another helicopter rotor into position above the steep hillside landing zone, hovering close to the ground to pick up support personnel returning to base. The men on the C&C copter could see men scurrying below, disappearing in and out of the scrub trees and bushes. The mechanical dragonfly wigwagged, impatient to leave.

Kaboom!

Suddenly the air burst with rockets. Puffs of white smoke from small firearms rose in dozens of places over the hillside. The copter near the ground recoiled left, as if stabbed in its side. A curling plume of gray scorpioned the back rotor, and the machine began to pitch wildly. The smoke grew black and full.

As the wounded machine continued to yaw and heave, Ken McGarity watched the scene from his right-gunner position in the C&C copter. He saw the other helicopter fall, slamming down onto the landing zone, its main rotor shattering. He spotted two helmets pop out. Then another. The three men ran for cover, one of them on fire.

The black smoke from the hit copter mushroomed, obscuring Ken's view. Rockets continued to shoot up through the smoke, though they didn't have the range to reach the C&C copter.

"We're going down!" screamed the C&C pilot. He shouted and waved at Ken to watch his side as they spiraled down.

Ken took his gun off its stand and knelt in the doorway, his right foot out on the skid. He leaned out as far as he could, straining to see. He had to know where their own men were before he could lay down a blanket of fire.

The colonel pushed his way to the open door, beside Ken, ready to throw out an extinguisher for the burning soldier on the ground. Their C&C copter had cleared the high bamboo and would soon be down to the scrub trees, but Ken still couldn't see where their guys were hiding. He couldn't see the enemy either.

Soon they were right over the landing zone. Why didn't the colonel throw out the extinguisher? They weren't supposed to be here more than seven seconds. They had been here at least twenty. *Throw the thing!*

No one saw the B-40 rocket coming.

Half the ship exploded on contact. Ken was catapulted into the air and fell from the height of the scrub trees onto the bare ground. . . .

When he regained consciousness, Otto Mertz, a buddy from the first downed copter, was dragging him through the mud to safety.

"My legs!" Ken screamed.

"They're broken," someone said.

His arms had been crossed over his chest. *They must be broken, too,* Ken thought.

He passed in and out of consciousness several times before he was finally hoisted onto a medevac helicopter. When he was secured into a transport stretcher, a woman's voice asked, "What's your name?"

"McGarity," he said. "Ken McGarity. Am I hurt bad?"

"We're going to take care of you," the nurse shouted as the thrashing blades lifted them away.[1]

.   .   .

WHEN THE WOUNDED men arrived at the Army's 71st Evacuation Hospital at Pleiku on September 21, 1968, Dr. Kenneth Swan was surgeon of the day. The thirty-three-year-old doctor had been in Vietnam only a month.

Two men had died at Plei Merong. All the others could be classified as "walking wounded," having sustained only minor injuries—all except the soldier identified as Army Specialist 4 Ken McGarity. The man was covered with dirt and bloodied mud. One leg hung by a thin strip of skin; the other was broken so badly that the femur protruded from what was left of his thigh. Shoelace tourniquets had stopped the arterial bleeding, but the wounds were plastered with mud and sticks. Both arms were badly fractured and pitted with shrapnel wounds. The man's right pinkie finger was gone, and one testicle had been blown away. Blood oozed from both eyes, and the left eyeball was shattered. The injuries to the eyes indicated shrapnel wounds, which could mean brain damage.

As Swan assessed the devastation before him, he had two choices. He could classify the soldier as "expectant," medicate him, and leave him to die, or he could devote the full resources of the hospital to treating him. Which call should he make?

By all rights, this soldier should have bled to death already. He had been in the field almost two hours before being airlifted out. But he was not only alive, he was conscious.

"How am I doing?" the man asked.

"You're in the hospital."

"I feel like I left my legs back on the helicopter. They're broken, aren't they?"

Dr. Swan knew the soldier's joke was closer to the truth, but the short exchange helped Swan make up his mind. As a Christian, how could he refuse to treat a man who was talking to him?

"We're going to take care of you," he promised.

X rays revealed what the surgeon already knew: The soldier's legs had to come off. As Swan worked on the amputations—both legs above the knee—he coordinated the activities of the team of doctors he had called in. The orthopedist treated the shrapnel wounds in McGarity's arms. The ophthalmologist removed the man's left eye and cleaned the wounds to the right eye, hoping to save it. When the orthopedist had done all he could on McGarity's arms, Swan amputated the ragged stump of the soldier's right pinkie finger. A urologist worked to limit the damage of the "shrapnel vasectomy."

Then, in a final delicate and involved surgery, the neurologist performed a craniotomy, cutting through the top of the soldier's forehead and lifting away the skull so that he could extract the shrapnel from the brain's frontal lobes—damage that might have a lobotomizing effect. Or worse.

For eight hours, the surgeons stood in their muddy boots on the concrete floor and did the best they could to repair Ken McGarity. A civilian photographer from Casualty Care hovered about—much to the surgeons' irritation—recording the soldier's wounds for a research study. In the background, providing a bizarre rhythmic accompaniment, the adjacent air base took incoming mortar fire.

When the surgeries were completed, Dr. Swan felt his team had done well. Their patient had a chance.

The next morning, however, Swan's commanding officer sat down with him in the mess hall and grilled him about the case. Why had he decided to treat the recent casualty so aggressively?

"There was no other way to treat his injuries," Swan replied, surprised at the question.

His superior looked him squarely in the eye. "Look, Ken, why send blind, double amputees with significant brain damage back to their parents? What were you thinking?"

Swan found himself responding from his gut. "I was trained to *treat* the sick. It's not up to me who lives and dies. That's God's decision."

"As the surgeon on duty, it *was* up to you," said his commanding officer. "The next time you make a call, ask yourself what kind of life you're condemning someone to." He paused. "Of course, he may die yet." He sounded grimly hopeful.

■   ■   ■

SEVERAL DAYS LATER, Rick Martin, a fellow enlistee from Alabama, stopped in the ICU to visit Ken McGarity. His friend's head was swathed in a giant bandage. His broken arms were restrained in tight wraps that allowed their wounds to be freshly dressed. A single sheet covered his bandaged leg stumps, each of which had swollen to the size of his waist.

"Hey, buddy," he said. "It's Rick Martin."

"Look at this, man—my legs are broke. My eyes must have got sandblasted, too."

The nurse had told Rick that Ken did not yet understand the severity of his injuries. But hearing how wrong Ken's impressions were, Rick became distraught, almost angry. Someone had to tell the guy the truth.

"No, man," Rick said. He paused a moment, gathering courage. "Your legs aren't broke. They were amputated."

"Really?"

"Yeah. You lost your legs."

"How about my eyes?"

"I'm sorry. You're going to be blind."

"My arms feel like they're there."

"Yeah, your arms are going to be okay. They're just broken."

Ken was silent for so long that Rick wondered if the drugs had lulled him back to sleep.

"Okay, then," Ken said finally. "Okay."

Rick didn't know what to make of his friend's resignation; he figured it was probably the morphine talking.

"I want you to do something for me, Rick," Ken said. "I really need you to do this. Write my mom and dad and tell them that I got my legs broken and that sand blew in my eyes. But tell them I'm going to be all right. I don't want them to know how bad it is. Will you do that?"

"Sure," said Rick. "Sure."

"You got a cigarette, man?" Ken asked.

"Yeah," he said, "but I don't think we'd better light up in here with all this oxygen around. We'll probably blow the place up."

"Get me out of here then," Ken said.

"I'm not sure—"

"Just load me in a wheelchair and take me out."

Rick scooped Ken up. The guy felt as light and frail as Rick's nine-year-old brother.

Outside, on the hardpan ground surrounding the ICU, Ken tilted his head back and took deep breaths.

"Feel that, Rick?" he asked. "Feel the wind? It feels good on my face."

Rick lit a cigarette and put it in Ken's mouth. He took a couple drags, then Rick took the cigarette back.

"I'm alive," Ken said.

"You're darn right," said Rick, starting to feel an odd glimmer of enthusiasm. "You're smoking."

"The wind feels good," Ken said again. He took a full breath. Then another. Then a shuddering came over him. "I'm going to pass out now, Rick."

"Okay. I've got you, buddy."

■　　■　　■

A MONTH LATER, the chaplain's assistant, another young man from Ken McGarity's hometown of Phenix City, Alabama, brought Dr. Kenneth Swan a piece of news. "Thought you would like to know, McGarity made it back. He's at Walter Reed."

Kenneth Swan should have been happy to hear those words, but he was not. He envisioned the damaged soldier living in a veterans hospital, heavily medicated against the violent rages or psychotic delusions brought on by brain damage. He saw the man half-curled in a wheelchair, stretching his neck and muttering in a drugged rage. These images burned in the surgeon's imagination, where they would remain for twenty years.

■   ■   ■

BY THE TIME Ken McGarity reached Walter Reed Army Medical Center in Washington, D.C., three weeks after being wounded, the nightmares had started. As additional surgeries were performed to repair the ligament damage in his right arm and his amputation wounds, pain exploded at every level of his consciousness.

In his dreams he saw North Vietnamese regulars running down the middle of the base's airstrip. . . . The bodies were being picked up after Tet. . . . He leaned out of the copter once more, desperate to identify his own men. . . . He was running down a road in the middle of a firefight wearing only a T-shirt, fatigues, and boots. "Never go anywhere without your weapon!" his sergeant barked. "Never!" A rocket exploded, and he woke screaming, covered with sweat.

The nurse whispered, "We let you sleep through your last meds. We won't do that again." She gave him another shot of morphine.

He wanted to tell her that he was afraid to sleep. Then the morphine took over once more.

In McGarity's rare moments of lucidity, something else scared him—as much or more than his nightmares, though in a completely different way. When he had re-upped for his second tour in Vietnam, requesting reassignment to helicopter duty from his relatively safe post in the 75th Engineering Battalion, he had gone home for a month's leave. While there, one evening he drove out by the lake to be alone with his thoughts.

At first he relaxed, lying back in the long grass, watching the stars come out. But soon the sky's immensity seemed to tilt, levering until it threatened to topple on him. Suddenly he was straining to breathe against a pressing sense of fear.

What was he afraid of?

Death.

That was the thought smothering him. He didn't want to die. Anything but that. He was too young to leave this world that he was just beginning to discover.

He sat up, as if throwing open his own coffin, and lifted his arms up to the skies. "God, if you are there and will be with me, let me know," he prayed. "Give me a sign."

What sign?

In an instant, he made the deal. "You can take my eyes, you can take my arms, my legs, my mind, but leave my life." Did he know what he was offering? He thought he did. Suffering didn't scare him. Death did.

So when Rick Martin had first told Ken that he had lost his legs and his sight, Ken's mind had instantly flashed back to that deal he'd made with God. When he had said okay to Rick, it was really God that Ken had been talking to.

Now, lying in Walter Reed Army Medical Center, it was clear that God was real. God had heard him and had taken almost everything he had offered—but had left him his life. Even in the midst of his living nightmare, Ken McGarity realized that his life was a gift from God. God had not taken his life. *Why not? And where do I go from here? What does God want from me?*

.   .   .

WHEN KEN ARRIVED at Hines Veterans Administration Hospital outside Chicago to begin his rehabilitation on the blind ward, orderlies wheeled his eighty-pound body into the hospital. In transport, he had sweated out every toxin his infection-riddled body could produce.

"He sure needs to be cleaned up," said the nurse during his intake.

"I don't know what I'm supposed to do with him," complained the psychiatrist. "Why didn't they let this guy die?"

Why did people assume that because he was blind he was also deaf, Ken wondered. They not only spoke past him, they talked as if saving his life had been a mistake.

On the blind ward at Hines, however, Ken discovered a new power. He didn't have to do anything he didn't want to do. He had always been independent to a fault. Now he could play out his rebellion with abandon.

Medical personnel told him he needed to begin learning how to live his new life. He needed to exercise his arms, develop his upper body strength. But Ken only wanted the pain to go away. So he decided he would just lie in his bed and let them take care of him until the pain diminished enough for him to think about such things as upper body strength.

But he hadn't allowed for Nurse Early. She never handed his water cup to him; she always placed it on the table that pivoted in front of him. She wanted him to learn to feel for a glass without knocking it over.

Once, he became so frustrated that he knocked the glass across the room with a sweep of his right forearm. He heard the splat of water and the skip and bounce of the plastic cup with supreme satisfaction.

But Nurse Early came back every day. During the morning hours, she stretched his arms, working first for mobility, then strength, letting him use a half-pound dumbbell.

"Give me more weight," he demanded. He wanted to exercise like a man. Early wouldn't allow it, so he quit lifting her half-pounder.

Their running battle continued for weeks. Secretly, Ken liked the nurse's perfume. Just to know a woman was nearby, just to smell her scent—he liked that.

One day, feeling particularly lousy, Ken refused to attend occupational therapy. "I ain't no basket weaver!" he complained.

"Oh yeah?" said Early, and plopped him down hard in his wheelchair. "You are going to occupational therapy!" she said. "And I'll tell you what else you are going to do. You are going to act like a soldier. Your injuries don't entitle you to anything more than the United States Congress is willing to pay for. And it's not paying me to pity you!"

She kept up this harangue during the struggle of getting him belted into his chair and wheeling him out of the ward. She kicked the door open for emphasis. Then, she hung a fast right into a room that smelled of freshly washed towels and linen.

"We're in the laundry room, Ken," she said. "We're alone." Now her voice was calm, lower. "I want to tell you something."

You've told me enough already, he thought.

"I know you're hurting," she said, her voice warming with compassion. "I know that's why you don't want to do any of this. But you have to try. You have to try now while it still hurts. When the pain's gone, the opportunity's gone. You won't be able to regain any mobility if much more time passes. Ken, put all that stubbornness to use. I know you can do anything you put your mind to. From now on, it's just going to take a whole lot more effort. You're going to have to find your own way to do things. But you can. You will. If you were a quitter, you would be dead by now. I need you to show me the courage that kept you alive."

"Nurse Early?" said Ken.

"What?"

"What size do you want your stupid basket?"

■   ■   ■

KEN'S WARD CONTAINED all the worst cases. He didn't need his eyes to know that. He was the only one among the half-dozen in the room who could scoot himself out of bed into a wheelchair. Still, he and his ward mates found ways to entertain themselves. On Friday nights, they called a fried chicken delivery service and ordered in buckets and beer.

One Friday afternoon they were kidding each other, feeling high, anticipating their big night of chicken and suds, when Dave Crowley suggested, "Hey, Ken, why don't you get us some munchies? You can get in that chair now. Go on down to the PX and buy out the store."

"Yeah, what else can we do with our money?" said another.

Ken had never been able to turn down a dare. "I'll do it," he said.

He was in his wheelchair and nearly past the nurse's station when the nurse on duty called, "Where you going, Ken?"

"To the PX. Going to get my friends some munchies."

"That's good," she said absently, as if talking to a three-year-old who said he was flying to the moon.

Ken kept rolling. He would show them all.

By the time he reached the end of the first hall, he was wondering how he would ever make it. He waited until he heard the familiar scraping slide of a doctor's surgical booties.

"Can you tell me how to get to the PX, sir?" Ken asked.

"Turn left here, then down this corridor, a right at the next, two more, another left, another right, and then you had better ask again."

"Okay, thanks."

Powering his wheelchair with his left hand and scraping the wall for guidance with his right, Ken worked his way past doorjambs, heating ventilators, abandoned IV stands, and laundry carts. Several steep ramps gave him more than a thrill, and he wondered how he would ever wheel his chair up again on his way back.

He remembered instructions for one or two corridors at a time, then asked again. Finally, he turned into an open space and smelled hamburgers and fries. A few more hand-pumps, and he hit a table and chair and knew he had arrived.

But how would he make his way along the cafeteria rail? How would he know what was in front of him? He was swiveling his head around, trying to take in as much as he could through his useful senses, when he heard someone talking close by.

"Soldier?"

Was the person speaking to him?

"Soldier?"

"Yes, sir?"

"I'm Colonel McDermott. Are you supposed to be here?"

"I'm doing rehabilitation on the blind ward, sir. My buddies asked if I would go to the PX and get them some munchies. I'm the only one who can get in a chair, so I came down."

"That ward's up on level 9, isn't it?"

"Yes, sir."

"Level 9. That's a long way. Did somebody bring you down?"

"No, sir. I came down by myself."

"What's your name, soldier?"

"Specialist 4 Ken McGarity, sir. I was a door gunner with the Ghostriders."

"Would you like me to help you find your snacks?"

"Yes, sir. Appreciate it, sir. I was wondering how I was going to manage."

"You don't mind if I wheel you through the line, do you?"

"No, sir. It's a long way down from level 9."

As Colonel McDermott wheeled Ken past the candy bars, pretzels, and potato chips, the room grew quiet. So quiet that when the cash register chinged on Ken's purchases, it sounded like a symphonic *ta-da!*

"How are you going to get that bag up to level 9 with you, private?" the colonel asked.

"Easy." Ken tucked his change in the front pocket of his hospital gown, then grasped the top of the grocery bag between his teeth. He couldn't hold the bag in his lap because his leg stumps were too short to balance anything. He took a big breath through his nose, preparing to roll.

"Private McGarity?" said the colonel.

Ken let loose of the bag to answer. "Yes, sir?"

"I'm saluting you, private."

"Yes, sir."

Suddenly, the quiet was broken as applause rang out around him.

"Carry on," said the colonel.

Outside the PX, Ken powered up the first ramp, a new energy in his hands and arms. He could do it. He had found his way down here; now all he had to do was find his way in life. Nurse Early had said he could do anything he put his mind to. Now, for the first time, he was sure that he could. He hadn't realized how tightly his doubts and fears had been gripping him, trying to suffocate the life that remained.

Relief teared in his eyes. He was truly going to make it!

■   ■   ■

TWENTY YEARS LATER, in 1989, Peter McPherson, a young freelance journalist, called Dr. Kenneth Swan, then a professor of surgery at the

University of Medicine and Dentistry of New Jersey. McPherson was writing about trauma care, and Swan was an ideal candidate to interview. Besides his experience in Vietnam, he was chief of surgery for trauma care at his university hospital; he also remained in the army reserves as a full colonel.

"Dr. Swan, what was the toughest case of your career?" the young journalist asked. A twenty-year-old memory, long suppressed, rose to the surface of Swan's mind. It was the memory of a soldier wounded so badly that Swan's colleagues had thought him better off dead.

"What ever became of the guy?" asked McPherson after he heard the story.

"He made it back to the States," said Swan. "That's all I know."

When Peter McPherson's article appeared, dozens of readers wrote letters to the editor, wanting to know what had become of the young soldier. McPherson called Kenneth Swan and suggested that they find out. Neither was sure he would like what they might find.

Their search became almost an obsession that carried them through many dead ends and bureaucratic runarounds. But two years later, in July of 1991, Dr. Swan finally learned that his former patient, Kenneth McGarity, was now living in Columbus, Georgia; that he had a wife and two daughters, had completed his high school education, attended Auburn University, and had learned to scuba dive.

"You must have the wrong guy," Swan said to the person at the Veterans Administration. "My patient had brain damage. He was a double amputee. How would he ever learn to scuba dive?"

"Doctor, this is your patient. If you want to call him, go ahead."

When Swan placed the call, an upbeat Southern male voice answered. It was Ken McGarity.

Swan explained about Peter McPherson, the story, his search. "I would like to meet you," he concluded.

"Fine," said McGarity. "You can fill in a lot of holes for me, Dr. Swan. There are a lot of things I would like to know about that day."

So it was that on September 25, 1991, almost twenty-three years to the day since their fateful encounter in Pleiku, Dr. Swan and Ken McGarity met outside the McGarity home in Columbus, Georgia, accompanied by McPherson and a photographer. When McGarity extended his hand in greeting, Dr. Swan recognized his own work, the amputated right pinkie finger. In that instant, he felt a bond with this man. And in the long conversation that followed, he was able to offer Ken McGarity reassuring answers to a host of troubling concerns. Like survivor's guilt. Maybe he should have been left to die, as so many had suggested to him. Perhaps there had been someone who needed medical attention more.

"No, no," Swan reassured him. Treating Ken had not meant denying treatment to anyone else.

Then Dr. Swan raised his own troubling questions. Had it been worth it? Was Ken happy to be alive?

"I'll tell you something," Ken said to the doctor. "Being blind in a wheelchair has its problems, I won't deny that. But really, it's not so bad, Dr. Swan. I would be dead if it weren't for you!"[2]

▪   ▪   ▪

PETER MCPHERSON'S STORY was published in the *Washington Post*, and soon ABC's *20/20*, the *New York Times*, *Good Housekeeping*, and even the *Times* of London came calling.

The mass media ate up the story on its most superficial terms—after twenty years, doctor finds worst-case patient living a full and happy life. What an inspirational tribute to the indomitable human spirit! But real life is always more complicated than it appears, and it certainly was for Ken McGarity. At the time of Dr. Swan's visit, Ken, his wife, Theresa, and their girls were living through the most difficult part of Ken's healing.

In 1989, two years before Dr. Swan met the McGaritys, Theresa had had a nervous breakdown and had been hospitalized. The two girls, Alicia and Elizabeth, had gone to live with Theresa's parents. When Theresa came out of the hospital, she knew she had to confront Ken about the problems that had been building since their marriage in 1971, problems that had contributed to her own illness. To do so, she had to return to the place she had once considered her dream house—a place where Ken now lived alone, a sickened ghost of the man she had married.

When she crossed the threshold, the familiar scent and atmosphere hit her with the chilling effect of a mausoleum's dead air. She knew she couldn't bear to stay here for more than a few minutes, but what she had learned in the hospital told her that she needed to do this, especially if she and Ken were going to have the slightest chance at a future.

"Theresa! Theresa!" Ken called, bumping his way out of the bedroom. "Theresa, you're back. Come here, and let me kiss you."

She bent down, but gave him only her cheek to kiss. Then she stepped away. "I'm not back, Ken. Not yet."

"They want to keep you longer at the hospital?"

"No. I'm getting better. But I'm not really going to be well until you get the help you need. And our marriage isn't going to work until you get the help you need."

"The help I need?"

"Ken," Theresa said, "you have post-traumatic stress disorder."

But Ken was so frightened of becoming a sedated zombie in a VA hospital that he drove Theresa out of the house rather than admit the truth. He knew he was addicted to Valium and alcohol, though neither delivered any relief from his anxieties. So he continued to live alone, desperate and despairing, haunting his back bedroom—his cave of refuge.

His fears went into a feedback loop: He didn't want to end up a zombie in a hospital, but if he sought help now, the doctors would put him exactly where he didn't want to be. He saw no way out, so he kept delaying, refusing to make a decision, refusing to take action.

He prayed, screaming out to God to rescue him. Once again, God answered. But this time, God declared clearly what was required of him.

You want your wife back? God asked. *You want your daughters back?*

"More than life itself," he told the Lord.

Then you're going to have to fight for them, Ken. You're going to have to get help.

■   ■   ■

KEN REMEMBERED HOW it all started. He hadn't become an addict and a recluse all at once, although he had known something was wrong almost from the moment he came home from the hospital. He had lasted only ten days with his parents before he knew he had to move out. He heard them whispering about him, talking past him, arranging what he would do and when. So he announced he was getting his own place, and within a day he had rented a one-bedroom apartment. His younger brother had been a big help, bringing his friends around to visit and taking Ken out joyriding, to the movies, to bars. Someone always wanted to hear the war stories of a garrulous, hard-drinking vet.

His mother came over occasionally to cook for him. The rest of the time Ken ate out of cans. He could survive on his own. The only problem was, he couldn't sleep. Away from his buddies and the booze, alone in his bedroom, the darkness closed in, like a circling sniper. He heard every sound. The cars passing his apartment building. Moths fluttering against the floodlight close to his window. Worse, the occasional airplane passing overhead sent him diving out of his wheelchair to the floor in sudden panic.

To save his sanity, he established a perimeter against the darkness. His bed was his bunker, and he kept his rifle beside him. Sometimes he spent hours working its bolt action, the oiled mechanism precise and secure. Sometimes he hypnotized himself to sleep that way. But the nightmares wouldn't stop.

After he met and married Theresa in 1971, he improved for a time. She could not understand why he kept a gun by his side at night. First she moved it out of the bed and set it beside the nightstand. Then under the bed. Finally, she persuaded him to put it in the closet.

Theresa's mother was a strong Christian, and at her encouragement, the newlyweds started attending church regularly. Married life cut way down on Ken's time hanging out in the bars, as well as his drinking at home with his buddies. Physically and emotionally, he began to feel much better. He even slept, with only the occasional nightmare throwing him into Theresa's arms.

A year after their wedding, despite Ken's partial "shrapnel vasectomy," Theresa came home with the news that they were going to be parents. After Alicia's birth, holding his perfect newborn daughter in his arms, Ken experienced the deepest possible joy. Six years later, he felt the same as Elizabeth came into the world.

Bolstered by Theresa's love, his delight in his daughters, and his increased sense of security, Ken studied hard and passed a high school equivalency exam, then began taking classes at Auburn University. He learned how to scuba dive, trusting the instructor enough to hold his hand and go down into the waters. Nothing seemed impossible—as Nurse Early had told him, he only had to find his own way of doing things.

But after about ten years of marriage, Ken began to go downhill. His moods grew dark and irritable, punctuated by violent rages. His wife and daughters became afraid of him after he threw a few punches their way, and they moved out.

Despite the nightmare their life became, Theresa never abandoned Ken. After she came home from the hospital and first confronted him about his post-traumatic stress disorder, she kept coming back to the house periodically to check on whether he had changed his mind about therapy.

Finally, after a year of separation from his family, Ken broke. "I want you back, hon," he told her. "I want the kids back. I know this is what God wants me to do. I'm willing. But I just don't want to get help from the VA."

Theresa knew that he meant it; she could hear it in his voice. She had gone back to college herself, majoring in counseling, and with access to psychological treatment resources, she soon found a psychiatrist qualified to treat Ken as an outpatient.

"Why do you think you feel a need to have a safe area around you?" Ken's counselor asked. "To 'keep the perimeter clear,' as you say?"

They had arrived at this question only after two months of therapy sessions. Now Ken knew the answer.

"The day the B-40 hit me, my whole world exploded. I suppose I'm trying to keep that from happening again."

"Exactly." [3]

.   .   .

THE PUBLICITY GENERATED by Ken's meeting with Dr. Swan caused other vets to get in touch with him, to share their own war stories and their problems as civilians. Ken realized he was not alone in his struggles. Many others had suffered post-traumatic stress disorder.

He was especially pleased to hear from guys in his old Ghostrider helicopter unit, like Otto Mertz, the soldier who had dragged him to safety in the midst of the firefight. As they renewed their friendship, Ken discovered that Otto was a strong Christian, and Ken spilled out the story of his prayer out by the lake and about waking up to find that it had happened—that God had taken his eyes and legs. He confessed that he had been running from God ever since, from God's sheer, terrifying power and the wrath of his judgment.

"Why does God seem to be wrathful?" Otto asked. "If you look at your life and see all the wonderful things you've got, don't you have to say that he's a loving God?"

Ken was brought up short. He had to acknowledge that God had given him a wonderful wife, two lovely daughters, and freedom from financial worries. God had preserved his life and had been nurturing it all along, despite his many failings.

From that point on, Ken began to accept this loving God as the lord of his life. He no longer wanted to run from God; he wanted to run toward him, into his embrace. While Ken had known God before, he was finally fully at peace with him.

How thankful Ken was that God, through Dr. Swan, had not left him to die that day at Pleiku.

CHAPTER 12

WHATEVER HAPPENED TO HUMAN LIFE?

I see no reason for attributing to man a significance different in kind from that which belongs to a baboon or a grain of sand.

OLIVER WENDELL HOLMES

Life is a miracle, a sacred gift from God. Nobody knows this better than Ken McGarity. Admittedly he did not live "happily ever after." Yet despite his pain and handicaps, Ken is thankful to be alive. He knows how precious life is.

What is the meaning of human existence? Why are we here? What is the value of human life? The most vexing cultural issues of our day—abortion, assisted suicide, euthanasia, genetic engineering—all turn on questions about what it means to be human, about the value of human life and how life should be protected. Which, in turn, center on the question of our origin.

Christians believe that God created human beings in his own image. And because human life bears this divine stamp, life is sacred, a gift from the Creator. He and he alone can set the boundaries of when we live and when we die. Against this, as we saw in earlier chapters, is the naturalistic belief that life arose from the primordial sea through a chance collision of chemicals, and that over billions of years of chance mutations, this biological accident gave rise to the first humans. Millions of people today accept this basic presupposition that we are little more than grown-up germs—just as Dave and Katy saw at Epcot—which logically leads to the conclusion that a person has no greater significance than a baboon, as Oliver Wendell Holmes so bluntly put it.

These two worldviews are antithetical, and this antithesis lies at the very heart of our present cultural crisis. The question of where life comes from is not some academic argument for scientists to debate. Our understanding of the origin of life is intensely personal. It determines what we believe about human identity, what we value, and what we believe is our very reason for living. It determines who lives and who dies. This is why ethical questions surrounding human life have become the great defining debate of our age.

The Christian's commitment to life cannot be dismissed as some "love affair with the fetus," as critics have charged, or as a desire to impose a repressive Victorian morality.[1] Instead, the Christian is driven by a conviction, based on biblical revelation, about the nature of human origins and the value of human life. That's why, confronted with a mangled soldier clinging to life, Dr. Kenneth Swan did not consult some ethics book or debate abstract principles. Having been brought up in a culture steeped in the Judeo-Christian tradition that human life has intrinsic value because it was made in the image and likeness of God, he simply did what came naturally. He saved the man's life.

But what was once a culture of life is today being overtaken by what John Paul II calls a "culture of death," a naturalistic ethic sweeping across the entire spectrum, from the unborn to the old and infirm, from the deformed and disabled to the weak and defenseless. Relentlessly pursuing its own logic, this culture of death denies that the human species is superior to all other biological species, and it ends by threatening life at every stage. It has advanced so far that assisted suicide (euthanasia) is now a protected constitutional right in one state, paid for by the state's Medicaid program, and infanticide is being openly advocated by respected professors and scientists, with hardly a ripple of public shock or dissent.

Surely this is hyperbole, you may say. Alarmist rhetoric. Well, let's take a look at how the most fundamental convictions upon which Western civilization has rested for two millennia are being replaced by a naturalistic ethic of pragmatism and utilitarianism.

IT'S MY BODY, ISN'T IT?

The shift from a culture of life to a culture of death has been like a shift in the tectonic plates underlying the continents—as sudden as an earthquake, when measured against the long view of history. It occurred largely in the 1960s, although as with so much else in American life, the fault lines were evident centuries earlier, in the Age of Reason and the Enlightenment.

The beginning point might be fixed in the seventeenth century, when French mathematician René Descartes resolved to doubt everything that could possibly be doubted. After intense inner questioning, Descartes concluded that he could doubt everything except the fact that he doubted, everything except his mental experience. This conclusion led to his famous statement: "I think, therefore I am." With this, Descartes unleashed the revolutionary idea that the human mind, not God, is the source of certainty; human experience is the fixed point around which everything else revolves.[2]

Ironically, Descartes was a sincere Christian, a devout Catholic, to the end of his life. But there is nothing Christian about his philosophy. By establishing the human mind as the judge of all truth, his philosophy eventually rendered God irrelevant. And since traditional notions of morality and social order are largely derived from Christianity, these moral conventions likewise crumble when God is dismissed as irrelevant or nonexistent.

The death of God means the death of morality. This logic was pressed by a decidedly odd prophet—Friedrich Nietzsche, a German who peered into the soul of our century and later went insane. "Whither is God?" Nietzsche asked in 1889. "I will tell you, *we have killed him*—you and I. All of us are his murderers!"[3] He was incensed that the majority of Westerners had not yet fathomed the devastating consequences of the death of God. He wanted them to understand that if they gave up belief in God, they must also give up biblical ideas of morality and meaning.

This is exactly what the twentieth century has done. If we were not created by God—and therefore are not bound by his laws—if we are simply the most advanced of the primates, why shouldn't we do whatever we choose? In the 1960s, the Age of Aquarius, such views exploded into popular consciousness, aided by inhibition-freeing drugs. Sexual liberation would be the means to create a new, open, egalitarian society where "nobody can tell us what to do with our bodies." As Christian apologist Peter Kreeft says in his brilliant satire "The World's Last Night," we have a society today in which the "one intrinsic good, self-justifying end, self-evident value, meaning of life, and non-negotiable absolute is sex."[4]

What makes this view possible, notes Professor Robert George of Princeton, is a radical dualism between body and soul, a dualism that can also be traced back to Descartes, who reduced the body to little more than a machine operated by the mind. It follows that the body is not really "me," but something separate from my real self—an instrument to be used, like a car or a computer, for whatever purposes I choose. Therefore, what I do with my body, whether I use it for physical pleasure or even discard it if it becomes inconvenient, has no moral significance.

Carried to its logical conclusion, this view implies that sexual acts between unmarried people or partners of the same sex or even complete strangers have no moral significance. Since the body is reduced to the status of a mere instrument of the conscious self, it can be used for any form of pleasure and mutual gratification as long as there is no coercion.[5] Even disposing of physical life is of no greater moral consequence than discarding an old set of ill-fitting clothes.

This logic is what caused the Supreme Court to decide in *Roe v. Wade* (1973) that a human fetus is not a person and can therefore legitimately be destroyed.[6] Justice Harry Blackmun, who wrote the majority opinion, acknowledged at the time that if a fetus were a person, then its right to life would be guaranteed under the Fourteenth Amendment (which instructs the states that they may not deprive "any person of life, liberty, or property"). In order to uphold the right to abortion, the Court had to argue that though the fetus is biologically human, it is not a legal person. What's more, if the justices acknowledged that the fetus changed from a nonperson to a person at any stage of pregnancy, then abortion would become an unlawful deprivation of life—in short, murder. The Court ruled that the fetus is a nonperson with no rights at all at any stage of pregnancy. Only the mother is a person, with a "right to privacy."

Roe v. Wade was the leading edge of a powerful social movement, fueled by sexual politics, to free the individual from the yoke of allegedly repressive moral restraints. "Choice" over what to do with one's own body became the defining value of the 1970s and 1980s—all the while ignoring the fact that choice in itself cannot possibly be a value and that value depends on *what* is chosen.

A CULTURE OF DEATH

Abortion has always been about more than abortion. It is the wedge used to split open the historic Western commitment to the dignity of human life. In 1973, when pro-life proponents warned that *Roe* was taking us down a slippery slope to all manner of horrors, they were mocked as alarmists. Later events proved them prescient.

With the "Baby Doe" case in 1982, in Bloomington, Indiana, the relentless demand for choice crossed the great divide—from the living fetus in the womb to the living baby outside the womb—and America moved from abortion to infanticide. Baby Doe was born with a deformed esophagus, making it impossible for him to digest food. Doctors proposed a fairly simple operation, a procedure that had proven to be 90 percent successful. But the parents refused to grant permission for the operation, even though they knew this meant certain death for their newborn infant. Their own doctor concurred. The reason? Infant Doe was also born with Down's syndrome.[7]

Two Indiana courts declined to intervene, and six days later Baby Doe had starved to death. Columnist George Will, who himself has a Down's syndrome child, declared flatly, "The baby was killed because it was retarded."

In the flurry of controversy over Baby Doe, something shocking came to light: Handicapped infants were quite routinely being allowed to die. As early as 1975, a poll of pediatric surgeons revealed that 77 percent favored withholding food and treatment in the case of defective babies. And in an Oklahoma hospital it was discovered that the pediatric staff weighed "quality of life" in deciding whether to treat handicapped children or let them die. Among their considerations of "quality" were race and family income.[8]

Even earlier, of course, the philosophical groundwork for eliminating defective babies was being laid by the abortion debate. In the 1960s, the American Medical Association (AMA) had passed a resolution endorsing abortion when "an infant [may be] born with incapacitating physical deformity or mental deficiency."[9] Several states had also already passed laws allowing abortion in such cases. When such a law was passed in New York, a commentator at WCBS radio hailed it, saying, "Abortion . . . is one sensible method of dealing with such problems as over-population, illegitimacy, and possible birth defects."[10]

The first public official to declare abortion a positive public health policy was Arkansas State Health Director Joycelyn Elders, later surgeon general of the United States. Abortion, she said, has "an important and positive public health effect," reducing "the number of children afflicted with severe defects."[11] Abortion was no longer treated as a wrenching tragedy, a decision reached with agonizing reluctance. Instead, it was a positive good—a means for improving the species.

To support her position, Elders cited a study showing that the number of Down's syndrome children born in Washington State in 1976 was "sixty-four percent lower than it would have been without legal abortion."[12] What Elders did not say is that most people with Down's syndrome are only moderately retarded and grow into adults who are capable of holding a job and living independently. And if the birth parents cannot cope, there is a waiting list of couples eager to adopt these children. Yet today, they are being targeted for elimination.

Because people with Down's syndrome have an extra chromosome, the condition can be diagnosed before birth by amniocentesis. Insurance companies readily agree to pay for these tests; often, if the test is positive, the insurance companies also cover abortion. But the same companies will not pay the $100,000 or more that is required to sustain the first year of the baby's life. How many couples facing such a choice can withstand the economic pressure? Not many. Studies show that 90 percent choose abortion—often under pressure from doctors.[13]

For any "unwanted" or "defective" baby who may manage to slip through this front line of defense, there is always the ultimate solution. Francis Crick, who along with James Watson won the Nobel prize for the discovery of the double helix structure in DNA, advocates that all newborns be screened to determine who should live. All who fail to reach a certain level on the Apgar test, used to determine the health of newborns, would be euthanized.[14]

Steven Pinker of MIT, who has replaced the late Carl Sagan as the nation's great science popularizer, is injecting these views into the mainstream. He is central casting's perfect choice for the job: glib and genial, just professorial enough to carry authority but friendly enough not to be threatening. Pinker is the most prominent proponent of evolutionary psychology, the latest version of sociobiology, which reduces living things to products of their genes.

The reason evolution has produced the human mind, Pinker claims, is merely to protect the genes and "maximize the number of copies of the genes that created it." Applying these concepts to the issue of infanticide, Pinker argues that the newborn is basically a gene carrier and that before bonding with their newborn children, parents have always "coolly assessed" the "biological value of a child (the chance that it will live to produce grandchildren)," based on its health and the parents' own resources. When mothers kill their own newborns, Pinker said, we must "understand" their actions, remembering that "the emotional circuitry of mothers has evolved" by natural selection to include "a capacity for neonaticide" in cases where the mother feels she lacks the resources to raise the child. In short, while denying that he supports the practice, Pinker suggests that infanticide is built into our "biological design," and we cannot blame people for doing it.[15]

The rationale for all of this is, again, a dualism between body and person. Rights belong only to persons, so if someone can be reduced to a nonperson, then he or she has no rights. Peter Singer, newly appointed Ira DeCamp Professor of Bioethics at Princeton, openly advocates permitting parents to kill disabled babies on the basis that they are "nonpersons" until they are rational and self-conscious. As nonpersons, he says, they are "replaceable," like chickens or other livestock. And Singer does not stop there. He goes on to advocate killing incompetent persons of any age if their families decide their lives are "not worth living."[16] (This is the unspeakably inhumane brand of ethics that students in some of our nation's most prestigious schools are now learning. And what will happen when these elite students move into positions of power?)

The baby in the womb, having been reduced to the status of a nonperson, is then demonized in pro-choice literature as a hostile aggressor against the mother, and abortion is dressed up as self-defense. Northeastern University professor Eileen McDonagh claims that the fetus "massively intrudes on a woman's body and expropriates her liberty," justifying the "use of deadly force to stop it," analogous to cases of rape, kidnapping, or slavery.[17]

Clearly, anyone who threatens our cherished right to do whatever we please with our bodies must be stopped, by whatever means necessary. Arguing that the fetus is a violent and dangerous intruder, and justifying the use of deadly force to repel it, are the functional equivalent of having Susan Smith justify the drowning of her children with the defense that they were interfering with her freedom to be with her new lover.

And yet many well-meaning Americans, including Christians, have bought into the "choice" argument. They don't see that abortion, infanticide, and euthanasia are all part of the same package. The logic that supports abortion as a "useful social policy" to prevent the birth of "defectives" or to reduce welfare and crime, applies with equal force at all stages of life. If the body is merely an instrument of the self, if it has no inherent dignity, then we are free to dispose of it at will—or others are free to dispose of it for us.

The abortion lobby understands very well that all these issues are interconnected, which is why feminist organizations fight relentlessly to defend even partial-birth abortion—a gruesome, barbaric procedure that the AMA has denounced and that even its practitioners have acknowledged is not medically necessary. This is also why the abortion lobby fights so furiously against any diminution of abortion rights—even minor limits such as parental notification. A school must obtain a parent's consent before giving a child an aspirin, but the abortion lobby fights tooth and nail against any statute requiring parental consent for abortion. Why do pro-choicers oppose even modest limits? Because they understand that abortion represents a worldview conflict: God and the sanctity of life versus the individual's moral autonomy. They can give no quarter.

But once the principle of autonomy and choice is established, there is no way to maintain any higher value for life. A few years ago, a former inmate whom I had discipled, and who had then gone on to become a gifted young pastor, took his own life. I was shattered when I received the news. In addition to grief, I blamed myself. I should have seen it coming, should have done something.

A friend, seeing my distress, sought to comfort me. "Don't blame yourself, Chuck," she said, gently gripping my arm, "and don't judge. It was, after all, *his* life."

His life. *His* choice! The well-intentioned remark drove me deeper into despair, because this middle-aged woman was reflecting the beliefs of a majority of Americans.

Opinion polls show consistent and growing public support for euthanasia—in the name of patients' rights and compassion, of course. In fact, one of the organizations aggressively promoting euthanasia is named Compassion in Dying. Even Dr. Kevorkian, who put his "patients" to death ignominiously in cheap trailers or motel rooms and then dumped the bodies at local hospitals, evaded prosecution again and again before finally being convicted and imprisoned.

In 1997, Oregon became the first state to legalize assisted suicide, enacted by public referendum. So far, challenges to the law have been successfully rebuffed. In the states of Washington and New York, referenda were passed barring the practice, but challenges to both were successfully sustained in lower courts. To grasp the connection between abortion and euthanasia, one need only look at the way these lower courts argued in favor of assisted suicide.

The judges in both cases relied on a 1992 decision, *Planned Parenthood v. Casey* (discussed more fully in chapter 39). In this decision, the Supreme Court, while upholding modest state restrictions on abortion, attempted to place the alleged constitutional right to abortion created by *Roe v. Wade* on a more secure legal footing. Its dictum defined liberty as the right to make "intimate and personal choices . . . central to personal dignity and autonomy. . . . [It] is the right to define one's own concept of existence, of meaning, of the universe, and of the mystery of human life."[18]

In the Washington assisted-suicide case, Federal District Judge Barbara Rothstein echoed *Casey's* definition of liberty. After all, what could be more "intimate and personal" than the choice of whether to live or die? Hence Rothstein argued that assisted suicide "constitutes a choice central to personal dignity and autonomy."[19] The Ninth Circuit Court of Appeals sustained her. (Although the Supreme Court eventually set this decision aside, it offered largely pragmatic reasons for not permitting assisted suicide at this time.)[20]

The Ninth Circuit Court decision sustaining Rothstein was written by Judge Reinhardt, a liberal activist, who, in his 109-page opinion, included a chilling footnote: In cases where patients are unable to give informed consent, a surrogate may be appointed to act for them in consenting to assisted suicide.[21] With a stroke of the pen, the court crossed the divide—from suicide to euthanasia, from voluntary death to involuntary death. This represented the first time a U.S. court has ever endorsed the private use of lethal force (outside the context of abortion), a move that undercuts the very essence of the American social contract in which individuals agree to renounce the use of lethal force in return for the state's preserving order. As moral theologian Russell Hittinger says, this is no longer the right to die; it's the right of some Americans to kill other Americans.[22]

The line between assisted suicide and euthanasia has become a legal fiction. Legislatures or courts may slow the process here or there, but the train is out of the station and roaring down the tracks. And even if euthanasia is not yet secure as a constitutional right (except in Oregon), its practice is on the increase.

We must be clear, however, that the Christian is not morally obligated to save life by all measures and at all costs. Many Christians believe that it is morally acceptable to withdraw life support when the technology is merely sustaining life artificially. Many also believe that it is morally acceptable to refuse extreme intervention or heroic measures to resuscitate a patient who is beyond recovery. But without a biblical view of human life, the distinction between refusing heroic measures and actually helping to hasten death can quickly become blurred.

■   ■   ■

IN THE END, these issues all hinge on the way a culture views human life. If human life bears the stamp of the divine Maker, it is infinitely precious. But if human life is simply a product of biology or nature, a utilitarian unit, then utilitarian values become the dominant determinant. Get the dying, the infirm, the disabled, the nonproductive out of the way of the living.

When two assisted-suicide cases were being heard in the U.S. Supreme Court, protesters gathered on the front steps of the building. Most of them were disabled Americans, many in wheelchairs, and many carried signs that proclaimed "We're Not Dead Yet." These protesters know that if the Court legalizes physician-assisted suicide, it will create tremendous pressure on the handicapped to take that option and stop being a burden on society. Looking at life through the eyes of a quadriplegic who requires vast sums of money and human resources for support, or through the eyes of a Ken McGarity, we see with laser-beam focus the deadly logic of a worldview that degrades life.[23]

The supremely tragic irony in all of this is that a supposedly exalted view of human reason has led to such a degraded view of human life. When Descartes declared, "I think, therefore I am," he had no idea his slogan would lead to a culture in which what I am is determined by what *other* people think.

BRAVE NEW BABIES

Descartes also did not anticipate where this degraded view of human life would lead us.

Aldous Huxley's prophetic novel *Brave New World* opens with a visit to a laboratory where rack upon rack of glass bottles clatter across conveyor belts. Each bottle contains a carefully fertilized human egg immersed in amniotic gel, predestined for a specific purpose, ranging from the alphas (the intellectuals) to the gammas (the manual laborers). Defects are eliminated, and most females are neutered.

In the story, this remarkable process creates an ideal species capable of living in complete harmony and stability, a species free of all antiquated encumbrances such as family and child rearing. To ensure the unfettered pursuit of happiness, free sex is encouraged, and an all-purpose drug called Soma is readily available. Life is perpetual bliss. When it becomes burdensome or inconvenient, it is gently and mercifully ended.

Huxley's vision was not some bizarre fantasy. He was expanding on ideas then being soberly discussed among his friends in the intelligentsia. Eugenics—the idea of improving the human race through selective breeding—did not originate in Hitler's laboratories. It originated in the 1920s and 1930s among respectable and sophisticated men and women in places like London, Philadelphia, and New York.

On the horizon of today's brave new world looms the specter of genetic engineering, the ultimate attempt to create a race free of defects. Hardly any obstacles remain in the path of this final expression of human autonomy. In March 1997, when Dolly, the first cloned sheep, was introduced to the world, scientists and doctors hailed the experiment as the dawn of a new era, promising great medical and commercial benefits. At a hastily called hearing in the United States Senate, scientists assured the legislative body that no one would attempt to clone human beings. Everyone nodded . . . until one

brash, outspokenly liberal senator shocked those gathered by asking the logical question: "Why not?"

Why not indeed? If life is simply the result of a chance naturalistic
process—molecules colliding and combining in a primordial soup—why
shouldn't we control our own genes or create new life forms? We are simply
adapting a natural process to its most advantageous use.

Achieving *Brave New World* technology is only a matter of time. Research called EG—for extracorporeal gestation—is now under way at the
Juntendo University in Tokyo and Temple University in Philadelphia and is
intended to create an artificial womb for severely premature babies.[24] If the
research is successful, the same technology will surely be developed further,
until the artificial womb can house a fertilized egg. There is almost no stop-
ping the technological imperative: If something *can* be done, it *will* be done.
Then, with the role of biological parents rendered superfluous, humanity
can take another important step along the road to total autonomy.

Truly our capabilities have exceeded our ethical and moral grasp.

Though most Christian ethicists support assisted reproduction if used
only to help restore natural function, the problem comes when we do things
never done in nature—for example, genetic combinations impossible in nature. The technology of in vitro or in vivo fertilization also makes possible a
host of morally dubious practices, such as the harvesting of fetal tissue for
medical purposes, the disposal of fertilized eggs that are capable of becoming
fetuses, and surrogate parenthood, which has already opened a Pandora's
box. We hear of a woman who is impregnated by her son-in-law and gives
birth to her daughter's child. A female Episcopal priest has the sperm from
three men mixed (so she will not know who the father is), is impregnated,
and gives birth. Gays and lesbians mingle at gatherings they call
"Sperm-Egg Mixers," where they examine one another with an eye toward
selecting good genes. Two lesbians may contract with a gay man for his
sperm for artificial insemination, or two men may contract with a lesbian
whom they chose to be a surrogate mother.[25]

There is little left in our culture to restrain or even slow the process.[26] In
Britain, a prestigious committee under the leadership of Dame Mary
Warnock, professor of moral philosophy at Cambridge, was organized to
provide moral guidance on these questions. But Dame Warnock herself says
that in these issues "everyone has a right to judge for himself." And who
could possibly object?

The answer, of course, is anyone who is truly human. Even in Huxley's
Brave New World, the great dramatic moment comes when the protagonist,

appropriately called "the savage," who was born the old-fashioned way, escapes the world of endless pleasures in pursuit of his natural parents.

Something within us stirs ceaselessly in search of meaning and purpose
and connection. Christians know this something as the soul, or the *imago
Dei*—the image of God within us. Because of the doctrine of creation, we
know life has worth. We know it is rooted in something beyond the test tube
or colliding atoms, even as many voices around us say otherwise.

IN WHOSE IMAGE?

It is not natural to see man as a natural product, it is not seeing straight to see
him as an animal. It is not sane. It sins against the light, against the broad
daylight of proportion, which is the principle of all reality.

G. K. CHESTERTON

Can anyone really live with a completely naturalistic view of human life, that human beings are just primates? Some people in Denmark thought so.

In 1996, the Copenhagen Zoo announced a new exhibit. In a glass-walled cage in the primate house, a pair of *Homo sapiens* would be on display. Since people can observe *Homo sapiens* just about anywhere, at any time, the exhibit seemed a strange choice. But zookeeper Peter Vestergaard had a specific agenda. The exhibit, he said, would force people to "confront their origins," causing them to "accept" that "we are all primates." After all, he added, humans and apes share 98.5 percent of the same chromosomes.[1]

Yet what an amazing difference that 1.5 percent seems to make. While their hairy neighbors were busy staring at the ceiling, swinging from bars, and picking lice from each other's pelts, the caged *Homo sapiens*—otherwise known as Henrik Lehmann and Malene Botoft—read books, worked on a motorcycle, checked E-mail on the computer, sent and received faxes, and, when necessary, adjusted the air conditioning. The *Homo sapiens* were also free to leave their cage whenever they encountered the primitive urge for a movie, a candlelight dinner, or a night at the opera. Unlike their animal neighbors, the humans on display refused to heed the call of nature in public, and when Lehmann was asked whether he and his female partner would display "intimate behavior" in front of the spectators, he sniffed, "That's not interesting."[2]

A few weeks later the exhibit was terminated, and both *Homo sapiens* departed the monkey house. Were they any the wiser for their experience? One would hope so. I suspect they were forced to recognize that they were qualitatively different from the apes in the surrounding cages.

The short-lived experiment certainly made a point—though not the one the zookeeper intended. Naturalistic philosophy holds unwaveringly to the proposition that we are descended from apelike creatures, making us primates in the highest stage—at least so far—of the evolutionary process. Yet the test of any worldview is whether it conforms to reality, to the way things really are. And the reality is that humans are fundamentally different from animals. The truth is *in* us, put there by the divine stamp of the Maker, and as hard as we may want to, we cannot dislodge it. In fact, every attempt to deny the truth about our nature is doomed.

Only the Judeo-Christian view of life conforms to reality, to the nature and character of the human condition as we actually experience it. Only the biblical view creates a sustainable and rational and truly liberating basis for human life. This becomes abundantly clear when we examine Christianity and naturalism from several perspectives: compatibility with the scientific evidence, human dignity, the ultimate meaning in life, our destiny, and service to others.

Which worldview corresponds with the scientific evidence? Respect for human life at all stages is supported by growing scientific data showing that even before birth, the fetus is fully human. Sonogram pictures show the unborn child clearly responding to stimuli; and due to advances in neonatology, doctors now consider the baby in the womb a real patient. Medicine is performing diagnostic and therapeutic wonders on unborn babies, including surgery. The growth of scientific knowledge "is causing us to regard the unborn baby as a real person long before birth," says Mike Samuels in *American Family Physician.*[3] The pro-life position is supported by empirical, rational arguments that are accessible to everyone.

Robert George of Princeton University has pressed these arguments among the nation's leading scholars, including well-known deconstructionist Stanley Fish of Duke University. In 1998, George was invited to debate Fish at a meeting of the American Political Science Association: The debate would be about the nature of the evidence for and against abortion. In earlier writings, Fish had dismissed arguments against abortion as based on "religious conviction" alone, while suggesting that the case for abortion is based on "scientific facts." George's position held that, on the contrary, the arguments against abortion are based on scientific data that a fetus is indeed human.

George sent his paper to Fish in advance, and then the two joined two hundred other scholars who had gathered for the debate. But the event was cut short at the start when Fish rose, threw his own paper on the table, and announced, "Professor George is right, and he is right to correct me. Today the scientific evidence favors the pro-life position."

The audience sat in stunned silence.[4]

Which worldview provides the strongest basis for human dignity? Scripture tells us that "God created man in his own image, . . . male and female he created them" (Gen. 1:27). This is a breathtaking assertion. Humans actually reflect the character of the ultimate Source of the universe. How could anyone even theoretically conceive of any more secure basis for human dignity?

The Christian worldview also tells us that humans have an eternal destiny, which likewise bolsters human dignity. Throughout history, most cultures have had a low view of the individual, subordinating the individual to the interests of the tribe or state. And if Christianity were not true, this would be quite reasonable. "If individuals live only seventy years," said C. S. Lewis, "then a state, or a nation, or a civilization, which may last for a thousand years, is more important than an individual. But if Christianity is true, then the individual is not only more important but incomparably more important, for he is everlasting and the life of a state or a civilization, compared with his, is only a moment."[5] This explains why Christianity has always provided not only a vigorous defense of human rights but also the sturdiest bulwark against tyranny.

And because we all stand on equal ground before God, Christianity gives a sound basis for social and political equality. Each individual stands directly accountable before the Creator, writes Abraham Kuyper; there are no intermediaries, no spiritual hierarchies between us and God. It follows, then, that we "have no claim whatsoever to lord [it] over one another, and that we stand as equals before God, and among men." Consequently, the Christian worldview "condemns not merely all open slavery and systems of caste, but also all covert slavery of women and of the poor."[6]

Multiculturalists insist that all cultures are morally equivalent.[7] But this argument blurs over genuine differences. For in a culture that truly upholds the God-given dignity of individuals, widows are not burned on their husband's funeral pyre (as they are in India), people are not sold into slavery (as they are in the Sudan and elsewhere), and life is not sacrificed to satisfy ancestors or an angry god (as still happens in some primitive cultures). No, for all of the faults of its adherents—and there have been many—Christianity has accorded men and women dignity unlike any other belief system in the world.

Since the Enlightenment, secular thinkers in the West have sought to ground human rights in human nature alone, apart from biblical revelation. The French Revolution was fueled by rhetoric about the "rights of man." Yet without a foundation in the Christian teaching of creation, there is no way to say what human nature is. Who defines it? Who says how it ought to be treated? As a result, life is valued only as much as those in power choose to value it. Small wonder that the French Revolution, with its slogan "Neither God nor master," quickly led to tyranny and the guillotine.

When the thirty-nine misguided members of the Heaven's Gate cult took their lives, broadcasting magnate Ted Turner dismissed the tragedy with the cynical comment: "It's a good way to get rid of a few nuts. There's too many people anyway."[8] His comments succinctly, if callously, sum up the beliefs of growing numbers of Americans who have succumbed to the notion that there is nothing special about human life, that we are all simply part of nature.

In that naturalistic worldview it is only logical to place the goal of population control above the dignity of human life and to resort to any means available to reduce the human population in order to preserve Mother Nature from being depleted and despoiled. From this perspective, humans are often seen as aggressors against a pristine nature. Of course, Christians believe we are responsible to protect God's creation, to be good stewards, and to exercise dominion. But naturalists go far beyond responsible environmentalism to outright reverence. In the movie *The River,* an all-American farm family sits around the dinner table, and the young children recite the blessing, which turns out to be a prayer to nature: "Thank you earth, thank you sun, we are grateful for what you have done. Amen."[9]

The same logic drives the animal rights movement, as it denigrates human life in its efforts to make the human species equal with all others. These attempts often turn nasty, with animal rights activists throwing paint on women wearing furs; nasty and destructive, strapping explosives around tree trunks to blow up loggers and save the spotted owls; nasty, destructive, and sometimes silly, raiding restaurants to liberate lobsters.

When animal rights proponents discover the inherent irrationality of their own belief system, as they sometimes do, this debased view of human life can produce a kind of schizophrenia. Such is the case when two trendy causes collide. Animal rights groups like PETA (People for the Ethical Treatment of Animals), popular among Hollywood stars, militantly oppose animal research, to the point of sometimes raiding and vandalizing laboratories and kidnapping laboratory animals.[10] But animal research, which was essential in developing the polio vaccine and hosts of other lifesaving breakthroughs, is also crucial to AIDS research, another favored cause in

Hollywood. So AIDS activists now find themselves eagerly supporting animal research, even while their political allies smash laboratories.[11]

The naturalistic view of human life is simply not rationally sustainable, yet the cultural elites cling to it with slavish devotion. Some years ago, an editorial in *California Medicine* stated that the traditional Judeo-Christian ethic "is being eroded at its core and may eventually be abandoned." The anonymous editorialist welcomed the shift from a "sanctity of life" ethic to a "quality of life" ethic, arguing that "it will become necessary and acceptable to place relative rather than absolute values on such things as human lives, the use of scarce resources, and the various elements which are to make up the quality of life or of living which is to be sought."[12]

It's hard to imagine anything more terrifying than living in a culture where human life is made relative to lesser values, such as material resources. The principle we see at work here is that any culture that kills God inevitably ends up worshiping some other deity—and will gladly sacrifice even life itself in the service of this new deity.

Which worldview gives a sense of meaning and purpose? One of the arguments often used for abortion is that children should not be brought into a world where they are destined to suffer poverty or abuse. Likewise, a common argument for euthanasia is that the gravely ill have no purpose for living. These views seem persuasive only because the purpose of life has been reduced to something woefully shallow, a simplistic sense of happiness as emotional fulfillment, career success, or wealth. Many modern Americans have lost any sense of a higher destiny. Their lives have no aim or goal.

It is as if a friend were to suggest that you load your family in the van and start out on a trip. No destination in mind, no time constraints, no limit to your choice of recreation. "Take as long as you wish, and return whenever you choose," your friend urges. "It's all yours. You're free. Go."

"You're crazy," you say. "Why would I want to take my family on some aimless journey?"

Yet that is exactly what modern humans are told to do in today's world: make our lives into aimless journeys; follow our whims and impulses. To be sure, the voices of the culture dress it up a bit. They celebrate the joys of autonomy, our right to create our lives and even our selves, our endless choices and conveniences, our freedom from all the quaint conventions and legalisms of a less enlightened era. Whether it be the chatter of the elite, the steady torrent of TV, or the politicians' babble, we constantly hear that personal choice is the only thing that will produce "happiness"—the most sacred goal of American life. We are cast free, only to drift helplessly, like someone embarking on a journey with no destination and no answer to the oldest philosophical question of all: What is the purpose of life?

I've seen examples of this in many places. My wife and I live in an area of Florida that, a few years ago, began attracting upscale retirees: presidents of auto companies, comptrollers of major corporations, and high-powered barons of Wall Street, who settle into their luxurious gated communities, surrounded by manicured golf courses, fine restaurants, and swaying palms. They enjoy the American dream come true: no worries, no work, and golf every day.

Many of them follow a predictable pattern. Like a man I'll call Charlie. Freed from the pressures of work, Charlie eagerly trots off to the golf course every morning, ends up on the nineteenth hole for a few relaxing drinks, and then arrives home in time to scan the *Wall Street Journal* and take a short nap. At five o'clock Charlie gets out his chartreuse sports jacket with matching checked pants, part of a new wardrobe he purchased at a local, pricey men's shop. No more navy pinstripes for Charlie. Then it's off to the club for a cocktail party thrown by his neighbors. (We'll call them the Hewitts.)

Different neighbors host the party each night, either at their home or at the club. After six weeks or so, the cycle comes back to the Hewitts, and around they go again.

After a cycle or two, Charlie begins to detect a certain sameness to the conversation. People grumble about taxes, share tidbits about the new neighbors, complain about the yard people or the plumber, compare their grand edifices . . . and, of course, comment on the weather.

"It's a good one today, eh, Charlie?"

"Oh yeah, but getting muggy."

Charlie even finds his enthusiasm for golf waning somewhat, which is strange because he's loved golf all his life. And he finds that when he skims the *Wall Street Journal,* he sometimes experiences a wave of nostalgia for the good old days when he *had* to read it—and when it often quoted him. He misses striding into the office every morning to begin a new day.

It's usually only six months, a year at the most, before the disillusion-ment sets in. Charlie is no longer interested in talking about books or current events; the banal cocktail chatter has hollowed out his brain. Besides, he's drinking too much, and his memory is slipping. He's short-tempered and easily angered, particularly by incompetent plumbers and yard people. When someone swings a car door open recklessly and dings his new Mercedes, he gets really depressed. He begins to wonder how many golf games he has left before he dies. In fact, thoughts like that begin to wake him up in the middle of the night.

Sadly, I know a lot of Charlies—once vital, productive people who have deteriorated into heavy-drinking bores. They long for a sense of fulfillment and dignity that no amount of pleasure can provide.[13]

The fact is, men and women cannot live without purpose. The *Westminster Shorter Catechism* asks:

"What is the chief end of man?

"To glorify God and enjoy Him forever."

It's a staggering thought that we can know and glorify and enjoy the sovereign God, fulfilling his purpose through our lives. This all-consuming purpose gives life meaning and direction in all circumstances.

This explains why quadriplegic Joni Eareckson Tada can live so joyfully even though she is confined to a wheelchair. Like Ken McGarity, she has known great pain and suffering and distress; but she also knows she has a purpose, and her work with handicapped people has touched the lives of millions. I've been with Joni many times and have never seen her anything but cheerful and bent on encouraging others. She is far more fulfilled than many people who are in robust health or surrounded by material abundance.

Pleasure, freedom, happiness, prosperity—none of these is ultimately fulfilling because none can answer that ultimate question of purpose. What is the purpose of human life? Knowing that we are fulfilling God's purpose is the only thing that really gives rest to the restless human heart.

Which worldview provides a sense of assurance about our ultimate destiny? Every view of human life is shaped by two great assumptions: our origin and our destiny—where we came from and where we are going. The latter asks, Is this life all there is? Is death the end of all our deepest aspirations and longings?

The existentialists pointed out that if there is nothing beyond the grave, then death makes a mockery of everything we have lived for; death reduces human projects and dreams to a temporary diversion, with no ultimate significance. But if our souls survive beyond the grave, as the Bible teaches, then this life is invested with profound meaning. Everything we do here has a significance for all eternity. The life of each person, whether in the womb or out, whether healthy or infirm, takes on an enormous dignity.

This is why death has always been surrounded by rituals and religious rites, for it is death that reminds us of our own mortality and forces us to ask disturbing questions about the meaning of our own life. I recall how this struck me in April 1994 at the funeral of Richard Milhous Nixon, thirty-seventh president of the United States, a man whose career profoundly defined my own life before my Christian conversion. Even after Watergate and my own prison term, I visited him often, for the truth is, I admired Nixon. He was a decent and caring man, at heart a true son of his Quaker mother, with an idealist's passion for peace. More important, he was a friend. For me, the funeral was especially poignant and painful.

For three days, thousands of visitors, oblivious to the cold rain, surrounded the Nixon Library in Yorba Linda, California, filing past the coffin in silent tribute. On the afternoon of the funeral service, the area was cordoned off for blocks around, as limousines brought in the great and near great from every continent. The library parking lot had been turned into an open-air sanctuary, with fifteen hundred chairs arranged in rows, marked off strictly according to protocol. Present were four former presidents and the incumbent president, cabinet members and presidential staff, diplomats and foreign dignitaries, and most members of the Congress of the United States.

As military pallbearers marched the coffin bearing the body of Richard Nixon to its resting place, the crowd fell silent and stared somberly at the proceedings, the silence broken only by the roar of jets overhead.

It had rained that morning, but as the crowd waited, evanescent shafts of light filtered earthward through the dark clouds. Minutes passed. The stillness became eerie. I looked around and saw that everyone was simply staring at the coffin. All the power in the world sitting there, mesmerized by a coffin—forced in those moments to come face-to-face with the one reality about which all their power could do nothing: their own mortality. It was a vivid picture of the great human quandary.

Then, standing before that audience, with millions more watching on television, Billy Graham preached one of the greatest and most timely messages that I have ever heard him preach. He preached about Christian hope, a hope that no other world belief system offers.

For the secularist, death is like stepping off a cliff into a black abyss of nothingness. The Muslim faces a fearsome judgment, and for many Eastern religions, the prospect is equally grim: After death, the law of karma decrees that people must pay the penalty for what they have done in this life, being reincarnated according to their past deeds. But for the Christian, assured of eternity with the Lord, "To die is gain" (Phil. 1:21).

Which view of life provides the most certain motive for service and care of others? This is a crucial question, for any society in which citizens care only for themselves cannot long endure. Such a group cannot even be called a society. Rather, it is a collection of self-centered individuals, destined to implode when their selfish pressures reach a certain point, which is exactly what we are moving toward in our own self-absorbed culture.

Scripture commands believers to love our neighbors as ourselves (Matt. 19:19), to care for widows and orphans (James 1:27), to be a Good

Samaritan (Luke 10:30-37), to feed the hungry, clothe the naked, visit the sick and imprisoned (Matt. 25:36). But where does this compassion, this compulsion to care for others, come from?

The answer is that if we know we are created by God, then we should live in a state of continuous gratitude to God. Gratitude, said G. K. Chesterton, is the mother of all virtues. Gratitude for every breath we breathe, every moment we have to enjoy the wonders of his creation and all that is ours—family, work, recreation. Gratitude that the Son of God took away our sins and paid our debt on the cross. Compelled by this gratitude, we desire to love him and live as he commands. "This is love for God: to obey his commands" (1 John 5:3).

People often ask me why I've continued to work with prisoners for more than twenty-five years, to go back to prison, to frequent places rampant with disease, violence, and massive depression. My answer is simple: Out of gratitude for what Christ did for me, I can do nothing less.

Obedience to Christ's commands changes our habits and disposition. That's why, through the centuries, so many of the great humanitarian causes have been led by Christians, from abolishing the slave trade to establishing hospitals and schools. At one point in the early nineteenth century in America, there were more than eleven hundred Christian societies working for social justice. Today, two of the world's largest private organizations caring for the hungry are Christian agencies: Catholic Relief Services and World Vision. And the Salvation Army alone does more for the homeless and destitute in most areas than all secular agencies combined.

To be sure, well-meaning secularists can show compassion, give generously to charities, and offer help to the downtrodden and the needy. As creatures made in the image of God, all human beings practice some of the virtues. But the critical question is, What motivates them? As sociobiologists have so persuasively argued, if humans are a product of natural selection, then even the most caring acts are performed, ultimately, because they advance our own genetic interests. Kindness is a disguised form of selfishness. What this means is that even the most conscientious secularists have no rational basis for being compassionate; they act on solely subjective motives—which could change at any given moment.

Of course, Christians often fail to follow their own convictions. But when believers are selfish, they are acting contrary to their own beliefs. By contrast, when secularists are compassionate, they are acting contrary to the internal logic of their own worldview.

There is also no basis for compassion in alternative worldviews like Eastern pantheism. While visiting a prison in Trivandrum, India, some years ago, I saw firsthand what the Hindu caste system does to human dignity. Our team was welcomed warmly to the old colonial-era structure by a group of well-dressed corrections officials, and we were immediately surrounded by a cordon of Indian guards in summer dress khaki uniforms: knee-length shorts, red epaulets on their shoulders, and swagger sticks tucked under their arms. As they marched us toward the flower-bedecked center platform, I could almost hear the strains of the "Colonel Bogey March."

In the field before us were at least a thousand inmates, most of them "untouchables." Their sweaty, dark skin contrasted with their white loincloths, their only clothing. They rested submissively on their haunches, their eyes fearfully darting from side to side. These men were not only condemned to this horrid institution, where they were caged in squalid holes with no toilets or running water, but even worse, they were totally dehumanized, treated as outcasts. No Hindu who lived by his own beliefs could care one whit for them.

I spoke that day through a Hindi translator, sharing my own testimony and the gospel of Jesus Christ. When I talked about forgiveness for sins, I saw many eyes open wide, startled. This was a radical thought. In Hinduism there is no forgiveness. Whatever wrong one has done in this life must be repaid in one's next incarnation according to the iron law of karma. As a result, no consistent Hindu would practice charity, for that would interfere with the law of karma.

A new life in Christ? Their sins washed away? Freedom? The inmates were astounded by these ideas. A thousand pairs of eyes riveted on me intently, many of them glistening with tears.

After the prayer of invitation, I startled the guards and dignitaries by jumping down off the platform and walking toward the crowd, thrusting out my hand to the first man I could reach. It was pure impulse; I sensed that I should let the men know that I wanted to touch them.

Suddenly, like a flight of birds, men rose to their feet and circled around me. For the next twenty minutes, I shook every hand I could. Most of the men just reached out and touched; I felt hands all over my arms and chest and back. They were desperate to "touch," to know that the love God offers is real. They kept swapping positions with one another, until virtually all had made some kind of physical contact with me.

Later, these men went back to their grim cells. No one can say how many of them submitted to Christ that night, but at least one message got through—that in Christianity they are not untouchable.

The Christian worldview compels us, in a way no other worldview can, to genuinely care for one another.

■   ■   ■

THE HIGH VIEW of human life offered by Christianity is not a veneration of mere biological life. The Christian understands that our real hope is in the spiritual realm, so that some things are more important than biological life. Obedience to God is one of those things. Like a scarlet thread, such obedience winds its way from the lions' den to the cross to Chinese house churches to services held underneath trees in the barren regions of southern Sudan. Justice and truth are values far dearer than biological life.

The naturalistic view of life pervades every area of Western culture, but nowhere with greater effect than among young people. At every turn, they are bombarded with hedonistic, self-gratifying messages. Day in and day out, they are bombarded with the message that life is all about toys and pleasures and satisfying every hormonal urge.

Yet deep within each of us is a truth that cannot be suppressed, even under such a relentless assault. It is in our very nature, the way we are created, no matter how hard we may try to suppress it. And it bursts out in the most unlikely places—even at a presidential press conference.

In 1993, Bill Clinton boldly seized an opportunity to identify with the young people of our country by holding a question-and-answer session on the MTV network with a group of high school students. The show is best remembered as the occasion when students asked the president whether he wore boxer shorts or briefs. But not all the questions were so trivial.

Near the end of the session, an eighteen-year-old from Bethesda, Maryland, raised her hand. "Mr. President," said Dahlia Schweitzer, "it seems to me that singer Kurt Cobain's recent suicide exemplified the emptiness that many in our generation feel. How do you propose to . . . teach our youth how important life is?"

Clinton's answer was what one would expect from a skilled politician and a child of the sixties. He told her that young people need improved self-esteem; they need to feel that "they're the most important person in the world to somebody."

But Kurt Cobain *was* important to somebody—to lots of somebodies. He was a star. Yet he still felt the "emptiness" that young Dahlia was talking about; nothing in his personal worldview could teach him "how important life is."

In reporting the exchange between Dahlia Schweitzer and the

president, the *New York Times* commented, tongue in cheek, that the president did not seem to have a legislative answer to the question.[14] Well, we should be grateful for small things, I suppose. One can only imagine some politician proposing a "meaning of life" bill.

Obviously, the question is not something that can be addressed by political measures or by our culture's dominant worldviews. As the existentialist philosopher Albert Camus argued, if God is dead, then "there is [only] one truly serious philosophical problem, and that is suicide. Judging whether life is or is not worth living amounts to answering the fundamental question of philosophy."[15]

Yet Augustine offered an answer that is as true today as it was sixteen hundred years ago: "You made us for yourself, and our hearts find no peace until they rest in you."[16] Only when we find God can we halt this restless search, because the very essence of our nature is the *imago Dei*—the image of God—implanted in us by the Creator.

Why have we dealt at such length with creation and the question of origins? Because the most important implication of creation is that it gives us our basic understanding of who we are; our view of origins determines our view of human nature. The dignity of human life is not only a burning issue of our day, it is intensely personal to me.

I know all the theological arguments and believe I can hold my own in any rational debate. But when all is said and done, I find the ultimate answer to the question of life in the smiling face of my grandson Max.

CHAPTER 14

GOD MAKES NO MISTAKES

Max is a handsome eight-year-old with dancing blue eyes and a shock of blondish hair that tosses about as he bounces up and down in his favorite spot in our home—my office chair. "Grandpa's chair, Grandpa's chair," he squeals with delight, his face breaking into a broad smile.

Max and I see each other a lot, and our times together are, to put it mildly, intense. Sometimes we go to a super McDonald's, the ones with the playland of slides and brightly colored boxes of plastic balls. No matter how many children are sliding and jumping among the balls, Max is always having the best time. If the other kids leave, he will continue jumping up and down, chanting, "More kids, more kids."

Everybody notices Max. Not only because he is so adorable, but because he is different. He is set apart by his sometimes moody, impenetrable stares, his failure to respond.

You see, Max is autistic.

Max arrived by way of a frightening and difficult delivery requiring an emergency cesarean section. So there was special joy in the Colson family when our daughter, Emily, came through the surgery and Max arrived safely, appearing to be a robust and healthy baby boy. But soon we noticed that Max was not behaving as expected. He was colicky and irritable. He would scream loudly, and he seemed especially bothered by unfamiliar noises. He didn't crawl when he should have and was late walking. Then there were the distant stares and the periods of withdrawal. We denied what was becoming evident for as long as we could, confidently assuring each other that he would grow out of it.

I confess that I prayed hard for some miraculous intervention. I also asked the tough questions. How could God let this happen to my beloved daughter's only child? *It isn't fair,* I told God many times. And at first I found it difficult to enjoy Max as much as I did our other grandchildren. I couldn't bounce him on my knee or get him to look at me. Often he would scream when I picked him up.

But as he got a little older, we noticed something else. Max has a special capacity for love.

Patty and I usually ask our grandchildren to accompany us when we make our annual delivery of Angel Tree gifts at Christmas. So when Max was only two, he was with us as we headed out into the country to visit a family who lived an hour from our home. As we drove, Emily and Patty and I talked about the two little girls we were going to see. Their father was in prison, and their mother was away working, so they were living with their grandparents. We vowed that when we got there, we would try as hard as we could to let these two girls know how much they were loved. All the while, Max sat in his car seat, sucking his thumb, his expression fixed in the distant, unconnected stare characteristic of his condition.

The grandparents were waiting in front of their home, a large trailer set back on a wooded lot. As we walked through the front door, Max, usually painfully shy with strangers, suddenly pulled free of Emily's hand and ran across the living room straight for the two little girls. He awkwardly embraced the younger one, a cute four-year-old with long blond pigtails, and then held his cheek against hers, smiling. He did the same thing with her six-year-old sister. Then, still smiling, he retreated to his mother's side.

Max had never done anything like this before. My only explanation is that he understood what we were talking about in the car—and he was determined to deliver the love for us.

One of the many great paradoxical truths of the Christian life is that the greatest adversity often produces the greatest blessings. I've certainly discovered in my own life the truth of James 1:2: "Consider it pure joy, my brothers, whenever you face trials of many kinds." And I've seen the truth of it in my daughter's life. Max was one of the stresses, we now surmise, that led to Emily's ending up as a single parent. But if she was discouraged by all this, she never showed it. And Max has changed my daughter from a lovely young girl into a mature Christian woman who sees her son as a gift from God.

On Max's sixth birthday, Emily wrote me a touching letter. "God created Max exactly the way he intended Max to be," she wrote. "Max was not a mistake in the way he was made. God had a definite purpose when he created Max as he did. I do not presume to know what God had or has in mind for his purpose, and I may never know all the intricacies of God's purpose for Max. What I do know is that Max is perfect in the way God created him."

Max hears things differently from other people, sees things differently, tastes things differently, and enjoys life differently. Yet his "joyous spirit and exuberance for life" are a great gift. "I've learned to look past the disability and see the individual," Emily wrote, "and now Max has become my greatest blessing."

Max is a blessing to others as well. "Max has an ability to affect people's lives more than anyone else I know," Emily continued. "When Max enters a room full of people, it's like dropping a spoon into a blender—everyone stops and reacts. Just when people's lives are running along smoothly, everything blending as it should, in comes Max, this sweet, energetic, beautiful child who doesn't fit into their recipe. Everyone reacts in some way, good or bad. But eventually they become aware of their own actions and feelings, and this profoundly affects them. It is a wonderful experience for me to see someone who has not felt comfortable with Max take the chance and reach out to him."

Emily summed up her experience with these words: "God knew when he created Max that he would need extra help in this world, so God keeps his hands cupped around Max. He doesn't let him go. I know that wherever Max is, God is holding him gently in his hands. How could a child who is held by God be anything but a gift?"

The fact is that Max has touched more lives than any other little guy I know. Yet Max is exactly the kind of child that the modern eugenics crowd would snuff out in the womb—or, if his "defect" couldn't be detected there, then on the delivery table. Or even, if Francis Crick had his way, in the first weeks of life.

The dreadful truth is that the culture of death has taken a firm grip on the minds and hearts of otherwise responsible people in every walk of life. But when it comes to Max, these people are going to have to deal with my daughter first—and with me. Christians need to form a frontline defense for the Maxes of this world.

．　　　■　　　■

THE REAL PROBLEM with this world is not deformity in the body; it's deformity in the soul. In a word, it's sin. Anyone who harbors an idealistic urge to improve the human race ought to look not to eugenics but to means for healing the sinful heart.

Yet the very notion of sin is unpalatable to the modern mind. As a result, many of the brightest Western thinkers have constructed a great myth to avoid facing the truth about sin and guilt. And ironically, this myth, more than anything else, has brought unimaginable havoc and misery into this century.

THE FALL: WHAT HAS GONE WRONG WITH THE WORLD?

CHAPTER 15

THE TROUBLE WITH US

*Certainly nothing offends us more rudely than this doctrine [of original sin],
and yet without this mystery, the most incomprehensible of all, we are
incomprehensible to ourselves.*

BLAISE PASCAL

The first and most fundamental element of any worldview is the way it
answers the questions of origins—where the universe came from and how
human life began. The second element is the way it explains the human
dilemma. Why is there war and suffering, disease and death? These
questions are particularly pressing for the Christian worldview, for if we
believe that the universe came from the hand of a wise and good Creator,
how do we explain the presence of evil? Or, to paraphrase the title of Rabbi
Kushner's best-seller, why do bad things happen to good people?[1] If God is
both all-loving and all-powerful, why doesn't he use his power to stop
suffering and injustice?

No question poses a more formidable stumbling block to the Christian
faith than this, and no question is more difficult for Christians to answer.

Yet the biblical worldview does have an answer, and it accounts for
universal human experience better than any other belief system. Scripture
teaches that God created the universe and created us in his image, created us
to be holy and to live by his commands. Yet God loved us so much that he
imparted to us the unique dignity of being free moral agents—creatures with
the ability to make choices, to choose either good or evil. To provide an
arena in which to exercise that freedom, God placed one moral restriction on
our first ancestors: He forbade them to eat of the tree of the knowledge of
good and evil. The original humans, Adam and Eve, exercised their free

choice and chose to do what God had commanded them not to do, and they rejected his way of life and goodness, opening the world to death and evil. The theological term for this catastrophe is the Fall.

In short, the Bible places responsibility for sin, which opened the floodgates to evil, squarely on the human race—starting with Adam and Eve, but continuing on in our own moral choices. In that original choice to disobey God, human nature became morally distorted and bent so that from then on humanity has had a natural inclination to do wrong. This is the foundation of the doctrine that theologians call *original sin,* and it haunts humanity to this day. And since humans were granted dominion over nature, the Fall also had cosmic consequences as nature began to bring forth "thorns and thistles," becoming a source of toil, hardship, and suffering. In the words of theologian Edward Oakes, we are "born into a world where rebellion against God has already taken place and the drift of it sweeps us along."[2]

The problem with this answer is not that people find it unclear but that they find it unpalatable. It implicates each one of us in the twisted and broken state of creation. Yet just as sin entered the world through one man, eventually implicating all humanity, so redemption has come to all through one man (Rom. 5:12-21). Righteousness is available to all through belief in Christ's atoning sacrifice.

The Christian view of sin may seem harsh, even degrading, to human dignity. That's why in modern times, many influential thinkers have dismissed the idea of sin as repressive and unenlightened. They have proposed instead a *utopian* view that asserts that humans are intrinsically good and that under the right social conditions, their good nature will emerge. This utopian view has roots in the Enlightenment, when Western intellectuals rejected the biblical teaching of creation and replaced it with the theory that nature is our creator—that the human race arose out of the primordial slime and has lifted itself to the apex of evolution. The biblical doctrine of sin was cast aside as a holdover from what Enlightenment philosophers disdainfully called the Dark Ages, from which their own age had so triumphantly emerged. No longer would people live under the shadow of guilt and moral judgment; no longer would they be oppressed and hemmed in by moral rules imposed by an arbitrary and tyrannical deity.

But if the source of disorder and suffering is not sin, then where *do* these problems come from? Enlightenment thinkers concluded that they must be the product of the environment: of ignorance, poverty, or other undesirable social conditions; and that all it takes to create an ideal society is to create a better environment: improve education, enhance economic conditions, and reengineer social structures. Given the right conditions, human perfectibility has no limits. And so was born the modern utopian impulse.

Yet which of these worldviews, the biblical one or the modern utopian one, meets the test of reality? Which fits the world and human nature as we actually experience it?

One can hardly say that the biblical view of sin is unrealistic, with its frank acknowledgment of the human disposition to make wrong moral choices and inflict harm and suffering on others. Not when we view the long sweep of history. Someone once quipped that the doctrine of original sin is the only philosophy empirically validated by thirty-five centuries of recorded human history.

By contrast, the "enlightened" worldview has proven to be utterly irrational and unlivable. The denial of our sinful nature, and the utopian myth it breeds, leads not to beneficial social experiments but to tyranny. The confidence that humans are perfectible provides a justification for trying to make them perfect . . . *no matter what it takes.* And with God out of the picture, those in power are not accountable to any higher authority. They can use any means necessary, no matter how brutal or coercive, to remold people to fit their notion of the perfect society.

The triumph of the Enlightenment worldview, with its fundamental change in presuppositions about human nature, was in many ways the defining event of the twentieth century, which explains why the history of this era is so tragically written in blood. As William Buckley trenchantly observes: Utopianism "inevitably . . . brings on the death of liberty."[3]

The reasons for this will emerge in the heartwrenching story that follows. To some people, at least initially, this might seem to be a story of misguided do-gooders or a crazy cult. But bear with us, for it is much more than that. It is a cautionary tale, revealing how easy it is to succumb to the great utopian myth, with all its horrifying consequences.

CHAPTER 16

A BETTER WAY OF LIVING?

A Lawyer's Office, San Francisco, 1977

The day Meg Broadhurst walked into my law office and said, "I want you to help me get my child back," she immediately had my attention.

"Has your husband abducted your child?" I asked.

"No, it's more complicated than that. My son, Jason, is at Synanon."

Having lived for the past twenty years in the Bay Area, I had heard of the organization called Synanon, mostly as a drug-rehabilitation program. Although the group had started out in Los Angeles in the late 1950s, they now had a center in Oakland and another up in Tomales Bay, an hour and a half north of the city.

As a family court lawyer, I had heard a lot of strange stories, but the one Meg told me took the prize. At first, after she admitted her own history of alcohol and drug abuse, I wondered whether she might be delusional. Could this really be happening less than two hours from San Francisco?

As much as Meg tried to conceal it, she had a desperate air about her—and a frightfully dark tale to tell. But let her tell her story. . . .

Meg's Story

Okay, I'll be honest with you. I got my family involved in Synanon. But first you need to know a little about me and my husband, Jack.

I met Jack at one of my parents' parties in Malibu. He wasn't like the surfers I had been hanging around with. He worked in real estate, and he had something more on his mind than shooting the curl on the north coast of Oahu. When we started dating, he treated me as if I expected more from him than drinking sangria and groping in sleeping bags. His style appealed to my serious side—the part that took me to UCLA to study English. That's where I was at the time, when I wasn't hanging out at the beach. The idea that I could date a man who had ambitions and who thought of the future—and please my parents at the same time—came to me like an epiphany. I could date Jack Broadhurst. I might even marry Jack Broadhurst.

Jack was always telling me how free I was. Maybe I was too young for my age, but he was definitely too old for his, and as we fell in love, it brought out his little-boy side. I think he married me out of gratitude for that. And I married him because I didn't see how else I would ever get my life organized. The rich kids I grew up with thought life would be one endless summer, but something kept telling me that couldn't be real. Besides, I admired Jack. He put on a suit, coped with the real world, and acted . . . well, like a man.

When we got married, we moved into this amazing place in the Malibu Colony. So there I was, still a senior at UCLA, but living in a house on the beach and driving a Porsche. Our first year was so much fun. I didn't have anything to do but study for my classes and cook dinner for my husband. When he came home, we ate, smoked dope, drank wine, and enjoyed each other.

But after I graduated, Jack wanted to go out more, especially to Hollywood parties where he could meet future clients for his high-end real estate business. I hated those parties, and the only way I got through them was to do a few lines of cocaine in the bathroom and then keep drinking tequila. I played the spacey surfer chick while Jack was off in the corner trying to score a one-nighter. By then, you see, Jack and I had settled on an "open marriage"—he could sleep around, and I could "use."

The problem was that when I drank, I didn't stop. And with enough money and enough Bloody Mary and Margarita mix, I really didn't have to—except to get a buzz from the Peruvian powder. Not until the night Jack found me crashed on the floor of someone's bathroom.

That's when we moved to San Francisco and Jack started selling commercial properties downtown. I *really* didn't know what to do with myself on Nob Hill, but I knew I couldn't drink or use, so I spent my time in Alcoholics Anonymous meetings and tried to do the organic health thing. I wanted to be an earth mother, or at least a regular mother, and that's when we had our son, Jason, my little boy that I want you to get back for me. My baby was so wonderful and such a handful, and I went back and forth between loving him to death and wanting to escape all the diapers and drudgery.

Then I heard about these Game Clubs—a kind of AA meeting run by a group called Synanon. People in AA didn't exactly know what to do with someone like me who was attracted to both alcohol and drugs, but Synanon did.[1]

Synanon's Game Club was like an AA meeting except that you could say anything you wanted. You didn't have to talk just about yourself. You could attack people for lying about their addiction or rationalizing their behavior—giving them a "haircut," it was called. No comments were off-limits in the Game.

Once I started talking at the Game Club, I just could not shut up, and those sessions were wild. I loved inviting Jack there and hearing people just blister him for his uptight, businessman ways. And it was amazing, you know, because he actually liked it, too. Somehow when he was inside the Game, he was able to tell me things about our relationship that he never could say otherwise. He needed to know that I really loved him, for one thing. And by that time, I did.

I guess having a kid was changing both of us, and I wanted us to be a real family—to love each other and be good parents to our child. I remember the night I told Jack in the Game, "No more open marriage. No more sleeping around. I don't want that anymore." The other Synanon Game Club members really affirmed what I was saying. They could see how much I wanted our marriage to work.

When we went home that night, Jack called me into Jason's room. As we looked at our five-year-old son sleeping so peacefully, all curled up and snug, Jack whispered to me, "I take thee, Meg, to be my lawfully wedded wife, to have and to hold. . . ." He gave the whole speech, all the vows, the traditional ones that we hadn't even used at our wedding.

After that, Jack and I became so tight. It was as if we fell in love all over again, only this time better, much better. And it was because of Synanon.

Then we heard that Synanon had formed live-in communities, and people like us from the Game Club were beginning to move into them, especially the Tomales Bay facility. The idea really appealed to me, but I never thought Jack would do it. He was Mr. Money. His idea of a high was taking a building with a bad leasing percentage and selling it within a year for twice what he paid. He could do it, too. Jack knows when a property is basically sound and just needs window-dressing upgrades, and he knows when a bad, old building is just a bad, old building. I have to admit he's a genius at what he does.

But Jack was starting to talk about wanting something more out of life, too, and one day he said to me, "You want to move to Synanon? I mean, like permanently?"

I couldn't believe he was serious. But he was.

The head of the San Francisco Game Club had told him that Synanon was interested in recruiting Gamers for executive positions. They needed someone like Jack to help them develop their properties. He would have to do the pots and pans for about a week, like all new members of the community, but then they would move him back into the work he loved.

"Meg," he told me, "why don't we move to a community where we can concentrate on us and on Jason? If there's really a better way of living, maybe we ought to try it."

I never thought I would hear those words come out of Jack's mouth. First the renewed wedding vows and now this! I agreed, and within three months, we moved to Tomales Bay. That was in March of 1973, and that's when this whole story really gets started.

The first time I saw Tomales Bay, I thought, *I'm going to be living in a Japanese landscape painting!* It's beautiful.

Synanon's property there overlooks the water, and up until a couple of years ago, Tomales was the organization's corporate headquarters. That's moved to Badger now, but the warehouse at the center of Synanon's main business, Advertising Gifts and Premiums (ADGAP), is still at Tomales. The place is like a little self-enclosed city. There are about five hundred people still living there, and it has medical clinics, a barbershop, sewage treatment plants, a movie theater, artists' studios—everything.

When Jack and I first arrived, I thought Charles Dederich, the founder of Synanon, was some kind of guru. He invited Jack and me to have a private conference with him, and we were so excited to meet with the old man himself. We had seen him before, of course, in the Game Temple, the special building devoted to the AA-like sessions at Tomales. But we had never met him in person.

That first meeting, he totally blew us away. He put his arm around Jack and said, "Now I know what you're asking yourselves. Have we made the right choice, moving in here with all these drunks and head-cases? Meg had a problem, I understand, but obviously she's now highly functional. So you're asking, Is this the right thing for our family?

"I'll tell you why you came here, Jack. You know what's inside you. You know that there's a desire to live as you've never lived before, and somehow you just can't get to do it in the world outside Synanon. You know you're alive inside the Game Club in a way you never are outside it.

"Let me tell you why that is. It's because the thing inside you, your real self, is total energy. It drives toward life in its highest sense. It's restless, and it stays restless until it finds fulfillment."

Then Dederich quoted his favorite lines from Ralph Waldo Emerson, the same ones we would always quote at the outset of every Game: "'As long as a man willingly accepts himself, he will continue to grow and develop his potentialities. As long as he does not accept himself, much of his energies will be used to defend rather than to explore and actualize himself.'

"Here at Synanon you're going to have a chance to accept yourself and use your energies to grow, to be positive, to become a self-actualized person," Dederich said. "Why can't you do that on the outside? Because our whole society fosters various forms of character disorders. When Synanon first got started back in Ocean Park in 1958, I thought the problem was addiction. But the real problem is character disorder, and it's something everyone suffers from—you, Jack, as much as Meg, even though she was the one with the addiction. You're addicted to other things. Like money and other women—right? There's no shame in it. We're all messed up because of the society we've been raised in.

"But here at Synanon you can tap your inner resources toward absolute fulfillment because you can see through your own disguises in the Game. We can help you be free from all those hang-ups, all those crusty old ideas of right and wrong that shackle your inner self. We're going to set you free from those outdated rules and conventions that hem you in, so you can finally be your true self. You're going to be free from all your character disorders, and together we can make a healthy community and show the whole world a better way of living."

I remember after that meeting, Jack said, "That man's a genius. No one's ever seen through me like that."

For a while our life at Synanon was everything we dreamed of. We worked ten-day shifts, which is called "being in Motion," and then we had ten days for "Growth," which meant we could go horseback riding, take a swim in Synanon's reservoir, sail on the bay, watch movies, use the libraries, do crafts. We didn't have much money, but we didn't need it.

When people joined, they often gave all their money to Synanon. That's how much they believed in what Synanon was doing. We all got a regular allowance from the organization—pocket money that we called WAM (Walking Around Money). And since we had free use of all Synanon's facilities, we lived as if we were rich.

There wasn't any crime there, either. We could leave our possessions right out in the open and not lock any doors. The whole place was run with

only two rules: no violence and no drugs, and that included alcohol and cigarettes. So we had all these people, most of them former addicts and lots of
them former criminals, and yet the place was completely peaceful. Dederich
kept talking about starting new "Synanon cities" all around the country so we
could spread this peaceful new way of life to everyone. We were excited
about being involved in such a noble mission.

Jack and I worried at first when people in the Game suggested that we
put Jason in the community's boarding school. He was only seven. But we
found out that it was common for parents to hand over their kids to the community schools when the children were as young as six months old. The
leaders told us it was much healthier for a child to be loved by the whole
community, where everyone functions as the child's extended family. That
sounded good, and anyway, we saw Jason every night. At least we did at first,
until they started night nurseries. We also turned over all of Jason's clothes to
the school because the kids there didn't own their clothes; they just took
them out of communal bins.

But with other people taking care of Jason, Jack and I did get to spend
more time together. That's what really hooked me—the chance for Jack and
me to be happy together.

I really became a Synanon fanatic the night Dederich started
"Gaming" Jack about his latest fling. You see, I thought Jack had stopped
that kind of thing when he recited the wedding vows that night. But he
hadn't. We were all in the Game Temple—Dederich in his big chair at the
front, wearing his overalls and plaid shirt, and his wife, Betty, next to him
in one of her long, flowing gowns.

"I want to introduce Jack Broadhurst," Dederich said to the guests,
who came to watch. "Jack's a square. He comes to us from a successful real
estate business. He sold it when he decided to join Synanon and invested
$100,000 in our corporation. Brought his wife, Meg, and his son, Jason,
here, too. I just appointed Jack the director of our Land Development Division." Then Dederich asked, "You like your new job, Jack?"

"What I like," Jack said, "is being part of Synanon Corporation. I think
it's the best investment anyone can make, not only with their money but
their lives as well."

Dederich heaved his weight around, away from Jack. "The man really
knows how to blow smoke, doesn't he?" Then Dederich asked me, "Meg, do
you know exactly why Jack is so pleased with being a big director?"

I knew right away where Dederich was headed. So did everyone else.

"Have you met Trina?" he asked.

"She's Jack's new secretary," I said, playing innocent.

"Trina," Dederich said, "stand up for us."

I had to admit she was pretty. Trina had these striking Italian features, oval eyes, full lips. She was wearing a halter top and miniskirt, and stood as if she was posing for *Vogue* or something, with one knee bent in.

"Tell me, Trina," said Dederich, "before you came to Synanon, what did you do?"

"I was on the road," she said.

"As a rock groupie, right?"

"I provided personal services," she said after a pause.

"Personal services?" said Dederich. "We can call it that if you like, sweetheart. But what it means is, you made yourself available for whatever 'personal services' the band members wanted, and in return, they supplied you with LSD, meth, and quaaludes. Right?"

She crumpled and sat down. "Look, I'm not proud of the way I lived," she muttered.

"None of us are," Dederich said. "But what I want to know is this: Why does my new land development director think *you're* qualified to be his secretary?"

"Hey, Chuck, there were only so many in the applicant pool," Jack said, jumping in.

Dederich bolted around to face Jack. "Hey, Mr. Director," he said mockingly. "I saw to it—I saw to it *personally*—that you had a legal secretary with twelve years of experience in your candidate pool. And yet you hired Trina instead. Now just why did you do that?"

Everyone in the Game Temple started to hoot and holler. You can't believe the obscene things people scream out in there.

"Okay, Okay," bellowed Dederich to calm everyone down. "The point is, Jack's not going to bring his middle-class, hit-on-the-secretary act here. He was given a responsible position, and the first thing he's done has been totally irresponsible. I think maybe it's back to washing kitchen pots for Jack."

That stopped Jack's cheating on me. He finally became Mr. Faithful. At least as long as Dederich wanted him to be. But that part of the story comes later.

Another good thing that happened in Synanon was that I became a teacher. They let me teach in the boarding school at Tomales, and I even became head of humanities for the junior high and high school students. Finally people were taking me seriously. And I liked teaching because it allowed me to be closer to Jason since all the schools were in one combined operation.

I remember back in high school, one of my boyfriends said to me, "You are such a scrumptious muffin." That was me all right, "the scrumptious muffin" girlfriend, the trippy wife—I played all these side-dish roles. Nobody knew that I had graduated from UCLA with honors. But in Synanon, I finally stopped feeling as if I had to hide my brains. I guess it's because I was pretty straight compared to everybody else there. For one thing, I hadn't been a prostitute, like almost half of the women there had been, including Dederich's wife, Betty.

The Synanon schools had been modeled after a sixties-style free school, like Summerhill, but by the time I started teaching, they had become rather traditional prep-school institutions. Except for one thing: We taught the kids to do their own version of the Game. They would tear into each other for things like not doing their homework or slacking off on their chores. I thought that was good because it meant the kids kept each other in line. The only thing that bothered me about the school was that Dederich's picture hung on the walls everywhere. It was spooky, like Lenin's picture hanging everywhere in the Iron Curtain countries. And after a while, there was even an expectation that we would teach the kids that they owed their whole lives to Synanon—that their first allegiance wasn't to their parents but to the organization.

In fact, many things began to change after Jack and I had been there about two years. A lot of it was because of the lawsuit.

You see, by that time Dederich had lost interest in helping druggies; he was much more interested in selling Synanon to the world as a new kind of ideal society. He had become an evangelist for the Synanon way of life. The problem is, we were still making a lot of our money by selling corporate give-away items that presented us as a drug-rehabilitation center. So the *San Francisco Examiner* did an exposé calling Synanon a "racket." Synanon's lawyers turned around and sued the newspaper's parent company, the Hearst Corporation, for using underhanded tactics in gathering their evidence, and we won. Hearst had to pay big bucks.[2]

But the negative publicity hurt the organization, and Dederich decided he would have to redefine its mission. His chief counsel, Dan Garrett, came up with what they thought was a great idea: They would declare Synanon a legal religion. They saw all kinds of advantages: It was better for taxes, and they didn't have to keep trying to bolster the "success rate" with addicts. The success rate really wasn't too good anyway. Most addicts didn't do well if they left Synanon, so most of them were staying on. But if Synanon were a religion, that no longer mattered. As Garrett used to say, "Nobody graduates from a religion." Besides, being a religion meant everyone would have to be a lot more committed and "obey the tenets of the faith"—Garrett actually wrote that in a memo.

In the Game, we spent hours discussing the idea of becoming a religion, and I had a hard time believing what some people said. They said Chuck was a "god" to them, and Betty was a natural "high priestess." For years, recruits had been welcomed with the slogan "Abandon all and follow Chuck," but I had taken that as a joke. Now I realized that a lot of the old-timers really looked up to Dederich as a Christ figure. We even had a Game where everyone decided Chuck could be called "Savior."[3]

Honestly, I didn't know quite what to think. I guess Synanon *was* like a religion for me in a lot of ways. For instance, in the Game, people frequently rehearsed their life histories—it was called "telling your rotten story"—talking about how hopeless and useless life had been before we joined Synanon. The histories were just like some religious testimonials. But things were going overboard, in my mind. Dederich wrote a book to define the group's beliefs; it was called *The Tao Trip Sermon*. He even wrote a prayer that we were supposed to recite—the Synanon Prayer. Betty got into the act, too, telling people that we were like a seminary, like priests in training, and that we had to accept the Synanon dogma "without any mental reservations"—that we were to "just say 'amen'" to any directive Chuck passed down.

Those were her exact words. She was even starting to *talk* like a high priestess. And anyone who wasn't willing to accept Synanon as a religion was promptly excommunicated.

The Game was really changing, too. Instead of being open and real about what we thought, we started getting pressure to "Game affirmatively." That meant once Chuck or Betty or their insiders had insinuated the Synanon line on anything, everyone was supposed to line up and agree with them. And if we criticized some policy, everyone would jump on us and talk about how grateful we should be for everything Chuck had done for us.

In fact, the group would start dragging up people's pasts, telling them what a mess their lives were before they came to Synanon and how Dederich had saved them. "And *this* is how you repay him?" the group would ask. The pressure was so bad that often the people being attacked would actually start agreeing with the accusations; they would even bring up new faults to confess to the group and start accusing themselves. Creepy. Just like what the communists used to do to break people, getting them to accuse themselves.

By this time, too, Dederich had hooked up an in-house radio network called "the Wire," that was broadcast into every building, every workroom, even the bathrooms, so that every member of Synanon could hear Dederich's thoughts on any subject, any time of the day. You hardly had a moment to think for yourself. Everyone was constantly listening for Chuck's opinion on anything that happened so they could be on the "right" side.

But that wasn't the worst of it. Next came the loyalty tests. Like shaving our heads. Synanon had various forms of punishment that were meted out when we broke the rules, and one of the punishments was having our head shaved. Then, suddenly, it was made clear that *everyone* had to get shaved—permanently—as a kind of proof of their commitment. This was in 1975, and I was still so much a part of things, I got buzzed without much protest. But some of my friends were really upset about losing their hair. Betty tried to make them feel better by telling them, "You cannot be ugly. You are Synanon. You wear the badge of the Religion."[4]

But Synanon was still getting a lot of bad publicity. The article in the *San Francisco Examiner* had tipped off other reporters, and donations began drying up. So Dederich decided he would simply reduce the population, pare it down to those who were absolutely loyal to him. He launched another loyalty test, what he called a "little emotional surgery." He started talking about how couples with children placed a great burden on the community. He told us that raising each child cost Synanon up to $200,000 and how, if we saved that money, we could help juvenile delinquents. "The world is already overpopulated," he would say. "Why should Synanon members go on breeding when they could selflessly help save children who were already in this miserable world?"[5]

So Chuck ordered all the pregnant women to have abortions. That's when I really started to pull back and wonder about Synanon. There were about five pregnant women there at the time, and one was my best friend, Jean, one of the other teachers. She had wanted a child for the longest time, and she had finally gotten pregnant when she was almost forty years old. She was about five months along when Chuck made his pronouncement, and she really didn't want an abortion. She held out for a while, but everyone kept Gaming her about her loyalty to Synanon, and she couldn't take the pressure.[6]

I tried to talk her out of it, but I remember the day I walked into the school building and knew she had done it. She had been out for a day, and when she came back, she wouldn't look at me, so I knew. She had gone to a Synanon doctor. Now she'll never have any children. And for what? Why?

Dederich knew how upset everyone was over the abortions, but he didn't back off. He let it be known that it would make him very happy if all the men got vasectomies. That meant anyone who wanted to stay in his good graces had better go along—because staying in Chuck's good graces meant better housing, better job assignments, and other perks. If you resisted, you could be demoted and forced to collect garbage or pull weeds.

This was the beginning of the end for Jack and me. I begged Jack, "Please don't do this. Don't get a vasectomy." I wanted to have another baby.

But he knew that his position as land development director was at stake. So he said, "Look, honey, we already have Jason. And besides, I'm getting too old."

"Old? Jack, you're all of thirty-six! Listen, Jack, please," I said. "We've made a mistake. This is completely crazy. We need to leave this place right now."

And the minute I said that—the minute I suggested leaving Synanon—I could see him turn against me. His face got really hard, and he wouldn't listen to me or talk to me. He just shut me out of his life. It was so awful. We had come to Synanon to make our relationship better, but now Synanon was coming between us. Jack is totally dependent on that organization; it's his whole life. He's going to fight me tooth and nail about getting Jason back. As far as he's concerned, Jason doesn't belong to him *or* me; he belongs to Synanon.

So, anyway, he got the vasectomy—I knew he would—and so did every other man in Synanon. Except Dederich himself, of course. Isn't that rich? I know he's laughing at the way he can coerce everyone else to do something he would never lower himself to do. Some couples left Synanon over it, but most of them stayed on, and they were even more committed because of the sacrifice they had made.[7]

But as bad as that is, it's not the worst of it.

After the suit against the Hearst Corporation, Dederich started having fantasies of revenge. Synanon facilities had had break-ins from time to time, especially in Oakland, where a street gang actually came in and started beating up our people for no reason. So Dederich told all the facilities to form security details. They were like volunteer fire departments at first, but in just a short time they got to be like internal police forces. Then Dederich started a group of guards, but really they're more like a small army. They're called the Imperial Marines, and they're made up mostly of juvenile delinquents that government social service agencies send us to rehabilitate.[8] These kids are mean, and they're well armed, too.

On top of this, Dederich started giving tirades over the Wire—the in-house radio network—saying how Synanon was not going to be messed with anymore. He would go on and on about the urban riots of the late 1960s and the crime wave of the 1970s. He would say that we have to counter violence with violence. Synanon would "break some legs and kneecaps," if it had to. That's what he actually said, this former guru of nonviolence.

He even made this part of the Synanon religion. He liked to say Synanon was becoming an "aggressive, militant" religion and that we weren't going to mess with turning the other cheek. Instead, the rule of our religion was "Don't mess with us—it can get you killed."

And to be fair, I have to warn you that if you take my case, I'm not sure what might happen, because Dederich gets rabid when lawyers help former Synanon members get their kids back. I've heard him say, "I am quite willing to break some lawyer's legs and next break his wife's legs and threaten to cut their child's arm off."[9] And he means it, too.

A lot of couples were like me and Jack—one partner wanting to leave and the other one wanting to stay. I think that's why Dederich came up with his idea for the biggest loyalty test of all. He decided marriage was getting in the way of total loyalty to him, so he decided to get rid of it. Just abolish marriage. To do this, he decided to split up all the married couples and force them to hook up with someone else—what he called a "love match." These would last about three years, and then everyone had to take a new love match. Dederich himself selected who went with whom most of the time.[10]

Dederich would hold these big separation ceremonies, where all the married couples were supposed to thank each other for the time they had had together and then pair off with someone new. He started off with his own grown children, to set an example. His daughter—her name was Jady—really loved her husband, but she left him to pair up with another man. His son had a harder time, and Dederich had to threaten to demote him. He said, "You're not going to get in the way of this movement." As if Synanon were still some idealistic movement to change the world! It may have started out that way, but by now it was nothing but personal tyranny. Dederich was stripping all of us of everything we loved, everything we cared about, trying to make us loyal only to him.

He told Jack and me to split, and he put Jack with Trina. Can you believe it? I think he did it to make the point that he could do anything he wanted, even reversing something he had done in the past. For me, Chuck picked Michael Tenney.

I owe Mike a lot, actually. I think he loves his wife, Diane, even more than I love Jack. A lot of people looked up to them as the ideal Synanon couple. Mike's a doctor, Diane's a nurse, and they took care of just about everybody at one time or another at Tomales. I think even Dederich regretted breaking up Mike and Diane, but he couldn't allow exceptions. Diane was so upset, she just walked out of Synanon and never came back. Dederich got on the Wire and ranted about how she was a "splittee"—that's what they call people who leave—and how she had no gratitude, no loyalty, how she was rotten, and on and on. He always did that when anyone left.

Anyway, the first night after I was matched with Mike, I went through the motions; I put on my nightie and waited for Mike to finish taking a shower. I kept thinking of that line from Huxley's *Brave New World:* "Let's do it for the state!" It was like Orwell's *1984,* too, because, I mean, what was the difference between Charles Dederich and Big Brother? Dederich was going for complete control.

Mike came back from the communal showers in his T-shirt and sport shorts, and he shut the door. I've never seen a man look sadder in my entire life, especially walking into a room with a woman waiting for him in bed, and I started laughing.

"What?" Mike asked.

"You. You look like you're about to be drawn and quartered."

He sat down on the side of the bed, and we began to talk. "I've decided to leave Synanon," he said. "I know this may go badly for you. Maybe they'll accuse you of driving me off or something. But I love Diane more than anything in this world, and I want to find her. I hope she'll get back together with me once I'm out."

"Do you know where she is?"

"I haven't talked to her, but she's probably over in Walnut Creek with her sister."

"Look," I said, "you don't have to do this, I know, but if you could just sleep in this room—over there on the couch—for two or three nights, then people would think our 'love match' is working. Then we'll both go at the same time. We'll just split."

Both of us knew how traumatic—even dangerous—it could be to leave Synanon. The Imperial Marines gave one splittee a serious beating. They have a huge cache of weapons, and anyone who leaves gets all kinds of threats. Dederich gets on the Wire and starts condemning splittees and gives out hints that he wouldn't mind if they were hurt. I know it sounds incredible, but the place has turned into an armed camp, a small totalitarian state. I had even heard a rumor about a prison camp they're running in the desert.[11]

Mike and I made our break at the same time, as we planned. Mike and Diane had liquidated all their assets and poured the money into Synanon, so they left with nothing but the clothes on their backs. They lost everything.

As for me, the past month I've been down in Malibu, back with my parents, getting myself together. I've called Jason, and they did let me talk to him. He's twelve now, very independent and, I'm afraid, very foul-mouthed. He thinks he's about to become a cowboy in the Imperial Marines or something, and says he doesn't want to see me anymore. You should hear him. "Mom," he told me, "you don't own me. I belong to Synanon, and that's where you should be, too. You should get your blankety-blank back here." It's as if he's joined the Nazi youth!

He's still a kid, though. He needs his mother. And I need him. I can't believe I gave up so much to be a loyal member of that organization! I've lost years of my life, and I've lost my husband and my child. I realize that Jack's gone, but there's still a chance for Jason. You have to help me get him back. You have to.

।   ।   ।

WHAT YOU'VE JUST read is a dramatized account, and Meg Broadhurst is a fictionalized character. But Synanon, its leader Charles Dederich, and the major figures associated with Synanon are real. The events described here all took place, and the experience of Meg and her family accurately represents the typical fate of those who became involved in Synanon, a countercultural organization devoted to what Dederich liked to call "a better way of living."

Two years after Meg would have been providing this account, a real-life custody battle, similar to the one described in this dramatization, provoked such violence from Charles Dederich that his criminal actions brought Synanon to an end. An attorney named Paul Morantz won a $300,000 judgment against Synanon for its interference in a child-custody case. Afterward, Morantz received so many anonymous threats that he began checking everywhere for traps. One day when he reached into his mailbox, his hand felt as if a nail gun had gone off straight into his palm. He whipped his hand away. Seconds later, a four-and-a-half-foot rattlesnake, its rattles clipped so that it would give no warning, slithered out of the box. Neighbors rushed him to the hospital. Eleven vials of antivenin serum saved his life, but the assault left him with permanent nerve damage.[12]

Through a neighbor's testimony, the attack on Morantz was traced back to Synanon. The two men who set the trap were eventually arrested, along with Dederich himself. All three were indicted, though Dederich was given only a fine and probation. But the convictions effectively ended Synanon's reign of terror. The community continued to struggle on through the early 1980s, but lawsuits against Synanon for its violent treatment of community members and outsiders, along with the complete collapse of its donation network, demanded that assets be sold off until nothing was left. One by one, former members left Synanon.

Sadly, for many families it was too late. Hundreds of children lost their childhood to Synanon's communal nurseries. Hundreds of parents lost their families, their children's love and affection, and years of their lives to Charles Dederich's "better way of living." It was a utopian dream for an ideal society, and it went the way of all utopian dreams . . . as we shall see.

CHAPTER 17

SYNANON AND SIN

If the experience of human history from Rousseau to Stalin means anything, it must be that we are stuck, like it or not, with a doctrine—nay the reality—of original sin.

EDWARD T. OAKES

Synanon is not just a tale of 1960s idealism gone awry in a small corner of northern California. It is a parable of what happens when men and women reject the biblical teaching of sin and evil and then embrace the great modern myth of utopianism: that human nature is intrinsically good and can form the basis of a perfect society. As political philosopher Glenn Tinder writes, if one acknowledges "no great, unconquerable evils in human nature," then it seems possible to create a heaven right here on earth.[1]

This was exactly the philosophy behind Synanon. And in the events of that small, coercive community, we can see in microcosm just how dangerous that philosophy is. For when we close our eyes to the human capacity for evil, we fail to build the moral boundaries needed to protect us from that evil.

Charles Dederich's desire to free addicts from their destructive behavior began with apparently good intentions. His approach was inspired, in large part, by the individualism of Ralph Waldo Emerson, who trusted that the isolated self could find within itself all the goodness and truth needed for a moral community. This is what Emerson meant by his celebrated notion of "self-reliance"—that the self, in its search for truth, must be freed from all external authority, whether divine revelation, the church, history, or tradition. Emerson announced the dawn of a new age of "every one for himself; driven to find all his resources, hopes, rewards, society, and deity within himself."[2]

This utopian vision of a new age shaped Dederich's strategy. To create isolated, Emersonian individuals among his flock, he mercilessly attacked all their preconceptions, belief systems, and moral loyalties. He broke down their emotional reserve in the vicious free-for-all exchanges of the Game; he severed loyalty to family and friends by recasting outsiders as "enemies"; he invaded the private boundaries of the mind with the Wire; and finally, he destroyed the family, with his enforced policies of communal nurseries, abortion and vasectomy, and temporary "love matches."

The idea was that old emotional ties, old loyalties, old thought patterns must be torn down to make way for new, positive, healthy patterns to emerge. But what really emerged was total dependence on a cultic authority figure. When moral convictions and personal commitments are destroyed, the result is not a great release of human goodness. Instead, the individual becomes malleable, controllable by anything or anyone who steps in to take the place of family, church, and village—and who can then impose his will and convictions on the isolated individual.

All utopians, no matter how well intentioned, adopt this strategy in one form or another. They start with the promise to liberate the individual from such things as economic oppression or crime-ridden streets or ancient superstitions. And the bargain is always the same: Give me power, and I'll use it to create an ideal society. But, as we saw in the Synanon story, the exchange only brings out the worst in those who have the power, while enslaving those they promised to liberate.

Does the modern utopian worldview, then, produce a rational, sustainable life system? Most emphatically not. It tells us we are good, but it unleashes the worst evil. It promises enlightenment, but it thrusts us into darkness.

The cautionary lesson we must derive from Synanon is that the same pattern can take hold anywhere the utopian myth is accepted. Contrary to comfortable contemporary assumptions, the threat of tyranny did not die in the rubble of the Berlin Wall. The utopian myth lives on. Admittedly there's an enormous difference between a totalitarian state and America's democratic republic, yet the same assumptions that led to the most destructive tyrannies of the twentieth century are at work in our own society. The only difference is the speed at which these ideas are being played out toward their inevitable consequences. While the totalitarian nations have completed the cycle, demonstrating the consequences of utopianism in all their horror, most Western nations are still somewhere in the earlier stages, still couching the utopian vision in humanitarian language.

For example, the denial of sin and responsibility is couched in therapeutic terms, such as the need to "understand" even the worst crimes as a result of a dysfunctional childhood or other circumstances. Symptoms of family breakdown—such as divorce, adultery, and abortion—are defended as expressions of the individual's freedom of choice. Social engineering schemes are dressed up as public compassion. But these are all window dressings, for beneath these explanations lies the same false utopian view we saw played out vividly in the story of Synanon. It is the same worldview that gave rise to modern totalitarianism. As Glenn Tinder writes, "Much of the tragic folly of our times, not only on the part of extremists such as Lenin but also on the part of middle-of-the-road liberals and conservatives, would never have arisen had we not, in our technological and ideological pride, forgotten original sin."[3]

Will the Western nations see through their delusions and change course before it is too late? That is a pressing question raised in the following chapters, where we will probe the consequences of the false worldview of human goodness, in both the totalitarian systems of the East and the welfare state of the West. We will trace this worldview's effects in politics, psychology, crime, welfare, and education, in order to reveal its fatal weaknesses. Against the utopian worldview, we will pose the Christian worldview, which we submit is demonstrably the only philosophy that fits universal human experience.

But first we must look at how the myth of utopianism was born and why it has such a grip on the modern mind. We cannot begin to counter the myth until we understand how the utopian vision came to replace what had been for sixteen centuries the settled understanding of human nature and society. In other words, whatever became of the biblical notion of sin?

. . .

WHATEVER BECAME OF SIN? In 1973, when psychiatrist Karl Menninger posed this provocative question in his best-selling book of that title, he sounded like an Old Testament prophet thundering against the moral relativism of our age.[4] Let's not talk about what's progressive or unprogressive, what's appropriate or inappropriate, he said, cutting through the fog of fashionable cover-up words like a brisk breeze. Let's talk about good and evil, right and wrong.

What did become of sin? Good question. To solve the mystery, we must travel back to the mid–eighteenth century and to the influential writings of a young Swiss-born philosopher named Jean-Jacques Rousseau. Persuasive ideas are typically launched in the writings of one person who captures and gives expression to what becomes a powerful trend. Such was the case when Rousseau burst upon the European intellectual scene, winning instant notoriety with an essay arguing a surprising thesis: that the progress of civilization had not been beneficial for human beings, but harmful. In its natural state, human nature is good, he contended; people become evil only when they are corrupted by society.

From the time of Aristotle, most philosophers had taught that humans are naturally social and that they fulfill their true nature by participating in the civilizing institutions of family, church, state, and society. But Rousseau turned this settled notion around. He insisted that human nature is at its best prior to and apart from social institutions; that people are naturally loving, virtuous, and selfless; and that it is society, with its artificial rules and conventions, that makes them envious, hypocritical, and competitive.

Rousseau's notion that civilization is artificial is perhaps less surprising when you realize that the society he lived in was just that. Picture the French aristocracy of the 1700s. Women concealed themselves beneath powdered wigs, pasty white makeup, and ornate dresses dripping with jewels and ribbons. Men pranced about in long, curly, powdered wigs; silk waistcoats and frilly cuffs; satin britches; clocked hose; and high-heeled, buckled shoes. Rousseau fled this powdered and polished society, denouncing it as false to the core, and he retreated to small country houses where he could be close to nature. He dressed in shabby, threadbare clothing, but he also delighted in shocking people by wearing bizarre flowing robes and caftans. He refused to practice accepted manners or social formalities, cultivating instead an intensely emotional and spontaneous style of behavior. He kissed his friends ostentatiously, often throwing himself around their necks. He enjoyed playing the part of the tactless, vulgar oaf.

Rousseau's odd dress and crude manners were a deliberate expression of his philosophy: If human nature is essentially good, if evil and corruption are created by a false and hypocritical society, then throw off the restraints of civilization and explore your natural, spontaneous self—the true self that underlies social forms. Free it from stultifying pressures to conform.

These same ideas appear in Rousseau's formal writing on philosophy. He rejected anything that limits the freedom of the inner self, which he saw as naturally good—or, at least, unformed and undefined and capable of being *made* good. Individuals must be free to create themselves by their own choices, free to discover their own identity, free to follow their own road (to quote the Saab advertisement mentioned in chapter 4). Rousseau's most influential work, *The Social Contract*, opens with the famous line, "Man is born free, and everywhere he is in chains."[5] He called on reformers to set people free from the chains of institutions, rules, customs, and traditions.

Yet ironically Rousseau's philosophy of radical and unbounded freedom spawned the most oppressive regimes of the modern world, inspiring revolutionaries like Robespierre, Marx, Lenin, Hitler, and Mao. Even Pol Pot and his cadre of Paris-educated terrorists were known to have studied Rousseau while their henchmen were slaughtering a quarter of the Cambodian population. How did this happen?

The key is that Rousseau did not define freedom as the assertion of rights against the *state;* freedom meant liberation from the forms and institutions of *society*—family, church, class, and local community. The state, in fact, would be the liberator. By destroying all social ties, the state would release the individual from loyalty to anything except itself. "Each citizen would then be completely independent of all his fellow men," proclaimed Rousseau, "and absolutely dependent on the state."[6]

This was the first time that the state was actually portrayed as a liberator. For Rousseau, the state "is the agency of emancipation that permits the individual to develop the latent germs of goodness heretofore frustrated by a hostile society."[7] And so was born what one historian calls "the politics of redemption," the idea that politics can be the means not only of creating a better world but of actually transforming human nature, creating "the New Man."[8]

Moreover, since human nature is essentially undefined, according to Rousseau, there are no moral principles limiting the state's ambitions. In the Christian worldview, we treat a thing according to its nature, the type of being it is, based ultimately on what God created it to be. That's why we treat a child differently from a dog. But if there is no such thing as human nature, then there is no justification for saying we should treat people one way rather than another. There is no basis for saying the state must treat its citizens justly instead of unjustly, and there are no moral limitations on the state's use of power.

This explains why Rousseau's philosophy gave birth to the modern concept of revolution, which involves not just political rebellion to overthrow a particular ruler but also the wholesale destruction of an existing society in order to build a new, ideal society from scratch. Whereas traditional social theory justified any given action by an appeal to the past—to the normative human nature created by God—modern revolutionaries justify their actions by an appeal to the future—to the ideal society they will create. The bloodiest atrocities can be justified by invoking the perfect society that the revolutionaries promise to build on the ashes of the old.[9] Thus modern revolutionaries moved ruthlessly and brutally, slaughtering millions of people.

Why didn't anyone in Rousseau's legions of disciples foresee these disastrous consequences? Why didn't anyone consider that absolute power is sure to corrupt?

Because utopianism creates a peculiar blindness. Believing the individual to be naturally good, Rousseau was confident that the all-powerful state would likewise be good, since in his view the state was simply a merging of individual wills into a "General Will." Rousseau actually believed that the state would always be right, always tending toward the public good—"always constant, unalterable, and pure."[10] And if some recalcitrant individuals failed to agree with the General Will? That merely proved that they had been corrupted and that they must be coerced into seeing that their true liberty lay in conforming to the General Will. As Rousseau put it, the individual must "be forced to be free."[11]

Robespierre, who led the Reign of Terror that overtook the French Revolution in 1793, grasped this logic all too well. He and his fellow Jacobins understood Rousseau's call for "force" to include condemnation and execution of all who opposed the new order, resulting in the imprisonment of 300,000 nobles, priests, and political dissidents, and the deaths of 17,000 citizens within the year. Of course, this was only the beginning of the rivers of blood that would flow from Rousseau's philosophy. For in practice, the utopian program of building a new and perfect society always means killing off those who resist, those who remain committed to the old ways, or those who belong to a class judged to be irredeemably corrupt (the bourgeoisie, the kulaks, the Jews, the Christians).

This same basic pattern can be seen in the philosophy of Karl Marx, whose vision of a perfect society has fueled one failed utopian experiment after another in nations around the globe. The fatal flaw in Marxism's utopian view of the state is once again the denial of the basic Christian teaching of the Fall. If one is to believe there is such a thing as sin, one must believe there is a God who is the basis of a transcendent and universal standard of goodness. All this Marx denied. For him, religion and morality were nothing but ideologies used to rationalize the economic interests of one class over another. Small wonder that the totalitarian states created by Marxism acknowledged no universal moral principles, no transcendent justice, and no moral limits on their murderous brutality. The party, like the General Will, was always right.

The same denial of sin explains the roots of fascism. In 1964, *Time* magazine was a latecomer in raising the question on its front cover, "Is God

Dead?" Back in the nineteenth century, German philosopher Friedrich Nietzsche had already declared the death of God and had etched out what that meant: the death of morality. He dismissed sin as nothing but a ruse invented by a wretched band of "ascetic priest[s]," Old Testament shamans who had achieved a magical hold over men and women by playing the "ravishing music" of guilt in their souls.[12] And he denounced Christian morality as a morality for slaves. Kindness, forgiveness, humility, obedience, self-denial—these were the characteristics of weak, repressed slaves who had rejected the joy of life. To Nietzsche, the biblical ethic was nothing less than a pathology, a life-killing prudery. He looked forward to the evolution of a race of superhumans imbued with an ethic of power. A century later, the Nazis, taking their cue from Nietzsche, tried to create just such a superrace.

It is paradoxical indeed that such horrors flowed from the idealistic-sounding philosophy of innate human goodness. French satirist Anatole France once observed that never have so many been murdered in the name of a doctrine as in the name of the principle that human beings are naturally good.[13] But if we look into the personal lives of the people who established the philosophy, we begin to see the dark flaw at the heart of their "idealism."

Take Rousseau. Why did he see oppression only in social institutions such as the family? And why did he paint the state as the great liberator?

Historian Paul Johnson offers an intriguing hypothesis. At the time Rousseau was writing *The Social Contract*, Johnson explains, he was struggling with a great personal dilemma. An inveterate bohemian, Rousseau had drifted from job to job and mistress to mistress, eventually living with a simple servant girl named Thérèse.[14] When Thérèse presented Rousseau with a baby, he was, in his own words, "thrown into the greatest embarrassment."[15] At that time, he was still trying to make his way into Parisian high society, and an illegitimate child was an awkward encumbrance.

Friends whispered to Rousseau that unwanted offspring were customarily sent to a "foundling asylum," and a few days later, a tiny, blanketed bundle was left on the steps of the local orphanage. Four more children were born to Thérèse and Rousseau, and each ended up on the orphanage steps.[16]

Records show that most of the babies placed in this institution died; the few who survived became beggars. Rousseau was quite aware of this unhappy fact; he knew he was abandoning his own children to almost certain death. In several of his books and letters, he even made vigorous attempts to justify his actions.

At first he was defensive, arguing that he could not work in a house "filled with domestic cares and the noise of children."[17] Later his stance became positively self-righteous. He insisted he was merely following the teachings of Plato, who had declared the state better equipped than parents to raise good citizens.

When Rousseau turned to writing political theory, his personal excuses seem to be sublimated into general maxims. His ideal state turns out to be one that liberates its citizens from troubling personal obligations. In particular, he urged that responsibility for educating children should be taken away from parents and given to the state. Was there a connection between Rousseau the man, fleeing from the obligations of fatherhood, and Rousseau the political theorist?

Of course, it's risky business to try to read a philosopher's personal motives from his theoretical writings. But we do know that right up to the end of his life, Rousseau struggled with guilt over his children. In his last book, he grieved that he had "lacked the simple courage to bring up a family."[18]

Ideas do not arise from the intellect alone. They reflect our whole personality, our hopes and fears, our longings and regrets. People who follow a particular course of action are inevitably subject to intellectual pressure to find a rationale for it. Theologians call this the "noetic" effect of sin, meaning that sin affects our minds, our thinking processes. The Reformers coined the phrase "total depravity," meaning that our sinful choices distort all aspects of our being, including our theoretical ideas.

Rousseau's story chillingly refutes the contemporary notion that personal morality has no public consequences. The world has paid dearly for Rousseau's personal choices, from the ovens of Auschwitz to the Game Temple of Synanon. And we're still paying today, in ways that are subtle and thus all the more insidious.

CHAPTER 18

WE'RE ALL UTOPIANS NOW

*The utopian illusions and sentimental aberrations of modern liberal culture
are really all derived from the basic error of negating the fact of original sin.*
REINHOLD NIEBUHR

When the Berlin Wall came tumbling down, the rejoicing on this side of the Atlantic had an almost smug ring to it. The Western model of democracy had triumphed, once and for all, over the great tyrannies that had dominated so much of the twentieth century. And indeed, the collapse of the communist behemoth was a profoundly significant political event. But what happened to the ideas that created communism in the first place? Have they quietly died as well?

Not at all. In fact, many Americans and other Western people continue to cherish the same utopian myth that produced such bitter fruit in the totalitarian nations: the same assumption that human nature is basically good, the same rejection of transcendent morality as confining and oppressive, the same grandiose dreams of social engineering. And unless we change these basic presuppositions, we are headed down our own path to tyranny in a form the great French statesman Alexis de Tocqueville called "soft despotism," an oversolicitous nanny state that debilitates its citizens just as thoroughly, but by coddling them instead of coercing them.[1]

American utopianism traces its ancestry to Rousseau's notion of human goodness, but it also exhibits a unique technological, pragmatic cast that is rooted in the scientific revolution and that appeals to the Yankee, can-do mind-set. Isaac Newton's dramatic discovery that a single law—the law of gravity—explained a variety of phenomena, both in the heavens and on the earth, led to an image of the universe as a vast machine, running by natural laws. Many people began to extend this machine image into every area of life, including society itself.[2]

In the eighteenth and nineteenth centuries, social thinkers fervently believed that science would not only explain the physical world but also show us how to order our lives together harmoniously. They searched for some principle that would explain society in the same way Newton's law of gravity explained motion—a principle that would reduce society to a unified, law-governed system. They sought an experimental physics of the soul that would enable them to craft a science of government and politics to conquer the age-old plagues of ignorance, oppression, poverty, and war.

Of course, nowhere has this vision of scientific utopianism become a reality. And the reason it continually fails is lodged in the logic of the scientific method itself. If we turn human beings into objects for scientific study, we implicitly assume that they are objects to be manipulated and controlled, like scientific variables. That means we have to deny things like the soul, conscience, moral reasoning, and moral responsibility. And when we apply these assumptions to real social problems, we inevitably dehumanize and demoralize people, placing them at the mercy of social scientists in the employ of the technocratic state. The end result is not utopia but another form of despotism.

FROM ANIMAL TO MACHINE

This line of logic can be seen clearly in the field of psychology, beginning in the nineteenth century with Sigmund Freud, who did more than anyone else to debunk the very notion of moral responsibility.[3] Freud reduced humans to complex animals, rejecting explanations of behavior couched in "old-fashioned" theological terms—such as *sin, soul,* and *conscience*—and substituting scientific terms borrowed from biology, such as *instincts* and *drives.* In Freud's theory, people are not so much rational agents as pawns in the grip of unconscious forces they do not understand and cannot control. A committed Darwinist, Freud proposed an evolutionary scheme in which our primitive impulses (the id) belong to the oldest, most animal part of the human brain, while the rational mind (the ego) is a later development from the more highly evolved cerebral cortex. Thus, the things that society labels "bad" are not really evil; they simply reflect the more ancient, animal part of the brain.

Later psychologists carried the process of reduction even further.

Human nature was modeled not on the animal but on the machine. The earliest book on experimental psychology was titled *Elements of Psychophysics,* as if psychology were a branch of physics. Its author, Gustav Fechner, another radical Darwinist, argued that humans are complicated stimulus-response mechanisms, shaped by forces in their environment.

After Fechner came Ivan Pavlov, whose name is familiar because of his experiments conditioning dogs to salivate at the ringing of a bell. Pavlov, an evolutionist and materialist, adamantly rejected any notion of soul, spirit, or even consciousness. All mental life, he declared (whether in his salivating dogs or in human beings), could be explained in entirely mechanical terms of stimulus and response.

In the 1960s, B. F. Skinner's *Walden Two* introduced millions of college students to behaviorism, a school of psychology that flatly denies the reality of consciousness or mental states. Because these things cannot be observed, Skinner argued, they cannot be described scientifically; therefore, they are not real. Only observable, external behavior is real.[4]

By denying the reality of the mind, Skinner and the behaviorists believed they were "purifying" psychology of all philosophical prejudices and rendering it completely scientific and objective. In reality, of course, they were simply injecting their own philosophical prejudices. They were creating a new brand of "scientific" utopianism, which said that the flaws in human nature are a result not of moral corruption but of learned responses—responses that can be *un*learned so that people can then be reprogrammed to be happy and adjusted, living in harmony in a utopian society.

RETOOLING HUMAN NATURE

One of the results of this utopian thinking was a shift in education. Classical education had always aimed at the pursuit of truth and the training of moral character. But if human nature was nothing more than a reactive mechanism, then it could be manipulated and shaped by the laws that science discovered. Thus, education became a means of conditioning, with the child being treated as essentially passive rather than as an active moral agent.

Of course, this dehumanizing philosophy is always presented in the language of utopian promise. In the words of J. B. Watson, the founder of behaviorism, "Give me the baby and . . . the possibility of shaping in any direction is almost endless."[5] Forget trying to reform behavior through religion and morality; these are merely forms of oppression. Through education the world can be "unshackled from legendary folklore . . . free of foolish customs and conventions . . . which hem the individual in like taut steel bands." Watson, sounding eerily like an early Charles Dederich, promised to bring up children with "better ways of living," who "in turn will bring up their children in a still more scientific way, until the world finally becomes a place fit for human habitation."[6]

The same ideas were applied to law. Traditionally in the West, positive law (or human law) was based on a transcendent standard of justice, derived ultimately from God's law. But in the late nineteenth century, legal thinkers like Oliver Wendell Holmes, influenced by Darwin and the rise of social science, began to shift these foundations (as we will see later). They reduced law to a summary of the social and economic policies proven scientifically to work best. The law was redefined as a tool for identifying and manipulating the right factors to create social harmony and progress.

The same scientific utopianism explains the rise of the welfare state. The idea that both law and government policy should be transformed into social engineering took root in the New Deal of the 1930s and blossomed in the Great Society programs of the 1960s. Many American politicians became enthusiastic converts, sincerely believing that all it would take to solve the problems of poverty and crime would be some well-designed, well-funded government programs. They were confident they could win President Lyndon Johnson's "war on poverty."

Well, today the war is over, and poverty won. The welfare state has backfired, creating both a near permanent underclass of dependency and a host of attendant social pathologies, from broken families and teen pregnancy to drug abuse and crime. What went wrong?

Novelist Dean Koontz discovered the answer through hard experience. In the 1960s, young, idealistic, and eager to change the world, Koontz signed up as a counselor in Title III of the Appalachian Poverty Program. His job was to work with problem students, giving them one-on-one tutoring and counseling to help them break out of the area's depressed economic situation. But when Koontz showed up for work, he discovered that many of the students had criminal records. In fact, the man who preceded him on the job had been beaten up by the kids he was there to help and had ended up in the hospital. Koontz soon realized these kids needed a lot more than a bit of tutoring. They needed forms of moral guidance and discipline, which they were not getting at home or school. By the end of his first year in the program, a discouraged Koontz realized that the notion of reforming society through government programs was itself misguided. The failed Great Society programs, he writes, are an illustration of "humanity's hopeless pursuit of utopia through government beneficence."[7]

Koontz puts his finger squarely on the problem: the "hopeless pursuit of utopia." The utopianism of the Great Society offered no real answer to the dilemma of moral breakdown—to crime and social disorder—because it redefined moral maladies as technical problems that could be solved by bureaucrats. Instead of treating human beings as moral agents who must be addressed in the language of duty and responsibility, the Great Society treated them as objects to be shaped and manipulated. As a result, its programs tended to undercut the moral dignity of their recipients, leaving millions dependent and demoralized.

Again we see the irony: When we deny the Christian worldview and reject its teachings on sin and moral responsibility in favor of a more "enlightened" and "scientific" view of human nature, we actually end up stripping people of their dignity and treating them as less than human.

Public housing is another example. In the 1920s, progressives began clearing city slums and replacing them with housing projects built to hygienic and sociological standards. These great, hulking structures reflected the utilitarian, technocratic vision. They were drab, stark towers of steel and concrete, impersonal and functional, designed to warehouse as many people as possible, as efficiently as possible.

The results? Walls that belonged to no one were soon defaced by graffiti. Hallways that belonged to no one were soon stalked by criminals and drug dealers. Grounds that no one was responsible for were soon dry, dusty, and littered with junk. The housing projects designed with such scientific care turned into seedbeds of crime and misery.

Many of these projects have even had to be demolished. When a housing project in Newark, New Jersey, was dynamited, former residents stood by cheering. By contrast, the city mayor mourned "the end of an American dream that failed."[8]

Yet the dream has *not* died. As housing projects collapse into rubble, plans for new social engineering schemes are on the drafting table. And these, too, will fail. Why? Because the source of the welfare-state crisis is not a few wrongheaded policies; it's the utopian philosophy behind the policies—a worldview that regards human beings as ciphers that can be molded and manipulated, tinkered with and retooled, to fit the visions of social planners.

The trouble with the technocratic vision is that it reduces individuals to passive recipients of the state's ministrations, thus robbing them of liberty and initiative. Small wonder that B. F. Skinner's vision of a technocratic utopia was set out in a book called *Beyond Freedom and Dignity*. The title pressed the point that the only way to force people to fit into any ideal blueprint for society is to jettison traditional notions of human freedom and dignity.

Moreover, when things go wrong, when poverty and crime prove intractable, the assumption is that the state is not doing enough. Thus we have bred an entitlement mentality wherein people believe that government owes them support even if they do not fulfill the basic duties of citizenship—or even if they engage in harmful or illegal behavior.

Do they use drugs? Are they alcoholics? Are they able-bodied but refuse to work? Are they having children without the slightest intention of supporting them? No matter. They are entitled to government benefits, no questions asked. Thus these dysfunctional patterns are reinforced, and the cycle continues. Citizens are offered no encouragement to assume moral or personal responsibility for their lives. It's no surprise, then, that welfare has spawned an underclass in which dysfunctional and illegal behavior is the norm. By ignoring the moral dimension, by reducing social disorders to technical problems to be addressed with scientific solutions, we have created moral chaos.

Scientific utopianism always backfires. It expands government control while gradually sapping citizens of moral responsibility, economic initiative, and personal prudence.

A MATTER OF THE SOUL

But welfare is not the only area of public policy that illustrates the pernicious effects of the utopian myth. When it comes to crime, America's criminal justice policy swings back and forth between liberal and conservative approaches: from an emphasis on rehabilitation and social engineering to an emphasis on tougher laws and harsher sentences. Yet both approaches exemplify, in different ways, the same utopian worldview.

Traditional liberalism fixes responsibility for crime on poverty and other social ills. Crime is not a matter of the soul, says the liberal; it is a technical problem that can be solved by engineering the right social conditions: devising the right public policies, distributing money to the right places, and arranging the right physical environment. This view was expressed at the dawn of the Great Society by then Attorney General Ramsey Clark. He enumerated the causes of crime in sordid detail: "the dehumanizing effect on the individual of slums, racism, ignorance and violence, of corruption and impotence to fulfill rights, of poverty and unemployment and idleness, of generations of malnutrition, of congenital brain damage and prenatal neglect, of sickness and disease, of pollution, of decrepit, dirty, ugly, unsafe, overcrowded housing, of alcoholism and narcotics addiction, of avarice, anxiety, fear, hatred, hopelessness and injustice."

Astonishingly, after reciting this horrendous litany, Clark concluded optimistically: "They can be controlled." Never mind how universal, how endemic, how intractable these problems are; they are all merely technical malfunctions that can be fixed by applying the right technical solution.[9]

Furthermore, since liberalism regards crime as the outcome of impersonal forces in society, it locates responsibility for crime outside the criminal. Already at the turn of the century, Clarence Darrow, the lawyer who achieved notoriety defending Darwinism in the Scopes trial, was portraying criminals as helpless victims of their circumstances. In 1902, in a widely published speech to the prisoners in Chicago's Cook County Jail, he declared that "there is no such thing as a crime as the word is generally understood. . . . I do not believe that people are in jail because they deserve to be. They are in jail simply because they cannot avoid it on account of circumstances which are entirely beyond their control and for which they are in no way responsible."[10]

Today, Darrow's heirs fill courtrooms across the country, wringing pity from juries by presenting wrongdoers as victims of forces beyond their control. This kind of defense has grown so common that it is now known as the "Twinkie defense," named for a 1978 case in which a man pleaded temporary insanity after shooting the mayor and the city supervisor in San Francisco's city hall. He insisted that a steady diet of junk food had raised his blood sugar and addled his brain. Twinkies made him do it.

While this liberal approach is often presented as caring and compassionate, the truth is that it is based on a low view of human nature. As Myron Magnet writes in *The Dream and the Nightmare,* liberalism treats people as passive products of the environment, like corn or alfalfa, that automatically grow or wilt depending on the rain and sunshine.[11]

Yet the traditional conservative approach is equally dehumanizing, for it treats crime as little more than a calculation of incentives. It proposes that crime increases when the benefits of criminal behavior outweigh the cost of punishment. Therefore, the solution is harsher punishments and longer sentences. I know this approach intimately, having written many of President Nixon's law-and-order slogans when I was in the White House. How we curried applause in conservative circles with that tough rhetoric!

Ultimately this approach stems from a mechanistic philosophy that reduces the world to mathematical relations and truth to calculation. It treats people not as moral agents who are disposed to sin but as complex calculating machines that total up incentives, weigh them against disincentives, and then decide whether to commit a crime.

America's staggering crime rate from the 1960s through the 1980s demonstrates that both liberal and conservative approaches to criminal justice have failed. Why? Because neither recognizes the dignity of the soul and its ability to make morally significant choices. Neither respects human beings as genuine moral agents, capable of both real good and real evil. And neither addresses the need for moral responsibility and repentance.

This denial of sin and loss of moral responsibility has spread across the entire spectrum of our culture, ushering in "The Golden Age of Exoneration."[12] When people are consistently told that they are controlled by outside forces, they begin to believe it. When things go wrong, someone else must be to blame.

Preposterous examples are legion. Like the woman who entered a hot-dog-eating contest in a Houston nightclub. In her rush to outdo the other contestants, she ate too quickly and began to choke. Did the woman shrug off the mishap as a natural consequence of her own zany behavior? No, she decided she was a victim. She sued the nightclub that sponsored the contest, arguing that the business was to blame because "they shouldn't have contests like that."[13]

The victim ploy can be attractive because it frees us from having to admit to wrongdoing. Yet it is in admitting guilt that we find our true dignity, for doing so affirms the moral dimension of human nature. For centuries, Western law codes and social morality were based on a high regard for individual responsibility. It was understood that human beings are moral agents capable of distinguishing right from wrong, and are, therefore, accountable for their actions.

Of course, acknowledging responsibility means attributing real praise and blame—and blame, in turn, implies the legitimacy of punishment. That's what makes moral accountability so bittersweet. Yet punishment actually expresses a high view of the human being. If a person who breaks the law is merely a dysfunctional victim of circumstances, then the remedy is not justice but therapy; and the lawbreaker is not a person with rights but a patient to be cured. The problem, said C. S. Lewis, is that "to be 'cured' against one's will . . . is to be put on a level with those who have not yet reached the age of reason or those who never will; to be classed with infants, imbeciles, and domestic animals. But to be punished, however severely, because we have deserved it, because we 'ought to have known better,' is to be treated as a human person made in God's image."[14]

.   ▪   ▪

DENIAL OF SIN may appear to be a benign and comforting doctrine, but in the end, it is demeaning and destructive, for it denies the significance of our choices and actions. It reduces us to pawns in the grip of larger forces: either unconscious forces in the human psyche or economic and social forces in the environment. Social planners and controllers then feel perfectly justified in trying to control those forces, to remake human nature and rebuild society according to their own blueprints—and to apply any force required toward that end.

"Of all tyrannies a tyranny sincerely exercised for the good of its victims may be the most oppressive," wrote Lewis. "Those who torment us for our own good will torment us without end for they do so with the approval of their own conscience."[15]

Utopianism can be maintained only by a kind of willful blindness to the reality of human sin. But when we succumb to that blindness, we lose the capacity to deal with sin, and in the end, we actually compound its effects. Therein lies the greatest paradox of all attempts to deny the Fall: In denying sin and evil, we actually unleash its worst powers.

CHAPTER 19

THE FACE OF EVIL

Sin cannot be overcome by human devices of the kind that governments wield but only by suffering and by grace.

GLENN TINDER

What does the face of evil look like?

A few years ago when I visited a South Carolina women's prison, I learned that Susan Smith had signed up to hear me speak. Smith is the woman who drowned her two small sons by letting her car slide into a lake with the children still strapped in their car seats. Her reason? She felt that the man she was dating had hinted that the children were obstacles to marrying her.

As I prepared to speak that day, I scanned the audience, wondering what this unnatural mother would look like. I imagined some kind of female Dorian Gray, her face marked by the soul-struggle she had waged with evil. Recalling photos from the newspaper, I searched for her face, but I couldn't pick her out.

After the meeting, I asked the local Prison Fellowship director whether Smith had even attended. "Oh, sure," he replied. "She was in the front row, staring at you the whole time."

The face of evil is frighteningly ordinary.

In Jonesboro, Arkansas, an eleven- and a thirteen-year-old pull the school fire alarm, assume sniper positions, and then shoot at students and teachers as they file out of the school. They kill four students and one teacher, wounding eleven others.[1]

In Oakland, California, a teenager with a knife chases a woman down

the street, while a crowd gathers and chants, "Kill her! Kill her!" like spectators at a sporting event. Someone in the crowd finally trips the frightened
woman, giving her assailant a chance to stab her to death.[2]

In Dartmouth, Massachusetts, three boys surround a ninth-grade
classmate and stab him to death. Afterward they laugh and trade high fives,
like basketball players celebrating after a slam dunk.[3]

In New Jersey, Brian Peterson takes his girlfriend, Amy Grossberg,
across the state line to a Delaware hotel room, where she gives birth. They
kill the newborn and dump him in the trash.[4]

Killers with freckled faces. Killers on the playground. Killers who do it
for sport.

What does the face of evil look like? It looks like the kid next door. It
looks like us.

How can we view this carnage, this unspeakable evil lurking behind the
wholesome grin of an eleven-year-old, and still cling to the myth that humans are basically good?

Media coverage of these heinous crimes offered all the conventional
answers. The problem is poverty. (But most of these killers were middle
class.) The problem is race—for there is a hushed racism in much of our perception of crime. (But most of these perpetrators were white.) The problem
is a dysfunctional childhood—the therapeutic catchphrase these days for all
abnormal behavior. (But millions of kids come from harsh circumstances
and never commit a crime.)

The only explanation not offered is the one that modern commentators
cannot bring themselves to utter: the dreaded "s word". . . *sin*. It is sin that
unleashes the capacity for raw evil. It is sin that blinds us to anything beyond
our own selfish desires. As the judge said to Amy Grossberg during her sentencing, "If there is a disturbing aspect to your character, . . . it was an
egocentricity that blinded you to the need to seek help, and to the intrinsic
value of the life of the child."[5]

Sin is choosing what we know is wrong. After he had interviewed Susan Smith's pastor, a reporter for the *New York Times Magazine* concluded
with this analysis: Smith "had a choice between good and evil. She had a
choice and knew what she was doing when she made it."[6] How rarely we hear
people acknowledge this stark, simple truth. We have a choice, and when we
sin, we choose to do evil.

How have we lost touch with such a fundamental truth? To begin with,
look at the way children are raised today. A generation ago, children and
adolescents were still subject to moral discipline at school, following a
long-standing tradition that regarded moral character as important as

academic ability. Teachers believed that part of their role was to encourage virtue and instill restraints against the ever threatening lure of sin and immorality. This tradition dates back to colonial days when little girls in aprons and little boys in knee britches learned how to read from the *New England Primer*, which taught the alphabet along with almost gloomy theological lessons.

> *A*—In Adam's fall,
>   we sinned all. . . .
> *I*—The idle fool
>   is whipt at school. . . .
> *X*—Xerxes did die,
>   and so must I.[7]

How different from the modern classroom, where children are taught, above all else, to like themselves. Where even grammatical errors go uncorrected lest a red mark damage the student's self-esteem. Where "guilt" is something hazardous to mental well-being, an artificial constraint from which we need to be liberated. As a result, today's younger generation does not even understand the vocabulary of moral responsibility. Is it surprising, then, that we now see kids who show no remorse when they violate the rights of others, from trivial things like stealing a sister's blouse to horrific crimes like gunning down a classmate?

The utopian myth has even taken hold in the home, where the same ideas are served up through magazines, parenting seminars, maternity classes, and books on child development. Back in the 1940s, in the most influential book ever written for parents, Dr. Benjamin Spock encouraged parents to reject the old puritan notion of children as savages, prone to evil and in need of civilizing. Instead, he urged them to understand children as evolving psyches in need of attention. For example, when a school-age child steals something, Spock suggests that parents consider whether their child might "need more . . . approval at home," and even a raise in his allowance![8]

The same message was advanced in the most popular parenting books of the 1960s and 1970s: Haim Ginott's *Between Parent and Child* and Thomas Gordon's *Parent Effectiveness Training*. These books aimed at transforming parents from stern moralizers into sympathetic therapists, who were to remain coolheaded, nonjudgmental, even professional in their demeanor, calmly leading their children to "clarify" their own values.[9]

Thus, even in the home, the heart and hearth of society, a sense of duty has been replaced by a sense of entitlement, a sense that we have a right to what we want, even if it means violating standards of proper behavior. Adults who once gave firm and unequivocal moral direction—parents, teachers, even pastors—have been indoctrinated with the idea that the way to ensure healthy children is not to tell them what's right and wrong but to let them discover their own values. As a result, many Americans have lost even the vocabulary of moral accountability. Sin and moral responsibility have become alien concepts.[10]

Just how deeply this has affected us was evident in an MTV network special news report on "The Seven Deadly Sins," which aired in August 1993. A description of the program looked promising enough—interviews with celebrities and ordinary teens talking about the seven deadly sins: lust, pride, anger, envy, sloth, greed, and gluttony. But what came across most forcefully was the participants' shocking moral ignorance.

Rap star Ice-T glared into the camera and growled, "Lust isn't a sin. . . . These are all dumb."

One young man on the street seemed to think sloth was a work break. "Sloth. . . . Sometimes it's good to sit back and give yourself personal time."

Pride was the sin the MTV generation found hardest to grasp. "Pride isn't a sin—you're supposed to feel good about yourself," one teen said. Actress Kirstie Alley agreed. "I don't think pride is a sin, and I think some idiot made that up," she snapped.

The program offered not one word about guilt, repentance, or moral responsibility. Instead, it was littered with psychotherapeutic jargon, as if sin were a sickness or addiction. Even the program narrator joined the chorus: "The seven deadly sins are not evil acts, but rather universal human compulsions."[11]

The utopian mind-set has become so pervasive that most people in Western culture have no intellectual resources to identify or deal with genuine wrongdoing. For example, when a respected historian wrote a book about mass murderers like Hitler and Stalin, all he could say was that they were subject to "mental disorders."[12] Every one of us is affected by this degeneration of moral discourse, to the point where even Christians are prone to use the vocabulary of therapy instead of the sterner language of morality.

The question of genuine evil was posed with brutal honesty in Thomas Harris's *The Silence of the Lambs,* a horror novel made into a grisly but riveting movie. In it, an imprisoned serial killer named Hannibal Lecter, a monster who cannibalizes his victims, is approached by a young female FBI agent who hopes he can give her information that will help catch another brutal killer.

"What possible reason could I have for cooperating with you?" asks Lecter.

"Curiosity," says Officer Starling.

"About what?"

"About why you're here. About what happened to you."

"Nothing happened to me, Officer Starling. *I* happened. You can't reduce me to a set of influences. You've given up good and evil for behaviorism, Officer Starling. . . . Nothing is ever anybody's fault. Look at me, Officer Starling. Can you say I'm evil? Am I evil, Officer Starling?"[13]

Hannibal Lecter's taunting question blows away the accumulated jargon that clogs our brains. We do know, both intuitively and from experience, that evil is real. We sense a force—in ourselves and in others—that has the power to dominate and destroy.

The fatal flaw in the myth of human goodness is that it fails to correspond with what we know about the world from our own ordinary experience. And when a worldview is too small, when it denies the existence of some part of reality, that part will reassert itself in some way, demanding our attention. It's like trying to squeeze a balloon in your hands: Some parts will always bulge out. Our sense of sin will always find expression in some form.

Take, for example, the enormous appetite Americans have for horror fiction. What explains this fascination? Part of the answer is that these books deal with gnawing questions about the depth of human evil. This may be one reason Stephen King's novels top the charts again and again. For in King's gruesome world, evil is threateningly real, and supernatural forces lurk everywhere, seeking whom they may devour. Normal people are drawn to these grim stories for the same reason a small child wants to hear the story of the "Three Little Pigs" over and over again, each time delighting in the way the resourceful third pig heats a pot of boiling water in his fireplace to scald the big bad wolf when he sneaks down the chimney.

Children love fairy tales, especially the classic ones recorded by the Brothers Grimm, because they're stocked with scary villains—evil stepmothers and wicked witches, ugly trolls and fierce dragons. Children instinctively know that evil exists, and they gravitate toward stories that symbolize the bad and scary things of life through fantasy characters—and then show those characters being soundly defeated by the good.

Psychologist Bruno Bettelheim says well-meaning parents who refuse to read these spine-tingling stories to their children are not doing the kids a favor. Instead, they're denying them a chance to face their very real fears within the safely sheltered realm of fantasy—in a story where the witches and goblins disappear with the words "happily ever after."[14]

For adults, fiction can provide a similar function: a way of confronting the dark side of reality. Novelist Susan Wise Bauer says adults living in a world of tragedy and pain "need a Grimm for grown-ups—a narrative that not only explains the presence of evil but offers a triumph over it."[15]

Horror/thriller writer Dean Koontz believes the popularity of his own novels about serial killers stems from readers' hunger for pictures of the world painted in vivid moral hues. In our therapeutic age, we have been taught that "one form of behavior is as valid as another," that even murder and destruction must not be condemned but understood, Koontz says. "In 'enlightened' thought there is no true evil." But in our daily life, we know this isn't true. This explains why "people gravitate to fiction that says there is true evil, that there is a way to live that is good, and that there is a way to live that is bad. And that these are moral choices." People have an "inner need to see what they really know on a gut level about life reflected in the entertainment they view or the literature they read."[16]

In a world where juries excuse the inexcusable, where psychologists explain away the most inexplicable evils, people are groping for a kind of realism that they find, ironically, in fiction.

■   ■   ■

THE FACT IS that a utopian framework has taken away the conceptual tools we need to grapple effectively with genuine evil. And when we cannot name or identify evil, we lose the capacity to deal with it—and ultimately we compound its deadly effects.

I saw this in a tragic way a few years ago during a visit to Norway. The prisons there resemble the snow-draped landscape: cold and white. Officials are proud of their prison system, with its expensive, up-to-date facilities. They brag that, along with the Swedes, they employ the most humane and progressive methods of treatment anywhere in the world, and many penologists agree.

The prison I visited just outside of Oslo was a model maximum-security facility. I was greeted by the warden, a psychiatrist with a clinically detached attitude. As she showed me through the sterile surroundings, which seemed more like a laboratory than a prison, she touted the number of counselors and the types of therapies given to inmates. In fact, we met so many other psychiatrists that I asked the warden how many of the inmates were mental cases.

"All of them, of course," she replied quickly, raising her eyebrows in surprise.

"What do you mean, 'all of them'?"

"Well, anyone who commits a violent crime is obviously mentally unbalanced."

Ah, yes. People are basically good, so anyone who could do something so terrible must be mentally ill. And the solution is therapy. I was seeing the therapeutic model fully realized. Tragically, I would also soon see its failure.

That day I spoke to an audience of inmates. Typically, prison is the one place where I don't have to belabor the message of sin; it's one biblical truth that men and women behind bars know well. But these inmates remained completely unmoved by anything I said, even the invitation to receive Christ. No response. Only glazed expressions.

As I was leaving, however, I was approached by an attractive young correctional officer who identified herself as a Christian. In perfect English she thanked me, then said, "I've prayed for this day, when these men would be confronted with a solid message of sin and salvation." She went on to describe her frustration at having to work within such a flawed system, where there was no concept of personal responsibility, and therefore no reason to seek personal transformation.

Only days later, her criticisms of the system were horribly borne out. By then, I had traveled on to Scotland, and while there, I received an urgent phone call from the Norwegian Prison Fellowship workers. They soberly informed me that the young officer I had met had been given the responsibility of escorting an inmate out to see a movie—part of the inmate's therapy—and on the way back, he had overpowered her, raped her, and then murdered her.

A sign of mental illness? A result of social or economic forces? How pale and ineffective such explanations appear beside the monstrosity of human cruelty and violence. When we embrace nonmoral categories to explain away moral evil, we fail to take it seriously, and we fail to constrain it. When we refuse to listen to the true diagnosis of the sickness of the soul, we will not find a true remedy, and in the end it will destroy us.

In any society, only two forces hold the sinful nature in check: the restraint of conscience or the restraint of the sword. The less that citizens have of the former, the more the state must employ the latter. A society that fails to keep order by an appeal to civic duty and moral responsibility must resort to coercion—either open coercion, as practiced by totalitarian states, or covert coercion, where citizens are wooed into voluntarily giving up their freedom. Given the examples cited at the beginning of this chapter, it's not much of a stretch to imagine Americans eventually so frightened of their own children that they will welcome protection by ever greater government control. That's why utopianism always leads to the loss of liberty.

The only alternative to increased state control is a return to biblical realism about the human potential for evil, a bracing willingness to look evil in the eye and not flinch. Sociologists are constantly searching for the root causes of crime and other dysfunctions in society. But the root cause has not changed since the temptation in the Garden. It is sin.

Human beings have revolted against God and his created order, throwing the entire creation out of joint. Everything is distorted by sin. Nothing is free from its effects. This is not merely a "religious" message, limited to some "private" realm of faith. It is the truth about ultimate reality. And as we examine that truth more closely, we will see clearly why the biblical worldview provides the only rational basis for living in the real world.

CHAPTER 20

A SNAKE IN THE GARDEN

[God] created the fact of freedom; we perform the acts of freedom. He made evil possible; men made evil actual.

NORMAN GEISLER AND RON BROOKS

The best diagnosis of the human condition is "all in the first few pages of Genesis," says theologian Nigel Cameron.[1] In those pages we learn where we came from, what our purpose is, and what has gone wrong with the world.

When God created the first two human beings, Adam and Eve, he set a moral limit: "You are free to eat from any tree in the garden; but you must not eat from the tree of the knowledge of good and evil, for when you eat of it you will surely die" (Gen. 2:16-17). Adam and Eve were free either to believe God and obey his law or to disobey him and suffer the consequences. This same choice has confronted every person throughout history.

Obedience to God is not just a matter of following rules arbitrarily imposed by a harsh master. Obedience to God is a means of entering into real life, a life rich in meaning and purpose: "See, I set before you today life and prosperity, death and destruction. . . . Now choose life, so that you and your children may live" (Deut. 30:15, 19).

And obedience is not simply about external acts. Obedience is an internal response to God as a personal being; it is choosing to know and "love the Lord your God with all your heart and with all your soul and with all your strength" (Deut. 6:5). At the core of God's commandments is not a set of principles or a list of expectations; at the heart of God's commandments is a *relationship*. We are to love God with our whole being.

To create personal beings capable of this kind of relationship, however,

God had to create beings capable of choice. These were not human puppets dangling from celestial strings but morally significant agents who are capable of altering the course of history by the choices they make.

This does not imply that the Bible endorses the contemporary notion of autonomous "choice," where whatever I choose becomes right for me by virtue of the fact that I choose it. The Bible teaches that there is a holy God whose law constitutes a transcendent, universally valid standard of right and wrong. Our choice has no effect at all on this standard; our choice simply determines whether we accept it, or reject it and suffer the consequences.

God is good, and his original creation was good. God is not the author of evil. This is a crucial element in Christian teaching, for if God had created evil, then his own essence would contain both good and evil, and there would be no hope that good could ever triumph over evil.[2] There would be no basis for any doctrine of salvation, for God could not save us from evil if the same evil were lodged in his own nature. There also would be no basis for fighting against injustice and oppression, against cruelty and corruption, for these, too, would be reflections of God's own nature and, therefore, inherent in the world as he created it.

The biblical teaching of the original goodness of creation solves two important philosophical problems: It explains the source of evil, and it grounds our hope of personal salvation. If we had been created with a fatal flaw, then salvation would require destroying us and starting over. But since we were created good, salvation means restoring us to what we were originally created to be. Redemption means the restoration and fulfillment of God's original purposes.

But if God is good and creation is good, what is the ultimate origin of evil? Again we turn to the early pages of Genesis, where we are told about the temptation of Eve by a powerful spiritual being who appeared in the form of a serpent and insinuated his destructive ideas simply by raising questions. "Did God really say, 'You must not eat from any tree in the garden'?" the serpent asked (Gen. 3:1). Then, having raised doubts, he moved in for the kill, issuing a direct contradiction to the divine word. The serpent boldly announced: "You will not surely die" (Gen. 3:4). He blatantly confronted the truth with a lie.

And where did this serpent—this evil being—come from? Throughout history, all cultures have had some concept of evil as a real entity, some force personified as a devil or an evil god—or what philosophers call "presence." Only in the Bible do we learn the true source of this evil force. There is an invisible realm of spiritual beings, both good angels and fallen ones (demons), and there is a moral battle going on in this invisible world, just as there is in the visible world. Occasionally Scripture pulls aside the curtain to give us a brief glimpse of that invisible battle.

One of the main characters in this battle is a fallen angel, a once-perfect being who made a moral decision to rebel against God. This being is called "the accuser" or "Satan" or "the devil."[3] In the first chapter of the Old Testament book of Job, Satan boasts that he goes freely "roaming through the earth and going back and forth in it" in his search for souls to corrupt (Job 1:7). Thousands of years later, the apostle Peter, apparently picking up this image from Job, warns that the devil "prowls around like a roaring lion looking for someone to devour" (1 Pet. 5:8). In the Gospels, we learn that after Judas made his fateful decision to betray Jesus, "Satan entered into him" (John 13:27), a hair-raising phrase that tells us an evil spirit can extend its grip deep into a person's soul once that person has made the decision to betray the Lord. Jesus warned that Satan's primary mode of operation is deceit: "He is a liar and the father of lies" (John 8:44).

Satan's own fall from grace began when he declared his intention to be like God: "I will make myself like the Most High" (Isa. 14:14). He then enticed Eve with the same temptation: If you eat from the tree, you will be like the Most High, able to determine good and evil. As Francis Schaeffer puts it, Satan is "the originator of The Great Lie"—that we have the capacity, like God, to create our own standard of right and wrong.[4] It is a lie repeated so often that it has become the accepted wisdom of our culture.

We can almost imagine the crowds of angels, knowing that all of human history hangs in the balance, watching in tense silence as Satan makes his offer to Eve. And we can almost hear then the collective groan of sorrow as Eve reaches out her hand and grasps the fruit. She has believed the lie!

"She also gave some [of the fruit] to her husband, who was with her, and he ate it" (Gen. 3:6). In these utterly simple words lies the explanation for the human dilemma that has bowed generations upon generations under a load of suffering and pain. Adam and Eve's sin was not eating a piece of fruit. Their sin was coveting godlike power, craving something that was not rightfully theirs. They rejected their nature as created, limited, finite beings, and they tried to be what they could never be—divine. They wanted to be their own god.

This single choice to disobey a divine command introduced the moral battle of the heavenlies into the earthly arena, with consequences that will reach to the end of history. The original sin in the Garden has affected all of humanity, so that every human being is born into a state of alienation from God.

A young convert once asked Nancy, "Aren't Adam and Eve just

symbols for all humanity, and isn't the Fall merely a symbol of the sin that traps us all?" No, this is not a mythical fable. These were real choices, made by real human beings. As the apostle Paul declares again and again in Romans 5, Adam and Eve's fall into sin was as historical as Christ's redemptive work on Calvary. And the reverse holds as well: Because the Fall was genuinely historical, the second person of the Trinity had to enter history and suffer a historical death and resurrection to bring about redemption.

The biblical explanation of evil is not some intellectual exercise or a theoretical way to explain what's wrong with the world. Instead, it carries an unavoidable personal message: that *each of us* has sinned against a holy God. As the apostle Paul writes, "There is no one righteous, not even one. . . . All have turned away" (Rom. 3:10-12). When we truly understand these words, we are gripped by a profound humility. We realize that we all come into this world on an equal moral standing before God; we all need the redemption that God alone can provide.

Virtually every other worldview draws the line separating good and evil between sets of people: between Jew and Gentile, between Aryan and non-Aryan, between Brahmin and untouchable, between bourgeoisie and proletariat. But the Bible teaches that the line between good and evil divides each human heart. The evil is within us. "Nothing outside a man can make him 'unclean' by going into him," said Jesus. "Rather, it is what comes out of a man that makes him 'unclean'" (Mark 7:15). We all stand guilty before the Judge of the universe. We are all responsible for the brokenness in our world.

Moreover, we all face the same profound consequences, both personally and cosmically. Many people are put off by the very idea of hell or by preaching about an eternal judgment. But the doctrine of hell is historic Christian orthodoxy. God is a God of love, but he is also a God of justice, and justice requires both heaven (reward for righteousness) and hell (punishment for unrighteousness). This divine judgment may sound harsh and inhumane, but the reality of hell is what makes our choices significant and what grants us full human dignity. For if our actions had no ultimate consequences, they would be meaningless. Furthermore, there would be no final moral accountability and therefore no reason for acting morally, which in turn means there would be no basis for a civilized society.

But, the skeptic asks, what about the person who never hears the gospel? The apostle Paul tells us that all are without excuse because "what may be known about God is plain to them" (Rom. 1:19-20). We are accountable for what we know (and by implication *not* for what we *don't* know). And when we rebel against what we know to be right and true, we eventually pay the consequences.

Even so, God always leaves us a way out. He is ready and willing to forgive and restore us. Full redemption, as we shall see in the next section, is God's provision for sparing us the consequences we rightly deserve.

BONDAGE TO DECAY

The consequences of sin affect the very order of the universe itself. Most people have a narrow understanding of the term *sin*. We tend to think it means that we have broken a few rules, made a few mistakes. So we apologize and get on with our lives, right? Wrong. Sin is much more than breaking the rules. God created an intricate, interwoven cosmos, each part depending on the others, all governed by laws of order and harmony. Sin affects every part of that order and harmony—twisting, fracturing, distorting, and corrupting it.

First, sin disrupts our relationship with God. What was the first thing Adam and Eve did after they ate the forbidden fruit? They tried to hide from God. Because of sin, humans feel guilty and afraid of God. This is not some neurotic, false guilt, some dysfunctional barrier to living a full, uninhibited life, as modern psychiatry often contends. No, real guilt is an internal signal that we have done something wrong, just as pain is a signal we have done something harmful to our body. When we put a hand on a hot stove, pain tells us that we need to change something we're doing. (We need to take our hand off the burner!) Guilt works the same way. It is an awareness in the core of our being that we have violated the law that governs the universe and have shattered our relationship with the Creator.

Second, sin alienates us from each other. Adam immediately began to blame Eve for his action; Eve, in turn, blamed the serpent for tempting her. ("The devil made me do it.") Evasion, blaming, finger-pointing, superiority, bitterness, and pride—all the elements of social breakdown are right there in the early chapters of Genesis.

Third, the Fall affects all of nature. Because Adam and Eve were given dominion over the rest of creation, their rebellion injected disorder into all of creation. This is a difficult concept to grasp in our scientific age, but Scripture clearly teaches that sin ruptured the physical as well as the moral order. God warned Eve that, as a consequence of sin, childbearing and family life would become a matter of pain and sorrow (see Gen. 3). Certainly it is in our intimate family relationships that we suffer the deepest heartbreak. Then God warned Adam that when he tried to cultivate the earth to grow food, it

would produce "thorns and thistles" (Gen. 3:17-19). Work, which was originally creative and fulfilling, would became a matter of drudgery and toil.

Finally, God told Adam and Eve that they would return to the dust
from which they were taken. In other words, death and its preliminar-
ies—sickness and suffering—would become part of the human experience.
Death "had no place in the original creation," writes C. S. Lewis; it entered
our experience because the physical world itself—including our physical
bodies—was damaged by the Fall. "It is not the soul's nature to leave the
body; rather, the body (denatured by the Fall) deserts the soul."[5] Creation itself is in "bondage to decay" until the final redemption (Rom. 8:21).

Clearly, the Fall was not just an isolated act of disobedience that could
be quickly mended. Every part of God's good handiwork was marred by the
human mutiny. This is why the Reformers described human nature as "totally depraved." They did not mean that human nature is completely corrupted, for in the midst of our sin, we still bear the image of God, just as a
child's sweet face shows through smudges of mud and dirt. Total depravity,
according to the Reformers, means that every part of our being—intellect,
will, emotions, and body—shows the effects of sin. No part remains un-
touched by the Fall.

For example, sexuality is good, created by God; but it is often distorted
by lust and unfaithfulness. Similarly, government was created to maintain
order; but it easily degenerates into tyranny and oppression. The human capacity for artistic creativity is good; but it can be twisted into messages of rebellion and license. At the Fall, every part of creation was plunged into the
chaos of sin, and every part cries out for redemption. Only the Christian
worldview keeps these two truths in balance: the radical destruction caused
by sin and the hope of restoration to the original created goodness.

PAYING THE PRICE

Only the Christian concept of sin and moral responsibility gives us a rational
way to understand and order our lives. An exchange in one of Nancy's college ethics classes illustrates this well. During a discussion on the nature of
moral responsibility, one student asked, "Who are we responsible *to?* After
all, the notion of responsibility makes no sense unless we are responsible to
someone."

"We're responsible to other people," another student volunteered. "For
example, if you run over a child, you're responsible to the child's parents."

"But who says?" persisted the first student. "Who will hold me accountable to those parents?"

"It's society we're responsible to," ventured a third student. "Society sets up the laws that we follow, and it holds us accountable."

"But who gives society that right?" asked the first student.

The answer lurking in many of the students' minds was that our ultimate responsibility is to God. Any other authority can be challenged. Only if there is an absolute Being, a Being of perfect goodness and justice, is there an ultimate tribunal before which we are all accountable. But in a secular university classroom, no one dared say that. So the students debated back and forth, hoping to find some basis for moral accountability that would not require them to acknowledge divine authority.

The university classroom is not the only place where "God talk" is taboo. In many parts of contemporary culture, it is acceptable to believe in God, but only if you keep your belief in a private box. Yet Christianity will not remain privatized. It is not merely a personal belief. It is the truth about all reality. Christians must learn how to break out of the box, to penetrate environments hostile to our faith, make people see the dilemma they themselves face, and then show them why the Christian worldview is the only rational answer.

Nonbelievers must be made to see that they are in an intolerable dilemma. On one hand, we all implicitly hope to live in a society where divine authority is respected, where we don't have to be afraid of being cheated, robbed, or murdered. Yet at the same time, many of us don't want to submit to that divine authority ourselves; we don't want to recognize an external, transcendent source of moral truth that restricts our own behavior. That would be a blow to human pride and self-centeredness, and a denial that choice is our ultimate right, that we are morally autonomous. What's worse, it would mean that when we fail to live up to that transcendent truth, we are in the very uncomfortable position of having not only to admit guilt before the divine tribunal but also to accept the consequences. This is the price we pay for accepting the Christian answer.

And yet the price for rejecting it is much higher. When morality is reduced to personal preferences and when no one can be held morally accountable, society quickly falls into disorder. Entertainers churn out garbage that vulgarizes our children's tastes; politicians tickle our ears while picking our pockets; criminals terrorize our city streets; parents neglect their children; and children grow up without a moral conscience. Then, when social anarchy becomes widespread in any nation, its citizens become prime candidates for a totalitarian-style leader (or leader class) to step in and offer to fix everything. Sadly, by that time many people are so sick of the anarchy and chaos that they readily exchange their freedom for the restoration of social order—even under an iron fist. The Germans did exactly this in the 1930s when they welcomed Hitler; so did the Italians, eagerly following Mussolini, who promised to make the trains run on time.

We must ask people to face the stark choice: either a worldview that maintains that we are inherently good or a worldview that acknowledges a transcendent standard and our accountability before a holy God for our sin. The first choice eventually leads to moral anarchy and opens the door to tyranny; the second choice makes possible an ordered and morally responsible society. When Jewish theologian Dennis Prager gives speeches, he often asks audiences to imagine that they are walking down a dark city alley at night and they suddenly see a group of young men coming toward them. Prager then asks: "Would you be frightened or relieved that they are carrying Bibles and that they've just come from a Bible study?" Audiences invariably laugh and admit that they would be relieved.[6] Commitment to biblical truth leads to more civil behavior.

By contrast, no one looking at the history of our own century should be able to swallow the notion that if only we liberate people from oppressive moral traditions and rules, they will be spontaneously good and generous. Every civilization from the beginning of time has known that lawlessness leads to cruelty and barbarism. Even thieves have codes of honor, as the saying goes. Moral laws are not stifling rules that repress and restrict our true nature; rather, they are directions for becoming the kind of beings God intended when he created us. When we understand this, we see that moral standards are life-giving, life-enhancing, life-enriching truths.

The case needs to be made that a realistic, biblical doctrine of sin is the only safeguard against both the personal tyranny of a Charles Dederich and the impersonal tyranny of an overbearing state. It was acceptance of the biblical doctrine of sin that gave Americans the historically unprecedented degree of freedom that we still enjoy today. Our founders built checks and balances on all branches of government because they recognized the need to contain ambition and greed. As James Madison put it, these structures "pit ambition against ambition and make it impossible for any element of government to obtain unchecked power."[7] Such limits on power protect us much better than any written document guaranteeing human rights. After all, the constitution of the former Soviet Union contained a list of rights even more extensive than our own Bill of Rights, but the document didn't do any good without limits on power.

We need to press our skeptical neighbors to spin out the logical consequences of their worldviews. Denying the reality of sin may appear to be enlightened and uplifting, but ultimately it is demeaning and destructive. It denies the significance of our choices and actions, and it unleashes our worst impulses. Christianity, on the other hand, enables us to address societal issues such as welfare, crime, human rights, and education. Christianity provides the basis for a welfare system that is both compassionate and morally challenging, reinforcing recipients' dignity and self-respect. Christianity undergirds a criminal justice system that holds people accountable for their actions rather than reduces their stature as moral agents through the psychobabble of victimization. Christianity affords the basis for a solid theory of human rights, regarding all individuals as equally created by God and equally fallen. Christian education treats children with the dignity of beings made in the image of God. In each of these areas, as we have seen in the preceding chapters, a comparison exposes the utter bankruptcy of modern utopianism and its central tenet of natural goodness.

TURNING THE TABLES

Of course, the notion of sin is not just a worldview issue; it is also intensely personal. On that level, a realistic grasp of human depravity drives us to God in our search for a solution to our personal guilt. Instead of trying to bury it under layers of psychological jargon—where it never stays buried—we can face our guilt head-on, knowing that God himself has provided a way out.

We frequently hear it said that religion is merely wish fulfillment. This was Freud's argument: Christianity is an illusion we invent to meet various personal needs. And it's true that there are psychological benefits to be derived from believing in God. But psychological reductionism is a game both sides can play. For it can be said that there are likewise certain psychological benefits from *not* believing in God. After all, the idea of God can be as disconcerting as it is comforting (at least in the short term). Who wants to abandon personal preferences and be held accountable to an absolute moral standard for every thought and action? Who wants to go beyond admitting to a few mistakes and actually confess to having sinned before a holy God? Who wants to give away one's wealth? Who wants to suffer for others?

Indeed, we could argue that the myth of human goodness to which modern culture has succumbed is best explained by the psychology of atheism, which is itself a form of wish fulfillment—a deep desire to be free from all external authority or from any transcendent source of morality. It can be much more pleasant to believe the dogma of the autonomous self, which reassures us that there are no objective truths making legitimate demands on us, that right and wrong are subject to our own choices, that by our own decisions we create values out of nothing. Each individual is a mini-god, creating his or her own private world. People can even consign their own children to death with impunity, as Rousseau did.

No God, no sin, no guilt. Humanity is on the throne, and all's well with the world. No wonder the utopian myth can appear, initially, to be so attractive.

By turning the tables in this way, we can show people that the strategy of relegating ideas to the game of mere wish fulfillment cuts both ways. And then we can steer the conversation back to the real issue: the straightforward claim that Christianity is true. It matches our own experience better than any other worldview. It fits reality. It makes sense. It answers the questions of existence.

And yet, there is one question that every sensitive soul raises at some point: How can God be good and still allow evil? In moments of distress, believers and nonbelievers alike face this seeming contradiction. Why would a loving God allow his creatures to suffer? Even the most brilliant mind of our century was stymied by this question, and in his case it formed a tragic barrier between him and the God that he knew must exist.

CHAPTER 21

DOES SUFFERING
MAKE SENSE?

*A God who did not abolish suffering—worse, a God who abolished sin
precisely by suffering—is a scandal to the modern mind.*

PETER KREEFT

The year was 1942, and the scene was the crowded front parlor of Albert
Einstein's home, where the famous physicist had arranged a tea party for three
clergymen: a young orthodox rabbi named Dov Hertzen, a middle-aged
Catholic priest named Brian McNaughton, and a liberal Protestant theologian
named Mark Hartman.[1]

"Rabbi Hertzen here 'provoked' this little party," Einstein began, as
soon as the men had sampled the tea and cookies. "He congratulated me on
my open-mindedness when I dropped my belief in a static universe. Not
long ago, I observed Hubble's red shifts for myself at Cal Tech."

Einstein leaned back in his chair and lifted his chin. "Of course, I have
known for a long time that one of the implications of general relativity is that
the universe is expanding. And if it is expanding, then clearly in the past it
was once smaller. Extrapolate backward in time, and you end up with a universe that began at some finite time in the past as a superdense ball.

"And so," Einstein concluded, folding his hands, "I have come to accept that the universe had a real beginning in time. But what are the consequences of this discovery? Does it have any metaphysical, or even religious,
implications? This is what Rabbi Hertzen asked me, and I thought perhaps
we could discuss it together."

He smiled briefly. With his tousled hair and bushy mustache, his old
sweater and slacks, Einstein was a master at creating the stereotype of the

gentle, absentminded professor. But he used his famous image ruthlessly, disarming people, then wielding his sharp logic to cut them to shreds.

Rabbi Hertzen fell for the ruse immediately. Perched on the edge of his chair, he plunged in eagerly. "Don't you think, if the universe itself had a beginning, there must be a cause behind it? A capital *C* Cause?"

"And why is this conclusion necessary?" Einstein gave the young rabbi a sharp look over his teacup, then added in a friendlier tone, "I know something of science, but when we begin to speak of a capital *C*, we have passed beyond the bounds of science."

"This much, at least, remains scientific," Father McNaughton broke in, calmly gesturing with the cigarette wedged between his fingers. "If we observe an effect, we infer a cause. If the universe had a beginning in time, that event must have a cause—a cause *outside* the universe."

"Bravo," Einstein said archly. "You have just reduced the question to a simple syllogism."

"Sometimes the truth is simple," McNaughton retorted with a smile. The group laughed nervously.

Rabbi Hertzen resumed his argument, his voice slightly shrill with agitation. "The findings of astronomers are giving scientific confirmation that there must be an almighty Being. As a Jew, Dr. Einstein, don't you have every reason to find out whether or not this Being is the One who gave Moses the Torah? The almighty One, blessed be He, of the Jewish people. Your own people," he finished triumphantly.

"How could any almighty being *not* be the God of the Jewish people?" Einstein asked dryly.

"So you do believe in a creator?" the rabbi pressed.

"I have said it before and I will say it again: I believe in Spinoza's God, a deity revealed in the orderly harmony of the universe."[2] He leaned forward for emphasis, warming to his subject. "As a scientist, whenever I find a way to reduce disparate events to some underlying unity of natural law, I am moved by reverence for the rationality at the heart of reality. For me, this attitude seems to be religious in the highest sense of the word. I call it cosmic religious feeling."[3]

The faces of his three guests brightened, while Einstein drew on his pipe, permitting them this momentary hope. "But what I *cannot* accept," he went on, "is the idea of a personal God who punishes or rewards people. My religion has no dogma, no personal God created in man's image. A real scientist must be convinced of the universal operation of the law of causation, and he cannot for a moment entertain the idea of a being who interferes in the course of events."

Einstein's voice grew louder. "Why do you religious leaders attach your conception of God to the myths of the past? I tell you, you do religion a disservice by keeping up this primitive notion. It's the major cause of conflict between science and religion."

He jabbed his pipe and glared from one man to another. "I know what it is. Your religion has been a tool for control. You use it to fill people with fear and concentrate power in the hands of priests. That's why you cling to it—to increase your own power."[4]

Taken aback, his three guests scrambled mentally for a response. Einstein took advantage of their silence.

"Forgive me for my vehemence. You are, after all, my guests. But please, consider—the argument is really simple. If this personal being is omnipotent, then every event everywhere in the universe is his work—including every human action, every human thought, every human feeling. So how is it possible to think of holding people responsible for their deeds and thoughts before such an almighty being?"

His voice dropped to a steely intensity. "You say God is a being of absolute goodness and righteousness. But think of this. If he is the one ultimately responsible for our actions, then he is behind all the harm we do each other. In giving out punishments and rewards, he is in a way passing judgment on himself. God himself is the source of the very evil he supposedly judges!"[5]

Father McNaughton was the first to recover. "But we have free will," he began.

"This I do not believe," Einstein interrupted. "Science reveals a universe utterly bound by natural laws, a rational universe. There is simply no room left for causes of a different nature."

"If we have no free will, how can there be morality?" asked Rabbi Hertzen.

"Free will. Free will. Don't you see, it's an illusion?" Einstein rubbed his forehead and closed his eyes briefly, beginning to weary of this fruitless exchange. "When science has probed the depths of the human mind, I am convinced we will find the laws that govern it, just like everything else. So, please, don't rest your arguments for God on arguments for free will. Your religion is constantly being forced to retreat before the advances of science."[6]

As Einstein picked up his teacup, Reverend Hartman finally found his opening. "Really," he said soothingly, "we don't have to argue science versus religion. Religion doesn't make any claims about the world known by science. Genuine religion is a feeling of dependence on the Absolute."

"Hmmm," Einstein said, crumbling a cookie. "I know you to be a progressive, forward-thinking man, Reverend. So how do you explain away the problem of a God who causes evil?" His eyes glinted.

"Oh, I have no quarrel with science or its teaching that we are part of a universe governed by natural laws. But religion belongs in the realm of human experience. We give meaning to suffering by believing in a God of love and redemption."

"I see," said Einstein evenly. "We know religion is false, but we believe anyway to meet our psychological needs."

"No!" exclaimed Rabbi Hertzen. "God allows suffering because we learn by it."

Einstein took a deep breath and raised his eyebrows cryptically. "Yes, I'm afraid we do," he said. "This has been a most interesting afternoon, gentlemen. But I have a headache and should rest before dinner."

After his guests had left, Einstein wandered over to his music stand and began shuffling idly through the sheet music. His eye caught the title of a piece he had played recently on his violin: Bach's "Jesu, Joy of Man's Desiring."

With a snort Einstein gave vent to the impatience and frustration that had been building all afternoon. He knew well what had motivated his little tea party. He had long nursed a smoldering anger about the suffering of the Jewish race through the centuries, and now ominous rumors were coming out of Germany. No, he could not accept the idea of a personal God who allowed such things to happen. And this afternoon's conversation had brought him no closer to an answer.

Better to escape into the world of science, where order and rationality offered an alternative to the chaotic pain of personal life. He opened his violin case and fingered the strings of his instrument. For that matter, music was almost as good an escape. In music he found the symmetry, the fundamental simplicity, the rational perfection that he craved—the same order he found in his scientific work.[7]

He took out his violin and started tuning up. Music would take his mind off these troubling questions that had no answers.

EINSTEIN'S DILEMMA

For Albert Einstein, the greatest scientist of this century, the toughest intellectual barrier to Christian faith was not the question of whether God created the world. He saw clearly that the universe is designed and orderly, and he concluded that it must, therefore, be the result of a mind, not merely of matter bumping around endlessly in space. As he put it, the order of the universe "reveals an intelligence of such superiority" that it overshadows all human intelligence.[8] His famous quip, "God does not play dice with the universe," though directed specifically against quantum theory, reveals his fierce commitment to a causal order unifying nature from top to bottom.

No, what stymied Einstein was something much tougher than the doctrine of creation: It was the problem of evil and suffering. Knowing there must be a designer, he agonized over the *character* of that designer. How could God be good yet allow terrible things to happen to people? And because Einstein could not reconcile the problem of evil and suffering with a good God, he turned away from the God of the Bible.

What tripped Einstein up was that he was a determinist. He viewed human beings as complicated machines, doing what they are programmed to do by natural forces, like windup toys. But if that is so, then there can be no such thing as morality, sin, or guilt. If a person's actions are determined, Einstein wrote, then "in God's eyes he cannot be responsible" for his behavior, any more than a stone is responsible for where it flies when someone throws it.[9]

Who *is* responsible then? God himself, Einstein had to conclude. If an omnipotent God exists, he reasoned, there must be a kind of divine determinism, where God winds us up and makes us act the way we do. But if God makes us do bad things as well as good, then he is directly responsible for evil. "In giving out punishments and rewards, he would to a certain extent be passing judgment on himself," Einstein wrote. "How can this be combined with the goodness and righteousness ascribed to him?"[10] If our actions are determined, then God himself must be evil.

Unwilling to accept the hopelessness of a belief system in which the ultimate reality is evil, Einstein concluded that the only God that exists is an impersonal cosmic mind giving the world its rational structure. In saying he believed in Spinoza's God, Einstein meant he believed in the principle of order in the universe. To Einstein, true religion was nothing more than rapture before the rational structure of the universe.[11]

Einstein was nothing if not logical. But a person's conclusion is only as good as his premise, and Einstein's premise—that humans are essentially robots—was seriously flawed. He missed the truth of Judaism (into which he was born) and of Christianity (which he also investigated) not because he was forced to by "the facts," but because he had already committed himself to a particular philosophy—a philosophy that prevented him from reconciling the existence of suffering and evil with the existence of a good God.

Many people share Einstein's predicament, finding the problem of evil a major stumbling block to Christian faith. So how can we respond? Does the Bible offer a sound answer that makes sense of suffering? Can Christianity answer the heart's demand for justice in a fallen universe?

THE PROBLEM OF EVIL

To see the problem clearly, let's state it in simple propositions. If God is both all-good and all-powerful, he will not allow evil and suffering to exist in his creation. Yet evil does exist. Therefore, either God is not all-good (that's why he tolerates evil), or he is not all-powerful (that's why he can't get rid of evil, even though he wants to). Throughout history, people have grappled with this apparent contradiction and have proposed a variety of solutions, all of which fall short of the biblical solution. Since we encounter these solutions again and again, it is important to know why they are inadequate and false. Let's examine five of the most common false solutions.

Solution #1: Deny that God exists at all. The atheist simply throws out the first proposition. If there is no God, then evil poses no problem. Or does it?

If we follow this proposal to its logical conclusion, the problem of evil is transformed into something even worse: that *nothing* is evil, and, by extension, that nothing is good. For if there is no God, then "good" and "evil" are nothing more than subjective feelings that reflect what our culture has taught us to approve or disapprove, or what we individually happen to like or dislike. For the atheist there is no answer to the question of evil because there is really no question. There *is* no such thing as objective evil; we are merely projecting our subjective feelings onto external events.

But does this satisfy the innate human outrage over evil and suffering? Of course not. Instead, it mocks us by reducing our deepest moral convictions to a trick of our minds. We may be robbed, our children may be murdered, we may die a lingering death, but none of this is genuinely evil. It is merely part of nature because nature is all that exists. We may cry out in the night for answers, but objective reality is indifferent to our tears. Poet Stephen Crane portrays this dilemma poignantly:

> *A man said to the universe,*
> *"Sir, I exist."*
> *"However," replied the universe,*
> *"The fact has not created in me*
> *A sense of obligation."* [12]

On its own terms, atheism simply has no answer, and the pointlessness of our suffering makes it all the more painful.

Ironically, though, when things go horribly wrong, even die-hard atheists shake their fists at heaven; even those who say God does not exist instinctively blame him for their sorrows. There are no atheists in foxholes, as the saying goes. So let's move on to various religious answers.

Solution #2: Deny that suffering exists. Some people attempt to solve the problem by casting evil and suffering as illusions created by our own minds. This is the strategy adopted by Christian Science and by some Eastern religions. The physical universe is an illusion (*maya* in Hinduism), and the suffering of the body is a misconception of the mind. If we train ourselves to think correctly, we can overcome suffering through realizing that it does not exist.

But can anyone really live consistently with such a philosophy of denial? The story is told of a boy who went to a Christian Science practitioner and asked him to pray for his father, who was very ill. "Your father only *thinks* he is sick," the man told the boy. "He must learn to counter those negative thoughts and realize he is actually healthy." The next day the boy came back, and the minister asked how his father was doing. "Today he thinks he's dead," replied the boy. The power of positive thinking cannot erase the objective reality of suffering and death.

During my White House days, I personally witnessed the futility of trying to pretend evil is not real. Among President Nixon's small circle of top advisors were four Christian Scientists, including Bob Haldeman and the late John Ehrlichman, the two men closest to the president during the critical months following the Watergate break-in, when the cover-up was being fashioned. One evening during the scandal, I met with Bob Haldeman and warned him that any cover-up would imperil the presidency. The tough-minded chief of staff swung around in his chair and glared at me.

"What would you do?" he demanded.

"Don't provide any money to the burglars who broke into the Watergate offices," I suggested. "It could be considered hush money."

Haldeman brushed aside my caution with a steely gaze. "Everyone has defense funds," he said.

I kept pressing. "Bob, the president needs a good criminal defense attorney to advise him."

"Nah," Haldeman replied. "We've done nothing wrong. What he needs is just a good PR man."

With Nixon's chief advisors assuring him that his only problem was public image, he was never forced to confront reality. Like King David, he needed a Nathan to be brutally honest with him. (How I wish I had done that.)

But could it have been their worldview that caused Haldeman and Ehrlichman to keep reducing wrongdoing to a problem of perception? In the words of Glenn Tinder, "A logical Christian Scientist does not deplore and try to eradicate sinful desires but tries simply not to notice them. Nor does a logical Christian Scientist who has committed a grave wrong suffer pangs of guilt and seek redemption; rather the whole matter is as far as possible erased from one's mind."[13] Or, perhaps, from the country's mind. Just hire that good PR man.

But the lessons of history tell us that if we do not believe in evil, we cannot cope with the reality when it hits us squarely in the face. The illusion theory simply cannot hold up under the weight of human experience.

Solution #3: Place God beyond good and evil. Some people hold the notion of a God so distant and transcendent that he cannot be defined by any concept in the human mind—a "God who is beyond good and evil." This may sound lofty and reverent, but if the terms *good* and *evil* do not apply to ultimate reality, then they are mere quirks of our own subjective consciousness. The idea of God as "wholly other" makes him so utterly transcendent that our moral outrage finds no echoing outrage in him. We are still left alone with our tears in the night.[14]

Solution #4: God's power is limited. The reasoning here is that an all-powerful God would not allow bad things to happen; since bad things do happen, God must not be all-powerful. This perspective is gaining popularity today through a school of thought known as *process theology,* which proposes a God who is still in the process of becoming—a God who is evolving with the world and is not yet omnipotent. This God has the best of intentions (he really would like to change things), but being finite, he is not able to get rid of the evil that plagues creation. We must direct our hope to the future, when God and the world will reach a glorious new stage of evolution and all ills will be overcome.

This is the theology promoted in Rabbi Kushner's best-seller *When Bad Things Happen to Good People,* which defends God's goodness by denying his omnipotence. "God wants the righteous to live peaceful, happy lives, but sometimes even He can't bring that about," Kushner writes. "It's too difficult even for God to keep cruelty and chaos from claiming their innocent victims."[15] This is a deity who struggles against the forces of chaos, winning some battles and losing others.

Now, such a theology might solve the problem of suffering for future generations, born after God has finally gotten his act together, but it certainly won't solve the problem of suffering and evil for us here and now. This deity is a kind but incompetent heavenly bumbler who has little to offer to the many generations who must suffer and die *before* heaven has evolved here on earth.

Solution #5: God has created evil to achieve a greater good. This is the position taken by philosopher John Hick in *Evil and the God of Love.* Only in a world where we have to struggle for the good can we freely choose God, Hick argues. The struggle itself is necessary to mature the soul and make us ready to enjoy God forever.[16]

This position contains a kernel of truth, for good does sometimes emerge from bad things, and struggle can, indeed, mature the soul. The problem is that if we propose that God created evil *for any reason,* even a good reason, then we are back to Einstein's dilemma: that God himself is evil and there is no escape, no salvation. For if evil is an intrinsic part of reality, it cannot ultimately be eliminated. Besides, if God created human beings in such a way that they require evil in order to mature, then he made them flawed rather than "very good," as Genesis 1 proclaims.

The poet and playwright Archibald MacLeish makes this point in his play *J. B.,* which retells the story of Job in a modern setting. A clergyman tells J. B. that his suffering is caused by the simple fact that he is a human being, for humans are intrinsically flawed. "Your sin is simple. You were born a man."

J. B. finds this explanation singularly uncomforting. "Yours is the cruelest comfort of them all," he responds, "making the Creator of the Universe the miscreator of mankind, a party to the crimes He punishes."[17]

Like Einstein, MacLeish realized that if we say that God created humanity sinful, the implication is that when he judges sin, he judges himself.

Moreover, the notion that God created evil to achieve a greater good is an obvious fallacy, for it is clear that many evil things do not lead to good results. The most gripping expression of this objection comes from the pen of the great Russian novelist Fyodor Dostoyevsky in *The Brothers Karamazov.*

In a challenge to his younger brother, who is a Christian, Ivan Karamazov tells the story of a little girl tormented by her parents. "This poor child of five was subjected to every possible torture by those cultivated parents. They beat her, thrashed her, kicked her for no reason till her body was one bruise." Then Ivan turns on his brother, demanding an answer. "Can you understand why a little creature who can't even understand what's done to her should beat her little aching heart with her tiny fist in the dark and weep her meek, unresentful tears to dear, kind God to protect her? Do you understand . . . why this infamy must be and is permitted?"[18]

For himself, Ivan insists, he will not accept a God who allows the pointless suffering of even one tiny child. "Imagine that you are creating a fabric of human destiny with the object of making men happy in the end, giving them peace and rest at last, but that it was essential and inevitable to torture to death only one tiny creature—that baby beating its breast with its fist, for instance—and to found that edifice on its avenged tears, would you worship the architect on those conditions?"[19]

The answer must be no. No sensitive person could respond otherwise. But the problem lies in the premise: the assumption that God requires evil, even as a temporary stage, to complete creation's destiny. The God of Scripture does not need to build a temporary hell in order to produce heaven. Of course, once evil exists, God can and often does wring good from it. But that is a very different point (as we will see later).

So why is there evil in the world? How do we find any meaning in our suffering? None of the alternatives described above satisfies the cry of the human heart. Every one of them either diminishes God or diminishes us. Only the biblical explanation is consistent with both reason and human experience, for it alone tells us how God can be God—the ultimate reality and Creator of all things—and yet not be responsible for evil.

FREEDOM TO CHOOSE

How does the Bible reconcile God's goodness and power with the presence of evil? Scripture teaches that God is good and that he created a universe that was "very good." It also teaches that the universe is now marred by evil, death, and suffering. Logically there is only one way to reconcile these two statements *without* denying any element in them: *There must be a source of sin outside of God.* And that is exactly what Scripture tells us.

God is good and created a perfect world. But one of the things that makes humans (and angels) intelligent beings is freedom. They had the freedom to obey God or to turn away from him. And to turn away from God, the source of all goodness, is to create evil. Evil does not have an independent existence, nor was it created by God. Evil is created by sin.

The decision to sin was made in the spiritual realm by Satan and other angels, who are intelligent beings capable of genuine moral choice; sin then entered our world through the free moral choices made by the first human beings, Adam and Eve. From there, the plague has spread through all of history because of the free moral choices humans continue to make.

People sometimes ask, What made Adam and Eve sin? But freedom means there *is* no external cause. We are not trapped in an endless chain of cause and effect, as determinists like Einstein believe. Instead, we can initiate a genuinely new chain of cause and effect. In making moral choices, we are genuine first causes; and logically you can't ask what caused a first cause. Thus we can resolve the apparent contradiction we began with: God is all-good, and he created a world that was good and perfect; but one of the perfect things he made was free creatures, and they have freely chosen to do wrong.

As we said earlier, it is vital that we recognize the historicity of the Fall. If the Fall is merely a symbol, while in reality sin is intrinsic to human nature, then we are back to Einstein's dilemma: that God created evil and is implicated in our wrongdoing. Scripture gives a genuine answer to the problem of evil only because it insists that God created the world originally good—and that sin entered at a particular point in history. And when that happened, it caused a cataclysmic change, distorting and disfiguring creation, resulting in death and destruction. That's why evil is so hateful, so repulsive, so tragic. Our response is entirely appropriate, and the only reason God can truly comfort us is that *he's on our side.* He did not create evil, and he, too, hates the way it has disfigured his handiwork.

But if God knew beforehand that we would make such a mess of things, says the skeptic, why did he let it happen? Why did he create us capable of sinning? Fair question. But think carefully about what it means. In order for God to ensure that we *could not* sin, he would have had to tamper with our freedom of will—to create us not as full human beings but as puppets or robots programmed to do only what he wanted. But that would have rendered us incapable of loving God or one another, for genuine love cannot be coerced. [20] Also, without free will, we would not be capable of moral responsibility, creativity, obedience, loyalty, or heroism. The only way God could create beings that are fully human was to take the risk that they would use their freedom to choose evil.

Then, once humans did choose evil, God's holy character required justice. He could not ignore it, overlook it, or simply wipe the slate clean and start over again. Once the scales of justice had been tipped, they had to be balanced. Once the moral fabric of the universe had been torn, it had to be mended.

In that case, says the skeptic, the human race should have ended with Adam and Eve. They should have been punished for their rebellion, cast into hell, and that would have been the end of human history. Ah, but God is merciful as well as just, and he devised an astonishing alternative: He himself would bear the punishment for his creatures. God himself would enter the world of humanity to suffer the judgment and death that sinful humans deserved. And that is exactly what he did, through the God-man, Jesus Christ.

This was not what anyone ever would have expected; it was not anything humans could have devised. Jesus met the demands of divine justice by accepting execution on a Roman cross. He beat Satan at his own game: He took the worst that Satan and human sin could mete out, and he turned it into the means of our salvation. "By his wounds we are healed," writes Isaiah (Isa. 53:5). Through his death on the cross, Jesus defeated evil and guaranteed the ultimate victory over it. At the end of time there will be a new heaven and a new earth, free of sin and suffering, where he will "wipe every tear from their eyes" (Rev. 21:4).

Until that time, God uses the "thorns and thistles" that have infested creation since the Fall to teach, chastise, sanctify, and transform us, making us ready for that new heaven and earth. This is something I well understand: The greatest blessings in my life have emerged from suffering, and I have seen the same process repeated in countless lives. Just as it hurts when the doctor sets a broken bone, so it can cause enormous pain when God resets our character. Yet it is the only way to be whole and healthy.

An ancient document describing the martyrs of the church in the first century says that they "attained such towering strength of soul that not one of them uttered a cry or groan."[21] Through suffering, God gives all who turn to him "towering strength of soul." Because we are fallen creatures, it often takes suffering to detach us from our wrong habits, our mistaken notions, and the idols we live for, so that our hearts are free to love God.

Friedrich Nietzsche, though himself an atheist, once uttered a profoundly biblical truth: "Men and women can endure any amount of suffering so long as they know the why to their existence."[22] The Bible gives us "the why," the wider context of meaning and purpose, an eternal perspective. God's purposes are the context that give suffering meaning and significance.

In his famous doctrine of "Blessed Fault," Augustine encapsulated the mystery of suffering: "God judged it better to bring good out of evil than to suffer no evil at all."[23] Better to endure the pain involved in redeeming sinners than not to create human beings at all.

Why did he do that? There is only one answer. Love. God loved us so much that even when he foresaw the sin and suffering that would darken and distort his creation, he chose to create us anyway. That is the most profound mystery of all, and one that inspires our hearts to worship.

REDEMPTION: WHAT CAN WE DO TO FIX IT?

GOOD INTENTIONS

The bank of operating-room lamps cast a glaring light over the patient as Dr. Bernard Nathanson surveyed the scene with a practiced clinical eye from beneath his bushy black eyebrows. Heavy white sheets covered the woman's upper body; her knees were bent, her feet in the stirrups. Forty minutes ago she had been prepped with a tranquilizer to ease her anxiety.

Nathanson positioned the speculum to hold open the vaginal canal, then administered a local anesthetic to the cervix with a hypodermic. He widened the cervical canal with a metal rod and inserted the curette (a long metal instrument with a sharp-edged steel loop at the end) into the uterine cavity. The patient was about nine weeks pregnant—far enough along that it took Nathanson an extra minute or two to be sure that all of the inner layer of the uterus was scraped away and the tissue collected for examination.

At the end of the ten-minute procedure, Nathanson carefully examined the lumps of bloody tissue on the tray to make sure that he could account for all the parts of the dismembered fetus. Having satisfied himself that the procedure was successfully completed, Nathanson turned away from the gurney, nodded to the nurse, and stripped off his surgical gloves. After dropping them in the disposal bin, he brushed his hands in a dismissive but satisfied gesture. He'd done a good job. Quite routine, yet one did want to maintain high standards.

He stepped over and looked down into the face of the woman under the white sheet.

"Everything's fine," he said. "Rest for a while in the recovery room; then I'll come check on you. You have someone to take you home, right?"

The woman nodded, licking her dry lips.

Nathanson headed for the swinging doors leading to the surgeon's rest area, where he would take a short break before returning to the table for the afternoon patients. Another lineup of terrified, often grief-stricken women.

No one watching the scene in the operating room would have guessed that the woman on the gurney was Nathanson's lover . . . or that he had just aborted his own child.[1]

■   ■   ■

FOR DR. BERNARD NATHANSON in the mid-1960s this scene typified the new world of reproductive freedom. He had campaigned vigorously for the legalization of abortion, and in his eyes, his intentions were good and reasonable. Even righteous. After all, when he had begun his residency at the obstetric and gynecologic clinic at New York's Woman's Hospital ten years earlier, he had seen hundreds of emergency cases resulting from illegal abortions. And the outcomes differed markedly, depending on the woman's social and economic situation.

Poor women arrived hemorrhaging badly, running high fevers, in shock. They had either attempted to induce abortion themselves, using crude instruments, or they had been butchered by quacks. The massive infections that often followed frequently resulted in sterility, and many times they led to the need for a hysterectomy. Some women even died.

By contrast, affluent private patients had it easy. Together with sympathetic doctors, they contrived ways of faking miscarriages, which meant that Nathanson and other residents would then perform a D & C (dilation and curettage, a procedure that scrapes the uterine wall). Or the women simply flew off to Puerto Rico, England, or Japan and had the procedure done there.

It was this social inequity that first motivated Bernard Nathanson to campaign for the legalization of abortion. In 1969, he teamed up with Lawrence Lader to found the National Abortion Rights Action League (then known as the National Association for the Repeal of Abortion Laws). The organization helped to enlist feminists, including Betty Friedan, in the cause of abortion on demand; but it was the two men, Nathanson and Lader, who crafted the movement's strategy against its most formidable opponents and did much to define abortion as a "woman's issue" on which only feminists are permitted to express an opinion. It was also Nathanson and Lader who determined that the Catholic hierarchy should be demonized as an elite club of white males who were insensitive to women's problems.

In 1970, when New York liberalized its abortion laws, Nathanson began running the nation's largest abortion clinic, the Center for Reproductive and Sexual Health (known to staff members by its acronym, CRASH). Located in Manhattan, the facility thrived on referrals from the Reverend Howard Moody's Clergy Consultation Service on Abortion, a network of Protestant ministers and Jewish rabbis. Nathanson took pride in the clinic's high professional standards and in the success of its outpatient surgical model.

In 1973, however, when *Roe v. Wade* made abortion on demand legal across the country, Nathanson decided to make a career change. He accepted a position as chief of obstetrical service at St. Luke's Hospital Center and went from tending mothers to tending babies (although he continued to perform abortions). His task was to organize a sophisticated perinatology unit, complete with electronic fetal-monitoring machines and other expensive equipment to treat ailing newborns.

At the time, one of the most exciting new gadgets was the ultrasound machine, which literally opened a window on fetal development. The first time Nathanson saw an ultrasound in action, he was with a group of residents gathered around a pregnant patient in a darkened examining room, watching a demonstration by a technician.[2]

The technician applied a conductive gel to the woman's abdomen and then began working a handheld sensor over her stomach. As the splatter on the video screen clarified, Nathanson was amazed. He could see a throbbing heart! When the technician focused closely on the image, Nathanson could see all four chambers pumping. It looked like an animated blossom, with such thickness and definition that it took his breath away. He could also see the major vessels leading to and from the cardiac rose.

The technician next brought the baby's forehead, eyes, and mouth into focus. Then, by zooming out, the technician showed that the baby had its hands folded over its face. Right hand, left hand. On each one, Nathanson counted four fingers and a thumb.

The view from above the crown of the baby's head showed the development of the brain, where the first folds could be seen. Then the technician scanned the elegant architecture of the spine.

Was it a boy or a girl? Just like expectant parents, the group couldn't help wondering. It was a girl. Then finally, the technician showed the bone structure of the legs, and each foot with five perfect toes.

During the course of the scan, Nathanson noticed that his mind had dropped the word *fetus* in favor of *baby*. Suddenly, everything he had been learning about the child in the womb since his entry into the field of perinatology snapped into focus. For example, he knew that a fertilized human egg becomes a self-directed entity very early, after it has multiplied into only four cells; that the heartbeat begins as early as the eighteenth day after conception; that at six weeks the major organ systems have formed. In fact, after only twelve weeks, *no* new anatomical developments occur; the child simply grows larger and more capable of sustaining life outside the womb.

All these had been only medical facts, but now they coalesced with the grainy image on the screen and crashed into Nathanson's consciousness. He felt a chill along his spine, and the air in the room seemed to grow denser, making it hard for him to breathe. His mood swung from the exaltation of new knowledge to a brow-sweating panic as the question hit him: How many babies just like this little girl had he himself cut to pieces? How many human lives had he taken?

■   ■   ■

BERNARD NATHANSON SOON became convinced that human life existed within the womb from the onset of pregnancy. In an article he wrote for the *New England Journal of Medicine,* he confessed that at CRASH he had presided over "60,000 deaths." In abortion "we are taking life," he wrote, "and the deliberate taking of life, even of a special order and under special circumstances, is an inexpressibly serious matter." While he did not conclude that abortion was wrong, he did say that physicians "must work together to create a moral climate rich enough to provide for abortion, but sensitive enough to life to accommodate a profound sense of loss."[3]

Nathanson's article caused heated controversy, and the public attention forced him to think even more closely about the morality of abortion.

The article also generated a new development that took Nathanson by surprise. He began receiving invitations to speak at pro-life gatherings—groups that consisted largely of devoutly religious people, whether Catholics, conservative Protestants, or Orthodox Jews. Although Nathanson accepted the invitations, he always made it clear that his objections to abortion were not based on any religious beliefs but proceeded from scientific facts and purely humanitarian conclusions. When his first book, *Aborting America,* was published in 1979, he even criticized what he saw as specious arguments and false rhetoric used by some pro-life activists.

Yet by this time, Nathanson had decided that abortion could be justified only when the life of the mother was threatened. The same year that *Aborting America* was published, Nathanson stopped performing abortions. He had always believed that a society's morality must be judged by its treatment of the weak and defenseless, and his own early work for abortion reform had been inspired by a concern for the poor. But ultrasound technology had revealed to him an even more vulnerable class: the unborn.

■   ■   ■

ONE DAY, NATHANSON had a brainstorm. Since ultrasound could reveal the baby in womb, it could also be used to witness an abortion. He asked a colleague who was performing several abortions a day to put an ultrasound device on a few of the patients and, with their permission, tape the procedure.

Nathanson knew quite well what happened in an abortion. Yet when he saw abstract concepts transformed into vivid images—when he actually witnessed tiny bodies being torn limb from limb—he was startled and revolted. Even more sickening, the ultrasound showed the babies desperately trying to wriggle away from the suction apparatus. One twelve-week fetus continued to struggle even after it had been severely maimed, opening his mouth in what looked horrifyingly like a scream of fear and pain.[4]

Nathanson made the tape of the twelve-week fetus into a film and titled it *The Silent Scream*.[5] When it was released in 1985, it instantly transformed the nature of the abortion debate. Pro-abortion forces raged, accusing Nathanson and the producers of faking the footage. When the authenticity of the tape was confirmed, they switched tactics and sidetracked the discussion into the question of whether a fetus is capable of feeling pain during an abortion—as the fetus so clearly appeared to in the film. Without proposing any theological position, Nathanson had forced abortion supporters to acknowledge that abortion is about taking human life.

■   ■   ■

AT THE SAME time, an internal "silent scream" began to dominate Bernard Nathanson's own life. Troubling questions played and replayed in his mind: How could I have been so blind to the true nature of abortion? How could I have presided over mass slaughter? And with such a crassly utilitarian attitude, as if it were nothing more than a matter of professional competence?

He began a profound examination of conscience, digging into his past to uncover the source of his skewed ideas. His father, Joseph Nathanson, a wealthy doctor, had sent him to Hebrew school while at the same time ridiculing the spiritual lessons taught there. Although the older Nathanson dismissed the religious claims of Judaism as superstition, he wanted his son to embrace Judaism as an ethnic identity. Joseph Nathanson, having escaped the poverty he grew up in, was driven by materialism. Now, looking back, Bernard Nathanson realized he had learned one overwhelming lesson from his father: *Don't let anyone get in your way.*

And he had learned the lesson well. He had even consigned not one, but two of his own children to death. The first time an unwanted pregnancy threatened to "get in the way," he was in medical school, and he gave his pregnant lover the money to get an illegal abortion. The second time was in the mid-sixties, when he was between marriages and his womanizing resulted in an inconvenient pregnancy. That was the abortion he had performed himself.

Like his father, Bernard Nathanson had grown materialistic and ruthlessly ambitious. His first marriage had been fashionable and without substance. His second marriage gave him his son, Joey, but Nathanson had neglected the boy for an ever more frantic swirl of professional activities and appointments. His idea of parenting was to send his son to expensive private schools. After that marriage ended, he played the swinging bachelor. Eventually, he destroyed his third marriage as well.

He had lived an "unspeakably shallow" life, as he wrote later, acquiring lavish homes, trendy autos, trophy wives, wine cellars, and horses. Then, as he aged, he sought desperately to recover his youth through cosmetic surgery, bodybuilding, and fashions designed for college kids. "I was dwelling in the suzerainty of the demons of sin," he wrote, "oblivious to all but the seemingly endless carnival of pleasures, the party that never ends (or so the demons would have you believe)."[6]

But the heaviest baggage Nathanson carried was abortion. Abortion, abortion, abortion. How ironic that his one great humanitarian cause had turned out to be nothing less than mass slaughter. Nathanson found himself face-to-face with guilt. Real guilt. Not a passing feeling of shame or a confused embarrassment, but a brutal, crushing, dogged knowledge of his own evil. He was a charred ruin.

Off and on during the late 1980s, Nathanson contemplated suicide. He would awake from fitful dreams at four or five o'clock in the morning, feeling as if he were being strangled by some nameless dread. His grandfather and sister had committed suicide, and he found himself asking, "Would the people closest to me find my death a relief?"

He turned to what he called the "literature of sin." He read St. Augustine's *Confessions* repeatedly and absorbed books by Kierkegaard, Tillich, Niebuhr, and Dostoyevsky—works that described the soul's tormented search for answers to guilt. "Your beauty drew me to you," Augustine wrote. "I had no doubt at all that you were the one to whom I would cling, only . . . my inner self was a house divided against itself."[7] Augustine wanted to turn to God, but he couldn't bring himself to do it. Nathanson's own cry echoed Augustine's agonizing meditations.

But was Augustine's ultimate solution available to him? Could Nathanson accept Christianity? Ever since his childhood, he had associated the name of Jesus Christ with the long history of Christian persecution of the Jewish people. So instead of turning to Christianity, he sought relief in therapy, self-help books, antidepressant drugs, counseling, and a hodgepodge of spiritual approaches, from theosophy to Swedenborgianism. All to no avail.

"I felt the burden of sin growing heavier and more insistent," Nathanson wrote. "I [had] such heavy moral baggage to drag into the next world. . . . I [was] afraid."[8]

•   •   •

THEN, IN 1989, Nathanson attended a pro-life rally in New York City to gather data for an article he was writing on the ethics of abortion clinic protests. Forbidden to participate himself because of a court order stemming from earlier protests (he had been convicted of trespassing), he stood apart as an objective observer. And what he saw there finally broke through his defenses.

The pro-life activists seemed to have an otherworldly peace. "With pro-choicers hurling the most fulsome epithets at them, the police surrounding them, the media openly unsympathetic to their cause, the federal judiciary fining and jailing them, and municipal officials threatening them—all through it they sat smiling, quietly praying, singing, confident," Nathanson wrote. They exhibited an "intensity of love and prayer that astonished me."

It was only then, with this vivid image of love pressing in on him, that Nathanson began "for the first time in my entire adult life . . . to entertain seriously the notion of God."[9]

Almost immediately, he turned from the literature of sin to the literature of conversion, especially to *Pillar of Fire,* an autobiography detailing the conversion of Karl Stern, one of Nathanson's former teachers. As a medical student, Nathanson had been fascinated by Stern, the leading figure in McGill University's department of psychiatry. In his book, Stern described his long intellectual journey from nominal Judaism to a highly intellectual and devout Christianity. In retrospect, Nathanson realized that Stern's religious beliefs were what had transformed mere medical technique into medical *care.* Nathanson had been drawn to Stern's methods without understanding their inspiration.

That's the kind of transformation I want in my own life and practice, he thought.

In 1993, Nathanson shut down his practice to pursue advanced studies in bioethics, first at Georgetown University, then at Vanderbilt, where bioethics students were allowed to incorporate religious studies in their programs. He also sought counsel from rabbis, for he had come to the point where he believed he would meet his Creator someday. How could he enter the presence of a just God? The rabbis taught that one can atone through performing good works, through hearing the declaration of God's forgiveness of Israel at Yom Kippur. But how, Nathanson wondered, can one know forgiveness personally and individually? How could he himself be delivered from death—the death of all the lives he had taken and the death of his own soul?

In the dim hours of early morning he sometimes felt that he had already entered a hell marked "No Exit," that his "good intentions" had led him to become, in his words, the "Mayor of Hell."[10] His own sense of justice haunted him. He stood condemned in his own eyes. Was there any hope for him?

CHAPTER 23

IN SEARCH OF REDEMPTION

He has rescued us from the dominion of darkness and brought us into the kingdom of the Son he loves, in whom we have redemption, the forgiveness of sins.

COLOSSIANS 1:13

One day in late autumn 1996, my secretary informed me of a surprising phone call. Dr. Bernard Nathanson was inviting my wife and me to his baptism at St. Patrick's Cathedral, with Cardinal John O'Connor presiding.

I was stunned. "Are you sure you've got the right name?" I asked. "Bernard Nathanson?"

"That's it," she said with a smile.

I had known that Nathanson was interested in Christianity; in fact, the two of us had been trying to meet for some time, but we had been unable to coordinate our schedules, and I had no idea he had come so far. I confess I experienced a twinge of disappointment that I hadn't introduced him to the Baptist tradition, yet I was overjoyed to learn that the man who had once been the nation's leading abortionist was now a Christian. It was an invitation I could not refuse.

A few weeks later, on a cold December morning, Patty and I stepped along briskly as we walked the few blocks from our Manhattan hotel to St. Patrick's for the 7:30 service. We had been told to go to the back entrance of the massive cathedral, where we were greeted by a smiling young man in a black coat and a broad-brimmed black hat. He introduced himself as Father John McCloskey and led us down a few steps to a basement entrance.

I knew of McCloskey, a charismatic young priest who had a powerful student ministry at Princeton University. He had also given Nathanson the good news of forgiveness that he so desperately sought and had guided him into the Christian faith.

Father McCloskey led us to a small basement chapel, chilly and damp, where about fifty people were seated on folding chairs. No pomp or ceremony, just a group of believers surrounding a small altar. We could have been the first-century church, gathered in the catacombs, about to witness the baptism of a new believer in the name of the resurrected Christ.

Standing before the altar, Cardinal O'Connor gave a short welcoming homily. Then Nathanson was escorted forward by a young woman whom I immediately recognized as Joan Andrews (now Joan Andrews Bell). How God delights in ironies, I thought. Andrews was a former nun who had spent five years in a Florida prison for nonviolent resistance at abortion clinics. In the prison, thieves and murderers came and went, while Joan—her parole consistently denied by a stubborn judge—sat silently in her cell praying. Eventually most people forgot who Joan Andrews was, and she might have wondered if her act of protest had been worth the cost. But God uses every act of faithful obedience, and here she was, guiding one of the world's leading abortionists to the baptismal font.

It was a striking moment of spiritual victory. Most of the time, we Christians fight in the trenches, seeing only the bloody warfare around us. But every so often God permits us a glimpse of the real victory. This was one of those rare, illuminating moments, as we watched Bernard Nathanson—a Jew by birth, a man who had been an atheist by conviction and a brilliant but amoral doctor by profession—kneeling before the cross of Christ.

My mind flashed back to a day three months earlier when I had joined a group of religious leaders to walk the corridors of Congress and plead with senators to override President Clinton's veto of a ban on partial-birth abortions. During the roll call of votes, I sat in the gallery, watching and praying. The atmosphere that day was unusually solemn; the senators seemed to move about the chamber in slow motion. The only sound was the secretary calling the roll, followed by "yea" or "nay" responses.

Suddenly the shrill cry of a baby pierced the eerie silence . . . probably the child of a tourist visiting the Capitol building. Was it my imagination, or did some of the senators turn ashen? The sound of a live baby in that chamber was a vivid reminder of what was at stake in this crucial vote.

Yet it made no difference. The vote to override failed.

Dejected, ashamed for my country, I made my way through the crowds and down one floor to the marble reception room just off the Senate chambers. There I saw Kate Michelman, a leader of the pro-abortion forces, and a group of her cohorts celebrating—embracing, cheering, and exchanging high fives. The

scene struck me as macabre. Here were well-dressed, professional women celebrating the right to continue an utterly barbaric practice: a procedure in
which a baby is removed from the birth canal backward, all except for its head,
then the base of the skull is punctured and the baby's brains are sucked out.

That day, the pro-choicers won an important political victory. And yet
it paled in comparison to what Patty and I were witnessing, just three
months later, at Bernard Nathanson's baptismal service. There before our
eyes was the real victory: God's ultimate triumph over sin through Christ's
sacrifice on the cross.

After the baptism, our small group gathered in an Irish pub on Second
Avenue. Bernard Nathanson, Father McCloskey, Joan Andrews, several
priests (most of whom also had been imprisoned for nonviolent demonstrations against abortion), and other Right to Life activists filled the half-dozen
tables, ordering late breakfasts of bagels and scrambled eggs. Speaking softly
and with deep feeling, Nathanson thanked everyone for coming.

"All I could think about while I was kneeling at the altar was my bar
mitzvah," he said. "That day I was so afraid." He hesitated, then looked up.
"Today I felt all that fear fall away. I experienced sheer grace."

■   ■   ■

BERNARD NATHANSON HAD been redeemed. He was a new man, taking his
first tentative steps into a new world of faith and hope, his fears relieved, his
tormented soul transformed, and the most vexing questions of life answered.
As I listened to him speak, I shivered with wonder at the transformation that
can take place in the human soul. Dorothy Sayers, mystery writer and friend
of C. S. Lewis, coined the phrase "The dogma is the drama," meaning that
the Christian teaching on salvation has all the artistic elements of a great
story.[1] Indeed, it is the best story ever told. No novelist, no playwright, no
movie scriptwriter has ever come up with a plot line so compelling. And it is
reenacted every time a person stops running from the Hound of Heaven and
gives in to his relentless pursuit of love.

Not all of us, of course, are driven to the depths of despair that
Nathanson was. Yet all human beings yearn, deep in their hearts, for deliverance from sin and guilt. Many try to suppress the longing, to rationalize it
away, to mute it with lesser answers. But ultimately, it is impossible to evade.
This is the great human predicament: Sooner or later, even the most decent
among us know that there is a rottenness at our core. We all long to find
freedom from our guilt and failures, to find some greater meaning and purpose in life, to know that there is hope.

This need for salvation has been imprinted on the human soul since the first couple went astray in the Garden. The desire is universal, and every religion and worldview offers some form of redemption. For the Buddhist, it is nirvana; for the Jew, it is the atonement of good works; for the Muslim, it may be heaven after the perilous walk across the sword of judgment.

But religions and philosophies are not the only ones offering redemption. Any belief system in the marketplace of ideas, any movement that attracts followers, anything that has the power to grab people's hearts and win their allegiance does so because it taps into their deepest longings. And those longings are, ultimately, religious.

Just as every worldview offers an answer to the question of how we got here (creation), and an analysis of the basic human dilemma (the Fall), so every worldview offers a way to solve that dilemma (redemption). But which offer of redemption is true? Which gives a genuine answer to the human dilemma? And which ones are crass counterfeits?

MORALITY PLAYS FOR TODAY

The siren that calls many people today is the one that claimed Bernard Nathanson's heart and soul for so long: the belief that the object of life is material gain, that achievement and advancement and sensual pleasure are "all there is." America has a highly developed, technologically advanced industry—the advertising industry—designed to entice us with the promise of redemption through materialism and commercialism.

Every time we turn on the television set or open a magazine or newspaper, we are bombarded with the gospel of commercialism: that for every need, every insecurity, every worry, there is a product for sale that can satisfy our need, pump up our self-esteem, soothe our worry. Advertisers devote huge budgets to hiring psychologists to probe the human psyche and pinpoint our deepest needs and longings. Then they craft seductive images and phrases designed to hook us, to beguile us into thinking that buying their product will satisfy those fundamental needs.

And since those deepest needs are religious, what ads really trade on is the universal longing for redemption.

This is no accident. According to sociologist James Twitchell, in his book *Adcult U.S.A.*, many of America's early advertisers were Christians, often sons of clergymen. As they developed the art of modern advertising, they simply translated their understanding of spiritual need into the commercial arena. The spiritual sequence of sin-guilt-redemption became the psychological sequence of problem-anxiety-resolution. That's why the typical television commercial is, in Twitchell's words, "a morality play for our time."[2] We see a man or woman in distress. He has a headache; she has a cold. A second figure appears on the screen promising relief, testifying to the power of the product being advertised. The seeker tries the product, and, hallelujah, the problem is solved. Life is blissful. From on high, the disembodied voice of an announcer presses home the advantages of the product.

"The powerful allure of religion and advertising is the same," Twitchell concludes. Both reassure us that "we will be rescued."[3]

This message takes various forms. Sometimes ads trade on themes of personal faith, with slogans such as "I found it!" "It's the right thing." "Something to believe in." Others offer a veiled substitute for a personal relationship with the divine: "Me and my RC" "You're in good hands." Still others suggest the blessings of the Promised Land: "We bring good things to life." "Be all you can be." Finally, some ads exploit the rhetoric of religious gratitude: "Thank you, TastyKakes." "Thanks, Delco." "I love what you do for me."[4]

In recent years we've even seen religion itself pop up in ads. After all, what is deeper than the need for God? Take an appeal to status or pleasure, combine it with an appeal to religion—or turn pleasure itself into a religion—and the allure is all but irresistible.

Picture this: A family battles desperately as floodwaters threaten to wash away their home. With the house on the verge of collapse, the father cries out for help. And behold, the heavens open and a giant hand descends from the sky to rescue the family from disaster.

Deliverance by God? No. Deliverance by Allstate Insurance Company. The ad co-opts the universal longing for security, which is, at core, a religious longing. One almost expects to see the family offer up a prayer: "We thank you, Allstate, for your protection in times of trouble."

Then there's the ad that shows a young woman in church "confessing" her miserly ways. "It's not a sin to be frugal," the preacher reassures her. And the young woman is released from guilt to enjoy her sporty but economical new Chevy Cavalier.

One IBM ad shows Catholic nuns walking to vespers while whispering about surfing the Net. Another IBM ad shows Buddhist monks meditating telepathically about Lotus Notes. Gatorade features Michael Jordan running in Tibet and meeting an Eastern holy man, who intones, "Life is a sport. Drink it up." Snickers shows a football team inviting a Catholic priest to bless the team, followed by a rabbi, a Native American, a Buddhist, and a long line of other spiritual leaders. "Not going anywhere for a while?" says the tag line. "Grab a Snickers." A Volvo ad shows a man being bathed in flowing, crystal-clear water. As he looks skyward, a soothing, ethereal voice says, "Volvo, it can help save your soul."[5]

Clearly, advertisers are attuned to the human yearning for salvation—and eager to exploit it. Novelist John Updike compares the effort put into commercials with the fanatical care medieval monks devoted to decorating sacred manuscripts. The goal of all this advertising artistry is "to persuade us that a certain beer, or candy bar, or insurance company, or oil-based conglomerate is, like the crucified Christ, . . . the gateway to the good life." Modern advertising makes "every living room a cathedral," and places within it, every six minutes or so, the icons of modern culture—"votive objects as luxurious and loving as a crucifixion by Grünewald or a pietà by Michelangelo."[6]

Calvin Coolidge, our thirtieth president, once told the American Association of Advertising Agencies that "advertising ministers to the spiritual side of trade." It is part of the "greater work of the regeneration and redemption of mankind."[7] Regeneration? Redemption? Through advertising, the "religion" of appetite and ego gratification is offered to us as a solution to the human dilemma, a comfort in our insecurities, a way of salvation. The most advanced tools of communication and persuasion are being used to press us into the service of America's most popular deity, the idol of consumerism.

But as Bernard Nathanson would tell you, material goods and consumer items offer no comfort when one enters the dark night of the soul. As some people have said, the poor are better off than the rich because the poor still think money will buy happiness; the rich know better.

Practicing the religion of consumerism is like drinking salt water: The more you drink, the thirstier you get. There is never enough wealth and power to satisfy, never enough material possessions to blot out guilt. And no matter how pleasant or attractive such things can make our brief existence here on earth, they cannot carry us beyond. For the old adage is apt: You can't take it with you.

Though consumerism is America's favorite substitute religion, it is not the only one. Others have proven equally seductive . . . and even more destructive.

DOES IT LIBERATE?

One of the most dangerous errors instilled into us by the nineteenth-century progressive optimism is the idea that civilization is automatically bound to increase and spread. The lesson of history is the opposite.

C. S. LEWIS

When Diane went off to college in 1967, she also went off the deep end. Within weeks she was smoking pot, flouting her childhood faith, and mouthing slogans about women's liberation.

Today, Diane has returned to her Christian faith and no longer calls herself a feminist. "I got tired of being a victim," she explains. "I used to read feminist books by the armload. Then one day it hit me. All those books were the same! Every problem a woman might have was explained by saying that someone, somewhere had done her wrong—as if women were weak, passive creatures. It was pathetic."

Diane has changed her mind, but millions still march behind the banner of women's liberation—along with a host of other liberation ideologies. Across the nation, groups gather around ideologies of gender, race, and sexual orientation, seething with rage over alleged oppressions of one kind or another.

To understand the appeal these groups exert, we need to understand their underlying worldview. According to these groups, what is the human dilemma, the source of suffering and injustice? Oppression by whites or males or heterosexuals or some other group. What is the solution, the way to justice and peace? Raising our consciousness and rising up against the oppressor. Thus, the promise of liberation is ultimately a promise of redemption.

All the liberation ideologies in the marketplace of ideas today are variations on a single theme that has been pervasive in Western thought since the nineteenth century: that history is moving forward toward a glorious consummation. This is sometimes dubbed the "myth of progress," or, in the words of British philosopher Mary Midgley, "the Escalator Myth," and it is a secularization of the Christian teaching of divine providence. Whereas Christianity teaches that history is moving toward the kingdom of God, the Escalator Myth reassures us that we are evolving toward an earthly utopia that is the product of human effort and ingenuity.[1]

Along with the denial of sin, the idea of inevitable progress has fueled the great utopian movements that we traced in the previous section. This idea first took hold through the work of the nineteenth-century German philosopher Georg Friedrich Hegel. Until that time, the world had been pictured as a static ladder of life. Everything had its niche on a rung on this great ladder—from rocks to plants to animals to humans to angels to God himself. But Hegel did something entirely new, something really breathtaking. He tilted the ladder of life on its side, so that instead of being a list of all the things that exist in the world at any one time, it became a series of *stages* through which the world passes during the course of history. Thus the ladder was transformed into a dynamic series of steps: Everything moves from one rung to the next in an endless progress toward perfection.[2]

As a result of Hegel's influence, everything was seen as subject to evolution—not just living things but also customs, cultures, and concepts. The universe was thought to be in a process of constant change, caught up in a great transformation from primitive beginnings to some exalted future. In every field, from biology to anthropology, from law to sociology, there was a fevered search for "laws of development" that would reveal the pattern of history and the direction of evolution, providing people with guidance on how to live in accord with that great movement toward a better world. There was great optimism that the best human minds could uncover the laws of progress and lead us forward into utopia—a substitute vision of heaven. Philosophers and thinkers began vying with one another to be the one to unveil the path to the earthly heaven, the means of redemption.

The Escalator Myth took various forms, some of which will be the topics of the following chapters, as we discuss the theme of redemption.

NEO-MARXISM IS ALIVE AND WELL

Hegel's best-known disciple was Karl Marx, and Marxism is best understood as a prime example of the Escalator Myth—of an effort by the modern mind to secularize the kingdom of God, to create a purely human heaven here on earth. Marxism may be discredited as a political theory in most parts of the world today, but it lives on in updated form in various liberation movements, as we noted at the beginning of this chapter. The cast has changed, but the plot is the same.

In the classic Marxist drama of history, the oppressed were the proletariat (urban factory workers); in the newer multiculturalist ideologies, the oppressed are women, blacks, or homosexuals. In classic Marxism, the proletariat will rise up against their oppressors—the capitalists; in the updated forms, people of various colors and genders are likewise called to harness their rage and do battle against their oppressors—usually white male heterosexuals.

The politically correct campus today offers countless variations on the Marxist theme, but the common core of all these variations is revealed by the way they overlap and complement one another. The University of California at Santa Barbara offers a course listed as Black Marxism, linking Marxism and black liberation. Brown University connects black and homosexual liberation in a course called Black Lavender: Study of Black Gay/Lesbian Plays. UCLA relates Hispanic ethnicity with homosexuality in a course listed as Chicana Lesbian Literature. Villanova combines feminism with environmentalism in a course titled Eco-feminism. And Stanford University mixes everything in a single cauldron with a course its catalog lists as Women of Color: The Intersection of Race, Ethnicity, Class, and Gender. As a result of this massive politicization of education, college students are being taught to apply Marxist categories to law, politics, education, family studies, and many other fields.

What all this means is that Marxism, though largely discredited as a political ideology, is still very much alive and well in Western intellectual life. Reborn as multiculturalism and political correctness, it remains one of the most widespread and influential forms of counterfeit salvation. Government-mandated group rights and other outgrowths of multiculturalism are even being read into the U.S. Constitution, so that though original Marxism never took over our nation, this reborn Marxism may yet do so.

A GULAG IN THE END

While Karl Marx hunched over his books in the British Museum in the mid–nineteenth century, feverishly philosophizing, what he eventually came up with was a full-blown alternative religion. In the beginning was a creator:

namely, matter itself. In Marxism the universe is a self-originating, self-operating machine, generating its own power and running by its own internal force toward a final goal—the classless, communistic society. Marx's disciple, Lenin, stated the doctrine in explicitly religious language: "We may regard the material and cosmic world as the supreme being, as the cause of all causes, as the creator of heaven and earth."[3]

Marxism's counterpart to the Garden of Eden is the state of primitive communism. And the original sin was the creation of private property and the division of labor, which caused humanity to fall from its early state of innocence into slavery and oppression. From this follow all the subsequent evils of exploitation and class struggle.

In this drama, redemption is wrought by reversing the original sin: destroying the private ownership of the means of production. And the redeemer is the proletariat, who will rise up against the capitalist oppressors. In the words of historian Robert Wesson, "The savior-proletariat [will] by its suffering redeem mankind and bring the Kingdom of Heaven on earth."[4]

The Day of Judgment, in Marxist theology, is the day of revolution, when the evil bourgeoisie will be damned.[5] It is significant that Marx called not for repentance but for revolution. Why? Because, like Rousseau, he regarded humanity as inherently good. He believed that evil and greed arise from the economic structures of society (private property), and therefore they can be eliminated by a social revolution that destroys the old economic system and institutes a new one.

Finally, like all religions, Marxism has an eschatology (a doctrine of the final events of history). In Christianity, the end of time is when the original perfection of God's creation will be restored, and sin and pain will be no more. In Marxism, the end of history is when the original communism will be restored and class conflict will be no more. Paradise will be ushered in by the efforts of human beings whose consciousness has been raised. Marx looked forward to this inevitable consummation of history as eagerly as any Christian anticipates the Second Coming.

"Marxism is a secularized vision of the kingdom of God," writes theology professor Klaus Bockmuehl. "It is the kingdom of man. The race will at last undertake to create for itself that 'new earth in which righteousness dwells.'"[6] Marxism promises to solve the human dilemma and create the New Man living in an ideal society.

These religious elements explain Marxism's puzzling powers of endurance. Most of Marx's specific theories have failed spectacularly, and his promise of a classless society has never come to pass, despite countless Marxist-inspired revolutions around the globe.[7]

Why, then, is Marxism still so popular? Why do so many liberation movements today adopt Marxist categories and analysis? Why have multiculturalism and political correctness cut a huge swath across the university campus, sweeping up students like Diane and teaching them to view the world through the lens of aggrieved self-righteousness? Precisely because Marxism aims at an essentially religious need, tapping into humanity's hunger for redemption.

Marx himself knew he was offering a militantly atheistic counterpart to Christianity. "Marx was confirmed at fifteen and for a time seems to have been a passionate Christian," says historian Paul Johnson. But ultimately he rejected the biblical God, denouncing religion as "the illusory sun around which man revolves, until he begins to revolve around himself."[8]

Marx's ultimate goal was autonomy. He wrote: "A *being* only considers himself independent when he stands on his own feet; and he only stands on his own feet when he owes his *existence* to himself." But a person cannot be independent if he is the creation of a personal God, for then "he lives by the grace of another."[9] So Marx determined to become his own master, a god to himself.

This is the root of Marxism, and it is the point where we must begin to critique it. How plausible is this insistence on absolute autonomy? Ironically, Marx himself admitted that it is highly *im*plausible. Belief in a creator, he acknowledged, is "very difficult to dislodge from popular consciousness"; at the same time, to most people the notion of absolute autonomy is "incomprehensible." Why? "Because it contradicts everything *tangible* in practical life."[10] In other words, in real life it is obvious that we are *not* completely autonomous. We do not create ourselves, and we cannot exist completely on our own. We are finite, contingent, dependent beings—tiny specks within a vast universe, a mere eddy within the ever flowing stream of history.

The conclusion is that Marx's worldview is fatally flawed; it does not match up with reality. And Marx himself admitted as much in acknowledging that his philosophy "contradicts everything" in "practical life." Marx is a living example of the apostle Paul's description of unbelievers: They *know* the truth, and still they suppress it (Rom. 1:18-32).

As a young man, Marx wrote poetry, much of it dwelling on themes of rage, destruction, and savagery. One of his surviving pieces includes these lines:

Then I will wander godlike and victorious
Through the ruins of the world
And, giving my words an active force,
I will feel equal to the creator.[11]

Here he reveals the ultimate religious motivation behind his philosophy: to be equal to the Creator, to give his own words the active force of God's creative words.

Marx's self-deification has had disastrous results for millions, leading to war, massacre, and labor camps. "Apply Marxism in any country you want, you will always find a Gulag in the end," says French philosopher Bernard-Henri Levi, himself a former Marxist.[12] Because revolutionaries are confident that the next stage in history will automatically represent progress, that any change will be for the better, they readily tear down and destroy the existing order—which historically has often meant killing off anyone who resists, from rulers to peasants. Moreover, because Marxism assumes that the reconstruction of social and economic institutions is enough to usher in harmony and peace, it puts no moral restraints on the leaders in the new order. Because it denies the evil in human nature, it does not recognize the need to place checks and balances on the individuals in power, allowing them to accrue absolute power. And we all know what absolute power does.

Marxism is a substitute religion that wreaks devastation and death. And today's liberation movements, which depend heavily on the Marxist worldview, are inherently religious as well. They may have dropped Marx's focus on economics in favor of race or gender or ethnicity, but the basic thought forms remain the same—and they are equally flawed and dangerous.

And for those who really believe in salvation through the Escalator Myth, the sexiest form of liberation is . . . sex itself.

CHAPTER 25

SALVATION THROUGH SEX?

All the intellectual and cultural breakthroughs of modernity were in some way or other linked to the sexual desires their progenitors knew to be illicit but which they chose nonetheless. Their theories were ultimately rationalizations of the choices they knew to be wrong.

E. MICHAEL JONES

In his 1967 novel *An Exile,* Madison Jones portrays a sheriff who is drawn into adultery with a young woman—and has an experience of transcendence. As they lie in bed together, moonlight falls on colored windowpanes in the turret above them, reminding the sheriff of a stained-glass window in the church he attended as a child.

"Figured in the glass, in dull colors of blue and yellow and red, was a picture of Jesus blessing the children," Jones writes, "and from that window there fell upon him just such a light as this—a light that was the color of grace, that was God's grace itself descending through the window upon them all."

Gazing at the young woman sleeping beside him, the sheriff muses, "It was grace, the preacher had said, that made sinless, sinful man; and there he sat bathed in it. New-born in grace. Was it not strange that now, with the sweat of his sin barely yet dry upon him, he should feel as he had felt then?"

Strange indeed. For the sheriff's relationship with this young woman is solely sexual. He does not love her, and she does not love him. In fact, as the reader later discovers, she has been coerced into the relationship by her father, who is engaged in criminal activity and hopes to corrupt the sheriff. Still, this loveless, utilitarian, purely physical encounter is portrayed as an avenue for a religious experience.

"Like new, [the sheriff] thought: purged of the old body and the old mind. So this was grace. . . ."[1] The sheer physical act of intercourse, even in a sinful, loveless relationship, is portrayed paradoxically as a means of grace.

Medieval mystics used meditation and self-denial to achieve transcendence and to commune with the sacred; modernists use sex.

Sex is a vital part of God's created order, a sacred part of the marriage covenant; and our sexual nature is a good gift from God. But for many modern thinkers, sexuality has become the basis for an entire worldview, the source of ultimate meaning and healing, a means of redemption. Sex has been exalted to the means of raising ourselves to the next level of evolution, creating a new kind of human nature and an advanced civilization. In short, sexuality has been transformed into another version of the Escalator Myth.

Where do these near mystical ideas of sexuality come from? In large measure, they stem from Rousseau, who taught that human nature was good and that evil was the result of the constraints of civilization, with its moral rules and social conventions. In the nineteenth century, Freud attributed neurosis to the constraints of moral rules and the guilt they produce. Then, as science learned more about the physiology of sexuality—for example, the action of the glands—these same ideas were dressed up in scientific garb.

For example, in the early twentieth century Margaret Sanger, who is generally remembered as an early champion of birth control, taught a broad philosophy of sexuality, a philosophy reinforced by science. She contended that sexual restraint suppresses the activity of the sex glands and thus injures health and dulls the intellect. Thus science itself, she argued, supports sexual liberation.

The drama of history, by Sanger's account, consists of a struggle to free our bodies and minds from the constraints of morality, the prohibitions that distort and impoverish human nature. She adamantly opposed "the 'moralists' who preached abstinence, self-denial, and suppression," and described Christian ethics as "the cruel morality of self-denial and 'sin.'" She hoped to replace it with her own morality of sexual liberation, promising that the release of sexual energies was "the only method" by which a person could find "inner peace and security and beauty."[2] And also the only method for overcoming social ills: "Remove the constraints and prohibitions which now hinder the release of inner energies, [and] most of the larger evils of society will perish."[3]

What Sanger offered was nothing less than a doctrine of salvation in which morality is the root of all evil and free sexual expression is the path to redemption. She even resorted to religious language, calling on a sexual elite to "remove the moral taboos that now bind the human body and spirit, free the individual from the slavery of tradition, and above all answer their unceasing cries for knowledge that would make possible their self-direction and salvation."[4] Salvation? In another passage, she promises that men and women will literally become geniuses through "the removal of physiological and psychological inhibitions and constraints which makes possible the release and channeling of the primordial inner energies of man into full and divine expression."[5] Divine? Here's a new twist on the serpent's promise in Eden: It's not eating the fruit from the tree in the Garden that will make us godlike; it's the release of sexual energies.

Sanger's philosophy is simply another version of the Escalator Myth in which sexual freedom is the means to transform human nature and create the New Man. It is in our power to "remodel the [human] race" and create "a real civilization," to "transmute and sublimate the everyday world into a realm of beauty and joy," she wrote euphorically. And she resorts again to religious language: "Through sex, mankind may attain the great spiritual illumination which will transform the world, which will light up the only path to an earthly paradise."[6]

One of Sanger's contemporaries, Alfred Kinsey, was equally influential in shaping sexual mores and sex-education theories, particularly with his books *Sexual Behavior in the Human Male* and *Sexual Behavior in the Human Female,* published in the 1940s.[7] Kinsey's impact was due in part to the pose he struck as an objective scientist, tabulating what Americans did in their bedrooms. But the truth is that he was neither objective nor scientific. Like Sanger, he was committed to an ideology that defined morality as a harmful force to be opposed and that elevated sexuality into a means of salvation.

To liberate sex from morality, Kinsey reduced sex to the sheer biological act of physical orgasm. He then claimed that all orgasms are morally equivalent—whether between married or unmarried persons, between people of the same or the opposite sex, between adults or children, even between humans and animals. His model was the animal world. Kinsey was a devout Darwinian who believed that since humans evolved from animals, there are no significant differences between them. He liked to talk about "the human animal," and if a particular behavior could be found among animals, he considered it normative for humans as well. For example, Kinsey claimed that certain mammals are observed to have sexual contact between males, and even across species; therefore, he concluded, both homosexuality and bestiality are "part of the normal mammalian picture" and are acceptable behavior for humans.[8]

So eager was Kinsey to drive home his philosophy that he employed highly unscientific research methods, such as relying on unrepresentative samples that included a disproportionate percentage of sex offenders and other deviants. It is hardly scientific to use such skewed samples to define "normal" sexuality, and yet, as biographer James Jones documents, Kinsey persistently studied people who were on the margins, or even beyond the pale, in their sexual behavior: homosexuals, sadomasochists, voyeurs, exhibitionists, pedophiles, transsexuals, and fetishists.[9]

Kinsey remained undeterred by criticism, however, for his sexual views were not based ultimately on science but on an intensely held personal belief system. In the words of Stanford professor Paul Robinson, a sympathetic critic, Kinsey viewed history "as a great moral drama, in which the forces of science competed with those of superstition for the minds and hearts of men."[10] By "superstition," Kinsey meant religion and its moral prescriptions. Kinsey sometimes spoke as if the introduction of Bible-based sexual morality was *the* watershed in human history, a sort of "Fall" from which we must be redeemed. For Kinsey, sexual expression was the means of saving human nature from the oppression of religion and morality.

Another major influence on American sexual attitudes was Austrian psychologist Wilhelm Reich, who became something of a cult figure in the 1960s. His contribution was the search for the "ultimate orgasm," which quickly became one of the fads of the human potential movement. Reich taught that nearly everyone is in some degree neurotic and that every neurosis is in turn a symptom of sexual failure. Therefore, the answer to all human dysfunction is to develop "the capacity for surrender to the flow of biological energy without any inhibition, the capacity for complete discharge of all dammed-up sexual excitation through involuntary pleasurable contractions of the body."[11] Reich believed that human beings are nothing more than biological creatures and that redemption comes through complete immersion in the sexual reflex.

The enemy in Reich's sexual Eden is, once again, traditional religion and morality, that "murderous philosophy" that creates guilt, distorts our drives, and gives rise to personality disorders.[12] He insisted that since nature knows nothing of morality, any moral restraints on the sexual impulse work like a slow poison on the entire personality. In a book aptly titled *Salvation through Sex,* psychiatrist Eustace Chesser says that for Reich, orgasm "is man's only salvation, leading to the Kingdom of Heaven on earth."[13]

Reich's ideas were incorporated by Robert Rimmer in his provocative novel *The Harrad Experiment,* published in 1966. The book sold three million copies and helped fuel the sexual revolution. For an entire generation of college-educated Americans, it became recommended reading in college courses on marriage and family, and many people credit the book with being instrumental in the sudden merger of male colleges with female colleges and in the creation of coed dormitories.

The novel portrays an experimental college where the students are expected to couple up in various combinations and permutations in order to develop a free and uninhibited approach to sexuality. The philosophy behind this sexual utopia is voiced by the professor who founded the college: "The premise is that man is innately good and can lift himself by his bootstraps into an infinitely better world." How? By sexual liberation. It is the means for taking "one more step up the evolutionary ladder," for "evolving into a new form of man and woman."[14]

Rimmer's view of sex is frankly religious, and he has the professor state openly that intercourse "is actually an act of worship." Or, as he has another character say (quoting philosopher Alan Watts), "What lovers feel for each other in this moment is no other than adoration in the full religious sense. . . . Such adoration which is due God, would indeed be idolatrous were it not that, in that moment, love takes away the illusion and shows the beloved for what he or she in truth is . . . the naturally divine." Sex is portrayed as the path to divinity.[15]

In a postscript added in the 1990 edition of the novel, Rimmer neatly summarizes his religion: "Can we lift ourselves by the bootstraps and create a new kind of society where human sexuality and the total wonder of the human body and the human mind become the new religion—a humanistic religion, without the necessity of a god, because you and I and all the billions who could interact caringly with one another are the only god we need? I think we can."[16]

Sexuality is clearly being presented as more than mere sensual gratification or titillation. It is nothing less than a form of redemption, a means to heal the fundamental flaw in human nature. Only when we see these sexual ideologies as complete worldviews, held with religious fervor, will we understand why Christians and moral conservatives find it so hard to reform sex-education courses in public schools. You won't find contemporary sex educators using words like *salvation;* nonetheless, many hold the same basic assumption that free sexual expression is the means to a full and healthy life.

For example, Mary Calderone, a major architect of contemporary sex education and former executive director of Sex Information and Education Council of the United States (SIECUS), tipped her hand in a 1968 article in which she said that the "real question" facing sex educators is this: "What kind [of person] do we want to produce" to take the place of human nature as we know it today? And "how do we design the production line" to create this advanced creature?[17]

The problem, as Calderone sees it, is that human nature is not evolving as quickly as technology; therefore we must remold human nature itself to fit the modern, ever-changing world. A new stage of evolution is breaking across the horizon, she writes, and the task of educators is to prepare children to step into that new world. To do this, they must pry children away from old views and values, especially from biblical and other traditional forms of sexual morality—for "religious laws or rules about sex were made on the basis of ignorance."[18]

In this new stage of evolution, all currently held values will fall by the wayside, making way for new values based on science alone. Therefore, says Calderone, the best thing we can do for our children is to prepare them to view all notions of right and wrong as tentative, changing, and relative. Then, loosed from the old values, they can be inculcated with the values of a scientifically trained elite (consisting of professionals like herself, of course), who know what makes a human being truly healthy. She calls on schools and churches to use sex education to develop "quality human beings by means of such consciously engineered processes as society's own best minds can blueprint."[19] Here sexual utopianism takes on almost frightening tones, for it ties sex education to a vision of social engineering according to a "blueprint" drawn up by a scientific elite.

■   ■   ■

WHEN WE TRACE the history of ideas about sexuality, it becomes clear that the founders of sex education never did seek simply to transmit a collection of facts about how our bodies work. Rather, they were evangelists for a utopian worldview, a religion, in which a "scientific" understanding of sexuality is the means for transforming human nature, freeing it from the constraints of morality and ushering in an ideal society. It is another form of the Escalator Myth.

Yet if we examine the lives of these self-appointed prophets, we find little grounds for believing their grandiose promises. Margaret Sanger was married twice and had numerous lovers—or, as she put it, "voluntary mates." She was addicted to the painkiller Demerol and obsessed with numerology, astrology, and psychics in a desperate attempt to find meaning. In her life, sexual liberation was not the high road to salvation that she had promised in her writing.[20]

Kinsey, too, had a secret life we rarely hear about. His goal was "to create his own sexual utopia," says biographer James Jones, and Kinsey built up a select circle of friends and colleagues who committed themselves to his philosophy of total sexual freedom. Since the results were often captured on film, we know that Kinsey and his wife both had sexual relations with a host of male and female staff members and other people. Kinsey was also a masochist, sometimes engaging in bizarre and painful practices.[21]

But Kinsey had an even darker secret. In *Kinsey, Sex, and Fraud*, researcher Judith Reisman argues convincingly that Kinsey's research on child sexual responses could have been obtained only if he or his colleagues were actually engaged in the sexual molestation of children. How else could "actual observations" be made of sexual responses in children age two months to fifteen years old?[22] And this is the man whose ideas have been so influential in shaping American sex education.

Wilhelm Reich's life likewise reveals the flaws in his own philosophy. Reich demanded complete sexual freedom for himself and conducted multiple affairs, but he couldn't stand the thought that his wife might live by the same sexual philosophy. His third wife writes that he was desperately jealous and forbade her from living as he did.[23] One test of whether a worldview is true is whether it corresponds to reality: Can we live with it? Obviously Reich could not.

The truth is that sexual liberation has been no high road to salvation for those who have worshiped at its shrine. Instead, the tragic results of sexual licentiousness have spread across our entire society, producing epidemics of abortion, sexually transmitted diseases (afflicting one out of four women), and children born out of wedlock, with all the attendant social pathologies, including school problems, drug and alcohol abuse, and crime. Yet for many Americans, sexual liberation remains a cherished right, and the utopian visions planted by Sanger, Kinsey, Reich, and Calderone continue to flourish. Their ideas still form the unspoken assumptions in the sex-education curricula used throughout our public school system.

■   ■   ■

WE ALL BASE our lives on some vision of ultimate reality that gives meaning to our individual existence. If we reject God, we will put something in his place; we will absolutize some part of creation. That's exactly what has happened with those who look to a sexual utopia for fulfillment and salvation. Biology takes the place of God as the ultimate reality, and sex becomes the path to the divine.

The irony is that those who reject religion most emphatically, who insist most noisily that they are "scientific," end up promoting what can only be called a religion. In fact, this seems to be a common malady among those who pride themselves on being scientific. Back in the Age of Reason, science was offered as a substitute for religion. But what few foresaw was that in the process, science would take on the functions of religion. And today, as we shall see, science itself has become one of the most popular forms of redemption.

CHAPTER 26

IS SCIENCE OUR SAVIOR?

Scratch an "altruist" and watch a "hypocrite" bleed.
M. T. GHISELIN

Wh_en the movie *Independence Day* hit the theaters in the late 1990s, many viewers had the feeling they had seen the story somewhere before.[1] In effect, they had. The film was essentially a remake of the 1953 science-fiction classic *War of the Worlds*—but with one significant difference.

While both versions feature aliens invading Earth, in the 1953 movie, scientists come up with a weapon that is eventually destroyed. The panicking population is forced to turn to God; churches are jammed with people praying. What's more, their prayers are answered: The aliens contract earthborn bacteria and suddenly die off. "All that men could do had failed," says a final voice-over; deliverance came from the hand of God alone. The film ends with a scene of people standing on a hillside, singing praise to God.[2]

The contemporary update is quite different—signaling a dramatic change in American culture within only a few decades. *Independence Day* nods politely in God's direction by showing people praying for help. But real deliverance comes through the deployment of advanced military technology: A few strategically placed bombs blow up the aliens and save the world. *Independence Day* is a celluloid expression of a widespread belief in science and technology as means of salvation.

The outline of this faith is neatly summarized in Daniel Quinn's best-seller *Ishmael,* which features a series of conversations between a disaffected 1960s idealist and a know-it-all gorilla, who offers to explain what's wrong with the world. The problem, says the gorilla, is that Western culture has bought into the myth of science as savior. The myth goes something like this: The universe started out about fifteen billion years ago with the big bang; our solar system was born about seven billion years ago; eventually, life appeared in the chemical broth of the ancient oceans, evolving first into simple microorganisms, then into higher, more complex forms, and finally into human beings. We humans are the apex of evolution, with the intelligence to control nature and bend it to serve our purposes. The solution to our social problems therefore lies in our own hands, through the exertion of human intelligence and ingenuity. Through our ever advancing science and technology, we will save ourselves.[3]

SCIENCE AS SALVATION

Quinn has put his finger squarely on the assumptions that float around in the minds of most Western people, many of whom hold this basic worldview without even realizing that they do. Because the worldview has no name, no label, no church, and no rituals, most people don't identify it as a religion or even as a distinctive belief system. It's simply part of the furniture of the Western mind. Yet it is nothing less than a vision of redemption, a surrogate salvation, a substitute for the kingdom of God, setting up science as the path to utopia.

Looking back over history, we find some of the first dabbling with this notion in the writings of the sixteenth-century scientist Francis Bacon. In a tale titled *New Atlantis,* Bacon depicts an imaginary civilization centered on a gigantic laboratory committed to perpetual progress through science—or, as he quaintly put it, to "the effecting of all things possible."[4]

More influential was the nineteenth-century philosopher Auguste Comte, who is honored today as the founder of sociology. Comte proposed that all societies pass through three stages of social evolution. The most primitive is the theological stage, where people seek supernatural explanations for events; the second is the metaphysical stage, where people explain the world through abstract philosophical concepts; and the highest is the scientific stage, where people find truth through scientific experimentation. Unlike most of his contemporaries, Comte admitted that what he was proposing was essentially a religion. He actually founded a Religion of Humanity, complete with churches and hymns and calendars listing special days for the "saints" of science and philosophy—with himself as the high priest.[5]

But the religion of progress through science really took off after Charles Darwin published his theory of evolution by natural selection. By providing scientific sanction for evolution, Darwin's theory gave enormous impetus to the idea of endless, universal progress.[6] English philosopher Herbert Spencer expanded evolution into a comprehensive philosophy covering all of reality—from stars to societies. In his system, the goal of evolutionary progress is the emergence of human beings, who, in turn, will help produce something new and better for the next stage of evolution. Spencer's gospel of evolution became a secular substitute for Christian hope. As Ian Barbour writes in *Issues in Science and Religion*, "Faith in progress replaced the doctrines of creation and providence as assurance that the universe is not really purposeless."[7]

Even certain strains of Marxism identify science rather than revolution as the source of salvation. In the early part of this century, physicist J. D. Bernal predicted that after the triumph of the proletariat and the rise of the classless society, there was still one more stage before a real utopia would appear—a stage when a new "aristocracy of scientific intelligence" would create a world run by scientific experts. In a burst of enthusiasm, Bernal predicted that scientists would actually evolve into a new, superhuman race that would "emerge as a new species and leave humanity behind."[8]

The idea of creating a new and improved race is a key component in many forms of scientific utopianism. In the early twentieth century, after Gregor Mendel's groundbreaking work on genes was rediscovered, many scientists began to place their hope in a vision of creating the New Man through genetic engineering. In the 1930s, the great geneticist H. J. Muller divided the history of life into three stages: In the first stage, life was completely at the mercy of the environment; in the second stage, human beings appeared and reversed that order, learning how to reach out and control the environment; and in the dawning third stage, humans would reach inside and control their own nature. Humanity will "shape itself into an increasingly sublime creation—a being beside which the mythical divinities of the past will seem more and more ridiculous," Muller wrote. This godlike being surveys the entire universe, and, "setting its own marvelous inner powers against the brute Goliath of the suns and planets, challenges them to contest."[9]

Muller was an excellent scientist, but what he is describing here is not science. It is science turned into a myth of salvation.

This same myth motivates much of the research done today in genetic engineering. Nobel prize–winner Francis Crick, codiscoverer of DNA, writes: "We can expect to see major efforts to improve the nature of man

himself within the next ten thousand years."[10] Some people even believe genetic science will eventually develop "supergenes" to produce human beings
with superintelligence or superstrength. This is salvation by genetics—the
creation of the New Man by gene manipulation.

REALITY TEST

But will such a salvation really save us? How does this vision of redemption
stack up in a test against reality? Not very well.

Science itself gives no moral guidelines for our genetic experimentation. How do we decide which traits we want? Do we want to create a
super-Einstein or a super–Mother Teresa, or even a class of subhuman slaves
to do our menial work? These questions presuppose a standard of values,
which science itself cannot provide.

More important, the sheer attempt to remake human nature geneti-
cally would strip people of their dignity and reduce them to commodities.
With technology offering greater choice and control over the embryo's traits,
having a child could become like purchasing a consumer product. And children themselves may come to be regarded as products that we plan, create,
modify, improve, and evaluate according to standards of quality control.
What happens if the "product" doesn't meet the parents' standard—if they
do not think they're getting their money's worth? Will the child be tossed
aside, like an appliance that stops working? As one theologian argues, human beings are "begotten, not made," and if we reverse that—if children become products that we manufacture—we do immeasurable damage to
human dignity.[11]

Unfortunately, objections like these are not likely to be raised in a climate where scientists hold a faith in inevitable progress, for the Escalator
Myth creates the expectation that change will always be for the better. This
explains why some scientists reveal a disturbingly uncritical acceptance of
genetic engineering. But clearly, change can be either an improvement or a
degeneration. New forms of technology can be used in the service of either
good or evil. The faith that we can save ourselves through science can be sustained only if we shut our eyes to the human capacity for barbarism.[12]

Many thoughtful scientists find it hard to go along with such a blind
faith. Yet rather than search for another form of salvation, they simply transfer the Escalator Myth to a different galaxy. Because planet Earth is so mired
in pollution, war, and other pathologies, they say, we are likely to destroy
ourselves before we manage to evolve to a higher stage. For example,

Stephen Hawking, author of the best-seller *A Brief History of Time,* warns that evolution will not improve the human race quickly enough to temper our aggression and avoid extinction.[13] Our only hope, then, is to link up with beings elsewhere in the universe—a civilization of extraterrestrials who have themselves successfully evolved to a more advanced stage and can help us.

These are not the rantings of wide-eyed UFO enthusiasts, mind you. Both the federal government and private foundations have poured huge amounts of money into the Search for Extra-Terrestrial Intelligence (SETI), scanning the heavens with powerful radio telescopes in the hope of picking up signals from another civilization. If we ever do discover another civilization in space, says Frank Drake, who heads up the SETI Institute, "it can tell us what we might evolve to, and how far we might evolve." These friendly extraterrestrials might even pass on their technological knowledge, handing over "scientific data which otherwise might take us hundreds of years and vast resources to acquire."[14]

The breathless enthusiasm that often accompanies descriptions of SETI is a dead giveaway that this search for an extraterrestrial solution is at core religious. And no one was a more enthusiastic supporter than the late Carl Sagan. For him, SETI was not just a scientific project; it would be, quite literally, the source of the world's redemption. His reasoning went like this: Any society capable of transmitting messages to us must be far more technologically sophisticated than our own. Therefore, the receipt of a message from space would give us "an invaluable piece of knowledge," telling us "that it is possible to live through [the] technological adolescence" through which we are now passing.[15]

No such message has ever been detected, of course, yet Sagan offered detailed descriptions of the wondrous secrets we might learn if we ever succeed in decoding one. "It is possible," he exclaimed, "that among the first contents of such a message may be detailed prescriptions for the avoidance of technological disaster, for a passage through adolescence to maturity." Sagan never explained how an alien race that has never had any contact with Earth, a race whose chemistry and brains and language would be completely different from ours, would just happen to know exactly what our problems are, or how they would be capable of giving "detailed prescriptions" for solving them. Still, he seemed certain that they would offer advice for "straightforward solutions, still undiscovered on Earth, to problems of food shortages, population growth, energy supplies, dwindling resources, pollution, and war."[16]

Though disguised as science, this is nothing more than a magical vision of heavenly extraterrestrials emerging from the unknown to lift us from our misery. A longtime critic of SETI puts the matter bluntly: "It's a dream based on faith—a technological search for God."[17]

So this is where the great promise of science and technology leads us—not to a glorious earthly utopia, but to a fantasy-world escape from this planet and from the horrors that this same technology has created. This view of salvation is no more rational than the demented dreams of the Heaven's Gate cult—thirty-nine intelligent, well-educated people who ingested cocktails of alcohol and drugs in the hope that, by leaving their bodies behind, their spirits would meet up with a comet and move on to the "Level Above Human." In their case, the Escalator Myth proved deadly.

None of this scientific optimism, one should note, involves a change of heart. It is assumed that humanity's problems are not caused by wrong moral choices but by lack of knowledge. For example, Sagan promises that the longed-for message from outer space will teach us "the laws of development of civilizations" that will enable us to control society, just as knowing the laws of physics and chemistry enables us to control nature. What need is there for an awkward and troublesome thing like morality when we can control society for its own good through inviolable laws of "cultural evolution"?[18]

Yet history offers no evidence that knowledge alone will save human society. To the contrary, the problem with the Hitlers and Stalins of the world was not that they were stupid or ignorant of the laws of cultural evolution; the problem was that they were evil. Bigger and better technology simply gives people bigger and better means to carry out either good or evil choices.

Having confidence in technology is a misguided form of salvation; some things are simply not amenable to a technical quick fix. It is the human heart that determines how we will use our machines—whether we will fashion them into swords or plowshares. Instead of scanning the skies for messages from other galaxies, it is far more realistic to seek the God who *made* those heavens and who came to reveal the truth by living among us. We don't need radio messages from extraterrestrials; we already have a message from God himself, and it is found in an ancient book that proclaimed the creation of the cosmos long before there were astronomers around to muse over such questions. The message begins: "In the beginning God created the heavens and the earth" (Gen. 1:1).

Properly understood, science is a wonderful tool for investigating God's world. But science cannot solve the human dilemma, and it cannot give us hope and meaning. And ultimately, those who exalt science into a religion discover this—which is why they finally give in to a profound pessimism, adrift on a space station called Earth, waiting for a beacon from beyond to save us from ourselves.

But for those less inclined to fantasy, there is no escape from the dreadful realization that a world without God can end only in despair.

CHAPTER 27

THE DRAMA OF DESPAIR

So far as the eye of science can see, man is alone, absolutely alone, in a universe in which his very appearance is a kind of cosmic accident.

JOHN HERMAN RANDALL

The more the universe seems comprehensible, the more it also seems pointless." With these startling words, Nobel prize–winning physicist Steven Weinberg concludes *The First Three Minutes,* his book about the origin of the universe.[1]

Science reveals that we live in an "overwhelmingly hostile universe," Weinberg explains. It existed long before human beings appeared, and it is not going to remain habitable forever. According to current predictions, the universe is headed for a fiery death, and it will take us with it. Nothing we do will outlast our temporary span on this globe. Life is meaningless, purposeless, "pointless."[2]

For many modern thinkers, the alternative to the Christian message of salvation is not any of the ersatz salvations we have discussed but a free fall into pessimism and despair. They have given up, deciding there *is* no transcendent purpose, no hope of redemption, no answer to life's most wrenching dilemmas, and the courageous person is the one who faces reality squarely and shakes off all illusory hopes. Yet, ironically, even this pessimism is often held with a fervor that resembles faith. Like the literary antihero, who is really the hero, this is an antifaith that actually functions as a faith.

What happened to the utopian dreams of the past two centuries, the vision of endless upward progress? For many people, those dreams crashed in the convulsions of two world wars that left a trail of horrors, from the blood-soaked trenches of Argonne to the ashes of Auschwitz. From 1918 to 1945, a little more than a quarter century, the world was shocked out of its complacent optimism by the inescapable reality of naked evil.

European intellectuals who experienced the madness firsthand, on their native soil, were the first to preach a philosophy of despair. "There are no divine judges or controllers," proclaimed French philosopher Jean-Paul Sartre. "The world is all there is, our existence is all we have." Thus was born the word *existentialism*. In Sartre's play *No Exit*, one character distills the existentialist creed to a catch phrase: "You are your life, and that's all you are."[3] There is no higher purpose or goal or meaning to life.

Albert Camus, another post–World War II existentialist, probed the problem of meaninglessness in *The Myth of Sisyphus*, based on a story from classical mythology in which Sisyphus is punished by the gods who require him to push a boulder to the top of a hill, only to have it roll down again. For Camus, this mythological figure represents "the absurd hero," the person who recognizes the absurdity of existence and rebels against it. Since the universe is "without a master," Camus writes, all that's left for the absurd hero is to exercise his free choice and rebel, thereby becoming his own master.[4]

In the 1960s, the works of Sartre and Camus became wildly popular among American intellectuals and university students, feeding into the antiestablishment mood of the Vietnam era. If naturalistic science leads to the conclusion that there is no ultimate meaning to life—that life is absurd—then why not seek alternative sources of meaning in sensual pleasure and mind-altering drug experiences?

Make no mistake. The sixties was not just an era of long hair and bell-bottoms. It was an intellectual and cultural upheaval that marked the end of modernity's optimism and introduced the worldview of despair on a broad level. Ideas concocted in the rarefied domain of academia filtered down to shape an entire generation of young people. They, in turn, have brought those ideas to their logical conclusion in postmodernism, with its suspicion of the very notions of reason and objective truth.

Of course, modernity has always had its dark underside. Already in the nineteenth century, sensitive people realized that science seemed to suggest an image of the universe that was hostile to human values. The world discovered by science was supposedly a world of mathematical entities: mass, extension, and velocity. The things that matter most to humans—purpose, meaning, love, and beauty—were relegated to the subjective realm of the mind, while human beings were reduced to an insignificant presence in an unthinking, unfeeling, purposeless world of masses spinning blindly in space. Science teaches us that mankind is no longer "the Heaven-descended heir of all the ages," said British philosopher Lord Balfour. "His very existence is an accident, his story a brief and transitory episode in the life of one of the meanest of the planets."[5]

It is a gloomy picture, but many people have found it all the more attractive for its gloom, shuddering "in delicious horror" before it, writes historian John Herman Randall. In fact, starting in the nineteenth century, "many believed it *because* it was so dreadful; they prided themselves on their courage in facing facts."[6]

A widely quoted example is from British philosopher Bertrand Russell's *A Free Man's Worship*. (With a title like that, Russell clearly understood that he was proposing an alternative faith). "Man is the product of causes which had no prevision of the end they were achieving; . . . his origin, his growth, his hopes and fears, his loves and his beliefs are but the outcome of accidental collocations of atoms." And finally, these proud, despairing words: "Only within the scaffolding of these truths, only on the firm foundation of unyielding despair, can the soul's habitation henceforth be safely built."[7] One almost pictures Russell standing on a craggy rock, bloody but unbowed, his chin raised to the impersonal skies, proclaiming his credo to the uncaring elements.

A more recent example is the work of Nobel prize–winning biochemist Jacques Monod. In his celebrated *Chance and Necessity*, Monod rejects the Christian faith and replaces it with the drama of the scientist as lonely hero, challenging an alien and meaningless universe. "Man must at last wake out of his millenary dream and discover his total solitude, his fundamental isolation. He must realize that, like a gypsy, he lives on the boundary of an alien world; a world that is deaf to his music, and as indifferent to his hopes as it is to his sufferings or his crimes."[8] This melodramatic portrait goes far beyond anything that could properly be called science. It clearly expresses a faith, or, more accurately, an antifaith: The world is hostile to all that makes us human, yet we will overcome our cosmic loneliness through heroic defiance.

The creeds of pessimism often take on a distinctly Darwinist cast. Darwin's theory suggests that human beings are merely advanced animals competing in the struggle for existence—that nature is "red in tooth and claw," in the words of Alfred, Lord Tennyson. All life-forms are driven to compete for the next rung on the evolutionary ladder, leaving the weak behind. In the late nineteenth and early twentieth centuries, these ideas were enshrined in social Darwinism—the idea that the rich and corrupt are in power because they've proven themselves the "fittest" in the struggle for survival and that there's nothing we can do about it because it's simply the law of nature.

Moral persuasion and spiritual redemption are irrelevant because we are trapped in an endless struggle to reach the top of the heap.

GENE MACHINES

This dark side of Darwinism remained an undercurrent, causing few ripples in the reigning myth of progress until recent decades, when it burst forth in what is known as *sociobiology*—today often called evolutionary psychology (discussed briefly in chapter 12). Sociobiology is an attempt to explain what evolution implies for human values. In doing so, it tends to take on the functions of religion, for it is impossible to discuss values without stumbling onto the most basic religious questions.

Starting with the Darwinian assumption that those who are most competitive come out on top, sociobiologists conclude that evolution requires ruthlessly selfish behavior. Even actions that appear to be aimed at the benefit of others are grounded in underlying selfishness: We are nice to others only so they will be nice to us. Love and altruism are illusions, cover-ups for underlying self-interest. In the words of one sociobiologist, there is "no hint of genuine charity" among humans or any other organism. Though an organism may sometimes find himself forced to act in ways that benefit others, still, "given a full chance to act in his own interest, nothing but expediency will restrain him from brutalizing, from maiming, from murdering—his brother, his mate, his parent, or his child."[9] In the cold light of science, we turn out to be selfish to the core.

What a ferocious picture of life—and taken at face value, it is a rather ridiculous one. No human society exists without altruism, charity, and cooperation. Yet these can be explained away, insists the sociobiologist. According to the theory, the real agents of evolution are the genes, and their only interest is in surviving and being passed on to the next generation. Even when we are engaged in apparently altruistic behavior, we are actually being duped by our genes, which are busily stacking the deck in their favor. Thus, the mother sacrifices selflessly for her child, but she does so only because her genes compel her to take care of the child, who is the vehicle for her genes to survive into the future.

Now, we might agree that taking care of our own family members has a tinge of self-interest. But what about cooperation and altruism that reach beyond family and kin? What about the heroic passerby who rescues a drowning child? Even that is reducible to genetic selfishness, says science writer Mark Ridley in *The Origins of Virtue*. He argues that any organism intelligent enough to remember individuals and keep tabs will discover that it is sometimes in our interest to help others—because they might someday help us in return. And if it's in our interest, then it will be preserved by natural selection. Even the most selfless behavior can be explained by selfish genes.[10]

But notice how the claims of sociobiology have moved far beyond science and into the realm of myth, where the gene is personified as the hero of the plot. In Ridley's account, for example, the genes weigh the pros and cons of cooperative behavior and "program" us accordingly, as if genes had the logical capacity of a computer expert.[11] British science writer Richard Dawkins insists that humans are nothing more than "machines created by our genes," as if genes were engineers capable of designing and building complex mechanisms.[12] Or consider a famous line from Edward O. Wilson, the founder of sociobiology: "The organism is only DNA's way of making more DNA," as if genes were capable of planning and making things. Wilson even argues that the ultimate source of human morality is the "morality of the gene," making genes capable of moral reasoning and choice.[13]

In short, sociobiology attributes consciousness, will, and choice to genes, while reducing humans to machines that carry out their orders. This is a worldview in which genes become the deity—the ultimate creators and controllers of life.

Of course, when pressed, sociobiologists will say this is all metaphorical, not intended to be taken literally. And yet, a consistent and pervasive metaphor eventually shapes the way we think. Even scientists themselves go back and forth, speaking sometimes as if they take the idea of selfish genes literally. "I shall argue that a predominant quality to be expected in a successful gene is ruthless selfishness," writes Dawkins. "Let us try to teach generosity and altruism, because we are born selfish."[14] Notice how he leaps from genes to humans, using the word "selfish" in exactly the same sense, with all its moral connotations. In the "religion of the gene," selfishness is the original sin.

"Like successful Chicago gangsters," Dawkins goes on, spinning his colorful tale, "our genes have survived, in some cases for millions of years, in a highly competitive world," and preserving our genes is "the *ultimate rationale* for our existence." Dawkins argues, "By dictating the way survival machines [that's us] and their nervous systems are built, genes exert *ultimate power* over behavior." Finally, Dawkins waxes positively lyrical. The gene "does not grow old. It leaps from body to body down the generations, manipulating body after body in its own way and for its own ends, abandoning a succession of mortal bodies before they sink in senility and death. The genes are the immortals."[15]

The immortals? Dawkins offers this as sober science, but to speak about an immortal force with "ultimate power" over our lives, giving us the "ultimate rationale" for living, is clearly a religious statement.

Indeed, sociobiology has all the essential elements of religion. It tells us where we came from: Random chemicals linked up to form the rudimentary DNA, until finally some DNA discovered how to construct bodies for themselves. It tells us what's wrong with us: The fatal flaw in human nature is that we are selfish—a selfishness that reaches far beyond our conscious moral choices and is firmly embedded in our genes. But whereas most worldviews go on to offer a proposal for remedying the basic flaw in human nature, sociobiology offers no remedy. It presents the human being as a puppet in the control of immoral, scheming genes, with no real hope of ever breaking free. It is a religion with no hope of redemption. Life is reduced to perpetual warfare, while the gene is transformed into an evil and destructive demon, driven to overcome all competitors in the struggle for existence.

Thus, sociobiology can be understood as a contemporary form of those fatalistic religions that tap into the human fascination with power, death, and destruction. After all, the Greeks and Romans worshiped the gods of death (Pluto) and war (Mars). The Babylonians worshiped Nergal, a god of death and pestilence. The Hindu god Siva and his wife, Kali, stand for death and destruction. Similarly, in sociobiology the "deity being worshipped is power," writes British philosopher Mary Midgley. Adherents "offer us a mystique of power" located in the genes.[16]

What could possibly be appealing about such a negative faith? Despite its pessimism, it offers one compensation: It gives adherents a way to debunk conventional religion and morality. It dispels the "illusion" that there is a loving, sovereign God and that human beings have dignity and significance as genuine moral agents.

If you wonder whether we are reading too much into sociobiology, just dip into the writings of Edward O. Wilson, founder of the movement. Wilson admits that he left his Baptist tradition at the age of fifteen and transferred his religious longings elsewhere: "My heart continued to believe in the light and the way . . . and I looked for grace in some other setting"—which turned out to be science. Having entered "the temple of science," Wilson shifted his faith to the "mythology" of scientific materialism, and then searched for a "single grand naturalistic image of man" that would explain everything "as a material process, from the bottom up, atoms to genes to the human spirit."[17]

Wilson is completely candid that his goal is to "divert the power of religion" into the service of materialism or naturalism. "Make no mistake about the power of scientific materialism," he warns. It is a philosophy that presents "an alternative mythology" that has repeatedly "defeated traditional religion."[18]

But has it, in fact, defeated traditional religion? Not at all, for sociobiology or evolutionary psychology itself fails a basic test of any truth claim: It is not an accurate portrayal of either human nature or human society. Common experience and common sense—bolstered by the findings of sociology and anthropology—easily debunk its excessively dark picture of unmitigated competition and slavery to the power of selfish genes.

It is seriously misleading to apply the word *selfish* to an object that has no self—namely, the gene. When we talk about changes in gene frequencies, that's science. But if we say that humans are helpless puppets whose strings are in the hands of calculating genes, that's mythology. When we say that humans are influenced by their genes, that's science. But if we say that genes are "selfish"—that they are "hidden masters" who have "programmed" us to "serve" them—that's mythology.

Science does not compel us to adopt sociobiology or any other pessimistic worldview that denies the reality of redemption and dramatizes nature as a stage for perpetual conflict. Indeed, many pessimists engage in circular reasoning: First they banish God and conclude that the universe is meaningless; then they argue that since the universe is meaningless, there cannot be a God. Atheism is presented as the *conclusion* when it is, in fact, the hidden *premise*.

And if your premise is rejection of the biblical God, then no matter how sophisticated your theories, they will end in despair. For these pessimistic myths are right about one thing: A universe without God is indeed impersonal, meaningless, and purposeless. It is, to echo Weinberg, pointless.

DEFYING DEATH

A full-page ad for Schwinn bicycles shows a young man leaping high into the air on his Schwinn; at the bottom of the page is a picture of a coffin being lowered into the ground. The ad copy taunts the reader: "What, a little death frightens you?" Schwinn is clearly marketing more than bikes; it is telling kids that it is cool to court death.

Since when did playing with death become chic? Since a pervasive sense of meaninglessness has left many people so jaded that it takes more than a whiff of danger to restore a sense of ultimacy. And what is more intense, more ultimate, than coming face-to-face with death?

This mind-set may explain the growing popularity of high-risk sports, from hang gliding to rock climbing, from street luge to skydiving. When *U.S. News and World Report* ran a cover story on the topic of high-risk sports, one subhead read: "The peril, the thrill, the sheer rebellion of it all."[19] Like Camus's absurd hero, this is rebellion against the absurdity, against the futility of life, where everything we love or live for ends in death. In a society reduced to sterile secularism, the only response left is to look death squarely in the face . . . and spit on it. This is the ultimate, heroic existentialist response.

Kristen Ulmer, an icon of the "extreme sports" crowd, says she took up "extreme skiing" (maneuvers that deliberately expose one to danger) to combat boredom. She insists she gets a thrill from any kind of risk or danger, and she suggests spicing up conventional sports by injecting more danger: "It's one thing to be a really good basketball player. But imagine if every time you missed a basket, somebody would shoot you in the head. It would be a lot more exciting, right?"[20]

In the Midwest, several companies offer to take tourists out to chase tornadoes. What's the attraction? The excitement of a brush with death. One man told NBC news that coming close to a tornado was "a religious experience."[21] This is all that's left for a culture that has plumbed the depths of absurdity: daredevil antics in the face of death.

And when the antics grow old, there is only death itself. Ernest Hemingway, one of this century's great novelists, held to the existentialist credo that life is "a short day's journey from nothingness to nothingness."[22] To give meaning to that nothingness, Hemingway invented his own code: He would taste life to the fullest—experience everything, feel everything, do everything. Even death could be overcome if he treated it as another experience, the most exciting and interesting experience of all.

And so, at age sixty-one, after a life of notoriety as a big-game hunter, adventurer, and womanizer, Hemingway deliberately embraced death. He could no longer prove that he was master of his own fate by his daredevil adventures or self-indulgent lifestyle, but he could prove it by controlling the time and means of his own death.

On Sunday morning, July 2, 1961, Hemingway loaded his favorite gun, seated himself in the foyer of his Idaho home, braced the butt of the gun on the floor, put the barrel in his mouth, and pulled the trigger.

Neurotic? Sick? Perhaps not. Given his worldview, Hemingway's action was eminently logical. After all, if life is meaningless and despair crouches like a lion at the gate, the best option might be to exit heroically on your own terms. Ernest Hemingway shook his fist at despair one last time by taking control of his own death.[23]

•   •   •

IN THE END, those who deny the God of the Bible and of history, and who find the myth of progress empty, have only two choices: They can either trivialize death by defying it or control death by embracing it on their own terms. Thus, Hemingway is the perfect icon for the failure of Western science and philosophy: Having played out the logical consequences of the Enlightenment's rejection of God, many people are brought to complete despair of any transcendent truth or meaning. The blazing, optimistic hope that humanity is moving ever upward and onward, boldly progressing to a new stage in evolution, has been replaced by bitter cynicism. Marooned on the rocks of reality, science itself now promises only the near comical fantasy that humanity might be rescued by extraterrestrials from outer space.

One might think that upon hitting the dead end of despair, men and women would be driven to return to the Creator. But, alas, although it is true that "our hearts find no peace until they rest in [God]," the basic human instinct is to flee him.[24] For finding God will cost us our cherished autonomy.

So where do many people turn? To the East.

CHAPTER 28

THAT NEW AGE RELIGION

Men and women have ultimately come up from amoebas, [and] they are
ultimately on their way towards God.

KEN WILBER

When the bright image of science and progress began to fade, and optimism gave way to disillusionment and despair, many people began to cast about for answers from other cultures. Asian religions, especially Hinduism and Buddhism, have always enchanted people from Western cultures to some degree, and today these religions have become popular alternatives to the dominant Western worldview.

And the attraction is powerful. Western secularism is materialistic, limiting reality to what can be tested scientifically. Eastern mysticism is spiritual, opening the consciousness to new levels of awareness. Western thought is analytical, leading to fragmentation and alienation. Eastern thought is holistic, promising healing and wholeness. Western science has destroyed the environment and polluted the air. Eastern pantheism proffers a new respect for nature.

In the 1960s, many young people turned to Eastern religion to fill their spiritual emptiness, giving rise to the New Age movement. Today the movement has become so mainstream that community colleges offer classes in yoga, tai chi, astrology, and therapeutic touch. The New Age movement is also a major commercial success. Local supermarkets carry free copies of slick New Age publications, advertising everything from holistic health practices to past-life therapy.

Buddhism swept the silver screen with *Kundun* (which is Tibetan for "the presence") and *Seven Years in Tibet*. In the latter, Brad Pitt donned a white sari and shaved his head for his role as Heinrich Harrer, an Austrian who escapes from a World War II British prison in India and reaches Lhasa, where he comes under the influence of the young Dalai Lama. Pitt reportedly asked for the role because he wanted the religious experience. After each day's shooting, Buddhist monks would pray for the set and invite the cast to sing with them. Pitt was often in tears.[1]

Actor Richard Gere is even more devout. In 1984, he converted to Tibetan Buddhism and now spends several months each year traveling and speaking on behalf of the Dalai Lama. Then there is Steven Segal, who has been recognized by the supreme head of the Tibetan-based Nyingma lineage as a *tulku* (a reincarnated lama), as well as a *terton* (a revealer of truth). Think of that the next time you watch Segal on film breaking an enemy's neck.[2]

It's not difficult to see why Eastern religion is such an attractive form of salvation for a post-Christian culture. It assuages the ego by pronouncing the individual divine, and it gives a gratifying sense of "spirituality" without making any demands in terms of doctrinal commitment or ethical living. And to make it even more palatable, the New Age movement reshapes Eastern thought to fit the Western mind, with its hunger for upward progress.

Whereas Eastern thinking is fatalistic and pessimistic—the cycle of karma is called the "wheel of suffering"—the New Age adaptation is optimistic and utopian. It promises that if we get in touch with the "Universal Spirit," of which we are all part, we will create a new consciousness and a new world. The New Age movement is premised on the promise that we are on the threshold of a great leap forward into, literally, a new age—of "harmony and understanding, sympathy and trust abounding," to quote the musical *Hair*.[3] The massive social upheavals of the past decades are not a warning of imminent disaster but the prelude to evolutionary transformation. As New Age writer Ken Wilber puts it, "Men and women have ultimately come up from amoebas, [and] they are ultimately on their way towards God."[4] Toward *becoming* God, Wilber means. Humanity, he suggests, is about to make a quantum leap forward, to emerge as an entirely new creature, to become divine. This is nothing but the Escalator Myth in spiritualized form.

It may seem that the New Age movement appeared out of nowhere in the 1960s, but the way had been prepared by the nineteenth-century romantic movement, which was a kind of counterculture in its own day. As we saw in the last chapter, back then sensitive people could already see that science was creating a picture of the world as a vast machine, inexorably grinding its gears, with no place for beauty or meaning or purpose. The romantics cast about for an alternative, just as the children of the sixties did, and they revived an ancient philosophy known as neo-Platonism, a blend of Greek thought and Eastern mysticism. They tossed out the metaphor of the universe as a machine and replaced it with the metaphor of the universe as an organism, a living thing, animated by a "Life Force."

Everything is alive, the romantics said. Even matter itself, they thought, has a rudimentary form of life or consciousness. And what is the major characteristic of life? Growth. Development. The romantics proposed that just as each organism unfolds in stages according to an inner law of development, so life itself unfolds in definite stages from simple to complex under the direction of the Life Force. The Life Force often took on the trappings of an immanent deity, so that God was conceived not as the transcendent creator, but as a spirit pervading nature. "The world was no machine, it was alive," writes historian John Herman Randall, "and God was not its creator so much as its soul, its life."[5]

The publication of Darwin's *Origin of Species* gave the concept of spiritual evolution a big boost. Most people who accepted Darwinian evolution were not atheists; instead, they tried to integrate it in some way with religion by identifying God with a force that gives purpose and direction to evolution. But the end result was often more akin to pantheism than to orthodox Christianity. This God was completely immanent in the world, compelling evolution to ever greater heights and leading mankind to some far-off divine perfection. As Alfred, Lord Tennyson wrote, there is "One God, one law, one element, / And one far-off divine event, / To which the whole creation moves."[6]

Spiritual evolution often reduced God to a participant in the process, a "God-in-the-making," who was gradually evolving along with the world into full divinity. In the early twentieth century, philosopher Henri Bergson reduced God to a vital force animating all life and driving evolution forward. The great philosopher Alfred North Whitehead pictured God as the soul of the world, changing as the world changes, striving toward perfection. And the role of humans is to help God actualize himself. As theologian Charles Hartshorne puts it, we are "co-creators" with God, not only in making the world but also in making God himself.[7] We have met some of these ideas before in chapter 21 under the label of process theology, the fastest-growing theology in America today.

What we see is that for a long time, in philosophy, the arts, and even theology, the Western world has been embracing ideas compatible with Eastern pantheism. All it took was a widespread disillusionment with Western culture to send these ideas hurtling into the mainstream.

NEW AGE IN THE CLASSROOM

Today, New Age thinking permeates Western society, spawning a host of techniques used in medicine, business, education, the military, and even—tragically—churches. Various meditation exercises are sold as means for resolving conflict and for enhancing relaxation, creativity, self-esteem, and even physical health. For example, at Stanford University's Graduate School of Business, a seminar listed as Creativity in Business includes meditation, chanting, "dream work," tarot cards, and a discussion of "the New Age Capitalist."[8] Government agencies as well as private businesses spend millions of dollars in contracts with consulting companies that use New Age techniques for management training.[9]

Of course, these programs rarely use overtly religious language. For example, the Universal Spirit (Brahma, in classic Hindu thought) is often called the Higher Self or some similar term. Yet beneath the secular rhetoric, these programs embody the basic Hindu doctrine that the individual human mind or spirit is part of a Universal Mind or Spirit, and that by using relaxation and guided imagery exercises, we can tap into that Mind as a source of wisdom and creativity.[10]

New Age programs have even permeated our elementary and secondary schools. A mother in Atlanta, Georgia, was concerned when her second-grade daughter failed to respond to her one day when they were driving in the car. The mother called the girl's name repeatedly and finally turned around to look in the backseat. Her daughter's eyes were closed and her head drooped forward. Alarmed, the woman stopped the car, opened the back door, and shook her daughter's arm. The girl jerked awake, as if startled out of a trance.

"What's wrong?" the mother asked anxiously. "You wouldn't answer when I called."

"Don't worry, Mom," the little girl replied. "I was with my friend Pumsy."

Questioning her daughter further, the mother discovered that the girl had been learning meditation techniques from the school's guidance counselor through a curriculum titled *PUMSY in Pursuit of Excellence*. Pumsy is a cute, fairy-tale dragon who discovers a wise guide named Friend, who teaches Pumsy (along with the children in the program) basic concepts of the Eastern worldview. For example, Friend tells Pumsy that her mind is like a pool of water: When she is tempted to think negative thoughts, her mind is muddy. But when she thinks positive thoughts, she can tap into a Clear Mind, which will help her solve her problems.[11]

There's a reason the term *Clear Mind* is capitalized: It's another cover-up term for Brahma, the god of Hinduism. One clue is the quasi-religious language used to describe it. For example, Friend tells Pumsy, "Your Clear Mind is the best friend you'll ever have. . . . It is always close to you, and it will never leave you." This sounds suspiciously close to biblical language: "I will never leave you nor forsake you" (Josh. 1:5). A few pages later in the story, we read, "You have to trust [your Clear Mind] and let it do good things for you."[12] Through this program, children are essentially being taught to place religious trust in a Hindu notion of God as a Universal Mind.

Of course, such New Age techniques are not sold to teachers as religion. They are marketed as ways to increase creativity and boost self-esteem. PUMSY teaches youngsters to chant slogans like "I can handle it," "I can make it happen," and "I am me, I am enough." Once again, we hear echoes of biblical themes: "I am who I am" (Exod. 3:14). This program is teaching self-worship, not self-esteem. It's teaching that we are saved not by trusting a transcendent God who reaches down to us in grace but by realizing that God is within us, that *we* are God. Salvation is not a matter of recognizing our sin; it's a matter of raising our consciousness until we recognize our inner divinity.[13]

Education is only one avenue for New Age ideas. They turn up in every outlet of popular culture. Books about the New Age, for example, enjoy a commanding position on bookstore shelves, often crowding out traditional religious works. If you opened a book and read, "I looked and saw a new heaven and a new earth," you might think you were reading the book of Revelation in the Bible. Instead, it is the opening of James Redfield's megahit *The Tenth Insight.* The words are indeed from Revelation, but that's the closest link to anything biblical. As the story unfolds, the author weaves his own New Age philosophy into the plot. We learn that, before birth, we are all part of a great spiritual force pervading the universe. We can reconnect to this force—or "achieve union with God"—by recalling what it was like to be part of God before we were born. That knowledge is recaptured by tuning into the "spirit within"—to the fragment of the Universal Spirit that remains in all of us. If enough people make this connection, Redfield claims, society will be transformed. Evil and crime will disappear; poverty and disease will be wiped out. We will live in perfect harmony—just as pictured in the book of Revelation.[14]

Even Christians can be disarmed by the subtleties of the New Age. "You must read this book," an enthusiastic friend told Nancy, handing her a copy of *The Secret Garden* by Frances Hodgson Burnett, first published in

1911. The friend was a thoughtful Christian mother, and the book is a children's classic. But Nancy was jolted when she discovered that the book is Hindu philosophy dressed up in a charming children's story.

In the words of ten-year-old Colin, one of the book's main characters, the world is made of a single spiritual substance, which he calls Magic (always capitalized). "Everything is made out of Magic, leaves and trees, flowers and birds, badgers and foxes and squirrels and people," says Colin.[15] "The Magic is in me. . . . It's in every one of us."[16] This is classic pantheism, and Burnett entwines it with language right out of the Christian creeds. "Magic is always . . . making things out of nothing," says Colin.[17]

The difference between this pantheistic deity and the biblical God is that this is an impersonal force that can be tapped, like an electric current. As Colin says, we need to learn how to "get hold of it [Magic] and make it do things for us—like electricity and horses and steam."[18] This is not a Lord to be obeyed but a force to be manipulated. And the way to do that is through spells and incantations. Thus, Colin chants, "The Magic is in me. . . . Magic! Magic! Come and help!"[19]

Ironically, a few years after Nancy read *The Secret Garden* and dissected its New Age themes, her son was assigned the book to read—in a Christian school. We must be on guard to know what our children are reading in school.

THE PRIMAL TEMPTATION

Clearly, the New Age movement should not be laughed off as a silly fad. It is the vehicle for disseminating a complete worldview, offering an answer to all three major life questions. *Where did we come from, and who are we?* We are somehow fragmented off from the Universal Spirit. *What has gone wrong with the world?* We have forgotten our true nature, forgotten that we are part of God. *What is the source of our salvation?* We must rediscover our true nature and link up to the God within.

Like all forms of the Escalator Myth, this one starts with utopian premises. There is no real evil, only ignorance: We have forgotten who we are. And by the same token, there is no real redemption, only enlightenment: We must recover a mystical knowledge of our inner divinity. This we do by various techniques, such as meditation, relaxation exercises, guided imagery, visualization, and use of crystals—all aimed at producing a state of consciousness in which the boundaries of the self dissolve and we gain a sense of unity with the divine. Through this higher consciousness, a person is said to tap into divine power and become more creative, more energetic, and even capable of healing illnesses through the power of the mind.

But like all forms of utopianism, this offer of salvation is hollow. By denying the reality of sin, it fails to address the crucial truth of our existence—that we are fallen creatures prone to evil. Proponents of the New Age reassure us that alienation and strife exist only on the superficial level of existence; at the deepest level, we are one with each other in God. As we become aware of this unity, they assert, we will begin to treat each other with kindness and charity.

However, this view of human nature simply doesn't stack up against reality. Mere knowledge is not enough to undercut the evil in the human heart. Simply *knowing* what is right doesn't enable us to *do* right.[20] This is the dilemma the apostle Paul wrestled with: The good that I want to do, I don't do (see especially Rom. 7:14-25). We don't need to raise our consciousness; we need to be saved.

The New Age deity cannot save us. It is an impersonal spiritual substratum of energy underlying all things. He—or rather, it—is more akin to electricity than to a deity. It is a power people try to plug into, not a personal God they can love and communicate with.

Moreover, for all its promises about raising self-esteem, the New Age gospel does nothing to affirm the worth of the individual; it offers no basis for human dignity and meaning. On the contrary, the goal of all meditation techniques is to lose the individual self, to dissolve it in the Universal Spirit, just as a drop of water dissolves in the ocean. How utterly unlike the biblical God, who created us as individuals, who watches over each of us and numbers "even the very hairs of [our] head" (Matt. 10:30).

Furthermore, New Age philosophy gives us no basis for morality. If God is in everything, God is in both good and evil; therefore, there is no final difference between them. Morality is reduced to a method for purifying the soul from desires so that it can attain mystical consciousness, like the eightfold path of Buddhism.[21]

But the ultimate failure of New Age thinking is its sheer implausibility. How many of us are capable of insisting, with a straight face, that we are perfect? Yet New Age proponents actually claim that "we are perfect exactly the way we are. And when we accept that, life works."[22] People who can swallow that have to be deliberately oblivious to their own failures, shortcomings, and sins.

And how many of us are capable of claiming, without sounding as if we've escaped from an asylum, that we are God, the ultimate reality, the absolute spirit? In a scene in Shirley MacLaine's television miniseries *Out on a*

Limb, the star shows how she had to be coached by her New Age counselor to shout, "I am God" over and over until she could say it with confidence.[23] It takes some doing to convince ourselves, against all the evidence, that we are divine. And those who succeed in doing so have simply given in to the oldest temptation in human history: the impulse to self-deification, humanity's primal temptation. "You will not surely die," the serpent promised. "You will be like God" (Gen. 3:4-5).

In short, spiritual evolutionism is not merely an error, a mistaken idea; it is religious rebellion against reality—against the sheer fact that God is the Creator and we are creatures. It is the empty boast of the pot that claims to make itself without the need of a Potter.

A GOD IN OUR OWN IMAGE

The pantheism that underlies New Age thought has appeared in so many periods of history and in so many guises that C. S. Lewis considered it the religion that we fall into naturally, apart from divine revelation: "the natural bent of the human mind . . . the attitude into which the human mind automatically falls when left to itself." Therefore, Lewis notes, pantheism is "the only really formidable opponent" to Christianity.[24]

And today it is making inroads even into Christian institutions. Mainstream churches hold "Re-Imagining" conferences denouncing the biblical God as patriarchal and holding worship services to "our mother, Sophia" (the Greek name for wisdom).[25] Christian apologist Peter Kreeft says that at Boston College, where he teaches, most students enter as pantheists: "Most of my Catholic college students believe we are parts of God and that God is in everyone." As a result, they don't believe we need to be saved; we "need only recognize our intrinsic value and accept ourselves as we are."[26] No wonder many people anticipate that the great confrontation of the next century will be between the New Age movement and orthodox Christianity (represented largely by evangelicalism, conservative Roman Catholicism, and the Orthodox church).

The danger is that as more and more Christians regard religion as therapy, we lower our defenses against worldviews that appeal primarily to our emotions while demanding nothing. The New Age is the perfect religious match for a culture driven by a therapeutic mind-set, hungry to fill the nothingness. It allows its followers to draw on ancient wisdom but to reshape it to fit the fashion of the moment.

By contrast, Christianity makes stringent moral demands on its followers. Critics often dismiss Christianity as mere wish fulfillment, a comforting illusion dreamed up by the ancients. But this characterization is patently foolish. Who, after all, would invent a religion that commands us to give up our lives for one another, to overcome evil with good, to love our enemies, to turn the other cheek, to give our possessions to the poor, to be just and merciful? Would anyone really design a religion devoted to an all-powerful, sovereign, omniscient God who demands righteousness and obedience? A God who dispenses severe judgment?

No. When people create their own religion, they create gods and goddesses in their own image. The ancient gods of mythology had limited powers, were subject to human interference, and displayed all the human weaknesses and vices. And the New Age god, who is little more than a warm feeling within or at worst a dabbling in occult powers, is merely a ratification of whatever the human ego wants.

In the final analysis, any religious worldview must pass the most crucial test: Can it make sense of the human predicament? Does it offer genuine redemption? Is it true? Applying this test to the New Age worldview, we detect its fatal weaknesses. It fails to correspond to reality as we experience it.

And if there is no answer in the West and no answer in the East, where does one turn?

CHAPTER 29

REAL REDEMPTION

The Bible is supported by archeological evidence again and again. . . . The fact that the record can be so often explained or illustrated by archeological data shows that it fits into the framework of history as only a genuine product of ancient life could do.

MILLAR BURROWS

Modern pluralistic society provides a smorgasbord of worldviews and belief systems, all clamoring for our allegiance. And whether their trappings are secular or religious, all are in essence offering means of salvation—attempts to solve the human dilemma and give hope for renewing the world. Today's most fashionable answers presume there is no kingdom of God on which to fasten our eschatological hopes, and therefore, they promise to create heaven here on earth—the Escalator Myth in its various forms. Alongside these are messages of heroic despair, challenging us to be courageous in facing life's meaninglessness.

It is easy to become bewildered by the array of answers available in to-day's marketplace of ideas, to throw up one's hands and declare them all valid options. That's why pluralism often leads to relativism—to the idea that there *is* no overarching, objective truth but only a variety of subjective beliefs. As Catholic scholar Ronald Knox once quipped, "The study of comparative religions is the best way to become comparatively religious."[1] Sadly, that maxim often holds true.

Yet a careful examination of competing worldviews can actually lead to the opposite effect: By lining up the Christian faith against other worldviews and religions, as we have done in the previous chapters, we see with aston-ishing clarity that Christianity offers the only real answers to the most basic questions of life and the best understanding of how we can be saved.

First, Christianity begins with an accurate diagnosis of the human dilemma. The basic problem is a moral one: our guilt before a holy God. God created us and established the moral dimensions for our lives. But we blew it. We have sinned, every one of us; we all have fallen short of God's perfect standard (Rom. 3:23). We have defied the moral order of the universe, and as a result, we are alienated from God.

Admittedly, people often do not *feel* guilty before God, since we are indoctrinated with the belief that guilt is merely a subjective feeling, a neurosis to be cured, and that we really ought to feel good about ourselves. As a result, many people come to Christianity on grounds other than guilt: a longing for inner peace and purpose, an attraction to the quality of love practiced in a local church, or a need to resolve some life crisis. But no matter what initially attracts us to Christianity, at some point each of us must confront the truth of our own moral condition: Guilt is objectively real, and *we* are guilty. We are sinners in the hands of a righteous God. The Holy Spirit can penetrate the hardest heart to convict us of our sinfulness. I know, because that is exactly what the Spirit did in my life.

Second, Christianity provides the only answer to the problem of sin. God himself has reached across the moral chasm that separates us from him in order to bring us back. The second person of the Trinity became a human being, lived a perfect life of obedience to the moral order, and in his death paid the price for our violation of the moral law, satisfying the demands of divine justice. God's solution reveals a marvelous economy, for the substitutionary atonement permits God to be both "just and the one who justifies" (Rom. 3:26). He remains "just" because he does not merely turn a blind eye to humanity's violation of the moral law, which flows from his own holy character. Yet at the same time he "justifies" those who have violated that law because its demands have been met by Christ's suffering on the cross.

Since it is humans who commit sin, only a human being can pay the penalty for it. But since sin offends an infinite Being, the penalty is infinite—which means only God can pay it. Thus the Incarnation is the only reasonable and fitting solution: God becomes man in order, as man, to pay the penalty for our sin.

But death of the God-man is not the end of the story, for Jesus was resurrected from the dead and lives forever. He overcame death, making it possible for us to be free from sin and death, from evil and destruction. By accepting his salvation, we become new creations and a new people. This is the "good news" (the literal meaning of *gospel*) that Christianity offers. And it is far more than a mere intellectual answer; it transforms our lives. For myself, I know that I could not live with myself if I hadn't experienced the overwhelming conviction one night in 1973, sitting in my car in a friend's driveway, that God had died *for me*. In a flood of tears, I felt released from a crushing sense of guilt and revived with a new sense of purpose and meaning. For the first time, I had a real reason for living.

All the ideologies we've examined in this section are pallid imitations of the Christian gospel. They promise to free people from oppression (or neurosis, or whatever else they define as the problem) and create the New Man, build the New Society, usher in the New Age. Clinging to the beauty of the gospel's hope but wanting none of the gospel's requirements, they re-cast it as the Escalator Myth, a fallacy of progress, promising that we can create a new life through politics, sex, science, or Eastern spirituality. But all of these worldviews are defective, inadequate substitutes for the real need of real people for real redemption.

Third, Christianity's offer of salvation is based on historical truth. The final element that sets Christianity apart from all other religions and worldviews is that it is based not on some evolutionary projection millions of years into the future or on some extraterrestrial fantasy, but on a historical event at a specific time and place: the crucifixion of Christ during the Jewish Passover in Jerusalem in the year A.D. 30 and his resurrection three days later.[2]

During the two thousand years since Christ's resurrection, the historical validity of this event has withstood every imaginable assault, ranging from the charge of "a cover-up" (by religious leaders of Jesus' day) to modern claims that it was a "Passover plot" or a "conjuring trick with bones." What skeptics overlook is that the empty tomb was a historical fact, verifiable by ordinary observation like any other historical fact. It was acknowledged by the soldiers who guarded the tomb (why else did they need to concoct an alternative explanation?). The resurrected Christ also appeared to five hundred eyewitnesses—too many people to dismiss the accounts as mass hysteria or the power of suggestion (1 Cor. 15:3-6).

Moreover, the original disciples refused to renounce Jesus, even though they were persecuted, tortured, and martyred. This defeated band of men, who had already returned to their fishing nets and boats, would never have been transformed into bold preachers of the gospel and defenders of the faith had they not seen Jesus' resurrected body and known him to be the living God. Had they attempted a Passover plot, they could never have kept it secret. People will die for something they *believe* to be true, but they will never die for something they *know* to be false.

I know how impossible it is for a group of people, even some of the most powerful in the world, to maintain a lie. The Watergate cover-up lasted only a few weeks before the first conspirator broke and turned state's evidence.[3]

A common stance, especially among theological liberals, is that the historicity of Jesus' resurrection doesn't matter—that even if the event didn't happen, Jesus is an important moral teacher. India's late, great spiritual leader Mohandas Gandhi expressed this attitude: "I may say that I have never been interested in an historical Jesus. I should not care if it was proved by someone that the man called Jesus never lived, and that what was narrated in the Gospels was a figment of the writer's imagination. For the Sermon on the Mount would still be true for me."[4]

But historical truth *does* matter. It is not enough to see Jesus' death and resurrection as a symbol, a parable, a myth, a purely subjective idea that can be "true for me," even if not true for others. The Christian message is the good news about what God has done. *But if the gospel is a myth, then God has not done anything.* "If religion be made independent of history, there is no such thing as a gospel," wrote the great Christian scholar J. Gresham Machen. "For 'gospel' means 'good news,' tidings, information about something that has happened. A gospel independent of history is a contradiction in terms."[5]

Jesus' resurrection is much *more* than a historical fact, of course, but it is nothing *less* than one. And the facts clearly support the gospel's claims. Critics used to argue that the New Testament was not written until hundreds of years after Jesus lived, by which time a jungle of myth and legend had grown up and distorted the original events. But we now know that the New Testament books were originally written a few decades after Christ's resurrection—far too short a period for legends to develop. Even many liberal scholars have come to agree that the New Testament was composed soon after the recorded events occurred, at a time when many people who knew Jesus were still alive and could dispute any false claims. "In my opinion," writes William F. Albright, "every book of the New Testament was written by a baptized Jew between the forties and eighties of the first century." [6]

Moreover, we have several thousand copies of the New Testament, many of them very old. (Generally, the older the copy, the closer it is to the original composition and therefore the more reliable it is considered to be.) Most of the New Testament books are preserved in manuscripts that are dated only a little more than a hundred years after the originals (and some fragments are dated even earlier). By contrast, we have only twenty copies of the works of the Roman writer Tacitus, and the earliest manuscript is dated a thousand years after he lived. The earliest manuscript we have of the work of

Aristotle is dated fourteen hundred years after he lived. The earliest copy of Caesar's *Gallic Wars* is dated a thousand years after he wrote it. Yet no one questions either the historicity of Tacitus or Aristotle or Caesar, or the authenticity of their writings.[7] The upshot is that today, Jesus' life is more thoroughly validated than that of virtually any other ancient figure.

The salvation attested to in the New Testament is the culmination of a long process of preparation in the Old Testament, which is also historically reliable, as archeological discoveries continue to confirm. For example, there was a time when critics said Moses could not have written the Pentateuch because writing had not yet been invented. Then archeologists discovered that writing was well developed thousands of years before Moses' day. The Egyptian and Babylonian cultures were highly literate cultures, with dictionaries, schools, and libraries.[8]

Critics once reserved their sharpest criticism for the early chapters of Genesis, dismissing the stories of the patriarchs as legend. But in recent years, archeological discoveries have repeatedly confirmed that Genesis gives highly accurate accounts of the names, places, trade routes, and customs of patriarchal times. Archeologists have found cuneiform tablets containing references to people such as Abraham and his brothers, Nahor and Haran. Tablets also explain puzzling customs, such as Abraham's and Jacob's practice of having children by a servant girl; the tablets show this was a common practice at the time. Yet, only a few centuries after the patriarchs lived, many of these names and practices and even some cities had completely disappeared. Contrary to what critics once claimed, it would have been impossible for the Bible writers to invent these stories later. They would have to have invented events that, by sheer chance, matched places and customs by then long forgotten.

The discovery of the Dead Sea Scrolls likewise provided confirmation for much of the Old Testament—even its supernatural character. Take Psalm 22, which predicts Christ's crucifixion in uncanny detail. Skeptics, rejecting the reality of divinely inspired prophecy, insisted that the psalm must have been written in the Maccabean Era, just before the birth of Christ, since before then, the practice of crucifixion did not exist in the Roman Empire. But when the Dead Sea Scrolls were discovered, they included copies of the Psalms dated centuries *before* the Maccabean Era.

And the evidence continues to mount. In the 1970s, archeological excavations confirmed the unique design of Philistine temples, with the roof supported by two central pillars about six feet apart. This discovery gives historical plausibility to the story of Samson, who grasped two pillars in the Philistine temple and brought it down.

Archeologists have also uncovered the ruins of the ancient city of Jericho and have found evidence that the walls of the city fell in an unusual manner—outward and flat, forming a perfect ramp for an invading army.[9] And in 1993, in Israel, archeologists uncovered a rock fragment inscribed with an ancient text referring to "the House of David," the first reference to King David and his royal family ever found outside the pages of the Bible.[10]

The historical data presses us to conclude that the stories in the Old and New Testaments are not made-up fables; they are accounts of real people and real events. As British journalist and historian Paul Johnson concludes, "It is not now the men of faith, it is the skeptics, who have reason to fear the course of discovery."[11]

THE MYTH BECOMES FACT

The old pagan world was littered with myths about a dying god who rises again, writes C. S. Lewis, but in Christianity, that myth became fact. "The dying god really appears—as a historical Person, living in a definite place and time."[12] Like a myth, the gospel is a colorful story that inspires our imagination, yet at the same time it is sober fact, something that happened in the real world. The story of Jesus, Lewis concludes, is "Perfect Myth and Perfect Fact: claiming not only our love and our obedience, but also our wonder and delight, addressed to the savage, the child, and the poet in each one of us no less than to the moralist, the scholar and the philosopher."[13]

But Christ's resurrection is only the beginning of the story of redemption. At Pentecost, the risen Christ sent forth the Holy Spirit into the lives of believers, to work out his purposes in their lives. Today as well, all believers receive the power to become children of God, to be transformed and restored to our true nature, people created in the image of God. And we live as the community of hope, in eschatological expectation, knowing that Christ will return and establish his rule over all.

God's redemption, then, does not change us into something different so much as it *restores* us to the way we were originally created. Virtually all of the words the Bible uses to describe salvation imply a return to something that originally existed. To *redeem* means to "buy back," and the image evokes a kidnapping: Someone pays the ransom and buys captives back, restoring them to their original freedom. *Reconciliation* implies a relationship torn by conflict, then returned to its original friendship. The New Testament also speaks of *renewal,* implying that something has been battered and torn, then restored to its pristine condition. *Regeneration* implies something returned to life after having died. As Al Wolters notes, "All these terms suggest a *restoration* of some good thing that was spoiled or lost."[14]

Being justified before God is a wonderful gift, yet it is just the beginning. Salvation empowers us to take up the task laid on the first human beings at the dawn of creation: to subdue the earth and extend the Creator's dominion over all of life.

■　　■　　■

ONLY CHRISTIANITY PROVIDES true redemption—a restoration to our created state and the hope of eternal peace with God. No other worldview identifies the real problem: the stain of sin in our souls. No other worldview can set free a tormented soul like Bernard Nathanson—or like me and you.

And having been liberated from sin, we are empowered to help bring Christ's restoration to the entire creation order.

RESTORATION: HOW NOW SHALL WE LIVE?

CHAPTER 30

THE KNOCKOUT PUNCH

Those first nights of his imprisonment in the Plymouth County Correctional Facility, Danny Croce couldn't settle into sleep. Couldn't even come close. He watched and listened as his fellow inmates muttered and the building's old pipes complained. The prison itself seemed restless. Vapory shadows swirled around the bare concrete ceiling, jaundiced by the low light in the hallway.

Wide awake on his bunk, Danny kept descending into deeper shadows, reliving the night that had brought him to this cell. A "village boy" from Brockton, Massachusetts, home of the famous middleweight fighter Marvelous Marvin Hagler, Danny had fought professionally himself. Now the scenes from that night hit him like short punches with plenty of leverage. A pounding he couldn't fend off.

Once again he saw the bus swinging into his lane, its high beams lighting up the curtain of falling rain. He swerved to the right. His car suddenly heaved into the air, the engine racing as the tires spun free. The night's quiet was sheared by the sound of scissoring metal. Danny peered into the sudden blackness, trying to search his way through it. *What's blocking my vision?* The Chevy Nova's wheels touched down at last, thumping into soft earth. The steering wheel played wildly in his hands. Still he could not see. *What is that?* He hit the interior dome light, which only intensified the nearness of the thick black covering across his windshield. His blindness lasted a moment's full horrible eternity before the windshield suddenly cleared and he skidded to a stop.

Stumbling out of his car, he saw a splintered police barrier and a man crumpled on the ground. He asked onlookers what had knocked the man down.

"You did," they said.

He looked again and felt a horrible stab of recognition. The man on the ground was police officer John Gilbert. The same John Gilbert who played pool with him in the bar and teased him about keeping in shape for the ring.

Danny's car had carried Gilbert thirty yards, they said. Splayed across the windshield in a black oilskin raincoat, it was Gilbert's body that had blotted out Danny's vision.

Remembering the episode, Danny felt as if that raincoat were covering his own face like a shroud, the rain running down like tears of remorse. Through the nights, the scene played over and over in Danny's head as if God, or maybe the devil, had looped the tape, setting it to replay without end. It was his own hell, which he knew he deserved. And in hell the "if onlys" go on forever.

If only he had left the bar after the first time he nodded off. *If only* his ironworker friend Sully hadn't been juiced up worse than he was and had been able to drive. *If only* it hadn't rained that day and he and Sully had been able to stay and finish out the eighth floor of that building they had been working on. *If only* they had been able to follow the motto of the ironworker: Look where you want to go, and let your feet follow. *If only* he had been able to see the consequences, he would never have followed where that day led. But he hadn't seen a thing.

Danny often wondered whether the freebasing had started the whole chain of events. That was something else he saw in the darkness. The pure white cocaine crystals left after the ethyl ether evaporated. The first of a series of bad choices that had landed Gilbert spread-eagled across Danny's windshield.

When Danny turned in his bunk to stare at the opposite wall, he saw Gilbert's family—his wife, his two kids, the empty chair at their dinner table. He had wanted to apologize to Jeanie Gilbert a thousand times before the sentencing, but his lawyers had said no. So he remained their ghost . . . and they remained his nightmare.

The video began to replay . . . midnight . . . 2:00 A.M. . . . 4:30. Sometimes it felt to Danny as if he were directing the scenes, looking for that undiscovered bridge to a different ending. Sometimes he could only cover up against the assault, both fists clenched over his brow. The memories swung at him—roundhouses, overhands, uppercuts.

Even before Danny got Sully's call about John Gilbert's condition, he had expected the bad news. The same way he had known how the bout would end that time he fought Tommy Rose. Tommy had been the number fourteen–ranked bantamweight at the time, and the matchup was Danny's one moment of boxing glory. Tommy Rose was a fighter going places.

At first Danny thought he had Tommy cornered, and he kept trying to cut him off. He tried to make Tommy think the right was his best shot; that way Tommy would counter weakly, and Danny could step through it and deliver his bomb of a left hook. He did connect with a few shots, but by the end of the third round—or was it the second?—Danny's arms and legs were gone. He kept standing, like a cow too stupid to fall after the slaughterhouse jolt, as Tommy gave him the most vicious beating of his life.

That's what Sully's telephone call was like: knowing his legs were gone, knowing what was coming.

"It's bad," Sully said.

"He's dead, isn't he?"

"Yeah, he's dead."

Except there was a difference. Danny couldn't remember Tommy's punch that put out his lights, but he would never forget the impatient way Sully said "dead"—as if he couldn't wait to clear out of Danny's life.[1]

■   ■   ■

DURING DANNY'S FIRST week in prison, he was assigned to a work detail out in the fields, cultivating the hard New England soil, still almost frozen in April. At the end of one shift, as the men drifted toward the water tower to be recounted and escorted back to their cells, Danny heard someone calling him.

"Hey, Croce! Come over here!" A guy by the hay cart. Danny didn't know him, so he kept on walking toward the water tower. But the guy moved out to block his way. He was big in the upper arms and thick through the gut. Danny saw other inmates glancing over their shoulders at the guards in the distance, then converging on the two of them.

"So, Croce, I heard you fought Tommy Rose. Heard you were tough. But the thing is, I don't remember any Croce fighting Rose."

"The promoter called me Rivaro for that one."

"Why? You ashamed of your name? Your wop name—Cro-chay. That's why your family says it's 'Crose,' I bet. Your whole family's ashamed, with a killer like you in it." The guy turned to grin at the onlookers. "A killer everywhere but in the ring."

Danny had known he would have to use his hands in prison. He was surprised only at how soon. "I know the game well enough," he said. "Get out of my way."

"I'm *in* your way, you puke. A real killer, you are. As long as you're driving a car."

The guys around them laughed, and the man rocked his weight back like a Goliath. Then he rushed Danny, throwing a looping right toward his temple.

He threw it as if he had a wrench in his hand, which gave Danny enough time to decide against the typical crossing counter. He didn't want any extra time tacked onto his sentence, so he hoped to take this guy down without marking him too much. He threw a triple combination into the guy's gut—*bm, bm, bm*—and the man's face drained.

He came back at Danny, though. This time he faked with a jab, or threw it so weakly Danny couldn't tell the difference.

Danny popped him in the side of the head with the right, then jabbed him with a left hook, lifting the oaf clean off the back of his heels. He fell dead out like concrete—not even a bounce.

Usually when a fight ended, whether in a bar or in the ring, there was cheering and shouting. But Danny's fellow inmates kept this one quiet. Then something even stranger happened. The onlookers began crowding closer. For a moment Danny thought he was going to have to fight them all. Then he understood. They were walking him away, protecting him.

"The water tower's got a spigot," someone said. They shielded him from view as he washed the blood from his hands. Then they all lined up for the count.

"O'Brien," the guard called out.

"He fell down," someone said. "Back by the hay cart."

"Always sleeping, that mick," the guard said.

Everyone laughed, hearty and false.

At least I won't have to fight again for a while, Danny thought.

.   .   .

UNABLE TO SLEEP at night, Danny was groggy during the day. He had to find a way to rest, or one of the new arrivals would challenge him, and he would lose his reputation. He dreaded the guards' call of lockdown, the haul and clang of the closing cellblock doors, and time slowing once more as the black moments in that car drained the sweat out of him.

One night, about three months into Danny's sentence, an inmate named John Dunn poked his head into Danny's cell just before lockdown. Danny was not overjoyed to see him. He knew Dunn thought of himself as spiritual.

"We're starting a vehicular-homicide group," Dunn said.

"Like an AA group?" asked Danny.

Dunn nodded. "You get 'good time' for it—time off your sentence," he added. "A day for an hour."

Danny thought about the eighteen-month stretch still ahead of him. "I guess you'll be seeing me, then," he said.

Eventually Danny told his story to the group. When he finished, several of the men said, in one way or another, "It was his time. Everyone's ticket gets punched."

The process was supposed to provide some relief, but Danny felt none. It *wasn't* John Gilbert's time. That was the whole point.

Afterward, a longhaired hippie type came up to him. "Have you ever prayed to God?"

Danny hadn't prayed since he was a kid. He hadn't even thought much about religion. But later that night, back in his cell, he found himself begging, more out of desperation than anything else, "Please, God, let me sleep."

That was the last thing he remembered. Suddenly it was morning, and for the first time in months, he had an appetite for breakfast.

The insomnia returned, though. He waited it out for several nights, then prayed once more, just as simply. "Please, God, let me sleep."

Again, the next thing he knew, it was morning.

This was so curious that he felt compelled to talk with the longhair. Danny knew almost nothing about religion. He knew only that whether it was Catholics, Jehovah's Witnesses, or the Four Squares, when they talked at you or handed you a tract, they were carrying "that Book." So he asked the hippie if he had a Bible, and the man loaned Danny his New Testament.

As Danny read the Gospels, he discovered that the Jesus they described appealed to him. Jesus was straight with everyone, and although he was always being set up, he stood his ground. He told people so clearly what was in their hearts that he knocked them out with his words, without throwing a punch—unlike Danny, who had been fighting ever since his family moved into the town of Brockton. "So you think you're too good for us," one of the bigger kids would shout. Or they would yell nasty things about his mother. Anything to start a fight. The first time, he had refused to fight, and they had dropped him into a garbage bin. So he had learned to use his fists. Now, reading the Bible reminded him of how he had become such a tough guy—and what an act it was.

The more Danny felt drawn to Jesus, the more he saw himself in a new light. He was used to comparing himself to the guy on the next bar stool, and that way he usually didn't look so bad. But when he compared himself to Jesus, he started to feel afraid. This man who never raised his fists scared him as nobody else ever had.

He also read the passages about people being "cast into outer darkness," where there was "weeping" and "gnashing of teeth." Danny knew something about darkness. In his mind, he was shut in that car, unable to see, unable to change directions, carrying death along with him—not only John Gilbert's death but also his own.

Lying on his bunk at night, Danny began to review his whole life, horrified by the person he had become. He saw himself living for his next drink, his next coke party; he saw himself using women. His last girlfriend had been good to him, but he would have thrown her away for the next quarter ounce of coke. In fact, he probably had.

That next Sunday, when the guard called out for people who wanted to be let out of their cells to attend chapel, Danny shouted, "Cell 16." But he sat like a stone through the service, hearing little. He was there to ask a question. Afterward, he approached Chaplain Bob Hansen and asked him if the passages he had read about outer darkness were really about hell.

"Yes," said the chaplain.

"Then I'm in big trouble," Danny said.

"When you get back to your cell, get on your knees by your bunk," said the chaplain. "Confess your sins to God, and pray for Jesus Christ to come into your heart."

Danny did just that. In his cell, he knelt, confessed that he was a sinner, and asked Christ to be his Lord. As he did, he kept remembering horrible things he had done, and the memories brought both pain and an eagerness to be forgiven. Talking to God seemed like carrying on a conversation with someone he had missed all along without knowing it. He could almost hear God replying through a silence that echoed his sorrow and embraced it. Danny not only felt heard, he also felt understood, received.

He slept that night. And every night afterward.

.   .   .

DANNY BEGAN WEARING a cross. He walked the cellblocks with a spiritual strut, a pugnacious witness to the truth he had found. He pumped along with a new confidence, asking everyone he met to come to chapel. Some prisoners even took a step back when he passed, as if he would slam them against a wall if they didn't become Christians.

Inside, Danny resolved that he wouldn't take any abuse for his new convictions. They could call him a Jesus freak, but no one was going to get in his face. He prayed that no one would touch him. He could control himself if they left him alone.

The only fights that broke out were the ones inside him—a war between his new convictions and his old habits.

One day when he was playing Ping-Pong, Danny flipped his usual cigarette into his mouth and flicked his lighter. Suddenly, something said, "Stop." The filter no longer tasted clean. He slipped the cigarette back in the pack and wondered what was going on.

Chaplain Hansen always said to look to the Bible for answers, so Danny actually did a concordance search that night. He found only one passage that said anything at all about smoking; it was in Isaiah and had to do with "smoking flax." Yet he didn't doubt that he had heard a voice say "stop."

Eventually, he discovered 1 Corinthians and gained an understanding that his body was God's house. He shouldn't deliberately damage it. So he prayed for the willpower to stop smoking. The first day he had to pray twenty times . . . as he sat in the mess hall having coffee . . . as he worked in the fields . . . as he played cards at a table in the yard—all the places and times that prompted him to light up again.

The next day he prayed nineteen times. The smoking battle kept him on his knees for weeks.

Danny soon heard that same voice countering most of his lifelong habits. It was a patient voice and said stop to only one thing at a time, but the list was long, beginning with smoking and drinking, then going on to using dope and swearing. He discovered that when he began to clean up his language, he lost half his vocabulary. He also discovered that his first victories produced an overconfidence born of spiritual pride.

One day while playing cards, he said to another Christian inmate, "What are you putting that cigarette in your mouth for, brother? Don't you know that God will deliver you from that if you ask?"

"Well, I believe it, Danny, but I'm not there yet," his friend said.

Not too long afterward Danny cruised by the showers, where guys smoked dope during the day, back in a hidden area. He could smell the sweet, heavy scent. An inner yearning taunted him, *What would it be like to take just a few more tokes?* He couldn't resist finding out.

When Danny ducked back out, the first person he saw was the brother he had just jumped on for smoking. "Hey, Danny," the guy grinned, gesturing with his cigarette, "guess you're not so perfect either."

Danny went to his bunk and cried out to God for strength. These inner battles with himself were tougher than anything he'd faced in the ring.

Eventually, though, after umpteen prayers a day, the old habits started to fade, and Danny began to feel something like the "new creation" spoken of in the Scriptures.

Then, just before he went into chapel one day, while he was still out in the yard, one of the new inmates started ragging a frail nineteen-year-old called Squeaky. The nickname was apt. The kid, who was in the joint for writing bad checks, really was a mouse. He even looked like one, with his colorless hair and flappy ears.

In contrast, the new inmate looked like a real bad boy, slim but muscled, with things to prove. He pushed Squeaky's shoulder hard with the butt of his hand.

Squeaky did nothing but grab for the place where it hurt.

"You're a tough guy," Danny said, stepping in.

"This punk's been looking at me like he's queer or something."

"He hasn't been looking at you. Squeaky never looks at anything but the ground."

"You calling me a liar?"

"You want to fight someone, fight someone who knows how. Me."

"This shrimp's your whore?"

Danny made no reply.

"Well, I'll fight you, you queer freak. You . . ." He loosed a flood of curses, working up a fighting rage.

His first jab snapped out with greater skill than Danny expected. It went through the block Danny put up and caught him on the side of the head. For a moment Danny anticipated another left, a right, whatever combination the guy's rhythm dictated.

But the newcomer just threw one and stepped away. Threw another and stepped away. Danny blocked and feinted.

When the newcomer yawed the next time, Danny stepped forward quickly and caught him with three close-in shots to the head—*bm, bm, bm.* That left the guy's face a blank, with blood trickling from the brow. The old fury rose up within Danny, and he cleaned the guy with a crossing right.

Totally pure. The guy fell on the seat of his pants, bleeding heavily from the mouth. He didn't get up.

"Squeaky's one of Danny's boys now," someone said. "You're gonna have to get born again, Squeaky."

"You don't owe me nothing, Squeaky," Danny said, suddenly feeling as if he had lost the fight.

The buzzer sounded. Time for chapel.

Danny sat through the service, preoccupied with his own thoughts. Afterward, he went up to Chaplain Hansen and asked what he should do.

"You know what you have to do," the chaplain said. "When you offend your brother, you have to make it right. You have to go to the guy."

When Danny appeared at the newcomer's cell, the guy snarled at him, and Danny could hardly bring himself to put his hand forward. "I came by to see how you're doing. I'm sorry for laying you out. I know what I'm doing—too much to hit you like that."

"You proved it," the newcomer said. His mouth was swollen and distorted.

"You don't need to make your rep on guys like Squeaky. Now that you fought me, people will leave you alone. You landed that first shot."

"Didn't slow you down much."

"Like I said, I know what I'm doing. We square?"

"Square," the newcomer said. He stood and shook Danny's hand quickly, then scrambled back to his bunk.

Danny thought of asking the guy to chapel, but he knew that was not the moment for invitations. *He'll be asking about me,* Danny thought. *There'll be other times.*

Back in the dormitory, where he had been permitted to live for the last several months, Danny stood and looked out the window. He could see the water tower and the fields beyond. The rows were filled with lettuce heads, the back fields with waist-high corn. The day was settling down as night came on with a watery blue sky, the clouds blushed with sunset.

All at once, Danny felt free. Standing in the middle of the Plymouth County Correctional Facility, with months still to serve, he felt unfettered as he never had on the outside. There, he had made a prison of his world. Here, in prison, God had set him free. *Look where you want to go, and let your feet follow.* He now saw where the old ways would lead him, and he was free to turn and walk the other way—free to choose the good, even when his old ways still called to him.

Looking at the water tower, he remembered his first fight here, remembered washing the blood off his hands after hammering O'Brien. But it had taken more than the whole water tower to wash John Gilbert's blood off his hands. It had taken Christ's blood—the living water.

.   ■   ■

TEN YEARS AFTER his release, Danny Croce once again entered the Plymouth County Correctional Facility. Although the government had closed the old building and built a new one, the Plymouth facility was essentially the same.

He stood in the lock, between the double doors operated by security. The first door had closed behind him. The second refused to open. He buzzed again.

"Who are you?" a voice said over the intercom.

For a panicky moment he wondered. He remembered being in the old prison. Was he the man who had killed John Gilbert? Yes.

Who else was he? Faces and events rushed through his memory like a video in fast-forward. The day he was released from prison. His marriage. His five children. The years working with troubled kids in Boston. Then the big break: being accepted at Wheaton College and receiving the Charles W. Colson Scholarship for ex-offenders. His graduation. His ordination. Yes, he remembered. Both who he had been and who he now was.

"Who are you?" the voice repeated.

"I'm the new prison chaplain," Danny answered.

CHAPTER 31

SAVED TO WHAT?

Culture in the broadest sense is the purpose for which God created man after His image . . . [which] includes not only the most ancient callings of . . . hunting and fishing, agriculture and stock raising, but also trade and commerce and science and art.

HERMAN BAVINCK

Danny Croce's "wake-up punch" is the perfect punch line for this book. Not because it's a heartwarming conversion story—though it is that—but because of what Danny did *after* his broken life was redeemed. It's the kind of wake-up punch that contemporary Christians urgently need, as well as an apt metaphor for the theme that will be woven through the rest of this book.

When Danny Croce became a Christian, he embarked on an adventure to change the world. First to be transformed was his own life: He cleaned up his act, got out of prison, got married, settled down into a respectable life, and earned a college degree. But changing his own life wasn't the end of things for Danny. After his graduation, he didn't tuck his Wheaton diploma under his arm and head off for the comfortable life that his education might have given him. No, he set out to transform the world he had known. He went back to prison.

And transform it he did. The Plymouth County Correctional Facility houses fourteen hundred inmates in twenty-two units, four of which are the "holes," the dreaded segregation and protective-custody units. In each unit, Danny located an on-fire Christian believer, or else he preached and witnessed until God converted someone. Danny then appointed these men to function as elders to help and lead others; to equip them, he continues to disciple and teach them, giving courses on theology and doctrine, often using seminary-level materials. He also holds weekly Bible studies throughout the prison, assisted by Prison Fellowship volunteers. And every day Danny talks with inmates one-on-one, teaching, encouraging, and helping them solve personal problems.

He helps inmates like Peter, who received a letter from his wife telling him she was filing for divorce. Danny prayed with Peter, then drove sixty miles to meet the estranged wife. Many meetings later, Peter and his wife were reconciled, and they are now growing together in Christ.

When God makes us new creations, we are meant to help create a new world around us, and Danny Croce's work at the Plymouth prison, like Jorge Crespo's at García Morena, offers a striking example. Again and again, I have witnessed this kind of transformation within a rotting prison culture, and the results are measurable in terms of reduced disciplinary problems and reduced recidivism.[1]

Yes, cultures can be renewed—even those typically considered the most corrupt and intractable. But if we are to restore our world, we first have to shake off the comfortable notion that Christianity is merely a personal experience, applying only to one's private life. No man is an island, wrote the Christian poet John Donne. Yet one of the great myths of our day is that we *are* islands—that our decisions are personal and that no one has a right to tell us what to do in our private lives. We easily forget that every private decision contributes to the moral and cultural climate in which we live, rippling out in ever widening circles—first in our personal and family lives, and then in the broader society.

That's because every decision we make reflects our worldview. Every choice, every action, either expresses a false worldview and thus contributes to a disordered and broken world, or expresses God's truth and helps build a world that reflects his created order. Our purpose in this final section of the book is to show you how to make genuinely biblical choices in every area of your life. The three worldview categories examined in the earlier sections—*creation, fall,* and *redemption*—provide a conceptual structure by which we can identify what is wrong with non-Christian ways of thinking and then formulate a Christian perspective on every subject.

The first task, then, is to be discerning, to examine various worldviews by measuring how well they answer the fundamental questions of life: *Creation*—Where did we come from, and who are we? *Fall*—What has gone wrong with the world? *Redemption*—What can we do to fix it? Trace out the way any worldview answers these three questions, and you will be able to see how nonbiblical ideas fail to fit reality. By contrast, the biblical worldview provides answers that are internally consistent and really work.

Finally, when we apply this three-part analysis, we learn how to put biblical principles into practice in every area of life. As we have seen with Danny Croce and Jorge Crespo, *transformed people transform cultures.* And that is what every believer is called to do, as Scripture makes clear.

THE CULTURAL COMMISSION

The scriptural justification for culture building starts with Genesis. At the dawn of creation, the earth is unformed, empty, dark, and undeveloped. Then, in a series of steps, God establishes the basic creational distinctives: light and dark, "above the expanse" and "below the expanse," sea and land, and so on. But then God changes his strategy.

Until the sixth day, God has done the work of creation directly. But now he creates the first human beings and orders them to carry on where he leaves off: They are to reflect his image and to have dominion (Gen. 1:26). From then on, the development of the creation will be primarily social and cultural: It will be the work of humans as they obey God's command to fill and subdue the earth (Gen. 1:28).

Sometimes called the "cultural commission" or "cultural mandate," God's command is the culmination of his work in creation. The curtain has risen on the stage, and the director gives the characters their opening cue in the drama of history.[2] Though the creation itself is "very good," the task of exploring and developing its powers and potentialities, the task of building a civilization, God turns over to his image bearers. "By being fruitful they must fill it even more; by subduing it they must form it even more," explains Al Wolters in *Creation Regained*.[3]

The same command is still binding on us today. Though the Fall introduced sin and evil into human history, it did not erase the cultural mandate. The generations since Adam and Eve still bear children, build families, and spread across the earth. They still tend animals and plant fields. They still construct cities and governments. They still make music and works of art.

Sin introduces a destructive power into God's created order, but it does not obliterate that order. And when we are redeemed, we are not only freed from the sinful motivations that drive us but also restored to fulfill our original purpose, empowered to do what we were created to do: to build societies and create culture—and, in doing so, to restore the created order.

It is our contention in this book that the Lord's cultural commission is inseparable from the great commission. That may be a jarring statement for many conservative Christians, who, through much of the twentieth century, have shunned the notion of reforming culture, associating that concept with the liberal social gospel. The only task of the church, many fundamentalists and evangelicals have believed, is to save as many lost souls as possible from a world literally going to hell. But this implicit denial of a Christian worldview is unbiblical and is the reason we have lost so much of our influence in the world. Salvation does not consist simply of freedom from sin; salvation also means being restored to the task we were given in the beginning—the job of creating culture.

When we turn to the New Testament, admittedly we do not find verses specifically commanding believers to be engaged in politics or the law or education or the arts. But we don't need to, because the cultural mandate given to Adam still applies. Every part of creation came from God's hand, every part was drawn into the mutiny of the human race and its enmity toward God, and every part will someday be redeemed. This is the apostle Paul's message to the Romans, in which he promises that "the creation itself will be liberated from its bondage to decay" (Rom. 8:21). Redemption is not just for individuals; it is for all God's creation.

Paul makes the point most strongly in Colossians 1:15-20, where he describes the lordship of Christ in three ways: (1) *everything was made by and for Christ:* "By him all things were created: things in heaven and on earth, visible and invisible . . . all things were created by him and for him"; (2) *everything holds together in Christ:* "He is before all things, and in him all things hold together"; (3) *everything will be reconciled by Christ:* "For God was pleased to have all his fullness dwell in him, and through him to reconcile to himself all things, whether things on earth or things in heaven." Redemption covers all aspects of creation, and the end of time will not signal an end to the creation but the beginning of a new heaven and a new earth: God will make all things new (Rev. 21:5).

The lesson is clear: Christians are saved not only *from* something (sin) but also *to* something (Christ's lordship over all of life). The Christian life begins with spiritual restoration, which God works through the preaching of his Word, prayer, the sacraments, worship, and the exercise of spiritual gifts within a local church. This is the indispensable beginning, for only the redeemed person is filled with God's Spirit and can genuinely know and fulfill God's plan. But then we are meant to proceed to the restoration of all God's creation, which includes private and public virtue; individual and family life; education and community; work, politics, and law; science and medicine; literature, art, and music. This redemptive goal permeates everything we do, for there is no invisible dividing line between sacred and secular. We are to bring "all things" under the lordship of Christ, in the home and the school, in the workshop and the corporate boardroom, on the movie screen and the concert stage, in the city council and the legislative chamber.

This is what we mean when we say a Christian must have a comprehensive worldview: a *view* or perspective that covers all aspects of the *world*. For every aspect of the world was created with a structure, a character, a norm. These underlying principles are God's "laws"—God's design and purpose for creation—and can be known through both *special revelation* (God's words given in Scripture) and *general revelation* (the structure of the world he made). They include both laws of nature and norms for human life.

This point must be pressed, because most people today operate on a fact/value distinction, believing that science uncovers "facts," which they believe to be reliable and true, while morality and religion are based on "values," which they believe to be subjective and relative to the individual. Unfortunately, Christians often mirror this secular attitude. We tend to be confident about God's laws for nature, such as the laws of gravity, motion, and heredity; but we seem far less confident about God's laws for the family, education, or the state. Yet a truly Christian worldview draws no such distinction. It insists that God's laws govern all creation. And just as we have to learn to live in accord with the law of gravity, so, too, we must learn to live in accord with God's norms for society.

The reason these two types of laws seem quite different is that norms for society are obeyed by choice. In the physical world, stones fall, planets move in their orbits, seasons come and go, and the electron circles the nucleus—all without any choice in the matter—because here God rules directly. But in culture and society, God rules indirectly, entrusting human beings with the task of making tools, doing justice, producing art and music, educating children, and building houses. And though a stone cannot defy God's law of gravity, human beings *can* rebel against God's created order—and they often do so. Yet that should not blind us to the fact that there is a single objective, universal order covering both nature and human nature.

All major cultures since the beginning of history have understood this concept of a universal order—all, that is, except postmodern Western culture. Despite the differences among them, all major civilizations have believed in a divine order that lays down the law for both natural and human realms. In the Far East it was called *Tao;* in ancient Egypt it was called *Ma'at;* in Greek philosophy it was called *Logos.*[4]

Likewise, in the Old Testament the psalmist speaks almost in a single breath of God's spreading the snow like wool and revealing his laws and decrees to Jacob, suggesting that there is no essential difference between God's laws for nature and those for people (see Ps. 147:16-19). Both types of law are part of a single universal order. John's Gospel borrows the Greek word for this universal plan of creation *(logos)* and, in a startling move, identifies it with a personal being—Jesus Christ himself. "In the beginning was the Word *[Logos]*," which is the source of creation (John 1:1). "Through him all things were made; without him nothing was made that has been made" (John 1:3). In other words, Jesus himself is the source of the comprehensive plan or design of creation.

As a result, obedience to Christ means living in accord with that plan in all aspects of life. Family and church, business and commerce, art and education, politics and law are institutions grounded in God's created order; they are not arbitrary in their configuration. A school is not a business and shouldn't be run like one; a family is not a state and shouldn't be run like one. Each has its own normative structure, ordained by God, and each has its own sphere of authority under God.[5] For the Christian, there must be no dichotomy between the sacred and the secular because nothing lies outside of God's created order. Our task is to reclaim that entire created order for his dominion.[6]

The world is a spiritual battleground, with two powers contending for the same territory. God's adversary, Satan, has invaded creation and now attempts to hold it as occupied territory. With the death and resurrection of Jesus Christ, God launched a counteroffensive to reclaim his rightful domain, and we are God's soldiers in that ongoing battle. "He has rescued us from the dominion of darkness and brought us into the kingdom of the Son he loves" (Col. 1:13). Redeemed, we are armed for the fight to extend that kingdom and push back the forces of Satan. The fighting may be fierce, but we must not lose hope, for what we are waging is essentially a mop-up operation. Because of the Resurrection, the war has been won; the victory is assured.[7]

The history of Christianity is filled with glorious demonstrations of the truth and power of the gospel. Through the centuries, when Christians have lived out their faith by putting both the cultural commission and the great commission to work, they have renewed, restored, and, on occasions, even built new cultures. They have literally turned the world upside down.

ALL TRUTH IS GOD'S TRUTH

In the first century, a tiny group of Jewish dissidents spread a preposterous message about a condemned felon who rose from the dead. From such ignoble beginnings, Christianity grew into a force that dominated Western culture and eventually the world. How? By believers' dramatic testimony under persecution. Witnessing the peace and joy shining from the faces of ordinary men and women put to death for their convictions, pagans were drawn to Christ and his church.

In the second century, the church father Tertullian even reproached the secular authorities for the failure of their harsh policies: "Your cruelty [against us] does not profit you, however exquisite. Instead, it tempts people to our sect. As often as you mow us down, the more we grow in number. The blood of the Christians is the seed [of the church]." As a result of their striking witness, Christians soon filled every corner of ancient society. "We have filled all you have—cities, islands, forts, towns, assembly halls, even military camps, tribes, town councils, the palace, senate, and forum," Tertullian said, mocking the Romans. "We have left you nothing but the temples."[8]

Even as Christians were growing in number, however, they were also working to transform the culture from within. Another second-century church father, Justin Martyr, showed the way.

As a young man, Justin decided to become a philosopher and studied with teachers of the various philosophical schools of the ancient world, from Stoicism to Aristotelianism to Platonism. Finally he realized that the truth he sought was found in Scripture, and he became a believer, but he did not abandon philosophy. By becoming a Christian, he argued, he had simply become a *better* philosopher: He was now able to gather all the individual truths discovered by various philosophers and make sense of them within the framework of the one perfect truth provided by divine revelation. "Whatever things were rightly said by any man, belong to us Christians," he wrote.[9]

Justin wasn't urging Christians to be complacent relativists, as if all paths lead to God. He was resolutely opposed to the paganism of his day, and he was even put on trial for being a Christian, where he refused to renounce his faith and was executed. No, Justin wasn't one to compromise the truths of Christianity. Yet he did believe that pagans perceive reality in part, and he taught that Christ is the fulfillment of all the partial truths embodied in pagan philosophy and culture.

Following Justin's lead, the early church sought to fulfill both the great commission and the cultural commission, to redeem both souls and society. And when the Roman Empire fell, it was Christians who saved civilization in one of the most inspiring chapters of Western history.

.   .   .

THE DARK AGES began with a cold snap. In A.D. 406 the Rhine River froze, forming a bridge of ice that allowed a band of barbarians to cross from the

Germanic territories into Roman territory. In the following years, successive waves of Vandals and Visigoths, Sueves and Alans, overran the Roman Empire and Europe, reducing cities to rubble and decimating populations. The entire substructure of Roman civilization was destroyed, to be replaced by small kingdoms ruled by illiterate, barbaric warrior-kings.

As the shadow of the Dark Ages fell over Western Europe, who emerged from the rubble? Who rebuilt Western civilization? The Christian church.[10]

In A.D. 401 a sixteen-year-old British boy named Patricius was seized by a raiding Irish war party, abducted from his Romanized homeland, and sold to a petty Irish chieftain named Miliucc, who sent the boy out to shepherd his flocks. Patricius spent months alone in the hills, hunger gnawing at his innards and the clammy cold biting into his limbs, until finally he sought help from the only source left: He began to pray.

Before this time, Patricius had not really believed in the God his Christian parents had taught him about, and he thought priests were fools. But he found in God a source of strength that helped him endure six long years of bitter isolation and deprivation. "Tending flocks was my daily work, and I would pray constantly during the daylight hours," he wrote later. "The love of God and the fear of him surrounded me more and more—and faith grew and the Spirit was roused."[11]

Then one night, Patricius was awakened by a mysterious voice telling him that he was going home. "Look, your ship is ready," said the voice. Although uncertain of the direction or distance, Patricius set out for the sea. More than two hundred miles later, he found a ship bound for England.

When he reached his homeland, however, Patricius discovered that he no longer fit in with his people. "Hardened physically and psychologically by unsharable experiences, hopelessly behind his peers in education, he cannot settle down," writes historian Thomas Cahill.[12] Then one night, the former slave boy heard Christ's voice again, this time telling him to return to Ireland. He entered theological training and eventually returned as Patrick, missionary to the Irish.

This was no romantic return, set to the tune of Irish ballads. When St. Patrick began his mission, he faced pagan Irish priests (druids) who still practiced ritual human sacrifice to their monstrous Celtic gods (often portrayed eating people). The fierce Irish warriors, believing that the human head was the seat of the soul, hung their enemies' skulls from their belts as trophies.

Into this bloodthirsty culture St. Patrick brought the Christian message of love and forgiveness and established monasteries throughout the land. The monastic movement in Ireland began to revolutionize the world, replacing the old values of a warrior society with the new values of Christianity. Within St. Patrick's lifetime, warriors cast aside their swords of battle, intertribal warfare decreased markedly, and the slave trade ended. A culture of battle and brute power was transformed by an ethic that sanctified manual labor, poverty, and service. A culture of illiteracy and ignorance became a culture of learning.

Moreover, after Rome fell, the Irish monasteries also became refuges for vast numbers of Christian scholars and monks fleeing the barbarians, streaming in from all across Europe and even from as far away as Egypt, Armenia, and Syria. As a result, says historian Kenneth Clark, surprising as it may seem, "for quite a long time—almost a hundred years—western Christianity survived by clinging to places like Skellig Michael, a pinnacle of rock eighteen miles from the Irish coast."[13] Yet survive it did, and eventually a flood of missionaries from Ireland fanned out across Scotland, England, and the European continent. All along the way the monks established monasteries and carried on their tradition of copying and preserving the Bible, along with every other book they could get their hands on—including the great classics of the Greeks and Romans, some of which had not been seen in Europe for centuries. They also taught their converts Latin, music, and painting.

To give some idea of their success, by the early 600s nearly seven hundred monastic communities had been established along the rocky coasts and mountains of Scotland alone, and between A.D. 650 and A.D. 850 more than half of all known biblical commentaries were written by Irishmen. Everywhere they went, the Irish monks carried their Bibles and books around their waists, just as the Irish pagans had once tied their enemies' skulls to their belts.

This is "how the Irish saved civilization," to use Cahill's words, for it was the disciplined labor of the monks that stanched the tide of barbarism across Europe, preserved the best of Greco-Roman culture, and infused new life into the decadent monasticism of the continent. The monastery became the center of culture, replacing the dying cities and expanding into a vast complex populated by monks, workers, servants, and dependents. Gradually, "the woody swamp became a hermitage, a religious house, a farm, an abbey, a village, a seminary, a school of learning, and a city," writes John Henry Newman.[14]

What's more, this astonishing feat was accomplished again and again throughout the Dark Ages. From the north, Vikings repeatedly swooped down on the coasts or sailed deep inland on the rivers to loot and destroy, murdering people, ruining fields, plundering wealth, and burning cities across Europe. From the east, the Magyars and Avars, the Huns and Mongols, swept successively across the steppes, leaving similar devastation and death in their wake. But each time, Christianity showed its unquenchable, supernatural power of spiritual regeneration. Each time, the monastic communities arose from the rubble to become islands of peace and spiritual order.

The monks' first concern, of course, was to nourish the inner life of faith. But spiritual reform inevitably led to social change as they fulfilled the call to defend the oppressed and to speak boldly against evil in high places. In the monks, says historian Christopher Dawson, "the lawless feudal nobles, who cared nothing for morality or law, recognized the presence of something stronger than brute force—a numinous supernatural power they dared not ignore."[15]

Lasting peace could not come to Europe, however, until the barbarians themselves were evangelized, and one of the most exciting chapters in the history of the Christian church is the transformation of the barbarians from bloodthirsty warriors into peace-loving farmers, determined to live by the work of their own hands instead of by theft and plunder.[16] As the barbarians were converted and the destructive invasions ceased, European society began to flourish. Cities grew, guilds emerged to protect the interests of the crafts and professions, and ideas of representative government took root.

In this setting, Christianity gave birth to a new institution, the university, which developed from schools attached to the great cathedrals in places such as Paris and Bologna, eventually replacing the monasteries as centers of learning and culture. Later, the Reformation would spark a quantum leap in culture formation, inspiring a new work ethic that would fuel the industrial revolution and create a political climate that made free democracies possible.

This is how Christianity is meant to function in society—not just as a private faith but as a creative force in the culture. The inner life of faith must shape our actions out in the world. In every choice and decision we make, we either help to overcome the forces of barbarism—whether medieval or modern—or acquiesce to those forces; we either help build a life-giving, peace-loving ethos, or fan the flames of egoism and destruction.

THE NEW MILLENNIUM

At the dawn of the third millennium, we face the same challenge and opportunity that the early church and the medieval monks faced: to build a culture informed by a biblical worldview. The most hopeful words from any Chris-

tian leader today have come from John Paul II, who urges believers everywhere to make the new millennium a "new springtime" for the gospel.[17] Is
this false optimism? On all sides I hear battle-weary evangelicals saying that
we have lost the culture war and that we might as well turn back to building
our churches instead. But in light of our historical heritage, we dare not give
in to despair. That would be not only a sin (lack of faith in God's sovereignty) but also a misreading of our times. To leave the cultural battlefield
now would be to desert the cause just when we are on the threshold of a great
opportunity.

In recent years, all the grand propositions advanced over the past century have fallen, one by one, like toy soldiers. The twentieth century was the
age of ideology, of the great "isms": Communism, socialism, Nazism, liberalism, scientism. Everywhere, ideologues nursed visions of creating the ideal
society by some utopian scheme. But today all the major ideological constructions are being tossed on the ash heap of history. All that remains is the
cynicism of postmodernism, with its bankrupt assertions that there *is* no objective truth or meaning, that we are free to create our own truth as long as
we understand that it is nothing more than a subjective dream, a comforting
illusion.

And as the reigning ideologies crumble, people are caught in an impasse: Having believed that individual autonomy was the holy grail that
would lead to liberation, they now see that it has led only to moral chaos and
state coercion. The time is ripe for a message that the social peace and personal fulfillment people really crave are available only in Christianity. The
church has stood unshaken through the ebb and flow of two millennia. It has
survived the persecutions of the early centuries, the barbarian invasions of
the Middle Ages, and the intellectual assaults of the modern era. Its solid
walls rise up above the ruins littered across the intellectual landscape. God
forbid that we, heirs of saints and martyrs, should falter at this pivotal
moment.

The new millennium is a time for Christians to celebrate, to raise our
confidence, to blow trumpets, and to fly the flag high. This is the time to
make a compelling case that Christianity offers the most rational and realistic hope for both personal redemption and social renewal.

But if we are to have an impact on our culture, the beginning point
must be to take our stand united in Christ, making a conscious effort among
all true believers to come together across racial, ethnic, and confessional
lines. In his high-priestly prayer, Jesus prayed fervently that we would be one
with one another, as he is one with the Father. Why? *So that the world will
know* that he is the Christ (see John 17:20-23). The unavoidable implication

of Jesus' words is that Christian unity is the key to evangelism and cultural renewal. Much of the church's weakness can be traced to its inability or unwillingness to obey the command to strive for unity in Christ.

This is difficult for many evangelicals (as well as Catholics and Orthodox) to accept, and understandably so. The bloody wounds inflicted in the Reformation and Counter-Reformation remain raw and painful, and deep doctrinal differences continue to divide believers. Conservative believers are distrustful of ecumenism because of the danger of glossing over those differences.

Focusing on worldview, however, can help build bridges. Protestants and Catholics who join together in pro-life demonstrations find that they do indeed share the deepest worldview convictions. They discover what one scholar calls "an ecumenism of the trenches."[18] It was in recognition of this common worldview that in 1992 Father Richard Neuhaus and I organized Evangelicals and Catholics Together (ECT), a nonofficial group seeking common ground in our witness to the world and our defense of Christian truth. ECT's joint statements have emphasized the great truths of the faith we hold in common without compromising the very real doctrinal differences that continue to exist.

Our efforts have been controversial, but they should not be. Abraham Kuyper, a committed Calvinist, saw more clearly than any other modern figure that the battle of our times is worldview against worldview, principle against principle, and that in this battle against the forces of modernity, Catholics and Protestants must stand side by side. More than a hundred years ago in his famous Stone Lectures at Princeton, Kuyper argued that when we understand Christianity as a worldview, we "might be enabled once more to take our stand by the side of Romanism in opposition to modern pantheism." For "what we have in common with Rome . . . are precisely those fundamentals of our Christian creed now most fiercely assaulted by the modern spirit." If Roman Catholics "take up the sword to do valiant and skillful battle" against the same enemy, Kuyper concluded, "is it not the part of wisdom to accept their valuable help?"[19]

Yet Kuyper was only echoing themes expressed back in 1541. In the very midst of the Reformation battles, a group of Catholic and Protestant leaders, including a cardinal from the Vatican, met at Regensburg, Germany, in the Colloquy of Ratisbon. The group reached agreement on the doctrine of justification, which had been the great opening wedge of the Reformation (though discussions foundered on other issues, such as the Mass). One of the Protestant participants wrote a letter to a friend, in which he said, "You will be astonished that our opponents yielded so much . . .

[they] have thus retained the substance of the true doctrine."[20] The writer of that letter was a young aide to the Protestant negotiators. His name was John Calvin.

Today we need the kind of stand Calvin sought and Kuyper so powerfully urged on us. We need what C. S. Lewis called *mere Christianity:* believers standing together, rallying around the great truths of Scripture and the ancient creeds. Only when such unity is visible in the world will we truly experience the power of the gospel.

Then, standing together as the people of God, we must obey the two great commissions: first to win the lost and then to build a culture. Christians must seize this moment to show the world, just as the Irish did centuries ago, that Christianity is not only true . . . it is humanity's one great hope.

CHAPTER 32

DON'T WORRY, BE RELIGIOUS

The Christian and the Materialist hold different beliefs about the universe.
They can't both be right. The one who is wrong will act in a way which simply
doesn't fit the real universe.

C. S. LEWIS

How do we redeem a culture? How do we rise to the opportunity before us at the start of a new millennium?

The answer is simple: from the inside out. From the individual to the family to the community, and then outward in ever widening ripples. We must begin by understanding what it means to live by Christian worldview principles in our own behavior and choices. Unless we do, we will interpret the biblical commands according to the spirit of the age and will therefore be conformed to the world rather than to God's Word.

Some years ago, in the middle of a doctrinal discussion, a young man differed with Nancy over a point the apostle Paul makes in 1 Corinthians.

"I disagree with you," he said.

"No, you disagree with Paul," Nancy corrected him gently.

"Okay, then, I disagree with Paul," he shrugged.

He went on to explain that as he saw it, the Bible was written long ago for a different age and that today the Holy Spirit can reveal new truth—truth that might even contradict what the Bible teaches. Now, this young man was a sincere Christian—president of a Christian campus group and a leader among his peers—but he had absorbed the mental framework of a secular culture and was reinterpreting Scripture in the context of that framework. He had lost his understanding of truth and revelation, of a worldview that roots Scripture in the God who is ultimate reality. This carried over into his personal choices, evidenced by the fact that he was sleeping with his girl-friend. He was not untaught in biblical ethics; and he was not deliberately backsliding. His honest convictions told him that the Bible consisted of nothing more than human documents and, therefore, was not normative for his life. Whenever he read Scripture, it was filtered through a mental grid set by a non-Christian worldview, resulting in a distorted understanding of doctrine and personal ethics.

If we want to transform our pagan culture as the monks did in the Middle Ages, we must start with ourselves, understanding what a Christian worldview means for our own moral and lifestyle choices. This is more important today than ever because individual moral choices determine the health of the entire society. Polls consistently show that Americans worry most about social and moral decay—crime, family breakdown, drug abuse, sex and violence in the entertainment media—all results of moral choices made ultimately by individuals.[1]

Given these facts, one might expect the nation's bully pulpits would be devoted to encouraging people to take responsibility for their lives, to exert the self-discipline needed to change their behavior. Instead, for the past few decades, the dominant cultural voices have argued that individuals have a right to live in any way they choose and that *society* has a responsibility to pick up the tab for any negative consequences that result.

This attitude was cleverly illustrated in the comic strip "Outland" during the controversial health-care debate in 1993. In the opening frame, the penguin Opus and his friends are perched precariously on a tricycle at the edge of a precipice. Posted all around are warning signs: Danger! Stop! A surgeon general's warning says "Plummeting down cliffs is hazardous to one's health." But the characters ignore the signs and go careening down. The tricycle topples over, of course, and they all fly off. From the mud, Opus reaches out his hand and demands, "Quick! Free unlimited health care!"[2]

Sadly, this is the attitude many Americans have taken toward the pathologies plaguing both our personal lives and society at large: that our behavior is our own business and that society has a duty to compensate for any negative consequences of our autonomous choices.

Sexual behavior is a prime example. Sexual relationships outside marriage are responsible for the spread of sexually transmitted diseases (STDs), for most abortions, for fatherless homes, and for chronic welfare dependency. But did this social wreckage cause sex educators to teach young people to refrain from sex outside marriage? Hardly. From the 1960s through the 1980s, public school sex-education programs and their advocates were adamant that sexual activity was entirely a matter of the student's personal choice. And when the inevitable consequences followed, these same educators pressed for government solutions to bandage over the negative effects. To avoid STDs, the government supplied condoms in the schools. When homosexual promiscuity led to fatal diseases, the government was blamed and shamed into picking up the tab for more research. When sex led to pregnancy, the government was expected to pay for abortions or supply welfare support to fatherless families.

This attitude began in the 1960s, when a new concept of public morality took hold, stated baldly in the words of sociologist Christopher Jencks. Speaking of fatherless families, Jencks argued that if people "truly prefer a family consisting of a mother, children, and a series of transient males, then it is hardly the federal government's proper business to try to alter this choice." What *is* the government's business then? It "ought to invent ways of providing such [single-parent] families with the same physical and psychic necessities of life available to other kinds of families."[3]

Note carefully what Jencks is saying: The government *must not* seek to help shape the nation's moral climate or discourage irresponsible behavior. Instead, its job is to "invent ways" to compensate for any disadvantages created by the bad choices people make. As psychiatrist David Larson puts it, the government is supposed to make sure people have their cake and eat it, too![4]

This attitude is not confined to the government. It's amazing how many ordinary Americans have fallen into the trap of expecting someone else to pick up the costs of their own irresponsibility. The American Medical Association says the growth in health-care expenses today can be traced largely to "lifestyle factors and social problems." Some studies indicate that up to 70 percent of all diseases result from lifestyle choices.[5] People know they should stop smoking, cut out junk food, and get regular exercise. But how many take these basic steps in preventive care? And when their unhealthy habits give them heart disease or lung cancer, they expect the health-care system to protect them from the consequences of their own bad habits.[6] The Opus cartoon is uncomfortably close to the truth.

Where did this idea of value-free lifestyles come from? What are its worldview roots? How do the categories of *creation, fall,* and *redemption* help us to diagnose what's wrong with the predominant secular view—and to see how a Christian worldview leads to a better, healthier, and more rational way of living?

In a nutshell, if we reject the biblical teaching about creation, we end up with nature as our creator. Morality then becomes something humans invent when they have evolved to a certain level. There is no transcendent source of moral standards that dictates how we should live. Each individual has the right to chart his or her own course. And if we reject the idea of sin and the Fall, nothing is objectively wrong, and there is no real guilt; there are only false guilt feelings that result from social disapproval. The logical conclusion of this thinking is that redemption means freeing ourselves from false guilt and restoring our natural autonomy by eliminating the stigma from all lifestyles. And the role of public authorities is to mobilize resources to make sure that no negative consequences follow from the choices any individual may make. For if all choices are morally equal, then no one should suffer for the choices he or she makes.

By contrast, Christianity claims that God created the universe with a definite structure—a material order and a moral order. If we live contrary to that order, we sin against God, and the consequences are invariably harmful and painful, on both a personal and a social level. On the other hand, if we submit to that order and live in harmony with it, then our lives will be happier and healthier. The role of public authorities is to encourage people to live according to the principles that make for social health and harmony.

Over the past four decades, our public discourse was dominated by the value-free model. Yet today, its disastrous consequences are becoming abundantly clear. Even determined secularists have begun to see that society simply can't keep up with the costs of personal and moral irresponsibility: Over those same four decades, abortion and teen pregnancy soared; the welfare system grew overloaded; crime rates shot up, especially among juveniles; health-care costs climbed so fast that the government keeps threatening to take over (even as Medicare projects bankruptcy in a few years). It is becoming increasingly obvious that the welfare state has *not* been able to "invent ways" to give fatherless families "the same physical and psychic necessities of life available to other kinds of families," as Jencks put it.[7] Instead, welfare has helped create a permanent underclass that is disordered and demoralized. By compensating for irresponsible behavior, government has, in essence, subsidized it, thus encouraging more of it.

Americans have reached "the modernist impasse": They were told they had a right to be free from the restrictions of morality and religion, yet as unrestricted choices have led to social breakdown, they have begun to long for the protection that morality once provided. After all, we didn't *have* epidemics of crime, broken families, abortion, or sexually transmitted diseases when Americans largely accepted biblical morality. Many are beginning to understand that morality is not merely an arbitrary constraint on individual choice but a protection against social disintegration.

That's why, after decades of public rhetoric about individual rights, we now hear cultural leaders struggling to find some common secular language to revive a sense of civic duty and virtue. Organizations like David Blankenhorn's National Fatherhood Initiative are emerging to halt family breakdown. Sex educators are beginning to talk about teaching kids to delay sexual involvement (if not until marriage, at least until adulthood). Character education is making inroads into classrooms.

This new openness to moral arguments gives Christians an extraordinary opportunity to make our case that living according to the biblical moral order is healthier for both individuals and society. And there's a growing body of scientific evidence we can use to back up our argument. Medical studies are confirming that those who attend church regularly and act consistently with their faith are better off, both physically and mentally. Consider a few recent findings. [8]

Alcohol Abuse: Alcohol abuse is highest among those with little or no religious commitment.[9] One study found that nearly 89 percent of alcoholics said they lost interest in religion during their youth.[10]

Drug Abuse: Numerous studies have found an inverse correlation between religious commitment and drug abuse. Among young people, the importance of religion is the single best predictor of substance-abuse patterns. Joseph Califano, former secretary of the department of Health and Human Services and an architect of Lyndon Johnson's Great Society, did an amazing about-face when he became head of Columbia University's Center on Addiction and Substance Abuse. In 1998, Califano invited me, along with General McAffrey, Clinton's antidrug czar, to join him at a press conference where he released the results of a three-year study showing the relationship between substance abuse and crime. The statistics were startling: In 80 percent of criminal offenses, alcohol or drugs were implicated.[11] Then Califano pointed at me and told the assembled press gathering, "He has the answer. Every individual I have met who successfully came off drugs or alcohol has given religion as the key to rehabilitation." Califano now vigorously supports public funding for drug-treatment programs that "provide for spiritual needs."[12]

Crime: There is also a strong correlation between participation in religious activities and the avoidance of crime. In one study, Harvard professor Richard Freeman discovered that regular church attendance is the primary factor in preventing African-American urban young people from turning to drugs or crime.[13] Another study revealed that regular attendance at a Prison Fellowship Bible study cut recidivism by two-thirds.[14]

Depression and Stress: Several studies have found that high levels of religious commitment correlate with lower levels of depression and stress.[15] In one Gallup survey, respondents with a strong religious commitment were twice as likely to describe themselves as "very happy."[16] Armand Nicholi, professor of psychiatry at Harvard Medical School and a deeply committed believer, argues from his lifelong experience that Christians are far less likely to experience mental disorders than their secular counterparts. Why? Because "the one essential feature that characterizes all types of depression" is "the feeling of hopelessness and helplessness," and Christians are never without hope.[17]

Suicide: Persons who do not attend church are four times more likely to commit suicide than are frequent church attenders. In fact, lack of church attendance correlates more strongly with suicide rates than with any other risk factor, including unemployment.[18]

Family Stability: A number of studies have found a strong inverse correlation between church attendance and divorce, and one study found that church attendance is the most important predictor of marital stability.[19] Religion has also shown itself to be an important factor in preventing teen sexual relations, babies born out of wedlock, discord between parent and child, and other forms of family breakdown.

The classic sociological research project "Middletown" studied the inhabitants of a typical American town three times, first in the 1920s and for the third time in the 1980s. The data over this extended period indicated a clear "relationship between family solidarity—family health, if you will—and church affiliation and activity."[20] In a study of the factors that contribute to healthy families, 84 percent of strong families identified religion as an important contributor to their strength. In yet another study, African-American parents cited church influence as significant in rearing their children and providing moral guidelines.[21]

Marital and Sexual Satisfaction: Lest one think these numbers mean that religious people are staying in unhappy marriages from a sense of duty, consider these statistics. Churchgoers are more likely to say they would marry the same spouse again—an important measure of marital satisfaction. A 1978 study found that church attendance predicted marital satisfaction better than any other single variable.[22] And the 1994 Sex in America study showed that very religious women enjoy a higher level of sexual satisfaction in their marriage than do nonreligious women.[23]

Physical Health: Studies have shown that maternity patients and their newborns have fewer medical complications if the mothers have a religious affiliation. Belonging to a religious group can lower blood pressure, relieve stress, and enhance survival after a heart attack. Heart surgery patients with strong religious beliefs are much more likely to survive surgery. Elderly men and women who attend worship services are less depressed and physically healthier than their peers with no religious faith. They are also healthier than those who do not attend worship services but watch religious television at home. People who go to church have lower blood pressure, even when risky behaviors such as smoking are factored in.[24]

Church attendance even affects mortality rates. For men who attend church frequently, the risk of dying from arteriosclerotic heart disease is only 60 percent of that for men who attend infrequently. The death rates of churchgoing men from pulmonary emphysema are less than half and from cirrhosis of the liver only 25 percent as high as for nonchurchgoing men.[25] Science seems to be confirming the teaching of Proverbs: "The fear of the Lord adds length to life" (Prov. 10:27).

■   ■   ■

THIS DOES NOT MEAN that every person of faith is healthy and happy, but the statistics do "make a powerful statement about the typical human condition," writes Patrick Glynn in *God: The Evidence*. Both clinical experience and research data suggest that "among the most important determinants of human happiness and well-being are our spiritual beliefs and moral choices."[26]

The statistics are so compelling that even a confirmed secularist ought to be convinced that religion is good for society. In fact, that's exactly what Guenter Lewy concludes in his recent book *Why America Needs Religion*. Lewy started out to write a book defending secularism, but after surveying the data, he ended up arguing, to his own surprise, that belief in God makes people happier and more fulfilled. "Whether it be juvenile delinquency, adult crime, prejudice, out-of-wedlock births, or marital conflict and divorce, there is a significantly lower rate of such indicators of moral failure and social ills among believing Christians."[27] In short, a person *can* live a moral and healthy life without God, but statistically speaking, the odds are against it.

Furthermore, the benefits of Christianity are not solely a matter of attitude and lifestyle. It is impossible to dismiss the frankly supernatural. Dr. Dale Matthews has documented experiments in which volunteers prayed for selected patients with rheumatoid arthritis. To avoid a possible placebo effect from knowing they were being prayed for, the patients were not told which ones were subjects of the test. The recovery rate among those prayed for was measurably higher than among a control group, for which prayers were not offered.[28]

It is time for the medical profession to recognize the healing potential of the spiritual dimension, says Harvard professor Herbert Benson. Though not a professing Christian himself, Benson admits that humans are "engineered for religious faith." We are "wired for God. . . . Our genetic blueprint has made believing in an Infinite Absolute part of our nature."[29] That is about as close as a nonbeliever can get to confirming the biblical claim that the human spirit was created in order to live in communion with God.

These findings do not mean, however, that just any kind of religion is beneficial. Gordon Allport, the great psychologist of religion, drew a distinction between *intrinsic* and *extrinsic* religion. Extrinsically religious people use religion for external purposes, like the politician who attends church to gain respectability or the person who prays for purely material benefits. But intrinsically religious people serve God without ulterior motive: They pray in order to commune with him and understand his truth; they give without any utilitarian calculation. In Allport's professional experience, improved mental health correlates only with intrinsic religion. The benefits go to those who genuinely believe, not to those who use religion for ulterior purposes.[30] These findings seem to shatter the Freudian stereotype of religion as mere wish fulfillment, something we make up to obtain certain benefits. For if we were to make up a religion for external purposes, we would be more miserable than ever.

Similarly, benefits accrue only to those who practice their faith, not to those who merely profess it. In fact, the Larsons' studies have found that it is extremely *un*healthy to hold strong religious beliefs without practicing them. People exhibit high levels of stress if they believe in God but neglect church attendance, fail to read and meditate on Scripture, omit prayer before meals, or fall into sin. One study of chronic alcoholics found that a surprisingly high number hold conservative religious beliefs but are not acting on them. The Larsons suggest that the stress caused by this contradiction between belief and practice may contribute to their alcoholism.[31]

In short, the inconsistent Christian suffers even more than the consistent atheist. The most miserable person of all is the one who knows the truth yet doesn't obey it.

■   ■   ■

THE GROWTH IN scientific evidence validating the Christian worldview has been greatly inspired by the work of one man, David Larson, president of the National Institute for Healthcare Research. Larson's story illustrates not only how Christians should persevere in their convictions but also what we can achieve when we do.

When Larson began his training in psychiatry, one of his professors tried to discourage him. "Tell me, Dave," the professor said. "Your faith is important to you, isn't it?"

"Yes," said Larson.

"Then I think you should put aside the idea of becoming a psychiatrist. For psychiatric patients, religion can only be harmful."

Larson's professor was stating the conventional wisdom among psychiatrists and psychologists, handed down from Sigmund Freud, the founder of psychoanalysis, who defined religion as "a universal obsessional neurosis," an "infantile helplessness," and "regression to primary narcissism." The terminology has changed since Freud, but most psychologists and psychiatrists retain the assumption that religion is a negative factor in mental health and that it is associated with mental pathologies.[32]

Yet Larson refused to be deterred. And as he continued his studies, he noticed a very interesting pattern: Religion was not associated with mental illness after all. In fact, quite the opposite: Religion actually helped protect *against* mental disorders.

This insight spurred Larson to conduct his own research, and today his work has begun to turn around an entire profession. "Growing numbers of psychologists are finding religion, if not in their personal lives, at least in their data," reports the *New York Times*. "What was once, at best, an unfashionable topic in psychology has been born again as a respectable focus for scientific research."[33] The data is showing that religion, far from being a mental illness, is actually beneficial to mental health, physical health, family strength, and social order.

This new scientific data provides a wonderful tool for apologetics, for it shows clearly that if we ignore biblical principles, we end up living in ways that run against the grain of our being, and we pay a steep price in terms of stress, depression, family conflict, and even physical illness. Rather than being an arbitrary set of rules and restrictions that repress and distort our true nature, Christianity actually describes our true nature and shows us how to live in accord with it. And when we do so, we enjoy the fruits of operating the way we were made to. "The fear of the Lord is the beginning of wisdom. . . . For through me your days will be many, and years will be added to your life" (Prov. 9:10-11). The evidence is a powerful validation of Proverbs; a biblical view of human nature does indeed conform to reality.

Recognizing these concrete benefits of faith, many Christians are joining together for their own financial, spiritual, and emotional advantage—as well as to provide an effective witness to the broader culture. For example, the Florida-based Christian Care Medi-Share Program offers members 100 percent coverage for far less than most conventional group insurance programs—a little under $200 per family, per month. In return, members commit to living a healthy lifestyle: no smoking, no illegal drugs, no sex outside marriage, moderation in alcohol use. They also pray for one another. When a group member suffers illness or injury, others pray and write letters of encouragement. John Reinhold, founder and president of Christian Care Medi-Share Program, says, "Our members believe in sharing and caring, but they do not wish to subsidize those . . . who choose to live in a way which inevitably leads to a premature breakdown in mind and body."[34]

We cannot escape the consequences of our own choices. In our bodies, we flesh out either the biblical worldview or a worldview that is in opposition to the Bible. And when we incarnate the truth of God in our lives and families, we help bring new life to our neighborhoods and churches, our cities and nation, in an ever widening circle.

CHAPTER 33

GOD'S TRAINING GROUND

If the family trends of recent decades are extended into the future, the result will be not only growing uncertainty within marriage, but the gradual elimination of marriage in favor of casual liaisons oriented to adult expressiveness and self-fulfillment. The problem with this scenario is that children will be harmed, adults will probably be no happier, and the social order could collapse.

DAVID POPENOE

Imagine your children bringing home a library book that assures them divorce is nothing serious, just a transition some families go through. Or *don't* imagine it. Go to the library yourself, and you'll find a rainbow of children's books that downplay the importance of an intact marriage.

"There are different kinds of daddies," one book for preschoolers reassures them. "Sometimes a daddy goes away like yours did. He may not see his children at all." In other words, divorce is just a normal variation on fatherhood. "Some kids know both their mom and their dad, and some kids don't," says another book. Still another treats divorce as an awkward moment that can be mastered by applying a few practical tips. "Living with one parent almost always means there will be less money. Be prepared to give up some things."[1]

The message? That daddies who stay and daddies who leave are just "different kinds of daddies" and that divorce has no moral significance.

The message does not end with picture books for young children. When the Institute for American Values surveyed twenty of the most widely used college textbooks in undergraduate courses on marriage and family, it uncovered a shockingly negative outlook on the subject.[2] The textbooks

emphasize problems such as domestic violence while downplaying the benefits of marriage. They warn women that marriage is likely to be psychologically stifling and even physically threatening. "We do know," states one
textbook, " . . . that marriage has an adverse effect on women's mental
health," an assertion that has no support in empirical data. In fact, most
studies find that both men and women report higher levels of happiness
when they are married.[3] Meanwhile, these volumes all but ignore the
well-documented negative effects of divorce on children, only half even
mentioning the fact that family breakdown correlates strongly with increased juvenile crime.

It would not have been surprising if the Institute for American Values
study had found a few ideologically biased textbooks. What is disturbing is
the finding that virtually *all* the textbooks used by students across the nation
are preaching the views of radical feminism and the sexual revolution to our
nation's future teachers, guidance counselors, and caseworkers.

Out of sheer self-interest, if for no other reason, nearly every civilization has protected the family both legally and socially, for it is the institution
that propagates the human race and civilizes children. Yet in postmodern
America, the family is being assaulted on many fronts, from books to popular magazines, on television and in movies, through state and federal policies. This systematic deconstruction of the oldest, most basic social
institution is a prime cause of the social chaos in America in recent decades.

As we move out from the range of individuals and their choices, the
first circle of influence is in the intimate relationships of the family. Nowhere is the clash of worldviews more pronounced than here. Nowhere are
its effects more disastrous. Nowhere does it touch more deeply on the natural order that underlies all civilizations. And nowhere is it more evident that
we Christians must take a worldview approach if we are going to make a difference. Many believers have become politically active over issues related to
the family, yet typically our efforts are reactive rather than proactive, largely
because we have failed to confront the underlying worldview assumptions.

THE FAMILY IN AN AGE OF MURPHY BROWN

Conflicting worldviews over the family were displayed sharply in 1992 when
then Vice President Dan Quayle delivered his infamous "Murphy Brown"
speech, which evoked howls of ridicule from one end of the country to the
other. Many Americans tuned in to the next season's opening show just to
hear Candice Bergen's response. And the star did not disappoint. As

Murphy Brown, she looked straight into the camera and lectured viewers that there is no normative definition of the family. All that matters, she intoned, is "commitment, love, and caring."

Shortly afterward, however, Bergen was interviewed in *TV Guide* and took quite a different line. "As far as my family values go," she said, "my child and my family have always been my top priority." Bergen even claimed that she had been one step ahead of Dan Quayle, having warned the show's producers not to "send out the message . . . to young women especially, that we're encouraging them to be single mothers." She ended by declaring that "I myself . . . believe the ideal is that you have a two-parent family. I'm the last person to think fathers are obsolete."[4] When speaking as cultural icon Murphy Brown, she insists there is no normative family structure. But as Candice Bergen, wife and mother, she enthusiastically supports the committed, two-parent family.

If we are to understand contemporary moral liberalism, we must dissect this puzzling inconsistency. We live in an age in which liberty has been defined as absolutely free choice. It doesn't matter *what* we choose; the dignity of the individual resides in the mere capacity to choose. So we are perfectly free to favor marriage and traditional values, just as long as we don't deny others the right to choose other values. That is, as long as we don't claim that our choice is based on an objective, normative standard of truth that applies to everyone.

So Bergen feels perfectly free to reveal her own adherence to traditional ideals for the family because all she's doing is expressing her own private, personal, subjective opinion. But when Dan Quayle expresses identical ideals, he is savaged in the media and ridiculed by late-night comedians. Even Bergen condemned him as "arrogant," "aggressive," and "offensive"—even though she apparently holds precisely the same views.[5] Why? Because Quayle is presenting these views not as personal preferences but as objective moral truths.

This subtle distinction is at the heart of the moral conflicts dividing our culture today. As a result, we cannot determine people's worldview simply by asking about their position on particular moral questions: Are you for or against abortion? Are you for or against homosexual marriage? Instead, we must ask how they *justify* their views. Many Americans retain traditional ideals but regard them as matters of personal choice, refusing to insist on them as objective, universal norms. The most familiar example is those who are "personally opposed" to abortion yet defend the right of others to make their own choice. In their own lives, many Americans practice exemplary ethical behavior, yet when asked to articulate objective principles to justify that behavior, they can offer nothing beyond, "It feels right for me."[6]

This is certainly true when it comes to family and sexuality. People use the traditional terms *marriage* and *family,* but the words no longer muster a sense of objective obligation. Many Americans no longer treat marriage as a moral commitment with its own definition and nature, a commitment that makes objective demands of us, regardless of what we might prefer. Instead, marriage is regarded as a social construction, as something one can define according to one's own preferences. Even some who wear the mantle of moral conservatism fall into this trap. At the 1992 Republican National Convention, former First Lady Barbara Bush came out with this fuzzy statement: "However *you* define family, that's what we mean by family values."[7]

It's important that we cut through the rhetoric and get to the root of this conflict, which again hinges on our basic assumptions about *creation, fall,* and *redemption.* The Christian worldview teaches that from the beginning, God created individuals in relationship. By creating human beings as male and female, God established the interrelatedness of human sexuality, the marital relationship, and the institution of the family, each with its own divinely given moral norms. While there can be great variety in the cultural expression of these institutions, when we enter into the covenant of marriage and family, we submit to an objective and God-given structure.

But during the Enlightenment, philosophers began rejecting the doctrine of creation and substituting a hypothetical presocial, prepolitical "state of nature." In this primeval state, individuals are the only ultimate reality; social bonds are created by the choices individuals make. That's why French philosopher Pierre Manent says the basic tenet of modern liberalism is that "no individual can have an obligation to which he has not consented."[8]

This radically changes one's view of marriage, for if it is not rooted in the way we were originally created, but only in individual choice, then it is also something we can *alter* by choice. What's more, all choices become morally equivalent, and there is no justification for favoring some choices over others. If someone wants a traditional marriage, that's fine. If someone else wants a same-sex marriage or some other variant, well, that's fine, too.

This moral equivalence has led to an aggressive defense of deviant practices. In Hollywood, for example, it's become normal to have children out of wedlock and to grow patchwork families from various couplings. For these people, foregoing marriage is not merely a matter of unrestrained sexual urges but an expression of genuine conviction, an assertion that cohabitation is as morally acceptable as marriage.

Film critic Michael Medved found that out when he commended the film production work of a particular Hollywood couple, referring to them as "married." This was a natural assumption, since they had been together more than fifteen years and had given birth to two children. Ah, but one can no longer assume such things, and Medved received an angry letter from a friend of the couple, saying that the two were certainly *not* married and that they would be "offended" to hear themselves described that way. [9]

Offended? Assuming that someone is married is now an insult? What we're seeing is that challenges to traditional morality are themselves treated as moral crusades. For if no choices are wrong, then no lifestyle may be criticized, and one must never be made to feel guilty. Indeed, doing so is positively wrong. Put in worldview terms, in modern liberalism, the only "sin" is hemming others in with oppressive rules and artificial moral codes; "redemption" means restoring the freedom once enjoyed in the original state of nature. As political philosopher John Stuart Mill once wrote, "the mere example of nonconformity, the mere refusal to bend the knee to custom, is itself a service."[10] Now, *there's* a positive spin on immorality: If you deliberately reject moral and social rules, you're actually performing a service, helping to free people from the grip of oppressive moral traditions.

This is the philosophy of the "unencumbered self," says Harvard political philosopher Michael Sandel, a worldview that depicts the isolated self as prior to all commitments or moral obligations. In traditional societies, a person's identity was found in and expressed through the social roles he or she played in the family, church, village, trade, tribe, and ethnic group. Today, however, roles and responsibilities are regarded as separate from, even contradictory to, one's essential identity, one's core self. The self can either accept or reject them in the process of defining itself.[11]

This may sound abstract, but it has intensely practical consequences. One of the themes of the radical feminist movement has been that women are stifled by the roles of wife and mother and must discover their true self *apart* from these relationships. As a result, the past few decades have seen a vast migration of women into the paid workforce, as personal fulfillment became more important than marriage and family to many women. The sharp rise in abortion can be seen as a strong indicator of a decreased interest in bearing children. Similarly, the increased use of day care reflects in part a lower commitment to being the primary caregiver for one's own children. Dr. Stanley Greenspan, pediatrics professor at the George Washington University School of Medicine, observes that this is the first time in history that there's been a growing trend for middle-class families "to farm out the care of their babies."[12]

The source of these trends, however, is not solely feminism. One reason women found the theme of autonomy so persuasive is that it had already been adopted by *men* for nearly half a century. In colonial times, manhood was defined in terms of responsibility for the family and the common good; today, "true" masculinity tends to be defined as individualistic, aggressive, and self-assertive. This new image emerged at the end of the nineteenth century in cowboy and adventure fiction that "celebrated the man who had escaped the confines of domesticity."[13] By the 1950s, *Playboy* came on the scene, warning that marriage is a trap that will "crush man's adventurous, freedom-loving spirit."[14] The roles of husband and father, instead of being God-ordained responsibilities that express a man's essential nature, came to be seen as restricting conventions that contradict a man's true self. This bore deadly fruit as men deserted their family responsibilities, a trend so wide-spread today that the dominant social problem in America is male flight from the family.[15]

The notion of the "unencumbered self" has caused both men and women to view family relationships as arbitrary and confining roles. That's why people like sexuality researcher Shere Hite can insist that "the breakdown of the family is a good thing," because it liberates us from restrictive roles and rules.[16]

This negative view of marriage has yielded consequences across the entire culture. If people dare to say that marriage is superior to other arrangements, they are accused of "discrimination." Elayne Bennett, founder of Best Friends, a program that teaches girls to delay sexual involvement until after high school, was once asked why she did not urge girls to delay sex until marriage. "If we talk about marriage," she said, "the schools won't let us in."[17] Let that sink in for a moment: Many public schools today *won't even consider* a program that holds up marriage as an ideal. (Since the first publication of this book, Elayne Bennett has reported some encouraging changes. Her excellent program is being allowed in some schools, even when they talk about delaying sexual involvement until marriage.)

In addition, many public policies no longer protect marriage as a unique social good. In tax law, there's the marriage penalty; in business, there are spousal benefits for people who are not married; in the courts, there are rulings that put homosexual unions on the same level as marriage.[18] The family is treated as a loose collection of rights-bearing individuals who hook up with others in whatever ways they choose to for their own benefit.

Popular culture echoes this message. The same people who bring us those heartwarming Hallmark family films also produced a wedding card that reads, "I can't promise you forever. But I can promise you today." Equally telling, a cartoon in a major magazine depicts a young man saying to his girlfriend, "It's only marriage I'm proposing, after all, not a lifetime commitment." Acclaimed novelist Toni Morrison has said the nuclear family "is a paradigm that just doesn't work. . . . Why we are hanging on to it, I don't know."[19] And popular entertainment consistently portrays divorce and adultery as forms of liberation. In the closing scene of the hit movie *Mrs. Doubtfire,* the central character reassures a young girl after her parents' breakup that after divorce some parents "get along much better . . . and they can become better people and much better mommies and daddies."[20]

How about a reality check here? Social science statistics show that divorced parents *don't* generally become "better mommies and daddies." Few fathers even see their children regularly, and mothers spend less time with their children, too, because of the emotional devastation they suffer and the increased responsibilities they bear. In fact, the negative consequences of divorce are being measured over and over again, and the findings are grim.[21]

Consider these statistics. Children in single-parent families are six times more likely to be poor, and half the single mothers in the United States live below the poverty line. Children of divorce suffer intense grief, which often lasts for many years. Even as young adults, they are nearly twice as likely to require psychological help. Children from disrupted families have more academic and behavioral problems at school and are nearly twice as likely to drop out of high school.[22] Girls in single-parent homes are at much greater risk for precocious sexuality and are three times more likely to have a child out of wedlock.[23]

Crime and substance abuse are strongly linked to fatherless households. Studies show that 60 percent of rapists grew up in fatherless homes, as did 72 percent of adolescent murderers and 70 percent of all long-term prison inmates. In fact, most of the social pathologies disrupting American life today can be traced to fatherlessness.[24]

Surprisingly, when divorced parents marry again, their children are not any better off, and some studies actually show that the children develop increased pathologies. Preschool children in stepfamilies, for example, are forty times more likely to suffer physical or sexual abuse.[25]

Adults are also profoundly harmed by divorce. A study that examined the impact of divorce ten years after the divorce found that among two-thirds of divorced couples, one partner is still depressed and financially precarious. And among a quarter of all divorced couples, *both* former partners are worse off, suffering loneliness and depression.[26]

Divorce affects even physical health. Children of divorce are more prone to illness, accidents, and suicide. Divorced men are twice as likely as married men to die from heart disease, stroke, hypertension, and cancer. They are four times more likely to die in auto accidents and suicide, and their odds are seven times higher for pneumonia and cirrhosis of the liver. Divorced women lose 50 percent more time to illness and injury each year than do married women, and they are two to three times as likely to die of all forms of cancer. Both divorced men and women are almost five times more likely to succumb to substance abuse.[27]

The impact of divorce on health, says David Larson, president of the National Institute for Healthcare Research, "is like starting to smoke a pack of cigarettes a day."[28]

And the effects don't stop with the families directly involved. When family breakdown becomes widespread, entire neighborhoods decay. Neighborhoods without fathers are often infected with crime and delinquency. They are often places where teachers cannot teach because misbehaving children disrupt classrooms. Moreover, children of divorce are much more likely to get divorced themselves as adults, so that the negative consequences pass on to the next generation. In this way, family breakdown affects the entire society.[29]

Generation Xers often sense these truths better than their babyboomer parents do. Many have suffered through their parents' divorce(s) and typically say they desperately hope for a marriage that will endure, while at the same time they are profoundly pessimistic about marriage. When grunge-rock star Kurt Cobain committed suicide, reporters digging into his private life discovered that when he was eight years old, his parents divorced, sending him into a sharp downward spiral. "It destroyed him," admits his mother, Wendy Cobain. "He changed completely." The experience was so painful that when Cobain made an earlier suicide attempt in 1994, he had a note in his pocket that said, "I'd rather die than go through a divorce."[30]

The time is ripe for Christians to make a persuasive case for a biblical view of marriage and family, using statistics like these to frame a convincing argument that people are happier and healthier in stable families. And then we must learn how to model the biblical view before a watching world.

MARRIAGE AS A MYSTIC MIRROR

What does the Christian worldview say about the family? The doctrine of creation tells us God made us with a definite nature (in his image) and gave us a definite task: to nurture and develop the powers of nature (fill the earth and subdue it) and to form families and create societies (be fruitful and increase in number). The image of God is reflected, in part, in the differentiation of humanity into two sexes: "God created man in his own image . . . male and female he created them" (Gen. 1:27). The implication is that to be a husband or wife, a father or mother, is not an artificial or arbitrary role separate from our "true" self, a threat to authentic personhood. Instead, these relationships form an intrinsic part of our fundamental identity, of what makes us fully human. Liberation is not found by escaping these roles but by embracing them and carrying out our responsibilities in a manner faithful to God's ideals.

In other parts of Scripture, we learn that marriage is also rich in spiritual symbolism and meaning—a mystical mirror of the relationship between God and his people. Ancient fertility religions often imagined God to be both male and female, and pagan theology was expressed in fertility celebrations involving ritual fornication in temple prostitution. That's why, in the Old Testament, idolatry is often called fornication. But biblical theology was expressed in marriage, with the faithful love between husband and wife as an image of God's faithful love for his people. In the New Testament, Paul likens the relationship between a husband and a wife to the "profound mystery" of Christ's union with his bride, the church (see Eph. 5).

As husband and wife come together, they form a family, the core institution of human society—the training ground, in fact, for all other social institutions. Human sexuality is not designed only as a source of pleasure or a means of expressing affection. It was designed as a powerful bond between husband and wife in order to form a secure, stable environment for raising vulnerable children to adulthood. Family life is the "first school" that prepares us to participate in the religious, civic, and political life of society, training us in the virtues that enable us to place the common good before our own private goals. Saying no to sex outside marriage means saying yes to this broader vision of marriage as the foundation of an enduring institution that not only meets personal needs but also ties us into a wider community through mutual obligations and benefits.

It's not enough to insist that sex outside marriage is sinful or that practicing homosexuality is wrong. We must learn to articulate in a positive way the overall biblical worldview that makes sense of these moral principles. We must explain what it means to live within an objective, created moral order instead of perpetuating the chaotic reign of the autonomous self.

HOW TO BE A MARRIAGE SAVER

How well has the church taught this biblical model and helped believers to live it? Some of the best work has been done by parachurch organizations such as James Dobson's Focus on the Family. Dobson's books, articles, and radio programs have been singularly effective, and we cannot know this side of heaven how much they have done to help strengthen families and increase their dedication to living by biblical principles.

Sadly, local churches have not always been as effective. Their response to the decline of marriage has often been helpless hand-wringing and haranguing against a decadent culture. Few clergy have been equipped to put the brakes on the destructive trends that have torn marriages apart at ever increasing rates, even within their own congregations.

What are some of the most important principles that churches can teach families? For starters, believers should be encouraged to treat their own families as a ministry—a mission to the surrounding culture. Many friends of mine have this kind of vision for their families, and one family in particular has achieved bountiful success. As a young couple, Jack and Rhodora Donahue decided that their job as Christians was to produce a strong family. Today, they have 13 children and 75 grandchildren, and all are committed Christians. Some are clergy, some are involved in starting Christian schools, and most are active in lay ministries such as Young Life and Prison Fellowship. And the Donahues continue to educate their children and grandchildren, often holding dinner parties where they invite speakers to address topical issues, then spend the entire evening discussing related theological, philosophical, and moral questions.

As a stirring historical model, consider Jonathan Edwards, the Congregational pastor, scholar, and leader of the First Great Awakening. He and his wife, Sarah, reared 11 children; and by the year 1900, the family had 1,400 descendants, among them 13 college presidents, 65 professors, 100 lawyers, 30 judges, 66 physicians, and 80 prominent public officials, including 3 governors, 3 senators, and a vice president of the United States.[31] With families of such learning and distinction, it's no wonder the Puritans did so much to shape the American mind and character. If modern evangelicals hope to leave the same powerful legacy, we need to realize that the task of culture building requires a long-term commitment, and we must focus on nurturing godly families to influence future generations.

Whether your family is small or large, whether your resources are sparse or extensive, every Christian parent is called to make the home a ministry. That means educating our children in a biblical worldview and equipping them to have an impact on the world. In the long run, this is the best way that Christians can restore and redeem the surrounding culture.

How can the church nurture such families? A few years ago, Washington journalist Michael McManus searched out the best programs for engaged couples, for marriage enrichment, and for rescuing seriously troubled marriages. What started out as research for writing columns has ended up as a ministry. Mike has organized an overall strategy he calls Marriage Savers, and the programs in this positive, biblically based approach are making a difference across the country. When several churches in a community agree to adopt the Marriage Savers strategy, it *does* lower the local divorce rate and make marriages stronger.[32]

Consider some of the effective programs that Marriage Savers brings together:

Smart Dating: A couple's habits of relating to one another are formed long before they walk down the aisle. That means the church must begin by helping dating couples, and the first message they need to hear is that if you want a good marriage, avoid premarital sexual relations. The National Survey of Family Growth found that women who were not virgins when they got married have a 71 percent higher divorce rate. Saying no to premarital sex means saying yes to a stronger marriage.[33]

Trial Is Error: Many couples regard living together as a sort of trial marriage, a way to test their compatibility, making for a better marriage later. But the reality is just the opposite: Cohabitation is almost certain to *destroy* their chances of a good marriage. About 90 percent of the couples who live together say they want to get married, but the National Survey of Families and Households found that almost half break up before signing a marriage license. Those who do marry are 50 percent more likely to divorce. Living together is not preparation for marriage; it literally sets up couples for failure.[34]

Engaging Couples: Many churches have become "blessing machines," willing to marry any couple that comes knocking, without giving them any training in how to have a strong marriage. In fact, three-quarters of all weddings are blessed in a church or synagogue, which means churches are implicated in the nation's staggering divorce rate. Yet churches have access to excellent and effective programs such as PREPARE (Premarital Personal and Relationship Evaluation), which helps couples identify their strengths and weaknesses so they can iron out major conflicts *before* saying "I do." Another effective program is Engaged Encounter, an intensive weekend program that teaches couples how to relate more effectively. Both can prepare couples to face the difficulties that beset even the best marriage.[35]

Wedding Shock: After the romantic enchantment wears off, many couples face the most critical time of marriage, for most divorces trace back to habits established in those early years. ENRICH is a program to support fledgling marriages by enabling couples to inventory their strengths and weaknesses, identifying key problem areas.[36] In Old Testament law, a recently married man was exempt from military and other duties for one year so he could "be free to stay at home and bring happiness to the wife he has married" (Deut. 24:5). Clearly, the biblical principle is to protect and nurture young couples.

Divorce Insurance: No church needs to stand by while couples in the congregation break up. One of the best programs available to help couples is Marriage Encounter, an intensive weekend retreat with a 90 percent success rate in strengthening marriages. And for seriously troubled marriages, there is Retrouvaille (a French word meaning "recovery"), which works on the Alcoholics Anonymous model, with personal counseling by couples who themselves have worked through serious marriage problems. Of the couples who have attended Retrouvaille, nearly half were already separated or divorced, yet 80 percent have reunited and stayed together.[37]

In fact, all Marriage Savers programs rely on older couples as mentors. Whether working with engaged couples, newlyweds, or seriously troubled marriages, the most effective counselors are couples who have successfully worked through their own difficulties.

Sometimes pastors are hesitant to require couples to undergo counseling, for fear they will simply go to another church down the street. To forestall that, McManus has established Community Marriage Policies, in which several churches in a city agree together to impose uniform minimal requirements on couples who want to marry. The results have been dramatic. The first city to adopt this policy was Modesto, California, where clergy from ninety-five churches agreed to require couples to undergo four months of marriage preparation, take a premarital inventory, and meet with a mentor couple. A decade later, the city's divorce rate had dropped 40 percent, despite a large increase in the population. In the two years that a Community Marriage Policy has been in effect in the Kansas suburbs of Kansas City, divorces have dropped by more than a third (while in the Missouri suburbs of the same city where there was no program, divorces increased). By the end of 1998, a hundred cities had adopted Community Marriage Policies, and nine have been in place long enough to produce a measurable drop in the local divorce rate.[38]

Community Marriage Policies have been so successful that in some places they have attracted attention outside the church. In Grand Rapids, Michigan, the mayor of Kentwood, a major suburb, persuaded more than two thousand leaders from local businesses, universities, and government to come together and examine how "current policies . . . may undermine marriage formation," and to outline changes that might "promote marriage and stable families." Mayor Bill Hardiman made his appeal not on the basis of religion but on the need to "improve the well-being of children."[39]

In another part of Michigan, District Court Chief Judge James Sheridan persuaded the clergy of sixty churches to sign a Community Marriage Policy. Then, in an unusual step, Sheridan also elicited a voluntary agreement among all the judges, magistrates, and mayors who perform civil weddings to require couples to go through premarital counseling. "Divorce is a community issue, not just a religious matter," Sheridan explains, and he is quite right. "Divorce affects my caseload as a judge, and that of every judge in the U.S." He cites the statistics: "The number of alcohol-related problems doubles as you go from married to divorced. The mortality rate of both men and women is much higher if you're divorced. People tend to have accidents or illnesses that cause community expense." Then, too, many divorced mothers need government assistance. "Where does the money come from to take care of kids on welfare? From taxes." The entire community pays the price of marriage breakdown, and as a result, the entire community has an interest in programs that make marriages stronger.[40]

Much of this renewed effort is the result of the pressure exerted by Michael McManus, and he is an inspiring example of the difference just one Christian can make. A friendly giant of a man, McManus and his wife, Harriet, a tiny woman who mirrors his enthusiasm, are changing the way churches minister to married couples. And the surrounding culture finally seems ready to hear what the churches are saying as well.

Back in the 1970s, books touted divorce as liberation, with titles like *Creative Divorce* and *Divorce: The New Freedom.*[41] The common presumption was that divorce creates only temporary distress and that individuals soon bounce back and go on to form new and more meaningful relationships. Divorce was even presented as a chance for inner growth and self-actualization. But the moral tides are turning, and people are showing a growing concern for the social cost of family breakdown, reflected in titles such as *The Case against Divorce* by Diane Medved, *Divorce Busting* by Michele Weiner-Davis, and *Rethinking Divorce* by William Galston.[42] There are even efforts under way to eliminate no-fault divorce, which gives all the legal power to those who walk away from their family commitments. Christians ought to line up behind efforts like these to build moral accountability back into family law.

The family is one arena where we as Christians can and must be a redemptive force. Yet as we work to incorporate biblical principles within our own families, we inevitably come up against the counterforce of public education. Nowhere has the secular worldview gained a firmer foothold than in our nation's schools, and since the education of our children shapes the future, we must begin to take our redemptive message right into the classroom.

CHAPTER 34

STILL AT RISK

What I want to fix your attention on is the vast overall movement towards the discrediting, and finally the elimination of every kind of human excellence—moral, cultural, social, or intellectual. And is it not pretty to notice how "democracy" (in the incantatory sense) is now doing for us the work that was once done by the most ancient Dictatorships?
        SCREWTAPE (a devil in C. S. Lewis's *The Screwtape Letters*)

In 1983, the National Commission on Excellence in Education published "A Nation at Risk," a shocking assessment of American education. Today the risk is even graver. American high school seniors are among the worst educated in the world. In one study covering twenty-one nations, American students placed nineteenth in math and science, and dead last in physics.[1] Even students in well-endowed Ivy League colleges show gaping deficiencies in their knowledge of American history and civics. For example, three out of four cannot identify the author of the Gettysburg Address. Facts every immigrant has to master in order to gain U.S. citizenship seem to elude the young people destined to become our nation's next generation of leaders.[2]

Even more disturbing is the decline in moral education. In a study by the Josephson Institute of Ethics, two-thirds of the high school students surveyed admitted to cheating on an exam within the past year, one-third said they had stolen something, and more than a third said they would lie on a job application.[3] Clearly, American public education is no longer successful at its two historic tasks: academic training and moral education.

What has caused this disastrous decline? It's a well-known fact, of course, that schools have replaced time-tested methods of teaching with trendy techniques, from values clarification to multiculturalism. But the basic question is *why*. Why did educators buy into these methodologies in the first place, and why do they cling to them when it is obvious they are not working?

We can start by looking at the schools that train the nation's teachers and administrators. The typical curriculum in colleges of education, says Rita Kramer, author of *Ed School Follies,* is "all too often a grab bag of pieties about the influence of race, ethnicity, and gender on learning." Future teachers do not take courses on the subject matter they will be teaching; instead, their schedules are crammed with courses that focus on self-esteem and social equity. One professor told future teachers of language arts: "More important than content or thinking [are] the students' feelings. You are not there to feed them information but to be sensitive to their need for positive reinforcement, for self-esteem." A UCLA professor cautioned a class of young teachers against correcting children's spelling and punctuation: "It's more important for them to create than follow rules."[4]

No wonder American kids score at the bottom in terms of skills but at the top in terms of self-esteem. We've made them feel good about doing badly.

Where have these ideas about education come from? Once again, the answer lies in a shift in worldview. Every educational method grows out of a broader philosophy that addresses certain fundamental questions: Who are we as humans? What is our task in life? How can we prepare ourselves to perform that task? The best way to critique contemporary education is to examine the answers that have been offered to these basic questions, using the framework of *creation, fall,* and *redemption.*

In earlier chapters about creation, we saw how John Dewey, America's most influential educational theorist, applied Charles Darwin's ideas to education. Dewey rejected the biblical view of the child as a creature of God and maintained instead that the child is nothing but a biological organism. Thus the mind is merely a complex organ, evolving through adaptation to the environment, trying out different responses until it finds something that works. These assumptions led to pragmatism, a philosophy that says there are no transcendent, unchanging truths but only pragmatic strategies for getting what we want. Applying this philosophy, Dewey came up with an educational theory that stressed process over content. Children should not be taught facts and truths; they should be taught how to conduct a process of inquiry.[5]

A current version of this philosophy is "constructivist" education, today's most popular pedagogical technique, which is based on the idea that knowledge is not objective but a social construction; therefore, children should not be given the "right" answers but should be taught to construct their own solutions through interaction within a group. In the words of education theorist Catherine Fosnot, "Constructivism does not assume the presence of an outside objective reality that is revealed to the learner, but rather that learners actively construct their own reality, transforming it and themselves in the process."[6] Children are taught to construct their own math rules, their own spelling systems ("invented spelling"), their own punctuation, and so on, and teachers are urged not to tell students whether their answers are right or wrong.

Dewey applied the same process view of knowledge to ethics. If we experiment by selecting different responses to particular conditions, he taught, then over time we will develop a "science" of ethics, identifying those actions that predictably lead to enjoyable and satisfying consequences. The hitch, of course, is that what satisfies me may not satisfy you. Thus, Dewey's philosophy inspired the relativistic methods of moral education in vogue in the classroom today, including Sidney Simon's method of "values clarification" and its seven-step process for choosing values—followed by Lawrence Kohlberg's method of "moral reasoning," Clive Beck's "reflective approach," and many others. What all such methods have in common is that teachers are rigorously instructed not to be directive in any way but to coach students in a process of weighing alternatives and making up their own minds. Students' choices are considered acceptable not because the choices agree with a transcendent standard but because the students have gone through the required process—regardless of the outcome.[7]

A faulty view of creation has led directly to the conceptual and moral relativism that plagues modern public education. Equally disastrous has been the loss of the biblical teaching on sin and the Fall. As we saw earlier, Jean-Jacques Rousseau shocked the world by pronouncing that human nature in its natural state is innocent—that people are made evil only by the constraints of civilization. And where do we see human nature in its spontaneous, natural state, he asked, before it is ruined by rules and inhibitions? Why, in the child. The child reveals the full range of human potential, the glory of the indeterminate self, open to all possibilities.

And so was birthed a utopian view of the child. "Trailing clouds of glory do we come, from God, who is our home: Heaven lies about us in our infancy," in the words of the romantic poet William Wordsworth.[8] Gone was the biblical notion that children are affected by the Fall, their nature distorted by original sin. Gone was the idea that children are capable of genuine wrongdoing and thus need moral boundaries and training. As a result, the romantics set about crafting radical new ideas about the way children should be raised and educated.

In the nineteenth century, for example, the German educational theorist Friedrich Froebel founded the first kindergarten, which literally means "children's garden," where he fleshed out a radically new utopian approach to education. Whereas the goal of classical education is to transmit a cultural heritage, in Froebel's utopian vision, education is seen as the means of humanity's passage to the next stage of evolution. Whereas in classical education children are taught to imitate the best of the past, in utopian education they are taught to reject the past and create something new. Whereas classical education teaches children to adapt their lives to eternal principles, utopian education seeks to free them to unfold and develop new ideas and ways of living out of their own experience. Froebel's kindergarten pictured the child as a plant whose growth must be allowed to proceed according to its own inner law of organic development, lest we stunt its evolution. Old standards of truth and virtue must be cast off to give freedom to the New Man, who is even now in process of evolving through our children.[9]

Another nineteenth-century educator, Francis Wayland Parker, went so far as to call the child divine: "The spontaneous tendencies of the child are the records of inborn divinity."[10] In Parker's child-centered theory of education, the most important thing is for the adult to get out of the way of the child's natural tendencies, to refrain from stifling the child with either academic requirements or moral demands.

Educators like Froebel and Parker assumed that children, left to themselves, would spontaneously tend toward love, selflessness, hard work, creativity, and all the other Christian virtues. In other words, they assumed that human nature is naturally good, and they saw no danger in getting rid of externally imposed training and objective standards.[11] Today the same utopianism is at work in nondirective values-education programs, which, as we saw earlier, are based on the assumption that if children are merely taught a process of inquiry to evaluate their options, they will choose wisely and rationally.

The rejection of the biblical view of the Fall has led to unrealistic and unworkable educational methods that are blind to our children's need for moral direction. Is it any wonder that many kids are cheating, stealing, and even assaulting one another in the classroom?

If a faulty understanding of the doctrine of the Fall has undermined moral education, what about the effects of a faulty doctrine of redemption? Redemption is certainly alive and well in the classroom today, but it's political redemption—a reflection of the kind found in wider society. Many children know more about acid rain and gay rights than they do about

Shakespeare and George Washington. Education is being turned into the means for lifting society to the next stage in social evolution.

In the 1930s, the influential educator George S. Counts explicitly called on teachers to begin "controlling the evolution of society." He urged them to "redeem" society, to stop being merely transmitters of the culture and become "creator[s] of social values." Educators should reach deliberately for power to "build a new social order," raising students' consciousness about social problems and encouraging them to come up with alternative ways of ordering society.[12] Today schools are doing just that . . . with gusto.

Increasingly, classroom time is taken away from studying the classics of Western culture and is devoted to politically correct causes, based on a philosophy of postmodernism that reduces truth to power politics and treats all ideas as expressions of race, class, or gender. Most educators no longer define education as fostering the search for truth and transmitting a valued heritage, says Frederic Sommers of Brandeis University; instead, they define education as a means to "empower students by alerting them to the need for struggle against patriarchy, racism, and classism."[13] Nancy's son discovered this recently when he entered a state university. His honors English course was taught by a radical feminist who devoted the entire curriculum to contemporary works by feminists and homosexual-rights activists. Instead of being an arena where students can learn to weigh conflicting ideas dispassionately, the classroom is becoming a place where students are indoctrinated in political radicalism and enlisted in the culture wars.

At the same time, education has been greatly influenced by a therapeutic model of redemption, in which teachers treat children's psyches while teaching them the ABCs. The source of this widespread trend is the philosophy of existentialism, which casts each individual as an *autonomous self.* According to this worldview, people must create their own purpose by making choices, even though there is no standard to tell them whether or not the choices they are making are right.[14] The resulting theory of education is sometimes called humanistic education, after the great humanistic psychologists of the 1970s—Carl Rogers, Rollo May, and Abraham Maslow—who pioneered the use of therapeutic techniques in the classroom as a way of freeing students from psychological barriers so they could become autonomous decision makers. Teachers became amateur psychologists, exploring the student's personality with techniques borrowed from encounter groups and sensitivity training.

But education is not the same as therapy, and the impact of existentialism in the classroom has been disastrous. Educator William Coulson, once a colleague of Carl Rogers, tells a fascinating personal story that illustrates why humanistic education fails. In 1967, Coulson and Rogers received a grant to conduct the first large-scale systematic study of the effect of encounter groups in the classroom. Their laboratory consisted of some sixty schools within the Catholic school system in Los Angeles, and they began by holding workshops for the nuns who taught in the schools (the Sisters of the Immaculate Heart of Mary). To Coulson's surprise and consternation, many nuns responded to the training by removing their habits and leaving the Catholic church. The message they got from the workshops was that to be "authentic" individuals, they must free themselves from all external authority and make their own choices. Of course, as Coulson points out, in leaving the church, the nuns were not really liberating themselves from external authority at all. They were simply trading in one authority (the Catholic church) for another (the workshop leaders).[15]

Coulson's experience was not unique. When Abraham Maslow translated his humanistic theory of psychology into educational practice, he discovered that his students developed an "almost paranoid certainty of their own absolute virtues and correctness."[16] Having been taught that they were autonomous selves who must make up their own minds about right and wrong, his students became unteachable. No wonder research shows that students who take "lifestyle" courses employing nondirective decision-making methods end up being *more* likely to engage in destructive behavior.[17]

Students who are taught to look only to their own feelings soon lose all sense of accountability to any external moral standard. One teacher found this out when she used a values-education program with her low-achieving eighth graders. The program required students to list the things they loved doing, which turned out to be "sex, drugs, drinking, and skipping school." The teacher was horrified but powerless. Her students had clarified their values, and the nondirective program gave her no way to challenge them to aim for something higher.[18]

The decline in American public education is not due to poor teaching or lack of funding; it is due to educational theories that deny the existence of transcendent truth and morality, that renounce standards of excellence, and that ultimately render children unteachable. If we hope to reform the educational system, we must learn to analyze and critique the worldviews that have spawned these disastrous teaching methods and then offer an alternative worldview that is decisively Christian—one that will yield a theory of education capable of improving the schools for all students.

TRUTH IN TEACHING

What is the Christian view? It was captured in a dramatic moment in the movie *Witness.*[19] In a powerful scene involving a big-city detective and an eight-year-old Amish boy named Samuel, the boy spots the detective's pistol in a drawer and reaches to pick it up.

"Samuel!" the detective says sternly. "Never play with a loaded gun!"

The detective doesn't ask Samuel how he feels about what he's doing. He doesn't allow the boy to make up his own mind about whether playing with a loaded gun is right for him. Instead, a knowledgeable adult in a directive manner informs the boy of the dangers of playing with guns.

This example illustrates an approach to teaching that is directive and objective, and we suggest that it also reflects the biblical model. Christian education is not utopian; it does not assume that children (or the rest of us) are capable of determining ultimate truth on their own in the vacuum of subjectivism. Instead, God has communicated with us through the Bible, revealing an objective standard of truth and morality for all people. Our lives are guided by revealed truths that are much greater than anything we could possibly conceive on our own.

What are those truths? First, children are not merely biological organisms adapting to the environment; they are created in the image of God and bear all the dignity of beings capable of recognizing truth, goodness, and beauty. The goal of education should be to feed children's souls through a directive presentation of these objective ideals.

But that's only part of the story. We must also take into account children's capacity for selfishness and willfulness. Moral education should likewise be directive, teaching the biblical virtues and enforcing them with consistent classroom discipline.

Finally, education is one of the ways we seek to reverse the effects of the Fall and restore humanity to its original dignity and purpose. The goal of learning, wrote the great Christian poet John Milton, "is to repair the ruins of our first parents."[20] Teachers should recognize the moral and spiritual drama taking place in their students' souls, helping them see how that same drama is the stuff of history and literature and philosophy. Education is a major arena in the spiritual battle raging in the world, a battlefield where we should be bringing a Christian worldview to bear: pushing back the power of the adversary and claiming for Christ the entire territory of the mind and spirit.

Christian Schools

Scripture constantly enjoins Christians to teach their children and to pass on the great truths of the faith from generation to generation. So it's not surprising that Christians have historically accorded great importance to education, founding schools and teaching literacy wherever they went around the globe. Almost every major college in the first two centuries of American history was founded by Christians. (In fact, Harvard, Princeton, and the other Ivy League universities were founded to train pastors.) Today Christians continue to establish schools, often with the goal of reaching out to a decaying culture. In city after city, Christian and parochial schools educate a substantial number of inner-city students, producing higher test scores at a fraction of the cost of public education.[21]

Christian education is not simply a matter of starting class with Bible reading and prayer, then teaching subjects out of secular textbooks. It consists of teaching everything, from science and mathematics to literature and the arts, within the framework of an integrated biblical worldview. It means teaching students to relate every academic discipline to God's truth and his self-revelation in Scripture, while detecting and critiquing nonbiblical worldview assumptions.

For those seeking guidance on how to do it right, good models abound. In Detroit, my close friend Mike Timmis heads a coalition of leaders from local churches, businesses, and community organizations that has founded four Christ-centered, ecumenical schools in urban neighborhoods. With an enrollment of nearly seven hundred students, Cornerstone schools run eleven months of the year, and parents must sign a "covenant" to actively support the school. Chapel attendance is mandatory, and every student participates in a Bible study group. Privately funded by corporations and foundations, the schools also draw in ordinary people as "partners," who not only contribute $2000 a year to support one student but also commit to forming a friendship with that student. The students, 98 percent of whom are minorities, finish far above the national average in standardized tests, and the number of disciplinary violations is far lower than in public schools.[22]

One of the more interesting experiments in recent years has been the growth of the Christian classical school movement. Classical education is based on the idea that in any subject there is a three-stage development of learning. Students must (1) know the basics of the subject (what the ancient Greeks called "grammar"); (2) be able to reason clearly about it ("logic"); and (3) apply it in a creative, persuasive manner ("rhetoric"). Classical education teaches students how to use these basic tools of learning to appreciate the best of Western culture's classical heritage. Students listen to symphonies, study paintings, and read great works of literature by Homer, Plato, Dante, Shakespeare, Dickens, and Dostoyevsky. This approach is having a dramatic effect in creating academically stellar Christian schools across the country.[23]

Homeschooling

The most radical alternative for Christian parents is to take on the task of educating their children themselves, becoming part of the fast-growing homeschooling movement. In earlier centuries, many of our outstanding national leaders were educated, at least partly, at home: Patrick Henry, William Penn, Daniel Webster, Wilbur and Orville Wright, Abraham Lincoln, and Thomas Edison. Today some 1.7 million American children are being homeschooled, and on the 1997 ACT test, the average score of home-schooled students was above the national average.[24]

Meg and Steve Garber of Burke, Virginia, are teaching their nine-year-old twins at home, and the Garbers demonstrate how a curriculum can be unified across several subjects for greater learning effect. Last fall, while studying a unit on Colonial America, the twins read books on the subject and practiced writing by composing a journal of the everyday life of a colonial child; they cooked colonial food and read about nutrition and farming; they sewed colonial-style clothing and took a field trip to colonial Williamsburg. At the same time they kept up with drills in math, phonics, and composition, not to mention soccer, basketball, ballet lessons, and raising chickens in the backyard.

Of course, many Christian families choose to send their children to public schools either because they cannot afford private school or because they are committed to working within the public school system. But these families also have an educational task to do at home, teaching their children an overarching Christian worldview by which to interpret and critique what they learn at school. In this sense, all Christian parents must be homeschoolers. And all need support from the church, which means local churches need to encourage youth group leaders to go beyond volleyball and pizza parties and begin to teach apologetics and worldview issues.

Summit Ministries in Colorado is pointing the way. Perched high in the Rocky Mountains, every summer Summit packs in high school students who want to learn how to defend their faith against the ideological trends of the day. Founder David Noebel has developed a curriculum that gives Christian kids a crash course in apologetics, teaching them how to deal with the intellectual challenges they face in high school and college. They learn how to analyze and critique the New Age movement, humanism, Marxism, feminism, evolutionism, and whatever other "ism" happens to be gaining a foothold in contemporary American culture. Churches and Christian schools ought to take a page from Summit's book (or use Summit's own book *Understanding the Times*) and begin preparing young people to face an increasingly hostile culture.[25]

Reforming Public Schools

But even as we shore up Christian education, we cannot retreat from the challenge to reform public education. The future of any society depends on the way it teaches its children. That's why one of the first measures taken by revolutionary governments is to place all educational agencies under the direct control of the state, giving schools a central hand in building the new society. That's also why one of the fiercest battles in today's "culture war" is over education. If Christians are going to be "salt," if we are going to restore order and justice throughout the culture, we must restore high-quality education.

We can begin by supporting curricular reforms that restore an objective focus to the public school classroom. In state schools we cannot push for an explicitly Christian approach to education, of course, but we *can* play an active role in promoting the teaching of general principles of truth and morality that, though ultimately derived from Scripture, can also be supported on rational grounds. Because of common grace, these principles are often recognized by people of other faiths (such as Jews, Muslims, Mormons, and the like) as well as by nonbelievers, allowing us to work together as allies in the fight. For example, we ought to support groups such as the Character Education Partnership Inc., which seeks to teach the virtues on which a majority of citizens can agree.[26]

Reform efforts can be effective, as evidenced by Piscataquis Community High School, an impoverished rural school in Maine. A decade ago, the school's scores on a state achievement test were among the lowest in the state. Today they are among the highest. The secret? Discipline and a demanding curriculum. Or, as Norman Higgins, who was principal for ten years, puts it, "High standards for students, high standards for teachers, high standards for schools." Higgins brought in a classical curriculum in which all students, not just those bound for college, are required to learn algebra, biology, chemistry, physics, and foreign languages. "We are a New England private school in a poor public school setting," Higgins says.[27]

Individual Christians working within the public school system can also have an enormous impact. For thirty years, an African-American woman named Barbara Moses was a public school teacher in Philadelphia, where she led thousands of kids to straighten up their lives by sharing God's love with them. She prayed with kids, invited them to accept Christ, visited their homes, got to know their families. Few individuals have had greater impact on their local schools, demonstrating what one Spirit-led believer can do.[28]

Charter Schools

One of the most creative means of reforming public education is the charter-school movement. Charter schools are public schools, but the difference is that teachers survive on merit, not tenure, and they don't have to teach the state curriculum. In exchange for this freedom, charter schools must meet strict performance standards. The idea is to allow a wide range of experimentation while subjecting the students to rigorous academic standards so the state will be able to determine which methods work best.

An example of what charter schools can accomplish can be seen at Wesley Elementary in the violent, drug-infested Acres Homes section of Houston, Texas. The school is surrounded by barbed-wire fencing and boarded-up houses, and several years ago, only 18 percent of Wesley's third graders were scoring at grade level in reading comprehension. But after Thaddeus Lott became the principal in 1975, that number shot up to 85 percent. To achieve this astounding turnaround, Lott got back to the basics: strict discipline, high expectations, and a curriculum that stresses drills and sequential learning (Direct Instruction). His approach was so successful that he was asked to take over several additional troubled schools. These became the first charter schools in Texas, and their success is being replicated in charter schools around the country.[29]

Supplemental Programs

Christians can also create ways to supplement the public school system. This was the tactic adopted by Jerry McNeely, an ordained minister in the African Methodist Episcopal church, who set his sights on William D. Hinton School, a public elementary school in south-side Chicago, where gunfire and sirens are common background noises and the sidewalks are littered with empty liquor bottles and crack vials. These days something astonishing happens at Hinton School. Twice a week, as soon as the last bell rings, several students rush to take over an empty classroom, pull out their homework, and start comparing notes. Then Jerry McNeely arrives, opens a large box of chemicals, and the students are soon engrossed in a science project.

These kids are participants in one of the hottest after-school programs in Chicago: the Urban Pioneers, a component of the Chicago Urban League's Black Churches Project. McNeely is the director of Urban Pioneers, with a vision to help inner-city kids go on to earn graduate degrees in science and math. As a result, hundreds of students in grades five through eight spend four hours a week exploring the world of science and mathematics in hands-on experiments.[30]

One of the best programs for helping students succeed in school is Kids Hope USA, a program founded by Virgil Gulker, who was horrified by rising rates of violence, gang activity, and suicide, even in the youngest grades. When he interviewed experts across the country, he repeatedly heard the same refrain: We don't need any more programs. What we need are more caring adults to put their arms around troubled children and say, "I love you."

So Gulker founded a program in which a church "adopts" a local elementary school, and members of the congregation conduct one-on-one tutoring. Each volunteer meets with his or her student on school grounds, then sends the teacher a progress report after each session. The academic goal is for the students to acquire basic skills in reading and computation, but the personal goal is to sustain a long-term, consistent, trusting relationship between a Christian volunteer and a needy kid—the only kind of relationship with a proven record of giving these kids the hope they need.[31] Kids Hope USA currently has sixty participating churches in six states.

School Choice

The best hope for reforming our public schools may be the voucher system, which provides low-income families with some choice over their children's schooling.

In Cleveland, Ohio, Delvoland Shakespeare was horrified when he visited the school his five-year-old son would attend in the fall. At the intersection outside the school, drug dealers occupied one corner, winos a second corner, prostitutes a third, and men shooting dice on the fourth. Inside the school, he saw students bouncing around without any discipline, and battered textbooks with no covers. In the boys' bathroom, a man tried to sell him drugs. "[My son] had to walk through this war zone, and once we get in the school grounds, he is still in a war zone," Shakespeare said. "No way was I going to send him into that school."[32] The young African-American father moved his family into an attic so he could afford to pay for a private Catholic school. Finally, two years later, when Ohio began a voucher program that permitted parents to use the vouchers at religious schools, the Shakespeares won vouchers for both of their sons. Freed from tuition expenses, the family was able to move out of the attic and into their own home.

Vouchers are perhaps the best route to educational equity, giving low-income parents equal opportunity to take their kids out of failing public schools and enroll them in good private schools. According to a Harvard study of the school-choice program in Milwaukee, Wisconsin, minority children improved their reading scores by 3 to 5 percentage points and their math skills by 5 to 12 percentage points. Opponents continue to challenge voucher programs in court, but in 1998, by a vote of 8 to 1, the Supreme Court refused to block Wisconsin's program.[33]

Vouchers are beneficial for public schools as well, for they create the competition needed to break the monopoly of the public school system and force the schools to improve. Yet school-choice measures are often blocked politically by powerful teachers' unions and educational lobbies. As a result, some innovative business people are organizing private voucher systems. In Indiana, Golden Rule Insurance Company established America's first private voucher program, the Educational CHOICE Charitable Trust. Funded through private donations from individuals, corporations, and foundations, the program contributes half the tuition for a child from a low-income family to attend a private or church-run school.

CHOICE has been so successful that it has attracted many imitators. For example, financier Ted Forstmann and Wal-Mart heir John Walton started the Washington Scholarship Fund, a privately financed scholarship program that enables about thirteen hundred children every year to escape one of the country's worst school systems (Washington, D.C.) and attend private schools. They also started the Children's Scholarship Fund, putting up $100 million to give scholarships to children in cities around the country.[34]

■   ■   ■

WHAT THE SCHOOLS do today determines what society will be tomorrow. That's why reforming education, from preschools to universities, is one of the most crucial cultural tasks that Christians face. We have an opportunity not only to have an influence on our public institutions but also to create Christian centers of education that will become sources of cultural renewal much as the monasteries did in the Middle Ages. Though secularists once condemned biblical faith as irrational and contrary to reason, ironically Christianity now stands poised to become the great defender of reason.[35]

But just a step beyond the schoolyard is the neighborhood, another arena ripe for renewal, as one man discovered in his efforts to bring restoration in the midst of crime and decay.

CHAPTER 35

ANYTHING CAN HAPPEN HERE

The first day at Special Post 1 on DeKalb Avenue, Bed-Stuy in Brooklyn, Officer Salvatore Bartolomeo keeps his eyes open, watches, gives himself time to learn the beat. In the early morning he marches past corner bodegas, brick tenements, storefronts with their iron gates still locked. One of the bodegas already has a line out the back. He's sure they're running numbers, not selling milk.[1]

It's a cold, overcast November day, and people on the street are digging their hands into coat pockets. He passes an abandoned car, its stripped carcass halfway out into the street. The whole neighborhood looks similarly scavenged. Twenty dilapidated, garbage-strewn, pot-bunkered blocks. Every street has its burned-out husk of a building, its sooty abscess. Officer Sal understands why nobody else wanted this job, why it remained unfilled for months. Anything can happen here. Anything does. Daily.

The Lafayette Towers, the high-rise projects, loom ahead. First-day jitters tell him that galleries of thousands are watching his every move as three teenagers in army fatigue jackets and baggy pants approach.

"Hello," says Officer Sal. "How you doing today?"

The kids look down and keep walking.

"You in a hurry to get to school?" he asks. "Can't wait to start algebra?"

They stop. One of them, more powerfully built than the other two, quirks his thick eyebrows and says to his friends, "We're only walking the street, and this cop has to be talking to us."

"I'm saying hello," Sal says. "Like in . . . hello, how are you?"

"Do you know me?" the youth asks, finally looking directly at the outsider.

"I'm the new beat cop. I'm trying to get to know the neighborhood. You live in the Towers?"

The leader says to the others, "I didn't think he knew us."

"There's no reason for him to know us," the tallest kid says.

"Look, don't be saying hello to us if you don't know us," the leader says. "We don't like cops. Especially beat cops that get busted out of their cars. What'd you do? Kill somebody on Long Island, so they sent you here?"

"Hey, Mr. Mayor, I volunteered for this job," Sal says.

The three grin widely. They call him "stupid," followed by an obscenity, then walk off in a hail of cursing and jackal laughter.

I'm Brooklyn just like you, Sal wants to say. *I grew up here. My father was raised right on these streets—at DeKalb and Marsey.*

For the rest of the morning he walks DeKalb, says hello, and learns his beat. He walks by a burned-out area behind the welfare building on Skillman Street, with two abandoned, half-charred houses that have fallen against one another, their roofs tangled in the telephone wires. His eyes survey the surrounding lots filled with weeds, garbage, and abandoned cars. These abandoned buildings get as much traffic as the bodegas. Mostly individuals, but occasionally a couple, with the woman dressed to party at ten in the morning.

Sal always sees a black-jacketed kid stationed beside the handball courts in Lafayette Towers—somebody who can see for several hundred yards in every direction. This sentry says a word or two to everyone who passes. When somebody stops to talk, the sentry shakes hands at their parting. *He's either running for office or dealing drugs,* thinks Sal. There are others like him at various locations around the precinct. They've all got a good long view, and they'd be long gone before he could get to them.

He could have that abandoned car towed, though. It would be a start at cleaning up the neighborhood. His assignment here is part of New York City's experiment with a new theory of crime reduction, and his job is to start with the simple things, the first steps in restoring public order. He'll figure out how to bring down the dealers later.

■   ■   ■

As Sal becomes familiar with his beat, he begins to time his movements according to the neighborhood's schedules and rhythms. In the morning, the kids are on their way to school, so he walks the streets close to one of the neighborhood schools, in random order. The grade-schoolers begin to come up and hold his hand and are soon calling him "Officer Sal." They're glad to see him; he scares off the big kids and bullies. The middle schoolers, hanging back on street corners, start threading their way toward their homerooms when he shows up. The high schoolers are sometimes more stubborn about standing their ground, but then he has a chance to go up and ask them, "How's it going?" He quickly becomes a celebrated pain in the neck, a favorite target for the put-down artists.

"Yo, Rocky, Mr. Italian Stallion. There ain't no Mona Lisas here. You go back to AA-drii-ann before she gets the idea you got jungle fever."

"Yo, MC Mickey Mouth," Sal says, "you the one got the fever. But there ain't no Minnie for rats like you!" Sal always gives as good as he gets. In a few weeks he can call dozens of the kids by name, and sometimes his greetings are actually returned.

By the time the merchants open up in the morning, he's back on DeKalb Avenue and stops in at all the shops. Most of the shopkeepers have a story to tell of break-ins and robberies, and they seem surprised when he listens. He asks about delivery times, whether they have a bank-run routine, what their security measures are like. In their embittered manner he can sense the question, "What makes you think *you're* going to make a difference?"

The bank gets busy at eleven-thirty in the morning and stays that way until one-thirty. The check-cashing store gets most of its traffic at the end of the business day.

The first time Sal posts himself by the check store, sipping coffee out of a paper cup, he sees a panhandler within a hundred feet, a tall, thin man whose bony knees have nearly worn through his jeans. The guy doesn't have any signs that promise work for food, or gimmicks like a cute pet dog. He squats on the stoop and whispers, reaching out his hand. He keeps at it until Sal is right over him.

"How you doing this afternoon?" Sal asks.

The whites of the man's eyes are clear. Either he hasn't been on the streets long, or begging isn't his only profession.

"I'm fine," he says. "Taking the sun." He tilts an eye up at the heavy cloud bank and grins.

"You could do with some exercise," Sal says. "I'd like you to step off now." He holds out an arm as if to usher the man through a door.

"No harm in sittin'," the man says.

"Step off," Sal repeats, "or I'll run you in for panhandling."

"This is the United States." The man's flat face goes hard. "Why you troubling me if I ain't doin' nothin'?"

"Loitering here is illegal. Panhandling here is illegal. What else you are doing in your spare time, I don't know, but I can make it my business to find out."

The man rises slowly to his feet, stretches his neck until it pops. "You miss your chance to join the gestapo or what? This is America."

"Yes, it is. A country where people can go into a store without fear of being knocked over the head when they come out."

"Have I knocked anybody over the head?"

"If I have to ask you for your identification, I'll find out. Then I won't have any choice about what to do."

The man's expression grows serious for a moment. He twists his mouth as if working a toothpick around in it. Then he sets his head back and regally strolls away.

Sal shoos off another panhandler as well, then walks back to the check-cashing store. He sees an elderly woman still fidgeting with her purse as she's walking out the door. She's about to turn in the direction the panhandlers went.

"Ma'am," says Sal.

She takes a quick, cringing look to see who's talking to her.

"Would you like me to walk along with you down that way?"

Her shoulders settle. She steps closer to him. "Is there trouble?"

"No, there's not going to be any trouble. Not today."

.   .   .

SAL NOT ONLY patrols the streets but also conducts "vertical searches," climbing the stairs of the walk-up tenements. On one such venture he finds the body of a young woman, sexually abused, then shot in the back of the head, execution-style. She is only one of the many young people who will die by violence on his beat. In Sal's years on DeKalb Avenue, the funeral home becomes almost another stop on his rounds. He always goes in, says a prayer. It doesn't matter what kind of gangster the young man or woman might have been. He kneels down and prays.

Sal also frequents the places where people congregate so he can meet neighborhood residents. He likes stories, and he tries to have a "joke of the day" ready. The young mothers congregate by the swing sets in Lafayette Gardens playground. When he spots a new mom, he always goes over and puts a ten-dollar bill in the baby's hand. With his jokes and his baby kissing, he's kidded about running for mayor.

Mothers with older children begin to notice the protection he gives their kids in the mornings on the way to school and afterward in the park. One day, outside one of the small grocery stores, Destin's mother asks, "Officer Sal? You any good at math? Can you look at Destin's math homework here?"

The boy has a workbook page crumpled in his hand.

Sal thinks of where he and the boy might go—a place they can sit down together, with at least a little privacy. "Come into the store," he says, leading them into Marvelous Mart. "Bernie, let me sit over here in the corner for a while. I'm checking Destin's homework."

Sal gets a look he takes for permission. The little desk in the corner becomes his tutoring station as Destin is joined by many others. Sal teaches Sam how to make his *B*s. He practices fractions with Monique and helps Saleesha with phonics. Checking the kids' homework becomes one more important part of his job.

He starts building a photo collection of "his kids." When school pictures are taken, the mothers come up to him and give him their children's pictures, signed by the child on the back. "You helped Destin with his homework." "You made sure Roderick made it all the way to school." "Clay thinks you hung the moon." "Natasha wants to be a cop now, too."

■   ■   ■

PICKUP BASKETBALL GAMES run year-round, and Sal uses the game to stay fit. He has to, the way the beat calls for him to hang out his gut every day, chasing down perps, subduing them one-on-one. When he has weekend duty, he spends time at the parks and the courts.

Eight-year-old Donzell always comes over and wants to watch his cap and nightstick for him. He lets the kid put the cap on and strut around with the stick while he plays basketball. Sal and his mostly teenage opponents play serious half-court games. Sal plays all comers and beats most of them, which irritates the losers so much he knows they would try to punch him out if he weren't a cop. He earns the nickname "Officer Bird"—after the famous basketball player Larry Bird—because of his athletic skills, light brown hair, and green eyes.

After one matchup, a teen named Shawn loses his temper, mostly because his friend Dennis becomes more and more derisive as "Whitey" keeps scoring. He shoves his friend hard, and they start beating on each other.

Salvatore retrieves the nightstick from Donzell, all the time thinking they'll get in a few punches and calm down on their own. But they don't, and they soon start drawing blood. When Sal rushes in, most of the punches in the melee miss him, but not the body shots.

"What are you doing? What are you doing?" he screams. "Shawn! Dennis! Stop fighting! Stop fighting! I mean it!"

They finally break apart, breathing hard, although they're still guarded, as if recovering for the next go.

"Look, you two, cut it out." Sal reaches into his pocket and fishes out a five from his money clip. "Here. Go have a drink together and cool down, or I'll arrest you both. Is that what you want? Huh?"

Sal watches them play his offer against what's happened. He can see that their last thought comes down to remembering he's a cop.

"Take it," he urges. "Or don't pass go and proceed directly to jail."

Their breathing slows. They slump into sullen and self-protective postures, arms folded, feet twisting.

"Uh, you want something to drink, Shawn?" Dennis asks.

"Yeah, I guess."

They walk off together, still keeping a cautious distance between them.

■   ■   ■

THE ABANDONED BUILDINGS on Skillman behind the welfare building—the ones that get all the traffic—become the site of Sal's first stealth operation. The buildings are close to another beat cop's area, and he persuades the officer, Joey Francioso, to help him find out what's happening in there.

They position themselves in what was the back room of a double parlor in the ground-floor unit. The rooms are filled with trash, fallen plaster, and nail-studded fretwork. It's so dark they hardly have to hide themselves. They crouch down on the floor and look through a hole in the back-parlor wall toward the front. The first time they stake the place out, time passes so slowly that Sal finds himself counting each *woosh* of a passing bus or truck. He hears litter rustling as the rats scamper along the floors.

Soon enough, though, there's a flare of light in the front parlor. A user's crack pipe is being lit. The ammonialike scent hits them. They turn on their big heavy flashlights and come down on the crackhead almost before he looks up.

They take him out the back way, see that he's processed, then return. A string of users and prostitutes is caught this way.

■   ■   ■

AT DEKALB and Tenth there's a stoplight where the street angles, allowing drivers to see in both directions. Another light sits only thirty feet beyond, and then there's not another light for three blocks. People habitually run the light at DeKalb and Tenth, even when Sal is right there, blowing his whistle.

One day when it happens, some of the neighborhood bad boys are hanging around, and they're on Sal immediately. "Hey, Robo Cop, you fast enough to catch that car? No one going to pay attention to you if you can't catch somebody running a red light! Nobody care about you and that little whistle!"

Then they laugh and carry on, and the people standing around shake their heads and look sour.

The next time Sal sees someone run a light there, he hops into the back of a Yellow Cab. "You know what they say in the movies!" he yells at the driver. "Follow that car. He'll have to stop at the next light."

"Officer, I—"

"Just pull two or three car lengths ahead of him, and then you can scram as soon as I get out."

With that, the chase is on. The cab swings wide into the left lane at the next light and stops three car lengths in front of the offender.

Sal gets out and strolls over to the rusted-out Chevy that's shaking on its frame as if it has a case of the D.T.'s. The driver can't go anywhere, so now he's "awfully sorry" that he "didn't hear the officer's whistle." Then he's even sorrier because his registration has expired. Much sorrier because he has no insurance. Sorrier still because his multiple outstanding tickets have long ago resulted in a warrant for his arrest. And truly distraught when he steps out of the car and Sal sees the bag of marijuana on the floor.

Before long, Sal finds cabs nearly as useful as his old cruiser. Almost everyone he catches running that light has multiple unpaid tickets—at the very least. Nabbing people who run red lights is netting him drug dealers and muggers.

■   ■   ■

SAL'S SUCCESSFUL USE of cabs gives him an idea of how he might take a run at the drug dealers by the handball courts. He asks the driver of a *New York Daily News* truck if he can hitch a ride. As the truck lurches down the street, Sal stands on the rear steel bumper and clings to the latches that lift the gate.

He catches a break when the truck has to stop for traffic and his perch winds up almost directly in front of the courts. A deal is going down, and for the moment the dealer's eyes are on his customer's hands and pockets.

Sal starts his rush. The dealer looks up. His face registers total shock. His mouth drops; his eyes grow big. The customer jets toward another building in the projects.

Sal goes after the dealer, registering where the vials drop, hoping a few are still on the ground after he grabs the kid.

The dealer runs for building 5. If the kid gets inside an apartment, Sal knows he'll never find him. The back entrances lead to multiple stairwells and elevators.

As they reach the building's terracelike entrance, the dealer jumps the low steps and stumbles. Sal dives and delivers a rolling tackle to the back of the dealer's thighs just as he leaps for the door. They fall together, and Sal catches an elbow to the side of his head. The dealer rises to his knees. Sal holds the kid's plaid Pendleton-like jacket in his left hand and pops the kid with a straight right. That finally stops him, but it makes the arrest ugly as the kid's nose pours blood over his mouth and down his chin.

People begin to gather as Sal stands the dealer up and puts cuffs on him. The crowd keeps growing, and their attitude is increasingly unfriendly. "What's he done? That's Jimmy. Jimmy ain't done nothin'. Why'd you beat him like that?"

Sal realizes he's one Italian cop in the midst of the Towers' thousands of African-Americans and Hispanics. He has to be cool. This is how riots start. An arrest becomes a brawl . . . a brawl becomes South Central L.A.

The building's security guard shows up, but he's a retirement-age rent-a-cop whose obvious fear only spurs on the dealer's defenders.

"Why you tossing Jimmy?" someone asks again. "Look here, he's bleeding all over. You the one who needs to be arrested. Jimmy be needin' an ambulance."

Sal turns on the crowd. "Jimmy's been dealing, and if the ones that are in it with him stick around, I'll take you in, too."

"He thinks Jimmy's some kind of drug dealer? Where are the drugs then? Where are the drugs?" Enough people echo the speaker that the crowd is on the verge of chanting.

By now, Sal's on the radio, calling for help. He'll stay in front of the building, waiting for the backup to arrive. He's safer here than he would be running the gauntlet back out to the street. He takes the dealer over to the steel bike rack, detaches one cuff, locks it down on the rack. Sal can face the crowd now, although he's conscious that parking the dealer almost invites someone else to get in his face.

"Now I told you, if you don't let me do my job here, I'll take somebody else in. My backup will be here in another minute."

A tall, graying man, in an old-fashioned overcoat and oversized wing tips that turn up at the toes, steps toward him and then turns around to the crowd. "What are you people giving the officer here a hard time for? You know this punk is dealing. I see him about every time I go to work. I know what he's doing. Everybody does. 'Cept my six-year-old son, Mattie. And I don't want Mattie *ever* to know. Of course he will soon enough. But if I can have one more day without his knowing, I'll take it. The ones of you that care about your children, your brothers and sisters, leave with me. Let the officer haul off the rest of the scum that don't."

Without ever turning around to face Sal, the man walks off. The citizens join him. The gangsters reluctantly follow.

Sal's backup finally walks through the dispersing crowd, glancing from side to side to see why everyone's leaving.

■   ■   ■

WITH TIME, SAL'S TACTICS become more sophisticated, and he knows how to take advantage of the neighborhood's layout as well as or better than the crooks. The bad guys are always checking out his movements, his schedule. One day he gets an inquiry that's more particular than most.

A dealer he knows as Sonny asks, "What time you getting off today, Officer?"

"You got a big deal going down, Sonny? You want to know when the coast's clear?"

"Officer, it's cold out here. I'm just worried 'bout you coming in from the cold."

"I'm off at four o'clock, Sonny. That doesn't mean the neighborhood's without a presence, you know."

"I hope not. Enough people getting killed already."

"You got that right."

"You have a nice day, Officer. You get out of the cold soon as you can."

Close to four o'clock, the time he told Sonny his shift would end, Sal makes sure he passes the same corner at DeKalb and Spencer where he and Sonny had their talk earlier. Then Sal walks around the block and enters the welfare building the back way. He takes the elevator, then an interior stairwell, and posts himself in an office where the view takes in Sonny's field of operation. The welfare building, where the blinds are always drawn, provides perfect cover.

Sal watches Sonny's crew set up. The dealer posts lookouts on each side of the street, both ways, and four more on the cross street. He must be getting ready to move more than just daily hits. Three more people appear with him, and then he moves away toward the curb as they recede into doorways. The three shadows must be carrying the product while Sonny handles diplomacy.

Sal hits his radio and says, "This is Beat 12, central. We've got drug dealing on the corner of DeKalb and Spencer. I want the SNEU [Streets Narcotics Enforcement Unit] team to set up here. The buys are going to be coming in soon, and they look to be heavy."

In short order, SNEU sets up its units two blocks away.

Sonny must have told his customers he was having a sale because within the next two hours, nearly a dozen buys go down. Sal sits in the welfare building, directing traffic, while SNEU picks up the buyers a block or more from the dealer's spot. They hold them, collecting evidence.

Suddenly Sal sees the lookouts start to drift away. "Now! Now! Now!" he shouts into his radio. SNEU swarms in on Sonny & Company from every direction, cars screaming, weapons drawn.

■   ■   ■

THE MAN WHO had supported Sal earlier begins to have quieter partners among the kids.

"You see that phone booth," says a gangly kid with his hair shaved close. "I left something in there. Read it carefully."

The note, tucked in the coin return, lists a place and a time. Sal knows there's nearly always a dealer stationed where he's being directed and figures a fresh supply of crack is being delivered. He takes the risk that the kid knows what he's talking about and has SNEU set up on it.

The delivery comes in right on schedule, only this time it's the cops, not the gangsters, who score big.

■   ■   ■

SAL RECEIVES a call from detectives at the 67th Precinct. "You see the papers about the drug hit in Flatbush? That family?"

"I think so. Yeah."

"What happened was, the father of this family ripped off his drug partners. So they came to the house to get him. When he wasn't there, the partners decided to send a message. They blindfolded the women and children, gagged them with duct tape, and then shot them. *Bing, bing, bing.* A .44

special. All dead except an older daughter, who played dead. She got up after they left and called 911. The father came home eventually, and we got him. He says his former associate, named Scanlon, must have been the hitter. Scanlon's from your territory, the 79th."

"Scanlon? There's a Scanlon I met at a block association meeting. He's in insurance. Maybe a relative?"

"Find out for us, would you?"

Sal makes preliminary inquires that establish the insurance agent as the accused hitter's father. Sal likes Mr. Scanlon and goes to the apartment with mixed emotions, keeping a hand on his gun as he knocks on the door, in case the son is there.

"Come in, come in, Officer Sal," Mr. Scanlon welcomes him. He urges Sal to sit and insists on bringing him a Coke.

"Here's the situation," Sal says. "We think your son Harvey might be involved in something. Something pretty bad. Has he been around here?"

"Just went out. He came back home last night and has been running around ever since. That's his bag right there, by that chair. He packed like there was no tomorrow. I expect him to breeze in here and breeze out again anytime."

"You mind if I take a look in his bag, Mr. Scanlon?"

"You have to ask?"

"Well, actually, I do."

"Go ahead, go ahead!"

Sal goes through the bag. He finds the .44 special stuffed in a sock. There's also lots of ammo, along with canned beans, corn, peas, and carrots. "Does your son have a room, Mr. Scanlon?"

"Through there."

Sal finds clothes piled on the bed. Obviously this guy is planning to head underground. Sal calls for his precinct's detectives to come over and keep watch with him. While they do, Mr. and Mrs. Scanlon keep wanting to serve them food.

Harvey never shows. Someone must have tipped him off. So Sal puts the word on the street. Anyone know where Harvey Scanlon might be?

Soon little eyes and ears want to know if he's heard about Harvey's girlfriend over in Flatbush. He gets an address. An accurate one. The detectives at the 67th find Harvey, only blocks from where the hit occurred.

Sal gets a letter of commendation, but what he's concerned about is the Scanlons. He goes back to visit.

Mr. Scanlon greets him just as warmly as before, if not more so. He even calls in his wife and daughters. "My son was out of control with those

drugs," Mr. Scanlon says. "We were afraid he'd hurt *us*. Thank you for finding him. He's going to be away for a long time, but at least he'll be alive.
Maybe he'll think about things."

"Sure. Sure he will," Sal says.

After that, when Sal sees the family on the street, the mother and
daughters always have a kiss for him.

■   ■   ■

As MANY TIMES as Sal rousts people out of the abandoned buildings on
Skillman, the users and the couples always come back. People even shoot up
and defecate in the abandoned cars that the empty lots breed.

One of Sal's jobs is to reduce crime by destroying its protective surroundings, so he goes to work with the sanitation department's Bob
Tolito—a nice guy who also cares about the neighborhood. It takes awhile,
because Bob can pull only so many strings.

One day, however, the neighborhood sees a transformation. The sanitation department arrives with a regular mechanized army. With the assistance of a crane and wrecking ball, the giant earthmovers raze the abandoned
buildings. The wrecked cars are towed at the same time. John Deere tractors
as big as the ones that ply Midwest wheat fields level the whole area and drag
it smooth. Then the earthmovers come back, this time with gigantic boulders that they station at the area's perimeter. The sanitation department
then installs a hurricane fence topped with barbed wire around the whole
area. The users and abusers have no place to hide anymore.

Anything *can* happen here! Sal thinks.

■   ■   ■

SAL GIVES SEMINARS to churches, schools, block associations, and senior
citizens' groups.

"If you want to show us you care, just dial the phone," he tells them.
"We won't ask what your name is. We don't have to know it. The phone
number you're calling from is going to come up on our screens, you know
that. But we're not going to give you up to the people we arrest. If you'd like a
code number as a block watcher, we have those, too. You can just say, 'I'm
0573.' You don't have to give your name."

A woman stands up in the back. Sal remembers her and wonders what
she will say.

"This doesn't have anything to do with what we're talking about," she
says. "But I just want the rest of you to know that this man saved my life."

He remembers the day. He had been hiding out in the welfare building again, directing traffic for another SNEU drug bust, when he saw her faint right there on the street below him. He dashed down the stairs and out the building. When he checked for a pulse, he found she had none. Zero. He thought she was gone. He radioed for help and started giving her CPR. He kept at it until the paramedics came.

Here she is, big as life, telling them all about it.

At the end of the session, he gives out a lot of code numbers.

■   ■   ■

LATE ON A THURSDAY NIGHT, Sal stops by the liquor store on DeKalb Avenue across from the welfare building. It's Mr. King's shop, and Sal keeps a close watch on his store at closing time. "How are you doing, Mr. King? Everything all right? Closing up?"

"We'll be out of here soon, Sal."

"Okay. I'll just be up the street."

Sal steps back through the door and . . . *boom, boom, boom.* By the time he uncovers from hiding, he sees a young man sitting on the ground, shot. Shot bad. The perp is walking away, not even running. He turns the corner.

Officer Sal starts to run. His leather soles slapping the pavement, along with his jingling keys and cuffs, finally signal the shooter that he'd better run, too. "Stop! Police! Don't move!"

The shooter turns and unloads his 9 mm in Sal's direction. Bullets whang against poles, thunk into cars, ricochet off the street.

Sal zigzags between the cars, ducking. He's got his own weapon out, and he gets the shooter in his sights. Sal looks beyond his target and sees people sitting out in their folding chairs, baby strollers parked beside front steps. It's dark. Sal knows that if he misses, he might hit a bystander. He slows, holsters his weapon, but stays in pursuit, walking now. He sees the shooter jump into an abandoned lot filled with bushes and shrubs, and by the time Sal reaches the lot, the guy is gone.

He calls in the situation, and he and his backup spend the rest of the night searching the area. They don't quit until one-thirty in the morning, by which time the temperature has fallen to twenty degrees. Tired and cold, Sal just wants to go home. But when everyone from the community has dispersed, bored now that the manhunt is over, four guys come up to him.

"We were watching you," the leader says. "We waited until the crowd cleared out. Meet us at the elementary school. On the playground. We got what you need."

"Okay, guys. Sure, all right. I'll take a stroll over there." Sal speaks coolly, casually. To any possible onlookers, he wants it to look like they're shooting the breeze—as unlikely as that might be, here at a crime scene at one-thirty in the morning.

When the four guys leave, Sal gathers the undercover officers and tells them about the invitation. "Look, guys, throw your radios on channel 10 and come up in your cars as quietly as you can. No lights. If I need you, you've got to be there before I ask! I don't know if I'm being set up or what, and I've been shot at enough for one day."

Sal walks the familiar route to the school. He can sense the undercover officers rolling through the streets behind him. He keeps his own radio open to channel 10. "This is Sal. C-Pop 12."

"We're here, Sal. We can see you."

The four young men are waiting in the schoolyard, as promised. He walks up to them as casually as he can.

"Listen, we know the guy," says the talker in the group. "He lives at his father's place over on Spencer."

"You got a number?" Sal asks, taking out his memo pad.

"It's the tan building right across from the dry cleaner's." After they give him the apartment number and the guy's name, they say, "We don't want anybody messing with you. You're okay, Robo Cop. Nobody needs to be shooting at *you.*"

Sal thanks the guys and strolls away, confident that they have more than a good chance of nabbing the shooter. Beyond that, he basks in something more personal. The community has been noticing the time and attention he's put in. It's making a difference.

The next day, when the stakeout team finally sees the shooter show up at his father's apartment, the detectives grab him.

.   .   .

WALKING DEKALB late one afternoon, Sal runs into Shawn and Dennis, the two guys he broke up in the basketball fight. They talk about the Knicks, whether Patrick Ewing is mobile enough to win a championship.

Suddenly, from across the street, they hear shouts. "Stop him! Stop him! He's got my purse. Somebody help me! He's got my purse!"

They see the snatcher headed toward Spencer Street. Sal dashes at an angle across four lanes of traffic, bringing the southbound lanes to a screeching halt.

"Stop! Police!" he shouts at the thief.

Behind him, he hears someone else running. By the time he reaches the far curb, Shawn and Dennis have pulled ahead of him and are flying after the snatcher like gazelles. They dodge past the folks who can't think fast enough to get out of the way. Dennis actually jumps all the way over a short man.

Sal's sore hips begin to slow him. He's been on this beat for many years now, and both of his hip joints are worn down painfully. The jolt of each stride jacks up the pain voltage. He's hobbling as he rounds a corner, and then he sees both Shawn and Dennis flatten out in the air, double-teaming the snatcher to the ground. Whoa! That's a citizen's arrest for you!

■   ■   ■

IN THE SPRING of 1993, Sal receives an invitation to a block party. The Marsey Street Mavens, as they style themselves (a neighborhood watch association), are cooking for the community on May 26. This is the first time anyone has dared to hold such an event, and Sal is glad to see it happen on the street where his dad used to live.

The first party is quickly followed by others. People are no longer frightened to be out on the streets, at least in the daytime. The neighborhood has gone from a living hell to at least a borderline place. Now anything truly *can* happen here, including community events.

■   ■   ■

BY 1994, Sal's hips and legs are telling him that his days as a street cop have come to an end. He applies to go back into a cruiser, and the transfer comes through. His beat will be close to DeKalb, though, so he'll be able to roll back through and see his friends.

On his last day, while he's making his tour through Lafayette Towers, a group of people come up to him. The elderly woman to whom he gave CPR. Two block-association presidents. The tough kid who mouthed off at him the first day on the job. About forty people in all. They are, almost to a person, his favorites, and he wonders how they know about each other.

The security guard in the Towers steps forward. He's carrying a trophy, a loving cup. "Officer Sal," he says, "we know you're being reassigned. But before you go, we want to say thanks. We got you this trophy. You won a lot of battles here, and you helped us win back our neighborhood."

Everyone cheers, applauds.

Sal looks at the inscription on the cup: "To Officer Salvatore Bartolomeo. 'Robo Cop.' Six Years' Dedicated Service."

Official commendations are one thing. This is different, and much better. Sal never heard of a beat cop being given a trophy before. "I don't deserve this," he says. "You made it so easy."

Everybody laughs. "Right, easy," they mutter.

"No, I mean it! I mean it!"

Yes, something good *is* happening here.

CHAPTER 3 6

THERE GOES THE NEIGHBORHOOD

The crumbling of order and resulting self-destruction of the community start with broken windows not being fixed; next prostitutes and vagrants are allowed to loiter; soon delinquents and youth gangs realize they can act with impunity; and by then the neighborhood is well on its way toward disintegration.

ANDREW PEYTON THOMAS

Salvatore Bartolomeo's policing of the streets of Brooklyn illustrates an exciting new approach to crime prevention. As Officer Sal pounded his beat, he dealt, of course, with serious crimes like murder, drug dealing, and robbery. But he also helped clear out the things that attract crime to a neighborhood: the signs of social disorder and decay, such as loitering, panhandling, graffiti, abandoned cars, vacant buildings, and littered lots. The success of this form of policing in New York City suggests that it may well be the key to restoring America's crime-ravaged inner cities. And significantly, it builds on the classic Christian understanding that civil peace comes only from a just and responsible social order—an insight sorely needed in our culture.

Over the past few decades, both crime and public disorder have risen sharply. High on the list of causes is the demographic shift that occurred when the baby boomers hit the crime-prone teen years. Another cause is the misguided policies of the 1960s and 1970s (described in part 3), shaped by the assumption that the cause of crime is poverty, an approach that seemed to excuse crime by blaming it on the environment.[1] At the same time, drug use was soaring, causing a domino effect of crime; and Great-Society welfare programs were weakening family structure, which led to gangs of poorly parented juveniles roaming the streets. The resulting social chaos turned America's inner cities into combat zones, and nothing seemed able to stop the downward spiral. Violent crime (per 100,000 persons) grew from 161 in 1960 to 758 in 1992, a 470 percent increase. Property crimes (per 100,000 persons) grew from 1,726 in 1960 to 4,903 in 1992, a 284 percent increase.[2]

Our inability to respond to crime effectively was often blamed on the sheer fact that in many cities the police were outnumbered and outgunned. But it wasn't just insufficient manpower and firepower that allowed crime to flourish. It was also a flawed worldview.

In the 1970s and 1980s, the courts introduced a novel concept of civil liberties that transformed disorderly and disruptive public behavior into a civil right. Most significant were two Supreme Court cases, one in 1972 and the other in 1983, striking down statutes against vagrancy and loitering. In the 1972 case, Justice William O. Douglas waxed colorful about the rights of "rogues and vagabonds" to roam the countryside as "loafers or litterers," as if drunks and panhandlers were merely romantic wanderers. The real culprits, the Court suggested, were the uptight middle-class moralists who were trying to force all dissenters to conform.[3]

In throwing out laws against vagrancy and loitering, however, the high court departed from a legal tradition that extended as far back as the Middle Ages, and even to ancient Athens. Historically, these laws were designed to discourage "the extreme individualistic license" that marks people who flout social convention and disrupt social order, explains attorney Andrew Peyton Thomas. The laws especially targeted those once referred to as "hobos," "tramps," or "bums"—drifters and transients who "rebel against family and career commitments" and prefer a rootless, roaming existence, sleeping in public places and begging from responsible citizens. "Vagrancy laws sought to uphold public order and personal responsibility by encouraging gainful employment and stable ties to family and neighbors."[4]

It was this attempt to "uphold public order" that was abruptly abandoned by the Court in its two landmark cases. Vagrants and drifters were no longer regarded as a danger to social stability but as a persecuted class deserving protection. It was civilized society that the Court condemned for shirking its obligations to misfits and miscreants.

A domino effect followed from these cases, as lower courts overturned state and municipal laws that had given police authority to restrain behavior in public places. Before long, the streets, parks, and subways of our major cities were filled with panhandlers, prostitutes, drunks urinating on the sidewalks, and people sleeping on heating grates.

The same concept of civil liberties captured the mental-health profession, as psychiatrists like R. D. Laing began to argue that there is no generally applicable standard of normalcy and that the mentally ill simply hold a different, but equally valid, perspective on life. Civil libertarians began to portray the mentally ill as just another oppressed group, while championing the absolute right of all people, sane or insane, to live by their own perceptions of reality. The American Civil Liberties Union pressed the point home with several lawsuits. The result was a massive movement to de-institutionalize the mentally ill, unleashing a flood of mentally unstable, disoriented people onto the streets of the nation's cities. Many promptly became homeless, often acting in ways that were menacing or intimidating to ordinary citizens.[5]

So at the same time that crime was soaring and the mentally ill were taking over parks and other public spaces, the courts were handcuffing the police in their ability to curb antisocial and disorderly behavior. The symbol of the times was "The Wildman of 96th Street," a crack-addicted veteran who for years stalked women, pushed people in front of cars, and generally terrorized people on Manhattan's Upper West Side because authorities were unable either to jail or institutionalize him. Repeated across the country, such incidents sent a clear signal that authorities were unable or unwilling to prevent minor forms of disorder—and therefore were unlikely to prevent major crimes as well. As a result, law-abiding citizens began to move out of the cities, while lawbreakers moved in.

If we hope to restore our cities, we must understand and critique the worldview that unleashed this disorder. This novel view of civil liberties was the direct result of rejecting the biblical doctrine of creation, which teaches that humans were created to live in community, and replacing the Garden of Eden with a hypothetical "state of nature" (see earlier discussion in chapter 33). In this secularized myth of human origins, individuals are the only ultimate reality, and individual rights trump all others; the requirements of public order are outweighed by the imperious demands of individual autonomy. Thus civil liberties came to be defined in excessively individualistic terms, denying the right of communities to promote their values or to insist on standards of public behavior. This definition was adopted by sociologists, aggressively promoted by civil-liberty organizations, enshrined in court decisions, and finally even accepted by the police themselves.

The solution, therefore, is not simply a matter of building more prisons and incarcerating more criminals. Indeed, America has tried that route. The 1970s saw the biggest prison-building boom in our nation's history. Speeches sprinkled with slogans about "law and order" and "getting tough on crime" were sure winners on the campaign trail. Arrests rose, prisons became overcrowded . . . and yet crime continued to rise.

Then, in the early 1980s, a breakthrough came when social scientists

George Kelling and James Q. Wilson advanced what became known as the broken-window theory. They discovered that if a broken window in a building is left unrepaired, soon all the windows are knocked out. Why? Because damage left untended sends a message that no one cares, that no one is in charge, and that further vandalism will incur no penalty. A single broken window soon attracts the kind of people who will smash more windows. Likewise, a city that allows pockets of public disorder, starting with graffiti and litter, sends a message that authorities are either unwilling or unable to enforce standards of behavior—to control their space and their citizens. And once a city sends that message, law-abiding citizens leave, and the criminal element is attracted—exactly the cycle that has ravaged America's major cities.[6]

In the early 1990s, New York Police Chief William Bratton took the broken-window theory to heart and persuaded New York's newly elected mayor and tough ex-prosecutor Rudolph Guiliani to give the theory a try. The order went out to police in Precincts 69 and 75 and to Brooklyn, where Officer Sal was stationed, to "fix broken windows"—that is, to arrest petty offenders and clean up the neighborhoods. The police adopted a policy of zero tolerance for any violation of public order, and in the process they soon discovered that there is indeed a "seamless web" between controlling petty crime and restraining major crime. Whereas before they had ignored turnstile jumping at subways, officers now nabbed the offenders, who, as often as not, turned out to be muggers. Whereas before they had turned a blind eye to minor traffic violations, they now stopped all traffic violators, which often led to the discovery of drugs and guns in the cars. They chased away loiterers and panhandlers, many of whom were drug dealers looking for a sale. In three years in Precinct 75, once one of the most dangerous places in America, the number of homicides dropped from 129 to 47.[7]

Civil libertarians attacked Bratton's crime-prevention program repeatedly and even sued the New York Police Department, citing the earlier Supreme Court decisions and arguing that the program targeted people simply because they were poor or homeless. But Bratton had framed his policies carefully to penalize behavior, not status (e.g., homelessness), and the courts denied the challenges of civil libertarians. (One suspects that judges were also responding to public clamor to end the chaos.)[8]

Cities around the country began imitating New York, with equally dramatic results. Politicians were quick to trumpet their successes anywhere they could find a camera or microphone. It was as if they had discovered the Holy Grail, the long-sought answer to crime. Yet all that Guiliani and the others have "discovered" is a well-established, fundamental biblical truth.

REAL SHALOM

Thousands of years before the broken-window theory, the Jewish people had already captured the idea in *shalom*. Although popularly translated "peace," the connotations of the term are actually much broader than the absence of hostilities. *Shalom* refers to peace in a positive sense, the result of a rightly ordered community. When people live together according to God's moral order—in *shalom*—there is civility and harmony. The best way to reduce crime is not to react after the fact with punishments and rehabilitation but to discourage it before it happens by creating an ordered and civil community life.

The biblical basis for this approach is the doctrine of creation, which tells us we were created for community. Contrary to the notion of a "state of nature," with its war of all against all, the Bible teaches that we are not autonomous individuals. Instead, we are created in the image of the One who in his very essence is a community of being—that is, the Trinity. God's very nature is reciprocal love and communication among the persons of the Trinity. We were created as inherently communal beings, and the God-ordained institutions of society make rightful, normative demands that we are morally obligated to fulfill.

These institutions are not impositions on our freedom but expressions of our inherently social nature. "God might have created men as disconnected individuals," writes Kuyper. Instead, he created an original couple, with the result that, by birth, each of us "is organically united with the whole race."[9] This social nature is expressed through our social institutions, and these institutions need some kind of authority structure to direct their activities to the common good. Thus to create and maintain order in our political communities, God has ordained the state. All of us have a moral imperative to obey proper authority and to work for justice and *shalom*.

In the fourth century, in his classic work *The City of God*, St. Augustine taught that peace *(shalom)* is "the tranquillity produced by order" *(tranquillitas ordinis)*. A political community can enjoy peace and harmony only by following the moral order, he wrote; for only an ordered civil life allows fallen human beings to "live and work together." Therefore, the primary role of the state is not to chase down criminals after the fact but to nurture the *tranquillitas ordinis*, using its unique powers of coercion to that end. Pursuing *tranquillitas ordinis* is also the duty of every Christian, for though our sights are set ultimately on the "City of God," as long as we live in the "City of Man," it is morally imperative for us to work for the peace of that city. This is not optional; it is the only way to keep evil in check.[10]

For centuries this biblical view of communal order dominated Western thought. In the last century, William Wilberforce, the great evangelical British statesman, noted that "the most effectual way to prevent the greater crimes is by punishing the smaller, and by endeavoring to repress the general spirit of licentiousness, which is the parent of every kind of vice."[11] The same philosophy influenced the original principles of policing laid out by Sir Robert Peel in 1829. The first job of the police, said Peel, is not fighting crime but keeping the peace.[12] Seventy years later, in the first New York City charter, the same principles were repeated: "It is hereby made the duty of the police department to especially preserve the public peace, . . . remove all nuisances in the public streets, . . . restrain all unlawful and disorderly conduct."[13] As a result, at the turn of the century it was the police who developed the first food and soup lines; they built police stations with extra space where migrants could stay until they found work; they referred beggars to charitable agencies; and yes, they even helped lost children find their way home. Officer Sal would have been right at home.

The success this approach has demonstrated in restoring America's major cities underlines the wisdom of the classic biblical view and provides powerful evidence that it is, in fact, true—true to our nature, true to who we are. By contrast, the chaos of the last few decades attests to the disastrous consequences of living by a false philosophy of human nature, one that denies the biblical teaching of creation and substitutes a secular myth of our origins and our nature. The secular view has been tried and found wanting, and its failure opens a wonderful opportunity for Christians to make a case for a biblical view of human nature and community.

FIXING BROKEN WINDOWS

What does the biblical approach look like in practice? In Newport News, Virginia, police grew weary of constantly answering calls about burglars and drug dealers in a run-down housing project, and the entire project was finally scheduled for demolition. In preparation for new construction, the officers decided to clean up the area: They carted away trash, removed abandoned cars, filled in potholes. To everyone's surprise, burglary rates suddenly dropped by 35 percent. The police had inadvertently stumbled on the broken-window theory. Similarly, Baltimore police worked with local agencies to clean up a housing project—to upgrade street lighting, trim shrubbery, clean alleys, groundand build a play—with the result that burglaries were reduced by 80 percent and auto larceny by 100 percent. Restoring order really does create "the tranquillity of order."[14]

One of the most successful examples is in Charleston, South Carolina, where Police Chief Reuben Greenberg decided to fight crime by cleaning up inner-city neighborhoods, getting rid of litter, used needles, and graffiti. To keep costs down, he employed prisoners from the local jail. Soon formerly crime-ridden areas were clean and neat, signaling that disruptive and disorderly behavior would not be tolerated.

Greenberg then went after open-air drug dealing, which had taken over entire sections of the city. He simply placed uniformed police officers on every corner where drugs were being sold. The officers didn't question anyone; they just stood there. Yet the impact on business was immediate. No one came near the drug dealers, not even to say hello. They were forced to leave the area or go out of business altogether.

Next Greenberg revived the original 1930s vision of public housing as a refuge for the poor, not a haven for crime. The housing authority began to screen tenants, refusing to accept violent criminals, and today public housing is one of the safest places to live in the entire city.

Finally, to fight soaring juvenile crime, Greenberg reintroduced truant officers. If school-age children were spotted anywhere in the city during school hours, a truant officer was dispatched to pick them up and return them to school. Results were immediate: a 24 percent permanent decrease in such daytime crimes as purse snatching, car theft, and shoplifting.[15]

In some places, citizens themselves are taking the initiative to restore neighborhoods. A good example is Bryant Park in New York City, once a haven for drug dealers and other lawbreakers, the site of one hundred fifty reported robberies and ten rapes a year. Finally, neighbors and property owners formed an association and leased the seven-acre park from the city. They tore down iron fencing and high hedges that made easy hiding places for criminals; they remodeled the rest rooms and kept them clean and safe; they hired unarmed security guards to patrol the park to deter small misdemeanors such as wading in the fountains or walking in the flower beds. Today, while remaining virtually free from crime, Bryant Park draws thousands of New Yorkers every week to sunbathe, picnic, and attend artistic events.[16]

Even kids can get in on the act. A few years ago, in Montgomery, Alabama, fifty Christian teenagers armed with hedge clippers and Weedwacker trimmers descended on a neighborhood of mostly elderly people. Determined to tackle the overgrown bushes that provided hiding places for vandals, burglars, and muggers, the kids trimmed towering hedges, thinned low-hanging tree branches, even replaced burned-out lights and installed peepholes in doors. The project was called Youth Cutting Down on Crime, and it was organized by Neighbors Who Care, a Prison Fellowship ministry that mobilizes churches to help crime victims.

Why does establishing order work so well as a crime preventive? Because it expresses an underlying moral order and shows that the community is willing to enforce it. Such is the finding of one of the largest studies ever undertaken into the causes of crime and delinquency. Researchers at Harvard University, the Kaiser Institute, and the University of Chicago joined together to survey 382 Chicago neighborhoods, all with different ethnic, racial, and economic characteristics. They could find no common thread in traditional demographics. In some minority communities crime was high, while in others it was low. The same was true of poverty. The only common pattern researchers found was that rates of violence were lower in areas that had a strong sense of community values and a willingness to impose those values on the public space—for example, where neighbors felt free to step in and discipline kids who skip school or scribble graffiti on the walls or hang out on the streets. In other words, even disadvantaged communities can overcome adverse conditions if they have common values and are willing to enforce them, especially among the young.[17] As a *Boston Globe* reporter put it, somewhat tongue in cheek, the level of violence is mostly influenced by "such things as being willing to look after other people's children and mind others' business."[18]

This is what Roberto Rivera, one of our Prison Fellowship colleagues, calls the "Mrs. Greene syndrome." Rivera grew up in a racially mixed, big-city neighborhood presided over by an imposing woman named Mrs. Greene. She had three children of her own, but she considered it her business to watch out for everyone else's kids, too. "If she saw you doing something stupid or dangerous, she would not hesitate to call you on it," Rivera recalls. "Even worse, you could count on her telling your parents. It was almost impossible to get away with anything when Mrs. Greene was around."

Social science is proving that it's the Mrs. Greenes of this world who enforce community values and keep neighborhoods safe. And values, in turn, derive ultimately from biblical religion. Several recent studies show a direct connection between the influence of Christian faith and crime reduction. Independent studies have shown that crime is highest in neighborhoods with the most bars and liquor stores, and lowest in areas with the most churches.[19] A landmark study by Richard Freeman of Harvard found that young people who are active in church are more likely to finish school, avoid out-of-wedlock pregnancies, keep a job, and stay out of trouble with the law. In preventing crime, church attendance rates even higher than family structure, a highly significant finding, given that growing up in a fatherless home has also been proven to have a severely negative impact. The power of religion comes from the fact that it instills a sense of purpose and value to life; it also teaches a standard of morality that acts as a restraint on antisocial and criminal behavior.[20]

The same effect has been proven historically as well. James Q. Wilson found that crime fell dramatically in the latter half of the last century despite rapid industrialization. He traced the cause to a widespread revival (the Second Great Awakening), when Christians created an extraordinary number of associations to help the poor, the needy, unemployed men, and abandoned women.[21] Their success in transforming society gives persuasive evidence that Christians can do the same today.

In fact, it is only Christians who have a worldview capable of providing workable solutions to the problems of community life. Thus, we ought to be in the forefront, helping communities take charge of their own neighborhoods. Whether it's mobilizing efforts to paint over graffiti and clean up vacant lots, or political activism to pass laws enforcing standards of public behavior, we should be helping to restore order in these smaller areas as the first step toward tackling major social ills.

We can take our lead from the stunning successes of inner-city churches that have assumed an active role in recapturing their neighborhoods. Take, for example, the Reverend Eugene Rivers, who leads Azusa Christian Community, a Pentecostal congregation in Boston's impoverished Dorchester area. Rivers, a former gang member who went on to graduate from Harvard, was inspired to restore his community after witnessing a shocking tragedy. In the spring of 1992, gang members entered a church in the middle of a funeral and stabbed a teenager from a rival gang, then shot up the church. Rivers, joined by more than forty other pastors, set out to rescue inner-city kids from gangs and drugs. The churches started offering after-school tutoring ("latchkey learning") and Bible studies; they formed neighborhood patrols to offer kids safe conduct to and from school; they counseled juveniles on probation; and they made contacts with Christian businessmen to help teens get jobs.[22] After Boston went two years without a single gun-related homicide among teens, even national magazines such as *The New Yorker* took notice: "You couldn't function effectively without the ministers in Boston," former Boston police commissioner William Bratton told the magazine. "Those churches and leaders like Gene Rivers were a very significant reason for our success."[23]

Princeton professor John DiIulio was so impressed with ministries like the one in Boston that he reduced his teaching load at Princeton and created an organization called PRRAY (Partnership for Research on Religion and At-Risk Youth) to research and help fund faith-based programs. DiIulio describes such ministries in dramatic terms: Church volunteers "go right on the street, right to the gangs, right to the heart of the action. Kids are stunned. Police don't even go in there." But committed Christians go where police fear to tread, bringing the bold message that "God loves you and has something better for you."[24]

In 1996, I visited the Allison Hill section of Pennsylvania's capital city, Harrisburg, a desperate ghetto, its alleys reeking of old garbage and its abandoned lots littered with bullet casings and used needles. I saw sidewalks stained with blood from drug deals gone bad.

But shortly afterward, the Reverend Ana Martinez, copastor of First Spanish Christian Church, opened a small storefront office of Neighbors Who Care, a Prison Fellowship ministry to victims of crime. One night Ana and her coworkers Rosalie Danchanko and Paulita Vido led a prayer march through Allison Hill. Volunteers wearing bright yellow T-shirts printed with "When Neigbors Care, Crime Goes Down" handed out hot dogs and balloons. Face-painters and clowns entertained the children. And the crowds grew. Spontaneously, five hundred people began walking together down the littered streets, holding hands, singing hymns, and praying out loud. "Shine the Light," the people sang, "Shine the Light on Harrisburg!"

As they marched, people poured out of the local bar to see what was happening. A young woman, high on drugs, stumbled after them. "I need help," she sobbed. (Rosie and the volunteers later connected her with a treatment program and led her to Christ.) Kids sailing by on skateboards joined the procession.

The crowd approached a corner where a cluster of black-clad gang members were milling around, edgy with tension, and Reverend Ana called out in a booming voice, "The Lord loves you. We love you. But we don't love what you're doing. Come join us!" One teenage boy, his young face already hard from years on the streets, slowly backed away from the gang on the corner and joined the Christians.

Meanwhile, carloads of teenagers tried to disrupt what was going on, gunning their motors, honking their horns, blaring their radios. The marchers prayed even more loudly. Men were crying, women shaking. The prayer rose like a great roar, filling the streets and alleys.

When you walk the streets of Allison Hill today, you will find the syringes gone, the ranks of the drug dealers thinned out. As the prayer warriors keep marching, there is hope in Harrisburg, signs of shalom.

"It was the soccer ball and the Bible that worked," says Kathy Dudley who, with her husband, founded Voice of Hope to restore neighborhoods in West Dallas. "We would go to a street, gather up all the kids, take them to a playground and play ball," she says. "Then we would tell them Bible stories." From that first soccer ball, Voice of Hope has grown into a successful community-development program with after-school tutoring, job training, housing rehabilitation, a dental clinic, a thrift store, and a gift shop.[25]

Underway at Chicago's Lawndale Community Church are similar efforts begun by Wayne Gordon, who founded the church with a group of teenagers in 1978, having sensed the call to revive one of the city's toughest inner-city neighborhoods. Lawndale Community Church has become a safe refuge for kids, with a gymnasium and after-school tutoring. In the College Opportunity Program, eighth-graders commit themselves to a five-year program of twice-weekly study sessions at the church's learning center. If they maintain a 2.5 grade-point average, they receive a $3,000-per-year, four-year college scholarship. If the kids or their family members get sick, they can go to the church's full-service medical center for a minimal fee, and Lawndale's job-training program helps the unemployed find work. The church also has a housing ministry to rehabilitate abandoned buildings and give the poor an opportunity to become homeowners.[26]

In Baltimore, Sandtown was once a neighborhood of boarded-up row houses and littered alleys, with drug dealers on every corner—that is, until New Song Community Church was founded. Now the church reaches people like Torey Reynolds, mother of four, who was addicted to crack and on welfare. With the church's help, she went through job training and is now employed as a community health-care worker. Her children attend New Song's Learning Center, and when they're sick, she takes them to New Song Family Health Center. Torey and her husband are also proud first-time homeowners of one of the row houses rehabilitated through the local Habitat for Humanity.

In Memphis, Tennessee, the same vision for restoring social and moral order inspires the members of Mississippi Boulevard Christian Church. The church runs a housing-rehabilitation ministry, a Christian school, the Manna Food Center for distributing food to the poor and elderly, and the Family Life Center with everything from youth basketball and volleyball teams to roller skating, a handball court, and a bowling alley. The church also has a clothing pantry, a job-placement program, a bookstore, and counseling services.

All of these examples were originally inspired by a vision for Christian community development that was first born in the hearts of my friends John and Vera Mae Perkins. John grew up picking cotton in Mississippi, suffered beatings during the civil rights movement, and then founded Voice of Calvary ministry in Mendenhall and Jackson, Mississippi. Today these ministries have grown to include housing rehabilitation, a thrift store, job training, a school, day care, a food co-op, and a medical center. The Perkins's model of Christian community development is now being imitated across the country.

In recent years, John and Vera Mae have taken their vision to the drug-infested northwest corner of Pasadena, California. The first time I visited the Perkins's new home, I saw drug dealers on the street outside, pulling up in their limousines to do street-corner deals amid the garbage and litter. I prayed with John and Vera Mae in their living room, sitting by a window that still had a bullet hole from a drive-by shooting.

But within months, the Perkinses had turned their backyard into a play area where neighborhood kids could play safely and listen to Bible stories. Soon they bought up adjoining properties and renovated them; they opened a youth center and additional family services. They encouraged other Christians to buy properties close by and open related ministries. Over time, the drug dealers disappeared, crime abated, and children were playing in their front yards once more. When I returned for another visit, I could not believe the transformation.

What is happening in Boston, Dallas, Chicago, Baltimore, Memphis, Mendenhall, Jackson, and Pasadena is what Christians should be doing everywhere: converting chaos into the *tranquillitas ordinis,* one house at a time, one block at a time, one neighborhood at a time, one community at a time. Although our citizenship is in the "City of God," we know that God has placed us in our cities and neighborhoods to reflect his character and to restore his righteous dominion in the midst of a fallen world. We begin with our personal lives and habits, move out from there to our families and schools and then into our communities—and from there into our society as a whole.

CHAPTER 37

CREATING THE GOOD SOCIETY

"Why, sir, if he really believes there is no distinction between virtue and vice,
let us count our spoons before he leaves."
SAMUEL JOHNSON (when told that a dinner guest believed morality was a sham)

What does it take to achieve the good life? Not the Budweiser "good life," but a life of virtue? Our Founding Fathers understood that this is a crucial question for any society, for virtue is essential to freedom. People who cannot restrain their own baser instincts, who cannot treat one another with civility, are not capable of self-government. "Our Constitution was made for a moral and religious people," said John Adams. "It is wholly inadequate to the government of any other."[1] Without virtue, a society can be ruled only by fear, a truth that tyrants understand all too well.

The same critical question, then, confronts us as we move beyond our families and neighborhoods to consider our common life together: How can we achieve the virtue necessary to maintain a good society and to preserve liberty? And how do the worldview categories of *creation, fall,* and *redemption* help us analyze the false views we confront in our culture today?

Sadly, in our relativistic age many people, even Christians, have lost the ethical categories of right and wrong. A few years ago, a young acquaintance of mine, who is a member of a good church, attended a four-week ethics course at Harvard Business School—a course that was started in response to the Savings and Loan scandals in the 1980s. On his return, he raved about the course.

"What kind of ethics are they teaching?" I asked.

"Well, the professor really summed it up the last day when he said,

'Don't do anything that will get you in the newspapers. It's bad for business.'"

"But that's pure pragmatism," I replied in astonishment. "'Don't get caught.' 'Don't get the company in trouble.' What's that got to do with ethics?"

"But that's the point, isn't it?" said the young man. "To stay out of trouble."

Unfortunately, this perspective is quite common. Yet I have no grounds for self-righteousness, for when I was in politics, I practiced similar principles. I would not do anything I knew to be illegal, but I felt entitled to do to our opposition whatever they had done to us when they were in power (a sort of reverse Golden Rule). That's why the Watergate scandal was so frequently defended with the excuse "Everyone does it." Why was a little bugging of the Democratic headquarters so bad when we knew that President Johnson had bugged the Nixon campaign plane in 1968? And President Clinton resorted to exactly the same defense when challenged on campaign abuses in 1995.

Is it any wonder our country has been in an ethical free fall for the past three decades? A generation ago, the Watergate scandal rocked the nation; today, countless "gates" later, the public treats such scandals as routine.

The problem is that relativism provides no sure foundation for a safe and orderly society. If all people are free to choose for themselves what is right, how can a society agree on, and enforce, even minimal standards? And if there is no ultimate moral law, what motivation is there to be virtuous? The result is the loss of community. If you thought your neighbors had no clear definition of right and wrong, would you sleep well at night or let your children play in their yard?

Throughout most of Western history, the moral consensus was largely informed by the Judeo-Christian tradition. But with the Enlightenment, intellectuals began to argue that since God was no longer needed to explain creation, he was no longer needed to establish moral laws. Reason alone would form the basis for morality. Since then, the great question that has faced Western society is the one posed by the great Russian novelist Fyodor Dostoyevsky: "Can man be good without God?"

Can reason alone come up with a viable moral system? The answer is no, and the failure of reason alone to generate moral norms was illustrated forcefully some years ago by the fate of the Conference on Science, Philosophy, and Religion. In the summer of 1939, with Nazi armies occupying Czechoslovakia and poised to strike at Poland, the last hopes for appeasing Hitler were finally shattered, and the world girded itself for the horrors of another world war. Realizing that the moral resolve of the Western world must somehow be reinforced, Louis Finkelstein, chancellor of the Jewish Theological Seminary in New York, began planning for a grand conference where the greatest scholars from every discipline would draw on their collective wisdom to devise a universal code of ethics to provide the moral foundation for democracy. The conference was announced in June 1940 in a statement signed by seventy-nine leading intellectuals, including Albert Einstein. The *New York Times* printed the announcement in full on page one, breathlessly hailing it as an "intellectual declaration of independence."[2] A week later the *Times* published an editorial, "To Defend Democracy," which concluded that "we need a new Social Contract, a new Declaration of the Rights of Man."[3]

When the group convened later that year, the goal was what Finkelstein called "corporate thinking"—that is, an effort to synthesize Judeo-Christian ethics with Enlightenment humanism and modern science, in order to create a new foundation for democratic societies. Yet even before the opening gun—during the organizing session—the battle lines were drawn between traditionalists and modernists. On the side of the traditionalists, Mortimer Adler, editor of the Great Books series, declared, "We have more to fear from our professors than from Hitler," referring to those intellectuals who had abandoned historically accepted moral truths. His adversary, Sidney Hook, responded that Adler was promoting a "new medievalism." "The only absolute is science," Hook contended, and called for a pragmatic approach to morality. The modernists contended that all values are relative—except, of course, the value of tolerance.[4]

Notwithstanding the difficulties of the first conference, hopes continued to run high for the second one. Surely the best minds of our nation could agree on universal norms of conduct so that out of the ashes of war would emerge a new world of hope. The press continued its effusive coverage.

It was not until the third conference that the optimistic fervor began to subside as the debate came to a stalemate over which morality should be adopted. Around the country, editorialists began to reduce expectations slightly with headlines such as "Scholars Confess They Are Confused."[5]

The Conference on Science, Philosophy, and Religion continued to meet through the war years and after, debating issues such as the atom bomb, one-world government, and the end of Western colonialism. By the 1948 meeting, reports Fred Beuttler of the University of Illinois, "the biggest fear of most academic intellectuals was dogmatism and indoctrination." In other words, the relativists had carried the day. "All absolutist thinking," they said, "has totalitarian potential." By the early 1960s the conference was disbanded. The original goal of defining "cultural universals" had proved impossible.[6]

Think of it: For two decades some of the world's greatest minds engaged in stimulating debate and produced . . . nothing. Why? Because they disagreed about the proper starting point of ethical knowledge. The traditionalists, like Adler, understood that in order to have objective, universal ethical principles, there must be an absolute source, a transcendent authority. The modernists started with the assumption that science is the only source of sure knowledge, that nature is all there is, and thus that morality is merely a human invention that can be changed to meet changing circumstances in an evolving world. The two sides started out with conflicting worldviews, and in their fruitless exchanges were merely playing out the logical consequences of their starting points.

The grandiose endeavor of Louis Finkelstein brings into focus the failure of efforts to derive ethical rules from reason alone. Today ethics has degenerated into relativism, with each individual carving out his or her own private truths to live by. In the words of Father Richard John Neuhaus, we are "herds of independent minds marching towards moral oblivion with Frank Sinatra's witless boast on our lips, 'I Did It My Way.'"[7]

In this climate, it is considered offensive to assert in polite company that Western civilization, under the influence of the Judeo-Christian tradition, might enjoy any moral advantage or that its historic beliefs might be drawn on to arrest our moral free fall. When one of the Bass brothers of Texas gave $20 million to his alma mater, Yale University, stipulating that the grant be used for the study of Western civilization, the university hemmed and hawed. The faculty wanted a multicultural curriculum, not one that favored the Western tradition, so they dragged their feet until Lee Bass finally asked that his gift be returned.[8]

In our public schools it has become nearly impossible to teach traditional precepts of right and wrong—which has led to disastrous consequences. "For generations," writes theologian Michael Novak, "the primary task explicitly assigned public schools of the nation was character formation."[9] No longer. A few years ago, a *New York Times* reporter visited a New Jersey high school classroom in which students were discussing the case of a woman who had found $1000 and turned it in. All fifteen students said she was a fool. But the real shocker came after class, when the reporter asked the teacher why she had not told the students they were wrong. The teacher replied, "If I came from the position of what is right and wrong, then I'm not their counselor."[10]

Don't educators understand where this kind of value-free teaching must lead? A nation without virtue cannot govern itself. "Our people are losing virtue," Novak says bluntly. "That is why we have been losing self-government."[11] And if we cannot govern ourselves, then we invite others to govern us. The death of virtue threatens our very liberty as a people.

At root, this great struggle is between worldviews, and it poses the question: How now shall we live—by the Judeo-Christian tradition or by the moral nihilism of today's relativistic, individualistic culture?

A SOCIETY GUARDED BY 250 MILLION POLICEMEN

By examining these conflicting worldviews through the analytical grid of *creation, fall,* and *redemption,* we see clearly the cause of our ethical malaise. Creation tells us that we owe our existence to a holy God, whose character is the standard of all righteousness, the measure of all morality. "Be holy because I, the Lord your God, am holy" (Lev. 19:2). The clear failing of the secular worldview is that it tells us we owe our existence to natural forces acting at random; therefore, there can be no ultimate source of moral norms.

The second category is just as crucial. The Fall tells us we are prone to evil and thus need moral restraints for society to function. "What comes out of a man is what makes him 'unclean'" (Mark 7:20). But secularism fails to understand the nature of our moral dilemma, leading to the false assumption that since people are basically good, a virtuous society can be formed by creating the right social, political, and economic structures.

But the truth is that a virtuous society can be created only by virtuous people, whose individual consciences guard their behavior and hold them accountable. Without conscience, a society can be held in check only through coercion. Yet even coercion ultimately fails, for there is no police force large enough to keep an eye on every individual. "This country ought to have, when it is healthy and when it is working as it is intended to work, 250 million policemen—called *conscience,*" says Michael Novak. "When there are 250 million consciences on guard, it is surprising how few police are needed on the streets."[12]

The emphasis on social justice at the expense of private virtue is not only mistaken but downright dangerous. People without personal morality inevitably fail in their efforts to create public morality. "There is no social sin without personal sin," writes Georgetown University professor James Schall. "Our youth today are almost invariably taught they must change the world, not their souls. So they change the world, and it becomes worse."[13] Moral crusaders with zeal but no ethical understanding are likely to give us solutions that are worse than the problems.

What's more, when we focus young people's moral attention solely on public issues and causes, they fail to treat the personal realm as morally serious. Some years ago, Christina Hoff Sommers, philosophy professor at Clark University, wrote an article entitled "Teaching the Virtues," in which she attacked higher education for teaching ethics as social justice rather than as individual decency and honesty. One of Sommers's colleagues chastised her, complaining that she was promoting bourgeois morality and ignoring the real issues, such as the oppression of women, the evils of multinational corporations, and the exploitation of the environment. But at the end of the semester, the same teacher came to Sommers's office, horrified that more than half her students had plagiarized their take-home exam. They had cheated in an ethics course!

"What are you going to do?" Sommers asked. Sheepishly, the woman asked for a copy of Sommers's article on the importance of individual virtue.[14]

The myth of human goodness has led to a massive disconnect between the public and private realms, until many Americans are fractured and compartmentalized, glibly saying, "It doesn't matter what the president does in private." Or, worse, "It doesn't matter what *I* do in private." As we saw in an earlier chapter, Americans have embraced a dualism between the body and the "person," which is most obvious in arguments defending abortion (the fetus may be biologically human but not a "person").[15] The same dualism affords the perfect rationalization for libertinism. For if the body is merely a tool for getting us what we want—pleasure or emotional gratification—then its actions are judged by purely utilitarian considerations, not moral ones. Our actions do not reflect the "person," which is a separate entity. Thus we rationalize that a person can behave as a rogue, a liar, or a cheat in private life but can still be trusted in public life.

This runs totally against the grain of the Christian view of human nature. A good tree will produce good fruit, Jesus taught. "Whoever can be trusted with very little can also be trusted with much, and whoever is dishonest with very little will also be dishonest with much" (Luke 16:10). Integrity of character runs through large and small matters, through public and private actions.

I reflected on this principle a few years ago when I lectured on the subject of ethics at Camp Lejeune, North Carolina, the same place where I started out as an infantry platoon commander during the Korean War. With a touch of nostalgia, I returned to address two thousand marine officers and noncommissioned officers. They sat attentively in starched fatigues and spit-shined boots, but when the question-and-answer period began, no one stirred . . . until the general, a rugged, six-foot-six officer, turned around and said in a booming voice, "There will be questions." Suddenly, hands popped up all across the auditorium. (Some things never change.)

The last question was the toughest by far. "Mr. Colson," said a master sergeant, "which is more important—loyalty or integrity?"

Now, a marine lives by the creed *semper fidelis*—"always faithful"—and when I was a marine, I learned that loyalty meant unquestioning obedience. Yet I wish I had pondered the young sergeant's question when I was in the Nixon White House. For now I know the answer.

"Integrity comes first," I said. Loyalty, no matter how admirable, can be dangerous if it is invested in an unworthy cause.

Integrity comes from the verb *to integrate,* which means to become united so as to form a complete or perfect whole.[16] Scripture teaches that spirit, mind, and body all come from the hand of God, and thus they ought to be united, functioning together as a whole. Our actions must be consistent with our thoughts. We must be the same person in private and in public. Only the Christian worldview gives us the basis for this kind of integrity.

Moreover, Christianity gives an absolute moral law that allows us to judge between right and wrong. Try asking your secular friends how they decide what they *ought* to do, what ethical principles to follow. How do they know those principles are right? On what authority do they rely? Without moral absolutes, there is no real basis for ethics.

An absolute moral law doesn't confine people in a straitjacket of Victorian prudery. People will always debate the boundaries of moral law and its varied applications. But the very idea of right and wrong makes sense only if there is a final standard, a measuring rod, by which we can make moral judgments.

Only the Christian worldview offers redemption from sin, giving power to overcome the single most powerful obstacle to becoming virtuous: the rebellious human will. Morality is not just about an intellectual acknowledgment of ultimate standards, of what ought to be; morality is also about developing virtue—that is, the full range of habits and dispositions that constitute good character. We must not merely assent mentally to certain principles; we must *become* people who are just, courageous, patient, kind, loyal, loving, persistent, and devoted to duty. And only the Christian worldview tells us how to develop virtuous character, to become moral persons.

In the movie adaptation of Tolstoy's *War and Peace,* the central character, Pierre, asks dolefully, "Why is it that I know what is right, but do what is wrong?" That is the human dilemma. We may know the right thing, but that is no guarantee that we will do it. As the Old Testament prophet Jeremiah laments, "The heart is deceitful above all things and beyond cure. Who can understand it?" (Jer. 17:9). Or, as the apostle Paul puts it: "I know that nothing good lives in me, that is, in my sinful nature. For I have the desire to do what is good, but I cannot carry it out. For what I do is not the good I want to do; no, the evil I do not want to do—this I keep on doing" (Rom. 7:18-19).

Even if Louis Finkelstein's grand vision had succeeded and a universal code of morality had been agreed upon, would people have been able to live by it? Could they have become moral persons? The optimist says yes, but both Scripture and empirical evidence say otherwise. The secular view of ethics offers no salvation, no power to change the human heart.

I can testify to this from personal experience. I was raised in a good family with almost puritanical standards. My father, whom I idolized, drilled into me the principles of duty, honor, and honesty. I can still remember sitting with him on the back steps of our home on Sunday afternoons, listening to him lecture on the evils of cheating or stealing.

In 1969, when President Nixon asked me to leave my lucrative law practice to serve as his special counsel, I saw it as my duty to do so, even though it meant a drastic pay cut. To guard against temptation, or even the appearance of impropriety, I put my law firm investments and all other assets into a blind trust and vowed never even to see former law partners or clients (who might seek government favors). Any gifts I received, even boxes of candy at Christmas, were immediately turned over to the drivers of my limousine or the operators at the White House switchboard. I was determined: *No one would corrupt me.*

Yet I went to prison for obstruction of justice.

What happened?

My problem was that I didn't understand the deceptiveness of the human heart. In college, I had studied the best of the world's moral philosophy, including Immanuel Kant's famous "categorical imperative," which is really a modified version of the Golden Rule, a near universal moral principle. So I *knew* well enough what was right. The problem was that I lacked the will to *do* it. For we humans have an infinite capacity for self-rationalization; we can justify anything. Which is exactly what I did.

C. S. Lewis explains the dilemma in my favorite of his essays, "Men without Chests." For a person to be moral, the "head," the seat of reason, must rule the "stomach," or the passions. But it can do this only through the "chest," which in Lewis's analogy represents the will, the moral imagination. The problem today, Lewis writes, is that modern rationalism has reduced morality to cognition; it has focused on moral reasoning while ignoring the role of the will and moral imagination; it has robbed us of our "chests." And then we wonder why morality is declining. In Lewis's unforgettable words, "We make men without chests and expect of them virtue and enterprise. We laugh at honour and are shocked to find traitors in our midst. We castrate and bid the geldings be fruitful."[17]

Moral reasoning and intellectual knowledge are not enough. A fallen human being can fulfill the moral law only if the will is transformed. "For what the law was powerless to do in that it was weakened by the sinful nature, God did by sending his own Son in the likeness of sinful man to be a sin offering," writes the apostle Paul. "And so he condemned sin in sinful man, in order that the righteous requirements of the law might be fully met in us" (Rom. 8:3-4). When we turn to God, the Holy Spirit empowers us to do what we cannot do on our own. This is the essence of the term *conversion:* The will is turned around; it is transformed. At the heart of Christianity is a supernatural transforming power that enables us not only to know what is right but also to do it—to become virtuous.

Although only a converted will is capable of virtue in a consistent manner, there is also a natural virtue spoken of in Romans 2 (conscience), which is a consequence of our creation in the image of God. And while Christians must work for the conversion of individuals, we also have a duty to help build a good society by cultivating ethical knowledge even among the unconverted.

Our most intractable social problems cannot be solved by public policies but only by the practice of virtuous behavior. Take crime, for example. Sociologists and policy experts endlessly debate the question, What causes crime? But as Michael Novak notes, even if we uncovered the answer to that question, how would it help us? It would merely enable us to produce *more* crime. What we really need to know is how to produce virtue. Society ought to concentrate on finding ways to encourage virtuous behavior, and then crime will begin to fall.[18]

Historically, societies have encouraged virtuous behavior positively through custom and convention, and negatively through social stigmas, taboos, and shame. Admittedly, the latter are difficult to exert in a culture where no moral stigma is permitted for fear of damaging someone's self-esteem. But Christians can cut through this fog and argue for the right of a healthy society to express moral disapproval of socially harmful behavior.

We cannot rely on the law alone, for not all immoral actions should be made illegal. In many instances, right behavior is better enforced by an informal social consensus that defines certain behavior as unacceptable or worthy of contempt. That's why campaigns against drunk driving or drug abuse are often more effective than any law against them. In fact, if we fail to impose social conventions, we invite the imposition of more and more laws, which, in the absence of popular support, have to be enforced with ever increasing severity.

What does it take to create the good life? A firm sense of right and wrong and a determination to order one's life accordingly. Not out of a grim sense of duty, but because it is what fits with our created nature and makes us happiest and most fulfilled. When men and women act in accord with their true nature, they feel a sense of harmony, contentment, and joy. This is happiness, the fruit of virtue. In fact, the ancient philosophers defined happiness as something one achieves only at the end of life, after spending a whole lifetime in character training.[19]

It was this definition that the American Founders had in mind when they declared that we have an inalienable right to life, liberty, and the pursuit of happiness. The last phrase did not mean a right to hedonistic pleasure, as many people believe today, but the pursuit of virtue, a life spent ordering our appetites and desires to the truth of who we are, which produces happy individuals and a harmonious society.[20]

When we know the secret to true happiness, we will seek virtue in every area of life, even those that are typically thought to be purely technical or utilitarian, such as economics. And when that happens, we will make the astonishing discovery that the Christian worldview enhances our economic well-being and gives genuine meaning even to our work.

THE WORK OF OUR HANDS

*In nothing has the Church so lost Her hold on reality as in Her failure to
understand and respect the secular vocation. She has allowed work and
religion to become separate departments. . . . She has forgotten that the
secular vocation is sacred.*

DOROTHY SAYERS

During the 1992 presidential election, a new phrase entered the
American vocabulary: "It's the economy, Stupid." The phrase turned out to
be politically potent. For although there is more to life than bread alone, we
are all concerned about our economic well-being. After all, earning an
income and supporting our families is a prime undertaking in our lives, and
we spend the majority of our waking hours working, whether in the
marketplace or at home. Yet how often have you heard a sermon about the
biblical view of work or economics? The church has largely abandoned these
topics, charges British essayist Dorothy Sayers, and the result is that many
believers feel as if their faith has nothing to do with their work. No wonder,
then, that some people even come to question the relevance of religion to
their daily life. "How can anyone remain interested in a religion which seems
to have no concern with nine-tenths of his life?" Sayers asks.[1]

But the fact is, God's Word has a great deal to say about work. And although the Bible may not endorse any particular economic theory, it does lay
out a basic blueprint for a society that is free, prosperous, and just. Indeed, in
many ways biblical principles inspired the development of our own system of
democratic capitalism, which has triumphed so dramatically in the closing
decades of the twentieth century. Around the globe, nations are casting off
the chains of socialism and eagerly embracing Western models of economic
freedom. And in the West, liberal and leftist political parties are scrambling

toward the political center. Even the most fervent socialist sympathizers have finally had to concede that the free-market system is better not only at lifting people out of poverty but also at recognizing human dignity.

Ironically, though, the collapse of the Soviet system and the discrediting of Marxism make it all the more important for us to understand the principles that undergird the Western free-market system. During the past half century, Americans have had before them a clear and menacing contrast between the free world and two regimes of terror: Nazism and Communism. Whatever the failures of our own system, it was obvious to all but the willfully blind that a free-market system was immeasurably superior to the alternatives. Yet today we can no longer simply point to that stark contrast, and as a result we must formulate a positive defense of the principles that undergird a free society.[2] We must articulate the biblical principles that support economic freedom and a sense of vocation.

THE FIRST JOB DESCRIPTION

A Christian worldview perspective on work and economic development clearly follows the basic contours of the categories of *creation, fall,* and *redemption.* In the opening chapters of Genesis, we learn that human beings were made in the image of God, to reflect his character; therefore, we are called to reflect his creative activity through our own creativity—by cultivating the world, drawing out its potential, and giving it shape and form. All work has dignity as an expression of the divine image.

When God placed the first couple in the Garden of Eden, he assigned them the first job description: Work the earth and take care of it (Gen. 2:15). Even in Paradise, then, in the ideal state of innocence, work was the natural activity of human beings. In the words of theologian T. M. Moore, "Labor and economic development, using minds and hands in a communal effort, are thus part of the original mandate from God."[3]

Yet Scripture is never romantic or naïve about the human condition. The world God originally created was soon marred by the Fall, and work is now under a "curse," as theologians put it. In Genesis 3:16-17 the same Hebrew word is used for both the "pain" in childbirth and the "toil" of work—a word that means "labor" or "travail." The implication is that because of the Fall, both of the central tasks of human life—making a living and raising a family—are fraught with pain and difficulty. Understanding this, we can be realistic about the agony and anomie of life in a broken world.

Yet the sorrow that sin injected into creation does not cancel out the way we were originally made or the mandate to work. And redemption enables us to restore the original meaning and purpose of work. It gives us the power to carry out the task we were created for—to develop culture and civilization. Indeed, in our work, we cooperate with God in the task of redemption, helping free the world from the effects of the Fall.

The Bible also gives the underlying principles of economics, ranging from private property to rules of commerce to economic justice. It speaks clearly to the first requirement of economic liberty: that is, the protection of private ownership of goods and property. One of the traits that makes humans unique, different from animals, is our ability to use our skills and talents to shape material things to reflect our individuality—and when we do this, we create property. Material things in and of themselves are not property; they become property only when humans creatively find ways to use them productively. An example is a sticky, black, smelly substance that was nothing but a nuisance until humans developed technologies for refining it—then, suddenly, oil became a source of wealth. Seen in this light, the defense of the right to property is not a defense of material things per se, but rather of the dignity of human creativity, ingenuity, and inventiveness.[4]

Throughout Scripture we find the right to private property recognized and defended. As a moral principle, this recognition and defense is implicit in the Ten Commandments: in the eighth commandment, which forbids stealing, and in the tenth commandment, which forbids coveting. And in the Mosaic law, those who stole another's property were required to make restitution (Exod. 22).

The accumulation of wealth in itself is not treated as evil in Scripture. Men like Abraham and Solomon were very wealthy. Sometimes wealth is even a reward for spiritual faithfulness, as was the case when God restored Job's property, giving him twice what he had had before disaster struck (Job 42:10-12). Scripture does, however, warn against seeking wealth as an end in itself or using oppression and cruelty as means for amassing it. Paul called "the love of money" (though not money itself) "a root of all kinds of evil" (1 Tim. 6:10), and Old Testament prophets warned that wealth easily leads to spiritual complacency and even disobedience to God (see, for example, Deut. 31:1-21; 2 Kings 20:12-18; Ps. 49; Amos 6:1-4). In other words, the right to private property does not mean we have the right to do whatever we please with our possessions.

Ultimately, of course, we do not own anything; we are only stewards of the things God has entrusted to us. It is God who owns all things: "The earth is the Lord's, and everything in it" (Ps. 24:1). We are to use our economic resources and our labor as he commands, according to his law of justice and mercy. That's why Scripture calls for just scales and balances (Prov. 11:1; 20:23; Amos 8:5) and warns of God's judgment against oppressors who withhold wages or who take advantage of the needy (Lev. 19:13; Amos 5:11-12; 8:5-6). Scripture condemns those who manipulate the economy for their own sinful purposes, whether by hoarding or by other forms of wickedness such as greed, indolence, and deception (Prov. 3:27-28; 11:26; James 5:1-6). Economic justice forbids those who extend credit from taking advantage of those who are in their debt; on the other hand, those who incur a debt must repay it (Exod. 22:14; 2 Kings 4:1-7; Ps. 37:21; Prov. 22:7).[5]

The underlying principle is that private property is a gift from God to be used to establish social justice and to care for the poor and disadvantaged. Repentant thieves were told to steal no more but work with their hands *so that they would "have something to share with those in need"* (Eph. 4:28, emphasis added). Few themes in Scripture are sounded more loudly or clearly than God's commandments to care for the less fortunate. "Learn to do right!" God thunders. "Seek justice, encourage the oppressed. Defend the cause of the fatherless, plead the case of the widow" (Isa. 1:17). Through the prophet Isaiah, God announces that a true fast is not an empty religious ritual but is "to share your food with the hungry and to provide the poor wanderer with shelter—when you see the naked, to clothe him, and not to turn away from your own flesh and blood" (Isa. 58:7). Jesus deepens our sense of responsibility by telling us that in helping the hungry, the naked, the sick, and the imprisoned, we are actually serving him (Matt. 25:31-46).

Yet the poor are never reduced to passive recipients of charity; the able-bodied are required to work in exchange for benefits. This principle is best embodied in Old Testament laws requiring landowners to leave generous margins unharvested around their fields so the poor would be able to glean enough to live on (Lev. 19:9-10; Deut. 24:19-22). In the New Testament, Paul chastises the able-bodied who refuse to work, urging that they "settle down and earn the bread they eat" (2 Thess. 3:12). The poor are to retain their dignity as competent and responsible people who are capable of helping themselves.

Both the Old and New Testaments were written in societies that practiced slavery, and critics have often attacked the Bible for not challenging the practice. Yet, considering the times in which they were written, the Scriptures are among the most radical documents ever penned. In the Old Testament, God provided a means for slaves to earn their freedom (Deut. 15:12), and in the New Testament, Paul tells slaves that "if you can gain your freedom, do so" (1 Cor. 7:21). More important, the Bible calls both masters and slaves to recognize their primary identity as servants of God: "He who was a

slave when he was called by the Lord is the Lord's freedman; similarly, he
who was a free man when he was called is Christ's slave" (1 Cor. 7:22). It is
not economic conditions that count so much as the condition of the
heart—and when the heart is transformed, that will inevitably change the
way people structure their external relationships. That's precisely why Christians in the West came to see slavery as incompatible with the God-given
dignity of all people, and why many believers became leaders of the abolition
movement.

SECULAR WORK IS SACRED

Turning to the testimony of history, we can trace a steady development in
the dignity accorded to the individual and to economic vocation. In the first
centuries after Christ, the early church was forced to define a biblical view of
work and economic development in contrast to the views inherited from ancient Greek culture, which equated the material world with evil and disorder. As a result, the Greeks denigrated anything related to material
things—including manual labor. Working with one's hands was relegated to
slaves and artisans, whose labor freed up the intellectual elite for what the
Greeks regarded as the "nobler" pursuit of culture and philosophy.

Against this backdrop, the early church defended a high view of the
material world as God's creation. "There has never been room in the Hebrew
or Christian tradition for the idea that the material world is something to be
escaped from and that work in it is degrading. Material things are to be *used*
to the glory of God and for the good of men," writes British philosopher
Mary Hesse. As a result, "in western Europe in the Christian era, there was
never the same derogation of manual work. There was no slave class to do
the work, and craftsmen were respected."[6]

Nevertheless, many early theologians were influenced by Greek philosophy, especially Platonism, with the result that a distinction came to be
drawn between sacred and secular realms. Full-time religious workers, devoted "to the service of God alone," embody the "perfect form of the Christian life," wrote Eusebius in the fourth century, whereas farmers and traders
may achieve only "a kind of secondary grade of piety."[7]

This attitude was challenged by Thomas Aquinas, who stood against
the Platonic stream in Christian thought and stressed the value of the created world. His philosophy stimulated the Scholastics to explore topics now
considered part of economics, such as property, trade, prices, and wealth
creation—culminating in the work of the sixteenth-century School of

Salamanca in Spain, praised by the great economist Joseph Schumpeter as the "founders" of scientific economics.[8]

The Reformers likewise protested vigorously against the dichotomy between the sacred and the secular and its implicit devaluation of creation. When we carry out our vocation in obedience to God's commands, wrote Martin Luther, then God himself works through us to his purposes. And this partnership with God includes *all* legitimate forms of work, not just spiritual vocations. Luther totally rejected the notion that monks and clergy were engaged in holier work than shopkeepers and housewives. "Seemingly secular works are a worship of God," he wrote, "and an obedience well pleasing to God."[9]

The division into sacred and secular had not only made secular work second-best but also held secular workers to a lower standard of devotion and spirituality. The Reformation challenged that concept, insisting that no believer is exempt from the highest spiritual standards. Looking through the biblical lens, Luther wrote, we see that "the entire world [is] full of service to God, not only the churches but also the home, the kitchen, the cellar, the workshop, and the field of the townsfolk and farmers."[10]

Drawing from passages such as Jesus' parable of the talents in Matthew 25:14-30, the Reformers also cast aside a common medieval belief that making a profit is immoral. "One of the simplest lessons from the parable," writes Father Robert Sirico, "is that it is not immoral to profit from our resources, wit, and labor." After all, the alternative to profit is loss, and loss due to lack of initiative "does not constitute good stewardship."[11] God expects us to use our talents—both our abilities and our money—toward productive ends in order to serve others.

These beliefs about the value of work and entrepreneurial talent shaped what became known as the Protestant work ethic. It, in turn, became the driving force behind the industrial revolution, which has raised the standard of living immeasurably for vast numbers of societies around the globe.[12] The impact of the work ethic is one of the great examples of the way a Christian worldview can revolutionize a culture.

■   ■   ■

THE CHRISTIAN VIEW of work, however, has been opposed by a variety of secular views, which began to emerge after the Enlightenment. The rejection of the biblical doctrine of creation led to a rejection of its doctrine of human nature (its anthropology). No longer were human beings seen as the handiwork of God, living for high moral and spiritual purposes—to love

God and serve their neighbors. Instead, they were seen as merely a part of nature, driven by self-interest and expediency. As a result, the Protestant work ethic was separated from its Christian context of stewardship and service, and degraded into a creed of personal success.

In the late eighteenth century, for example, Adam Smith, the founder of capitalism, defined work solely as a means of fulfilling one's self-interest. No one acts out of benevolence, he argued, but only out of enlightened concern for personal advancement: "It is not from the benevolence of the butcher, the brewer, or the baker, that we expect our dinner, but from their regard to their own interest. We address ourselves, not to their humanity but to their self-love."[13] Whereas both classical and Christian ethics had regarded self-interest as a vice to be overcome for the common good, Smith contended that self-interest was actually good for society. His theory of capitalism turned an attitude once thought to be evil into a virtue. "The paradox," writes theologian Michael Novak, "consisted in attaining a highly moral outcome [getting rid of hunger and poverty] by placing *less* stress on moral purposes" and greater stress on rational self-interest.[14]

For Smith, the economy was an amoral, autonomous mechanism, grinding along apart from the moral influence of law or church or family. Indeed, he urged that the best thing for the economy is for everyone to stand out of its way and give free reign to "the invisible hand," which ensures that supply and demand will always balance. This vision of a self-regulating system of production and exchange is a secularization of the Christian doctrine of providence, replacing it with an interlocking order of nature.

Focusing on self-interest proved very effective, for in a fallen world, it is one of the strongest forms of motivation. But instead of raising the moral bar, challenging people to go beyond self-interest, Smith's system seemed to accommodate our sinful state. The system demanded the very impulses Christianity had traditionally renounced as immoral: self-interest instead of concern for the common good, personal ambition instead of altruism, and drive for personal gain instead of self-sacrifice and charity. Smith's system seemed to glorify those impulses by treating them as the driving force for a healthy economy, thus paving the way for a new ethic of ambition, aggression, and self-advancement.

Moreover, Smith was mistaken in thinking that an autonomous free market would operate most beneficently. Quite the opposite. As the early days of industrialism proved, an autonomous, secularized capitalism exploits both workers and the environment, creating new forms of slavery in what poet William Blake called the "dark Satanic Mills."[15] Capitalism is astonishingly efficient at generating new wealth, but it operates beneficently only when the market is shaped by moral forces coming from both the law and the culture—derived ultimately from religion.

How do we bring these moral forces to bear on today's economy? This is the major issue facing Christians in this area. How do we transform a secularized, *de*moralized capitalism into a morally responsible free-market system?

·   ·   ·

THE MOST IMPORTANT point we need to make is that an economy is not an autonomous mechanism. It depends, first of all, on a juridical framework: on a system of laws to maintain a sound currency, protect private property, enforce contracts, and clamp down on corruption. Government acts as a referee, making sure everyone follows the rules and plays fair. Business transactions cannot be carried out in a society where people cannot trust one another, where graft and corruption are the rule, where contracts are made to be broken. We have only to look at the current situation in Russia to see what happens when capitalism is introduced without the rule of law and the judicial infrastructure to maintain order in commerce: Ruthless businessmen, like the "Russian Mafia," pillage the country. Similar examples of "crony capitalism" abound in the Third World, where those in power steal from the people with impunity.

Humane capitalism also depends on a sound moral culture, for a free market readily caters to the moral choices we make, supplying whatever consumers want—from Bibles to pornography. Only a virtuous citizenry will refuse to manufacture or buy products that are immoral and destructive. Interestingly, the idea of a command economy was concocted to bypass this very requirement: It was thought that the only way to guarantee the production of socially beneficial products was by taking economic decisions out of the hands of private citizens and placing them in the hands of the state. But state-run economies didn't work. And we now know there are simply no shortcuts: Morality in the marketplace depends on the decisions made by each individual economic agent. This is why the Christian's role is indispensable, for we alone have the spiritual resources to help create a healthy moral climate.

Even entrepreneurship itself requires the practice of moral virtues. Those who invest their time and money in enterprises in which the rewards are not immediate must practice hard work, self-sacrifice, and delayed gratification, says Michael Novak.[16] They must also cultivate sensitivity and courtesy to others, because if you don't please the customer, you're out of business. It is said that when McDonald's first set up shop in the Soviet Union, the company had to teach cashiers to smile and say thank you—courtesies not required back when all stores were government monopolies.

All this can be summed up by saying that economic success depends on morality—strange as that may sound to some economic conservatives. I am sometimes told by Republican members of Congress that they struggle to hold together religious conservatives and corporate interests in the same party. For example, religious conservatives have pushed for sanctions against nations that practice religious persecution, while business interests oppose sanctions for fear they would hurt trade. My response is always that these two groups are not enemies but allies, who in fact need each other. For "businesses are plants that do not grow in just any soil," Novak writes. As we have shown, they thrive best in a culture that is both politically free and morally virtuous. Novak uses the image of a three-legged stool: A healthy democracy comprises political liberty, economic freedom, and moral responsibility. Weaken any leg, and the stool topples over.[17]

As societies around the world shake off the chains of communism and socialism, it is more imperative than ever that Christians make a case for the moral and spiritual basis of a free economy. For if a thoroughly secularized capitalism is adopted, it will surely lead not to freedom but to new forms of slavery, just as early capitalism created its "dark Satanic Mills." Capitalism provides the best opportunity for economic growth and human freedom only if it is tempered by compassion and regard for social justice.

HOW NOW SHALL WE WORK?

The modern tendency to regard economics as an arena of amoral forces and mechanisms has had a profound effect on the way ordinary people order their work lives. Torn out of a Christian context, the meaning of work has been distorted. Bereft of a vision of eternity and driven by an ever more acquisitive culture, many people have become obsessed with success in the here and now, resulting in a major shift in social priorities.

For many Americans, weakened ties to family and church mean the workplace has become the primary social environment. Coworkers have become the new family, the tribe, the social world. "We become almost citizens of our companies," says *Time* correspondent Lance Morrow, "living under the protection of salaries, pensions, and health insurance."[18] Many corporations consciously seek to become the center of employees' lives, offering child care, health centers, drug and alcohol counseling, and an array of social services. As sociologist Robert Schrank notes, "The workplace performs the function of community."[19]

Indeed, some people even *prefer* it to real community. In her provocative book *The Time Bind,* sociologist Arlie Hochschild suggests that many parents are actually choosing to overwork as an escape from family life. Back in the nineteenth century, home was pictured as a haven from the stress and pressure of the workplace. But for many of the parents Hochschild interviewed, home is a place filled with the incessant demands of noisy children, endless piles of laundry, and few tangible rewards—while at work they enjoy adult sociability and feel that their hard work is appreciated. One mother of three told Hochschild, "I usually come to work early just to get away from the house."[20]

Yet at the same time, evidence is mounting that institutional child care has negative effects on children, both in terms of frequent illnesses and unruly behavior.[21] As a result, many Americans feel a gnawing unease about the trade-offs they are making for work—a concern the popular press has been quick to pick up on: "The Myth of Quality Time," blazed a headline in *Newsweek,* and *U.S. News and World Report* titled a recent article "Lies Parents Tell Themselves about Why They Work."[22]

All this is symptomatic, however, of a more fundamental problem—which is that Americans have lost a sense of a higher purpose for work. In our materialistic culture, work is reduced to a utilitarian function: a means of attaining benefits for *this* world, *this* life—whether material gain or self-fulfillment. Work no longer has a transcendent purpose as a means of serving and loving God. No wonder, then, that many are questioning the very meaning of work. As Morrow writes, people today are asking, "Is there some inherent worth in work?"[23]

This offers Christians a rich opportunity to make the case that work is truly fulfilling only when it is firmly tied to its moral and spiritual moorings. It is time for the church to reclaim this crucial part of life, restoring a biblical understanding of work and economics. A biblical theology of work should be a frequent subject for sermons, just as it was during the Reformation, when establishing one's vocation was considered a crucial element in discipleship.[24] Churches should organize classes on business ethics and biblical work principles for those in the workplace.[25] Finally, they should set up programs to help the able-bodied poor become self-sufficient instead of dependent on government welfare.

The record shows that only the church can impart the work ethic and sense of purpose that lifts people out of poverty. When Allen-Edmonds Shoe Corporation set up a new factory in inner-city Milwaukee, company president John Stollenwerk contacted pastors at several neighborhood churches. When asked why he had not contacted local, state, and federal job-training programs to recruit new employees, Stollenwerk replied, "It just never occurred to us." Government training programs may impart specific skills, he explained, but they cannot provide the moral habits of reliability, hard work, and commitment to family that make good workers. Churches, on the other hand, impart precisely these fundamental values.[26]

Beyond that, many churches are providing outstanding models of programs that spur economic self-sufficiency. They are establishing job-training programs to help the poor become employable; they are setting up credit unions, job banks, and business fairs. In Brooklyn, New York, for example, Father Ronald Marino set up a program called Resources, Inc. to train immigrants in work and management skills. Then he started his own companies to employ them.[27]

In Portland, Oregon, the Union Gospel Mission started Life Change, a job-training program for convicted felons and drug addicts. One twenty-four-year-old man who was homeless and on drugs is now a college student in electrical engineering with a 3.8 grade-point average. A thirty-eight-year-old woman who was a prostitute is now the manager of a local Subway sandwich shop.[28]

Voice of Hope, a Christian community-development program in West Dallas (mentioned in chapter 36), uses its housing-rehabilitation project as a way to teach job skills to ghetto teens. The young people learn carpentry, painting, roofing, landscaping, and practical money management.[29] Mississippi Boulevard Christian Church in Memphis, Tennessee, encourages economic development in the surrounding low-income neighborhood by holding weekly minimalls on the church parking lot. Minority businesses and entrepreneurs sell their products and network with one another. The church also runs an annual Trade Expo.[30]

West Los Angeles Church of God in Christ operates a community-development corporation that aims at "economic empowerment" of the poor in its neighborhood. Its programs include job training and entrepreneurial development, and it also partners with major corporations and businesses to provide employment for neighborhood residents.[31]

As welfare reform reduces the government's role in helping the poor, the church has a great opportunity to step into the gap. Many Christians are already mobilizing to help welfare recipients make the shift from dependence to work, as the following success stories illustrate.[32]

In Mississippi, the Faith and Families program, which matches families on welfare with church members, has reached 350 families. More than half are now off cash welfare, and the program is being copied in other states.

In Texas, 219 churches have joined Pathfinder Families, helping 230 welfare recipients who are trying to find work under the state's strict time limits.

In Michigan, nearly 60 churches in Ottawa County have helped 60 families leave welfare in just over a year. The county is the first locality in the United States to move every able-bodied welfare recipient into a job—an astonishing success.

In Maryland, 21 congregations in Anne Arundel County have helped 30 families obtain jobs and leave public assistance.

And in Florida, a coalition of 70 churches has helped 700 elderly and disabled legal immigrants adversely affected by welfare reform.

Similar principles of economic development are being applied by Christians around the world to combat Third-World poverty. In Manila, the capital of the Philippines, one section of the city houses more than 65,000 people in shacks that are nothing more than wood and corrugated metal lean-tos. With no sewers, no plumbing, and no city water, the stench is sickening. Children run naked in the streets while adults sit on the sidewalk, staring vacantly.

In the midst of these desperate conditions, Prison Fellowship International has started a microenterprise project that takes people out of the nearby Mantalupa Prison, mentors them in a church, and then loans them $120 to buy a pedicab (a bicycle with a cab on the side, used for ferrying passengers and packages through crowded streets). The loan program has become a stunning success: 95 percent of those who receive loans repay them within nine months.

I visited the program and saw the parking lot where thirty brightly painted pedicabs, all bearing the Prison Fellowship logo on the front, were lined up like automobiles in a showroom, polished and gleaming in the sun. Greeting us were the proud pedicab owners (all former inmates) and their families, along with the pastors who mentored them.

The former inmates had put together a concert, and as they stood on the stage singing, one little girl, perhaps four years old, with brown button eyes, pulled herself up onto the platform and walked toward her father, who was standing in the front row. She clutched his legs and looked up with an adoring expression; he looked down and began to caress her hair. That picture is frozen in my mind's eye; everything I have done in the ministry over twenty-five years was worth that one moment—to see an ex-prisoner, ex-gang member with a loving family, a job, and hope.

The church's goal in all these programs is to meet a need far deeper than the need to make a living: The programs are addressing the need to be creative, a need imprinted in every human heart by the Creator. Alexander Solzhenitsyn captured this truth brilliantly in *One Day in the Life of Ivan Denisovich,* his classic novel describing life in the Gulag. There, despite the starvation rations, the brutality of the guards, and the backbreaking labor, the main character, Shukhov, discovers that the truly human elements of life can still break through: friendship, generosity, faith . . . and work. Even with his body abused and aching, Shukhov feels a stab of pride in his ability to build a wall of bricks with a fine, even line. As the guards muster the prisoners to march back to camp, Shukhov takes one final look at his work. "Not so bad!" he thinks. Then "he ran up and looked the wall over from right to left. He had an eye like a mason's level. It was straight. His hands had skill in them yet."[33] Even in the harshest of circumstances, work is still a gift of God that imparts a sense of personal fulfillment and useful service.

■   ■   ■

CONTEMPORARY CONCERNS over economic issues reflect a profound confusion in secular society—whether it is welfare reform, tensions over work and family commitments, or the relationship of morality to economic policy. Only Christianity holds the key to this dilemma. For only the Christian worldview provides the moral foundation essential to preserving free economic systems; only the Christian worldview provides a high view of work that gives meaning and dignity to human labor. Once again we see that Christianity offers the truth about reality, providing a road map to find our way amidst the confusions and perplexities of everyday life.

Christianity even gives us the basic presuppositions needed to run a nation through just and fair-minded laws and to foster a political system that is both free and well ordered. In fact, Christianity played a definitive role in shaping the character of our own government, as we will see in the following chapter.

CHAPTER 39

THE ULTIMATE APPEAL

The very idea of freedom presupposes some objective moral law which overreaches ruler and ruled alike. Subjectivism about values is eternally incompatible with democracy . . . if there is no Law of Nature, the ethos of any society is the creation of its rulers, educators, and conditioners.

C. S. LEWIS

The place was Birmingham, Alabama. The year, 1963. The date, just days before Easter weekend.

It was nine years since Rosa Parks had refused to sit in the back of the bus in Selma, Alabama, and nearly as long since the Freedom Riders made their harrowing journeys on Greyhound and Trailways buses to challenge segregated seating. A group of civil rights leaders—Martin Luther King Jr., Ralph Abernathy, Andrew Young, and others in the Southern Christian Leadership Conference (SCLC)—had gathered downtown in the "war room" suite in the Gaston Hotel to make their most significant strategy decision yet.

The group had launched a civil rights campaign in Birmingham, and it was taking off, with thousands of young people joining their elders in peaceful marches. A boycott of downtown stores was making an impact. And the strategy of nonviolent resistance was working: They were filling the jails to overflowing, making it impossible to suppress the movement by sheer force.

This much progress in Birmingham was remarkable. Birmingham—a city so racist that the authorities had shut down parks and city baseball leagues rather than integrate them. A city whose leaders had declared that blood would flow in the streets before they complied with the Supreme Court's decision to integrate schools. A city where serving food to whites and blacks at the same lunch counter was still illegal. A city that in the past six years had seen seventeen bombings—all unsolved—of black churches and homes of civil rights leaders. A city where racist terrorists had castrated a man and left his body on a deserted road.

Perhaps it was no surprise, then, that Birmingham officials had decided to fight the civil rights movement, adopting tactics that had already been used all too successfully a year earlier in Albany, Georgia. They had found a federal judge to issue a restraining order against King and other leaders of the movement who had announced plans to march on Good Friday. If the leaders obeyed the restraining order, as they had in Albany, they would miss the march—and they had seen what happened then. Without leadership, the movement had lost momentum and fizzled. Yet if they disobeyed the order, they would be defying a federal court, taking civil disobedience to new levels. Was that morally justifiable?

King's advisers urged him to forgo the march so he could raise the money to bail the other marchers out of jail. But how could he ask others to sit in prison unless he was willing to join them? Besides, his pledge to march on Good Friday had been made repeatedly in public rallies. If he didn't show up, supporters would be demoralized and enemies would think he had backed down.

What to do? King went into one of the suite's bedrooms to pray through his decision. When he reemerged after more than an hour, he was wearing a new pair of overalls he had bought to wear to jail.

"I'm going to march," he said. "We can't know what lies ahead. We just have to fulfill our promises as best we can. We're in God's hands now."

"Son," said his father, Dr. Martin Luther King Sr., "I've never gone against any of your decisions. But this time I think you'd better stay home. I wouldn't disobey that injunction."

For a moment the agony of the decision seized King once more. He thought for a moment, then said, "No. I'm determined."

"All right then," his father said, nodding.[1]

·   ■   ■

A PHOTOGRAPHER caught the moment of King's arrest in a photograph that became famous—the great civil rights leader in handcuffs, glancing back toward his supporters, his face haunted. Inside the Birmingham jail, he was locked in solitary confinement in a room the size of a monk's cell, narrow and windowless. Imprisonment was made even more bitter when his lawyers brought in a copy of the Birmingham *News* containing a statement signed by eight white clergymen criticizing his strategy of civil disobedience.

But suddenly King had an inspiration. He was going to compose a rebuttal to those clergy in the form of an open letter—a defense of the civil rights movement that would appeal to the conscience of all America. On scraps of toilet paper and writing paper later smuggled out page by page, King wrote a lyrical epistle on why it is sometimes justifiable to break the law.

The civil rights movement, he acknowledged, had gained much of its leverage from urging people to obey the Supreme Court's 1954 decision outlawing segregation in the public schools. Thus, "at first glance it may seem rather paradoxical for us consciously to break laws. One may well ask: 'How can you advocate breaking some laws and obeying others?' The answer lies in the fact that there are two types of laws: just and unjust. One has not only a legal but a moral responsibility to obey just laws. Conversely, one has a moral responsibility to disobey unjust laws. I would agree with St. Augustine that 'an unjust law is no law at all.'

"Now, what is the difference between the two? . . . A just law is a man-made code that squares with the moral law or the law of God. An unjust law is out of harmony with the moral law. To put it in the terms of St. Thomas Aquinas: An unjust law is a human law that is not rooted in eternal law and natural law."[2]

The tradition of civil disobedience, King noted, goes back to Old Testament times—to Shadrach, Meshach, and Abednego, three young Jewish men who for the sake of conscience disobeyed the laws of the Babylonian monarch Nebuchadnezzar. It goes back to the reformer Martin Luther, who declared, "Here I stand; I can do no other. God help me." Back to John Bunyan, who was imprisoned for his beliefs: "I will stay in jail to the end of my days before I make a butchery of my conscience." And Thomas Jefferson, who justified the American Revolution with these ringing words: "We hold these truths to be self-evident, that all men are created equal."

King would always remember this incarceration as the moment when his beliefs were put to the severest test. His "Letter from Birmingham Jail" became one of his greatest testaments of faith.

A great burden was lifted from his mind when he learned that the money had been quickly raised to secure the release of all civil rights workers. He was surprised and relieved, and at that moment, as he later wrote, he became "aware of a feeling that had been present all along below the surface of consciousness," a feeling that "I had never been truly in solitary confinement; God's companionship does not stop at the door of a jail cell. I don't know whether the sun was shining at that moment. But I know that once again I could see the light."[3]

A LAW ABOVE THE LAW

Martin Luther King Jr. secured his place in American history when the pop-
ulist movement he led finally convinced the nation to affirm that the principles of the Declaration of Independence truly apply to all Americans. But
just as important as the success of his crusade is the principle on which it
rested, for that principle is the most fundamental basis for our republican
form of government: that government is not simply a social contract between
the people and those who govern, but a social contract made under the authority of a higher law.

The greatest moral struggle in our nation's history—the campaign to
end slavery—turned on the same principle. Abolitionists denounced the fu-
gitive-slave bill (by which Congress required people to return escaped slaves)
as contrary to a "higher law," even though it carried out an express provision
of the Constitution.⁴ Lincoln employed the same argument in opposing the
Supreme Court decision condoning slavery.⁵ He wrote passionately about
"the duty of nations as well as of men to own their dependence upon the
overruling power of God."⁶ Only a deep conviction about our obligation to
submit to a higher authority could have steeled this humble country lawyer
to oppose slavery when it was a legally established institution.

The most significant moral debate of our own day—the debate over
abortion, euthanasia, and related life issues—is fueled by the same conviction. The pro-life movement refuses to accept current abortion law on the
grounds that no human law is valid as long as it is contrary to a higher law.

This understanding of a transcendent law above human law (or positive law) is critical to the preservation of liberty and justice. As the Declaration of Independence puts it, there exist certain "unalienable rights" that are
beyond the authority of government either to grant or to deny; it can only
recognize them as preexisting. For if the government confers these rights,
then they are *not* unalienable, for the government can also take them
away—and any group out of favor can be crushed by the self-interest of the
majority or the naked force of the state.

Professor Robert George of Princeton University made the point in a
colorful way in a civil-liberties course by reading to his students the opening
words of the Declaration of Independence: "We hold these truths to be
self-evident, that all men are created equal, that they are endowed by their
Creator with certain unalienable rights." Then he looked out at the sea of
students in the packed lecture hall and said: "These are the foundational
words of the American doctrine of civil liberties, and in light of the content
of that doctrine as expressed in the Declaration, perhaps it wouldn't be

inappropriate to begin our deliberations by offering thanksgiving to the Creator who endowed us with these rights. So let us in silence, each according to his own tradition and in his own way, give thanks to the Creator for our precious rights and liberties." And then he added, impishly, "Those of you who are not believers might take this opportunity to reflect in silence upon the source of our most important rights and liberties, which I believe you too cherish." When he looked up again, he saw two hundred fifty undergraduates with their heads bowed (and to the side, a handful of teaching assistants looking pale and horrified).[7]

The idea of a transcendent law has deep historical roots, as even a cursory survey makes clear. In ancient Jewish culture, the law (Torah) was revered as divine revelation. Among the ancient Greeks, Plato and Aristotle contended that human justice is defined by higher truths, or ideals, accessible to human reason and knowable through natural law—the moral principles that are in tune with our nature as human beings. The Romans likewise appealed to an eternal source of law, as reflected in Cicero's statement that "law is not the product of human thought, nor is it any enactment of peoples, but something eternal which rules the whole universe."[8] By A.D. 380 Christianity was the official religion of the Roman Empire, and from then on, Western law was largely shaped by the Christian conception of law, based on the doctrine of creation. Theologians like Augustine and Aquinas contended that human law must reflect the moral order created by God—knowable by believer and nonbeliever alike, since it is the "law written on the heart." A law that does not reflect this natural law, as King was to write from the Birmingham jail, is an unjust law—which is no law at all.

Thus the Western political tradition has generally assumed that in order to be valid, human laws must be grounded in the natural law by which God orders his creation, which is in turn a participation in his eternal law.[9] This assumption was expressed in the Magna Carta of 1215, a groundbreaking charter guaranteeing certain rights and privileges to the nobles against the king. It was also the foundation of English common law.

"The law of nature dictated by God Himself . . . is binding in all countries and at all times," wrote the great eighteenth-century jurist Sir William Blackstone. "No human laws are of any validity, if contrary to this; and such of them as are valid derive all their force and all their authority mediately or immediately, from this original." Blackstone understood that the genius of Western common law was that it reflected the customs, beliefs, and traditions of the people as written by "men infused with the Spirit of Christ."[10]

But then, with the rise of nationalism, there arose ideas of national sovereignty and political absolutism, such as the doctrine of the divine right of kings, which states that the king reigns with direct authority from God—that the law is whatever the king decrees. Many Christians rose up to oppose these ideas and to reassert the primacy of natural law. In the late 1500s, Jesuit theologian Robert Bellarmine published several pamphlets arguing against the divine right of kings and in favor of natural rights and popular sovereignty. His writings were so influential that King James I felt forced to respond in a series of pamphlets of his own.[11] In the 1600s, Scottish cleric Samuel Rutherford wrote a book titled *Lex Rex* ("the law is king"), asserting that the law stands above the king and that he is subject to it like all other citizens. The book was banned in Scotland and publicly burned in England, and Rutherford was arrested. But his ideas lived on and profoundly influenced the American Founding Fathers through the work of John Witherspoon and John Locke.[12] In the new republic, citizens would be ruled not by men but by law.

Yet the government was to be limited not only by the rule of law but also by the scope of its authority over society. In Catholic social thought the idea of limited government was developed through the concept of *subsidiarity,* and in Reformed thought through the concept of *sphere sovereignty.*

Subsidiarity (the Latin *subsidium* means "help, support, assistance") holds that the higher social institutions, like the state, exist only to help subordinate institutions, like the family. The implication is that if the state goes beyond helping them—if it destroys them or absorbs their functions—then it is acting illegitimately and disturbing the social order.[13]

Sphere sovereignty grew out of the rallying cry of the Reformation—*coram deo* ("in the face of God")—meaning that the individual is accountable to God directly, no longer approaching him only through the mediating structure of the church. The consequence is that all spheres of society—including the state, family, school, corporation, as well as professional and voluntary associations—stand not under the church but directly under God's authority. This understanding was greatly liberating because it meant that no sphere may properly dominate the others; all are responsible to God directly, through the conscience of the individuals involved. Moreover, the power of each sphere is limited by the power of the others. As Dutch theologian Abraham Kuyper explained in the nineteenth century, the sovereignty of the state is limited "by another sovereignty, which is equally divine in origin"—namely, the sovereignty of the other spheres of society.[14]

Thus the Reformation heritage passed on a balanced view of the state as ordained by God yet limited by the other divinely ordained social institutions. The function of the state is to restrain the force of sin unleashed by the

Fall. Genesis 3:24 tells us that God stationed angels with a flaming sword to guard the tree of life—the first cops on the beat. By thus preserving social order, the state allows liberty to flourish. But the liberty of the other spheres in turn limits the state. Their liberty is, as Kuyper wrote, "the God-ordained means to bridle the authority" of the state, which could otherwise degenerate into despotism.[15] In this balanced conception we see the roots of what the American Founders called "ordered liberty."

Another contribution of Christianity was the notion of separation of powers, based on the doctrine of the Fall. The Founders realized that since everyone is prone to sin, it is a fatal mistake to entrust too much power to any individual or group. As a result they established three branches of government—the judicial, legislative, and executive—based on the biblical teaching that God is our judge, lawgiver, and king (Isa. 33:22). The Founders also established a federal system in which state governments were to keep a check on the national government. This is why the Constitution originally reserved to the states the right to appoint senators, and even the election of the president was made the task of electors from the states (the electoral college). The states were to have real power, not function merely as administrative units of the national government.

Finally, the Founders built a system that would protect against direct democracy—against any system where "the voice of the people is the voice of God." Such democracies, James Madison warned, "have ever been spectacles of turbulence and contention."[16] Hence the Founders built a republican system, where the will of the people is sifted through elected representatives, intended to be persons of virtue and concern for the common good, capable of rising above the passions of the moment. At the same time, the representatives remain accountable to the people, achieving a marvelous balance.

What an ingenious plan! I never cease to marvel at it and to be grateful for this historical expression of a Christian worldview. For more than two centuries, the American experiment has provided a dramatic illustration of the way biblical principles successfully sustain both order and liberty.[17] Yet in recent decades, those principles have come under withering assault from increasingly aggressive forces of modern secularism—so much so that the rule of law and the very character of our political order is now threatened.

JUDICIAL IMPERIALISM

The idea that human (or positive) law must reflect a higher law was seriously challenged in the latter part of the nineteenth century—especially after the work of Charles Darwin. His theory of evolution implied that there is no created moral order that functions as the basis for law; rather, life is the result of a process of trial and error, with new structures being preserved if they help the organism get what it needs to survive. This new view, appearing with the imprimatur of science, seemed to suggest that truth itself is found by a process of trial and error—the "true" idea being the one that works best at getting the results desired. Thus was born the philosophy of *pragmatism.*

Pragmatism was formulated when several prominent university professors organized a group oddly named the Cambridge Metaphysical Club. These leading intellectuals—among them Oliver Wendell Holmes, Charles Pierce, and William James—defined truth as the hypothesis that works best. Or, as James succinctly put it, "Truth is the cash value of an idea."[18]

What pragmatism meant for law was stated baldly by Holmes in 1897 when he advised an audience of law school students to put aside notions of morality and look instead at the law as a science—the science of state coercion.[19] His crassest summary of what this means is captured in his famous dictum that law is the "majority vote of that nation that can lick all others."[20] In other words, without divine law as the final moral authority, the law is reduced to sheer force.

More recently, the authority of the law received another blow at the hands of *deconstructionism,* which began as a method of literary criticism but is now applied to all types of texts, including legal texts. According to deconstructionism, language does not reveal meaning (which would imply that there is a transcendent realm of truth); rather, language is a social construction. Any text reflects several (often conflicting) social and cultural forces, aimed ultimately at enhancing some social group's power. Interpretation does not mean identifying what the author meant but "unmasking" the underlying power relationships.[21]

In recent years, these radical views of the law have begun to filter down to shape actual court decisions—initially, in cases involving religious rights. There was no anti-Christian conspiracy at work here, contrary to what many Christians have believed; rather, religious cases were the most obvious target because they most clearly relied on what now had to be discredited—the authority of a higher law.

The courts moved swiftly and dramatically. As recently as 1952, Justice William O. Douglas had described America as a "religious people whose institutions presuppose a Supreme Being" and urged that the state should therefore "accommodate the public service to their spiritual needs."[22] Douglas was not defending any particular religion but simply stating that religion is good for people and that the state ought to respect it. But only two decades later, in 1973, the Court breezed right past the people's deepest religious and moral concerns, claiming to discover in the Constitution an implied right to "privacy" protecting a woman's right to abortion (*Roe v. Wade*). In one swoop, the Court sought to extinguish a political debate then being carried out in fifty state legislatures regarding a sensitive moral question—the legal status of the early stages of human life. It was an act of judicial hubris that could only call into question the law's authority, thereby assuring that the abortion debate would continue and grow ever more rancorous. Which, of course, it has done.

But *Roe* was only the most influential in a swelling stream of cases—involving prayer, religious displays, and sexual rights—in which judges cavalierly usurped the legislative process and showed an increasing hostility to the religious and moral traditions that have historically informed American law. Indeed, in some cases judges actually ruled that religious motivation behind a law serves to disqualify it. For example, in 1987 the Supreme Court struck down a Louisiana statute mandating the teaching of creation alongside evolution.[23] Why? Because the Court decided that the legislature's claimed secular purpose (namely, academic freedom) was a "sham," covering over what was really an attempt to promote biblical religion. This represents a stunning turnaround: Whereas biblical principles were once considered the authority that undergirds the law, now they disqualify a law.

One of the most destructive decisions in recent years was the 1992 case *Planned Parenthood v. Casey*.[24] While upholding some modest state restrictions on abortion, the Court sought to place the right to abortion created in *Roe* on firmer constitutional ground. It abandoned the old tactic of justifying abortion by an implied right to "privacy" lurking in the "penumbras" of the Fourteenth Amendment and instead went straight for the explicit right of "liberty."[25] The Court then chastised pro-life supporters for having the effrontery to challenge their decisions, and in essence admonished them to be quiet and go home. So after having summarily overridden the democratic debate about abortion in 1973, twenty years later the Court decreed that even to challenge abortion is an affront to the rule of law.[26]

The majority then defined the "liberty" of the Fourteenth Amendment in breathtakingly sweeping terms: "At the heart of liberty," wrote Justice Anthony Kennedy, "is the right to define one's own concept of existence, of meaning, of the universe, and of the mystery of human life." In short, the Court placed the isolated individual, constructing his or her own sense of meaning, at the center of gravity for constitutional law. Collective self-government by the people according to a common moral code was rejected as "majoritarian intolerance."[27]

Indeed, the Court has rejected *any* belief in a transcendent ethic as "intolerance," thereby rejecting the idea of a higher law above the Court. In 1992 in *Lee v. Weisman,* the Court decreed that even an innocuous, to-whom-it-may-concern prayer offered by a rabbi at a junior high school commencement was unconstitutional because it infringed on a fifteen-year-old's right not to have to listen respectfully to religious expression with which she disagreed.[28] What would have been considered a mark of civility a mere generation ago was transformed into a constitutional grievance. More disturbing, however, the religious expression disallowed by the Court covered not just the traditional faiths but any "shared conviction that there is an ethic and a morality which transcend human invention."[29] In other words, the Court was saying that no transcendent morality is to be permitted in the public square, only the postmodernist view that regards morality as a "human invention."

And if no appeal to transcendent authority is permitted, then the justices themselves become the supreme authority. In the 1995 case *Romer v. Evans,* the justices struck down a referendum, democratically enacted by the citizens of Colorado, barring special civil rights protections and preferences based on "sexual orientation." Admittedly the referendum was not carefully drafted, but Justice Kennedy, writing for the majority, completely discounted the voters' stated purpose, presuming to have an uncanny ability to know their minds better than they did. "Laws of the kind before us," he wrote, "raise the inevitable inference that the disadvantage imposed is born of animosity toward the class of persons affected."[30] In a single disdainful sentence, a basic moral position long shared by Christians, Jews, Muslims, and people of other faiths—and, moreover, a position democratically enacted into law—was reduced to nothing more than personal "animosity." The justices no longer merely disagreed with the biblical ethic; they didn't even recognize it as an ethic but dismissed it as bigotry.

The same attitude soon filtered down to lower levels of the judiciary. Writing for the Ninth Circuit Court of Appeals in 1996, overturning a state referendum banning assisted suicide, Judge Stephen Reinhardt slammed the courthouse door on people "with strong moral or religious convictions." He wrote: "They are not free to force their views, their religious convictions, or their philosophies on all other members of a democratic society."[31] Yet what is the democratic process but an attempt by like-minded citizens to join together and pass laws in conformity with their best judgment of right and wrong? And on what basis can a judge say that all citizens are free to participate in this process *except* those "with strong moral and religious convictions"?

This judicial coup d'état culminated in the 1997 decision *Boerne v. Flores,* the first challenge to the Religious Freedom Restoration Act (RFRA) of 1993. The purpose of RFRA was to reestablish a strict standard for protecting free religious exercise, which had been struck down by the Court three years earlier. Significantly, RFRA was passed unanimously in the House, had only three dissenting votes in the Senate, and was enthusiastically signed by President Clinton. If ever a piece of legislation reflected the will of the people, it was RFRA.[32] Nevertheless, in *Boerne* the Supreme Court declared RFRA unconstitutional on the grounds that the express authority of Congress to enforce the basic civil rights guaranteed by the Fourteenth Amendment is not "substantive" but merely "remedial." In other words, Congress cannot use its power to expand constitutional protections except for the sake of rectifying violations of rights that the Supreme Court itself has deigned to recognize. Thus two major trends by activist courts converged in this single case: one against the transcendent right of religious liberty and the other against self-government. Not only was the free exercise clause emasculated, but also a vote reflecting the nearly unanimous will of the American people was overruled.

Furthermore, the Court decreed that it has the supreme authority to define constitutional liberties and establish their scope, an arrogant grab for power that would have horrified the Founders. The right of judicial review is not in the Constitution, and Jefferson actually warned against "judicial oligarchy," while his frequent adversary, Alexander Hamilton, was equally resistant to unrestrained judicial power.[33]

Tragically, conservative judges seem unable to stand against the juggernaut of judicial imperialism. Prominent conservatives such as Robert Bork, Edwin Meese, and Supreme Court Justice Antonin Scalia have sought to resist judicial activism with various forms of legal positivism (for example, original intent jurisprudence) that reject appeals to natural law. Scalia goes so far as to insist that judges must not consider morality, custom, or even legislative intent in making decisions, but only the literal meaning of the text. For example, Scalia has argued that it is not up to judges to consider morality; rather, it is up to the people to enact their moral convictions into law. But of course those are exactly the kinds of laws that liberal judges are striking down as illegitimate. Thus we are caught in a catch-22, where conservative judges say the courts may not consult morality, that it's up to the people to encode morality into the law—while at the same time liberal judges are striking down democratically enacted laws that express the people's moral convictions, even disqualifying those convictions as mere personal "animosity."[34]

The result of these trends is that today the courts, unrestrained by higher law and disdainful of majority will, are the dominant force in American politics. As law professor Russell Hittinger writes, in *Casey* the Court has laid down a "new covenant" by which it agrees to give citizens the right to decide for themselves the meaning of life, to decide what is right and wrong, to do as they please. In exchange for this guarantee, the Court asks only that the people accept the Court's assumption of ultimate power.[35] Or as Notre Dame's Gerard Bradley puts it, the Court has said: "We will be your Court, and you will be our people."[36]

But this new covenant with the Court is inherently unstable and will give way in time to either anarchy or sheer power. Imbalance of power among the three branches of government has always been the great vulnerability of the American system. From time to time, the scales have tilted precariously; but providentially, we may say, each time the balance has been restored. Until today. Judicial imperialism now threatens to destroy the delicate balance that guarantees our liberty. The late historian Russell Kirk once warned that the Supreme Court's "power to do mischief would become almost infinite" were it to become the dominant force in American public life, for it would "abolish America's democracy."[37] Precisely. This is why it is so urgent for Christians with a biblical worldview of law and justice to alert our neighbors to the serious threat facing our system of government.

TAKING DOWN THE TEN COMMANDMENTS

The Christian understanding of law as based on a higher moral law has parallels in most civilizations throughout history. As C. S. Lewis pointed out, all major religions and moral systems assume the existence of an objective morality (which he called the Way or the Tao).[38] We all, whether Christians or not, intuitively sense that there must be some ultimate moral justification for the law, something that makes it right. Otherwise, any law can be shot down with the defiant barroom expression "sez who?" So argued the late Arthur Leff of Yale Law School in a celebrated 1979 speech. Unless there is a God who is himself Goodness and Justice, Leff said, there can be no ultimate moral basis for the law. For if there is no God, nothing can take his place. No human standard—no person, no group of people, no document—is immune to challenge.[39]

Leff deftly captured the consequences of a secular worldview. Once the Enlightenment began to deny the reality of divine creation and revelation, the basis of law was eroded. Enlightenment thinkers optimistically assumed they would find an alternative basis in human reason and experience. But as

Leff so colorfully points out, the moral beliefs of any group or individual are open to challenge. And the logical conclusion of all efforts to ground the law in something less than God's transcendent law is moral skepticism—the great "sez who?"

The consequences of this are shaking the very foundations of our government and society today.

First, the loss of moral authority in the law removes restraints on individual behavior. Americans seem strangely oblivious to the connection between the loss of moral authority in the law and the social chaos that results: crime, corruption, the loss of civility. I discovered just how oblivious they are when I was invited to talk about criminal-justice issues with a group of community leaders some years ago.

In get-acquainted conversation over lunch, one tall, distinguished man assured me of his company's commitment to religious liberty. "We led the campaign in our city to take the Ten Commandments off classroom walls," he boasted.

"Why did you do that?" I asked.

"We must be sensitive to all faiths," he said confidently.

"But Christians, Jews, and Muslims all believe in the Ten Commandments. Even Buddhists and Hindus don't object to them," I responded.

"Separation of church and state," he said.

"Of course." I nodded. "But the Decalogue and the *Lex Divina* are the historical roots of our legal system. That's why Moses is included among the great lawgivers whose faces are represented in the fresco that adorns the walls of the House of Representatives chamber."

"Tolerance, sir. Times have changed. We must recognize that." He drew himself up in his chair, a solid pillar of the community.

After our meal, as I began speaking on the subject of justice reform, many took notes as I reeled off the chilling statistics.

The same man then interrupted me, asking whether I had seen some of the latest surveys regarding crime in the schools. "Two-thirds of our kids cheat in school," he said. "And a third admit that they steal. What can we do about it?"

I couldn't help smiling. This was the same man who insisted we take the Ten Commandments off the classroom walls. And this is precisely the postmodernist impasse: We want freedom from rules and transcendent moral principles, but we hate the moral chaos that ensues.

Second, the loss of moral authority in the law means government is reduced to utilitarian procedures. Aristotle said that at the heart of politics is the question How shall we order our lives together? The question presupposes that there is some common good around which we should order our lives, a moral imperative proper to government. But today, as the logic of *Casey* suggests, the task of government is simply to protect individual autonomy—people's right to do whatever they choose. In the Court's new vision, writes Gerard Bradley, good government is secured by the liberation of the atomistic individual from the constraints of the common morality held by traditional religions.[40] As a result, the government has no positive moral task; rather, it functions as little more than a traffic cop, keeping people from bumping into each other as they do their own thing. The government has become what Harvard professor Michael Sandel calls a "procedural republic," its laws nothing more than procedures for helping people get what they want.[41]

Third, the loss of a moral basis for law means we can no longer engage in moral debate. If politics is only about who gets what, then politics becomes an interminable shouting match, with endless bickering over competing demands for rights—settled ultimately by whoever has the loudest voice or the most votes. Issues are settled not by principle but by power. In these circumstances, individuals feel increasingly helpless and eventually give up on the political system—a particularly dangerous trend in a democratic society, which depends on the participation of an informed and active citizenry.[42]

Finally, the loss of moral authority in the law means we have forfeited the rule of law and reverted to arbitrary human rule. The rule of law cannot survive unless there is an unchanging and transcendent standard against which we can measure human laws. Otherwise, the law is whatever the lawmakers or judges say it is—which can only result, eventually, in the collapse of free government.[43] The postmodernist assault on objective moral truth has put us on the road to tyranny.

Yet we must not give up hope, for Christian truth still offers us a way out of the postmodernist impasse. Christians everywhere can help revitalize our political culture and reestablish the rule of law by advancing a biblical view of law and politics.

THE ART OF PERSUASION

How should Christians work to renew our political and legal structures? If we have learned anything in recent decades, it is that we should not roll out heavy-handed political movements that recklessly toss around God-and-country clichés and scare off our secular neighbors. Our goal is not to grab power and impose our views. Instead, we should act through principled persuasion and responsible participation.

Principled Persuasion

The rule of law. Persuasion means our first task is apologetics—striving to convince our neighbors that the Christian worldview provides the best way to order society. We can assume most of our neighbors do not understand the necessity of something even so basic as the rule of law. When I was in school, that was covered in the first civics lesson; today, civics courses are more likely to address the exploitation of Native Americans by European settlers.

The public good. We also need to press home the importance of the idea of the common or public good. Take the illustration of a stoplight: For the public good, all people are required to stop at stoplights; otherwise, there would be chaos and death on the streets. This law applies to Christians, agnostics, Hindus, and New Age proponents alike; whether or not they are offended by the law, they must obey it for the public good.

We need to apply the same reasoning to other laws, such as those recognizing marriage only between two persons of the opposite sex. There are important reasons why protecting heterosexual marriage is in the interest of society: It recognizes a social pattern that every civilized society has adopted in order to propagate the human race and raise children. Christians need to argue that such laws do not "impose" a religious belief but are based on rational moral principles and historical evidence showing that protection of the family promotes the public interest. This is why decisions like *Casey* and *Romer* are so disastrous, for they make determination of the public good impossible. Finally, we can argue that the Christian worldview provides the most reliable standard for determining the public good and encouraging responsible personal behavior.

Perhaps the toughest sell today is persuading people that they *ought* to govern their personal behavior for the sake of the public good. Individualism has grown so rampant that most people think society exists to serve them, and they do not feel they owe anything to society. We need to argue that unless individuals voluntarily restrain their own behavior for the common good, government will have to restrain them by coercive measures—at the cost of our liberty.

Witness the coercion that already characterizes efforts to maintain political correctness. As people disregard the voluntary restraints of civility and social convention (the outdated customs of courtesy), the state begins to micromanage behavior by passing increasingly oppressive laws. For example, witness the often ridiculous attempts to define what is or what is not sexual harassment. Antioch College has published a code requiring students who are dating to give and get verbal consent from one another at each stage of escalating physical involvement.[44] Even more absurd, a six-year-old child was penalized by his public-school teacher for planting a friendly kiss on the cheek of another six-year-old, and the principal handed the miscreant's mother a copy of the school's sexual harassment policy.[45] And a Kansas bank was fined because it did not have Braille instructions on the ATM in its *drive-through* banking lanes![46]

We may dismiss such things as signs of temporary national insanity, but they are not illogical. They are the inevitable consequence of the loss of voluntary restraints. At one time, hurling a racial epithet would have been considered a lack of civility and would have been suppressed through social disapproval and ostracism; today, in the absence of such informal sanctions, it has to be an actionable hate crime. At one time, well-behaved young men did not "take advantage" of the "fairer sex"; today, in the absence of such social conventions, women must be protected by laws against sexual harassment. We have been "freed" from the older rules of courtesy and morality only to be hemmed in by new rules imposed by law. To reverse this erosion of freedom, we must make the case that self-government in the political sense depends on self-government in the personal sense—that is, governing our own speech and behavior by the norms of civility and respect.

The defense of liberty. The Bible is not a political document, yet it has profound political implications that are important to the general welfare of all citizens. Those who say Jesus and the apostles ignored politics miss the political implications of the maxim "Give to Caesar what is Caesar's, and to God what is God's" (Matt. 22:21). The first-century Christians knew exactly what Jesus' words meant—and it was because of a political act (they would not say, "Caesar is Lord") that they were crucified, tortured, and thrown to the lions.

What is the fundamental scriptural teaching on the state? On one hand, we are to live in submission to the state. For our benefit God has appointed kings and rulers to carry out the ordained duties of the state: to restrain evil, to preserve order, and to promote justice. Thus, we are to "honor the king" and to submit ourselves "to the governing authorities, for . . . the authorities that exist have been established by God" (Rom. 13:1; see also Dan. 2:21; Rom. 13:1-7; Titus 3:1; 1 Pet. 2:13-14, 17).

Some people have interpreted these passages as an absolute grant of authority, meaning that government is to be obeyed at all times and in all circumstances. But the injunction to obey is conditioned on the assumption that officials and magistrates are carrying out the purposes for which God has ordained government (in Romans 13:4 the ruler is called "God's servant"). Thus if rulers act contrary to their delegation of authority, if they do not act as God's servants, then Christians are not bound to obey them; indeed, believers may be morally obligated to resist. For example, if the state prohibits the preaching of the gospel, it is clearly acting contrary to the commandments of the One who granted government its authority in the first place. If the state practices injustice, like massacring Jews or engaging in systematic tyranny, it loses its claim to divine authority.

Through the ages, this principle has been affirmed by people such as Augustine, Aquinas, Calvin, Knox, and, as we have seen, Martin Luther King Jr. The church must hold the state morally accountable before the transcendent judgment of God, though this principle must be exercised with solemn judiciousness as the body of Christ collectively seeks the leading of the Holy Spirit.[47]

Deciding *which* actions result in a loss of state's legitimacy is a difficult and sensitive issue. In the early days of Hitler's regime, Christians in Germany struggled with this question, which led, in 1934, to the publication of the Barmen Declaration, a document protesting the Nazis' attempt to control the church and insisting on the church's independence. Those who agreed with the declaration called themselves the "Confessing Church" and engaged in escalating resistance to Hitler's oppressive policies; its most prominent leaders were jailed or even executed.

Christianity has historically proven to be the most dependable defender of human liberty. The commitment to a higher law means that Christians have been on the front lines in resisting laws or actions contrary to that law. The biblical view was argued eloquently by the British statesman Edmund Burke during a famous 1788 debate in the House of Lords over the impeachment of the governor general of India. The governor general had claimed a right to arbitrary authority over the unruly nationals, arguing that they were, after all, used to despotism. Burke replied with these wonderful words: "My lords, the East India Company have not arbitrary power to give him [the governor general]. The king has no arbitrary power to give. Neither your lordships, nor the Commons, nor the whole legislature, have arbitrary power to give. Arbitrary power is a thing which no man can give. . . . We are all born, high as well as low, governors as well as governed, in subjection to one great, immutable, preexisting law. . . . This great law does not arise from our combinations and compacts; on the contrary, it gives to them all the sanction they can have."[48]

Precisely. Neither king nor parliament holds absolute authority over even the lowliest subject of the British Empire. That bedrock Christian conviction gives us a basis for resistance to earthly authority when that authority is unjust, which is why the great roll call of those who have given their lives to defend liberty features predominantly believers.

Tyrants recognize this all too clearly, which explains why the Chinese government persecutes religious believers so fiercely, jailing pastors, burning churches, outlawing home meetings. It's not simply that communists are atheists and want to stamp out religion; it's that they cannot tolerate anyone who worships a King who stands above the kings of this world. For that higher allegiance gives a basis for demanding freedom and rights from the earthly king.[49]

The rule of law, the promotion of the public good, and the defense of liberty—these are the principles we must learn to articulate in making the case for a Christian view of politics, engaging in "backyard apologetics" over the barbecue grill with friends. But though our beliefs derive ultimately from Scripture, in a pluralistic society we must also translate them into terms non-believers can understand. For example, when we work to change abortion laws, we must not only appeal to divine revelation but also point out that the most fundamental duty of government is to defend the defenseless. When we oppose the legalization of assisted suicide and eugenics, we can note that the very purpose of government is to prevent the private use of lethal force. (Government wields the power of the sword precisely so individuals *won't*.) We must advance public and persuasive arguments that appeal to reason and evidence.[50]

Walking the Walk

We must also make the case by the way we live. Others will see the truth of what we believe most clearly if we live out our convictions as responsible citizens in our communities.

First, Christians must be good citizens. The most elementary requirement of any society is that its citizens behave responsibly, obey the law, and carry out their civic duties. Christians should be the best of citizens, as Augustine said, because we do out of love for God what others do only because they are forced to by law. This means that we vote, pay taxes, care for our neighborhood, and live peaceably with others. We honor and obey our leaders and civil magistrates, and we pray for those in authority. We can also support groups that seek to protect religious liberty, such as the Beckett Fund, the American Center for Law and Justice (ACLJ), the Center for Law and Religious Freedom, the Rutherford Institute, and the Alliance Defense Fund.[51]

Second, Christians must carry out their civic duty in every walk of life. When Alexis de Tocqueville came to this country in the early nineteenth century, he was startled by the extent to which citizens helped their neighbors, organizing all manner of voluntary associations to meet social needs and carry out projects for the common good. He commented that he did not know ten men in all of France who would do what ordinary Americans do every day as a matter of course.[52] Most of the associations that so impressed the French statesman were founded and run by Christians, following the command to love our neighbors.

The same remains true today. People may make light of the "Jesus Saves" banner across the door of the mission shelters and soup kitchens, but they can't deny that these places are dispensing mercy and compassion to the destitute. Visit our inner cities, and you will discover that the Salvation Army, gospel missions, and Catholic charities provide the vast majority of private relief services. In poverty-stricken areas, volunteer organizations like Habitat for Humanity are building homes and providing other relief for the poor. Through Prison Fellowship, thousands of volunteers minister to the outcasts of society—those behind bars. And through Prison Fellowship's Project Angel Tree, hundreds of thousands purchase and deliver gifts to the children of inmates every Christmas.

Just doing our duty within our own sphere of influence can produce surprising results. In early 1998, Barbara Vogel told her fourth grade class at Highline Community School in Aurora, Colorado, about the civil war in Sudan, where Christians in the south are being rounded up by Muslim slavers and sold into slavery in the north. Mrs. Vogel's kids began to cry. "We thought slavery didn't happen anymore," they said.

The children decided to do something about it. They formed a group called Slavery That Oppresses People, known as STOP. They learned about Christian Solidarity, an organization that redeems slaves—literally buys them back and returns them to their families. Though many of Vogel's pupils live in public housing, they saved their allowances and sold lemonade, T-shirts, and old toys. Soon they had enough money to free one hundred and fifty slaves!

But the students didn't stop there. They then launched a letter-writing campaign, sending fifteen hundred letters to newspapers and public officials. The story spread. A homeless man living out of his car sent his last $100. A class of handicapped children raised money through a bake sale. A truck driver told people all across the country about the kids and collected funds. Within nine months, more than $50,000 in donations had poured in, and more than five thousand slaves had been set free.

The U.S. Congress recognized Barbara Vogel's kids as America's "Little Abolitionists" and hung a flag over the capitol in their honor. "As a public-school teacher, I cannot say [in class] that Christ is the most important thing in my life," says Vogel, "but that doesn't mean that I can't model my faith."[53]

As we engage in civic affairs, we are making an eloquent witness for the faith. And in the process, we are strengthening self-government and limiting the state, for when intermediate structures are vibrant, government finds less occasion to become intrusive.

Third, Christians must be engaged directly in politics. As already noted, this begins with voting; beyond that, it includes joining civic groups and political organizations, and perhaps even running for public office. As we do so, we must be ever vigilant to keep our priorities in order, not compromising our commitment to Christ or putting partisan agendas first. Christian organizations active in politics need to set distinctively Christian goals and be uncompromising in biblical fidelity, never allowing themselves to be in the hip pocket of any political party. This is a narrow line to walk, but it can be done.

A good example is Justice Fellowship (JF), the public-policy arm of Prison Fellowship, which organizes task forces to work for biblically based reforms in the criminal-justice system. JF's approach follows the outlines of a Christian worldview. On the basis of *creation,* it says that because there is a holy God, there is a transcendent standard of justice; therefore, to qualify as just, all human law must be based on divine law. This is why JF works to defend religious liberty and protect transcendent principles expressed in the law. On the basis of the *fall,* it says that because we are morally responsible beings, justice must address our conscience. We must define crime as a moral problem, requiring a moral and spiritual solution. This is why Prison Fellowship goes behind bars to hold Bible studies and other faith-based programs. On the basis of *redemption,* it says that criminals are called to repent of their crimes and, as far as possible, to restore what they have damaged. Society, for its part, is called to restore both the criminal and the victim to the community. And how do we restore the civil order that has been damaged by crime? JF advocates what is known as *restorative justice,* which includes principles such as promoting the rights of victims in the legal process, encouraging offenders to reconcile with their victims, and requiring offenders to work and pay restitution to their victims. The object of restorative justice is to repair the moral and social order God has called us to live in. JF's agenda often cuts across party lines, and the organization has had remarkable success without compromising biblical principles.

Christians also can and should seek political office—and the best strategy is to shatter the common stereotypes. I know scores of men and women who do this successfully on both state and national levels. For example,

Mark Earley is a former missionary and unapologetic evangelical, who as a state senator in Virginia was uncompromising on moral issues yet also won respect for his careful work on a variety of issues. When he announced that he would run for state attorney general in 1997, the chattering class in adjacent Washington, D.C., predicted that voters would turn against this "religious zealot." But Earley waged a strong campaign on the issues, and he not only won, but he also won with the biggest victory margin for any Republican in the state's history.

Fourth, the church must act as the conscience of society, as a restraint against the misuse of governing authority. Corporately, the church must zealously guard its independence, keep its prophetic voice sharp, and resist the allure of worldly power. It should hold government morally accountable to live up to its delegated authority from God (along with holding all other spheres of society accountable to fulfill the functions ordained to them by God).

This is not to say that Christians go about "imposing" their beliefs on an unwilling populace. Whenever the church speaks to public issues, some secularists will mutter darkly that what Christians really want is a theocracy, where they are in charge. That is not true. Historically, it was Christians who first formulated the principle of separation of church and state, starting with Augustine's distinction between the City of God and the City of Man. Christians recognize that God has ordained government as a separate institution with its own distinctive purposes. Government is a civil function, not a church function. That's why Christians have often been the staunchest defenders of religious liberty—for all faiths. One need only compare the Western polity, shaped historically by Christianity, with, for example, an Islamic polity, which recognizes no distinction between church and state and which often mercilessly oppresses and persecutes religious minorities.[54]

In addressing the state, we must do so not on the basis of power, as special interests do, but on the basis of principle. This is a crucial distinction, yet it is one that secular politicians and journalists frequently miss. For example, in early 1998 James Dobson of Focus on the Family met with Republican congressional leaders in Washington to confront them for failing to promote the social issues they had promised to support. For Dobson, this was a matter of principle—and a valid one. Yet journalists interpreted Dobson's action as a power play, warning in apocalyptic tones that religious conservatives were "marching on Washington" and demanding their due. Newspaper articles described Christians as a powerful voting bloc that had delivered 45 percent of the vote in the 1994 Republican sweep of Congress and warned that they were now demanding "their place at the table." Christians were depicted in the same terms as those applied to a labor union or any other special-interest group.[55]

Of course, we do have a right to a place at the table, just as any other citizens do. And yes, we do have political clout, but only because millions of Americans share our moral concerns. Yet these facts are not the basis of our political stance. We contend for certain truths in the political arena because they are crucial to liberty and public justice—and we would do so whether we had 45 percent of the vote or 5 percent.

So our message is not, We put you in office, now pay up. Rather, we are saying, This should be done because it is right, because it is a principle that undergirds any well-ordered civil society, and because it is a proper duty of the state as ordained by God.

■　　　■　　　■

ALL THIS CAN be summed up by saying we should exhibit the best of Christian patriotism, always holding dear our own land and yet holding it up against the standard of divine justice. The United States, for all her faults and flaws, remains history's best hope for achieving morally ordered liberty. It is still the great beacon of hope for emerging nations as they witness the remarkable blessings brought forth by religious, political, and economic freedom. But if it is to remain so, we must be at our posts, "the king's good citizens but the Lord's first," as Thomas More said as he went to his death for opposing Henry VIII.[56] We must always be ready to show our fellow citizens the way to restore truth and moral authority to American law and politics.

And we must begin by returning to the foundation of the Christian worldview—the principle of creation. For as we have seen, it was the rejection of the idea of creation that led to the loss of the concept of an eternal law above the law. And this, in turn, was the result of a new view of science that turned the very definition of knowledge on its head.

CHAPTER 40

THE BASIS FOR TRUE SCIENCE

Materialism gave us a theory which explained everything else in the whole universe but which made it impossible to believe that our thinking was valid.
C. S. LEWIS

Darwin's Dangerous Idea, the title of a recent book, could easily fool an unsuspecting browser at the local bookstore. One might expect that the author, Tufts University professor Daniel Dennett, wants to warn readers of the dangers of Darwinism. But in reality, Dennett hopes to persuade readers to *embrace* the "dangerous" implications of Darwin's theory. He argues that Darwinism, rightly understood, is a "universal acid" that dissolves away all traditional moral, metaphysical, and religious beliefs. For if human beings have evolved by material, purposeless causes, then there is no basis for believing in a God who created us and revealed moral truths. Dennett even suggests that traditional churches and rituals be relegated to "cultural zoos" for the amusement of onlookers.[1]

The book is one of the more colorful examples of a common tactic—using science as a weapon to shoot down religious faith. The standard assumption is that science constitutes objective knowledge while religion is an expression of subjective need. Religion, therefore, must accommodate its claims about the world to whatever science decrees. In this way, science is elevated to an overall philosophy—often called *scientism* or *scientific naturalism*—which assumes that the only things that are real are those that can be known and measured by experience and observation. Everything else is unreal, a product of subjective fantasy, including things like love and beauty, good and evil, God and conscience.

David Hume, an eighteenth-century Scottish philosopher and critic of Christianity, exposed the real agenda of scientism in dramatic prose. He recommended that library shelves be purged of any book dealing with religion, ethics, metaphysics—anything that cannot be reduced to empirical facts. Take the book in hand, he urged, and ask, Does it contain reasoning based on mathematics? Does it contain reasoning based on facts and experiments? If the answer is no, then "commit it to the flames." If any book does not deal with mathematics or empirical facts—that is, with science—then "it can contain nothing but sophistry and illusion."[2]

Like Hume, many intellectuals today assume that science is the source of all genuine knowledge. Whether it travels under the banner of scientism, positivism, materialism, or naturalism, this is the dominant worldview of Western culture. Science, which originally simply meant the study of the natural world, has been conflated with scientific naturalism, the philosophy that the natural world is all that exists. As early as 1922, G. K. Chesterton warned that scientism had become a "creed" taking over our institutions, a "system of thought which began with Evolution and has ended in Eugenics."[3] And in 1955, one educator warned that while America's public schools are ostensibly neutral, they are "propagating a particular dogmatic faith, namely, scientific naturalism."[4]

That "dogmatic faith" aggressively seeks to subsume everything else under naturalistic categories. Even human beings are reduced to "objects" or "things" that can be inspected, experimented on, and ultimately controlled. Philosopher Arthur Koestler denounced this as "the ratomorphic fallacy," arguing that it treats humans as though they were a species of laboratory rat.[5] Similarly, the great Christian apologist C. S. Lewis warned that the rise of scientific naturalism would lead to "the abolition of man," for it denies the reality of those things central to our humanity: our sense of right and wrong, of purpose, of beauty, of God.

And if we deny the things that make us truly human, then we will create a culture that is, by definition, *in*human. If we treat morality as subjective feeling, then moral ideals will be relegated to the private realm, and the public realm will be stripped of all morality. If we deny the reality of the virtues that make us superior to the beasts, then those virtues wither away, reducing us to the level of beasts. Thus while science has created technological advances that make life easier and healthier, when science is confused with the philosophy of scientific naturalism, it destroys the very things that make life worth living. We gain control over the natural world at the cost of our own souls.

Lewis foresaw this predicament clearly. "For the wise men of old," he wrote, "the cardinal problem had been how to conform the soul to reality, and the solution had been knowledge, self-discipline, and virtue." The purpose of life was defined in terms of the growth of the soul, and there was an abiding moral standard to which to conform. But for the contemporary technical mind-set, "the problem is how to subdue reality to the wishes of men: the solution is a technique." This mind-set acknowledges no abiding standards, so there is nothing to check the human desire for control and domination.[6]

Watch a good TV interviewer interact with today's scientists, and you quickly realize that ethical subjectivism has stripped many scientists of the ability to evaluate the implications of even their own work. Their ethical understanding has not kept pace with their brilliant discoveries. As a result, science and technology blunder on without clear moral guidance, creating more sophisticated gadgets but also creating confusion as to what purposes, goals, or values they should serve.[7]

Yet despite these ominous weaknesses, it is no easy task to dislodge scientific naturalism from its position of intellectual dominance, for it has invested scientists with enormous power. If science is the only source of knowledge, then their own discipline trumps all others, and they alone speak with authority to the culture at large. Therefore, if we are to stand against attacks on Christian faith made in the name of science, our first target should not be specific theories, such as Darwinian evolution, but the underlying philosophy of scientific naturalism.

Christians ought to argue that scientific naturalism is incoherent and self-contradictory, for scientists must exempt themselves from the very framework they prescribe for everyone else. All human beings are reduced to mechanisms operating by natural causes—*except* scientists themselves. Why? Because to carry out their experiments, they must assume that *they*, at least, are capable of transcending the network of material causes, capable of rational thought, of free deliberation, of formulating theories, of recognizing objective truth. They themselves must form the single glaring exception to their own theory. This is the fatal self-contradiction of naturalism.

Lewis pointed out another contradiction that is equally devastating. The naturalist assumes that everything that exists can be explained in terms of natural forces. But that assumption itself cannot be the result of natural forces or it would not qualify as a genuine truth claim. For if an idea is simply the product of particles bumping around in our brains, then it is neither true nor false but merely a natural phenomenon. If, for example, a man tells us his room is on fire but we know that he just swallowed a hallucinogenic drug, then we probably will not call the fire department. If we think an idea is the result of physical, chemical causes in the brain, then we discount it and don't even credit it as a rational thought.

Now, scientific naturalism necessitates the conclusion that *all* ideas are products of natural causes in the brain—*including the idea of scientific naturalism itself.* Thus, if it is true, then it is not a rational thought and ought to be discounted. "Every theory of the universe which makes the human mind a result of irrational causes is inadmissible," Lewis wrote. For "in order to think, we must claim for our reasoning a validity which is not credible if our own thought is merely a function of our brain and our brain a byproduct of irrational physical process."[8]

The task for Christians, then, is clear: *to expose the flaws in scientific naturalism, which has invested science with ultimate intellectual authority.* We must do this not because we are against science but because we want to restore science to its proper role as a means of investigating God's world and alleviating suffering. And Christians are the ones to lead the way because the original conception of science was developed in the context of the biblical worldview, and only in that context can it function properly. In fact, surprising as it may be to many people, without Christianity there would be no science.

THE NATURE OF NATURE

The method of investigation that we now know as modern science first emerged in Christianized Europe, a culture steeped in biblical faith, and most of the key figures in the scientific revolution were believers, working from a basis of faith. In fact, contemporary historians of science, both Christians and non-Christians, agree that Christianity provided the underlying attitudes and intellectual presuppositions that made modern science possible in the first place.[9] Consider some of the most important elements of the Christian worldview, contrasting it to alternate worldviews:

The physical world is real, not an illusion. Most Eastern cultures embrace pantheism, which teaches that the physical world is an illusion (maya). But the Bible teaches that God created the material world; it is real and can be known. This assumption primed Western thinkers to value the physical world and to consider it worthy of study.

Nature is good but not divine. Many pagan cultures hold to *animism,* which teaches that the world is the abode of the divine or an emanation of God's own essence. Consequently, they believe that nature is alive with sun gods, river goddesses, and astral deities. This ancient belief is being revived in our own day. For example, in Disney's film *Pocahontas,* the young Indian maiden scolds the white man for thinking the earth "is just a dead thing," admonishing him that "every rock and tree and creature has a life, has a spirit, has a name." This is a startlingly clear expression of animism.[10]

But Genesis 1 stands in stark contrast to all this. It teaches that nature is not divine; it is God's handiwork. The sun and moon are not gods; they are lights placed in the sky to serve God's purposes. Historians describe the effect of this doctrine as the "de-deification" of nature, and it was a crucial precondition to science. For when nature commanded religious worship, then digging too closely into her secrets was thought to be irreverent. By "de-deifying" nature, Christianity turned it from an object of fear and worship into a possible object of scientific study.

Nature is orderly and predictable. Another unique contribution of Christianity was the idea of laws of nature. No other religion or culture, Eastern or Western, has ever used the word *law* in relation to nature. In fact, before modern times, most people regarded nature as mysterious, dangerous, and chaotic. As a result, notes historian Carl Becker, the idea of natural law did not arise from ordinary experience but only from the biblical teaching that God is both Creator and Lawgiver.[11] The early scientists had to act on *faith* that nature is orderly, long before they had amassed enough scientific evidence to prove it.

Humans can discover nature's order. Moreover, early scientists had to act on faith that the order in nature can be discovered by the human mind—a conviction grounded in the biblical teaching that we are created in the image of God. Again, a cross-cultural comparison shows how unique this conviction is. The ancient Chinese believed in some kind of order in nature, but they conceived of it as an inherent necessity, inscrutable to the human mind. That's why the Chinese, despite their great technical achievements, never developed science as a self-correcting, experimental enterprise (as we know it). By contrast, the biblical teaching of the image of God was taken to mean that human rationality reflects in some manner the rationality of God himself—the rationality by which he made the world. Therefore, we can "think God's thoughts after him" (to use a phrase popular with the early scientists) and discover the order he built into creation.

We need to experiment. But *how* do we think God's thoughts? The answer to that question was crucial for science. The ancient Greeks had defined science as intuition into the rational structure inherent in things, which implies that the world is the way it is because it is rationally necessary. Therefore, true knowledge of the world is gained primarily by logical analysis.

But near the end of the Middle Ages there emerged a form of Christian theology known as *voluntarism,* which taught that rational order is not something inherent *in* nature but is imposed *on* nature by God's will and design. Voluntarism helped inspire experimental methodology in science, for if the world is not structured by rational necessity but is a creation of God's free choice, then we cannot gain knowledge by sitting in an ivory tower and conducting logical analysis, as the Greeks had taught. Instead, we have to go out and see what God has actually done. We have to observe and experiment.

Many of the early scientists drew an explicit connection between voluntarist theology and scientific method. For example, Roger Cotes, a friend of Isaac Newton, wrote that the world arose from "the perfectly free will of God," and "therefore" we must investigate the world by "observations and experiments."[12]

Galileo made similar arguments and then gave a memorable example of what they meant. When he wanted to find out whether a ten-pound weight falls to the ground faster than a one-pound weight, he didn't ask philosophical questions (in his day he was much criticized for not cogitating on the "nature of weight"). Instead, he dropped two balls from the leaning tower of Pisa and watched what happened.

The order in nature is mathematically precise. Modern science depends on the idea that the order in nature is precise and can be expressed in mathematical formulas. This, too, was a contribution of Christianity. In all other religions, the creation of the world begins with some preexisting material, which the gods cannot fully control. For example, in the West, the Greeks believed that matter existed from eternity and that it was capable of resisting the rational order imposed by the creator (who was an inferior deity—a demi-urge). As a result, the Greeks expected to find a certain lack of precision in nature, a fuzziness around the edges, frequent anomalies and irregularities.

By contrast, the Bible teaches that God alone is eternal, that there is no preexisting "stuff" that is either beyond his control or capable of resisting him. The world comes completely from God's hand (creation *ex nihilo*, from nothing) and is completely at his command. As a result, Christians expected the order in nature to be precisely what God wanted it to be—mathematically precise.

For example, when Copernicus proposed that the planets go around the sun instead of the earth, he actually had no empirical evidence for the new hypothesis. Before the invention of telescopes, observations of the planets fit an earth-centered system just as well as a sun-centered system. The sole factor favoring a heliocentric system was that it was mathematically simpler; it didn't require as many adjustments in the equations. And since Copernicus was convinced that God had made the world mathematically precise, getting better formulas was good enough for him. Of course, when telescopes were invented, it turned out that Copernicus was right. But standing at the threshold of the scientific revolution, Copernicus was inspired not by the scientific facts available to him but by his Christian faith.

The same faith inspired Johannes Kepler, the man famous for discovering that the orbits of the planets are not circles, as people thought at the time, but ellipses. Kepler noticed a slight mismatch between mathematical calculations of the orbit of Mars and actual observations of the orbit. The difference was so tiny that other scientists shrugged it off, but Kepler was convinced that everything in creation is precisely the way God wants it to be. If God had wanted the orbits to be circular, they would have been *exactly* circular; since they were not, then they must be *exactly* something else. Kepler struggled for years to reconcile the equations with the observations until he finally hit on the discovery that the orbits are ellipses. Through those difficult years, it was his Christian faith that spurred him on—his conviction that the biblical God has complete control over matter and, therefore, it will be mathematically precise.[13]

"The possibility of an applied mathematics," writes historian R. G. Collingwood, "is an expression, in terms of natural science, of the Christian belief that nature is the creation of an omnipotent God."[14]

SCIENCE AS APOLOGETICS

We hear from all sides that science has disproved Christianity, but today the historical evidence gives us a clear response: On the contrary, it was Christianity that made science possible. Instead of being intimidated by attacks made in the name of science, we can show that the very existence of the scientific method, and all it has accomplished, is a great apologetic argument for the truth of Christianity.

Historically, many believers have done just that. Isaac Newton, often considered the greatest of the early scientists, was a devout Christian whose pursuit of science was strongly motivated by his desire to defend the faith.[15] He firmly believed that scientific study of the world would lead straight to the God who created that world. Science shows us "what is the first cause, what power he has over us, and what benefits we receive from him," Newton wrote, so that "our duty towards him, as well as that towards one another, will appear to us by the light of nature." And why does science show us all this? Because the business of science is to "deduce causes from effects, till we come to the very first cause, which certainly is not mechanical." In other words, the world may operate by mechanical causes, but as we trace them back, we deduce that the first cause must be an intelligent and rational Being.[16]

"This most beautiful system of sun, planets, and comets could only proceed from the counsel and dominion of an intelligent and powerful Being," wrote Newton.[17] Small wonder that his friend Roger Cotes proclaimed that Newton's work "will be the safest protection against the attacks of atheists, and nowhere more surely than from this quiver can one draw forth missiles against the band of godless men."[18] This is precisely the approach we must recover today.

Standard school textbooks still treat the rise of science as the cause of the demise of religion, which puts Christian young people on the defensive in the classroom. This stereotype is the legacy of the first modern historians such as Voltaire and Gibbon, who were Enlightenment rationalists eager to discredit Christianity. As a result, they composed histories of Western civilization that cast religion as an enemy of science and progress.[19] This is now so thoroughly ingrained in conventional wisdom that even Christians who are not trained scientists must be aware of the arguments in this chapter, learn to see through the stereotypes, and be able to make a defense of our faith.

I will confess that though I achieved moderate academic honors in college, I nearly flunked physics, so I cannot hold myself out as an expert in science (though Nancy has written extensively on the subject). But I can follow the reasoning of scientific apologetics, and I submit that most ordinary Christians can as well. Our case is strong and gives us the tools to challenge the reigning naturalistic orthodoxy and present a persuasive apologetic.

Many Christians are doing just that. Consider the story of Phillip Johnson, a professor on the law faculty at the University of California at Berkeley, a hotbed of 1960s radicalism. During a 1987 sabbatical in England, Johnson bought several books about Darwinian evolution. Reading them with his sharp lawyer's eye, he was astonished to discover how flawed the reasoning was, how flimsy the evidence. It dawned on him that Darwinism is dominant today not because of the strength of the scientific evidence but because Darwinism bolsters a worldview—one that rejects God and depicts humans as morally autonomous. He realized that the question of design versus Darwinism is at heart a battle between contrasting worldviews.

So today, dressed in baggy tweeds and peering through rimless glasses, Johnson breaks up his teaching schedule by accepting frequent invitations to present the case for design to lecture halls jammed with the world's most illustrious scientists. His books are best-sellers, and he's mentoring a cadre of bright young scholars who are working out the scientific details of the design argument.[20]

One doesn't have to be a professor to take up the case. In Colorado in 1996, fifteen-year-old Danny Phillips protested a classroom video on human reproduction from the PBS series *NOVA,* which opened with the sweeping statement that life originated billions of years ago when "powerful winds gathered random molecules from the atmosphere." Danny approached school authorities, arguing that the video violated a local school policy requiring teachers to present evolution as theory, not fact. He presented his case respectfully and persuasively, pointing out that the video's opening statement was unnecessary and doctrinaire—that it asserted without any evidence that life on earth is the outcome of natural laws operating purely by chance. A review committee from the school board agreed to discontinue using the video. Immediately, like vultures swooping down for the kill, representatives from the ACLU descended on the board, breathing threats of lawsuits, and school authorities reversed their decision.[21]

Danny was one young student alone against stiff opposition, so perhaps the reversal was predictable. Yet just raising the issue responsibly is an important starting point. And the way he went about it provides a good model for approaching public school officials. Danny acted completely on his own, so critics could not dismiss him as a pawn of outside groups. He limited his complaint to a clear case of naturalistic philosophy presented as scientific fact. And he politely offered for classroom use an educational video called *Darwinism: Science or Naturalistic Philosophy?* featuring debaters with impeccable academic credentials in an event held at Stanford University.[22]

If Christians intelligently raise issues in the classroom and the media, using reason and evidence, eventually we can shift the balance. Already there are signs that the scientific establishment is becoming nervous. The *Washington Post* reported on recent school controversies in an article titled "Creationism Makes a Comeback."[23] What's worse, warned *Science* magazine, it's coming back armed with a "shrewd new strategy."[24] That new strategy involves promoting critical thinking skills and helping people distinguish genuine science from naturalistic philosophy taught under the guise of science—as in the video Danny protested.

We need to communicate that what is at issue is not the specifics of evolution versus the specifics of Genesis. Rather, at issue is the worldview claim that life is the product of impersonal forces versus the claim that life was designed by an intelligent agent. We must fight worldview with worldview.

Consider the stark, dogmatic assertions made by typical school textbooks: "You are an animal, and share a common heritage with earthworms."[25] "Evolution is random and undirected . . . without either plan or purpose."[26] Our public schools are supposed to be neutral with regard to religion, but these statements are clearly not neutral; they are antagonistic to any and all theistic religions. They go far beyond any empirical evidence (how could anyone prove that evolution has no purpose?) and therefore are more philosophical than scientific.

Our first goal in dealing with schools, then, should be to get educators to separate philosophical claims from scientific theories. In other words, we must get them to stop treating philosophical statements as if they were science. Most teachers are fair-minded and are responsive if the issue is raised intelligently and respectfully.

Second, we should press for teaching science honestly. That is, educators should teach not only the examples that confirm evolution but also those that contradict it, the anomalies and unsolved questions. In *Education or Indoctrination?* science educator Norris Anderson illustrates how dogmatically naturalism is presented in textbooks. For example, "Darwin gave biology a sound scientific basis by attributing the diversity of life to natural causes rather than supernatural creation."[27] Or again, "Today, the evidence for evolution is overwhelming. . . . Evolution is no longer merely a theory." The same text takes a preemptive strike against troublesome critics by denouncing them as know-nothings: "There have always been those who resisted the appeal of evolution and every now and then declare 'Darwin was wrong,' in the hope of some profitable publicity, usually revealing that they do not understand Darwinism."[28]

Yet Anderson himself understands Darwinism better than most. Formerly a textbook writer, he helped prepare the infamous BSCS series (Biological Sciences Curriculum Study), which inaugurated the current dogmatic approach to teaching evolution. "I was practically an evangelist for evolution," Anderson says wryly. But he experienced a turnabout when a colleague told him privately, "I believe human evolution happened, but there's absolutely no evidence for it." Anderson was appalled and suggested that the textbooks be rewritten to reflect the real state of the evidence. His proposal was vehemently rejected.

"That's when my idealism began to crumble," Anderson says. "I saw that scientists close ranks to present a false image of scientific certainty."[29] His response was to spearhead a successful campaign in his home state of Alabama to paste an insert on the inside front cover of biology textbooks listing some of the anomalies and ambiguities in evolutionary theory. Several other states are now considering similar inserts.

This is a good start, for we must help people see that the deck has been stacked, that the presentations are completely one-sided. We need to press for an honest approach that shatters that "false image of scientific certainty" and openly weighs the evidence for and against any completely naturalistic account of life and the universe.

Perhaps the most important thing we can do is encourage Christian young people to go into science as a profession and to demonstrate in practice the viability of a biblical framework for science. Most Christians don't think of science as a mission field, as I discovered when a friendly young man introduced himself to me on a cross-country plane flight. He told me how much my books meant to him in his spiritual growth and then explained that he was studying molecular biology; as soon as he had his degree, however, he was planning to go to the mission field in South America.

"In that case, I see that my books have fallen short in guiding your spiritual growth," I responded.

The young man looked startled.

"Why do you feel you have to go to South America to serve God?" I asked. "How many Christian molecular biologists do you suppose there are?"

"Not many," he admitted.

Before the plane landed, he came by my seat one more time. "I've been thinking," he said, "I can be a missionary as a molecular biologist."

Precisely. If we are going to craft a winning strategy for extending Christ's lordship over all of life, we need missionaries in science and in every other discipline and vocation.

And the time is right. Though scientific naturalism has separated religion and science into antagonistic categories, the human urge for a unified vision of the world is spilling over those artificial boundaries. The Center for the Renewal of Science & Culture at the Discovery Institute in Seattle funds and publicizes research uncovering evidence for design in fields such as physics, cosmology, and biology. The Templeton Foundation has encouraged research into the relationship between science and religion, building bridges between them. As a result, religious issues are being hotly debated at scientific meetings.

The critical question is this: *What kind* of religion will receive the official approval of science? At the 1993 annual meeting of the American Association for the Advancement of Science (AAAS), participating scientists were somewhat startled to hear a clear, sweet voice rising above the group in a hymn as they assembled on Sunday morning. The singer was Nancy Abrams, wife of cosmologist Joel Primack, and the hymn was "The Handwriting of God," which celebrated the residual cosmic background radiation from the big bang. "God's secrets are written in the first light," announced the refrain. "Soon we'll be reading God's journal of the first day."

The performance highlighted a session on the relationship between science and religion, where participants flocked to discuss such topics as "The Religious Significance of Big Bang Cosmology" and "Scientific Resources for a Global Religious Myth." Not surprisingly, given that this is the age of do-it-yourself "god kits," many speakers argued that traditional faiths must give way to "a science-based myth." They urged their listeners to elevate cosmic evolution into a "compelling 'religious' narrative" with "the power to bind humans together in a new world order."[30]

What these priestly pronouncements miss is that Western science grew out of, and presupposes, not some "science-based myth" but Christianity, as we have seen in this chapter. As scientists grow more interested in these questions, it is crucial for Christians to seize the opportunity to demonstrate what the true basis of science is.

God calls us to "demolish arguments and every pretension that sets itself up against the knowledge of God" and to "take captive every thought to make it obedient to Christ" (2 Cor. 10:5). We must not fail to heed this call when it comes to modern science, for otherwise there's no telling what "compelling" but false new myths scientists may concoct to feed our society's deep spiritual hunger.

The reformation of science—and the way we think about reality—is not just a matter for ivory-tower academicians. It affects our entire worldview—not only ideas about religion and ethics but also about the arts, music, and popular culture, as we will see in the following chapters.

CHAPTER 41

BLESSED IS THE MAN

Headed to his mother's house north of Malibu, the young movie producer was driving along Pacific Coast Highway when the low buzzy ring of his car phone sounded. He snatched it up and listened to the panicky voice at the other end.

"No," he said. "No . . . no . . . I told them. . . . Look, if we're ever going to get this picture made, we have to have a star who can open it. . . . No, it's not something we can talk about. The script is just not that strong. If it doesn't open big here and do well internationally, we could find ourselves on the streets. . . . Yes, yes, that we can do. We're prepared to talk power numbers. No, I don't want just her agent. I want her at that meeting personally. I want her to feel . . . Okay . . . Okay . . . but just do it *now,* all right? . . . Okay, talk to you."

After the success of *Pretty Woman,* every Hollywood studio was hot to recycle the hooker-with-a-heart-of-gold scenario. They were preparing to roll out screens full of the stuff, "sanitized" by the woman's point of view: brutal men, the lonely struggles of single moms, and a woman's hallowed right to choose her own lifestyle. Meanwhile, men could overlook the "message" for the obvious titillating attractions, feeding their own fantasies. This was sexual politics, Hollywood style.

How did I end up here? the young producer wondered. He had started out with such high ideals, thinking he would write and produce serious films for adults, not adult-only schlock.

He tuned the radio to his favorite classical station, as he often did when his own life grew dissonant, and heard a faint, distant throbbing of double basses. Outside the window, the houses screening his view of the Pacific began to be spaced farther apart, and between them he glimpsed turquoise sea-foamed bays within surrounding arms of brown cliffs.

The theme started by the double basses grew stronger and more intense as other strings joined, pitting long, low strains against one another in a dirgelike progression. Somehow the music kept drawing his attention toward the cradling bays on the left. It seemed to speak with the power of the sea rumbling against the land and climbed in a steady progression that lifted his eyes to the blue, cloud-gauzed heavens. It made him long for . . . for what?

Suddenly a soprano began to sing, and her voice made him think of his mother, who was waiting for him. He was late and knew he might find her testy. But then again, he had waited for her his entire childhood. Waited for her to come back from the studio. Back from location. Back from his father's funeral after the plane crash—which, he had been told, he was "too young to understand."

But he had understood the loss of his father only too well. What he still did not understand was why his mother had pushed him away from her at that moment. Or in the following years, while she conducted numerous affairs and he was shunted off to boarding school.

Now both of them were trying to recapture something, and yet he went to their weekly dinners together with a guardedness he had not been able to shake off.

He didn't recognize the language in which the soprano was singing, but as the music ascended, he was gripped by her magnificent, yearning song. Suddenly, at its height, when the music turned bright and bittersweet, he found himself in tears, longing for something he couldn't even name.

People used to speak of being "ravished" by music. That must be what was happening to him. The music was releasing such an enormous store of emotions that he felt utterly at its mercy. He pulled over to the side of the road and gave in to the mourning and ecstasy that the music evoked, resting his head against the steering wheel. In the background, he heard traffic passing, but the music's strange hold on him kept him motionless as he cried his heart out for every loss he had ever suffered.

The strains began to subside into the patterns out of which they had emerged, easing the sorrow. He looked up at the sandy, pumpkin-brown cliff to his right, then to the ocean across the highway, where a group of coral-prickly boulders marched out to meet the waves. He knew he would remember this roadside spot, this holy ground of nowhere. He would never be able to pass those sea-marching boulders without remembering the first time he had heard this powerful piece of music.

As the music quieted to a point where he thought it must end, he turned up the volume to hear the name of the piece and its composer. Instead, another movement began.

He wasn't going anywhere, he decided, until he knew what he was listening to, for this music expressed exactly what the real artist in him had always wanted to create in film. Fidelity to contemporary experience yet with an unabashed capacity to address the deepest human sentiments. Before the second movement ended, he picked up his cellular phone and dialed information. Then he called KMCB.

"What are you playing?" he asked. "What's the piece on right now?"

"Górecki's Third."

"What? How do you spell that?"

"Not like it's pronounced. He's Polish. Henryk Górecki. You say 'Goo-*rets*-kee,' but it's spelled G-O-R-E-C-K-I."

"Is it available? Can you get it on CD?"

"Is this the first time you've heard it?"

"Yes, I'm calling from my car. I've never heard anything like this."

"You and everybody else. It's at the top of *Billboard* magazine's chart. The classical chart. It's even at number seven on the pop chart. It's a phenomenon."

■   ■   ■

IN 1993 THE WORLD discovered Henryk Górecki and his Symphony no. 3, *Symphony of Sorrowful Songs,* a work composed more than fifteen years earlier. Though the movie producer in our story is fictional, his reaction is based on news accounts of radio station managers who say they were inundated by calls from listeners—many of whom did pull over to the side of the road to weep, overwhelmed by the music.

In a world where serious contemporary music often has been dominated by the jarring dissonance of experimental music, how does this composition manage to be truly contemporary and yet so full of pathos? Why does the *Symphony of Sorrowful Songs* communicate to such a vast audience? And perhaps most mysteriously, to what unnamable reaches of the human spirit is Górecki speaking? Who is this composer, and how does he do it?

Henryk Mikolaj Górecki was born in Poland in 1933.[1] His mother, Otylia, played the piano, and his father, a railroad employee, was an amateur musician. Henryk's mother died when he was two years old, and after his father remarried, Górecki received no musical encouragement and was even forbidden to play his mother's piano. He taught himself to play in secret and eventually insisted on being allowed to study. But his musical progress had been set back so much that he was turned down the first time he applied to the Intermediate School of Music in Rybnik—a type of performing-arts high school.

Yet by 1955, when Górecki entered the Higher School of Music conservatory in Katowice, he was already an accomplished composer, and before he graduated, his music was being featured at national festivals. He went on to win international music festival awards in Paris in the early 1960s and became head of the Higher School of Music in Katowice. But what best explains Henryk Górecki's genius was the part he played in one of the late twentieth century's defining moments.

In 1977 the cardinal of Krakow, Karol Wojtyla, commissioned Górecki to compose a work for the upcoming anniversary of St. Stanislaw's martyrdom nine hundred years earlier. From the beginning, this commission carried grave risks for a musician in Communist Poland, for St. Stanislaw represented the moral authority of the Christian faith over secular rulers. Back in 1079, St. Stanislaw was a bishop who incurred the wrath of King Boleslaus II by opposing the king's adulteries and unjust wars. At first the king repented, but later he returned to his old ways and ordered his henchmen to kill the bishop. When they refused, the king did the job himself. While Bishop Stanislaw was celebrating Mass in the cathedral one day, the king split the holy man's skull with a sword.

The martyred Stanislaw became the patron saint of Poland, an emblem of the moral authority of the church and a rebuke to all the tyrants who have ruled Poland through its long, sad history. To compose a work in honor of St. Stanislaw in Communist Poland was to declare oneself in open opposition to the government.

Yet Górecki's acceptance of the commission cannot have surprised the authorities. As head of one of Poland's most respected educational institutions, Górecki had for several years conducted a running battle with the "yapping little dogs"—as he referred to Communist Party officials—who constantly tried to interfere in the workings of the school. In the West, the arts are often seen as a nonpolitical force, but the Communists always understood that the arts can have political implications—and they strongly "preferred" that their artists express an allegiance to Marxist-Leninism.

Górecki was also known as a devoted Roman Catholic. He taught his students the great canon of sacred music not merely as a historical artifact but as a living, vital tradition. His own compositions reflected the same conviction, with much of his work based on traditional sacred chant melodies. Official Communist ideology insisted that Christianity was a thing of the past—a religion for old people, soon to die out. Yet here was Górecki, the head of a state institution and already one of Poland's most celebrated composers, drawing his inspiration from this supposedly dry well. His work served as a rebuke, just as St. Stanislaw's work had done nine hundred years earlier. Now he was poised to create what would surely be a magnificent choral tribute to this saint—and just at the time when Solidarity had begun to shake the foundations of Communist Poland. A rumbling to which the Kremlin's political seismographers were exquisitely attuned.

Then, in the midst of Górecki's work on the new composition, something amazing happened. In 1978, a year after commissioning the piece, Karol Wojtyla, cardinal of Krakow, became Pope John Paul II. The following year, the pope was scheduled to visit his homeland to commemorate the anniversary of St. Stanislaw, and Communist Party officials knew that his visit would be watched by the entire world. As a result, they began pressuring Górecki to stop work on his commission.

A running battle ensued. Górecki's phone was tapped, his mail intercepted, his meetings secretly taped. Students he had nurtured were denied positions, and he was prevented from appointing the best of the younger composers to teaching positions. Communist Party members on the faculty were encouraged to plot against him. At an important anniversary of the conservatory, he was airbrushed out of all the photographs. Television news programs about the anniversary omitted any footage of him. Górecki became a nonperson. Officially, he ceased to exist. How long would it be until he was arrested . . . or worse?

Eventually, the party made it impossible for Górecki to continue as head of the Higher School of Music in Katowice, and in 1979 he resigned from this position. He would take his chances living by his music alone.

When John Paul II arrived on June 2 of that year, the Polish government did its best to suppress all news of the event. Officials put up checkpoints along all roads leading to papal appearances, blacked out television coverage in adjoining districts, made sure no television shots of the event revealed the massive crowds in attendance, sent jets streaking low overhead to intimidate the crowds, and in every other conceivable way tried to minimize the impact of the pope's visit. Yet everywhere in Poland, even in districts far removed from John Paul's personal appearances, people placed posters of their champion in their windows and even laid floral tributes at newsstands showing his picture. The essential freedom of the human spirit had not been eliminated by Gulags, secret police, or economic deprivation during the long, dark years of the Cold War; it had been harbored and nurtured by an ever living Christian faith. Now that faith reemerged—vigorous, joyous, hopeful.

Plans also went forward for Górecki's composition, now completed and titled *Beatus Vir* (Blessed Is the Man), and it was scheduled to be played several days later at John Paul II's final appearance in Poland. The Communist Party brought increasing pressure to bear on Górecki, even pressuring other musicians not to participate in the performance. As a result, no one was available to conduct *Beatus Vir*.

All right, said Górecki, he would conduct the choral work himself.

As a last resort, the Communists turned to physical intimidation. They hired a gang of thugs to "demonstrate" outside Górecki's house. The "demonstrators" marched back and forth, waving placards protesting Górecki's "antiproletarian compositions." When Górecki gave no sign of caving in to this pressure, the goons broke into his house and looted it.

Undaunted, Górecki and his family journeyed to Krakow. There, on the evening of June 9, *Beatus Vir* was premiered in the Franciscan Basilica before John Paul II and a packed congregation—with the composer conducting a magnificent orchestra and choir.

"Dominus!" the choir sang. "Dominus! Dominus! Dominus!" ("Lord! Lord! Lord! Lord!")

Through the opening bars, the choir called on God again and again in unison, voicing the earnest plea of the millions praying on this occasion. They echoed the prayer that must have been stilled in St. Stanislaw's throat nine hundred years earlier, as the king's sword split his skull.

"Lord! Lord! Lord!" the choir sang yet again, each call stealing into the silence, for the voices sang without accompaniment at this point.

Where is God? the silence asked. *Where was he when the saint cried out? Where is he now that all of Poland is crying out?*

"Lord!" the choir sang, with all the urgency of Poland's suffering millions and their compatriots in other Eastern European countries—and beyond, to every cry of human desperation for divine mercy.

A longer silence followed, and then the orchestra began to play long, low strains, strangely reminiscent of the events of that week. On Wednesday, John Paul had visited the concentration camps of Auschwitz and Birkenau. There he commemorated the deaths of two Christians—Father Maximilian Kolbe and Edith Stein—whose martyrdom spoke in a representative way of all those who have been slaughtered at totalitarian hands in the twentieth century.

A baritone voice began singing, "O Lord, listen to my prayer. Listen. Listen."

A rocking, cradling rhythm suggested a repetitive, even monotonous plea for help. "O Lord," sang the choir, "hear my prayer. In your justice, hear me."

The choir and the baritone joined together and rose toward the mid-point climax of the piece. "O Lord! You are my God."

Here the trudging tones suddenly swung up, as if the world itself were turned right side up once more, and the swinging movement of history became no longer a monotonous death knell but the pealing of church bells ringing out the joy of "Christ with us."

> *Make me quick to heed your mercy,*
> *Teach me to do your will,*
> *For you are my God.*
> *May your spirit lead me into the land of righteousness.*

After this splendor came a pause, and then the baritone returned to the low strains of the beginning, but with the certain knowledge that . . .

> *O Lord, you are my God.*
> *My fate is in your hands.*
> *Lord God, you are my salvation.*

For what, after all, had changed? Political power had merely switched hands: The Nazis had been succeeded by the Soviets and their Polish collaborators. Salvation would have to be inspired by something other than the will to power. Our fate remains in God's hands, the music insisted, in spite of those who hold the weapons of violence in theirs.

Then the music became surpassingly lovely.

"O taste and see that the Lord is good."

After all, was not John Paul II beyond the authority of all state power, free to articulate the hopes of oppressed peoples everywhere? Free and willing to remind the world that truth cannot be changed, that beyond the weapons of violence is a much more significant struggle waged in the hearts of men and women, the struggle between good and evil?

The orchestral bells rang out, recognizing that throughout history Christ has raised up champions for the truth. The bells pealed that Christ would always raise up champions to remind the world where ultimate authority lies.

"Blessed is the man who trusts in him."

This day of spiritual triumph would pass, giving way to many difficult days. But the hope that Henryk Górecki had conveyed in his powerful musical witness would not be forgotten.

■   ■   ■

AFTER THAT HISTORIC moment, Górecki retreated into private life and might have escaped the world's notice—had it not been for his *Symphony of Sorrowful Songs*. Composed in 1976, his Symphony no. 3 was recorded three times but with little impact. Then, in 1993, the London Sinfonietta recorded the *Symphony of Sorrowful Songs* once more, this time with soprano Dawn Upshaw. The recording became an international phenomenon. Perhaps the Lord wanted to reward this musician who showed such dedication and courage.

The movie producer who pulled over to the side of the road was thinking of his mother and their alienated relationship. Henryk Górecki may well have been thinking of his own mother when he composed Symphony no. 3. The text sung by the soprano consists of three songs, the first of which is a fifteenth-century monastic lamentation of Mary at the foot of the cross. The second is a prayer found scratched on the wall of a cell in a gestapo headquarters in Poland; the prayer is signed by an eighteen-year-old girl, urging her mother not to weep for her and asking Christ's mother to remember her. The third sorrowful song borrows the words of a Polish folk song, in which a mother bewails the loss of her soldier son. Since Górecki lost his own mother at an early age, we can imagine that long before he expressed the sorrow of the human condition in his compositions, he had himself turned to the One who could assuage his grief and longing.

From the personal to the universal, Henryk Górecki shows what the courage of one man can do against massive evil. He shows us the incredible power of music to reach into the soul of a jaded world. And through Górecki's music, Christ teaches us to sing despite our tears.

CHAPTER 42

SOLI DEO GLORIA

*Since Christians, artists as well as evangelists, have within them the power of
the Holy Spirit, it is only logical to conclude that artists, who bring everything
into captivity for Christ, write, just as they live, under the direction of the
Holy Spirit. . . . Their poems are not private; they are images incarnated for
themselves and for the community in which they live.*

JOHN LEAX

Henryk Górecki's Symphony no. 3 may be the first music ever to top
both classical and pop charts. Solemn clerks in classical music stores were
startled to see punk rockers with spiky orange hair coming in to ask for the
piece. People of all ages and backgrounds are drawn to Górecki's hauntingly
beautiful, near liturgical sound, which borrows from both medieval music
and folk melodies.

But the primary significance of Górecki's work is that it represents a return to tonal music—music based on the major and minor scales. In most
classical music composed in the latter half of the twentieth century, those
scales have been tossed aside, and composers are producing atonal music
(based on the twelve-tone scale of Arnold Schoenberg or the "chance music"
of John Cage). The trouble is, atonal music was rejected by the public from
the very beginning for its sheer unpleasantness. For example, Sir Harrison
Birtwistle's dissonant style has been described by reviewers as "extremely violent," capable of inflicting "an almost physical pain."[1]

Why are contemporary composers producing music with such harsh
dissonance? The answer reveals a shift in the very definition of art. The musical language of tonality was traditionally thought to represent the natural
law of sounds (based on the overtones that accompany any naturally produced sound). It goes back to the ancient Greeks, who discovered that if you
divide a string into pure mathematical lengths in simple ratios such as 2:1,

3:2, or 4:3, you get "pure"-sounding intervals (consonance).[2] But contemporary composers view tonality as an arbitrary construct that can be discarded so that new musical languages can be invented. In parallel fashion, artists in other fields have given up the traditional notion that art reflects nature or objective reality in some way, and they have substituted the idea that artists create their own autonomous, abstract, and artificial world from which they can cast down thunderbolts on the world of ordinary folk. Indeed, much contemporary art seems intended primarily to shock, to destroy traditions and conventions.

A few years ago on CBS's *60 Minutes,* Morley Safer engaged in a blistering critique of contemporary art. The program highlighted Robert Gober, who creates sculptures shaped like urinals; Robert Ryman, who paints entire canvases plain white; and Jeff Koons, whose work is exemplified by two basketballs floating in a fish tank. "Is this art?" Safer asked.[3]

It is an important question, for the way we define art has the power to shape our culture. As we saw in the work of Górecki, art affects us at the deepest level of the soul. It can shape our thoughts, move our emotions, enlarge our imaginations. The music we listen to, the images we plant in our minds, the stories we tell—all have enormous power over the kind of people we are. They both express and shape our beliefs and values.

Just think of the effective way Jesus used images and stories. He could have just said, "Take care of people who are hurt and victimized." Instead, he spun the story of the Good Samaritan. He could have just said, "God forgives your sins." Instead, he told the parable of the Prodigal Son. Why? Because a story gets at aspects of the truth that are beyond the power of didactic teaching. Symbols, metaphors, allegories, and images move the whole person—the emotions and senses as well as the intellect. The rich, evocative words of literature are far more powerful than factual description.

For the Christian, the arts are also an important way to understand God and his creation. The arts give us ears to hear and eyes to see more clearly. We know from Scripture that creation is God's handiwork and that it reveals his glory; but often our ears are deaf, and our eyes are blind to that revelation. Artists are gifted with a special sensitivity to the glories of creation, and through their work, they can bring these glories into sharper focus for others.[4] Think of the music of Bach, the paintings of Rembrandt, the sculpture of Michelangelo.

Why, then, has art been so degraded in our own day? How have we moved from Bach to Birtwistle's dissonances? From Rembrandt to Ryman's blank canvases? From Michelangelo to Gober's urinals? How have we lost a sense of art's high dignity and purpose?

THE HARMONY OF THE SPHERES

The answer is an underlying philosophical shift from objectivism to subjectivism, and as we examine the history of ideas about art, we will see how this change in worldviews has led to disastrous consequences.

The classical understanding is that the arts are a powerful means of communicating something significant about reality, a means of representing truth. Not that a work of art has to capture events in a photographic manner. After all, a painting may depict invisible things, such as angels, or abstract ideals, such as justice portrayed as a blindfolded woman with a scale; yet these images still convey something that is real. A novel is fictitious, yet it may represent profound realities about the human condition. Music is the most abstract of the arts, yet as we have seen, the traditional musical scale is rooted in an objective reality, based on mathematical relationships among sound frequencies found in nature.

From the time of the ancient Greeks, music was thought to reflect an orderly, mathematical structure built into the universe itself. With the rise of Christianity, these ideas were absorbed into a biblical worldview. Art was seen as rooted in the orderly structure and harmony of the universe God had created. Therefore, the basic justification for art is in the doctrine of creation.

Moreover, when God created the world, he cared enough to make it beautiful. There is no more convincing argument that God himself is pleased with beauty than to gaze at the delicate hues of a wildflower against dark green moss, the blue expanse of a Montana sky, the sharp outlines of the Swiss Alps. What's more, when God communicated his Word to us, he did so in a variety of literary styles: history, poetry, liturgical formulas, ethical principles, hymns, letters, maxims and proverbs, and even a love song.

Since God made human beings in his image, our capacity for aesthetic enjoyment is part of the way he created us—one of his good gifts to us. An engaging story, a majestic symphony, a beautiful landscape painting—these works of art give us aesthetic pleasure and cause us to contemplate not only the beauty of the world God created but also the eternal beauty of God himself. "One thing I ask of the Lord," says the psalmist, ". . . that I may . . . gaze upon the beauty of the Lord" (Ps. 27:4). In Scripture we find commands to make the temple beautiful and to make it ring with music. God wants us to use our best artistic skills in the worship of him.

Throughout history, believers have done just that, using the arts to glorify God and edify one another. The early church raised its voice in praise in a variety of chant styles (some of which have recently been turned into best-selling CDs). The medieval period gave us awe-inspiring cathedrals, designed to lift the mind to divine truth and to give "delight in the beauty of the house of God," in the words of twelfth-century Abbot Suger, architect of the great cathedral of St. Denis in France.[5] Indeed, in every period of Western history, many of the enduring artistic treasures have been produced by Christians.

Music

In music, the Renaissance produced the sublime treasure of sacred polyphony: the serene harmonies of Palestrina, the seamless textures of John Taverner, Thomas Tallis, and William Byrd. This is music that creates a sense that one is standing in a cathedral, the sound rising like high vaults towering overhead.

The baroque period gave us Antonio Vivaldi, a man of the cloth, nicknamed "The Red Priest" because of his wild red hair. Johann Sebastian Bach was a Lutheran, with an intense evangelical commitment, and signed most of his works "Soli Deo Gloria"—to God alone be the glory. When Bach was composing the majestic *St. Matthew Passion,* which depicts the suffering and death of Christ, he was so deeply moved that tears rolled down his face. The work is punctuated with devotional arias in which the composer pours out his intense sorrow and gratitude over Christ's suffering.

George Frideric Handel, also a Lutheran, was fifty-six years old when, at a time of crisis in his life, he closeted himself in his room to compose his famous *Messiah.* During that time, he reportedly underwent such an overwhelming spiritual experience that he sobbed with emotion, later telling his startled servant, "I did think I did see all Heaven before me, and the great God Himself."[6]

In the classical period, Franz Joseph Haydn, a Catholic, used prayer to break through writer's block. If a piece "does not make progress," he said, "I try to find out if I have erred in some way or other, thereby forfeiting grace; and I pray for mercy until I feel that I am forgiven."[7]

Among the Romantic composers, Felix Mendelssohn was a Lutheran of profound personal faith, (his father converted from Judaism). Mendelssohn wrote many works celebrating the Christian faith, including his 1830 "Reformation" symphony, which ends with a ringing rendition of Martin Luther's hymn "A Mighty Fortress Is Our God."[8] Antonín Dvořák, with his lively Slavic melodies, was a sturdy believer who penned invocations in his manuscripts: They begin with the phrase "With God," and end with "God be thanked."[9]

Literature

Many of the greatest masters in Western literature have been Christian poets. Think of Dante, whose *Divine Comedy* paints a rich mural of the soul's encounter with sin (hell), suffering (purgatory), and glory (heaven). Think of John Donne, with his memorable lines "Death be not proud," "No man is an island," and "Never send to know for whom the bell tolls; it tolls for thee." Or think of John Milton, who composed the magnificent epic *Paradise Lost* to "justify the ways of God to men."

There are others we might not immediately think of, such as Samuel Taylor Coleridge, who was elevated to an icon in the drug culture of the 1960s because he composed some of his visionary poems under the influence of opium. What literature textbooks rarely mention is that Coleridge sought freedom from his opium addiction by turning to Jesus Christ.[10]

Many of the traditional stories and fairy tales of Western culture were either written by Christians or at least reflect the ethos of a Christian culture, as Vigen Guroian shows in *Tending the Heart of Virtue*. For example, the well-known story of *Pinocchio* (the original, not the Disney version) features a wooden puppet that becomes a real boy by overcoming his proclivity for lying and self-indulgence. The story expresses the profound Christian truth that those whose hearts are "wooden" with sin can become "flesh" through a process of moral regeneration.[11]

Likewise, many of the classic works of literature clearly reflect a Christian worldview. *The Count of Monte Cristo* by Alexandre Dumas traces complex themes of revenge and forgiveness. *The Swiss Family Robinson* by Johann D. Wyss, the adventures of a Swiss clergyman and his family, is rich in Christian piety. Robert Louis Stevenson's novels such as *Kidnapped* and *Treasure Island* reveal a biblical worldview. And few people raised Christian themes and the great moral questions of life more brilliantly than Fyodor Dostoyevsky.

Visual Arts

Moving to the visual arts, we can trace throughout history a variety of styles that have been used to express a Christian vision. Many medieval paintings are lovely but symbolic, composed of two-dimensional images and stylized figures against a flat gold background. Beginning with the Renaissance, painting became more natural. In the thirteenth century, theologian Thomas Aquinas rejected the otherworldliness of the Middle Ages and stressed the importance of the natural world as God's creation, arguing that "grace does not deny nature but perfects it." Aquinas's philosophy was quickly felt in the arts, exemplified by Cimabue and Giotto, who began to paint more realistically, transforming the stiff medieval icons into living individuals. [12]

The Reformation brought a greater appreciation of everyday life and work. Artists began to paint ordinary people—farmers and housewives—plying their trades against real landscapes. Painters like Albrecht Dürer, Jacob van Ruisdael, and the incomparable Rembrandt wove spiritual themes deeply into the fabric of their masterpieces of everyday life.

The Counter-Reformation produced ornate, grandiose baroque art, inspired by a new appreciation of the Incarnation—that in Christ, God was manifest in the flesh. This led to a greater appreciation for creation, especially the physical body, as a revelation of God. Artists like the Flemish painter Peter Paul Rubens depicted heavy, fleshy, solid figures to convey the idea that God reveals himself in the physical world—that it carries a weight of spiritual glory.

Among more recent artists, nearly everyone is familiar with the Dutch painter Vincent van Gogh, and the intense, swirling lines of his trees, starry skies, and sunflowers. But few know that van Gogh, son of a Protestant pastor, at first believed he had a religious vocation. He worked as a missionary in the slums of London and then in the mining districts of Belgium. It was only as he began to show signs of mental instability and lost the financial support of his mission society that he turned to painting. In one fascinating work, he paints himself as Lazarus raised from the dead—a clear testimony of his faith.

■   ■   ■

FROM EVEN THIS sketchy historical survey, we can see that Christians have played an important role in creating and sustaining the great art of our culture. Yet you would never guess it from most secular books, for they often scrub out references to the artists' religious faith. This makes it easy for secular critics to belittle Christians wrongly as artistic know-nothings.

Indeed, some historians have even accused the church of being opposed to the arts. To answer that charge, we must look again at the testimony of history. It's true that at various points through the centuries Christians have had to stand against art in various forms—not because they were against art itself, but because they opposed its misuse. For example, the church has always condemned lewd, vulgar, coarse, or immoral content in art; it has also disapproved of grandiose art projects used for display and status.

The use of images within the church has also sparked recurring controversies.[13] During the Reformation, for example, Protestant extremists rampaged through cathedrals, knocking over statues and smashing stained-glass windows. As a result, some historians have criticized the Reformation; Kenneth Clark, in his influential television series *Civilisation,* denounced it as "an unmitigated disaster" to art.[14] But even the iconoclasts must be understood within their historical context. The medieval mind attributed great spiritual power to images. Icons were venerated, kissed, and addressed in prayer. Statues of the saints were said to bleed, weep, perform miracles, and even grant indulgences, exempting sinners from the pains of purgatory.[15] Eager to fight what they saw as idolatry, the iconoclasts mistakenly thought the way to end worship of the saints was to smash statues of the saints.

But this was not the true spirit of the Reformation. Its true spirit was exemplified by Martin Luther, who, after being condemned by the emperor, risked his life by coming out of hiding to *stop* the riots that burned images and smashed statues. Luther's own favorite art form was music, and he composed many hymns, including the much-loved "A Mighty Fortress Is Our God." Luther said that "the gift of language combined with the gift of song was given to man that he should proclaim the Word of God through music."[16] John Calvin, likewise, held a high view of some of the arts: "Because sculpture and paintings are gifts of God, I seek a pure and legitimate use of each."[17]

Throughout history, believers have pursued the same search for a "pure and legitimate use" of art. How, then, was this tradition eventually pushed out of the mainstream? How did art become so secularized that today it is sometimes pursued for little more than shock value?

FROM ART TO ANTI-ART

To understand why art has lost its high purpose, we must place it in the context of a broader worldview shift (noted in chapter 40), when modern science was elevated to an idol, the sole source of knowledge. The assumption took hold that anything science cannot detect and measure must not be real, leading to an assault not only on religion but also on the realm of the imagination and intuition expressed in the arts.

It began with rationalist critics looking with disdain on all the mythological creatures so beloved of poets and painters, saying, in essence, "Come now. Science proves there are no such things as unicorns and centaurs, witches and fairies, dragons and Cyclopes. Away with these myths and superstitions!" Eventually, rationalists concluded that art, by its very nature, is a falsification of reality. Isn't literature comprised of imaginary stories? Doesn't poetry employ metaphor and hyperbole? The artist might paint a sunset in all its glorious hues, but the scientist knows that a sunset is "really" nothing but the refraction of white light through dust particles in layers of air of variable density.[18] To many people it began to seem that if science is true, then art must be false, or at best merely an expression of personal emotion.

Not surprisingly, this all-out attack put artists on the defensive, and they began to question the meaning and purpose of what they did. If art did not express the truth in some way, what *did* it do? Some artists capitulated to the imperialism of science and tried to signify in their work the generalized principles that were said by science to underlie what we see and hear. This produced a trend toward ever more abstract art. Cubism, for example, with its geometrical shapes and angles, can be understood as an attempt to portray the mathematical structures underlying the physical world. In architecture, movements like the Bauhaus in Germany and de Stijl in Holland produced stark, boxlike buildings in an effort to base their art on "numbers, measurements, and abstract line."[19]

But the more typical response by artists was to concede the physical world to science and relegate art to a wholly separate world—one that it would create for itself. In fact, this was when artists first began to speak of their work in terms of "creating." Today this usage is so familiar that we do not realize that only four centuries ago it would have been shocking to speak of a poet or painter as "creating" something new. Such language seemed to equate the artist with God in his unique role as the Creator.

Understood in a biblical context, of course, there is nothing wrong with claiming that human creativity reflects the creativity of God, in whose image we are made. But torn out of that context, the notion quickly became idolatrous. In defending their work, artists began to overcompensate by claiming that art is actually *superior* to science. They contended that it is the imagination, not scientific reason, that is most godlike. And they insisted that art finds its highest form not in representing reality but in creating something completely new and imaginary. In every poem, every painting, the artist was conceived as the creator of a new universe, a microcosm in which his or her decisions were absolute. The artist's creativity, says literary scholar M. H. Abrams, was modeled on the "absolute fiat of Jehovah in the book of Genesis."[20]

Beginning in the nineteenth-century Romantic movement, the artist became idolized, and art itself became a surrogate for religion. In George Bernard Shaw's 1908 play *The Doctor's Dilemma*, a painter on his deathbed recites this credo: "I believe in Michelangelo, Velásquez, and Rembrandt, in the might of design, the mystery of color, the redemption of all things by Beauty everlasting. . . . Amen. Amen."[21] And if art was a religion, then the artist's work was beyond criticism, for "the appropriate attitude to Divinity, of course, is one of adoration," writes Abrams.[22] Ordinary people were no longer qualified to hold an opinion on whether works of art were good or bad, and art became the realm of an elite.

Thus "art inherit[ed] all the duties of the church," writes historian Jacques Barzun.[23] Artists were elevated to prophetic status in both senses of the word: as people gifted with unique insight, offering a vision of an ideal world, and as people who denounced the sins of the real world. In the first function, artists were heralded as the avant-garde of society, those who see farther than the rest of us. This attitude produced styles such as symbolism, abstraction, and expressionism—all attempts to free art from contamination by the everyday world and to construct an ideal, autonomous, quasi-spiritual world. In the second prophetic function, artists took it upon themselves to denounce the ugliness of the bourgeois, materialistic, industrialized society that had made the artists' own role so precarious. This attitude produced naturalism in art: the attempt to portray the ills of society with stark, ruthless accuracy.

Yet both prophetic functions—the vision of the ideal and the denunciation of the real—were united by a common theme: hostility toward the real world.[24] And in the end that hostility became the dominant theme as both approaches collapsed into protest, criticism, and attacks on established morality and social structures. For the autonomous world that the idealist artists were attempting to create was quite beyond their power. "It takes an omniscient God" to bring good out of evil, to make the last into the first, to bring down rulers and lift up the humble, writes Barzun. Therefore, "to a godless age, the negative part of the inversion alone remains potent."[25] All that was left was to attack and destroy, to subvert and "transgress"—or, in the poet Baudelaire's phrase, to "shock the bourgeoisie."

But art that attacks all standards ends up destroying itself—because eventually even artistic standards are attacked and cast aside. Which is why in the twentieth century Marcel Duchamp could exhibit a commercially produced urinal and call it art. Jackson Pollock dripped paint randomly on a canvas. Andy Warhol reproduced Campbell's soup cans, and Roy Lichtenstein painted images from comic strips. Today, artists exhibit "junk art" or "found art," consisting of bricks, broken glass, and crushed aluminum cans stuck on canvas or stacked into a sculpture. The common theme in all these examples is that there is no special standard distinguishing art from objects in the everyday world.

A parallel development in music is John Cage's "chance music," composed by tossing dice or some other chance mechanism. Cage has even offered "musical" pieces with no sound. In a performance of his work "4-33," the pianist sits at the piano, gazing at an open score, his hands suspended above the keyboard as if ready to begin. He does this for 4 minutes and 33 seconds, then shuts the score and leaves the stage.

The musical parallel to "found art" is "noise music," recordings of the background noise of the city. For example, Luigi Russolo recorded "the palpitations of valves, the coming and going of pistons, the howl of mechanical saws, the jolting of the tram on its rails" and then signed his name to the racket.[26]

The very concept of quality, of standards, is rejected by many of today's artists as a "paternalistic fiction," says art critic Robert Hughes.[27] The wholesale rejection of standards has led to the anti-art movement, exemplified by a 1993 exhibit titled "Abject Art" at the Whitney Art Museum in New York City. The exhibit featured what its catalog described as "abject materials such as dirt, hair, excrement, dead animals, menstrual blood, and rotting food." The display included a three-foot mound of synthetic excrement, a dismembered sculpture of two women engaged in sexual acts, and a film depicting Jesus Christ as a naked woman.

What was the point of all this? "To confront taboo issues of gender and sexuality" and other subject matter "deemed inappropriate by a conservative dominant culture," explained the catalog.[28] The show also included works that had sparked public controversy earlier: Andres Serrano's photo of a crucifix in a jar of urine, a homoerotic photograph by Robert Mapplethorpe, and a film by porn star Annie Sprinkle called *Sluts and Goddesses: How to Be a Sex Goddess in 101 Easy Steps.* In other words, the artists had no higher aim than denouncing the beliefs and standards of ordinary people, especially those who had had the audacity to voice moral protest in the past. Thus an influential branch of late-twentieth-century art has degenerated into expressions of rebellion on a par with eight-year-olds who giggle at bathroom jokes.

When even prestigious art museums display anti-art, it is clear that no one can say what art is any longer. And if art cannot be defined, then it will be destroyed. A few years ago the Manchester Academy of Fine Arts held a competition where an award was given to a watercolor entitled *Rhythm of the Trees.* The work displayed "a certain quality of color balance, composition, and technical skill," the judges decided. To their chagrin, the artist turned out to be a four-year-old child whose mother had submitted the work as a joke.[29] Artistic standards have been so thoroughly debunked that art critics honestly cannot tell the difference between the work of a trained artist and the dabbling of a small child.

And so we return to Morley Safer's question, "Is this art?" For the secular world today the answer is, "Who knows?" There are no standards by which art can even be defined.

The decline of the arts illustrates the staggering impact of a false view of *creation, fall,* and *redemption.* As we have seen, the process began when artists accepted the dogma of scientific naturalism, which set up science as the only source of genuine knowledge and relegated beauty to the subjective realm. In defense, artists claimed that realm itself as an arena where they could reign godlike in their capacity for creativity. Art became a surrogate religion, with artists hurling prophetic denunciations at "sinners." But it is a religion with no power of redemption, and so in the end it has degenerated into little more than assaults on mainstream society's beliefs and values.

FOR GLORY AND FOR BEAUTY

Christianity alone has the resources to restore the arts to their proper place, for Christianity is a worldview that supports human creativity yet does so with appropriate humility. Made in the image of the Creator, humans find fulfillment in being creative in their own sphere. Yet unlike God, the human artist does not create out of nothing. "Human creativity is derivative and reflective, working within the bounds of what God has formed," writes Os Guinness.[30] As C. S. Lewis put it, "an author should never conceive of himself as bringing into existence beauty or wisdom which did not exist before, but simply and solely as trying to embody in terms of his own art some reflection of that eternal Beauty and Wisdom."[31] Because of the Fall, we do not have a clear glimpse of Beauty or Wisdom; we see only a poor reflection. But because of Christ's redemption, the arts can be restored.

Scripture treats the arts as a divine calling. In his book *State of the Arts: From Bezalel to Mapplethorpe,* Gene Edward Veith tells of a great Old Testament artist named Bezalel. God chose Bezalel and "filled him with the Spirit of God, with skill, ability and knowledge in all kinds of crafts" (Exod. 31:3). Typically when we think of people being chosen by God and filled with the Spirit, we think of people sent into the ministry or to the mission field. But Bezalel was called to work as an artist, filled with the Spirit "to make artistic designs for work in gold, silver and bronze, . . . in all kinds of craftsmanship," in order to beautify the tabernacle, the early Hebrew tent of worship (Exod. 31:4-5). And Bezalel was not alone. Repeatedly in Exodus we find references to people to whom "the Lord had given skill" as craftspeople.[32]

Similarly, the Lord tells Moses to make garments for the priests "for glory and for beauty" (Exod. 28:2, 40, NASB). This ought to be the slogan of every Christian artist, musician, or writer: to work for the glory of God and the creation of beauty.

Given these scriptural principles, Christians have a responsibility to support artists and promote the arts. Sadly, many believers never think much about the arts until they discover that their taxes are being used by the National Endowment for the Arts to fund some blasphemous or indecent project. Even then, our response tends to be economic or political (boycotts and protests) rather than aesthetic. This makes it easy for critics to paint us as anti-intellectual, anticultural reactionaries.[33]

But God does not call his people simply to run around putting out fires after the secular world has lighted them. He calls us to light our own fires, to renew culture. And the best way to drive out bad art is to encourage good art. "If you do not read good books, you will read bad ones," said Lewis. "If you reject aesthetic satisfactions, you will fall into sensual satisfactions."[34] Since human beings are created in the image of God, they *will* create culture of one kind or another. The only question is whether it will be a decadent culture or a godly one.

To make it a godly culture, we must start by finding ways to reconnect with our own literary and artistic heritage. Go to concerts, read classic literature, visit art museums. Get to know the composers, writers, and painters who have been inspired by Christian faith. Enjoy the arts not only as art but also as media that speak to us spiritually. Louise Cowan, coeditor of *Invitation to the Classics,* tells how she lost her childhood faith in university courses on religion—only to regain it later in courses on literature. Tracing the Christian themes in Shakespeare spoke to her heart in a way that discursive theological treatises had failed to do.[35]

If the classics seem remote, begin with more recent or contemporary artists who have faced the challenge of standing against the tide of a secular culture and who give a powerful witness to Christian truth in our own century. For example, among twentieth-century composers who have created musical masterpieces reflecting their Christian faith is Francis Poulenc, who was a witty playboy of French music until a friend's death plunged him into despair and then a profound religious experience, which inspired his music from then on. Igor Stravinsky shocked the world with his strange, discordant music, but later in life he experienced a religious conversion and wrote compositions such as *Credo,* the Nicene Creed put to music. Among contemporary composers, acquaint yourself with John Tavener (not to be confused with the Renaissance composer Taverner mentioned on page 442) and Arvo Pärt, Orthodox believers who express the church's ancient musical heritage in a modern idiom. Sample the new renditions of ancient and medieval sacred music that have become a widespread fad today. What an irony that while many churches are striving to be relevant by imitating secular styles, the church's own musical heritage has taken the secular world by storm.[36]

In literature, the twentieth century has given us T. S. Eliot, often celebrated in literature textbooks as the first modernist poet. But few books mention that Eliot became a Christian in middle age, after which he wrote such significant works as "Ash Wednesday" and *Four Quartets.* The spangled language of the Jesuit priest and poet Gerard Manley Hopkins calls us to worship: "The world is charged with the grandeur of God. It will flame out, like shining from shook foil."[37] Christians should also be familiar with contemporary poets such as Luci Shaw, John Leax, Paul Mariani, and Irina Ratushinskaya.[38]

Among fiction writers, Christians should explore the riches of C. S. Lewis, especially his space trilogy and Narnia stories; the romances of George Macdonald (Lewis's mentor); the detective fiction of Dorothy Sayers; the supernatural novels of Charles Williams; and the fantasy of J. R. R. Tolkien, especially his incomparable *Lord of the Rings* trilogy. On this side of the Atlantic, the works of Walker Percy, Flannery O'Connor, and Allen Tate represent the Catholic literary renaissance of the 1940s. Among contemporary writers, Christians should get to know Larry Woiwode, Frederick Buechner, Ron Hanson, Annie Dillard, Walter Wangerin Jr., and Stephen Lawhead, to name a few. And we must not ignore the powerful novels of Alexander Solzhenitsyn—works that not only expose the horrors of the Soviet prison camp system but also reveal the response of the human heart to unspeakable suffering.

Visual artists have likewise expressed the classic Christian faith in modern forms. Among twentieth-century painters, some of the most beautiful and tender works have been rendered by Georges Rouault, who as an adult became an evangelical Catholic. He used the language of modern art to paint images that are reminiscent of stained-glass windows, with stark black lines and luminous colors, an exceptional balance of tradition and innovation. Contemporary artists who express the drama of divine grace in powerful images include Sandra Bowden, Ted Prescott, and William Congdon.

Corporately, the church can take a role in supporting the arts by involving artists in their services: They can invite musicians to write and play music; ask poets and writers to create dramatic presentations for religious holidays; encourage artists to design banners and bulletins and other works of beauty for the sanctuary. One Christmas, my colleague T. M. Moore, president of Chesapeake Theological Seminary, organized a powerful dramatization of John Milton's ode "On the Morning of Christ's Nativity." The production involved the choir and other musicians, painters (who prepared backdrops and staging), a stage crew, dancers, and actors.

Some churches focus on the arts by holding annual arts festivals that feature workshops, displays, readings, and concerts. Other churches designate a room or hallway as an art gallery, where they display the work of congregation members or of traveling art shows. We should also make a point of supporting organizations of Christian artists such as the Lamb's Players and the Washington Performing Arts Group.

Finally, every Christian family can make the home a place where art and culture are nurtured. When children are surrounded by the best in music, art, and literature, they grow up learning to appreciate the best. Play classical music in your home. Hang reproductions of historic works of art on your walls. Involve your children in reading literature that inspires their moral imagination. Good stories do what scolding or lecturing can never do: They make us *want* to be good. As child psychologist Bruno Bettelheim notes, children's moral choices are based not on abstract standards of right and wrong but on the people they admire and want to emulate. "The question for the child is not, 'Do I want to be good?'" Bettelheim writes, "but 'Who do I want to be like?'"[39] As children read, they encounter characters they can admire and identify with, and as children vicariously make choices along with the characters, their own character is shaped.

No one should grow up without the arts, for they move us as whole persons, not just our cognitive faculties. I discovered the joys of classical literature only after becoming a Christian, when my conversion gave me a hunger for truth in all its forms. My all-time favorite novel is *The Brothers Karamazov* by Fyodor Dostoyevsky, which raises the great moral dilemmas debated by philosophers through the ages and boils them down to one unforgettable dictum: "If there is no God, then everything is permitted." Recently I also determined to educate myself on classical music, and as a start, purchased a set of CDs of famous masterpieces. Although I have always had something of a tin ear, these recordings have opened a new world to me.

Music, literature, and art offer us a window through which we can appreciate God's truth more fully.

.   .   .

SEVERAL YEARS AGO, a nun in a black habit appeared on television talking about famous works of art. At first, viewers were taken aback, but today *Sister Wendy's Odyssey* is an immensely popular series. And why *shouldn't* a nun be an art critic? Who more than Christians have good reason to appreciate and create works of art?

It's time for the church to reclaim its artistic heritage and to offer the spiritual direction that contemporary artists need if they are to create works "for glory and for beauty," works that inspire and ennoble a culture. For what happens in high culture soon filters down to shape popular culture. The degradation of classical art and music has caused a parallel degradation of television and popular music—but even here, in what seems to be a moral wasteland, Christians can bring renewal and redemption.

One Christian is doing just that, with surprising results.

CHAPTER 43

TOUCHED BY A MIRACLE

Martha first came to the immortal hosts' attention one night when I was assigned to *In Extremis* (At the Point of Death) Watch. The galleries opened up to a view of a suburban California kitchen where a young woman was actually prostrating herself on her Mexican tile floor, her face to the ground, her arms spread wide in humility and penitence, as she gave her career over to God. Acting out of spiritual yearnings so deep that they overcame her self-consciousness about making dramatic gestures, the young woman was expressing her desire with her whole body—her entire being. She definitely wanted God to see, hear, and answer.

"This one is serious," the Glory announced. "Pay attention."

That single moment in eternity marked the beginning of a miracle. Or perhaps it was the miracle itself. I still can't decide.

Before I tell you about this miracle, I should probably tell you who *I* am. Imagine me as a guardian angel. A trustworthy guide. A means of viewing Martha's experience with both the telescopic wide-angle lens of eternity and the telephoto close-ups of life on earth.

What confuses me about miracles is the human factor. Otherwise, I know well enough what they are. Miracles occur when God acts in human history, crossing the boundary from eternity into time, bringing about what can't be caused in any other way. Across the millennia, I've seen my share of such events, often in times and places so dark that only a divine light could reach them. But how God enfolds the human will into these actions confounds and puzzles me. Perhaps that's why I was told to pay attention to Martha: to learn more about how God chooses to work through men and women.

Martha made this gesture of total surrender relatively early in her Christian life, only three years after her conversion. Perhaps her desperation stemmed from the fact that she works in Hollywood, where God's voice sounds very much like a voice crying in the wilderness. Perhaps she was crumbling under the pressure of a life lived on the free-fall terms of "the industry," where there's no guarantee of work, no regular paycheck, no company benefits, no health plan, no nothing. It's an industry like no other.

So Martha needed a peace like no other, a confidence with no illusions. Realizing that only the God who hung the world could lift her up, she surrendered herself that night to a God who can make even Hollywood holy ground.

■   ■   ■

MARTHA WILLIAMSON came to Hollywood straight out of college. She paid her dues and plenty of them, working as a personal assistant to various producers. She did everything from making coffee to picking up the producer's laundry, from tracking down talent to fending off wanna-bes. Long after most of the industry had discovered computers, Martha was still typing multiple scripts on an ancient typewriter for a highly successful weekly variety show.[1]

By the time she became a Christian in 1981, she was a trusted associate producer, helping to make real production decisions—and her change of heart immediately declared itself in the workplace. The company head who had taken her under his wing began calling her "the Jesus girl."

During the early 1980s, Martha joined a professional association of Hollywood directors and writers who met regularly for Christian fellowship and encouragement. The association prayed regularly that God would perform a miracle in Hollywood, that he would empower a clear Christian witness out of the heart of the entertainment industry itself.

People actually stood up in these prayer meetings, scripts in hand. They had acquired the rights to C. S. Lewis's *The Magician's Nephew* or some other piece of Christian allegory and wanted the group to pray that they would get a movie produced and help change the direction of the entire motion-picture industry. The group would then pray specifically for the success of the project.

Although Martha muttered "amen" to these prayers, she was really thinking, *Fat chance*. She doubted that these dreams would ever come true. She was already a Hollywood insider, taking "pitch-meetings" so fast she could hardly remember their content. She knew the people who ran the studios, and she knew they didn't work the way her well-intentioned friends hoped. A project conveying a Christian message would have to succeed in the larger culture *before* any Hollywood movers and shakers would consider doing it. Maybe someone would produce a story on, say, the civil rights movement, highlighting the faith dimension, but never *The Magician's Nephew*. The powers that be had no sense of mission. They were there to make money.

And frankly, so was Martha. While others talked of transforming the Hollywood culture, she had to admit that most of the time she just wanted to get paid. That was hard enough in this town.

Yet she did have her own dreams. She believed she had the talent to write funny, ironic comedy and drama. She also believed she could produce scripts for network television. She did not want to go to work for a Christian film company. She did not want to write about biblical characters, creating celluloid to fill up dead TV hours on Sunday mornings. She wanted to write prime-time shows from a Christian perspective.

She determined that she would give it a try, and she made the move from associate producer to writer. And it was shortly after becoming a writer that she lay facedown on her floor, acknowledging her utter dependence on God. She had quickly come to understand that planning her own career would prove maddening, and she vowed to God that she would not make any extraordinary efforts to hustle after work. She would not plan complicated strategies. She would do what God put before her and let him take her where she was meant to go. She believed that he knew the deepest desires of her heart and that he knew what he wanted for her. She would entrust everything to God's care.

■   ■   ■

AS WE IN THE heavenly hosts see things, the miracle was Martha's inner transformation. But what most humans would see as the miracle began when the CBS television network offered Martha a chance to be the executive producer of a show called *Angel's Attic*. She turned them down—primarily because CBS had just turned her down on another project and she was angry about it.

Martha had spent the past weeks working as a "fixer" for a television pilot called *Under One Roof.* The show had great potential. It starred the illustrious James Earl Jones and dealt with the realistic issues of one family living in Seattle. Just the type of dramatic series Martha had always wanted to work on. The pilot had turned out well, and it was just the quality programming that network executives always say they're looking for.

Yet, incredibly, CBS had turned it down. Then, only four hours later, they sent Martha the pilot for *Angel's Attic.*

The network was determined to do "an angel show." Polls showed that 70 percent of the American public believe in angels and that almost any product about angels could be marketed successfully. But when Martha watched the tape CBS had sent over, she discovered that it featured angels who quarreled among themselves and complained about the Almighty. The show was patterned after a cop show as much as anything, with God as the thickheaded superior and the angels as renegades who got the job done only by breaking bureaucratic rules. The old formula was to be bolstered, supposedly, with special effects showing the angels hovering in the air—wings and all. Even worse, the angels weren't even real angels. They were recently deceased people sent to earth for unknown reasons.

Martha respected the executives at CBS. They had nurtured her career for many years, challenging her to write from her heart, supporting her work on *Jack's Place* starring Hal Linden. So she couldn't fathom how they could turn down high quality like *Under One Roof* yet be determined to pick up a trite, formulaic show like *Angel's Attic.*

That night on her way to a dinner appointment, Martha carried on a furious mental debate with herself. Clearly, she would have to rethink her working relationship with CBS. Another network had already offered her a job, which represented a bird in the hand. Yet she had been hanging on to hopes that *Under One Roof* would be picked up so that she could continue on with CBS, doing her own kind of show.

Martha grabbed her car phone and dialed the vice president who had sent her the *Angel's Attic* tape. The network's offer was making her crazy, she told him, and she just wanted to get the issue out of the way. Then she could sort out whether she had a future at CBS (which she probably didn't) or whether she would write for the other network (which she probably would).

"I'm sorry," she told the vice president. "I know you've invested a lot in this show, and you've got a promising cast. But it's just not the kind of thing I want to do."

"But that's why we sent it to you, Martha. It needs to be turned into the type of program you and other talented people *will* want to do."

"No. I'm sorry, but no. We can have lunch next week, and I'll give you whatever advice I can to pass along to the person you hire."

The following week Martha talked with her agent, who reassured her that the writing job for the other network looked like a done deal, although in her business nothing was really nailed down until the electronic transfer rolled the digits into your account. To bring closure to her working relationship with CBS, she had lunch with the executives there. She felt somewhat dejected at ending such a good working relationship, and right up until the last moment, even as she was stepping into her car and saying good-bye to her CBS colleagues, she found herself giving them advice about their angel show.

That afternoon her agent called to say that the details for the job at the other network were being worked out, although the producers wanted to change her title, signaling that they were bargaining away some of the creative control they had promised. But it was the same money. Maybe even more money. All this was business as usual.

The next morning everything changed.

. . .

IF I WERE A TV angel instead of a real one, right at this point in the story I would make a dramatic entrance. I would say to Martha, "I am an angel, sent by God," and tell her what God wanted her to do. But as it was, she had no idea I was watching over her. She only knew, with a sudden but absolutely certain conviction, that God wanted her to work on that angel show.

During the twelve years of her Christian experience, Martha had grown more and more attentive to the Lord's voice, to the point where she thought she could usually distinguish God's leading from her own wishes. For her, a word from God did not announce itself gradually. It did not rise up over time like an intuition or insight. For her, a word from God came all at once . . . and then it kept demanding obedience. Unless she obeyed at once, she knew she would be miserable. If Martha had made any progress at all in her spiritual life, it was learning to minimize the time between hearing God's direction and acting on it.

That's what happened on this crucial morning. At some point during the time she got out of bed, drank her morning coffee, and brushed her teeth, she simply *knew* that God wanted her to do *Angel's Attic*. She even suspected that the angel show was the lifetime opportunity for which God had been preparing her.

She realized that she hadn't prayed about it before turning it down.

Always a mistake. With that, she confessed to God that she had been wrong and told him that she heard him now.

Was this a genuine miracle? With so little fanfare? No sound and light show? No special effects? Yet what else can explain the perfect alignment of the public's angel craze, the clumsy pilot, the network's enthusiasm, Martha's relationship with the network, and her relationship with God?

Martha called her agent but was informed that she would now have to "candidate" for the CBS job, which only yesterday had been hers for the asking.

"Okay," she said. "Set up the meeting."

Her agent called back. "Martha, the CBS people can't see you until next Wednesday. The agreement with the other network is buttoned up, but you have to sign it tomorrow. It's good for only twenty-four hours. You're going to have to take this now."

"I can't."

"Are you crazy? You're turning down a great show and a whopping paycheck for a chance at producing what everyone agrees is a turkey? This isn't like you. This isn't smart."

"Set up the meeting with CBS. I'm sure I'm going to get the job with them."

"Martha, you threw that show back in their face. Why would they give it to you now?"

"I know this all sounds crazy, but it's a God thing. Just set up the meeting."

Martha didn't scribble down her notes about how to fix *Angel's Attic* until the morning of her CBS meeting. Still, she went into the meeting supremely confident. If God had told her to candidate for the show, she reasoned, he was going to give her the job.

At the meeting, the executives sat at a semicircular table, including the then president of entertainment, Peter Tortorici. These were not people who had any affinity for spiritual things. How would they take to what she had to say?

"We're surprised, Martha," Tortorici said, after introductions, "but we're glad you decided to rethink your decision about being involved in the project. What would you do with the show?"

"Every successful show has its own dramatic rules," she began, "but the pilot doesn't demonstrate what those rules are. Or if it does, the rules aren't working. For example, you can't have angels who disagree with God's orders. Angels are messengers of God. They do only what he says."

She sensed the executives bracing at her confident tone, her assumption that she knew what angels do.

"Will we see God giving the angels their orders?" one executive asked tentatively.

"No," Martha said. "No one sees God. That's why, if God wants someone to see a celestial being, he sends angels. And angels aren't people who have recently died. They're angels from the beginning of time."

"But why would people want to watch a show about angels if they can't imagine becoming one?" The men and women around the table looked troubled by this thought.

"Because the show shouldn't be about the angels. That's the whole problem. The show has to be about whether the people they appear to are willing to do what God wants. That's where the drama is," she said firmly. "And we have to confront all the big questions. Why did God let my baby die? Where is God in the midst of terminal illness? Why doesn't God take care of the poor? Why doesn't God stop evil people from victimizing the defenseless?"

"You think we can take on issues like that?" they asked, surprised.

"We have to," she said. "And we have to do it from the standpoint that God loves everyone and wants the best for them. That he's intervening through his angelic messengers so that our characters, who are in critical situations, will know he loves them and will then do the right thing. You know I'm a Christian, but I'm not proposing we make this a Christian show. What I am proposing is that the dramatic rules of the show follow what all the major religions believe about God—that he loves us and cares for us."

She was on a roll now. "And there's no doubt that there's an audience for this," she said. "Religious people are tired of seeing themselves portrayed as fanatics, hucksters, serial killers, or just plain stupid. The audience for this show could use some real *inspiration* for a change."

The executives suddenly turned to specifics. *A good sign or a bad one?* Martha wondered.

"Can you reshoot some scenes and adapt the original pilot?"

"No."

She watched their faces as they tried to swallow a two-million-dollar loss.

"What about the cast?"

"That's your strongest point. Roma Downey and Della Reese are great, but you've got to take Roma's sincerity and Della's authority and give it a chance to brew its own kind of chemistry. There's got to be a tough sympathy there, a mentoring relationship. They can't be antagonists."

"Martha, why don't you wait in the office next door for a few minutes," said Peter Tortorici. "We need to discuss a few things here."

When he called Martha back to the meeting, he said, "We want you to do everything you just said. But we need a first episode in three weeks. As of right now, you've got an office and a parking space, and you'd better get started. Deal?"

■   ■   ■

WHETHER OR NOT the CBS executives were subject to divine influence, not even an angelic voice can say. Martha chalked up their openness to desperation. They needed the show, but they knew it wouldn't work without someone who had a real vision for it. Yet Martha could not have known this beforehand. So perhaps the real miracle here was her determined obedience even in the face of losing her immediate prospects for employment, along with her willingness to play a divine long shot. I would like to claim credit myself for Martha's being *Touched by an Angel*, as her show came to be titled, but to be honest, God sent me only to be an observer in this case.

For more than a year, *Touched by an Angel* remained a long shot. The terrible original pilot had produced a media "buzz" that nearly sealed the show's death warrant before Martha's efforts saw the light of a cathode-ray tube. Even then, CBS couldn't find the right time slot for the show. For an entire season they moved it around the television schedule, with the result that its ratings were dismal.

When the show finally went on hiatus (the seasonal break in production), it looked as if *Touched by an Angel* would be canceled after only one season. Martha was dead tired from pulling together scripts, cast, and crew, and she only wanted to rest and regather her energies. But she received another word from the Lord: She needed to campaign for the show's renewal with every bit of energy she could muster.

With the help of coworkers and Hollywood friends, Martha jetted around the country, conducting a media blitz to raise the show's viewership for the final two episodes, which had not yet aired. The viewer ratings didn't rise significantly for those two episodes, but they didn't slip either. Television people would recognize that as a positive sign: The show's viewership was loyal, hunting out the show whenever and wherever it appeared on the schedule.

Still, at its best *Touched by an Angel* attracted only a twelve share in the Nielsen television ratings. No one except Martha and her loyal supporters believed it would be picked up for another season.

Finally, Martha went to New York and trolled the halls of the network, grabbing anyone who would talk to her about the show's fate. Eventually she gained access to the network president, and while her appeals in other venues had been to the bottom line, here she spoke to the man's soul.

"When you are lying on your deathbed," she ventured to say, "you won't be thinking how glad you were that you renewed *Walker, Texas Ranger.* But you'll never forget renewing *Touched by an Angel,* and you'll always be glad."

The president made no promises, and to this day Martha does not know what finally tipped the balance. That part of the miracle remains hidden in someone else's heart. But the network's unexpected decision to renew *Touched by an Angel* for a second season gave it the chance it needed to become the enormously popular show it is today.

Martha Williamson's life was touched by a miracle. And so are the millions of people who watch the results of her work every week.

■   ■   ■

WHAT HAS THIS celestial observer learned from all this? God's unending determination to make his love known to human beings. What strange cultural forces God will use—even an angel fad to bring about his will. And what unlikely opportunities he will seize—even an ill-conceived TV show—to proclaim his love.

CHAPTER 44

DOES THE DEVIL HAVE ALL THE GOOD MUSIC?

Every generation of Christians faces unique challenges. . . . The challenge of living with popular culture may well be as serious for modern Christians as persecution and plagues were for the saints of earlier centuries.

KENNETH A. MYERS

Several years ago I was the speaker at a prayer breakfast held during the National Association of Broadcasters Convention. The young woman seated next to me at the table was pleasant and engaging—a writer, she told me—determined to produce a successful prime-time television show boldly expressing Christian themes. I smiled, thinking, *How noble . . . but how naïve.* And I wondered how many bright, young, open-faced midwesterners have had their idealism smashed on the rocks of Hollywood.

"Well, you hang in there," I said, intending to bolster her hopes a bit before she gave up and retreated to some safe Christian publishing house.

"Oh, I will," she replied cheerily. "In fact, I had one trial run for my show, and then the network bumped it. But I'm pounding on doors to get it back on the air. I know God is in this."

Suddenly she had my attention. "What did you say your name was?"

"Martha Williamson," she smiled. "And I'm going to do it. Really."

Oh me of little faith.

Many Christians grumble about television trash and the lack of wholesome fare for families, but Martha Williamson rolled up her sleeves and did something about it. Her story is all the more remarkable for the fact that there is nothing to set her apart from the many talented, creative people in Hollywood—nothing except her dogged faith. She is a great example of how

Christians are called to use their gifts to make a difference in shaping American popular culture.

THE MEDIUM IS THE MESSAGE

The call to redeem popular culture is surely one of the most difficult challenges Christians face today. For, thanks to modern communications technology, popular culture has become intrusively pervasive. It is virtually impossible to avoid the culture's influence through advertisements, tapes, CDs, television, radio, movies, magazines, computer games, video arcades, and the Internet. Popular culture is everywhere, shaping our tastes, our language, our values.

When I was a kid, my exposure to popular culture was limited—the occasional Saturday afternoon Western at the local movie theater, the Green Hornet radio serials, the Hardy Boys adventure series, and the *Saturday Evening Post*. That was it. But today popular culture beckons from every billboard, blares from the television on countless channels around the clock, pops up on our PCs, blasts from the car radio, and bedecks our T-shirts and tennis shoes. None of us can escape it.

As popular culture has spread, its content has coarsened shockingly. No one needs to be told that over the past three or four decades the level of sex and violence has risen sharply in movies, music, television, and even comic books. Of course, Christians have always had to deal with things that were vulgar, lewd, or coarse, but for the most part, we could simply avoid them. Today that is virtually impossible.

But while most of us realize how dangerous it is to expose ourselves to immoral *content*, we often fail to realize that the *form* of popular culture affects us just as much—not only *what* is said but also *how* it is said. This is what educator Marshall McLuhan meant by his famous adage, "The medium is the message."[1] The best way to grasp this is by a comparison to high culture. A sonnet or a symphony has a complex structure that takes some effort to understand. It challenges us; we have to work to appreciate it. That's why we study Shakespeare in English classes and Mozart in music-appreciation courses. But who takes courses to understand Madonna? Who needs to? Who takes Soap Opera 101? Who needs Cliff's Notes to understand a Harlequin romance?

These forms require virtually no intellectual discipline or effort. If anything, popular culture strives to *avoid* making the audience work. It's intended to be simple, entertaining, and easy to understand, offering immediate gratification. It grabs our attention with catchy lines, loud intrusive music, and sensational visual effects, all designed to bypass the mind and appeal directly to the senses and emotions. Moreover, popular books and television shows are often written to a formula, with predictable plots and stereotypical characters, so we all know what's going to happen. Readers and viewers glide along without having to think much about where they are going—they just enjoy the scenery along the way. This is cotton candy for the mind.

Now, there's nothing wrong with a little cotton candy in an otherwise balanced diet. But there *is* danger in a steady consumption of junk food. For starters, you may lose your taste for more wholesome food. And with mental cotton candy, that is perilously easy to do. Popular culture easily becomes addictive, destroying our taste for more substantial fare. It may become so handy to let the kids watch cartoons and videos that we no longer discipline ourselves to read classic literature to them. We may get so used to hearing a steady backdrop of popular music on the radio that we no longer put on CDs of Bach and Mozart and learn to appreciate classical music.

Worse, popular culture can break down even our ability to tackle more challenging mental tasks. By focusing on immediate experience, it erodes the skills needed for sustained attention. By offering easy consumption and emotional gratification, it discourages us from analyzing what we see and hear. What we must understand is that each form of media encourages a different kind of mental process, as Neil Postman explains in *Amusing Ourselves to Death*. In reading, for example, the printed page unfolds its narrative line by line, training us in a coherent, linear, rational thought process. By contrast, television reduces complex events to fast-moving images, fostering a short attention span, disjointed thinking, and emotional responses.[2] Popular culture is like a narcotic: Over time it can actually impair the brain's capacity.

Most troubling, however, is the impact popular culture may have on our spiritual lives. Attention to the spiritual realm requires an entirely different set of skills and sensibilities than do the easy distractions of pop culture. Studying God's Word takes mental concentration and discipline. Prayer and meditation require focused recollection and the ability to shut out the jangle of everyday events. Thus, pop culture (even Christian versions of it) may erode the skills and disciplines needed for a robust spiritual life.

Scripture suggests this principle in the second commandment, when it warns against making graven images. When Postman read the Bible as a young man, he writes, he wondered why God would prohibit his people from representing the deity in visual images. "It is a strange injunction to include as part of an ethical system," he says, "*unless its author assumed a connection between forms of human communication and the quality of a culture.*"[3] Precisely. In the ancient world, each nation had its own tribal deities, represented in statues and images. By contrast, the Bible teaches the existence of a universal deity—a concept so abstract that it simply cannot be expressed in concrete images. "The God of the Jews was to exist in the Word and through the Word, an unprecedented conception requiring the highest order of abstract thinking." This radical conception of God, Postman conjectures, could enter the culture only if concrete representations of God were banned.[4]

In other words, a culture's forms of communication are a major influence in shaping the way people think—even the way they think about God.

What this means is that as long as the content is not immoral, there's no harm in popular culture itself. Watching a good television drama, tapping our feet to the latest Christian pop music, or losing ourselves in a paperback novel for light entertainment can be a pleasant diversion. Many works of popular culture even express genuine moral or spiritual truths, as we shall see later. There *is* harm, however, in making a steady diet of pop culture, because it encourages an unreflective, emotional response to life instead of disciplined thought and analysis—which can lead, in turn, to a simplistic spiritual life. Popular culture fits under the category of things the apostle Paul referred to when he said, "'Everything is permissible'—but not everything is beneficial" (1 Cor. 10:23). We can enjoy cultural "junk food" as long as we have trained ourselves to be selective, as long as we don't fall into habits of escapism and distraction, and as long as we set limits so that the sensibilities of popular culture do not shape our character.

The dangers of modern popular culture were foretold by Aldous Huxley in his classic anti-utopian novel *Brave New World*—which contrasts sharply with another anti-utopian novel, George Orwell's *1984*. Orwell warned of a communist government that would ban books; Huxley warned of a Western government that wouldn't *need* to ban them—because no one would read serious books anymore. Orwell predicted a society deprived of information by government censors; Huxley predicted a society oversaturated by information from electronic media—until people lost the ability to analyze what they saw and heard. Orwell feared a system that concealed the truth under government propaganda and lies; Huxley feared a system where people stopped caring about the truth and cared only about being entertained. Orwell described a world where people were controlled by inflicting pain; Huxley imagined a world where people were controlled by inflicting pleasure.[5] Both novels have proven to be uncannily accurate—

Orwell describing the totalitarian plague of our century, Huxley the sickness of affluent free societies.

Huxley goes on to castigate the civil libertarians in the West who are ever on the alert against an externally imposed tyranny but who have failed to realize how easily we can be seduced into a mindless oppression by technology: These guardians of liberty, he says, have "failed to take into account man's almost infinite appetite for distraction."[6] And nowhere is the appetite for distraction more seductively tantalized by the banal, mindless entertainment of pop culture than in America.

How, then, can we protect ourselves and our children against this soft oppression? Only by understanding where popular culture came from, how it developed, what worldview it expresses, and what underlying ideas and trends have led us to this point.

MENTAL JUNK FOOD

The first step in examining the worldview behind popular culture is to find a workable definition of the term. Many people think of pop culture as the contemporary form of folk culture, but that is not accurate. Folk culture consists of the stories and myths, tales and songs that emerge from a particular people's way of life. America's authentic folk culture harks back to colonial days and includes such forms as square dancing, spirituals, banjo tunes like "Oh My Darlin' Clementine," tall tales about Davy Crockett and Paul Bunyan, arts and crafts. Pop culture, on the other hand, is relatively new, without roots in any ethnic or folk tradition; it is mass produced and standardized, shaped more by marketing surveys than by the spontaneous expression of a people's experience.

Kenneth Myers offers a helpful analogy in *All God's Children and Blue Suede Shoes,* comparing cultures to cuisine.[7] Folk culture, with its songs and tales, is like ethnic food—German sausage, Norwegian lutefisk, Russian borscht—arising out of a traditional way of life. But pop culture is like fast food, heavy with salt, sugar, and artificial colors and flavors. It looks attractive, has a strong flavor, but offers little real nutrition. Fast foods like Coke and McDonald's burgers are not rooted in America's distinctive cultural heritage but can be imposed wholesale onto any existing culture—and indeed *have* been transplanted across the globe. By analogy, pop culture belongs to no particular ethnic group but rather invades all cultures. For example, when refugees from southern China were rescued from shark-infested waters by the U.S. Coast Guard, the only English word they knew was *MTV*.

Where did this new, mass-produced, standardized form of popular culture originate? In large measure it is the result of the same theories of art traced in chapter 42. As we explained there, when science was anointed as the only path to truth (scientism), art was demoted to subjective fantasy, and artists were put on the defensive. They responded by crafting a philosophy that eventually cast art as a tool of subversion, a means of thumbing their noses at conventional society. This philosophy of art-as-rebellion migrated from Europe to America, where it infiltrated our own folk traditions. In music, for example, our ethnic culture had produced jazz, blues, folk, and gospel music, but as avant-garde philosophy invaded, the result was rock 'n' roll, Elvis, the Beatles, the Rolling Stones . . . and the rest is history. And as the new philosophy of art gained the upper hand, the relentless attack on mainstream values built to such a fever pitch of profanity and perversity that today we have lyrics that glorify death and violence.

The important point is that the decline in popular culture was not merely a result of declining public taste; it was a direct result of a change in worldview. Art began to champion everything opposed to the Enlightenment and science: It exalted emotion over reason, instinct over rationality, sensation over thinking, primitivism over civilization. Taught first in art colleges, this avant-garde philosophy eventually found its way into recording studios. In fact, a number of influential British rock musicians actually started out as art students, among them Keith Richards, Peter Townshend, Eric Clapton, and John Lennon. As a result, the Beatles, the Rolling Stones, the Who, Cream, and many of the other British bands were deliberately creating music that expressed the philosophy of the artist as a romantic hero who smashes established culture to create a new culture of moral freedom, emotional release, animal energy, and vivid sensation. The sheer energy of rock—the pounding beat, the screams, the spectacle—is intended to bypass the mind and appeal directly to the sensations and feelings.[8]

Thus rock music, by its very form, encourages a mentality that is subjective, emotional, and sensual—no matter what the lyrics may say. This is why Christians must learn to analyze not only the content of pop culture but also the art form itself, the mode of expression.

The danger is that Christian popular culture may mimic the mainstream culture in style, while changing only the content. The music market is overflowing with Christian rock and rap, Christian blues and jazz, Christian heavy metal. Bookstore shelves are filled with "Christian fiction," from children's adventure stories to almost-steamy romances. Christian theme parks offer an alternative to Disney, and Christian videos for children and exercisers are top sellers. In many ways, this is a healthy development, but we must always ask: Are we creating a genuinely Christian culture, or are we simply creating a parallel culture with a Christian veneer? Are we imposing Christian content onto an already existing form? For the form and style always send a message of their own.

For example, a few years ago Nancy read a startling video review in *Time* magazine: "Provocative images fill the TV screen. Over a driving, syncopated rock beat, a woman's voice—urgent, seductive—tells a story of possession and salvation." No, this was not a new Madonna video. It was a contemporary retelling of the Bible story of Jesus casting out the demons called Legion.[9]

Nancy ordered a copy of the video and discovered that the review was no exaggeration. The almost surrealistic style was so vivid that for all practical purposes it drowned out any biblical teaching. The "message is overwhelmed by the medium," the *Time* review had said, and that was quite true. The producers' goal was admirable—reaching out to young people raised on MTV—but if even a secular reviewer can sense a discrepancy between the biblical message and the style in which it is communicated, then surely we, too, must become more aware.

When we create Christian popular culture, we must take care not simply to insert Christian content into whatever style is currently on the market. Instead, we should cultivate something distinctly Christian in both content and form.[10] We must learn how to identify the worldviews expressed in various art forms in order to critique them and craft an alternative that is soundly biblical.

WHATEVER IS TRUE, WHATEVER IS NOBLE . . .

The way to reverse the degradation of pop culture is once again to link art to truth. We must challenge the scientism that reduces truth to what can be known only by the scientific method and argue for the first plank in the Christian worldview: creation. The world is the handiwork of a God who is himself Truth, Goodness, and Beauty. Thus, beauty is as objective and real as the scientists' particles of matter. The first step in redeeming popular culture, then, is to craft a biblically based view of the arts (the outlines of which are suggested in chapter 42).

Second, there are practical steps all of us can take, beginning with disciplining our personal habits to say no to the worst of popular culture. It has so infiltrated our homes, our schools, and our churches that we must start reining it in. Churches that use mostly contemporary music in their services should consider the effects of a steady diet of simple choruses and pop-style worship songs while neglecting the classic hymns of the faith.

In the home, parents need to have the courage of their convictions with their children—to turn off the television, unplug the earphones, and refuse to let teenagers wear T-shirts bearing airbrushed images of the latest grunge band. I have even "bribed" my grandchildren, offering them $100 toward their college fund for each month that they do not watch TV.

Dr. Ben Carson, the world-renowned pediatric neurosurgeon at Johns Hopkins, was once an angry ghetto kid headed nowhere. He credits his astonishing turnaround to his encounter with God and the discipline of his mother, who turned off the television and made him read the classics and write book reports on them. "How did your mother manage to do that?" he is often asked. To which he replies, with irrepressible wit, "Oh, that was back at a time when parents still controlled families." A family dynamic that Christian parents need to restore.[11]

Christians can also make a difference in what's offered in the marketplace by voting with our dollars. Refuse to purchase music with obscene or indecent lyrics. Refuse to patronize movies or rent videos that glorify immorality. Refuse to buy romance novels that cheapen the relationship between men and women and even border on soft porn. Boycotts—whether organized or merely individual—may not always get a product taken off the market, but they make an important moral statement.

Currently, for example, several Christian groups, including my own denomination, the Southern Baptists, are boycotting Disney products. I support their decision, for whether or not the boycott has a significant economic effect on Disney, it does serve an important educational function in the church and for the public at large. Until this boycott was publicized, many people—including many Christians—did not know that lurking behind Disney's family-friendly image is a secular, naturalistic philosophy hostile to Christianity. The corporation offers spousal benefits to employees' homosexual partners, and its theme parks hold a special "Gay Day." Disney owns the Miramax film company, which has produced movies like *Priest* and *Sirens,* which viciously attack Christianity. Disney owns ABC, which openly celebrated homosexuality on its program *Ellen* and mocked Christianity in the sitcom *Nothing Sacred.* Parents may still decide to let their children watch Disney films or take their families to Disney World, but at least they should be aware of the anti-Christian worldview their children are being exposed to so they can deal with it appropriately.

But boycotting bad products is only the beginning. The best way to overcome banality is to cultivate something better. We must seek out, as the apostle Paul writes in Philippians, "whatever is true, whatever is noble, whatever is right, whatever is pure, whatever is lovely, whatever is admirable—if anything is excellent or praiseworthy—think about such things" (Phil. 4:8). Notice that Paul doesn't limit that principle to spiritual things; he says if *anything* is excellent. Paul is telling us to train our tastes to love the higher things—things that challenge our mind, deepen our character, and foster a love of excellence—and this includes the music we listen to, the books and magazines we read, the films we watch, the forms of worship we employ.

If we are selective, we can find high-quality popular culture that deals with profound moral dilemmas in ways that teach us new dimensions of good and evil through a gripping story—even if the themes of that story are not overtly Christian. Stephen Spielberg's movie *Saving Private Ryan*, for example, inspires in many viewers a sense of gratitude for the bloody sacrifice made by their parents and grandparents during World War II. Spielberg's *Schindler's List* reminds us of the reality of evil and the need to resist it. *Dead Man Walking* is a powerful portrayal of Christian love and repentance; and my latest favorite, *The Spitfire Grill*, produced by a group of enterprising nuns, is a moving tale of redemption and new life. Mel Gibson, a devout Catholic, has started his own film company, Icon Productions, to create movies that reflect a Christian understanding of good and evil, of honor and courage. One of the company's most successful movies is *Braveheart*, with a script by Randall Wallace, a former Duke Divinity School student who decided he could have a greater impact telling stories than standing in a pulpit.[12]

Among somewhat older films, there is *Chariots of Fire*, based on the inspiring true story of a Scottish athlete willing to put God before an Olympic gold medal. Italian filmmaker Franco Zeffirelli recommitted himself to the Christian faith after a near fatal automobile accident, and since then he has given us films such as *Brother Sun, Sister Moon* (about St. Francis of Assisi), *Jane Eyre* (based on Brontë's classic novel), and his television miniseries *Jesus of Nazareth*. Even a non-Christian filmmaker like Woody Allen sometimes treats moral themes in a serious and thoughtful way, as in his *Crimes and Misdemeanors*, which probes the problem of guilt.[13] (Some of the films listed in these paragraphs have rough language or nudity or violence, so watch them yourself before letting your children see them.)

For family fare, check out the classics section at the video store—films from several decades ago. Many of these will open up a refreshing world to you and your children, for in these films, plot and character were more important than breathtaking special effects. Many of us can never get enough of the well-loved films by Frank Capra, such as *It's a Wonderful Life* and *Mr. Smith Goes to Washington.*[14] Capra successfully portrayed characters who stood for the traditional moral values of honesty, courage, and sacrifice—characters who turned to prayer as naturally as breathing. Capra, who was a practicing Catholic, said, "I deal with the little man's doubts . . . his loss of faith in himself, in his neighbor, in his God." And then, "I show the overcoming of doubts, the courageous renewal of faith."[15]

Ultimately, to be a redemptive force in popular culture, we must encourage Christians to go beyond being critical and start being creative. A surprisingly large number of Christians are seeking to do just that. Martha Williamson was not alone as she faced the trials of working in Hollywood; she was encouraged along the way by a supportive fellowship of believers working there. One such group is Inter-Mission, which is made up of writers, producers, directors, and actors who meet quarterly, with offices in New York and Hollywood; another group is Catholics in Media.[16] The Los Angeles Film Studies Center, a program of the Council for Christian Colleges and Universities, places interns—Christian college students—in the offices of powerful media companies. They work as production assistants and office personnel, learning what it takes to navigate their way through this minefield. And the program is working: Of the Center's two hundred seventy graduates, more than seventy are now working in Hollywood in some capacity, many in strategic positions—an almost incredible percentage.[17]

Some businesspeople are willing to put their own fortunes on the line to make a difference. Norman Miller, who made his mark as the entrepreneurial genius behind Interstate Batteries, has started a fledging film production company to create high-quality, wholesome films subtly interwoven with Christian themes. His first film, *The Joyriders,* is opening in theaters as we write.

One pocket of pop culture that retains a strong religious component, according to Dave Shiflett writing in the *Wall Street Journal,* is country music. "Most of the players of my generation are from church," says mandolin virtuoso Ricky Skaggs, who has been known to do a bit of stage preaching between numbers. "We usually stop our concerts and explain that bluegrass was birthed from church music."[18]

In popular culture, as in every field, the best way to reach a nonbelieving audience is not so much by works that preach Christianity explicitly as by works that express a Christian worldview indirectly. "We can make people attend to the Christian point of view for half an hour or so," said C. S. Lewis, "but the moment they have gone away from our lecture or laid down the article, they are plunged back into a world where the opposite position is taken for granted." Therefore, "what we want is not more little books about Christianity, but more little books by Christians on other subjects—with their Christianity latent."[19]

What would happen if the best popular music on the market were composed by Christian musicians? If the best books in the bookstores were written by Christian authors? If the best television shows implicitly communicated a Christian worldview? Nonbelievers would quickly see that Christianity is not something that can be relegated to a separate part of life labeled "religion" but is a viable worldview that makes better sense of all the things they care about.

Does the devil have all the good music? By our choices, you and I can make sure he doesn't.

HOW NOW SHALL WE LIVE?

He himself is our peace, who has made the two one and has destroyed the
barrier, the dividing wall of hostility. . . . His purpose was . . . to reconcile
both of them to God through the cross, by which he put to death their hostility.
EPHESIANS 2:14-16

From Jorge Crespo in Ecuador to Officer Sal in New York to Henryk Górecki in Poland to Martha Williamson in Hollywood, there emerges a common pattern: Christians who understand biblical truth and have the courage to live it out can indeed redeem a culture, or even create one. This is the challenge facing all of us in the new millennium.

As we have sought to demonstrate in these pages, the Christian worldview is more consistent, more rational, and more workable than any other belief system. It beats out all other contenders in giving credible answers to the great questions that any worldview must answer: Where did we come from? *(creation);* What is the human dilemma? *(fall);* and What can we do to solve the dilemma? *(redemption).* And the way we *see* the world guides the way we work to *change* the world *(restoration).*

No worldview is merely a theoretical philosophy. It is intensely practical, affecting the way we live our lives, day in and day out, as well as the way we influence the world around us. If we adopt a false worldview, we will inevitably find ourselves going against the grain of the universe, leading to consequences we cannot live with—as millions of Americans are discovering. If, however, we order our lives in accord with reality, we will not only find meaning and purpose but also discover that our lives are healthier and more fulfilled. Christianity is the only accurate road map of reality, and we must be ready to make the case to those who are growing increasingly aware of the futility of all other worldviews.

But there are five billion people on this planet, you say, and we live amid seemingly endless suffering, conflict, and war. Can we ever hope to help solve the intractable problems that set nation against nation? Our world is fractured by unfathomable chasms between people—by centuries-old enmities, by generations of mistrust and hostility, by all "the sin that so easily entangles" us (Heb. 12:1). Aren't these events shaped by large-scale international forces, far beyond the reach of anything you or I can do?

The answer is that even in these cases God can use acts of faith and faithfulness to heal the ugliest wounds and reconcile the deepest conflicts between people and even between nations.

■   ■   ■

ON THE MALL in Washington, D.C., people can always be seen clustered in front of The Wall that commemorates the soldiers who died in the Vietnam War. Every season of the year, every hour of the day and night, people gather there. Mothers and fathers, now grandparents, trace the names of sons and daughters long dead; children, now adults, search for the names of fathers they barely remember; veterans mourn their buddies; tourists puzzle over the war that never quite made sense. Always people, with their private grief, unanswered questions, and quiet awe in front of the rolls of the dead etched into the polished black marble.

Of course, weather-beaten monuments are scattered across the entire country—memorials to people who died in the Civil War, Spanish American War, World War I, World War II, and the Korean War. Yet it is the Vietnam War that haunts Americans as no other war ever has.

As a nation, we still can't clearly answer why our young people had to march the Ho Chi Minh trail or why so many had to die. Those of us who are old enough still remember the news photos of black body bags at the Saigon airport, the innumerable troop escalations, the talk of soldiers shooting their commanders, and the ugly confrontations at home between police and antiwar demonstrators. And then that last glimpse of our soldiers fleeing, jumping onto helicopters from the Saigon embassy roof—a sight that filled Americans with shame.

In 1996, in an effort to find some resolution to these questions, several men who had been high-ranking U.S. officials responsible for policy decisions during the war decided to meet with their Vietnamese counterparts. A conference was scheduled in Hanoi, initiated by Robert McNamara, who had served as secretary of defense in the Kennedy and Johnson administrations.[1] Two years earlier, McNamara had published *In Retrospect: The*

Tragedy and Lessons of Vietnam, in which he admitted, after a twenty-seven-year silence, that the decisions he and other White House officials had made regarding Vietnam were "wrong, terribly wrong." Yet clearly, he was still struggling to understand *why* U.S. actions had miscarried so disastrously. Perhaps this conference would provide the answers that had eluded everyone for so long.[2]

But it yielded nothing of the sort. From the opening moments the Vietnamese, though smiling politely, lectured the Americans sternly for interfering in what they regarded as a campaign for national reunification. "North Vietnam" had never been a separate country, they insisted; nor had it considered itself to be "intervening" in "South Vietnam's" affairs, any more than the American North considered itself to be intervening in the affairs of the South during our own Civil War. The Americans were stunned and frustrated.

For days, participants went back and forth in heated discussions. McNamara even tried to speak privately with General Vo Nguyen Giap, the general who had defeated both French and U.S. forces in his country. But the general lectured him nonstop on the true history of Vietnam, and McNamara couldn't get in a word.

At the end, former CIA analyst Chester Cooper stepped wearily to the lectern, his necktie loosened, his shoulders slumped, and sarcastically summed up Vietnam's unyielding stance—that "everything we did after the 1954 Geneva agreement was wrong and immoral and everything you [the Vietnamese] did was right and moral." And then he sighed. "I'm tired of saying we were wrong about everything."[3] Later, news photos showed Cooper and McNamara at the Hanoi airport waiting to board their flight home, their suits rumpled in the oppressive heat, their faces exhausted and dejected. Their mission had been an utter failure.

The problem was that McNamara was looking for technical solutions to apply to complex human and spiritual dilemmas. He was the quintessential technocrat: He came to prominence as a supermanager who had produced small miracles at the Ford Motor Company, and later at the Department of Defense, by introducing statistically based planning controls. Better planning and management would solve any problem, he was convinced, especially if it could be rationalized in quantifiable terms and manipulated in formulas.

But the wounds of war are not healed by mathematical analysis and statistics. The real healing must come in a very different way.

■   ■   ■

I HAVE MY OWN memories of the horror of Vietnam and certainly understand the longing for a solution. As part of the Nixon administration, I listened for years to the briefings of generals and admirals, to then National Security Advisor Henry Kissinger's daily reports, and to many of the president's late-night monologues about Vietnam. At times I helped the president make some of the most agonizing decisions, like the mining and bombing of Hanoi harbor in May 1972, and was involved in the secret negotiations after the election that same year. I was one of the president's men, and I supported his position right down the line. Still, the agony of the war came home to me in various ways. I knew that our decisions were putting my own former marine classmates in harm's way. Yet one image of the war was seared into my memory, and to this day, it remains poignant and painful. . . .

Before sunrise on June 9, 1972, I climbed into my limousine for my daily commute to the White House. En route, I planned to read intelligence and news summaries, as well as briefing memos in preparation for a senior staff meeting that morning. First, though, I flipped open the *Washington Post* to scan the headlines.

Suddenly I felt as if I had received a body blow. On page one, above the fold, was a photo from Vietnam showing the aftermath of a bombing. But something was terribly wrong: the wounded in the picture were not soldiers but children. A weeping boy in dark shorts. Two children running hand in hand. And then the girl. In the center of the photo was a young girl running directly toward the camera, her arms stretched out, her clothes burned off. Her skin was blackened by napalm, and her hands drooped lifelessly, while her mouth screamed in pain, her eyes reflecting the horror of the black exploding sky behind her.

Instinctively, my horrified mind wanted to help this child. I thought involuntarily of my own precious daughter Emily. *What if she had been hurt like this?*

Worse, I couldn't avoid a sinking sense of my own responsibility for this young girl's suffering. Her silent scream made me wince. My own skin burned with guilt and shame.

■   ■   ■

THE DAY THE PHOTO was shot, two journalists, Chris Wain from England and Vietnamese photojournalist Nick Ut, were accompanying a ground unit on patrol outside the village of Trang Bang on Highway 1, which ran between Saigon and Cambodia. A North Vietnamese offensive had briefly overrun the village, and then the South Vietnamese had bombed it heavily for three days. The population had taken refuge in a double-spired pagoda in an oasis-like setting of palms, silhouetted against deep-blue mountains. The temple was considered a holy place, and no soldiers, not even the Americans, would ever target it.

Suddenly, the firing grew more intense, and a colored signal fell out of the sky toward the pagoda, designating it as a target. South Vietnamese soldiers on the ground saw the signal and immediately began to hustle the villagers out of the temple, telling them to run for their lives. Chris and Nick looked up to see two planes. One banked and wheeled around, passing in front of the pagoda, right over the fleeing villagers.

As the plane screamed lower and lower, four canisters dropped from its hold. The journalists caught their breath. They knew those tumbling specks in the distance were filled with huge quantities of jellied gasoline. Napalm. In the moment before the canisters hit, everything seemed frozen.

Then, all at once, a tidal wave of fire swept over the road, incinerating everything in its path. The tarmac leading toward the pagoda melted into surging flame. The wind thrown off by the fire was so strong, it snapped the huge palm fronds around the temple.

Then the parade of death began. Out of the flames ran several women and children, strangely silent. An old woman carrying a dying three-year-old boy, his flesh hanging like tattered rags. A brother and sister running hand in hand. Then a young girl appeared, naked, her arms outstretched. The children running at her side began screaming, "Please help! Please help!"

Quickly, instinctively, photojournalist Nick Ut snapped a photograph of the scene. Then the two men caught the girl in their arms and gave her a drink of water. "So hot," she kept saying. "So hot." After emptying a canteen of water over the girl's burning shoulder, they put a rain slicker lightly around her and drove her to the hospital in their jeep. Somewhere along the way she lapsed into unconsciousness.

Chris and Nick were both longtime war correspondents, but neither had ever witnessed anything like this. The next day, Chris and his video cameraman, Michael Blakey, visited the young girl in the hospital. She lay facedown, unconscious, suffering from third-degree burns over her entire back and along her arms, especially her left arm. Her dark hair had been chopped off, her wounds bandaged. What looked like a roll of toilet paper was propped at the side of her mouth. Her mother sat at the end of the bed, fanning her. They learned that the girl's name was Kim Phuc, a name that means "Golden Happiness."[4]

Chris asked a male nurse for the girl's prognosis.

"Oh, her?" the nurse said indifferently. "She die, maybe tomorrow, maybe next day."

The callous tone was more than Chris could bear after the trauma of witnessing the bombing the day before. As it happened, he carried a bayonet at his back—a macho good-luck charm. He took it out and pressed the hilt into the male nurse's hand. "Why don't you just do the kind thing then and kill her now!" he said. "Take this, and kill her. It's more merciful than what you're doing. Letting her die a slow death this way!"

The nurse rushed off to find the doctors, and Chris talked to them fast, loud, and long. Finally they agreed to transfer the girl to Barsky Hospital in Saigon, a facility founded by an American doctor who first developed surgical techniques to treat Hiroshima victims. The hospital now specialized in plastic surgery for children.

At Barsky, the surgeon of the day, Dr. Mai Lee, took up Kim Phuc's cause, arguing against her own head nurse, who claimed the hospital lacked the personnel to care for a recent burn victim whose condition might not stabilize. But Dr. Mai Lee insisted, and she prevailed.

■   ■   ■

AFTER FOURTEEN MONTHS in the hospital and seventeen surgeries, Kim Phuc was released and returned home. For years afterward, she was just an anonymous teenage girl who always wore long sleeves to cover her twisted scars and who worried that they were so ugly that no one would ever want to marry her.

But Nick Ut's photo had left a legacy. I wasn't the only one struck by it; it won a Pulitzer prize and became an emblem for an entire nation questioning its reason for being in Vietnam. So in 1980, as the world observed the fifth anniversary of the end of the Vietnam War, journalists began asking what had happened to the young girl in the famous photograph. Vietnamese government officials took note and decided Kim Phuc could be played as a propaganda card, so they tracked her down. By that time, she was studying medicine in Saigon, but officials yanked her out of school and made her work as a secretary in the government offices of her own province, Tei Ling, so she would be on hand to parade before visiting media and dignitaries. Regularly they would ask her to roll up her sleeves and display her scars, making her act as a poster child for the horrors of American aggression.

Kim hated her propaganda role and ran away to Saigon to resume the medical studies she loved. The government retaliated by destroying her academic records. Even then, Kim would sneak away to Saigon at night to study English.

Eventually, she was sought out by journalists interested in telling her story (among them Perry Katz of the German magazine *Stern* and England's William Shawcross). They photographed her in her parents' restaurant and snapped her bowing and praying in the same twin-spired pagoda she had been running from in the famous photo. Her family worshiped in the Cao Dai tradition: a mixture of world religions, with spiritualist practices, including séances where messages were solicited from the dead.

When talking with interviewers, Kim always smiled, but inwardly she desperately wanted to lead her own life. To protect her family, she said nothing, however, for the government could destroy far more than her school records. To prove the point, officials took away all her family's possessions—the restaurant, their large home, everything but their lives. And who knew how long they would spare even these?

■   ■   ■

KIM BECAME INCREASINGLY depressed. And yet there was one compensation to holding a "show job" with few responsibilities: It allowed her to spend time in a local library, where she read voraciously. And it was there she read the New Testament for the first time. Its portrait of Jesus differed radically from what she had learned about him in Cao Dai, and eventually she began to question her childhood faith. Cao Dai seemed powerless to relieve her depression, even though she prayed more than four times a day at the temple.

Eventually Kim was invited to attend a Baptist church with her sister's brother-in-law, a strong Christian. She was greatly attracted to the Christian faith but reluctant to leave her family's religion. Finally, one Sunday before church she prayed for the first time, asking Jesus Christ for a small but significant favor. "I need one girlfriend I can talk with. If I see a girl sitting alone in the church, that is who will be my girlfriend."

When Kim walked through the church doors, sure enough, she saw one woman sitting alone. She approached her, and they quickly became friends. "I felt very happy," Kim says. "I just tried, and God answered my prayer right away!"

Not long afterward, Kim went forward to the altar and accepted Jesus Christ as her personal Savior. "It was the fire of the bomb that burned my body, and it was the skill of the doctor that mended my skin," she says, "but it took the power of God to heal my heart."[5]

▪   ▪   ▪

KIM WAS FINALLY allowed to resume her medical studies in 1986, this time in Vietnam's sister communist state, Cuba. The students lived on the twenty-fourth floor of a high-rise, without running water or a working elevator. This was a problem for Kim, because her burns still required daily washing and medication. A fellow Vietnamese student named Toan offered to carry buckets of water up to her apartment, and it wasn't long before he was touched by the loveliness of Kim's spirit.

Yet Kim remained noncommittal. Toan smoked cigarettes, drank excessively, and still embraced the communist ideology in which he had been raised. She began witnessing to him about Jesus Christ, but his intellectual barriers to faith seemed insurmountable. Gradually, however, Toan did give up both smoking and drinking and eventually asked Kim to marry him. Kim warned him that her injuries made it unlikely that she could ever have children, but he repeatedly reassured her that he truly wanted to marry her anyway. More important, he assured her that he understood and respected her faith. They dated for six years and finally married in 1992.

Kim and Toan honeymooned in Moscow, and on their return flight to Cuba, their Aeroflot jet was scheduled to refuel in Newfoundland. The couple had spoken before about defecting, but Toan was afraid of being caught by communist authorities. He also feared reprisals against their families. As the plane descended into the Gander International Airport in Newfoundland, Kim began praying.

"What are you doing?" Toan asked.

"Toan," she whispered, "if God opens the way, we should stay and live in Canada. I have peace about it."

"Kim, no. We'll never get away with it."

"Toan, I go by faith. If you love me, follow me, because I follow God."

"If they catch us, they'll send us back to Vietnam, and you know what happens then. They'll kill us." He was so worried that he even considered letting her defect without him, if it came to that.

"I know the risk. I love you, Toan, but I love God, too, so I follow him."

When the plane landed, the passengers entered the airport to wait during refueling. Kim had no idea how to go about defecting, and she was frightened. Should she simply hide out in the bathroom? No, when the secret police traveling with them counted the number of passengers, they would see that she was missing and come back for her. "Oh God, how can I stay?" she prayed desperately. "Give me a sign, please. I don't want to go back to Cuba or Vietnam anymore."

When she opened her eyes, her gaze was drawn to a small room off the central waiting room. The door was ajar, and inside she could see a group of people, some of whom she recognized from their community in Cuba. She walked over, put her head inside, and asked them in Spanish, "What are you doing here?"

"We want to stay."

"Me, too. How can I do it?"

"You just give your passport to the officer right up there, at the front of the room."

Providentially, Kim had walked right to the immigration office! Quickly she summoned Toan, and they handed their passports to the officer. "We want to stay in Canada," they said.

"Yes," said the officer. "Okay."

So easy? Kim marveled. *Praise the Lord!*

But then the official said, "Just wait about ten minutes. Another officer will come to interview you."

Ten minutes . . . even that small a delay could mean life or death for the frightened couple. Refueling was almost finished, and time was running out. Kim and Toan stood in the doorway, watching, waiting. Finally, the other officer arrived and asked them to follow him back into the office. Just as they crossed the threshold into freedom, they heard the boarding announcement.

All their belongings were still on the plane; they had nothing but the clothes on their backs. But it didn't matter. "I just say, 'Bye-bye,'" Kim says, "and I feel very happy. I am free!"[6]

Kim and Toan settled into a thriving Vietnamese immigrant community in Toronto, and soon another blessing was in store for them. Kim became pregnant—truly a miracle!—and the couple became the proud parents of a healthy baby boy.

In a recent film about Kim's life, two-year-old Thomas and Kim face each other across a table. Kim touches Thomas's face, first here, then there. "Cheeks," they say together. "Lips. Ears." Then they put their faces right up close and rub noses.[7] A loving mother and son, happy, fulfilled—so far away from that terrible day in 1972, when the sky rained napalm.

Yet Kim Phuc's spiritual healing was eventually to reach out beyond her own home and lead to a much wider healing.

In 1996, Kim agreed to speak at Veterans Day ceremonies held at The Wall in Washington, D.C. She took her place on the rostrum, flanked by U.S. military dignitaries, before a huge crowd of veterans. No one could tell how much it cost her just to stand there and face that sea of uniforms, a sight that brought back terrifying memories of the war.

"As you know, I am the little girl who was running to escape from the napalm fire. I do not want to talk about the war because I cannot change history. I only want you to remember a tragedy of war in order to do things to stop fighting and killing around the world."

Her voice dropped. "I have suffered a lot from both physical and emotional pain. Sometimes I thought I could not live, but God saved my life and gave me faith and hope."

And then she uttered healing words of grace and forgiveness: "Even if I could talk face-to-face with the pilot who dropped the bomb, I could tell him we cannot change history, but we should try to do good things for the present and for the future to promote peace."

When she finished her brief but moving remarks, the veterans rose to their feet and broke into an explosion of applause, many of them in tears. "It's important to us that she's here," one veteran said. "For her to forgive us personally means something."

One man, overcome with emotion, rushed to a patrolman and scribbled out a note, asking him to deliver it to Kim. *"I'm the man you are looking for,"* the note read.[8]

Intermediaries asked if she was willing to see him. Yes, she said, if they could arrange a meeting away from the crush of people. Officials brought the man over to her car.

When the reporters cleared away, Kim turned and looked straight into the man's eyes and then held out her arms . . . the same arms she had held out as she ran along the road, in agony from her burning skin. She hugged the man, and he began to sob.

"I am sorry. I am just so sorry!" he said.

"It is okay. I forgive. I forgive," said Kim Phuc, echoing her favorite Bible verse, "Forgive, and you will be forgiven" (Luke 6:37).

■   ■   ■

THAT DAY THE famous photo of thirty years ago, of the terrified little Vietnamese girl fleeing the napalm flames, was replaced in the national consciousness by a photo of a young mother embracing an ex-GI, silhouetted against the shimmering black memorial. The words of forgiveness Kim extended that Veterans Day helped heal the consciences of thousands of veterans gathered there; and as news reports carried the story far and wide, her words and the striking photo helped heal the nation's wounds as well. She brought the resurrection power of Christ to a place that serves as a collective memorial for 58,000 Americans, showing how the bitterness of war can be overcome with love.

I can't help but contrast Kim Phuc's message of reconciliation to the ongoing, fruitless efforts by Robert McNamara and so many others, still seeking technocratic solutions to the war. They want so desperately to see, but they remain blind. The only real solution is spiritual: It is forgiveness, repentance, and making restitution, actively pursuing good for our former enemy. Only Christianity provides the power to transform the world.

And so we come full circle, back to the questions with which we began this book. Can Christians really make any difference in the world? Does the Christian worldview give us the map we need for living? Can a culture be rebuilt so all the world can see in its splendor and glory the contours of God's kingdom? Can we really make the world "a new creation"? Kim Phuc, along with all the others we have met in these pages, show us that the answer is emphatically yes.

Every day you and I are making decisions that help construct one kind of world or another. Are we co-opted by the faddish worldviews of our age, or are we helping to create a new world of peace, love, and forgiveness?

How now shall we live?

By embracing God's truth, understanding the physical and moral order he has created, lovingly contending for that truth with our neighbors, then having the courage to live it out in every walk of life.

Boldly and, yes, joyously.

WITH GRATITUDE

W̲e̲ trust that these pages have equipped you to answer the question, How now shall we live? Our goal has been to give you the tools to analyze and respond to false worldviews, and to defend and live out the glorious truth of the Christian faith.

This book is the result of a conviction born in my life in the early 1980s and in Nancy Pearcey's life following her conversion in 1971. We believe that Christianity is a full worldview covering all of life, giving a framework for every human endeavor. Since 1985 I have been writing a worldview column for *Christianity Today,* and Nancy has coauthored that column with me since 1994. And in 1991 I went on the air with *BreakPoint,* a daily radio program commenting on current affairs from a Christian worldview perspective, with Nancy as executive editor. We have developed a close working relationship and frequently have been startled by how our minds have followed similar paths. This book emerges out of the day-to-day process of grappling with the application of biblical principles to current events and trends, steadily deepening our conviction that Christianity gives the only viable foundation for intellectual understanding and practical living.

We owe an immense debt of gratitude to those who have contributed to this project. Harold Fickett was a major collaborator (as he was in *Loving God*), offering his extraordinary gift of narrative to draft the story chapters, bringing abstract principles to life. Harold is a talented writer and an incisive conceptual thinker who helped shape the book's overall structure as well.

It is impossible to say enough in praise of Judith Markham of Blue Water Ink. Her editing skills brought clarity and grace to often clunky prose. This is my seventh book that Judith has edited, and as always it has been a joy to work with her. She is not only without peer as an editor, but she is also a gracious and loving Christian.

T. M. Moore, president of Chesapeake Theological Seminary, lent us his theological expertise, running the text through a tough grid of theological orthodoxy. He has been urging me for years to write this kind of book.

We are especially grateful to those who allowed us to tell their stories throughout the book to illustrate the key principles of Christian worldview, including Jorge Crespo, Kenneth and Theresa McGarity, Dr. Kenneth Swan, Dr. Bernard Nathanson, Danny Croce, Officer Salvatore Bartolomeo, and Martha Williamson. Many took time from demanding schedules to give us interviews and other assistance. We're also grateful to Dutch TV for film footage of their interview with Kim Phuc.

Thanks as well to those who gave generously of their time to read and critique various chapters, including Jay Budziszewski, Donald Drew, Chester Finn, Robert George, Patrick Glynn, Russell Hittinger, David Larson, Joe Loconte, Steve Meyer, Paul Nelson, Albert Quie, the Rev. Robert Sirico, and Gene Edward Veith. Special thanks to Fred Buettler, who alerted us to his extraordinary research on the Conference on Science, Philosophy, and Religion (described in chapter 37). Our appreciation goes also to Doug Griffin, who provided helpful information early on in the project.

Very special thanks are due to Research Associate Kim Robbins, who undergirded the writing task by tirelessly tracking down information in libraries and on Nexis, and also put in hours of painstaking work to find sources and complete the citations. Her dedication and dogged determination are unparalleled.

Thanks as well to the *BreakPoint* staff, whose work researching and drafting radio scripts on a variety of subjects contributed to our understanding of worldview issues: Managing Editor Anne Morse, Associate Editors Roberto Rivera and Eric Metaxas, and Research Associate Douglas Minson. Special mention must be made of the careful, meticulous work of my secretarial staff, Nancy Niemeyer and Diana Longenecker, who typed revision after revision—miraculously, without ever losing track or getting them mixed up.

For that matter, we are indebted to all our colleagues in the wonderful ministry of Prison Fellowship for their patience and understanding of our creative eccentricities. We especially thank Tom Pratt, who so ably keeps the ministry on track so that I am free to write.

Crucial to any literary enterprise is the publisher, and Tyndale's Ken Petersen is among the best. He took a keen interest in the ideas in the book from the start, worked patiently through the editorial process, and endured with special grace the last-minute panic of missed deadlines. It is a great encouragement to have a publisher who shows a real passion for the book's message. We owe much as well to Lynn Vanderzalm's sharp eye and scrupulous care in editing the text for Tyndale.

Most of all, we thank our families, whose support and love make all this effort worth it. Patty has been my steadfast rock, as always, my partner in every sense of the word, without whom I could not undertake my ministry. Nancy's husband, Rick, is her greatest inspiration, along with her sons, Dieter and Michael. Christianity is a worldview meant to be lived out in the crucible of a fallen world, and it comes most alive in the relationships in which we grapple to apply it day by day.

There are no words to describe our deep gratitude to God, the author of all truth. We are overcome by sheer wonder that God has given us not only salvation but also a basis for living out all of life in the grace of his presence. God's Word is not only Truth; it is surely also Goodness and Beauty.

NOTES

INTRODUCTION
HOW NOW SHALL WE LIVE?

1. Ezekiel 33:10, KJV.
2. Richard John Neuhaus, "The Religious Century Nears," *Wall Street Journal*, 6 July 1995.
3. Richard Nadler, "Glum and Glummer: Positive Change in U.S. Culture Helped by Conservatives," *National Review* 50, no. 18 (September 26, 1998): 26.
4. Abraham Kuyper, from his Stone Lectures delivered at Princeton in 1898, now abridged as *Christianity: A Total World and Life System* (Marlborough, N.H.: Plymouth Rock Foundation, 1996), 46.
5. The challenges Kuyper poses, especially in his masterful Stone Lectures on Calvinism, remained uppermost in our minds through the two years we labored over this manuscript. The Christian "does not for a moment think of limiting himself to theology and contemplation, leaving the other sciences as of a lower character, in the hands of unbelievers," Kuyper writes. On the contrary, "looking upon it as his task to know God in all His works, he is conscious of having been called to fathom with all the energy of his intellect, things terrestrial, as well as things celestial" (*Christianity: A Total World and Life System*, 84). As Kuyper put it, not one square inch of the universe should remain outside the claim of Christ. This is surely what the apostle Paul meant when he told the church at Corinth to take "every thought captive to the obedience of Christ" (2 Cor. 10:5, NASB).

CHAPTER 1
A NEW CREATION

1. In addition to my trip to García Moreno Prison, we obtained information for this chapter from later interviews with Dr. Jorge Crespo de Toral and from records he supplied. Additional background for the story was provided by Prison Fellowship staff members and by Ellen Santilli Vaughn's pamphlet on the work in Ecuador, *Lights in the Darkness: The Church behind the Wall in South America*, published by Prison Fellowship.

CHAPTER 2
CHRISTIANITY IS A WORLDVIEW

1. Read the story of my conversion in *Born Again* (Old Tappan, N.J.: Chosen, 1976).
2. Abraham Kuyper, *Christianity: A Total World and Life System* (Marlborough, N.H.: Plymouth Rock Foundation, 1996), 39–40.
3. Ibid., 41.
4. Cornelius Plantinga Jr., "Fashions and Folly: Sin and Character in the 90s," (presented at the January Lecture Series, Calvin Theological Seminary, Grand Rapids, Michigan, January 15, 1993), 14–15.
5. Richard M. Weaver, *Ideas Have Consequences* (Chicago: University of Chicago Press, 1984).

CHAPTER 3
WORLDVIEWS IN CONFLICT

1. Samuel Huntington, "The Clash of Civilizations," *Journal of Foreign Affairs* (summer 1993): 22. Huntington identified the major power blocs as the Western, Islamic, Chinese, Hindu, Orthodox, Japanese, and possibly African regions.
2. James Kurth, "The Real Clash of Civilization," *Washington Times,* 4 October 1994.
3. Jacques Toubon, cited in "Living with America," *Calgary Herald,* 6 October 1993.
4. William Orville Douglas, *Zorach v. Clauson,* 343 US 306 (1952).
5. Antonin Scalia, as quoted in John Pickering, "Christian Soldier in a Secular City," *Washington Post,* 12 May 1996.
6. Happily, this decision was overruled after being exposed in the conservative Washington journal *Human Events,* which led to congressional pressure spearheaded by Republican Senator Spencer Abraham from Michigan. See *BreakPoint* commentary, September 23, 1997.
7. George Weigel, "John Paul II in America," *Crisis* (December 1995).
8. Stanley Fish, "There's No Such Thing As Free Speech and It's a Good Thing, Too," in *Debating P.C.: The Controversy over Political Correctness on College Campuses,* ed. Paul Breman (New York: Delta, 1992), 244.
9. The discussion in the following paragraphs is based on a study reported by Paul H. Ray in "The Emerging Culture," *American Demographics* (February 1997): 28. This research was sponsored by the Fetzer Institute and the Institute of Noetic Sciences, the latter a sophisticated New Age foundation.

CHAPTER 4
CHRISTIAN TRUTH IN AN AGE OF UNBELIEF

1. These studies are described in greater detail in chapter 18, "We're All Utopians Now."

2. Shortly thereafter, in the political upheaval of 1997, the minister of justice was removed from office. Father Nikolai and other Christians have continued to minister to him. The story is not finished yet.

3. J. Gresham Machen, "Christianity and Culture," *Princeton Theological Review* 13, no. 3 (July 1913): 7.

4. Harry Blamires, *The Christian Mind: How Should a Christian Mind Think?* (Ann Arbor, Mich.: Servant, 1963), 80.

5. Ibid., 3.

6. Thanks to Frank Brock, president of Covenant College, for developing this thesis, which has such profound implications for the church. There was a time when the pastor was the best-educated person in the congregation. As recently as the 1940s, only a small percentage of Americans attended college, and those who did often attended schools with strong Christian traditions, almost all of which (at least among the older institutions) were founded by Christians. (Even Brown University, when I attended in the 1950s, still had mandatory chapel, astonishing as that might seem today.) While there were certainly skeptics a generation or two ago, they were not a major influence in most congregations. As a result, pastors could focus primarily on developing their flock's spirituality. Preaching was often subjective and emotional, particularly among fundamentalist and Pentecostal churches. All of that began to change after World War II. The GI bill provided the opportunity for almost universal higher education, and over the next years millions who never dreamed of going to college flooded our nation's institutions of higher learning. New colleges sprouted up, old ones expanded to meet the demand, and the emerging middle class began to view a college degree as an American right. Community and regional colleges are now available in every part of the country, and government programs provide widespread scholarship assistance. The result is that today a majority of church members and attendees are college educated.

7. Machen, "Christianity and Culture," 14.

8. Abraham Kuyper, *Christianity: A Total World and Life System* (Marlborough, N.H.: Plymouth Rock Foundation, 1996), 3.

9. The church's primary biblical mission is not to restore or create the culture but to be faithful in serving God. As Kuyper put it, "The church exists merely for the sake of God" (*Christianity: A Total World and Life System,* 38). But in serving God, the church works toward the regeneration of the elect and testifies to the glory of God in his work among all people. So when the church is faithful, it affects all of life. It does, indeed, rejuvenate culture. See Charles Colson with Ellen Santilli Vaughn, *The Body* (Dallas: Word, 1992).

10. Russell Kirk, "Civilization with Religion," The Heritage Foundation Report (July 24, 1992). Political philosopher Eric Voegelin and historian Arnold Toynbee, among others, make the same point.

11. Kirk, "Civilization with Religion."

CHAPTER 5
DAVE AND KATY'S METAPHYSICAL ADVENTURE

1. Dave and Katy Mulholland are characters we created for this book, but their story is based on real events. The exhibits at Disney World and Epcot Center are described accurately, based on a visit in 1997. In a sense, Dave is Everyman, and Katy is Everyman's Teenager.

CHAPTER 6
SHATTERING THE GRID

1. The following discussion owes much to Norman Geisler's book *Cosmos: Carl Sagan's Religion for the Scientific Mind* (Dallas: Quest, 1983).
2. Carl Sagan, *Cosmos* (New York: Random, 1980), 4.
3. Carl Sagan, *Broca's Brain* (New York: Random, 1979), 282.
4. Ibid., 287.
5. Sagan, *Cosmos,* 242.
6. Ibid., 5.
7. Ibid., 243.
8. Ibid.
9. Ibid., 345.
10. Sagan, *Broca's Brain,* 271–75.
11. Carl Sagan was one of the scientists who formed the SETI Institute (Search for Extra-Terrestrial Intelligence). Sagan wrote the novel *Contact,* on which the movie *Contact* was based.
12. Sagan, *Broca's Brain,* 275.
13. Stan and Jan Berenstain, *The Berenstain Bears' Nature Guide* (New York: Random, 1984), 11.
14. Ibid., 10.

CHAPTER 7
LET'S START AT THE VERY BEGINNING

1. Ludwig Büchner, as quoted in Gordon H. Clark, *The Philosophy of Science and Belief in God* (Nutley, N.J.: Craig Press, 1964), 50.
2. Lincoln Kinnear Barnett, *The Universe and Dr. Einstein* (New York: William Morrow, 1968), 114 (emphasis in the original).
3. Paul C. Davies, *The Edge of Infinity: Where the Universe Came From and How It Will End* (New York: Simon & Schuster, 1982), 169.
4. Arthur Eddington, as quoted in Hugh Ross, "Astronomical Evidences for a Personal, Transcendent God," in *The Creation Hypothesis,* ed. J. P. Moreland (Downers Grove, Ill.: InterVarsity Press, 1994), 145–46.
5. Robert Jastrow, *Until the Sun Dies* (New York: Norton, 1977), 51.
6. Carl Sagan, *Cosmos* (New York: Random, 1980), 259.

7. The energy described here is energy available for work, not total energy.
8. William Lane Craig and Quentin Smith, *Theism, Atheism, and Big Bang Cosmology* (New York: Oxford University Press, 1993), 135.
9. M. A. Corey, *God and the New Cosmology: The Anthropic Design Argument* (Lanham, Md.: Rowman & Littlefield, 1993), 105.
10. Paul C. Davies, *The Accidental Universe* (Cambridge: Cambridge University Press, 1982), 90.
11. Heinz Pagels, "A Cozy Cosmology," *The Sciences* (March/April 1985): 38. See also Nancy R. Pearcey, "A Universe Built for Us: The Anthropic Principle," *Bible-Science Newsletter* (October 1990): 7; "The Anthropic Principle: The Closest Atheists Can Get to God," *Bible-Science Newsletter* (November 1990): 7.
12. George Wald, as quoted in Dietrick E. Thomsen, "A Knowing Universe Seeking to Be Known," *Science News* (February 19, 1983): 124.
13. Freeman Dyson, as quoted in Martin Gardner, "Intelligent Design and Phillip Johnson," *Skeptical Inquirer* (November 21, 1997): 17.
14. George Greenstein, *The Symbiotic Universe: Life and Mind in the Cosmos* (New York: William Morrow, 1988), 197.
15. Patrick Glynn, "The Atheistic Assumptions of Modern Society Are Being Challenged by the New Science," *National Review* 48, no. 8 (May 6, 1996): 32. See also Patrick Glynn, *The Evidence: The Reconciliation of Faith and Reason in a Postsecular World* (Rocklin, Calif.: Prima, 1997).
16. William A. Dembski, *The Design Inference: Eliminating Chance through Small Probabilities* (Cambridge: Cambridge University Press, 1998), chapter 2.

CHAPTER 8
LIFE IN A TEST TUBE?

1. *The Land Before Time* video series, Universal Pictures (1988).
2. The following discussion draws heavily from Charles B. Thaxton, Walter L. Bradley, and Roger L. Olsen, *The Mystery of Life's Origin: Reassessing Current Theories* (Dallas: Lewis & Stanley, 1992). See also Stephen C. Meyer, "Explanatory Power of Design," in *Mere Creation: Science, Faith, and Intelligent Design,* ed. William A. Dembski (Downers Grove, Ill.: InterVarsity Press, 1998), 113.
3. Stanley L. Miller, *From the Primitive Atmosphere to the Prebiotic Soup to the Pre-RNA World* (Washington, D.C.: National Aeronautics and Space Administration, 1996).
4. Fred Hoyle, *The Intelligent Universe* (New York: Holt, Rinehart, and Winston, 1983), 11.
5. Dean H. Kenyon and Gary Steinman, *Biochemical Predestination* (New York: McGraw-Hill, 1969).
6. From an interview quoted in Nancy R. Pearcey and Charles B. Thaxton, *The Soul of Science: Christian Faith and Natural Philosophy* (Wheaton, Ill.: Crossway, 1994), 230.

7. See Michael J. Behe, *Darwin's Black Box: The Biochemical Challenge to Evolution* (New York: Free Press, 1996), 210–16.

8. Arthur Fisher, "New Search for Life in Space," *Popular Science* 225 (October 1984): 44.

9. *Reunion in France*, MGM (1942).

10. See Thaxton, *The Mystery of Life's Origin*; Pearcey and Thaxton, *The Soul of Science*; and Stephen C. Meyer, "The Origin of Life and the Death of Materialism," *Intercollegiate Review* 31, no. 2 (spring 1996).

11. Richard Dawkins, *The Blind Watchmaker: Why the Evidence of Evolution Reveals a Universe without Design* (New York: Norton, 1996), 150.

12. Stuart A. Kauffman, *At Home in the Universe: The Search for Laws of Self-Organization and Complexity* (London: Penguin, 1996), 74.

13. Nancy R. Pearcey, "DNA: The Message in the Molecule," *First Things*, no. 64 (June/July 1996): 14.

CHAPTER 9
DARWIN IN THE DOCK

1. Douglas Futuyma, *Evolutionary Biology* (Sunderland, Mass.: Sinauer, 1986), 3.

2. "NABT Unveils New Statement on Teaching Evolution," *The American Biology Teacher* 68, no. 1 (January 1996): 61. The NABT statement created such an uproar that the organization subsequently dropped the words "unsupervised" and "impersonal." The change was largely cosmetic, however, since the remaining words "unpredictable" and "natural" were understood to mean essentially the same thing.

3. In technical language, Darwinism assumes that microevolution (minor change) is the engine for macroevolution (major transitions). This section draws on Nancy R. Pearcey, "Everybody Can Know: The Most Powerful Evidence Against Evolution," *Bible-Science Newsletter* (June 1987): 7.

4. Charles Darwin, *The Origin of Species* (New York: Penguin, 1958), 41–47.

5. Rick Weiss, "Mutant Moniker: A Tale of Freaky Flies and Gonzo Genetics," *Science News* 139, no. 2 (January 12, 1991): 30; and Dan L. Lindsley and Georgianna Zimm, "The Hard Life of a Mutant Fruit Fly," *Harper's Magazine* 284, no. 1703 (April 1992): 24.

6. Darwin's depiction of evolution as resulting from the gradual accumulation of countless infinitesimally minute variations demands that the fossil record preserve an unbroken chain of transitional forms from one species into another. But that is not the overall pattern that emerges from the fossil record. Instead, major groups of organisms appear in the fossil record suddenly, fully formed, without transitional forms leading up to them. See Jeffrey H. Schwartz, *Sudden Origins: Fossils, Genes, and the Emergence of Species* (New York: Wiley & Sons, 1999), 3.

7. Phillip E. Johnson, *Reason in the Balance: The Case against Naturalism in Science, Law, and Education* (Downers Grove, Ill.: InterVarsity Press, 1995). See also

Nancy R. Pearcey, "Naturalism on Trial," *First Things*, no. 60 (February 1996): 64.

8. Jerry A. Coyne, "Not Black and White," *Nature* 396 (November 5, 1998): 35–36; Jonathan Wells, "Second Thoughts about Peppered Moths," http://www.trueorigin.org/pepmoth1.htm.

9. Luther Burbank, as quoted in Norman Macbeth, *Darwin Retried* (New York: Delta, 1971), 36.

10. Michael J. Behe, *Darwin's Black Box: The Biochemical Challenge to Evolution* (New York: Touchstone, 1996), 40–48. The functional integration of parts is a classic argument against Darwinism; it was first developed in the nineteenth century by George Cuirer. See Michael Denton, *Evolution: A Theory in Crisis* (Bethesda, Md.: Adler and Adler, 1985). See also Nancy R. Pearcey, "The Biochemical Challenge to Evolution," *Books & Culture* (November/December 1996): 10.

11. Charles Darwin, *The Origin of Species*, (New York: New York University Press, 1988), 154.

12. Behe, *Darwin's Black Box*, 18–21, 36–39.

CHAPTER 10
DARWIN'S DANGEROUS IDEA

1. Stephen Gould, as quoted in Phillip E. Johnson, *Reason in the Balance: The Case against Naturalism in Science, Law, and Education* (Downers Grove, Ill.: InterVarsity Press, 1995), 31. See also Stephen J. Gould, *Rocks of Ages: Science and Religion in the Fullness of Life* (New York: Ballantine, 1999).

2. William B. Provine and Phillip E. Johnson, "Darwinism: Science or Naturalistic Philosophy?" (videotape of debate held at Stanford University, April 30, 1994). Available from Access Research Network, P.O. Box 38069, Colorado Springs, CO 80937-8069, phone: (888) 259-7102.

3. Johnson, *Reason in the Balance*, 46–47.

4. Calvin Coolidge, as quoted in *The Journal*, (a Summit Ministries newsletter), 7.

5. Richard Rorty, "Trotsky and the Wild Orchids," *Wild Orchids and Trotsky: Message from American Universities*, ed. Mark Edmundson (New York: Viking, 1993), 38.

6. Richard Rorty, "Untruth and Consequences," *New Republic* (July 31, 1995): 27.

7. Richard Rorty, as quoted in Roger Lundin, *The Culture of Interpretation: Christian Faith and the Postmodern World* (Grand Rapids: Eerdmans, 1993), 15.

8. Richard Dawkins, *The Blind Watchmaker: Why the Evidence of Evolution Reveals a Universe without Design* (New York: Norton, 1987), 6.

9. The following discussion of Darwin and his contemporaries is based on Nancy R. Pearcey, "You Guys Lost," in *Mere Creation: Science, Faith, and Intelligent Design*, ed. William A. Dembski (Downers Grove, Ill.: InterVarsity Press, 1998): 73.

10. Nora Barlow, ed., *The Autobiography of Charles Darwin 1809–1882 with Original Omissions Restored* (New York: Norton, 1958), 87.

11. Ibid.

12. William Darwin, as quoted in John Durant, "Darwinism and Divinity:

A Century of Debate," in *Darwinism and Divinity: Essays on Evolution and Religious Belief,* ed. John Durant (New York: Basil Blackwell, 1985), 18.

13. Francis Darwin, ed., *Life and Letters of Charles Darwin,* vol. 2 (New York: D. Appleton, 1899), 155.

14. David Duncan, *Life and Letters of Herbert Spencer,* vol. 2 (New York: D. Appleton, 1908), 319.

15. Leonard Huxley, *Life and Letters of Thomas Henry Huxley,* vol. 1 (New York: Macmillan, 1903), 246.

16. Thomas Henry Huxley, "Science and Religion," *The Builder* 17 (1859): 35.

17. Charles Hodge, *What Is Darwinism? And Other Writings on Science and Religion,* ed. Mark A. Noll and David N. Livingstone (Grand Rapids: Baker, 1994), 85, 155.

18. Richard Lewontin, "Billions and Billions of Demons," *New York Review of Books* (January 9, 1997): 31.

19. Ibid.

20. William Steig, *Yellow & Pink* (New York: Farrar, Straus & Giroux, 1984).

21. Carl Sagan, "In the Valley of the Shadow," *Parade* (March 10, 1996): 18.

CHAPTER 11
A MATTER OF LIFE

1. This story is based not only on interviews with Ken and Theresa McGarity as well as with Dr. Kenneth Swan, but also on information found in the following sources: Peter MacPherson, "The War Surgeon's Dilemma: Confronting His Vietnam Past: Was the Life He Saved Worth Living?" *Washington Post,* 7 January 1992; Colonel Kenneth G. Swan, MC USAR, "Triage: The Path Revisited," *Military Medicine* 161 (August 1996): 448–52; "Doubt Gone, Doctor Glad He Saved GI," *Chicago Tribune,* 28 November 1991; Joan Sanchez, "Army Doctor Tracks Down His Patient," *Los Angeles Times,* 8 December 1991.

2. Dr. Kenneth Swan stayed in touch with Ken McGarity, and soon after their first meeting, Swan called with extraordinary news. He had arranged for McGarity to receive the medals he had never been awarded because of a mix-up in record keeping. On January 30, 1992, at Fort Benning, Georgia, Kenneth McGarity finally received his Purple Heart, an Air Medal, and four additional prestigious awards.

3. Theresa and the girls returned home to stay in 1992. As a family, they worked through the anger and pain each of them had to deal with, and by the following year the McGaritys were doing well.

CHAPTER 12
WHATEVER HAPPENED TO HUMAN LIFE?

1. Joycelyn Elders, former surgeon general, accused pro-lifers of carrying on a "love affair with the fetus" at an abortion rights rally in January 1992.

2. Medieval philosophers had argued from the existence of God to the reality of the world. Descartes reversed that, and from then on philosophers argued from the certainty of the self to the reality of God and the world. From human reason alone, philosophers would discover all truth. This was the birth of the autonomy of human reason.

3. Friedrich Nietzsche, *The Gay Science,* trans. Walter Kaufmann (New York: Random, 1974), 125.

4. Peter Kreeft, "The World's Last Night," *Crisis* (July/August 1994): 39.

5. Robert P. George, "Why Integrity Matters," speech given at the National Prayer Breakfast, February 7, 1998. Professor George subjects naturalistic ideas about sexual morality to searching philosophical criticism in his new book *In Defense of Natural Law* (New York: Clarendon Press, 1998), chapters 8, 9, 15, 16.

6. *Roe v. Wade,* 410 US 113 (1973).

7. Nearly a decade earlier, two eminent pediatricians at Yale-New Haven Hospital had supported the parents' right to let their severely handicapped children die in such cases and suggested that doctors present the option if parents don't bring it up themselves. See Raymond S. Duff and A. G. M. Campbell, "Moral and Ethical Dilemmas in the Special-Care Nursery," *New England Journal of Medicine* 289, no. 17 (October 25, 1973): 890–94.

8. Richard A. Gross, Alan Cox, Ruth Tatyrek, Michael Polly, and William A. Barnes, "Early Management and Decision Making for the Treatment of Myelomeningocele," *Pediatrics* 72, no. 4 (October 4, 1983): 450–58.

9. Tucker Carlson, "Eugenics, American Style," *The Weekly Standard* 2, no. 12 (December 2, 1996): 20.

10. Nat Hentoff, "Abortion as Self-Defense," *Washington Post,* 1 February 1997.

11. Carlson, "Eugenics, American Style," 20.

12. Christopher Scanlan, "Elders: I'm Willing to Be a Lightning Rod," *Houston Chronicle,* 17 December 1992.

13. Carlson, "Eugenics, American Style," 20.

14. See C. Everett Koop, "Life and Death and the Handicapped Unborn," *Issues in Law & Medicine* 5, no. 1 (June 22, 1989): 101.

15. Steven Pinker, "Why They Kill Their Newborns," *New York Times,* 2 November 1997. See also Andrew Ferguson, "How Steven Pinker's Mind Works," *The Weekly Standard* (January 12, 1998): 16.

16. As quoted in Cal Thomas, "Who Cares about Living When the Good Times Are Rolling," *Naples Daily News,* 16 July 1998.

17. Eileen I. McDonagh, *Breaking the Abortion Deadlock: From Choice to Consent* (New York: Oxford University Press, 1996), 7.

18. *Planned Parenthood v. Casey,* 112 S Ct 2791 (1992).

19. *Compassion in Dying v. Washington,* 850 F Supp 1454 (WD Wash 1994).

20. This decision was handed down in 1997. Despite the Supreme Court's unanimity in reversing the Ninth Circuit Court's ruling, there are reasons for concern that some justices are biding their time, awaiting an opportunity to manufacture a right to assisted suicide akin to the abortion right in *Roe*.

See Robert P. George, "The Supreme Court's 1997 Term," *First Things,* no. 77 (October 1997).

21. *Compassion in Dying v. Washington,* 79 F 3d 790 (9th Cir 1996).

22. Charles Colson and Russell Hittinger, "Private Liberty . . . Public Chaos," *Washington Times,* 22 April 1996. In 1991 a survey in the *New England Journal of Medicine* revealed that in the Netherlands as many as 1,000 patients had been euthanized annually without giving consent; and in 4,500 cases, excessive medication leading to death was given without patient consent. But a new study shows that these numbers vastly underrepresent the true extent of euthanasia practice there. A 1991 report published by the Dutch government said that in 1990 approximately 8,100 additional people were killed by their doctors by intentional overdose of morphine. In February 1999, a study in a British medical journal found that 59 percent of the deaths by either euthanasia or assisted suicide in the Netherlands go unreported. Wesley J. Smith, "Suicide Pays," *First Things* (June/July 1999): 14–16.

23. Tony Mauro, "Disabled Plan Protest against Assisted Suicide," *USA Today,* 6 January 1997.

24. Eric Zorn, "'Brave New World' Awaits Debaters of Abortion Rights," *Chicago Tribune,* 9 March 1997.

25. "Michael Has Four Parents: The Politics of Childbearing," *BreakPoint* commentary, June 21, 1995.

26. I strongly recommend reading Richard John Neuhaus, "The Return of Eugenics," *Commentary* (April 1988): 18–26.

CHAPTER 13
IN WHOSE IMAGE?

1. Steve Weizman, "Copenhagen Zoo Displays the Most Dangerous Animals," 12 September 1996, on-line Reuters North American Wire.

2. Ibid.

3. Mike Samuels and Nancy Samuels, as quoted in Robert D. Orr and Walter L. Larimore, "Medical Abortion Is Not Just a Medical Issue," *American Family Physician* 56, no. 2 (August 1997): 351.

4. Stanley Fish later disavowed much of what he said in Boston, or at least what most participants thought he said. Fish claimed that he has never been pro-choice, so what he said was no reversal of his position. He also claimed that he was not endorsing the pro-life position; he was merely acknowledging that he was mistaken in saying that pro-life arguments are religious, while pro-choice arguments are rational. In subsequent correspondence with me, he revealed the utterly self-refuting character of his own view. He argued that no moral position can be supported rationally—but of course he arrived at that position by thinking rationally. See also Stanley Fish, "Why Can't We All Get Along?" *First Things,* no. 60 (February 1996): 18.

5. C. S. Lewis, *Mere Christianity* (New York: Touchstone, 1996), 73.

6. Abraham Kuyper, *Christianity: A Total World and Life System* (Marlborough, N.H.: Plymouth Rock Foundation, 1996), 14.
7. See chapter 4 of Alvin J. Schmidt, *The Menace of Multiculturalism: Trojan Horse in America* (Westport, Conn.: Praeger, 1997).
8. Ted Turner, as quoted in Pat Buchanan, "Sermon from Ted Turner," *Washington Times*, 2 April 1997.
9. *The River*, Universal Pictures (1984).
10. Douglas Sadownick, "Choosing Sides," *LA Weekly*, 20 December 1996.
11. This is the same conflict Carl Sagan confronted when he was given the choice between certain death or submitting to a lifesaving treatment perfected through animal research (see chapter 10).
12. "A New Medical Ethics," *California Medicine* 113 (1970): 67–68.
13. A study done by Marv Miller shows that the inner state of emptiness among the elderly leads to an alarmingly high rate of suicide—especially older men after retirement (four times greater than the average rate for the U.S.). Marv Miller, *Suicide after Sixty: The Final Alternative* (New York: Springer, 1979), 11–12, 19.
14. Elizabeth Kolbert, "Frank Talk by Clinton to MTV Generation," *New York Times*, 20 April 1994.
15. Albert Camus, "Absurd Reasoning," *The Myth of Sisyphus*, trans. Justin O'Brien (New York: Alfred A. Knopf, 1969), 3.
16. Saint Augustine, *Confessions*, book 1, paragraph 1, trans. R. S. Pine-Coffin (New York: Penguin, 1961), 21.

CHAPTER 15
THE TROUBLE WITH US

1. Harold S. Kushner, *When Bad Things Happen to Good People* (New York: Schoken Books, 1980).
2. Edward T. Oakes, "Original Sin: A Disputation," *First Things* (November 1998): 21.
3. William F. Buckley Jr., *Nearer My God: An Autobiography of Faith* (New York: Doubleday, 1997), 232.

CHAPTER 16
A BETTER WAY OF LIVING?

1. David U. Gerstel, *Paradise, Incorporated: Synanon* (Novato, Calif.: Presidio Press, 1982), 36. In 1977, AA old-timers were often suspicious of younger people coming out of the drug culture. Today, Narcotics Anonymous (NA) and Cocaine Anonymous (CA) help people with drug problems.
2. Synanon reached a $600,000 out-of-court settlement with the *San Francisco Examiner* in 1976. See Betsy Carter, Michael Reese, and Martin Kasindorf, *Newsweek* (November 20, 1978): 133. In addition, to the Hearst settlement,

Time, Inc. paid $2 million to defend itself against Synanon's libel suit. See Fred Barbash, "Alton Telegraph Libel Judgment Sends Fearful Message to Press," *Washington Post*, 25 August 1981. In the 1970s, Synanon sued the American Broadcasting Company for slander (against one of their radio programs). ABC paid Synanon $1.25 million to drop its suit. See Nanette Asimov, "Life after Synanon for Radio Veteran Dan Sorkin," *San Francisco Chronicle*, 1 May 1990.

3. William F. Olin, *Escape from Utopia: My Ten Years in Synanon* (Santa Cruz, Calif.: Unity Press, 1980), 209–11.

4. Gerstel, *Paradise*, 185.

5. Olin, *Escape from Utopia*, 247.

6. Gerstel, *Paradise*, 211. "Jean" is based on a woman who was five months pregnant at the time of Dederich's pronouncement and who submitted to an abortion.

7. Gerstel, *Paradise*, 216–24.

8. Some states sent offenders to Synanon as an alternative to state-run correctional facilities.

9. In a recording made from "the Wire," which later became key evidence in the critical case against Synanon, Dederich declared these and other violent intentions. See Gerstel, *Paradise*, 268.

10. Gerstel, *Paradise*, 244.

11. A few "deadbeats" who had voiced criticisms of Dederich's "emotional surgery" were forced into the Mojave Desert to load rocks into wheelbarrows under the scorching sun. At night they huddled together in a tent, trying to stave off hypothermia. Fortunately, after only nine days of this, an heiress who was putting much of her wealth into Synanon visited the camp and objected to the conditions. The workday was shortened, decent quarters were built, and the fact that it was still a forced-labor camp was muted. See Gerstel, *Paradise*, 236–37.

12. "Kenton Son Sought in Snake-Bite of Anti-Synanon Lawyer," *Washington Post*, 13 October 1978.

CHAPTER 17
SYNANON AND SIN

1. Glenn Tinder, *Political Thinking: The Perennial Questions* (New York: HarperCollins, 1995), 199.

2. Ralph Waldo Emerson, as quoted in Roger Lundin, *The Culture of Interpretation: Christian Faith and the Postmodern World* (Grand Rapids: Eerdmans, 1993), 111.

3. Glenn Tinder, "Birth of a Troubled Conscience," *Christianity Today* (April 26, 1999): 37.

4. Karl Menninger, *Whatever Became of Sin?* (New York: Hawthorn Books, 1973).

5. Jean-Jacques Rousseau, *The Social Contract* (Boston: Charles E. Tuttle, Everyman's Classic Library, 1993), 181.

6. Jean-Jacques Rousseau, as quoted in Robert Nisbet, *The Quest for Community: A Study in the Ethics of Order and Freedom* (San Francisco: ICS Press, 1990), 127. As Nisbet explains, Rousseau felt that "the State is the means by which the individual can be freed of the restrictive tyrannies that compose society" (*The Quest for Community*, 128).

7. Tinder, *Political Thinking*, 200.

8. Nisbet, *The Quest for Community*, 127.

9. Historian Glenn Tinder puts it well: "Political leaders claim that power that the Old Testament attributes to God alone—that of erasing and avenging all injustice and of guiding humanity to its destined fulfillment" (Tinder, *Political Thinking*, 201).

10. Rousseau, *The Social Contract*, 275.

11. Ibid., 195.

12. Friedrich Nietzsche, *The Birth of Tragedy* and the *Genealogy of Morals*, trans. Francis Golffing (New York: Doubleday, 1956), 277–78.

13. Edward T. Oakes, "Original Sin: A Disputation," *First Things* (November 1998): 16.

14. Paul Johnson, *Intellectuals* (New York: Harper & Row, 1988), 22–23.

15. Jean-Jacques Rousseau, *Confessions*, vol. 1 (New York: Dutton, 1904), 314.

16. Ibid., 316.

17. Rousseau, as quoted in Paul Johnson, *Intellectuals*, 22.

18. Will Durant and Ariel Durant, *Rousseau and Revolution: A History of Civilization in France, England, and Germany from 1756, and in the Remainder of Europe from 1715 to 1789*, vol. 10 of *The Story of Civilization* (New York: Simon & Schuster, 1967), 886.

CHAPTER 18
WE'RE ALL UTOPIANS NOW

1. Alexis de Tocqueville, *Democracy in America*, trans. George Lawrence, Great Books of the Western World, ed. Mortimer Adler (Chicago: Encyclopedia Britannica, 1991), 374–77.

2. Nancy R. Pearcey and Charles B. Thaxton, *The Soul of Science: Christian Faith and Natural Philosophy* (Wheaton, Ill.: Crossway, 1994), 71–73.

3. The following discussion about Freud, Fechner, and Pavlov is based on "Evolution and the Humanities," a presentation made by Willem J. Ouweneel at the National Creation Conference, August 1985. See also Nancy R. Pearcey, "Sensible Psychology: How Creation Makes the Difference," *Bible-Science Newsletter* (February 1996): 7.

4. B. F. Skinner, *Walden Two* (New York: Macmillan, 1976).

5. J. B. Watson, *The Way of Behaviorism* (New York: Harper, 1928), 35ff.

6. John B. Watson, *Behaviorism* (New York: The People's Institute, 1924), 248. American philosopher and educator John Dewey used even stronger utopian language, heralding the teacher as "the prophet of the true God and the

usherer in of the true kingdom of God" (John Dewey, *My Pedagogic Creed* [Washington, D.C.: The Progressive Education Association, 1929], 17).

7. Dean Koontz, as quoted in Nick Gillespie and Lisa Snell, "Contemplating Evil: Novelist Dean Koontz on Freud, Fraud, and the Great Society," *Reason* 28, no. 6 (November 1996): 44.

8. Mike Swift, "Raising Hopes by Razing Housing," *Hartford Courant*, 19 March 1995.

9. Ramsey Clark, *Crime in America: Observations on Its Nature, Causes, Prevention, and Control* (New York: Simon & Schuster, 1970), 17–18.

10. Clarence Darrow, *Attorney for the Damned*, ed. Arthur Weinberg (New York: Simon & Schuster, 1957), 3–4.

11. Myron Magnet, *The Dream and the Nightmare: The Sixties' Legacy to the Underclass* (New York: William Morrow, 1993), 197–98. Moreover, evidence from social science shows this approach to be wrong. In the 1950s, Samuel Yochelson, a psychiatrist, and Stanton Samenow, a psychologist, set out to prove the conventional wisdom that crime is caused by such environmental forces as poverty and racism. But at the end of their seventeen-year study, they concluded that crime cannot be traced to social or economic causes. Instead, in every case the criminal act "was the product of deliberation." In short, the person "made choices." In their book *The Criminal Personality* they say that the answer to crime and the criminal personality is a "conversion to a whole new [responsible] lifestyle" (Samuel Yochelson and Stanton E. Samenow, *The Criminal Personality: A Profile for Change*, vol. 1 [New York: Jason Aronson, 1982], 19–20, 36).

12. John Leo, "The It's-Not-My-Fault Syndrome," *U.S. News and World Report* 108, no. 24 (June 18, 1990): 16.

13. George Flynn, "Woman Sues Houston Nightclub over Hot-Dog Eating Contest," *Houston Chronicle*, 25 March 1997. Victoria Franks Rios dropped her suit against the nightclub in December 1997. See George Flynn, "Woman Drops Her Lawsuit over Hot-Dog Eating Event," *Houston Chronicle*, 23 December 1997.

14. C. S. Lewis, "The Humanitarian Theory of Punishment," *God in the Dock* (Grand Rapids: Eerdmans, 1970), 292.

15. Ibid.

CHAPTER 19
THE FACE OF EVIL

1. Tammy Busche, "Parents Question Security in Wake of Student Arrests in Shooting Plot," *St. Louis Post-Dispatch*, 28 May 98.

2. "Police Seek Onlookers Who Cheered Killer," *Naples Daily News*, 15 August 1993.

3. Ed Hayward, "Second Teen Suspect to Be Tried," *Boston Herald*, 25 September 1994.

4. Karl Vick, "Delaware Seeks Death Penalty against Teens in Infant's Death," *Washington Post*, 19 November 1996.

5. Arianna Huffington, "Amy and Brian's Shameful Excuse Factory," *New York Post*, 14 July 1998.

6. Ron Rosenbaum, "Staring into the Heart of the Heart of Darkness," *New York Times Magazine* (June 4, 1995): 36.

7. *The New England Primer* (Hartford, Conn.: John Babcock, 1800).

8. Benjamin Spock, as quoted in Dana Mack, *The Assault on Parenthood: How Our Culture Undermines the Family* (New York: Simon & Schuster, 1997), 33.

9. Haim G. Ginott, *Between Parent and Child: New Solutions to Old Problems* (New York: Macmillan, 1965); and Thomas Gordon, *P.E.T., Parent Effectiveness Training: The No-lose Program for Raising Responsible Children* (New York: P. H. Wyden, 1975).

10. For Spock "the 'good' parent was no longer the parent who got his children to behave, but rather the parent who understood why his children might not behave" (Mack, *The Assault on Parenthood*, 33).

11. "Seven Deadly Sins," MTV (August 1993).

12. Alan Bullock, as quoted in Charles Maier, a review of *Hitler and Stalin: Parallel Lives*, by Alan Bullock, *New Republic* (June 15, 1992): 42.

13. Thomas Harris, *The Silence of the Lambs* (New York: St. Martin's Press, 1988), 19 (emphasis in the original).

14. Bruno Bettelheim, *The Uses of Enchantment: The Meaning and Importance of Fairy Tales* (New York: Alfred A. Knopf, 1977).

15. Susan Wise Bauer, "Stephen King's Tragic Kingdom," *Books & Culture* (March/April 1997): 14.

16. Nick Gillespie and Lisa Snell, "Contemplating Evil: Novelist Dean Koontz on Freud, Fraud, and the Great Society," *Reason* 28, no. 6 (November 1996): 44.

CHAPTER 20
A SNAKE IN THE GARDEN

1. Personal conversation with Nancy Pearcey (May 22, 1997).

2. Such a philosophy was held by an ancient Persian religion called Manichaeism, which taught that good and evil are both eternal principles, locked in an eternal conflict in which neither would ever triumph.

3. See Job 1 and 2, for example, as well as Job 31:35. Beginning in the New Testament, Satan is referred to as "the devil."

4. Francis A. Schaeffer, *Genesis in Space and Time* (Downers Grove, Ill.: InterVarsity Press, 1972), 80–83.

5. C. S. Lewis, *The Discarded Image: An Introduction to Medieval and Renaissance Literature* (Cambridge: Cambridge University Press, 1994), 155.

6. Dennis Prager, as quoted in "Religious Right Takes Heat for Salting and Lighting Cultural Debate," *Orlando Sentinel*, 26 August 1995.

7. James Madison, *The Federalist*, no. 48 (February 1, 1788).

CHAPTER 21
DOES SUFFERING MAKE SENSE?

1. While we tell this story about Einstein, Hertzen, McNaughton, and Hartman in a fictionalized dramatic form, it accurately represents Einstein's published views. The key ideas in this story are based on two books: Albert Einstein, *Out of My Later Years: The Scientist, Philosopher, and Man Portrayed through His Own Words* (Princeville, Ore.: Bonanza Books, 1990), 30–33; and Albert Einstein, *The World As I See It*, trans. Alan Harris (New York: Citadel Press, 1995), 24–29.

2. Spinoza was a seventeenth-century philosopher who used the word *God* to refer simply to the principle of order in the universe. See Robert Jastrow, *God and the Astronomers* (New York: Warner Books, 1980), 17.

3. This idea is expressed in Einstein, *Out of My Later Years*, 30–33; and *The World As I See It*, 24–29.

4. Ibid.

5. Ibid.

6. Albert Einstein, *Science, Philosophy, and Religion: A Symposium*, (New York: The Conference on Science, Philosophy, and Religion in Their Relation to the Democratic Way of Life, Inc., 1941).

7. Gerald Holton and Yehuda Elkana, *Albert Einstein: Historical and Cultural Perspectives* (Princeton, N.J.: Princeton University Press, 1982), 209.

8. Albert Einstein, as quoted in Ronald W. Clark, *Einstein: The Life and Times, An Illustrated Biography* (New York: Wings Books, 1995), 19.

9. Einstein, *The World As I See It*, 27–29.

10. Ibid., 24–29.

11. Jastrow, *God and the Astronomers*, 17.

12. Stephen Crane, as quoted in James W. Sire, *The Universe Next Door: A Basic Worldview Catalog*, 3rd ed. (Downers Grove, Ill.: InterVarsity Press, 1997), 13.

13. Glenn Tinder, "Birth of a Troubled Conscience," *Christianity Today* (April 26, 1999): 30.

14. Paul Helm, "Faith and Reason: Stained with the Blood of Suffering," *The Independent*, 23 April 1994.

15. Harold S. Kushner, *When Bad Things Happen to Good People* (New York: Schoken Books, 1981), 42–43.

16. John Hick, *Evil and the God of Love* (London: Collins, 1968).

17. Archibald MacLeish, *J. B.: A Play in Verse* (Boston: Houghton Mifflin, 1958), 126.

18. Fyodor Dostoyevsky, as quoted in Peter Kreeft, *Making Sense out of Suffering* (Ann Arbor, Mich.: Servant, 1986), 8.

19. Ibid., 9.

20. Norman Geisler and Ronald Brooks, *When Skeptics Ask: A Handbook of Christian Evidence* (Wheaton, Ill.: Victor, 1998), chapter 4.

21. *The Martyrdom of the Holy Polycarp*, as cited in Eberhard Arnold, *The Early Christians: After the Death of the Apostles* (Rifton, N.Y.: Plough, 1972), 66.

22. Friedrich Nietzsche, as quoted in Melvin Tinker, *Why Do Bad Things Happen*

to Good People?: A Biblical Look at the Problem of Suffering (Fearn, UK: Christian Focus, 1997), 4.

23. Saint Augustine, *Enchiridon,* 27, as quoted in *The Book of Catholic Quotations,* ed. John Chapin (New York: Farrar, Straus and Cudahy, 1956), 313.

CHAPTER 22
GOOD INTENTIONS

1. This story is a dramatic reconstruction based on a true event. Dr. Nathanson did abort one of his own children, and in our interview with him he described his attitude throughout as cold and clinical. In *The Hand of God* he writes: "The procedure went on without incident, and I felt a fleeting gratification that I had done my usual briskly efficient job and left the operating room while she was still struggling up from general anesthesia. Yes, you may ask me: That was a concise terse report of what you *did,* but what did you feel? Did you not feel sad—not only because you had extinguished the life of an unborn child, but, more, because you had destroyed your *own* child? I swear to you that I had no feelings aside from the sense of accomplishment, the pride of expertise. On inspecting the contents of the bag, I felt only the satisfaction of knowing that I had done a thorough job. You pursue me: You ask if perhaps for a fleeting moment or so I experienced a flicker of regret, a microgram of remorse? No and no. And that, dear reader, is the mentality of the abortionist: another job well done, another demonstration of the moral neutrality of advanced technology in the hands of the amoral" (Bernard N. Nathanson, *The Hand of God: A Journey from Death to Life by the Abortion Doctor Who Changed His Mind* [Washington, D.C.: Regnery, 1996], 58–61 [emphasis in the original]).

2. This ultrasound scene is a composite of many experiences Dr. Nathanson had with ultrasound scans. While this is an accurate description of the impact of that first ultrasound on Nathanson, it also incorporates recent technology. Nathanson would not have been able to see quite this much with the first ultrasound machines.

3. Bernard N. Nathanson, "Sounding Board, Deeper into Abortion," *New England Journal of Medicine* 291, no. 22 (November 28, 1974): 1188–90.

4. The colleague who performed the procedures that day later saw the tapes and vowed he would never again do another abortion.

5. *The Silent Scream* can be viewed on-line at http://www.silentscream.org or can be ordered from American Portrait Films, 503 East 200th Street, Cleveland, OH 44119, phone: (216) 531-8600.

6. Bernard N. Nathanson, *Why I'm Still Catholic,* ed. Kevin and Marilyn Ryan (New York: Riverhead Books, 1998), 281.

7. Augustine, *Confessions* (New York: Penguin, 1961), 151, 170.

8. Nathanson, *The Hand of God,* 187–88, 195–96.

9. Ibid., 193.

10. Nathanson, *Why I'm Still Catholic,* 282.

CHAPTER 23
IN SEARCH OF REDEMPTION

1. Dorothy L. Sayers, *Creed or Chaos* (Manchester, N.H.: Sophia Institute Press, 1974), chapter 3.
2. James B. Twitchell, *Adcult U.S.A.: The Triumph of Advertising in American Culture* (New York: Columbia University Press, 1996), 38.
3. Ibid.
4. Ibid., 45.
5. Jennifer Harrison, "Advertising Joins the Journey of the Soul," *American Demographics* (June 1997): 22.
6. John Updike, as quoted in Twitchell, *Adcult U.S.A.*, vii.
7. Calvin Coolidge, as quoted in Twitchell, *Adcult U.S.A.*, vii.

CHAPTER 24
DOES IT LIBERATE?

1. Mary Midgley, *Evolution as a Religion: Strange Hopes and Stranger Fears* (New York: Methuen, 1985), 30–35. This chapter draws extensively on Nancy R. Pearcey, "Religion of Revolution: Karl Marx's Social Evolution," *Bible-Science Newsletter* (June 1986): 7.
2. Nancy R. Pearcey and Charles B. Thaton, *The Soul of Science: Christian Faith and Natural Philosophy* (Wheaton, Ill.: Crossway Books, 1994), 107.
3. Vladimir Lenin, as quoted in Francis Nigel Lee, *Communism versus Creation* (Nutley, N.J.: Craig Press, 1969), 28.
4. Robert Wesson, *Why Marxism? The Continuing Success of a Failed Theory* (New York: Basic Books, 1976), 30.
5. Throughout their lives, Marx and his colleague Frederick Engels looked expectantly for the *Dies Irae,* as they themselves called it, when the mighty would be cast down. The *Dies Irae* (literally "day of wrath") is a medieval Latin hymn about the Day of Judgment and is sung in requiem masses.
6. Klaus Bockmuehl, *The Challenge of Marxism* (Leicester, England: InterVarsity Press, 1980), 17.
7. Modern historians do not accept Marx's stages of social and economic evolution—from primitive communism to slavery to serfdom to capitalism to communism.
8. Paul Johnson, *Intellectuals,* (New York: Harper & Row, 1988), 53, 56.
9. Karl Marx and Frederick Engels, "Private Property and Communism," in *Collected Works,* vol. 3 (New York: International Publishers, 1975), 304 (emphasis in the original).
10. Ibid.
11. Karl Marx, as quoted in Thomas Sowell, *Marxism* (New York: William Morrow, 1985), 166.
12. Bernard-Henri Levi, as quoted in Ronald Nash, *Social Justice and the Christian Church* (Milford, Mich.: Mott Media, 1983), 102.

CHAPTER 25
SALVATION THROUGH SEX?

1. Madison Jones, *An Exile* (Savannah, Ga.: Frederic C. Beil, 1990), 56.
2. Margaret Sanger, *The Pivot of Civilization* (New York: Brentanos, 1922), 238–39. This section draws heavily on Nancy R. Pearcey, "Creating the 'New Man': The Hidden Agenda in Sex Education," *Bible-Science Newsletter* (May 1990): 6.
3. Ibid., 232.
4. Ibid.
5. Ibid., 233.
6. Ibid., 270–71.
7. Alfred C. Kinsey, *Sexual Behavior in the Human Male* (Philadelphia: W. B. Saunders, 1948); and Alfred C. Kinsey, *Sexual Behavior in the Human Female* (Bloomington, Ind.: Indiana University Press, 1998).
8. Kinsey, *Sexual Behavior in the Human Male*, 59.
9. Alan Wolf, review of *Alfred C. Kinsey: A Public/Private Life*, by James H. Jones, *New Republic* 217, no. 21 (November 24, 1997): 31.
10. Paul Robinson, *The Modernization of Sex* (New York: Cornell University Press, 1988), 83–86.
11. Wilhelm Reich, as quoted in Eustace Chesser, *Salvation through Sex: The Life and Work of Wilhelm Reich* (New York: William Morrow, 1973), 44.
12. Wilhelm Reich, *Ether, God and Devil: Cosmic Superimposition* (New York: Farrar, Straus and Giroux, 1973), 9.
13. Chesser, *Salvation through Sex*, 67.
14. Robert Rimmer, *The Harrad Experiment* (Amherst, N.Y.: Prometheus Books, 1990), 13, 46, 145.
15. Ibid., 157, 167.
16. Ibid., 264.
17. Mary Calderone, "Sex Education and the Roles of School and Church," *The Annals of the American Academy of Political and Social Sciences* 376 (March 1968): 57.
18. Mary S. Calderone and Eric W. Johnson, *The Family Book about Sexuality* (New York: Harper & Row, 1981), 171.
19. Calderone, "Sex Education," 59.
20. Madeline Gray, *Margaret Sanger: A Biography of the Champion of Birth Control* (New York: Richard Marek, 1979), 416–18.
21. James H. Jones, "Annals of Sexology," *New Yorker* (August 25, 1997): 98.
22. Judith A. Reisman and Edward W. Eichel, *Kinsey, Sex, and Fraud: The Indoctrination of a People* (Lafayette, La.: Huntington House, 1990), 29–30.
23. Chesser, *Salvation through Sex*, 71.

CHAPTER 26
IS SCIENCE OUR SAVIOR?

1. *Independence Day*, Twentieth Century Fox (1996).
2. *War of the Worlds*, Paramount Pictures (1953).

 3. Daniel Quinn, *Ishmael* (New York: Bantam Books, 1992).
 4. Francis Bacon, as quoted in John Herman Randall, *The Making of the Modern Mind* (New York: Columbia University Press, 1976), 204.
 5. See Auguste Comte, *Religion of Humanity: The Positivist Calendar of Auguste Comte, and other Tables* (London: The London Positivist Society, 1929); and Auguste Comte, *The Religion of Humanity: Love, Order, Progress, Live for Others, Live Openly* (Liverpool, England: Church of Humanity, 1907). See also T. R. Wright, *The Religion of Humanity: The Impact of Comtean Positivism on Victorian Britain* (Cambridge: Cambridge University Press, 1986).
 6. Mary Midgley, *Evolution as a Religion: Strange Hopes and Stranger Fears* (New York: Nethuen and Co., 1985), 34. Ironically, Darwin himself admitted that he could see "no innate tendency to progressive development."
 7. Ian Barbour, *Issues in Science and Religion* (New York: Harper Torchbooks, 1966), 94.
 8. J. D. Bernal, as quoted in Mary Midgley, *Evolution as a Religion*, 35.
 9. H. J. Muller, as quoted in Mary Midgley, *Evolution as a Religion*, 34.
10. Francis Crick, *Life Itself, Its Origin and Nature* (New York: Simon & Schuster, 1981), 118.
11. Oliver O'Donovan, *Begotten or Made?* (London: Oxford University Press, 1984).
12. Beyond this, when you consider that the supposed evolutionary process requires several million years to accomplish even minor changes, the idea that we can predict anything at all about the end result is preposterous. This is utter pie-in-the-sky, blind faith.
13. Stephen Hawking, *A Brief History in Time* (New York: Bantam Books, 1988).
14. Frank Drake, interviewed by Bob Arnold in "Frank Drake Assesses the NASA Search," *SETI News* (first quarter, 1993).
15. Carl Sagan, *Broca's Brain* (New York: Random, 1979), 276.
16. Ibid.
17. Cited in Terence Dickinson, "Critics Scoff but Cool ET Hunt Carries On," *Toronto Star*, 24 August 1997.
18. Sagan, *Broca's Brain*, 276.

CHAPTER 27
THE DRAMA OF DESPAIR

 1. Steven Weinberg, *The First Three Minutes: A Modern View of the Origin of the Universe* (London: André Deutsch, 1977), 155.
 2. Ibid., 1–2.
 3. Jean-Paul Sartre, *No Exit and Three Other Plays* (New York: Random, 1949).
 4. Albert Camus, *The Myth of Sisyphus and Other Essays* (New York: Alfred A. Knopf, 1955).
 5. Lord Balfour, as quoted in John Herman Randall, *The Making of the Modern Mind* (New York: Columbia University Press, 1940), 581–82.
 6. Randall, *The Making of the Modern Mind*, 581–82 (emphasis added).
 7. Bertrand Russell, as quoted in Randall, *The Making of the Modern Mind*, 582.

8. Jacques Monod, *Chance and Necessity,* trans. Austryn Wainhouse (London: Fontana, 1974), 160.

9. Michael T. Ghiselin, *The Economy of Nature and the Evolution of Sex* (Berkeley, Calif.: University of California Press, 1974), 247.

10. Mark Ridley, *The Origins of Virtue: Human Instincts and the Revolution of Cooperation* (New York: Viking, 1996).

11. Ibid.

12. Richard Dawkins, *The Selfish Gene* (London: Oxford University Press, 1976), 2–3.

13. Edward O. Wilson, *Sociobiology: The New Synthesis* (Cambridge, Mass.: Harvard University Press, 1975), 3.

14. Dawkins, *The Selfish Gene,* 2–3.

15. Ibid., 2, 64 (emphasis added).

16. Mary Midgley, *Evolution as a Religion: Strange Hopes and Stranger Fears,* (New York: Nethuen and Co., 1985), 131, 140. See also Nancy R. Pearcey, "What Do You Mean: 'Evolution Is a Religion'?" *Bible-Science Newsletter* (April 1988): 7.

17. Edward O. Wilson, as quoted in Howard L. Kaye, *The Social Meaning of Modern Biology* (New Haven: Yale University Press, 1986), 169–79.

18. Ibid.

19. Brendan I. Koerner, "Extreeeme," *U.S. News and World Report* (June 30, 1997): 50.

20. Kristen Ulmer, as quoted in Koerner, "Extreeeme," 50.

21. "NBC Nightly News" (June 19, 1998).

22. "Hero of the Code," *Time* (July 14, 1961): 87.

23. See chapter 2 in Colson's *Kingdoms in Conflict* (New York: William Morrow; Grand Rapids: Zondervan, 1987).

24. Saint Augustine, *Confessions,* book 1, paragraph 1, trans. R. S. Pine-Coffin (New York: Penguin, 1961), 21.

CHAPTER 28
THAT NEW AGE RELIGION

1. R. Ascher-Walsch, et al., "October," *Entertainment Weekly* (August 22, 1997).

2. K. K. Campbell, "Getting Your Kicks on the Net," *Toronto Star,* 29 May 1997.

3. *Hair* opened off Broadway in 1967, then made its Broadway debut in 1968.

4. Ken Wilber, as quoted in Robert Burrows, "New Age Movement: Self-Deification in a Secular Culture," *Spiritual Counterfeit Project Newsletter* 10 (winter 1984–1985).

5. John Herman Randall, *The Making of the Modern Mind* (New York: Columbia University Press, 1976), 419.

6. Alfred, Lord Tennyson, *In Memoriam,* LV–LVI.

7. For a discussion of these ideas, see Randall, *The Making of the Modern Mind* and Ian Barbour, *Issues in Science and Religion* (New York: Harper Torchbooks, 1966).

8. Robert Lindsey, "Spiritual Concepts Drawing a Different Breed of Adherent," *New York Times,* 29 September 1986.

9. Martha M. Hamilton and Frank Swoboda, "Mantra for a Company Man: New Age Approaches Increasingly Popular in Management Training," *Washington Post,* 30 June 1996.

10. For example, yoga is sold as a means of relaxation or physical exercise. Yet the word *yoga* literally means "yoke," and the actual purpose of the exercise is to yoke, merge, or unite the individual spirit with the Cosmic Spirit.

11. Jill Anderson, *PUMSY in Pursuit of Excellence* (Eugene, Ore.: Timberline Press, 1987).

12. Ibid.

13. Deborah Rozman writes in *Meditating with Children:* "Meditation takes us back to the Source of all Life. We become one with ALL." What PUMSY teaches coyly, Rozman teaches openly: that we all are God, that salvation consists in realizing our divine nature. She even encourages children to apply biblical phrases to themselves, such as "I and my Father are one," "Before Abraham was, I am," and "I am that I am." Deborah Rozman, *Meditating with Children: The Art of Concentration and Centering* (Boulder Creek, Calif.: Planetary Publishing, 1994), 143.

14. James Redfield, *The Tenth Insight: Holding the Vision* (New York: Warner Books, 1996). The same views were expressed in Redfield's earlier best-seller, *The Celestine Prophecy: An Adventure* (New York: Warner Books, 1993), in which God is described as a "universal energy source" or the "Higher Will."

15. Frances Hodgson Burnett, *The Secret Garden* (New York: Dell, 1987), 230.

16. Ibid., 233.

17. Ibid., 230.

18. Ibid., 229.

19. Ibid., 233.

20. See also chapter 37, "Creating the Good Society."

21. Peter Kreeft, *Fundamentals of the Faith: Essays in Christian Apologetics* (San Francisco: Ignatius Press, 1988), 90.

22. *Spiritual Counterfeit Project Newsletter* 10 (winter 1984–85).

23. Shirley MacLaine's television miniseries *Out on a Limb,* which aired in 1987, was based on her book *Out on a Limb* (New York: Bantam Books, 1983).

24. C. S. Lewis, *Miracles: A Preliminary Study* (London: Fount, 1974), 86–87.

25. Jennifer Caternini, "Feminists Still 'Re-Imagining' God," *Faith and Freedom* 16 (fall 1996): 6.

26. Kreeft, *Fundamentals of the Faith,* 93.

CHAPTER 29
REAL REDEMPTION

1. Ronald Knox, as quoted in Peter Kreeft, *Fundamentals of the Faith: Essays in Christian Apologetics* (San Francisco: Ignatius Press, 1988), 74.

2. While it is difficult to pinpoint the exact date of Christ's crucifixion, most

biblical scholars agree that it is either A.D. 30 or A.D. 29. For information about the dating of Jesus' birth, see William Hendriksen, *The Gospel of Luke* (Grand Rapids: Baker, 1993), 139–41.

3. For a fuller explanation of this argument, referring to the Watergate cover-up, see Colson, "Watergate and the Resurrection," chapter 6 in *Loving God* (Grand Rapids: Zondervan, 1983).

4. Mahatma Gandhi, "Address on Christmas Day, 1931," as quoted in A. R. Vidler, *Objections to Christian Belief* (London: Constable, 1963), 59.

5. J. Gresham Machen, *Christianity and Liberalism* (New York: Macmillan, 1923), 121.

6. William F. Albright, as quoted in Norman L. Geisler, "Toward a More Conservative View," *Baker Encyclopedia of Christian Apologetics* (Grand Rapids: Baker, 1999), 529.

7. Paul Johnson, "A Historian Looks at Jesus," (a speech first presented at Dallas Theological Seminary in 1986), *Sources,* no. 1 (1991).

8. Joseph P. Free, "Archaeology and Biblical Criticism," *Bibliotheca Sacra* (January 1957): 23. See also Joseph P. Free, *Archaeology and Bible History* (Grand Rapids: Zondervan, 1992).

9. Charles R. Pellegrino, *Return to Sodom and Gomorrah: Bible Stories from Archaeologists* (New York: Random, 1994).

10. John Noble Wilford, "From Israeli Site, News of House of David," *New York Times,* 6 August 1993.

11. Johnson, "A Historian Looks at Jesus," *Sources,* no. 1 (1991).

12. C. S. Lewis, *God in the Dock: Essays on Theology and Ethics* (Grand Rapids: Eerdmans, 1970), 58.

13. Ibid., 67.

14. Al Wolters, *Creation Regained: Biblical Basics for a Reformational Worldview* (Grand Rapids: Eerdmans, 1985), 58 (emphasis in the original).

CHAPTER 30
THE KNOCKOUT PUNCH

1. While Danny Croce's remarkable story is true, some of the secondary characters in this story are composites or fictional. The story is based on interviews with Danny Croce.

CHAPTER 31
SAVED TO WHAT?

1. After a two-week evangelistic crusade through every prison in North Carolina, disciplinary violations dropped precipitously, and most wardens reported reduced tensions and better inmate behavior. Even months later, Bible studies were crowded, and lives continued to be changed. In New York state prisons, recidivism (the rate at which released prisoners return to prison)

was dramatically reduced—from an average of 41 percent to 14 percent— among men who participated in at least ten Prison Fellowship programs a year. See B. R. Johnson, D. B. Larson, and T. C. Pitts, "Religious Programs, Institutional Adjustment, and Recidivism among Former Inmates in Prison Fellowship Programs," *Justice Quarterly* 14, no. 1 (March 1997): 145.

2. Critics sometimes contend that Genesis gives two creation accounts, the second one beginning in Genesis 2:4, but this is a misunderstanding of the literary structure. The first chapter of Genesis and the first few verses of chapter 2 function as a prologue, setting the cosmic stage and raising the curtain. The drama itself actually begins in chapter 2 as Adam and Eve, the first husband and wife, begin societal life. Their tasks of tending the Garden and naming the animals mark the beginning of cultural life. True, the author uses a flashback technique to give more details on how Adam and Eve were created, but that does not make this a second creation story. Instead, this passage relates how the cultural mandate begins to be fulfilled in actual history.

3. Al Wolters, *Creation Regained: Biblical Basics for a Reformational Worldview* (Grand Rapids: Eerdmans, 1985), 36. The following discussion relies heavily on Wolters, who in turn popularized Dutch philosopher Herman Dooyeweerd. See Dooyeweerd, *A New Critique of Theoretical Thought* (Lewiston, N.Y.: Edwin Mellen Press, 1997).

4. C. S. Lewis, *The Abolition of Man* (New York: Touchstone, 1975).

5. Dutch theologian and statesman Abraham Kuyper developed this argument of the spheres of authority. See Abraham Kuyper, *Christianity: A Total World and Life System* (Marlborough, N.H.: Plymouth Rock Foundation, 1996). One of the most striking passages in Scripture on the God-given character of the order of creation is Isaiah 28:23-29, where we learn that the Lord teaches the farmer his business. There is a right way to plow, to sow, and to thresh, depending on the kind of grain the farmer is growing. A good farmer knows that, and this knowledge is from the Lord, for the Lord teaches him. This is not a teaching from the Scripture, from special revelation, but a teaching through the structures of creation, from general revelation. And it comes to us by experience with soil, seeds, and plow.

6. Al Wolters writes, "It is by listening to the voice of God in the work of his hands that the farmer finds the way of agricultural wisdom" (Wolters, *Creation Regained*, 28). The same is true in economics, politics, the arts, medicine, communications, and education—in every area of society. We learn how to take care of God's creation by familiarizing ourselves with the creational structures and living in tune with them, and we formalize that knowledge in a Christian worldview.

7. See Wolters, *Creation Regained*, chapter 4; and Charles Colson with Ellen Santilli Vaughn, *Kingdoms in Conflict*, (New York: William Morrow; Grand Rapids: Zondervan, 1987), chapter 7.

8. Tertullian, as quoted in Henry Chadwick, *The Early Church* (New York: Penguin, 1993), 65.

9. Justin Martyr, as quoted in Chadwick, *The Early Church*, 74–83.

10. This dramatic story is told in Christopher Dawson's *Religion and the Rise of*

Western Culture (New York: Doubleday, Image Books, 1991) and Thomas Cahill's *How the Irish Saved Civilization: The Untold Story of Ireland's Heroic Role from the Fall of Rome to the Rise of Medieval Europe* (New York: Doubleday, 1995).

11. Saint Patrick, as quoted in Thomas Cahill, *How the Irish Saved Civilization,* 102.

12. Cahill, *How the Irish Saved Civilization,* 105.

13. Kenneth Clark, *Civilisation: A Personal View* (New York: Harper & Row, 1969), 8.

14. John Henry Newman, as quoted in Christopher Dawson, *Religion and the Rise of Western Culture,* 53–54. Newman goes on to explain how the monks accomplished all this: "Silent men were observed about the country, or discovered in the forest, digging, clearing, and building; and other silent men, not seen, were sitting in the cold cloister, tiring their eyes and keeping their attention on the stretch, while they painfully copied and recopied the manuscripts which they had saved."

15. Dawson, *Religion and the Rise of Western Culture,* 126.

16. An eyewitness account describes the transformation of Scandinavian culture in these words: "But after their acceptance of Christianity, they have become imbued with better principles and have now learned to love peace and truth and to be content with their poverty. . . . Of all men they are the most temperate both in food and in their habits, loving above all things thrift and modesty" (Dawson, *Religion and the Rise of Western Culture,* 98).

17. Pope John Paul II, *Redemptoris Missio,* Encyclical Letter on the Permanent Validity of the Church's Missionary Mandate (December 7, 1990).

18. Timothy George, "Catholics and Evangelicals in the Trenches," *Christianity Today* 38, no. 6 (May 10, 1994): 16.

19. Kuyper, *Christianity,* 69, 110. Kuyper argued strenuously for the kind of cooperation sought in current efforts by Evangelicals and Catholics Together. "Rome is not an antagonist, but stands on our side, in as much as she also recognizes and maintains the Trinity, the Deity of Christ, the Cross as an atoning sacrifice, the Scriptures as the Word of God, and the Ten Commandments as a divinely imposed rule of life" (Kuyper, *Christianity,* 110).

20. Letter from John Calvin to William Farel written from Ratisbon, 11 May 1541. See John Calvin, *Letters of John Calvin,* ed. Jules Bonnet, vol. 1 (Philadelphia: Presbyterian Board of Publication, 1858), 260.

CHAPTER 32
DON'T WORRY, BE RELIGIOUS

1. For example, a 1996 poll showed that 59 percent of Americans were worried about "our country's ethical and moral condition" (James Davison Hunter, *The State of Disunion: 1996 Survey of American Political Culture,* vol. 2 [Ivy, Va.: In Medias Res Educational Foundation, 1996], table 46 F).

2. Berkeley Breathed, "Outland," 17 October 1993.

3. Christopher Jencks, as quoted in William Voegel, "Poverty and the Victim Ploy," *First Things* (November 1991): 37.

4. David Larson, personal interview with Nancy Pearcey (March 1999). We are not denying that government has a role to play in providing a safety net to families in trouble. What is objectionable is the value-free assumption that all family forms are morally equal and that the government's role is to make them equal in all other respects as well.

5. Louis W. Sullivan, "Foundation for Reform," (Washington, D.C.: Department of Health and Human Services, 1991): 15.

6. Judy Mann, "Going Up in Smoke," *Washington Post,* 26 February 1993.

7. See note 3 above.

8. Most of the following studies are based on the objective measure of church attendance (with response options ranging from "daily" to "never"). Some studies also ask subjects how important religion is to them (with response options ranging from "very important" to "not important at all"). Some studies were limited to Christians, while others included people of all faiths (though given the demographics of the American population, the majority would identify themselves as Christians).

9. D. B. Larson and W. P. Wilson, "Religious Life of Alcoholics," *Southern Medical Journal* 73, no. 6 (June 1980): 723–27.

10. David B. and Susan S. Larson, *The Forgotten Factor in Physical and Mental Health: What Does the Research Show?* (Rockville, Md.: National Institute for Healthcare Research, 1992), 68–69. The Larsons have collected and/or conducted a host of studies on the impact of religion on mental and physical health.

11. Joseph A. Califano Jr., *Behind Bars: Substance Abuse and America's Prison Population* (New York: The National Center on Addiction and Substance Abuse at Columbia University, 1998), 27.

12. Joseph A. Califano Jr., (speech given at the National Press Club, Washington, D.C., January 8, 1998).

13. Richard R. Freeman and Harry J. Holzer, eds., *The Black Youth Employment Crisis* (Chicago: University of Chicago Press, 1986), 353–76.

14. B. R. Johnson, D. B. Larson, and T. C. Pitts, "Religious Programs, Institutional Adjustment, and Recidivism among Former Inmates in Prison Fellowship Programs," *Justice Quarterly* 14, no. 1 (March 1997): 145–66.

15. Larson and Larson, *The Forgotten Factor,* 76–78.

16. George Gallup Jr., "Religion in America," *Public Perspective* (October/November 1995).

17. Armand Nicholi Jr., "Hope in a Secular Age," *Finding God at Harvard: Spiritual Journeys of Thinking Christians,* ed. Kelly K. Monroe (Grand Rapids: Zondervan, 1996), 117.

18. Larson and Larson, *The Forgotten Factor,* 64–65.

19. Ibid., 72.

20. Howard M. Bahr and Bruce A. Chadwick, "Religion and Family in Middletown, USA," *Journal of Marriage and the Family* 47 (May 1985): 407–14.

21. See N. Stinnet, et al., "A Nationwide Study of Families Who Perceive Themselves as Strong"; and Velma McBride Murry, "Incidence of First Pregnancy among Black Adolescent Females over Three Decades." Both studies are quoted in Patrick Fagan, "Why Religion Matters," *The Heritage Foundation Report*, no. 1064 (January 25, 1996): 8. Fagan's excellent report is a collection of studies showing the importance of religion to a healthy society.

22. Both studies are from Larson and Larson, *The Forgotten Factor*, 73.

23. Robert T. Michael, et al., *Sex in America: A Definitive Survey* (New York: Little, Brown & Co., 1994), 127.

24. Larson and Larson, *The Forgotten Factor*, 73–79, 109–23. Bob Condor, "Can Faith Heal?" *Chicago Tribune*, 4 December 1996.

25. Larson and Larson, *The Forgotten Factor*, 110. These findings show a positive association between religious commitment and physical health. This does not appear to be merely a correlation but an actual causal relationship. As Larson and Larson point out, in discussing lower blood pressure among smokers with a high religious commitment: "These findings are striking because the benefits of religion on health are often assumed to be the result of religious motivation for following healthier practices, such as not smoking, avoiding alcohol, and abstaining from harmful dietary practices. In this study, however, it was among the smokers that religious importance made the biggest difference in blood pressure. *Consequently the health benefit of religious commitment was beyond avoiding health-risk behavior*" (116, emphasis in the original). What was the connection then? Larson and Larson quote the authors of the study as saying, "This may reflect a preferentially greater moderating effect for religion on blood pressure among more tense or nervous individuals who may also be more likely to smoke" (116). In short, religious commitment itself appears to be the cause of the health benefits.

26. Patrick Glynn, *God: The Evidence: The Reconciliation of Faith and Reason in a Postsecular World* (Rocklin, Calif.: Prima Publishing, 1997), 67.

27. Guenter Lewy, *Why America Needs Religion: Secular Modernity and Its Discontents* (Grand Rapids: Eerdmans, 1996), 112.

28. Dale A. Matthews with Connie Clark, *The Faith Factor: Proof of the Healing Power of Prayer* (New York: Viking, 1998), 77–80.

29. Herbert Benson, *Timeless Healing* (New York: Scribner, 1996), 197, 208.

30. Larson and Larson, *The Forgotten Factor*, 86.

31. Ibid.

32. David B. Larson, "Physician, Heal Thyself!" *Guideposts* (March 1993): 41–43.

33. Daniel Goleman, "Therapists See Religion As Aid, Not Illusion," *New York Times*, 10 September 1991.

34. Other Christian cost-sharing groups include Samaritan Ministries in Greenfield, Indiana; the Christian Brotherhood Newsletter in Barberton, Ohio; All Saints in Tyler, Texas; and Helping Hands in Oklahoma City, Oklahoma. See Joe Maxwell, "Medical Cost Sharing," *Philanthropy, Culture and Society* (June 1996).

CHAPTER 33
GOD'S TRAINING GROUND

1. David Blankenhorn, "Where's Dad?" *Atlanta Journal and Constitution*, 19 March 1995; and Barbara Dafoe Whitehead, "Dan Quayle Was Right," *Atlantic Monthly* 271, no. 4 (April 1993): 47. We are not criticizing books that genuinely help children of divorce—only those that treat divorce as morally insignificant.
2. See Norval D. Glenn, *Closed Hearts, Closed Minds: The Textbook Story of Marriage* (New York: The Institute for American Values, 1997).
3. Ibid., 5.
4. Candice Bergen, interviewed in "Candy Is Dandy, but Don't Mess with Murphy," *TV Guide* (September 19, 1992): 8.
5. Ibid.
6. See Robert N. Bellah, *Habits of the Heart: Individualism and Commitment in American Life* (Berkeley, Calif.: University of California, 1985).
7. Barbara Bush, (speech given at the Republican National Convention, August 19, 1992).
8. Pierre Manent, "Modern Individualism," *Crisis* (October 1995): 35.
9. Michael Medved, "Hollywood Chic," *Washington Post*, 4 October 1992.
10. John Stuart Mill, *On Liberty* (Indianapolis: Hackett, 1978), 12.
11. Michael J. Sandel, *Democracy's Discontent: America in Search of a Public Philosophy* (Cambridge, Mass.: Belknop Press, 1996), 113.
12. Stanley Greenspan, as quoted in Don Feder, "Day-Care Study Defies Common Sense," *Boston Herald*, 8 March 1999. For a history of women and the family, see Nancy R. Pearcey, "Is Love Enough?: Recreating the Economic Base of the Family," *The Family in America* 4, 1 (January 1990): 1.
13. Steven Mintz and Susan Kellogg, *Domestic Revolutions: A Social History of American Family Life* (New York: Free Press, 1988), 117. For a discussion of these historical trends and a definition of masculinity and fatherhood, see Nancy R. Pearcey, "Rediscovering Parenthood in the Information Age," *The Family in America* 8, no. 3 (March 1994).
14. Cited in Barbara Ehrenreich, *The Hearts of Men: American Dreams and the Flight from Commitment* (New York: Doubleday, 1983), 47. See also Pearcey, "Rediscovering Parenthood in the Information Age."
15. David Blankenhorn, *Fatherless America: Confronting Our Most Urgent Social Problem* (New York: HarperPerennial, 1996).
16. Shere Hite, "The Case against Family Values," *Washington Post*, 10 July 1994.
17. Elayne Bennett, "If She's Facing Adolescent Girls Today," (lecture given at the Heritage Foundation, February 1995).
18. A recent Hawaii Supreme Court decision permitting gay "marriage" is often portrayed as simply opening up traditional marriage to gays. Rather than broaden traditional marriage, however, the decision denies the existence of traditional marriage altogether by redefining "marriage" purely in terms of legally protected economic benefits, leading to the logical conclusion that these benefits ought to be available to any and all people, regardless of gender or sexuality. In the same way, the legal definition of the family has been so

watered down that it no longer bears any resemblance to traditional notions, as when a New Jersey judge said that six college kids on summer vacation constituted a family. See Gerard Bradley, "The New Constitutional Covenant," *World & I* (March 1994): 374.

19. Bonnie Angelo and Toni Morrison, "The Pain of Being Black," *Time* (May 22, 1989), 120.

20. As quoted in William R. Mattox, "Split Personality: Why Aren't Conservatives Talking about Divorce?" *Policy Review*, no. 73 (summer 1995): 50.

21. Ibid.

22. Whitehead, "Dan Quayle Was Right," 47.

23. Michael McManus, "Voters Should Care about Divorce Reform," *Detroit News*, 19 September 1996.

24. David Popenoe, *Life without Fathers: Compelling New Evidence That Fatherhood and Marriage Are Indispensable for the Good of Children and Society* (New York: Free Press, 1996), 63.

25. Whitehead, "Dan Quayle Was Right," 47.

26. Judith S. Wallerstein and Sandra Blakeslee, *Second Chances: Men, Women, and Children a Decade after Divorce* (New York: Ticknor & Fields, 1989), 21–31.

27. James J. Lynch, *The Broken Heart: The Medical Consequences of Loneliness in America* (New York: Basic Books, 1977), 69–86, 87–90, 41–50, appendix B.

28. David Larson, as quoted in Mattox, "Split Personality," 50.

29. Allan Carlson is president of the Howard Center for the Family, Religion, and Society, which analyzes the status of the family today and disseminates research that empirically validates marriage as the foundation to a healthy society. These findings are published in *The Family in America*, available from the Howard Center for the Family, Religion, and Society, 934 North Main Street, Rockford, IL 61103, phone: (815) 964-5819.

30. Karl Zinsmeister, "The Humble Generation," *American Enterprise* 9, no. 1 (January/February 1998): 4.

31. Elisabeth D. Dodds, *Marriage to a Difficult Man: The "Uncommon Union" of Jonathan and Sarah Edwards* (Philadelphia: Westminster Press, 1971), chapter 14.

32. See Michael J. McManus, *Marriage Savers: Helping Your Friends and Family Avoid Divorce* (Grand Rapids: Zondervan, 1995).

33. "The National Survey of Family Growth," as cited in McManus, *Marriage Savers,* 93. A number of good programs are available to help churches teach strategies for abstinence. For more information, write or call True Love Waits, 127 Ninth Avenue North, Nashville, TN 37234, phone: (800) LUV-WAIT or (800) 588-9248. See also Josh McDowell, *Why Wait? What You Need to Know about the Teen Sexuality Crisis* (Nashville: Nelson, 1994); and Josh McDowell, *Why Say No to Sex?: The Case for Teaching Sexual Abstinence outside Marriage* (Eastbourne, England: Kingsway, 1995).

34. "The National Survey of Families and Households," as cited in McManus, *Marriage Savers,* 39.

35. PREPARE, P.O. Box 190, Minneapolis, MN 55440-0190.

36. ENRICH, P.O. Box 190, Minneapolis, MN 55440-0190.

37. Retrouvaille, 231 Ballantine, Houston, TX 77015, phone: (713) 455-1656.

38. See http://www.marriagesavers.org/fourchurches.htm, (March 10, 1999).

39. Roger Sider, "Grand Rapids Erects a Civic Tent for Marriage," *Policy Review* (July/August 1998): 6.

40. James Sheridan, as quoted in Michael J. McManus, "Judge Makes Sure Couples Are Prepared for Marriage," *Fresno Bee,* 12 April 1997. In Chattanooga Tennessee, a broad cross section of civic leaders formed a community-wide organization called First Things First in order to rebuild, renew, and revitalize the city. Chattanooga's divorce rate is 50 percent higher than the national average, so First Things First quickly started working on the problem of divorce. Within just one year, Hamilton County saw a 14 percent drop in divorce filings. Other initiatives include a Fathering Summit to help teach the importance of fathers, and a program called Reading, Writing, and Responsibility, where community leaders and school personnel teach students nine shared values: respect, responsibility, perseverance, caring, self-discipline, citizenship, honesty, courage, and fairness. 41. Mel Krantzler, *Creative Divorce* (New York: M. Evans, 1973); and Esther Oshiver Fisher, *Divorce: The New Freedom* (New York: Harper & Row, 1974).

42. Diane Medved, *The Case against Divorce* (New York: Ivy Books, 1990); Michele Weiner-Davis, *Divorce Busting: A Revolutionary and Rapid Program for Staying Together* (New York: Simon & Schuster, 1993); and William A. Galston, *Rethinking Divorce* (Minneapolis: Center for the American Experiment, 1996).

CHAPTER 34
STILL AT RISK

1. Third International Math and Science Study, conducted by the National Center for Education Statistics, Michigan State University, Boston College, National Science Foundation, and the International Association for the Evaluation of Educational Achievement (February 24, 1998).

2. Survey conducted by the National Center for Education Statistics (Washington, D.C., 1993). See http://www.nces.ed.gov./timms for further information.

3. Josephson Institute of Ethics, "1998 Report Card on the Ethics of American Youth" (Marina del Ray, Calif.: Josephson Institute of Ethics, 1998).

4. Rita Kramer, "Inside the Teacher's Culture," *Public Interest* (January 1997): 64.

5. John Dewey, *Democracy and Education* (New York: Macmillan, 1992); and John Dewey, *Quest for Certainty* (New York: Putnam, 1929). See also Nancy R. Pearcey, "What is Evolution Doing to Education?" *Bible-Science Newsletter* (January 1986): 6.

6. Catherine T. Fosnot, "Constructivism: A Psychological Theory of Learning," in *Constructivism: Theory, Perspectives, and Practice,* ed. C. Fosnot (New York: Teachers College Press, 1996), 8–13. See also James R. Gavelek and Taffy E. Raphael, "Changing Talk about Text: New Roles for Teachers and Students," *Language Arts,* 73, no. 3 (1996): 182.

7. See Sidney B. Simon, *Beginning Values Clarification: A Guidebook for the Use of*

Values Clarification in the Classroom (San Diego: Pennant Press, 1975); and Sidney B. Simon, Leland W. Howe, and Howard Kirschenbaum, *Values Clarification: A Handbook of Practical Strategies for Teachers and Students,* rev. ed. (Sunderland, Mass.: Values Press, 1978).

8. William Wordsworth, "Ode: Intimations of Immortality from Recollections of Early Childhood."

9. Friedrich Froebel, *The Education of Man* (New York: Appleton, 1891). The section is based on two articles by Nancy R. Pearcey: "The Evolving Child: John Dewey's Impact on Modern Education, part 1," *Bible-Science Newsletter* (January 1991): 5; and "The Evolving Child: John Dewey's Impact on Modern Education, part 2," *Bible-Science Newsletter* (February 1991): 6.

10. Francis Wayland Parker, as quoted in Richard Hofstadter, *Anti-Intellectualism in American Life* (New York: Random, 1963), 366.

11. Perhaps many children in the 1800s, brought up in an environment permeated by a Christian ethos of hard work and moral excellence, *did* blossom when given some freedom for self-direction. Today, when children are brought up in an environment of self-absorption and moral relativism, of course, the result is quite different.

12. J. Crosby Chapman and George S. Counts, *Principles of Education* (Boston: Houghton Mifflin, 1924), 598; and George S. Counts, *Dare the Schools Build a New Social Order?* no. 11 (New York: John Day Pamphlets, 1932).

13. Frederic T. Sommers, "A Campus Forum on Multiculturalism," *New York Times,* 9 December 1990.

14. For the impact of existentialism on education see George R. Knight, *Philosophy and Education: An Introduction in Christian Perspective* (Berrien Springs, Mich.: Andrews University Press, 1980).

15. William R. Coulson, "We Overcame Their Traditions, We Overcame Their Faith," *Latin Mass,* 3, no. 1 (January/February 1991): 14–22. In Carl Rogers's last book, *Freedom to Learn for the Eighties* (Columbus, Ohio: Merrill, 1983), he included a chapter entitled "A Pattern of Failure," in which he describes this and other failures of his educational methods.

16. A. H. Maslow, *The Journal of A. H. Maslow,* ed. Richard J. Lowry, 2 vols. (Monterey, Calif.: Brooks-Cole, 1979).

17. Richard Blum of Stanford University found that students who take drug-education courses actually use alcohol, tobacco, and marijuana in greater amounts and at an earlier age than control groups. See Richard H. Blum, et al., *Drug Education: Results and Recommendations* (Lexington, Mass.: Lexington Books, 1976); and Richard H. Blum, et al., "Drug Education: Further Results and Recommendations," *Journal of Drug Issues* 8, no. 4 (fall 1978): 379–426. A Lou Harris poll commissioned by Planned Parenthood in 1986 found that teens taking sex-education courses reported higher rates of sexual activity than did their peers who had not taken such courses. See Louis Harris and Associates, "The Planned Parenthood Poll," *American Teens Speak—Sex Myths, TV, and Birth Control* (New York: Louis Harris and Associates, 1986).

18. Story told by William Kilpatrick in *Why Johnny Can't Tell Right from Wrong* (New York: Touchstone, 1993), 81.

19. *Witness,* Paramount Pictures (1985). The use of this scene to illustrate the

directive approach to education is from William R. Coulson, "Sex, Drugs, and School Children: What Went Wrong," *Adolescent Counselor* (September 1991): 27–31.

20. John Milton, "Of Education," *Complete Poems and Major Prose,* ed. Merritt Y. Hughes (New York: Macmillan, 1957), 631.

21. For example, in Connecticut in 1996, the Scholastic Assessment Test scores for East Catholic High School were well above the national average: Verbal: East Catholic 545 compared to a national average of 505; Math: East Catholic 517 compared to a national average of 508 ("East Catholic High School's Scholastic Assessment Test Scores," *Hartford Courant,* 6 September 1996). A 1995 study by scholars from the University of Maryland School of Economics revealed that for inner-city children, attending a Catholic high school raises the probability of finishing high school and entering college by 17 percent. Having a Catholic school in the neighborhood is good for public schools, too. Harvard economist Caroline M. Hoxby showed that competition from Catholic schools actually raised the academic performance of surrounding public schools. Both studies cited in Nina Shokraii, "Catholic Schools Hold the Key to the Future for At-Risk Students," *News and Record* (Greensboro, N.C.), 28 September 1997.

22. In 1997, Cornerstone Schools Association students scored far above the national average on the Stanford Achievement Test: Reading: Cornerstone 60 percent compared to the national average of 50 percent; Math: Cornerstone 52 percent compared to the national average of 50 percent; Language: Cornerstone 61 percent compared to the national average of 50 percent.

23. Many of these schools have been inspired by Douglas Wilson's book *Recovering the Lost Tools of Learning: An Approach to Distinctively Christian Education* (Wheaton, Ill.: Crossway, 1991), which pays homage to Dorothy Sayers's seminal essay "The Lost Tools of Learning." See also Gene Edward Veith and Andrew Kern, *Classical Education: Toward the Revival of America's Schooling* (Washington, D.C.: Capitol Research Center, 1997).

24. In March 1999, a report was released by Lawrence M. Rudner, professor at the University of Maryland, who conducted the largest nonpartisan study on homeschooled students. Rudner, whose own children attend public schools, tracked the test results of 21,000 students and was shocked to find that the homeschooled students were substantially ahead of their peers in public school. Homeschoolers perform an average of one grade level above their counterparts in public and private schools in the elementary grades. By the eighth grade, the gap amounts to four grade levels (Philip Walzer, "Home Schooling Passes Test," *Virginia-Pilot,* [24 March 1999]).

25. David A. Noebel, *Understanding the Times: The Story of the Biblical Christian, Marxist/Leninist and Secular Humanist Worldviews* (Manitou Springs, Colo.: Summit Press, 1991); and Summit Ministries, P.O. Box 207, Manitou Springs, CO 80829, phone: (719) 685-9103; fax: (719) 685-5268.

26. The Character Education Partnership, 918 16th Street, NW, Suite 501, Washington, D.C. 20006, phone: (202) 296-7743.

27. Norman Higgins in an interview with Kim Robbins (February 26, 1999);

see also Susan Young, "The Right Direction,"
http://www.bangornews.com/Innovative/day1.html (February 26, 1999).

28. Barbara Moses is now a principal of a Philadelphia inner-city Mennonite high school.

29. Tyce Palmaffy, "No Excuses," *Policy Review* (January/February 1998): 18. Direct Instruction is an alternative to today's popular "constructivist" method of teaching. The constructivist method allows children to be in charge of their learning by experimenting and exploring. The Direct Instruction method puts the teacher in charge of the students' learning. Children are "guided through sequential lessons that provide the foundation for understanding content. Repetition of lessons is frequent to reinforce past learning, and errors are immediately pointed out in verbal recitation." Wesley principal Thaddeus Lott, in commenting on Direct Instruction, says: "We teach them the 'how.' The 'what' and 'why' will come later." He goes on to say that "by giving them the basics, we make it possible for them to do independent work when we turn them loose" (Lott, "Direct Instruction/Constructivist: Models for Learning," *Daily Report Card* [March 1, 1995]).

30. Margaret Bonilla, "Be Fruitful and Multiply," *Policy Review* (summer 1994): 73–76.

31. See Virgil Gulker, *A World without Welfare*, ed. David M. Wagner (Washington, D.C.: Family Research Council, 1997), 107. See also Amy L. Sherman, *Restorers of Hope: Reaching the Poor in Your Community with Church-Based Ministries That Work* (Wheaton, Ill.: Crossway, 1997), 151–54. This doesn't take a lot of specialized knowledge; mostly it takes the kind of love and initiative that Hannah Hawkins offers children in her low-income Anacostia district in Washington, D.C. There, Hawkins, a retired African-American woman, runs an after-school program for several dozen neighborhood children. Every evening they flock to her home, where she oversees their homework. Though simple and homegrown, such programs are helping grades go up and disciplinary incidents decline.

32. Amity Shales, "A Chance to Equip My Child," *Wall Street Journal*, 23 February 1998.

33. Cal Thomas, "Milwaukee's 'School Choice' Experiment Shows That Competition Works," *Wisconsin State Journal*, 13 November 1998.

34. "In Defense of School Vouchers," *The Hill*, 6 May 1998; and Robert Holland, "Free Markets and Technology Will Transform K–12 Education," *Richmond Times Dispatch*, 2 December 1998. There are eight applicants for every scholarship granted, indicating how much low-income families want for their kids the same break that the rich can get. On January 26, 1999, the Arizona Supreme Court upheld a tax credit for people who donate money for scholarships at private schools ("Can You Spare a Million?" *Washington Times*, 18 January 1998).

35. Pope John Paul II, *Fides et Ratio*, Encyclical Letter to the Bishops of the Catholic Church (October 1998).

CHAPTER 35
ANYTHING CAN HAPPEN HERE

1. The details of Officer Salvatore Bartolomeo's story were gleaned through several interviews and through assistance from Eddie Cordelia and John Stewart. Some of the secondary characters in this story are composites of real people Officer Sal knew on his beat. Additional background information about community policing came from articles that include James Q. Wilson and George L. Kelling, "Making Neighborhoods Safe," *Atlantic Monthly* (February 1989): 46–52; Myron Magnet, "Saving the Homeless from Some Bad Ideas," *San Diego Union-Tribune,* 18 February 1990; John Leo, "A New Fight against Urban Decay," *Courier Journal,* 2 February 1992; and William D. Eggers and John O'Leary, "The Beat Generation: Community Policing at Its Best," *Policy Review,* no. 74 (fall 1995): 4.

CHAPTER 36
THERE GOES THE NEIGHBORHOOD

1. Ramsey Clark, the attorney general under Lyndon Johnson, wrote, "The crowding of millions of poor people with their cumulative disadvantage into the urban ghettos of our affluent and technologically advanced society not only offers the easy chance for criminal acts—it causes crime" (Clark, *Crime in America: Observations on Its Nature, Causes, Prevention and Control* [New York: Simon & Schuster, 1970], 29). Similarly, when widespread looting occurred in the late 1970s during a blackout in New York City, then President Jimmy Carter explained it as the result of poverty, though later studies showed that most of those looters were employed and stole things they didn't need.

2. These figures from the Federal Bureau of Investigation; the Bureau of Alcohol, Tobacco, and Firearms; and the National Center for Health Statistics were cited in Ted Gest, Gordon Witkin, Katia Hetter, and Andrea Wright, "Violence in America," *U.S. News and World Report* 116, no. 2 (January 17, 1994): 22.

3. George L. Kelling and Catherine M. Coles, *Fixing Broken Windows: Restoring Order and Reducing Crime in Our Communities* (New York: Free Press, 1996), 55–56.

4. Andrew Peyton Thomas, "The Rise and Fall of the Homeless," *Weekly Standard* 1, no. 29 (April 8, 1996): 27. See also Andrew Peyton Thomas, *Crime and the Sacking of America: The Roots of Chaos* (Washington, D.C.: Brussey's, 1994).

5. To read more about this, see Rael Jean Isaac, *Madness in the Streets: How Psychiatry and the Law Abandoned the Mentally Ill* (New York: Free Press, 1990).

6. James Q. Wilson and George L. Kelling, "Broken Windows," *Atlantic Monthly* (March 1982): 29.

7. John Carlin, "How They Cleaned Up Precinct 75," *The Independent*, 7 January 1996.
8. See Kelling and Coles, *Fixing Broken Windows*, chapter 4.
9. Abraham Kuyper, *Lectures on Calvinism* (Grand Rapids: Eerdmans, 1983), 79.
10. Saint Augustine, *The City of God* (New York: Modern Library, 1950), 690. In the Middle Ages, Thomas Aquinas gave Augustine's insight a more positive interpretation, arguing that the state is not only a remedial institution established to curb sin but that it is also a good thing in itself, an expression of our social nature. Living within social institutions is essential to fulfilling our own nature.
11. William Wilberforce , as quoted in Garth Lean, *God's Politician: William Wilberforce's Struggle* (London: Darton, Longman & Todd, 1980), 74.
12. Robert Peel, as quoted in Fred Siegel, *The Future Once Happened Here: New York, D.C., L.A., and the Fate of America's Big Cities* (New York: Free Press, 1997), 192.
13. Eric Monkkonen, *Police in Urban America: 1860–1920* (Cambridge: Cambridge University Press, 1981), as quoted in Siegel, *The Future Once Happened Here*, 192.
14. James Q. Wilson and George L. Kelling, "Beating Criminals to the Punch," *New York Times*, 24 April 1989.
15. Reuben Greenberg, "Less Bang-Bang for the Buck," *Policy Review* (winter 1992): 56.
16. Andrew Heiskell, with Ralph Graves, "Soapbox: Struggling to Save Bryant Park," *New York Times*, 13 September 1998.
17. Robert J. Sampson, "Neighborhoods and Violent Crime: A Multilevel Study of Collective Efficacy," *Science* 277, no. 5328 (August 15, 1997): 918.
18. Delores Kong, "Study Shows Cohesiveness Curbs Neighborhood Violence," *Boston Globe*, 15 August 1997.
19. John J. DiIulio, "Broken Bottles: Liquor, Disorder, and Crime in Wisconsin," Wisconsin Policy Research Institute Report 8, no. 4 (May 1995).
20. Richard R. Freeman and Harry J. Holzer, eds., *The Black Youth Employment Crisis* (Chicago: University of Chicago Press, 1986), 353–76.
21. James Q. Wilson and Richard J. Herrnstein, *Crime and Human Nature* (New York: Simon & Schuster, 1985), 432. In the early 1980s, Wilson sought to discover why crime decreased in the middle of the last century and then, after some fluctuations (up in the 1920s, down in the 1930s), shot up dramatically in the 1960s and has been climbing ever since. He checked all the standard explanations of criminal behavior but found that none correlated with the historical pattern. Poverty, for example. If poverty causes crime, why was crime so low during the Depression, when more than a quarter of the population had no income at all? And why did it rise during the affluent 1960s and 1970s?

Then Wilson stumbled on the fact that the decrease in crime in the last century followed the Second Great Awakening. As repentance and renewal spread across the country, church membership rose steeply, Christians formed voluntary associations devoted to education and moral reform, and

American society as a whole came to respect the values of sobriety, hard work, and self-restraint—what sociologists call the Protestant ethic. And as the Protestant ethic triumphed, the crime rate plummeted.

Beginning in the 1920s through the late 1930s, however, the Protestant ethic began to fall out of favor among the educated classes. "Freud's psychological theories came into vogue," explains Wilson, and the educated classes began to view religion and ethics as oppressive. Their cause was no longer freedom for religion—a classic American liberty—but freedom from religion.

The attitude of these educated classes was restrained by the Depression and two world wars, but in the 1960s it finally percolated through to popular consciousness, resulting in a widespread cultural shift away from an ethic of self-discipline toward an ethic of self-expression. The result was a sudden and dramatic increase in crime. See James Q. Wilson, "Crime and American Culture," *Public Interest* (winter 1983): 22.

22. John Leland, with Claudia Kalb, "Savior of the Street," *Newsweek* (June 1, 1998): 20.
23. Joe Klein, as quoted in Joe Loconte, "The Bully and the Pulpit: A New Model for Church-State Partnership," *Policy Review* (November/December 1998): 28.
24. Leslie Scanlon, "From the PEWS to the Streets: More Churches Are Going beyond Their Walls to Fight Drugs and Crime," *Courier-Journal,* 27 July 1997.
25. Roy Maynard, "Voice of Hope," *Loving Your Neighbor: A Principled Guide to Personal Charity,* ed. Marvin N. Olasky (Washington, D.C.: Capital Research Center, 1995), 57.
26. This story about Chicago and the following stories about Baltimore, Memphis, and Montgomery are told in John Perkins, with Jo Kadlecek, *Resurrecting Hope: Powerful Stories of How God Is Moving to Reach Our Cities* (Ventura, Calif.: Regal Books, 1995).

CHAPTER 37
CREATING THE GOOD SOCIETY

1. From President John Adams's October 11, 1798, address to the military, as quoted in *The Works of John Adams—Second President of the United States,* Charles Francis Adams, ed., vol. 9 (Boston: Little, Brown & Co., 1854), 229.
2. "79 Leaders Unite to Aid Democracy," *New York Times,* 1 June 1940.
3. "To Defend Democracy," *New York Times,* 9 June 1940.
4. Fred W. Beuttler, "For the World at Large: Intergroup Activities at the Jewish Theological Seminary," in *Tradition Renewed: A History of the Jewish Theological Seminary—Beyond the Academy,* vol. 2 (New York: The Seminary, 1997), 667. See also Sidney Hook's address reprinted in the *New Republic,* 2 (October 28, 1940): 684.
5. "Scholars Confess They Are Confused," *New York Times,* 1 September 1942.
6. Beuttler, "For the World at Large," 667. We are indebted to Beuttler, who

has performed a great service in studying the history of the conference, and we have drawn extensively on his research. In the course of his study, he discovered a fascinating and revealing historical footnote. In 1956, Nelson Rockefeller launched an ambitious special-studies project to define national goals for America's future. Rockefeller engaged a young Harvard professor, Henry Kissinger, to staff the project. Kissinger shrewdly saw that such an effort would have to have a moral framework for national purpose. Kissinger called in Finkelstein, then heading the Institute of Ethics at the New York Seminary, for advice, specifically in formulating a moral justification for the use of limited nuclear weapons. The question Kissinger put was, What are we "willing to die for in terms of values"? The Institute, under Finkelstein's direction, began extensive discussions, but it soon broke down, just as the conference had earlier. The panelists began to dodge Kissinger's insistent questions as he pushed them to deal more with the role of religion and natural law. Finkelstein's panel eventually gave up trying to reach a consensus, in effect telling Rockefeller and Kissinger that they could only help them clarify their values.

7. Richard John Neuhaus, "The Truth about Freedom," *Wall Street Journal,* 8 October 1993.

8. Dan Shine, "Yale OKs Return of Gift to Billionaire Lee Bass: Clash over $20 Million for Program," *Dallas Morning News,* 15 March 1995.

9. Michael Novak, *Character and Crime: An Inquiry into the Causes of the Virtue of Nations* (Notre Dame, Ind.: Brownson Institute, 1986), 107.

10. Jonathan Friendly, "Public Schools Avoid Teaching Right and Wrong," *New York Times,* 2 December 1985.

11. Michael Novak, "The Conservative Momentum" (speech given at the Center for the American Experiment, March 24, 1993).

12. Michael Novak, "The Causes of Virtue" (speech given in Washington, D.C., January 31, 1994, reprinted by Prison Fellowship in *Sources,* no. 6 [1994]).

13. James Schall, "Personal Sin and Social Sin," *Crisis* (June 1997): 57.

14. Christina Hoff Sommers, "Teaching the Virtues," *Chicago Tribune,* 12 September 1993.

15. Robert P. George, "Why Integrity Matters" (speech given at the National Prayer Breakfast, Washington, D.C., February 7, 1998).

16. Webster's defines *integrate* as "to unite (parts or elements), so as to form a whole; also, to unite (a part or element) with something else, esp. something more inclusive" (*Webster's New International Dictionary,* 2nd ed.).

17. C. S. Lewis, *The Abolition of Man* (New York: Macmillan, 1947), 35.

18. Michael Novak, *Character and Crime,* 38. Novak draws a significant parallel with economics. For centuries people sought the cause of poverty. But the most profound change for the economic betterment of the world came about when the eighteenth-century economist Adam Smith reversed that question, asking instead, What is the cause of *wealth?* See Adam Smith, *The Wealth of Nations: An Inquiry into the Nature and Causes Of* (New York: Modern Library, 1994).

19. Deal W. Hudson, *Happiness and the Limits of Satisfaction* (Lanham, Md.: Rowman & Littlefield, 1996).
20. Ibid.

CHAPTER 38
THE WORK OF OUR HANDS

1. Dorothy L. Sayers, *Creed or Chaos?* (Manchester, N.H.: Sophia Press, 1949), 77.
2. Richard John Neuhaus, *Doing Well and Doing Good: The Challenge to the Christian Capitalist* (New York: Doubleday, 1992).
3. Theologian T. M. Moore in a memo entitled "Economic Aspects of the Biblical Worldview" (August 12, 1998).
4. Robert A. Sirico, "The Enterpreneurial Vocation," available from The Acton Institute for the Study of Religion and Liberty, 1611 Ottawa NW, Suite 301, Grand Rapids, MI 49503, phone: (616) 454-3080. Elsewhere Sirico writes, "By themselves, brilliant ideas do not serve humankind; to be brought into service to man, they must be transformed through complex processes of design and production. The talent to perform this transformation is as rare and as humanly precious as talent in any other field" (See Sirico, *Toward the Future: Catholic Social Thought and the U.S. Economy* [New York: American Catholic Committee, 1984], 28).
5. Theologian T. M. Moore suggests that this balance of private property and social justice can be seen in the description of the godly wife in Proverbs 31. She enters freely into enterprises designed to enrich herself and provide for her family (vv. 13, 16, 19, 24). She is generous to the needy (v. 20), yet she makes certain that the needs of her own household are met (vv. 21, 27). As a result of her labors, she dresses well, and she is not looked down on for this (v. 22). Her industry and productivity reflect well on her husband in the eyes of the city fathers (v. 23). The secret of her success is her fear of God and her determination to live for him (v. 30). And she is deserving of every cent she makes (v. 31)!
6. Mary Hesse, *Science and the Human Imagination: Aspects of the History and Logic of Physical Science* (New York: Philosophical Library, 1955), 263 (emphasis in the original).
7. Eusebius, as quoted in Leland Ryken, *Work and Leisure: In Christian Perspective* (Portland, Ore.: Multnomah, 1987), 66.
8. See Robert A. Sirico, "The Late-Scholastic and Austrian Link to Modern Catholic Economic Thought," *Markets and Morality* 1, no. 2 (October 1988): 122–29.
9. Martin Luther, as quoted in Ryken, *Work and Leisure*, 95, 97. This principle applies to all forms of work, not just paid employment: All our tasks and duties, including those as parents or as citizens, Luther regarded as a call from God.
10. Luther as quoted in Ryken, 135.

11. Robert A. Sirico, "The Parable of the Talents," *Freeman* 44, no. 7 (July 1994): 354.

12. For further discussion about this issue, see Chuck Colson and Jack Eckerd, *Why America Doesn't Work* (Dallas: Word, 1991).

13. Adam Smith, *The Wealth of Nations* (New York: Modern Library, 1994), 15.

14. Michael Novak, *The Spirit of Democratic Capitalism* (New York: Simon & Schuster, 1982), 79 (emphasis in the original).

15. William Blake, *Milton*.

16. Michael Novak, *Business as a Calling: Work and the Examined Life* (New York: Free Press, 1996).

17. Michael Novak, "Profits with Honor," *Policy Review* (May/June 1996): 50. See also "Sweet Vindication: Award of 1994 Templeton Prize to Michael Novak for Progress in Religion," *National Review* 46, no. 6 (April 4, 1994): 22; and Walter Isaacson, "Exalting the City of Man," *Time* (May 10, 1982): 38.

18. Lance Morrow, "What Is the Point of Working?" *Time* (May 11, 1981): 93.

19. Robert Schrank, as quoted in Morrow, "What Is the Point of Working?" 93.

20. Arlie Hochschild, *The Time Bind: When Work Becomes Home and Home Becomes Work* (New York: Metropolitan Books, 1997), 37. A July 2, 1997 *Wall Street Journal* article asked, Are today's parents neglecting their kids in favor of the "ego high they get from work"?

21. See Maggie Gallagher, "Day Careless," *National Review* (January 26, 1998): 37; Karl Zinsmeister, "The Problem with Day Care," *American Enterprise* 9, no. 3 (May/June 1998): 26; and William Dreskin and Wendy Dreskin, *The Day Care Decision: What's Best for You and Your Child* (New York: M. Evans, 1983).

22. Laura Shapiro, et al., "The Myth of Quality Time," *Newsweek* (May 19, 1997): 42; and Shannon Brownlee, et al., "Lies Parents Tell Themselves about Why They Work," *U.S. News and World Report* (May 12, 1997): 58.

23. Morrow, "What Is the Point of Working," 93. Even Christians have absorbed secular attitudes toward work. A book-length study surveying attitudes among young people enrolled at Christian colleges and seminaries found that they hold an appallingly secular view of work. James Davison Hunter, who directed the survey, concludes that "work has lost any spiritual and eternal significance and that it is important only insofar as it fosters certain qualities of the personality" (James Davison Hunter, *Evangelicalism: The Coming Generation* [Chicago: University of Chicago Press, 1987], 56).

24. Os Guinness, *The Call: Finding and Fulfilling the Central Purpose of Life* (Nashville: Word, 1998), chapter 4.

25. Many of these ideas are discussed in Chuck Colson and Jack Eckerd, *Why America Doesn't Work* (Dallas: Word, 1991).

26. John Stollenwerk, as quoted in Spencer Abraham and Dan Coats, "Hard-Working Churches," *American Enterprise* 8, no. 4 (July/August 1997): 13.

27. Ronald Marino (in a speech given at the symposium on welfare by the Family Research Council), *A World without Welfare*, ed. David M. Wagner (Washington, D.C.: Family Research Council, 1997), 86–91.

28. Don Michele (in a speech given at the symposium on welfare by the Family Research Council), *A World without Welfare*, ed. David M. Wagner (Washington, D.C.: Family Research Council, 1997), 91–93.

29. Marvin N. Olasky, ed., *Loving Your Neighbor: A Principled Guide to Personal Charity*, (Washington, D.C.: Capital Research Center, 1995), 64.

30. John Perkins, with Jo Kadlecek, *Resurrecting Hope* (Ventura, Calif.: Regal Books, 1995), 95–97.

31. See Virgil Gulker (in a speech given at the symposium on walfare by the Family Research Council), *A World without Welfare*, ed. David M. Wagner (Washington, D.C.: Family Research Council, 1997), 107.

32. The following examples are taken from Amy L. Sherman, "Little Miracles," *American Enterprise* 9, no. 1 (January/February 1998): 64.

33. Alexander Solzhenitsyn, *One Day in the Life of Ivan Denisovich* (New York: Dutton, 1963), 100.

CHAPTER 39
THE ULTIMATE APPEAL

1. The details of King's story are taken largely from Stephen B. Oates, *Let the Trumpet Sound: A Life of Martin Luther King, Jr.* (New York: HarperPerennial, 1994).

2. Martin Luther King Jr., *Why We Can't Wait* (New York: Harper & Row, 1964), 84–85.

3. Ibid., 75.

4. Russell Hittinger, introduction to *Rights and Duties: Reflections on Our Conservative Constitution* by Russell Kirk (Dallas: Spence, 1997), xxvii.

5. The decision was *Dred Scott v. Sandford*, 60 US 393 (1857).

6. Abraham Lincoln, "Proclamation for Appointing a National Fast Day" (March 30, 1863), as quoted in Mark Noll, *One Nation Under God?: Christian Faith and Political Action in America* (San Francisco: Harper San Francisco, 1988), 98.

7. Robert P. George, *A Preserving Grace: Protestants, Catholics, and Natural Law*, ed. Michael Cromartie (Washington, D.C.: Ethics and Public Policy Center; Grand Rapids: Eerdmans, 1997), 94.

8. Marcus Tullius Cicero, *The Great Legal Philosophers: Selected Readings in Jurisprudence*, ed. Clarence Morris (Philadelphia: University of Pennsylvania Press, 1971), 50.

9. See Willmoore Kendall, *The Conservative Affirmation in America* (Chicago: Henry Regnery, 1963), chapter 5. The church played a major role in making this tradition explicit. In the eleventh century, Pope Gregory VII set out to reform the primitive tribal societies of Europe with laws drawn directly from Scripture. The first German law book, written in 1220, stated that "God is Himself law; and therefore law is dear to Him." (H. J. Berman, "Religious Foundations of Law in the West: An Historical Perspective," *Journal of Law and Religion* 1, no. 1 [summer 1983]: 3–43).

10. William Blackstone, *Commentaries on the Laws of England,* vol. 1 (Chicago: University of Chicago Press, 1979), 41.

11. John C. Rager, *The Political Philosophy of St. Robert Bellarmine: An Examination of Saint Cardinal Bellarmine's Defense of Popular Government and the Influence of His Political Theory upon the Declaration of Independence* (Spokane, Wash.: Apostolate of Our Lady of Siluva, 1995).

12. John Whitehead, *The Second American Revolution* (Elgin, Ill.: David C. Cook, 1982), 28–30.

13. John Finnis, *Natural Law and Natural Rights* (New York: Oxford University Press, 1980), 146; Robert P. George, *Making Men Moral* (New York: Oxford University Press, 1993), 47; and Robert A. Sirico, "Subsidiarity, Society, and Entitlements," *Notre Dame Journal of Law, Ethics and Public Policy* 11, no. 2 (1997): 549.

14. Abraham Kuyper, *Christianity: A Total World and Life System* (Marlborough, N.H.: Plymouth Rock Foundation, 1996), 60.

15. Ibid., 46. "Calvin personally preferred a republic," notes Kuyper, in which there would be cooperation between the spheres of society "under mutual control." He also considered it most ideal "where the people themselves choose their own magistrate," and admonished people to take seriously their responsibility to choose their own leaders: "see to it that ye do not forfeit this favor by electing to the positions of highest honor, rascals and enemies of God" (49–50).

16. James Madison, "Federalist No. 10," *New York Packet,* 23 November 1787.

17. Historians are quick to point out that some of the Founders were not Christians but Enlightenment deists, including Jefferson and to some degree Madison. Yet deist and Christian alike agreed that the rule of law is rooted in a higher law, objectively true and binding—what Jefferson called "the law of nature and nature's God."

    Among the Founders, a minority held the Lockean idea of individuals with natural rights based in their personhood coming together and entering a political contract, by which they consent to be governed. The majority held that a political contract is made within the context of a higher law and that the contract reflects the natural order of things ordained by God.

18. William James, as quoted in R. C. Sproul, *Lifeviews: Understanding the Ideas That Shape Society Today* (Old Tappan, N.J.: Revell, 1986), 89.

19. Phillip E. Johnson, *Reason in the Balance: The Case against Naturalism in Science, Law, and Education* (Downers Grove, Ill.: InterVarsity Press, 1995), chapter 7.

20. Oliver Wendell Holmes, "Natural Law," *Harvard Law Review,* 30–32 (1918): 40.

21. Gene Edward Veith, *Postmodern Times: A Christian Guide to Contemporary Thought and Culture* (Wheaton, Ill.: Crossway, 1994).

22. William Orville Douglas, *Zorach v. Clauson,* 343 US 306 (1952). See also Richard John Neuhaus, *The Naked Public Square* (Grand Rapids: Eerdmans, 1995), introduction and chapter 3.

23. *Edwards v. Aguillard,* 482 US 578 (1987).

24. *Planned Parenthood v. Casey,* 505 US 833 (1992).

25. In making this ruling, the Court could not have been unaware that only once in American history (and that in a contract case) had the Court ever reversed a right protected by the Fourteenth Amendment.

26. The Court followed *Casey* with a series of unusually harsh decisions. It ruled, for example, that pro-lifers may not demonstrate within a bubble zone surrounding an abortion clinic, though pro-choicers remain free to do so (*Madsen v. Women's Health Center, Inc.,* 512 US 753 [1994]).

27. Gerard V. Bradley, "The New Constitutional Covenant," *World & I* (March 1994): 361. In its expansive definition of liberty in *Casey,* the Court was talking about the liberty of whether to define oneself as a mother. But taken to its logical conclusion, this definition of liberty could undercut all law. All laws restrain someone's behavior, and all behavior expresses in some way a worldview, a belief about the meaning of existence and the universe.

28. *Lee v. Weisman,* 505 US 577 (1992).

29. Ibid.

30. *Romer v. Evans,* 517 US 620 (1996).

31. *Compassion in Dying v. Washington,* 79 F 3d 790 (9th Cir 1996). What is even more frightening is the argument the justices used to reach their decision. *Compassion in Dying v. Washington,* the infamous assisted-suicide case of 1997, reached the Supreme Court when appellate courts overturned a referendum passed by the voters of the State of Washington banning assisted suicide. Since the appellate courts had reversed the referendum based on the Supreme Court's own decision in *Planned Parenthood v. Casey,* which defined liberty as the right to decide for one's self the meaning of life, to be consistent the Supreme Court should have affirmed the lower court. But even the insulated Supreme Court judges weren't ready to face the degree of moral outrage this might have triggered. (Contrary to popular opinion, the justices *do* read newspapers and polls.) So what did they do? Examine the Constitution or the law? Research legislative history? Not at all. Instead, they mused aloud from the bench and wrote in their opinion that as a nation we simply haven't had enough experience with assisted suicide—or euthanasia—to know whether we are ready for it.

These men and women were not speaking in juridical terms; they were using the language of social scientists. This decision was not based on principled opposition but on the sociological fact that America might not be ready to face it. Their only moral concern was reduced to pure pragmatism: Let's see how things work out. Let's see indeed.

32. *Boerne v. Flores,* 521 US 507 (1997); *Employment Division v. Smith,* 494 US 872 (1990). At issue was the expansion of a growing Catholic parish in Boerne, Texas, a suburb of San Antonio. City authorities objected to the expansion, contending that the church was an historic monument and that its quaint charm was important to an area being redeveloped for tourism. So a line was drawn in the sand: Was the church a museum to draw tourists or a sanctuary for worship? The answer the Court handed down was that tourism was more important.

33. Though most Americans are unaware of the fact, the power of judicial review is nowhere in the Constitution. The Court assumed the power in an 1803 case, but only for limited circumstances (*Marbury v. Madison*). Not until the *Boerne v. Flores* case in 1997 did the Court assert unchallengeable authority to interpret the Constitution (though something close to this claim was asserted in the 1958 case of *Cooper v. Aaron*).

    Furthermore, had the *Boerne* decision been the prevailing law in the nineteenth century, this country would still have slavery, for it would have held not only that slavery is a constitutional right, as the *Dred Scott* decision held, but also that Congress had no power to restrict slavery even in federal territories. (In fact, Lincoln refused to recognize the *Dred Scott* decision as a binding rule on the legislative and executive branches of the federal government.)

34. Antonin Scalia, "Of Democracy, Morality, and the Majority," *Origins* 26, no. 6 (June 27, 1996). In an unpublished speech at Gregorian Pontifical University in Rome in 1996, Scalia said that while he believes in natural law, it has no place in judicial decision making. In ruling on the Constitution, he said the justices are bound by the literal meaning of the words of the text; they should not take moral truth into account in giving effect to constitutional guarantees. So if the "people want abortion," Scalia concluded, "the state should permit abortion in a democracy."

    If we substitute *slavery* or *incest* or *anti–Semitism* for *abortion* in Scalia's statement, would the conclusion be different? Logically, no. For in Scalia's view, the majority always rules "and the minority loses, except to the extent that the majority . . . has agreed to accord the minority rights." (Scalia made it plain in his speech that, in his view, the democratic majority should, for the sake of justice, enact legal protections against abortion, but that does not mitigate his judicial positivism.)

35. In the *Casey* case, the Court actually referred to the Constitution as a covenant. See Russell Hittinger, "A Crisis of Legitimacy," *Loyola Law Review* 44 (1998): 83.

36. Bradley, "The New Constitutional Covenant," 374.

37. Russell Kirk, "The 'Original Intent' Controversy," *The Heritage Foundation Report*, no. 138, (October 15, 1987).

38. See C. S. Lewis, *The Abolition of Man* (New York: Touchstone, 1975) and *Mere Christianity* (New York: Touchstone, 1996).

39. Arthur Leff, "Unspeakable Ethics, Unnatural Law," *Duke Law Journal* (speech given at Duke University Law School on April 2, 1979): 1229.

40. Bradley, "The New Constitutional Covenant," 359.

41. Michael Sandel, *Democracy's Discontent: America in Search of a Public Philosophy* (Boston: Harvard University Press, 1996).

42. According to a 1996 Gallup survey of American political culture, 32 percent of Americans have "a great deal of confidence" in the federal government generally, but just 13 percent in the presidency and only 5 percent in the Congress (comparable figures for 1966 were 41 percent for the president, 42 percent for Congress). Eighty percent believe "our country is run by a close network of special interests, public officials and the media." Only one in five

Americans is satisfied with the quality of political debate. One-quarter of all Americans believe the nation's government works against the interests of the citizenry; three-quarters believe the government is run by a "few big interests looking out for themselves"; and one in five Americans believes that the people who run our nation's institutions are "involved in a conspiracy!" These figures are based on a study done by James Davison Hunter. See Hunter, *The State of Disunion: 1996 Survey of American Political Culture*, vol. 2 (Ivy, Va.: In Medias Res Educational Foundation, 1996).

43. This is why Pope John Paul II said, "Moral relativism is incompatible with democracy," for rights cannot exist apart from a moral law (in a speech to U.S. Bishops at the Vatican, October 1998).

44. Clarence Page, "On Today's Campus: Consent for a Kiss Is Romance 101," *Orlando Sentinel,* 16 September 1993. See also Martin Gross, *The End of Sanity: Social and Cultural Madness in America* (New York: Avon Books, 1998); and James Hannah, "Applications Up after College Enacts Sex Rules for 'Every Step of the Way,'" *Rocky Mountain News,* 15 January 1995.

45. Meg Greenfield, "Sexual Harasser?" *Washington Post,* 30 September 1996.

46. George F. Will, "The Popcorn Board Lives!" *Newsweek* (October 13, 1997): 88.

47. I have written on this at length in other forums. See *Kingdoms in Conflict* (New York: William Morrow; Grand Rapids: Zondervan, 1987); *Against the Night* (Ann Arbor, Mich.: Servant, 1991); *End of Democracy* (Dallas: Spence, 1997); and *We Hold These Truths* (a pamphlet of "A Statement of Christian Conscience and Citizenship," drafted by forty-four people on July 4, 1997; distributed by Prison Fellowship).

48. Daniel Ritchie, ed., *Edmund Burke: Appraisals and Applications* (New Brunswick, N.J.: Transaction Publishers, 1990), 222.

49. In late 1997, Chinese president Jiang Zemin defended his government's persecution of Christians on the grounds that he could not permit them to incite movements for freedom in China as they did in Eastern Europe. See Diane Knippers, "How to Pressure China," *Christianity Today* (July 14, 1997): 52.

50. See, for example, Robert P. George, "God's Reasons," (speech given at the 1998 American Political Science Association Convention; published by Prison Fellowship, Reston, Virginia). For example, five colleagues and I, all critics of judicial overreach, wrote on the crisis in the law in a symposium that proved to be enormously controversial. See "The End of Democracy?" *First Things* (November 1996): 18–42. It was reported that this material was read by supreme court justices as they debated the recent assisted-suicide cases.

51. Beckett Fund for Religious Liberty, 2000 Pennsylvania Ave., NW, Suite 3580, Washington, D.C. 20006, phone: (202) 955-0095; American Center for Law and Justice, P.O. Box 64429, Virginia Beach, VA 23467, phone: (757) 226-2489; Center for Law and Religious Freedom (founded by the Christian Legal Society), 4208 Evergreen Lane, Suite 222, Annandale, VA 22003, (703) 642-1070, clrf@clsnet.org; Rutherford Institute, P.O. Box

7482, Charlottesville, VA 22906, phone: (804) 978-3888; Alliance Defense Fund, 7819 East Greenway Rd., Suite 8, Scottsdale, AZ 85260, phone: (602) 953-1200.

52. Alexis de Tocqueville, *Democracy in America* (New Rochelle, N.Y.: Arlington House, 1966), 114. For additional material on the extensive social ministries run by Christians in the nineteenth century, see Gertrude Himmelfarb, *Victorian Minds* (Chicago: I. R. Dee, 1995); and Marvin N. Olasky, *The Tragedy of American Compassion* (Washington, D.C.: Regnery Gateway, 1992).

53. Barbara Vogel, in an interview with Anne Morse, managing editor of *Break-Point Radio* (January 1999).

54. Institutional separation does not mean that religious truth must never influence public policy, however, which is where the Christian conception of separation of church and state differs from the liberal conception.

55. One of the many examples was Andrew Marshall, "Christians Out to Reclaim GOP Agenda," *Arizona Republic*, 5 July 1998.

56. Sir Thomas More, as quoted in Peter Ackroyd, *The Life of Sir Thomas More* (New York: Doubleday, 1998), 405.

CHAPTER 40
THE BASIS FOR TRUE SCIENCE

1. Daniel Dennett, *Darwin's Dangerous Idea: Evolution and the Meanings of Life* (New York: Simon & Schuster, 1995), 520.

2. David Hume, as quoted in John Herman Randall Jr., *The Making of the Modern Mind* (New York: Columbia University Press, 1940), 273.

3. G. K. Chesterton, *Eugenics and Other Evils* (New York: Dodd, Mead, 1927), 98.

4. Philip H. Phenix, as quoted in Michael D. Aeschliman, *The Restitution of Man: C. S. Lewis and the Case against Scientism* (Grand Rapids: Eerdmans, 1983), 50.

5. Arthur Koestler, as quoted in Aeschliman, *The Restitution of Man*, 55.

6. C. S. Lewis, *The Abolition of Man* (New York: Touchstone, 1975), 83.

7. Christian sociologist Jacques Ellul warned that the contemporary state of mind is so completely dominated by technical values that we are becoming unfamiliar with any other values. See Jacques Ellul, *The Technological Society* (New York: Alfred A. Knopf, 1976).

8. C. S. Lewis, *God in the Dock: Essays on Theology and Ethics* (Grand Rapids: Eerdmans, 1970), 136.

9. The following discussion relies heavily on Nancy R. Pearcey and Charles B. Thaxton, *The Soul of Science: Christian Faith and Natural Philosophy* (Wheaton, Ill.: Crossway, 1994).

10. *Pocahontas*, Walt Disney Productions (1995).

11. Carl Becker, *The Heavenly City of the Eighteenth-Century Philosophers* (New Haven: Yale University Press, 1932), 55.

12. Roger Cotes, preface to the second edition of Newton's *Principia*, in *Newton's Philosophy of Nature: Selections from His Writings*, ed. H. S. Thayer (New York: Hafner, 1953).

13. See Pearcey and Thaxton, *The Soul of Science*.

14. R. G. Collingwood, *An Essay on Metaphysics* (Chicago: Henry Regnery, 1972), 253–57.

15. Newton's theology was not fully Trinitarian, but no historian questions that he was fervent and sincere in his belief or that in most respects his belief was fully Christian.

16. Isaac Newton, as quoted in Pearcey and Thaxton, *The Soul of Science*, 72.

17. Ibid., 91.

18. Cotes, preface to Newton's *Principia*, 134.

19. Becker, *The Heavenly City*, 55.

20. Johnson's books include *Darwin on Trial, Reason in the Balance*, and *Objections Sustained*. Michael J. Behe *(Darwin's Black Box)* and William A. Dembski *(The Design Inference)* demonstrate that design is a rigorously scientific concept. The professional journal *Origins and Design*, edited by Paul Nelson, draws together evidence from a range of scientific fields showing that design is empirically detectable.

21. As we write, the *NOVA* video is still used by the Wheat Ridge High School (Jefferson County) in the Denver, Colorado, area. The only difference in district policy, as a reporter says, is to "ensure that no previously approved materials are removed without board review." See Cate Terwilliger, "Words of Controversy: Changes in Biology Teachers' Platform Rekindles Evolution vs. Creationism Fire," *Denver Post*, 29 January 1998.

22. William B. Provine and Phillip E. Johnson, *Darwinism: Science or Naturalistic Philosophy?* (videotape of debate held at Stanford University, April 30, 1994). To order videotape, contact Access Research Network, P.O. Box 38069, Colorado Springs, CO 80937, phone: (888) 259-7102.

23. Jessica Mathews, "Creationism Makes a Comeback," *Washington Post*, 8 April 1996.

24. Karen Schmidt, "Creationists Evolve New Strategy," *Science* 273, no. 5274 (July 26, 1996): 420. For a good discussion of the modern design movement, see Nancy R. Pearcey, "The Evolution Backlash: Debunking Darwin," *World* 1 (March 1997): 12–15.

25. Johnson, *Biology* (New York: Holt, Rinehart, and Winston, 1994), as quoted in Norris Anderson, *Education or Indoctrination?: Analysis of Textbooks in Alabama* (Colorado Springs, Colo.: Access Research Network, 1995), 6.

26. Miller and Levine, *Biology* (New York: Prentice Hall, 1995), as quoted in Anderson, *Education or Indoctrination?*, 7.

27. Campbell, *Biology* (Reading, Mass.: Addison-Wesley, 1993), as quoted in Anderson, *Education or Indoctrination?*, 12.

28. Arms and Camp, *Biology*, 4th ed. (New York: Holt, Rinehart and Winston, 1995), as quoted in Anderson, *Education or Indoctrination?*, 22.

29. Norris Anderson, as quoted in Nancy R. Pearcey, "The Evolution Backlash: Debunking Darwin," *World* 11, no. 38 (March 1, 1997): 12.

30. Quoted in the program and abstracts from the annual national meeting of the American Association for the Advancement of Science, held in Boston, February 1993.

CHAPTER 41
BLESSED IS THE MAN

1. The account of Górecki's life and accomplishments is based on sources that include the following: Adrian Thomas, *Górecki* (Oxford: Clarendon Press, 1997); Joseph McLellan, "Górecki's Symphonies and Sympathies," *Washington Post,* 5 March 1995; John Rockwell, "Górecki: A Trendy Symphony and Beyond," *New York Times,* 30 August 1992; "Top of the Pops: A Symphony?" *Time* (March 8, 1993): 64; and Karen L. Mulder, "Move Over, Madonna: Composer Henryk Górecki Has Found Top 40 Status, but Defers Accolades to God," *Christianity Today* 39, no. 8 (July 17, 1995): 66.

CHAPTER 42
SOLI DEO GLORIA

1. Norman Lebrecht, "The Arts," *Daily Telegraph,* 10 April 1996.
2. See Martha Bayles, *Hole in Our Soul: The Loss of Beauty and Meaning in American Popular Music* (New York: Free Press, 1994), 39.
3. Morley Safer, "Yes . . . But Is It Art?" *60 Minutes* (September 1993).
4. Calvin Seerveld, interview with Nancy R. Pearcey, "Christianity and the Arts," *Perspective* 18, no. 3 (June 1984). See also Calvin Seerveld, *A Christian Critique of Art and Literature* (Toronto: Tuppence Press, 1995).
5. Abbot Suger, *The Book of Suger, Abbot of St. Denis,* as quoted in Elizabeth Gilmore Holt, ed. *A Documentary History of Art,* vol. 1 (Princeton, N.J.: Princeton University Press, 1981), 30.
6. Christ Pasles, "Music/Dance: Hallelujah Appeal of 'Messiah' Is Enduring," *Los Angeles Times,* 26 December 1991; Nan Robertson, "A 'Messiah' Cast of Thousands," *San Diego Union-Tribune,* 14 December 1987; and J. Lee Anderson, "'Messiah' a Religous Experience," 5 December 1985. In the words of John Hale, Louisville Bach Society education director, Handel "told people after he composed 'Messiah' that he had a vision as he was writing the Hallelujah Chorus. . . . He thought he saw heaven open and God Himself sitting in the middle, with all His angels around Him" ("All Church Music, All the Time?" *Courier-Journal* [Louisville, Ky.], 24 December 1995).
7. Franz Joseph Haydn, as quoted in Patrick Kavanaugh, *Spiritual Lives of the Great Composers* (Grand Rapids: Zondervan, 1996), 39.
8. Derrick Henry, "Arts and Entertainment," *Atlanta Journal and Constitution,* 27 July 1995; and "Columbia Orchestra Takes Up Mozart, Mixes in Mendelssohn," *Baltimore Sun,* 28 January 1999.

9. Antonín Dvořák, as quoted in Kavanaugh, *Spiritual Lives of the Great Composers,* 153.

10. Coleridge became a Christian as he struggled with his addiction. While it is not known whether he was actually freed from addiction, when he was converted, he was certainly freed spiritually. He then underwent years of medical treatment (personal correspondence from Gene Edward Veith, author of *State of the Arts: From Bezalel to Mapplethorpe* [Wheaton, Ill.: Crossway, 1991]).

11. Vigen Guroian, *Tending the Heart of Virtue: How Classic Stories Awaken a Child's Moral Imagination* (New York: Oxford University Press, 1998).

12. Thomas Aquinas, as quoted in Jade A. Hobbs and Robert L. Duncan, *Arts, Ideas, and Civilization* (Englewood Cliffs, N.J.: Prentice Hall, 1989), 274. See also Francis A. Schaeffer, *Escape from Reason* (Downers Grove, Ill.: InterVarsity Press, 1968), 9–13.

13. In the eighth and ninth centuries, in what is called the iconoclast controversy, the church debated the proper use of icons in worship. To the Byzantines (the Eastern branch of the church) the icon was more than a mere picture or mosaic. It was the "window" through which human beings apprehended the divine. As such, an icon itself was often believed to possess a divine presence. The faithful would offer flowers, candles, and incense before their icons; they carried them in processions and kissed them as part of liturgical rites. For some, this was too much like idolatry. In 726, Emperor Leo II declared that all images were idols and ordered their destruction. But theologians such as St. John of Damascus argued that images were made acceptable by the Incarnation, when the Son of God, a spirit, took on a human form, and became the "Living Image of the invisible God" (Carl A. Volz, *The Church of the Middle Ages: Growth and Change from 600 to 1400* [St. Louis, Mo.: Concordia, 1970], 134–35).

14. Kenneth Clark, *Civilisation: A Personal View,* 13 videocassettes (New York: Ambrose Video Publishing, 1969).

15. Gene Edward Veith, *State of the Arts: From Bezalel to Mapplethorpe* (Wheaton, Ill.: Crossway, 1991), 58–63.

16. Martin Luther, as quoted by Donald J. Drew (in a lecture given at L'Abri Conference in Rochester, Minnesota, August 1996), 21. Luther also held literature in high esteem. There should be "as many poets and rhetoricians as possible," he wrote, for by the study of literature "people are fitted for the grasping of sacred truth and for handling it skillfully and happily" (as quoted in Veith, *State of the Arts,* 62).

17. John Calvin, as quoted in Veith, *State of the Arts,* 59.

18. Jacques Barzun, *The Use and Abuse of Art* (Princeton, N.J.: Princeton University Press, 1975), 53.

19. Bayles (quoting the founder of de Stijl), *Hole in Our Soul,* 39.

20. M. H. Abrams, *The Mirror and the Lamp: Romantic Theory and Critical Tradition* (New York: Oxford University Press, 1953), 285. Similarly, art critic Clement Greenberg writes, "the avant-garde poet or artist tries in effect

to imitate God by creating something valid solely on its own terms"
(Greenberg, *Art and Culture: Critical Essays* [Boston: Beacon Press, 1961], 6).

21. George Bernard Shaw, as quoted in Barzun, *The Use and Abuse of Art*, 46.

22. Abrams, *The Mirror and the Lamp*, 275.

23. Barzun, *The Use and Abuse of Art*, 39.

24. Ibid., 38.

25. Ibid., 51.

26. Luigi Russolo, as quoted in Bayles, *Hole in Our Soul*, 43.

27. Robert Hughes, as quoted in Thomas Ewens, "Rethinking the Question of Quality in Art," *Arts Education Policy Review* (November 1994): 2.

28. Joyce Price, "Art Turns Heads, Stomachs," *Washington Times*, 6 July 1993.

29. John Simon, "Art or Child's Play? A Four-Year-Old Could Do It," *Sunday Telegraph*, 14 February 1993.

30. Os Guinness, "The Purpose of Invitation to the Classics," in *Invitation to the Classics: A Guide to Books You've Always Wanted to Read*, eds. Louise Cowan and Os Guinness (Grand Rapids: Baker, 1998), 14.

31. C. S. Lewis, as quoted in Guinness, *Invitation to the Classics*, 15.

32. Veith, *State of the Arts*, 106–13.

33. "There is more talk about de-funding the National Endowment for the Arts than there is about funding creative work that could be a healthy cultural force," says Ken Myers (personal conversation with Kim Robbins [May 1999]). Myers is the host of *Mars Hill*, a bimonthly audio magazine of contemporary culture and Christian conviction. Mars Hill, P.O. Box 7826, Charlottesville, VA 22906, phone: (800) 331-6407.

34. C. S. Lewis, "Learning in War Time," *The Weight of Glory and Other Addresses* (New York: Macmillan, 1980), 23.

35. Louise Cowan, "The Importance of Classics," in *Invitation to the Classics*, eds. Cowan and Guinness, 19–20.

36. Listen to Soeur Marie Keyrouz, a Lebanese nun who renders ancient Byzantine chants in a rich, throaty voice—a vivid reminder that the church emerged from Near Eastern culture. Re-create fourth-century sound by listening to the serene Ambrosian chants or the noble sonorities of the liturgy of Saint John Chrysostom, sung by the Greek Byzantine Choir. Several musical groups have also revived medieval music, both Gregorian chant and the lively songs of the visionary twelfth-century Hildegard von Bingen, becoming surprise best-sellers. And there's the astonishing commercial success of Anonymous 4, four women who sing medieval music with transparent tones and ethereal vocal blending.

37. Gerard Manley Hopkins, "God's Grandeur."

38. An account of Irina Ratushinskaya's conversion in a Russian prison camp is told in Charles Colson with Ellen Santilli Vaughn, *The Body: Being Light in Darkness* (Dallas: Word, 1992), chapter 6.

39. Bruno Bettelheim, *The Use of Enchantment: The Meaning and Importance of Fairy Tales* (New York: Alfred A. Knopf, 1976), 10.

CHAPTER 43
TOUCHED BY A MIRACLE

1. The authors are grateful to Martha Williamson for a personal interview in January 1998. Additional details for this story were taken from Martha Williamson and Robin Sheets, *Touched by an Angel: Stories from the Hit Television Series* (Grand Rapids: Zondervan, 1997).

CHAPTER 44
DOES THE DEVIL HAVE ALL THE GOOD MUSIC?

1. Marshall McLuhan, *The Medium Is the Massage* (New York: Simon & Schuster, 1967).
2. Neil Postman, *Amusing Ourselves to Death* (New York: Penguin, 1985), 10, 62, 86.
3. Ibid., 9 (emphasis in the original).
4. Ibid., 9.
5. Ibid., see also chapter 11.
6. Aldous Huxley, *Brave New World Revisited* (New York: Harper & Brothers, 1958), 44.
7. Kenneth A. Myers, *All God's Children and Blue Suede Shoes: Christians and Popular Culture* (Westchester, Ill.: Crossway, 1989), 89.
8. Ibid., 134–35.
9. "Short Takes," *Time* (December 7, 1992): 83.
10. Ken Myers describes an attempt by a Christian broadcasting network to produce a Christian soap opera. The program was marked by the same melodramatic music, stock characters, and tear-jerking plots as secular soaps. The only thing that distinguished it from its secular counterparts was that "a few of the characters were Christians, who occasionally spoke of the role their faith played in meeting soap opera crises." The Christian message was a thin veneer, while the real tone was set by the soap opera form—"You'll love our Christian soap opera villain . . . because she gets saved sometime next season. But meanwhile she's just as nasty as her 'secular' counterpart." The soap opera form is inherently contrary to Christian values, Myers concludes, because it depends on "the dramatic equivalent of gossip" (Myers, *All God's Children and Blue Suede Shoes*, 21).
11. You can read more about Ben Carson's dramatic story in his autobiography, *Gifted Hands* (Grand Rapids: Zondervan, 1996).
12. *Saving Private Ryan*, Paramount Pictures (1998); *Schindler's List*, Universal Pictures (1993); *Dead Man Walking*, Gramercy Pictures (1995); *The Spitfire Grill*, Columbia Pictures Corporation (1996); John Meroney, "'Live' with TAE, Randall Wallace," *American Enterprise*, (May/June 1998): 21.
13. *Chariots of Fire*, 20th Century Fox (1981); *Brother Sun, Sister Moon*, Luciano Perugio, producer (1973); *Jane Eyre*, Miramax Films (1996); *Jesus of Nazareth*, Sir Lew Grade (1977); *Crimes and Misdemeanors*, Orion Pictures (1989).

14. *It's a Wonderful Life,* Liberty Films (1946); *Mr. Smith Goes to Washington,* Columbia Pictures (1939).

15. Frank Capra, *Frank Capra: The Name above the Title: An Autobiography* (New York: Macmillan, 1971). Every Christian family ought to buy a copy of *The Family New Media Guide,* in which authors highlight the films that tell inspiring stories, the audio books that bring the classics alive for children, the computer games that stimulate the imagination while avoiding blood and gore. See William Kilpatrick and Gregory and Suzanne Wolfe, *The Family New Media Guide: A Parents' Guide to the Very Best Choices in Values-Oriented Media, Including Videos, CD-Roms, Audiotapes, Computer Software, and On-Line Services* (New York: Touchstone, 1997). Ted Baehr publishes a newsletter critiquing current films from a Christian perspective. To order the newsletter, contact Movieguide, 6695 Peach Tree Industrial Blvd., Suite 101, Atlanta, GA 30360, phone: (770) 825-0084.

16. Inter-Mission, First Presbyterian Church of Hollywood, 1760 North Gower Street, Hollywood, CA 90028, phone: (323) 462-8460; Catholics in Media Message Line, phone: (818) 907-2734.

17. Los Angeles Film Studies Center, 3800 Barham Blvd., Suite 202, Los Angeles, CA 90068, phone: (323) 882-6224.

18. David Shiflett, "God, What a Hit," *Wall Street Journal,* 21 August 1998.

19. C. S. Lewis, *God in the Dock: Essays on Theology and Ethics* (Grand Rapids: Eerdmans, 1970), 93.

CHAPTER 45
HOW NOW SHALL WE LIVE?

1. The conference, held in June 1996, was called "Missed Opportunities?: Former U.S. and Vietnamese Leaders and Scholars Reexamine the Vietnam War, 1961–1968."

2. Robert S. McNamara with Brian VanDeMark, *In Retrospect: The Tragedy and Lessons of Vietnam* (New York: Vintage Books, 1996).

3. Norman Boucher, "Thinking Like the Enemy," *Brown Alumni Monthly,* (November/December 1997): 36–45.

4. Sources for Kim Phuc's story include David Usborne, "Veterans of Vietnam Weep as the Girl Who Became a Symbol of Suffering Comes to Forgive 22 Years Later," *Independent,* 14 November 1996; "Portrait of Forgiveness," *Sarasota Herald-Tribune,* 14 November 1996; Elaine Sciolino, "A Painful Road from Vietnam to Forgiveness," *New York Times,* 12 November 1996; Elaine S. Povich, "A Prayer for Peace," *Newsday,* 12 November 1996. Further background information was provided by Linh D. Vo and Major Ronald N. Timberlake through private telephone conversations and correspondence. These two men were especially helpful in correcting mistaken impressions created by the initial story.

5. Interview conducted by EO (Dutch) Television, 6 December 1998.

6. Ibid.

7. *Kim's Story,* a documentary film produced by Bishari Films Inc. (1997).
8. The man who approached Kim Phuc was John Plummer. Later investigation determined that he was not, in fact, either the pilot who dropped the bomb or the commander who ordered the air strike, as he claimed. The attack on Kim's village was a South Vietnamese operation with no American involvement. Nevertheless, he symbolically represents all of us who feel directly or indirectly responsible, and his exchange with Kim Phuc that day speaks poignantly of the real solution to war and conflict between nations.

RECOMMENDED READING

WORLDVIEW

Bellah, Robert. *The Good Society.* New York: Alfred A. Knopf, 1991.

Berger, Peter and Brigitte Berger, and Hansfried Kellner. *The Homeless Mind: Modernization and Consciousness.* New York: Random, 1974.

Blamires, Harry. *The Christian Mind.* Ann Arbor, Mich.: Servant, 1978.

Brown, Harold O. J. *The Sensate Culture.* Dallas: Word, 1996.

Carson, D. A., and John D. Woodbridge, eds. *God and Culture: Essays in Honor of Carl F. H. Henry.* Grand Rapids: Eerdmans, 1993.

Colson, Charles, with Anne Morse. *Burden of Truth: Defending Truth in an Age of Unbelief.* Wheaton, Ill.: Tyndale House, 1997.

Colson, Charles, with Nancy Pearcey. *A Dance with Deception: Revealing the Truth Behind the Headlines.* Dallas: Word, 1993.

Colson, Charles, with Ellen Santilli Vaughn. *The Body.* Dallas: Word, 1992.

Dawson, Christopher. *Religion and the Rise of Western Culture.* New York: Doubleday, 1991.

Dockery, David S., ed. *The Challenge of Postmodernism: An Evangelical Engagement.* Grand Rapids: Baker, 1997.

Dooyeweerd, Hermann. *Roots of Western Culture: Pagan, Secular, and Christian Options.* Toronto: Wedge, 1979.

———. *In the Twilight of Western Thought: Studies in the Pretended Autonomy of Philosophical Thought.* Lewiston, N.Y.: E. Mellen, 1999.

Eliot, T. S. *Christianity and Culture.* New York: Harcourt, Brace and Jovanovich, 1968.

Geisler, Norman L., and Ronald M. Brooks. *When Skeptics Ask: A Handbook of Christian Evidence.* Wheaton, Ill.: Victor, 1998.

Glover, Willis B. *Biblical Origins of Modern Secular Culture: An Essay in the Interpretation of Western History.* Macon, Ga.: Mercer University Press, 1984.

Grisez, Germain G. *The Way of the Lord Jesus.* Vol. 1, *Christian Moral Principles.* Chicago: Franciscan Herald Press, 1983.

————. *The Way of the Lord Jesus.* Vol. 2, *Living a Christian Life.* Quincy, Ill.: Franciscan Press, 1993.

————. *The Way of the Lord Jesus.* Vol. 3, *Difficult Moral Questions.* Quincy, Ill.: Franciscan Press, 1997.

Gunton, Colin. *Enlightenment and Alienation: An Essay Toward a Trinitarian Theology.* Grand Rapids: Eerdmans, 1985.

Halton, Eugene. *Bereft of Reason: On the Decline of Social Thought and Prospects for Its Renewal.* Chicago: University of Chicago Press, 1995.

Henry, Carl F. H. *The Christian Mind-set in a Secular Society: Promoting Evangelical Renewal and National Righteousness.* Portland, Ore.: Multnomah, 1978.

Heslam, Peter S. *Creating a Christian Worldview: Abraham Kuyper's Lectures on Calvinism.* Grand Rapids: Eerdmans, 1998.

Hoffecker, W. Andrew, and Gary Scott Smith, eds. *Building a Christian Worldview.* Vol. 1, *God, Man, and Knowledge.* Phillipsburg, N.J.: Presbyterian and Reformed, 1986.

Holmes, Arthur. *All Truth Is God's Truth.* Grand Rapids: Eerdmans, 1977.

Holmes, Arthur, ed. *The Making of a Christian Mind: A Christian World View & the Academic Enterprise.* Downers Grove, Ill.: InterVarsity Press, 1985.

Kuyper, Abraham. *Christianity: A Total World and Life System.* Marlborough, N.H.: Plymouth Rock Foundation, 1996.

Machen, J. Gresham. *Christianity and Liberalism.* Grand Rapids: Eerdmans, 1990.

Moreland, J. P. *Love Your God with All Your Mind: The Role of Reason in the Life of the Soul.* Colorado Springs: NavPress, 1997.

Noll, Mark. *The Scandal of the Evangelical Mind.* Downers Grove, Ill.: InterVarsity Press, 1994.

Runner, H. Evan. *The Relation of the Bible to Learning.* Toronto: Wedge, 1970.

Schaeffer, Francis. *The Complete Works of Francis A. Schaeffer: A Christian Worldview.* Westchester, Ill.: Crossway, 1982.

————. *25 Basic Bible Studies: Including Two Contents, Two Realities.* Wheaton, Ill.: Crossway, 1996. Also in *The Complete Works of Francis A. Schaeffer: A Christian Worldview.* Vol. 3, *A Christian View of Spirituality.* Westchester, Ill.: Crossway, 1982.

————. *Art and the Bible.* Downers Grove, Ill.: InterVarsity Press, 1973. Also in *The Complete Works of Francis A. Schaeffer: A Christian Worldview.* Vol. 2, *A Christian View of the Bible as Truth.* Westchester, Ill.: Crossway, 1982.

————. *Back to Freedom and Dignity.* In *The Complete Works of Francis A. Schaeffer: A Christian Worldview.* Vol. 1, *A Christian View of Philosophy and Culture.* Westchester, Ill.: Crossway, 1982.

————. *Basic Bible Studies.* In *The Complete Works of Francis A. Schaeffer: A Christian Worldview.* Vol. 2, *A Christian View of the Bible as Truth.* Westchester, Ill.: Crossway, 1982.

————. *A Christian Manifesto.* Wheaton, Ill.: Good News, 1982. Also in *The Complete Works of Francis A. Schaeffer: A Christian Worldview.* Vol. 5, *A Christian View of the West.* Westchester, Ill.: Crossway, 1982.

————. *The Church at the End of the Twentieth Century: Including, the Church Before the Watching World.* Wheaton, Ill.: Crossway, 1994.

————. *Death in the City.* In *The Complete Works of Francis A. Schaeffer: A Christian Worldview.* Vol. 4, *A Christian View of the Church.* Westchester, Ill.: Crossway, 1982.

————. *Genesis in Space and Time.* Downers Grove, Ill.: InterVarsity Press, 1972.

————. *The Great Evangelical Disaster.* Wheaton, Ill.: Good News, 1984.

————. *He Is There and He Is Not Silent.* Wheaton, Ill.: Tyndale House, 1972. Also in *The Complete Works of Francis A. Schaeffer: A Christian Worldview.* Vol. 1, *A Christian View of Philosophy and Culture.* Westchester, Ill.: Crossway, 1982.

————. *How Should We Then Live?* Westchester, Ill.: Crossway, 1983. Also in *The Complete Works of Francis A. Schaeffer: A Christian Worldview.* Vol. 5, *A Christian View of the West.* Westchester, Ill.: Crossway, 1982.

————. *Joshua and the Flow of Biblical History.* In *The Complete Works of Francis A. Schaeffer: A Christian Worldview.* Vol. 2, *A Christian View of the Bible as Truth.* Westchester, Ill.: Crossway, 1982.

————. *The Mark of the Christian.* In *The Complete Works of Francis A. Schaeffer: A Christian Worldview.* Vol. 4, *A Christian View of the Church.* Westchester, Ill.: Crossway, 1982.

————. *The New Super-Spirituality.* In *The Complete Works of Francis A. Schaeffer: A Christian Worldview.* Vol. 3, *A Christian View of Spirituality.* Westchester, Ill.: Crossway, 1982.

————. *No Final Conflict.* In *The Complete Works of Francis A. Schaeffer: A Christian Worldview.* Vol. 2, *A Christian View of the Bible as Truth.* Westchester, Ill.: Crossway, 1982.

————. *No Little People.* In *The Complete Works of Francis A. Schaeffer: A Christian Worldview.* Vol. 3, *A Christian View of Spirituality.* Westchester, Ill.: Crossway, 1982.

————. *True Spirituality.* Wheaton, Ill.: Tyndale House, 1979. Also in *The Complete Works of Francis A. Schaeffer: A Christian Worldview.* Vol. 3, *A Christian View of Spirituality.* Westchester, Ill.: Crossway, 1982.

Schaeffer, Francis A., and C. Everett Koop. *Whatever Happened to the Human Race?* Westchester, Ill.: Crossway, 1983. Also in *The Complete Works of Francis A. Schaeffer: A Christian Worldview.* Vol. 5, *A Christian View of the West.* Westchester, Ill.: Crossway, 1982.

Schaeffer, Francis A., and Udo Middelmann. *Pollution and the Death of Man.* Wheaton, Ill.: Crossway, 1992. Also in *The Complete Works of Francis A. Schaeffer: A Christian Worldview.* Vol. 5, *A Christian View of the West.* Westchester, Ill.: Crossway, 1982.

Sire, James W. *The Universe Next Door: A Basic Worldview Catalog.* 3rd ed. Downers Grove, Ill.: InterVarsity Press, 1997.

Smart, Ninian. *Worldviews: Crosscultural Explorations of Human Beliefs.* 2nd ed. Englewood Cliffs, N.J.: Prentice Hall, 1995.

Sorokin, Pitirim A. *The Crisis of Our Age.* 2nd rev. ed. London: Oneworld, 1992.

Sproul, R. C. *Lifeviews.* Grand Rapids: Baker, 1990.

Vander Goot, Henry. *Life Is Religion: Essays in Honor of H. Evan Runner.* St. Catherines, Ontario: Paideia, 1981.

Veith, Gene Edward. *Postmodern Times: A Christian Guide to Contemporary Thought and Culture.* Wheaton, Ill.: Crossway, 1994.

Walsh, Brian J., and J. Richard Middleton. *The Transforming Vision: Shaping a Christian World View.* Downers Grove, Ill.: InterVarsity Press, 1984.

Wells, David F. *No Place for Truth, or, Whatever Happened to Evangelical Theology?* Grand Rapids: Eerdmans, 1993.

Wolters, Albert M. *Creation Regained: Biblical Basics for a Reformational Worldview.* Grand Rapids: Eerdmans, 1985.

APOLOGETICS

Chapman, Colin. *The Case for Christianity.* Grand Rapids: Eerdmans, 1984.

Craig, William Lane. *Reasonable Faith: Christian Truth and Apologetics.* Wheaton, Ill.: Crossway, 1994.

Evans, C. Stephen. *Why Believe? Reason and Mystery as Pointers to God.* Rev. ed. Grand Rapids: Eerdmans, 1996.

Geisler, Norman. *Christian Apologetics*. Grand Rapids: Baker, 1976.

Kreeft, Peter, and Ronald K. Tacelli. *Handbook of Christian Apologetics*. Downers Grove, Ill.: InterVarsity Press, 1994.

Lewis, C. S. *God in the Dock: Essays on Theology and Ethics*. Grand Rapids: Eerdmans, 1970.

―――. *Mere Christianity*. New York: Touchstone, 1996.

―――. *Miracles: A Preliminary Study*. Hammersmith, London: Fount, 1974.

McCallum, Dennis, ed. *The Death of Truth: What's Wrong with Multiculturalism, the Rejection of Reason, and the New Postmodern Diversity*. Minneapolis: Bethany, 1996.

McDowell, Josh. *Evidence That Demands a Verdict: Historical Evidences for the Christian Faith*. Vols. 1 and 2. San Bernardino, Calif.: Here's Life Publishers, 1990.

Moreland, J. P. *Scaling the Secular City*. Grand Rapids: Baker, 1987.

Novak, Michael. *Will It Liberate?: Questions about Liberation Theology*. Mahwah, N.J.: Paulist Press, 1986.

Phillips, Timothy R., and Dennis I. Okhom, eds. *Christian Apologetics in a Postmodern World*. Downers Grove, Ill.: InterVarsity Press, 1995.

Pinnock, Clark. *Set Forth Your Case: Studies in Christian Apologetics*. Chicago: Moody Press, 1971.

Schaeffer, Francis. *Escape from Reason*. Downers Grove, Ill.: InterVarsity Press, 1968. Also in *The Complete Works of Francis A. Schaeffer: A Christian Worldview*. Vol. 1, *A Christian View of Philosophy and Culture*. Westchester, Ill.: Crossway, 1982.

―――. *The God Who Is There*. Downers Grove, Ill.: InterVarsity Press, 1968. Also in *The Complete Works of Francis A. Schaeffer: A Christian Worldview*. Vol. 1, *A Christian View of Philosophy and Culture*. Westchester, Ill.: Crossway, 1982.

Sproul, R. C. *Objections Answered*. Glendale, Calif.: Regal Books, 1978.

Sproul, R. C., John H. Gerstner, and Arthur Lindsley. *Classical Apologetics: A Rational Defense of the Christian Faith and a Critique of Presuppositional Apologetics*. Grand Rapids: Zondervan, 1984.

CREATION

Aeschliman, Michael D. *The Restitution of Man: C. S. Lewis and the Case against Scientism*. Grand Rapids: Eerdmans, 1983.

Behe, Michael. *Darwin's Black Box: The Biochemical Challenge to Evolution*. New York: Touchstone, 1996.

Corey, M. A. *God and the New Cosmology: The Anthropic Design Argument.* Lanham, Md.: Rowman & Littlefield, 1993.

Craig, William Lane, and Quentin Smith. *Theism, Atheism, and Big Bang Cosmology.* New York: Oxford University Press, 1993.

Davis, Percival, and Dean Kenyon. *Of Pandas and People: The Central Question of Biological Origins.* 2nd ed. Dallas: Haughton, 1993.

Dembski, William A. *The Design Inference: Eliminating Chance through Small Probabilities.* Cambridge: Cambridge University Press, 1998.

Dembski, William A., ed. *Mere Creation: Science, Faith, and Intelligent Design.* Downers Grove, Ill.: InterVarsity Press, 1998.

Denton, Michael. *Evolution: A Theory in Crisis.* Bethesda, Md.: Adler & Adler, 1985.

Johnson, Phillip E. *Darwin on Trial.* 2nd ed. Downers Grove, Ill.: InterVarsity Press, 1993.

———. *Defeating Darwinism: By Opening Minds.* Downers Grove, Ill.: InterVarsity Press, 1997.

———. *Objections Sustained: Subversive Essays on Evolution, Law, and Culture.* Downers Grove, Ill.: InterVarsity Press, 1998.

———. *Reason in the Balance: The Case against Naturalism in Science, Law, and Education.* Downers Grove, Ill.: InterVarsity Press, 1995.

Macbeth, Norman. *Darwin Retried.* New York: Delta Books, 1971.

Moreland, J. P. *Christianity and the Nature of Science.* Grand Rapids: Baker, 1990.

Overman, Dean. *The Case against Accident and Self-Organization.* New York: Rowman and Littlefield, 1997.

Pearcey, Nancy R., and Charles B. Thaxton. *The Soul of Science: Christian Faith and Natural Philosophy.* Wheaton, Ill.: Crossway, 1994.

Polanyi, Michael. *Science, Faith and Society.* Chicago: University of Chicago Press, 1964.

Thaxton, Charles B., Walter Bradley, and Roger Olsen. *The Mystery of Life's Origin: Reassessing Current Theories.* Dallas: Lewis and Stanley, 1992.

LIFE

Burtchaell, James. *Rachel Weeping and Other Essays on Abortion.* Toronto: Life Cycle Books, 1990.

Crutcher, Mark. *Lime 5: Exploited by Choice.* Denton, Tex.: Life Dynamics, 1996.

Grisez, Germain G. *Abortion: The Myths, the Realities, and the Arguments.* New York: Corpus Books, 1970.

Jacoby, Kerry. *Souls, Bodies, Spirits: The Drive to Abolish Abortion Since 1973.* Westport, Conn.: Praeger, 1998.

Larson, Edward, and Darrel Amundson. *A Different Death: Euthanasia and the Christian Tradition.* Downers Grove, Ill.: InterVarsity Press, 1998.

Lee, Patrick. *Abortion and Unborn Human Life.* Washington, D.C.: Catholic University Press, 1996.

Marshall, Robert, and Charles Donovan. *Blessed Are the Barren: The Social Policy of Planned Parenthood.* San Francisco: Ignatius, 1991.

Massè, Sydna, and Joan Phillips. *Her Choice to Heal: Finding Spiritual and Emotional Peace after Abortion.* Colorado Springs: Chariot Victor, 1998.

Olasky, Marvin. *Abortion Rites: A Social History of Abortion in America.* Wheaton, Ill.: Crossway, 1992.

INDIVIDUAL CHOICES

Glynn, Patrick. *God the Evidence: The Reconciliation of Faith and Reason in a Postsecular World.* Rocklin, Calif.: Prima Publishing, 1997.

Larson, David B., and Susan S. Larson. *The Forgotten Factor in Physical and Mental Health: What Does the Research Show?.* Rockville, Md.: National Institute of Healthcare Research, 1994.

Lewy, Guenter. *Why America Needs Religion: Secular Modernity and Its Discontent.* Grand Rapids: Eerdmans, 1996.

Matthews, Dale. *The Faith Factor: Proof of the Healing Power of Prayer.* New York: Viking, 1998.

Tournier, Paul. *The Whole Person in a Broken World.* New York: Harper & Row, 1981.

MARRIAGE AND FAMILY

Blankenhorn, David. *Fatherless America: Confronting Our Most Urgent Social Problem.* New York: HarperCollins, 1995.

Carlson, Allan C. *Family Questions: Reflections on the American Social Crisis.* New Brunswick, N.J.: Transaction, 1988.

Christensen, Bryce J. *Utopia Against the Family: The Problems and Politics of the American Family.* San Francisco: Ignatius, 1990.

Dobson, James C. *Coming Home: Timeless Wisdom for Families.* Wheaton, Ill.: Tyndale House, 1998.

————. *Children at Risk: The Battle for the Hearts and Minds of Our Kids.* Dallas: Word, 1994.

Gallagher, Maggie. *The Abolition of Marriage: How We Destroy Lasting Love.* Washington, D.C.: Regnery, 1996.

Horn, Wade. *The Fatherhood Movement: A Call to Action.* Lanham, Md.: Lexington Books, 1999.

Larson, David B. *The Costly Consequences of Divorce: Assessing the Clinical, Economic, and Public Health Impact of Marital Disruption in the United States: A Research-Based Seminar.* Rockville, Md.: National Institute for Healthcare Research, 1995.

Mack, Dana. *The Assault on Parenthood: How Our Culture Undermines the Family.* New York: Simon & Schuster, 1997.

McManus, Michael J. *Marriage Savers: Helping Your Friends and Family Avoid Divorce.* Rev. ed. Grand Rapids: Zondervan, 1995.

Popenoe, David. *Disturbing the Nest: Family Change and Decline in Modern Societies.* New York: A. de Gruyter, 1988.

————. *Life Without Father: Compelling New Evidence That Fatherhood and Marriage Are Indispensable for the Good of Children and Society.* Cambridge, Mass.: Harvard University Press, 1999.

Satinover, Jeffrey. *Homosexuality and the Politics of Truth.* Grand Rapids: Baker, 1996.

Stanton, Glenn T. *Why Marriage Matters: Reasons to Believe in Marriage in Postmodern Society.* Colorado Springs: Pinon Press, 1997.

Wallerstein, Judith S., and Sandra Blakeslee. *Second Chances: Men, Women, and Children a Decade After Divorce.* New York: Ticknor and Fields, 1989.

EDUCATION

Finn, Chester, Diane Ravitch, and Robert Fancher, eds. *Against Mediocrity: The Humanities in America's High Schools.* New York: Holmes and Meier, 1984.

Garber, Steven. *The Fabric of Faithfulness: Weaving Together Belief and Behavior During the University Years.* Downers Grove, Ill.: InterVarsity Press, 1996.

Knight, George R. *Philosophy and Education: An Introduction in Christian Perspective.* Berrien Springs, Mich.: Andrews University Press, 1998.

Kramer, Rita. *Ed School Follies: The Miseducation of America's Teachers.* New York: Free Press, 1991.

Malik, Charles Habib. *A Christian Critique of the University.* 2nd ed. Waterloo, Ont.: North Waterloo Academic Press, 1987.

Marsden, George M. *The Outrageous Idea of Christian Scholarship.* New York: Oxford University Press, 1998.

———. *The Soul of the American University: From Protestant Establishment to Established Nonbelief.* New York: Oxford University Press, 1994.

Nash, Ronald. *The Closing of the American Heart: What's Really Wrong with America's Schools.* Dallas: Word, 1990.

Veith, Gene Edward, and Andrew Kern. *Classical Education: Towards the Revival of American Schooling.* Washington, D.C.: Capital Research Center, 1997.

Wilson, Douglas. *Recovering the Lost Tools of Learning: An Approach to Distinctively Christian Education.* Wheaton, Ill.: Crossway, 1991.

NEIGHBORHOOD

Bennett, William J., John J. DiIulio, and John P. Walters. *Body Count: Moral Poverty—and How to Win America's War against Crime and Drugs.* New York: Simon & Schuster, 1996.

Kelling, George L., and Catherine M. Coles. *Fixing Broken Windows: Restoring Order and Reducing Crime in Our Communities.* New York: Free Press, 1996.

Kunstler, James Howard. *The Geography of Nowhere: The Rise and Decline of America's Man-Made Landscape.* New York: Touchstone, 1993.

Magnet, Myron. *The Dream and the Nightmare: The Sixties' Legacy to the Underclass.* New York: William Morrow, 1993.

Olasky, Marvin, ed. *Loving Your Neighbor: A Principled Guide to Personal Charity.* Washington, D.C.: Capital Research Center, 1995.

Perkins, John, with Jo Kadlecek. *Resurrecting Hope: Powerful Stories of How God Is Moving to Reach Our Cities.* Ventura, Calif.: Regal Books, 1995.

Sherman, Amy L. *Restorers of Hope: Reaching the Poor in Your Community with Church-Based Ministries That Work.* Wheaton, Ill.: Crossway, 1997.

Van Ness, Daniel W. *Crime and Its Victims: What We Can Do*. Leicester, England: InterVarsity Press, 1989.

Van Ness, Daniel W., and Karen H. Strong. *Restoring Justice*. Cincinnati: Anderson Publishing, 1997.

WORK AND ECONOMICS

Bernbaum, John, and Simon Steer. *Why Work? Careers and Employment in Biblical Perspective*. Grand Rapids: Baker, 1987.

Colson, Chuck, and Jack Eckerd. *Why America Doesn't Work*. Dallas: Word, 1991.

Gay, Craig M. *With Liberty and Justice for Whom?: The Recent Evangelical Debate over Capitalism*. Grand Rapids: Eerdmans, 1991.

Goudzwaard, Bob. *Idols of Our Time*. Downers Grove, Ill.: InterVarsity Press, 1984.

Guinness, Os. *Winning Back the Soul of American Business*. Burke, Va.: Hourglass, 1990.

Kuyper, Abraham. *The Problem of Poverty*. Grand Rapids: Baker, 1991.

Middelmann, Udo. *Pro-Existence*. Downers Grove, Ill.: InterVarsity Press, 1974.

Nash, Ronald. *Poverty and Wealth: The Christian Debate over Capitalism*. Westchester, Ill.: Crossway, 1986.

Neuhaus, Richard John. *Doing Well and Doing Good: The Challenge to the Christian Capitalist*. New York: Doubleday, 1992.

Novak, Michael. *Business as a Calling: Work and the Examined Life*. New York: Free Press, 1996.

———. *The Spirit of Democratic Capitalism*. New York: Simon & Schuster, 1982.

———. *Toward a Theology of the Corporation*. Washington, D.C.: American Enterprise Institute, 1981.

Roepke, Wilhelm. *A Humane Economy: The Social Framework of the Free Market*. Wilmington, Del.: Intercollegiate Studies Institute, 1998.

Ryken, Leland. *Redeeming the Time: A Christian Approach to Work and Leisure*. Grand Rapids: Baker, 1995.

Schumacher, E. F. *Economic Development and Poverty*. London: Africa Bureau, 1966.

Sirico, Robert A. *A Moral Basis for Liberty.* London: Institute of Economic Affairs, Health and Welfare Unit, 1994.

ETHICS

Bellah, Robert. *Habits of the Heart: Individualism and Commitment in American Life.* Berkeley, Calif.: University of California Press, 1985.

Eberly, Don, ed. *The Content of America's Character: Recovering Civic Virtue.* New York: Madison Books, 1995.

Finnis, John. *Fundamentals of Ethics.* New York: Oxford University Press, 1983.

Grisez, Germain G. *Beyond the New Morality: The Responsibilities of Freedom.* Notre Dame, Ind.: University of Notre Dame Press, 1988.

Himmelfarb, Gertrude. *The De-Moralization of Society: From Victorian Virtues to Modern Values.* New York: Alfred A. Knopf, 1995.

Kreeft, Peter. *Back to Virtue.* San Francisco: Ignatius, 1992.

Lewis, C. S. *The Abolition of Man.* New York: Simon & Schuster, 1996.

MacIntyre, Alasdair. *After Virtue: A Study in Moral Theology.* 2nd ed. Notre Dame, Ind.: University of Notre Dame Press, 1997.

Neuhaus, Richard John. *America Against Itself: Moral Vision and the Public Order.* Notre Dame, Ind.: University of Notre Dame Press, 1992.

Plantinga, Cornelius, Jr. *Not the Way It's Supposed to Be: A Breviary of Sin.* Grand Rapids: Eerdmans, 1995.

Plantinga, Theodore. *Learning to Live with Evil.* Grand Rapids: Eerdmans, 1982.

Sproul, R. C. *Christian Ethics.* Orlando: Ligonier Ministries, 1996.

Thielicke, Helmut. *Theological Ethics.* Vol. 1, *Foundations.* Grand Rapids: Eerdmans, 1966.

LAW AND POLITICS

Alison, Michael. *Christianity and Conservatism.* London: Hodder and Stoughton, 1990.

Arkes, Handley. *First Things: An Inquiry into the First Principles of Morals and Justice.* Princeton, N.J.: Princeton University Press, 1986.

Bloesch, Donald. *Crumbling Foundations.* Grand Rapids: Zondervan, 1984.

Budziszewski, J. *Written on the Heart: The Case for Natural Law.* Downers Grove, Ill.: InterVarsity Press, 1997.

Canavan, Francis. *The Pluralist Game: Pluralism, Liberalism, and the Moral Conscience.* Lanham, Md.: Rowman & Littlefield, 1995.

Colson, Charles; with Ellen Santilli Vaughn. *Kingdoms in Conflict.* New York: William Morrow; Grand Rapids: Zondervan, 1987.

Cromartie, Michael, ed. *A Preserving Grace: Protestants, Catholics, and Natural Law.* Grand Rapids: Eerdmans, 1997.

———. *Caesar's Coin Revisited: Christians and the Limits of Government.* Grand Rapids: Eerdmans, 1996.

Ellul, Jacques. *The New Demons.* New York: Seabury, 1975.

———. *The Political Illusion.* New York: Vintage, 1972.

Finnis, John. *Natural Law and Natural Rights.* New York: Oxford University Press, 1993.

Fitzpatrick, James K. *God, Country, and the Supreme Court.* Washington, D.C.: Regnery, 1985.

George, Robert P. *In Defense of Natural Law.* New York: Oxford University Press, 1999.

———. *Making Men Moral: Civil Liberties and Public Morality.* New York: Oxford University Press, 1996.

Goudzwaard, Bob. *Capitalism and Progress: A Diagnosis of Western Society.* Grand Rapids: Eerdmans, 1979.

Grant, George Parkin. *English-Speaking Justice.* Sackville, New Brunswick: Mount Allison University, 1974.

Hittinger, Russell. *A Critique of the New Natural Law Theory.* Notre Dame, Ind.: University of Notre Dame Press, 1989.

Jouvenel, Bertrand de, *On Power: The Natural History of Its Growth.* Indianapolis: Liberty Fund, 1993.

Kendall, Willmoore. *The Conservative Affirmation in America.* Chicago: Regnery Gateway, 1985.

Kirk, Russell. *Rights and Duties: Reflections on Our Conservative Constitution.* Dallas: Spence, 1997.

Manent, Pierre. *An Intellectual History of Liberalism.* Trans. Rebecca Balinski. Princeton, N.J.: Princeton University Press, 1994.

————. *The City of Man.* Trans. Marc A. LePain. Princeton, N.J.: Princeton University Press, 1998.

Murray, John C., and Walter Burghardt. *We Hold These Truths: Catholic Reflections on the American Proposition.* Kansas City, Mo.: Sheed and Ward, 1985.

Nash, Ronald. *Social Justice and the Christian Church.* Milford, Mich.: Mott Media, 1983.

Neuhaus, Richard John. *A Strange New Regime: The Naked Public Square and the Passing of the American Constitutional Order.* Washington, D.C.: The Heritage Foundation, 1997.

————. *The Naked Public Square: Religion and Democracy in America.* 2nd ed. Grand Rapids: Eerdmans, 1984.

Neuhaus, Richard John, and Michael Cromartie, eds. *Piety and Politics: Evangelicals and Fundamentalists Confront the World.* Washington, D.C.: Ethics and Public Policy Center, 1987.

Nisbet, Robert. *The Quest for Community: A Study in the Ethics of Order and Freedom.* San Francisco: Institute for Contemporary Studies, 1990.

————. *Twilight of Authority.* New York: Oxford University Press, 1975.

Noland, James, Jr. *The Therapeutic State.* New York: New York University Press, 1998.

Noll, Mark. *One Nation Under God? Christian Faith and Political Action in America.* San Francisco: Harper San Francisco, 1988.

O'Donovan, Oliver. *The Desire of Nations: Rediscovering the Roots of Political Theology.* Cambridge: Cambridge University Press, 1999.

Olasky, Marvin. *The Tragedy of American Compassion.* Washington, D.C.: Regnery, 1995.

Sandel, Michael. *Democracy's Discontent: America in Search of a Public Philosophy.* Boston: Harvard University Press, 1996.

Skillen, James W. *The Scattered Voice: Christians at Odds in the Public Square.* Grand Rapids: Zondervan, 1990.

Smith, Gary Scott, ed. *God and Politics: Four Views on the Reformation of Civil Government.* Phillipsburg, N.J.: Presbyterian and Reformed, 1989.

Thielicke, Helmut. *Theological Ethics.* Vol. 2, *Politics.* Philadelphia: Fortress Press, 1969.

Tinder, Glenn. *The Political Meaning of Christianity: An Interpretation.* Baton Rouge, La.: Louisiana State University Press, 1989.

Voegelin, Eric. *From Enlightenment to Revolution.* Ed. John H. Hallowell. Durham, N.C.: Duke University Press, 1975.

THE ARTS

Cowan, Louise, and Os Guinness, eds. *Invitation to the Classics: A Guide to Books You've Always Wanted to Read.* Grand Rapids: Baker, 1998.

Gallagher, Susan V., and Roger Lundin. *Literature through the Eyes of Faith.* San Francisco: Harper San Francisco, 1989.

Guroian, Vigen. *Tending the Heart of Virtue: How Classic Stories Awaken a Child's Moral Imagination.* New York: Oxford University Press, 1998.

Jeffrey, David Lyle. *People of the Book: Christian Identity and Literary Culture.* Grand Rapids: Eerdmans, 1996.

Kavanaugh, Patrick. *Spiritual Lives of the Great Composers.* Grand Rapids: Zondervan, 1996.

———. *A Taste for the Classics.* Nashville: Sparrow Press, 1993.

Lundin, Roger. *The Culture of Interpretation: A Christian Encounter with Postmodern Critical Theory.* Grand Rapids: Eerdmans, 1993.

Lundin, Roger, ed. *Disciplining Hermeneutics: Interpretation in Christian Perspective.* Grand Rapids: Eerdmans, 1997.

Ritchie, Daniel E. *Reconstructing Literature in an Ideological Age: A Biblical Poetics and Literary Studies from Milton to Burke.* Grand Rapids: Eerdmans, 1996.

Rookmaaker, H. R. *The Creative Gift: Essays on Art and the Christian Life.* Westchester, Ill.: Cornerstone Books, 1981.

———. *Modern Art and the Death of a Culture.* Downers Grove, Ill.: InterVarsity Press, 1970.

Ryken, Leland. *The Liberated Imagination: Thinking Christianly about the Arts.* Wheaton, Ill.: Harold Shaw, 1989.

———. *Realms of Gold: The Classics in Christian Perspective.* Wheaton, Ill.: Harold Shaw, 1991.

Sayers, Dorothy. *The Mind of the Maker.* San Francisco: Harper San Francisco, 1987.

Schaeffer, Franky. *Sham Pearls for Real Swine.* Brentwood, Tenn.: Wolgemuth and Hyatt, 1990.

Seerveld, Calvin. *Rainbows for the Fallen World: Aesthetic Life and Artistic Task.* Toronto: Tuppence Press, 1980.

Veith, Gene Edward. *Reading Between the Lines: A Christian Approach to Literature.* Westchester, Ill.: Crossway, 1990.

———. *State of the Arts: From Bezalel to Mapplethorpe.* Wheaton, Ill.: Crossway, 1991.

Walhout, Clarence, and Leland Ryken, eds. *Contemporary Literary Theory: A Christian Appraisal.* Grand Rapids: Eerdmans, 1991.

Wolterstorff, Nicholas. *Art in Action.* Grand Rapids: Eerdmans, 1980.

POP CULTURE

Bayles, Martha. *Hole in Our Soul: The Loss of Beauty and Meaning in American Popular Music.* New York: Free Press, 1994.

Drew, Donald. *Images of Man: A Critique of the Contemporary Cinema.* Downers Grove, Ill.: InterVarsity Press, 1974.

Gelernter, David. *Mirror Worlds: The Day Software Puts the Universe in a Shoebox . . . How Will It Happen and What Will It Mean?* New York: Oxford University Press, 1991.

Jones, E. Michael. *Dionysius Rising: The Birth of Cultural Revolution Out of the Spirit of Music.* San Francisco: Ignatius, 1994.

Kilpatrick, William, Gregory Wolfe, and Suzanne Wolfe. *The Family New Media Guide: A Parents' Guide to the Very Best Choices in Values-Oriented Media, Including Videos, CD-Roms, Audiotapes, Computer Software, and On-Line Services.* New York: Touchstone, 1997.

Myers, Ken. *All God's Children and Blue Suede Shoes: Christians and Popular Culture.* Westchester, Ill.: Crossway, 1989.

Schultz, Quentin J. *Redeeming Television: How TV Changes Christians—How Christians Can Change TV.* Downers Grove, Ill.: InterVarsity Press, 1992.

———. *Dancing in the Dark: Youth, Popular Culture, and the Electronic Media.* Grand Rapids: Eerdmans, 1990.

INDEX

ABOUT THE AUTHORS

CHARLES W. COLSON graduated with honors from Brown University and received his Juris Doctor from George Washington University. From 1969 to 1973 he served as special counsel to President Richard Nixon. In 1974 he pleaded guilty to charges related to Watergate and served seven months in a federal prison.

Before going to prison, Charles Colson was converted to Christ, as told in *Born Again.* He has written and published *Life Sentence, Crime and the Responsible Community, Who Speaks for God, Kingdoms in Conflict, Against the Night, Convicted* (with Dan Van Ness), *The God of Stones and Spiders, Why America Doesn't Work* (with Jack Eckerd), *The Body* (with Ellen Vaughn), *A Dance with Deception* (with Nancy Pearcey), *A Dangerous Grace* (with Nancy Pearcey), *Gideon's Torch* (with Ellen Vaughn), *Burden of Truth* (with Anne Morse), and *Loving God,* the book many people consider to be a contemporary classic.

Colson founded Prison Fellowship Ministries (PF), an interdenominational outreach, now active in eighty-three countries. The world's largest prison ministry, PF manages over fifty thousand active volunteers in the U.S. and tens of thousands more abroad. The ministry provides Bible studies in more than a thousand prisons, conducts over two thousand in-prison seminars per year, does major evangelistic outreaches, and reaches more than half a million kids at Christmas with gifts and the love of Christ. The

ministry also has two subsidiaries: Justice Fellowship, which works for biblically based criminal-justice policies, and Neighbors Who Care, a network of
volunteers providing assistance to victims of crime. Also a part of the ministry is the Wilberforce Forum, which provides worldview materials for the
Christian community, including Colson's daily radio broadcast, *BreakPoint,*
now heard on a thousand outlets.

Colson has received fifteen honorary doctorates and in 1993 was
awarded the Templeton Prize, the world's largest cash gift (over $1 million),
which is given each year to the one person in the world who has done the
most to advance the cause of religion. Colson donated this prize, as he does
all speaking fees and royalties, to further the work of PF.

NANCY R. PEARCEY studied under Francis Schaeffer at L'Abri Fellowship in
Switzerland in 1971 and 1972 and then earned a master's degree from
Covenant Theological Seminary and did graduate work at the Institute for
Christian Studies in Toronto. She is coauthor with Charles Thaxton of the
book *The Soul of Science: Christian Faith and Natural Philosophy* and has
contributed chapters to several other books, including *Mere Creation, Of
Pandas and People,* and *Pro-Life Feminism.* Her articles have appeared in
journals and magazines such as *First Things, Books and Culture, The World &
I, The Family in America,* and *The Human Life Review.*

Pearcey is currently a fellow with the Discovery Institute's Center for
the Renewal for Science and Culture, in Seattle, and managing editor of the
journal *Origins and Design.* She is policy director of the Wilberforce Forum
and executive editor of Colson's *BreakPoint,* a daily radio commentary program that analyzes current issues from a Christian worldview perspective.
She is also coauthor with Colson of a monthly column in *Christianity Today.*

If you are interested in further information about Prison Fellowship or
BreakPoint, write to Prison Fellowship, P.O. Box 17500, Washington, D.C.
20041-0500.

RESOURCES THAT SUPPORT THE *HOW NOW SHALL WE LIVE?* WORLDVIEW MESSAGE

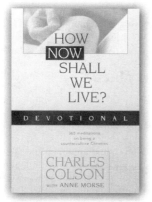

How Now Shall We Live? Devotional
365 meditations on how to be
a countercultural Christian
ISBN 0-8423-5409-3

Answers to Your Kids' Questions
A guide to help parents
know how to talk to their kids
about the worldview issues
they face every day
ISBN 0-8423-1817-8

  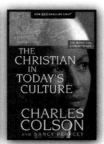

Developing a Christian Worldview series
How Now Shall We Live? worldview issues in a format for individual and group study:
    Science and Evolution ISBN 0-8423-5583-9
    The Problem of Evil ISBN 0-8423-5584-7
    The Christian in Today's Culture ISBN 0-8423-5587-1

COMING SOON

HOW NOW IN REAL LIFE SERIES:

How Now Shall We Live as Parents?
ISBN 1-4143-0164-2

How Now Shall We Live in the Workplace?
ISBN 1-4143-0165-0

Lies That Go Unchallenged: Popular Culture
ISBN 1-4143-0166-9

Lies That Go Unchallenged: Government
ISBN 1-4143-0167-7

**Complete How Now Shall We Live?
adult and youth video curriculum**

Available from **LifeWay Church Resources**:
LifeWay Church Resources
Customer Services, MSN 113
One LifeWay Plaza
Nashville, TN 37234-0113

Fax (615) 251-5933
Catalog orders (800) 458-2772
Order from online catalog at www.lifeway.com/shopping

OTHER TYNDALE BOOKS BY CHARLES COLSON

Burden of Truth
Practical help for handling difficult issues that collide with culture
ISBN 0-8423-0190-9

Justice That Restores
Charles Colson's legacy statement about criminal justice
ISBN 0-8423-5245-7

CONTENTS

HOW TO GET THE MOST
OUT OF THESE STUDY GUIDES

The lessons that follow are designed to guide you through a detailed and practical study of *How Now Shall We Live?*, which we think you will find to be a provocative and informative, disturbing and hopeful, challenging and inspiring book. It is a call to arms for the members of the Christian community to break free of the intellectual and spiritual constraints that have pushed the church to the margin of society. The goal of these study guides is to equip us to begin the work of renewing and restoring the culture.

Study Guide 1 covers the three worldview questions:

• Where did we come from, and who are we?
• What has gone wrong with the world?
• What can we do to fix it?

It explores the Christian worldview and demonstrates its superiority to the opposing worldviews of naturalism, Darwinism, moral relativism, multiculturalism, pragmatism, utopianism, existentialism, and post-modernism.

Study Guide 2 addresses the follow-up question: How now shall we live? It challenges us to take seriously our responsibility to engage the world and be God's redeeming force to influence the family, education, the neighborhood, work, law and politics, science, the arts, and popular culture.

WHAT YOU WILL FIND IN EACH LESSON

With the exception of the last lesson, all the lessons follow the same format. The section marked **Observe** is designed to lead you in your reading of the assigned parts of *How Now Shall We Live?* Read through the questions *before* you begin reading the book because they will guide you in knowing what to look for in the chapters.

The section headed **Reflect** will take you through a study of one or more Scripture passages that will help you to think biblically about the subject, and to ensure that your growing Christian worldview is firmly established on the foundation of God's Word.

The section marked **Apply** will help you to think about what the ideas in the chapters mean for your life. Here you will have an opportunity to be honest about your own needs for Christian growth and to chart paths for a more powerful experience of the gospel of Jesus Christ.

The final lesson in Study Guide 2 is designed to help you review what you have learned in this study and to establish a comprehensive plan for personal growth and ministry.

WHO CAN USE THESE GUIDES

We have designed these study guides with enough flexibility to be used by either individuals or groups. Some people will want to use the lessons for their personal study of the book.

Others will study the book with a group, whether that be a church group, a book group, or a group of neighbors. In such a setting, the study guides provide questions not only for personal preparation but also for group discussion and response.

We encourage you to study this book with a group, which will provide a forum for discussion, a springboard for action, and a tool for accountability. We don't expect you to agree with everything we say in *How Now Shall We Live?* But we do anticipate that the book will provoke lively discussion about a variety of themes and issues. We hope that your group wrestles with ideas presented in the book. We also hope that you come to a deeper understanding of your worldview. But most of all we hope that you are moved to act, to map out goals and strategies for becoming God's redeeming force in a new millennium.

As we said in the introduction to *How Now Shall We Live?*, the book is merely a beginning point for you to pursue what it means to live out a Christian worldview. Take a serious look at the list of resources in the recommended reading section at the end of the book. Choose several titles to deepen your understanding of specific topics that interest you.

Our prayer is that God will bless this project and use it to bring profound renewal and revival in his church and our world.

STUDY GUIDE
ONE

CHRISTIANITY IS A WORLDVIEW

Christianity is a *worldview*, that is, a way of understanding every aspect of the world and human life. For many of you, this is a new way of thinking about faith in Jesus Christ. But it is the *biblical* way, and once you grasp and begin to make use of it, a worldview understanding of Christianity will bring new excitement, enthusiasm, and power to your relationship with Jesus Christ.

Read the introduction and chapters 1 and 2.

OBSERVE

1 According to the introduction, how has failing to see Christianity as a worldview crippled Christians?

2 What is the difference between saving grace and common grace?

3 What is the purpose of *How Now Shall We Live?*

4 Summarizing from chapter 1, make a list of the differences between the Detainees Pavilion of the García Moreno Prison and the wing that had been given over to the Prison Fellowship (PF) leaders:
   - Conditions in the Detainees Pavilion
   - Conditions in the PF Wing

5 To what may we attribute these differences?

6 In what ways is the García Moreno Prison a parable of God's kingdom at work in the midst of a fallen world?

7 According to chapter 2, what is a *worldview?*

8 What are the three questions that form the grid through which all worldviews can be evaluated?

9 What is the basis for the Christian worldview?

10 What is the "false dichotomy" that plagues much of contemporary evangelicalism?

11 What are the great commission and the cultural commission? How do we "engage the world"?

REFLECT

12 The Bible uses many contrasts to show that the Christian life is very different from life in the world. For example, Ephesians 2:1-5 speaks of the contrast between being dead in sins and being alive in Christ. What other contrasts can you find in Scripture?

13 Read Ephesians 4:17-24, a classic passage comparing life in sin with life in Christ. How does Paul describe the effects of sin on those who still live in it (vv. 17-19)?

14 Verse 20 is pivotal. What event in our lives cuts us off from the life of sin and sets us on a new course? Have you come to experience this?

15 What differences should new life in Christ make in our lives (vv. 21-24)?

16 What is the role of the mind in helping us to begin realizing this new life in Christ (compare vv. 17-19 with vv. 22-24)?

17 In what ways would people who have been "made new in the attitude of [their] minds" look at life differently from people who are "darkened in their understanding"?

APPLY

18 What new insights have you gained from these first two chapters?

19 How do you hope that reading this book will enrich or enhance your relationship with Christ?

20 In what areas of your life do you see your worldview having an impact? To help you respond to this question, make a list of the places you go and the kinds of activities you are involved with during a typical week. Be comprehensive and specific. Place a C next to the involvements that you can honestly say are shaped by a Christian worldview.

21 Which of these areas still need to be influenced by a Christian worldview? Place an X next to each item that could use more "renewing of your mind" (Rom. 12:2).

22 How can your life begin to change as a result of renewing your mind according to a Christian worldview in these areas and activities?

23 What prayer requests come to mind as a result of studying these chapters?

2

THE BATTLE OF THE AGE

The spiritual warfare in which we as Christians are constantly engaged is often played out on the stage of relationships and history, where our view of life comes into conflict with the views of those who are still darkened by their sin. To be prepared to do effective battle we need to understand the nature and scope of this worldview conflict.

Read chapters 3 and 4.

OBSERVE

1 According to chapter 3, what is naturalism? How is it opposed to theism?

2 What is relativism, and why is it a component in a naturalistic worldview?

3 What is pragmatism?

4 What is utopianism?

5 In what sense are we living in a *post*-Christian world?

6 How are existentialism and postmodernism related to multiculturalism?

7 How are these ideas opposed to the Christian worldview?

8 According to chapter 4, what is pre-evangelism?

9 What is apologetics?

10 What is the role of the mind in the life of discipleship? What is the state of the "Christian mind" today?

11 What is the mission of the church?

REFLECT

12 Perhaps nowhere in Scripture is the clash of worldviews more powerfully observed than in the story of the temptation of Christ in Matthew 4:1-11.

Read these verses carefully. Who are the opponents here, and what is at stake in the outcome?

13 In what ways do Satan's temptations appeal to pragmatism? to relativism?

14 How is Satan tempting Christ to "live for the moment" (existentialism)?

15 In each case, how does Christ protect himself against Satan's wiles and frustrate the Tempter?

16 How can you see Christ's mind at work correcting Satan's false thinking and asserting a biblical worldview?

APPLY

17 In which of the areas and activities that you listed in the first lesson do you find that you are confronted by such things as naturalism, relativism, multiculturalism, pragmatism, utopianism, existentialism, and postmodernism? Give some examples.

18 Do you feel tempted to go along with these ways of thinking when they confront you? What makes that temptation so strong?

19 How can these ways of thinking actually be Satan's instruments in the spiritual warfare? What is his purpose as he confronts us with these ideas?

20 How can you prepare yourself to be victorious in the Lord in the face of such temptations?

21 How can you use the tools of pre-evangelism, apologetics, and discipleship to strengthen your ability to have a positive influence on your world?

22 In what ways are you fulfilling the great commission? In what ways are you fulfilling the cultural commission?

23 How does your personal "mission statement" line up with the mission of the church as expressed in this chapter?

24 What prayer requests come to mind as a result of studying these chapters?

3

THE RELIGION OF NATURALISM—PART I

The modern world owes much to science and technology. Every day our lives are enriched and made easier by the discoveries, inventions, and products that have been developed by thousands of brilliant and well-meaning men and women. As long as science and technology function within proper limits, they are one of God's great blessings. But when they exceed their limits and reach into areas typically left for such disciplines as theology, philosophy, and ethics, then real problems can ensue—as Dave Mulholland discovered.

Read chapters 5–7.

OBSERVE

1   In chapter 5 we find Dave Mulholland on a trip to Disney World with his daughter, Katy. This trip was an eye-opener for Dave in three ways. What shocking realization did he make about each of the following?

- The place of God in the scientific worldview
- Katy's view of religion in relation to science
- Dave's ability to talk with his daughter about the biblical perspectives of what they heard and saw

2   According to chapter 6, in what ways is the dominant view in our culture today "radically one-dimensional"?

3   Is naturalistic science neutral and objective? Why not?

4   How does naturalistic science, like religion, begin with certain faith assumptions?

5   In what ways did Carl Sagan's *Cosmos* attempt to provide a substitute for the Christian religion?

6   In what ways are Americans today being encouraged to believe in science as a religion?

7   According to chapter 7, what is big bang theory, and how can Christians use it to encourage belief in God?

8 What is the anthropic principle, and how does it help you to express your confidence in God's creation of the world?

9 How does the world as it presently exists strongly suggest that it was designed by the Creator?

REFLECT

10 Take a look at 2 Peter 3:3-9. It's almost as if the apostle Peter could see ahead to our day and to the challenge that would be raised by naturalistic science. Those mocking believers' faith in Christ in Peter's day were *uniformitarian* in their view of the natural world. They said, "All things continue as they always have, so where's your God?" How is this like Dave's experience?

11 In verse 4 Peter warns that mockers will deny God's promises by appealing to the stable course of nature. In what ways is this like the philosophy of naturalism?

12 According to verses 5-6, what do these mockers deliberately ignore in order to make their argument?

13 How does Peter account for the fact that the promise of the Lord's return has not yet been realized (vv. 7-9)? Why is he tarrying?

14 What does this suggest about why we are here during this time when the gospel is being mocked and marginalized by the religion of science?

15 Read 2 Corinthians 10:3-5. How are we to fight the battle with false philosophies, such as naturalism?

APPLY

16 In what ways have you observed that modern science claims to be the only genuine form of knowledge?

17 How would you engage a proponent of naturalism in a discussion? How would you articulate your worldview?

18 What prayer requests come to mind as a result of studying these chapters?

4

THE RELIGION OF NATURALISM—PART II

The more carefully we look at contemporary science, the more it confirms what the Bible teaches about life and the world.

Read chapters 8–10.

OBSERVE

1 According to chapter 8, how do scientists' attempts to create life in a test tube demonstrate that life is not a product of chance interactions of molecules?

2 How does the discovery of DNA support the idea of design and creation?

3 What is information theory? How does it affect the argument for design?

4 What is complexity theory? Does it establish a naturalistic account of life's origin?

5 According to chapter 9, what is Darwinism?

6 How have studies in animal breeding actually served to discredit Darwinism instead?

7 How do studies in genetic mutations discredit Darwinian thinking?

8 How does the concept of irreducible complexity discredit Darwinism?

9 In the face of so much contradictory evidence, why do naturalistic scientists continue to hold on to Darwinism?

10 According to chapter 10, why is Darwinism a dangerous idea? What "non-scientific" areas of life does it threaten to subvert?

11 On what does the authority of science rest today? How has Richard Lewontin helped to expose this false wizard?

12 Summarize the four points in the case for creation and design.

REFLECT

13 The best way of combating the religion of naturalism is by defeating it on its own turf, then bringing the gospel and the Word of God into the void that has been created. This is a biblical strategy, which can be seen by observing how the apostle Paul addressed some citizens of Athens. Read Acts 17:16-34. According to verses 32-34, what three reactions did listeners have to Paul's message in Athens?

14 What does Paul do in verses 16-18? What verbs describe his manner of speech among the Athenians?

15 On Mars Hill, did Paul begin with the Bible or something else (vv. 22-23)? What does he propose to do for the Athenians (see the last part of v. 23)?

16 Briefly trace the steps Paul took to get from his observation about their gods (v. 22) to the proclamation of coming judgment and the resurrection of Christ (v. 31).

APPLY

17 What steps can you begin to take to defend your children and the young people of your church against the false teachings of Darwinism and naturalism?

18 What kinds of results can you expect if you will take this challenge seriously? And if you don't?

19 Whose help will you enlist in doing this?

20 How can you engage the naturalistic scientists whom you know?

21 What approach and reasoned arguments will you use?

22 What prayer requests come to mind as a result of studying these chapters?

5

LIFE WORTH LIVING

Socrates once said, "The unexamined life is not worth living." We may go a step further and say that life is worth living only when it is seen in the light of God's mercy and grace. And, from that perspective, *every* life is worth living.

Read chapters 11–14.

OBSERVE

1 According to chapter 11, in what ways did God show his mercy and grace to Ken McGarity?

2 How did Ken finally come to realize that mercy and grace?

3 According to chapter 12, what are the main differences between the Christian and the naturalistic views of human life?

4 In what ways might we say that ours has become a "culture of death"? How did we become this way?

5 What is meant by "a radical dualism between body and soul," and why is this a problem?

6 What do we mean when we say, "Abortion has always been about more than abortion"?

7 What's wrong with the "choice" argument?

8 According to chapter 13, in what ways does the Christian worldview provide a basis for the dignity of human life?

9 How does the Christian worldview provide meaning and purpose for life?

10 How does the Christian worldview provide hope for the future?

11 How does the Christian worldview motivate us to serve others?

12 How does the story of Max (chapter 14) help us to see that every life is worth living when it is recognized as having been made in the image of God?

REFLECT

13 The first chapters of Genesis give an account of the creation of human life. Let's take a look at Genesis 1:26-28, along with Genesis 2, where the details of Genesis 1:26-28 are elaborated. First, describe the significance for us, the bearers of the image of God, that God himself is

- spiritual
- rational
- moral
- social
- aesthetic ("good")
- creative
- active

14 From these passages, what mandates did God give human beings? How would our first parents have understood what God expected of them?

15 How did the mandates that God gave to Adam and Eve require them to use every aspect of their image-bearing potential? Refer to each of the attributes of that image outlined in question 13. Look back over the list of attributes that reflect God's image in us. How is each of these necessary for fulfilling the mandates that God has given to us? How are you using these different attributes in fulfilling these mandates?

APPLY

16 In which of the seven aspects of God's image do you believe you need to grow? Explain:

17 How would growing in these areas prepare you to be more effective in fulfilling the great commission and the cultural commission?

18 What are the primary obstacles in the way of your acting more fully as one of God's image-bearers? What will you do to start overcoming these obstacles?

19 In what ways do you think your community would benefit if all the Christians in it lived fully as God's image-bearers?

20 Having studied the first worldview question—Where did we come from, and who are we?—what difference does it make to you that God created you in his image and has called you to carry out his work in the world?

21 Having studied chapters 1–14, in what ways are you better equipped to articulate and defend your worldview?

22 What prayer requests come to mind as a result of studying these chapters?

6

BUT FOR SIN

Have you ever heard someone say, "This would be a great place if it weren't for the people"? We could say the same thing, with far greater truth, about sin: This world and its people, societies, and cultures, would be a great place if it weren't for sin.

Read chapters 15–18.

OBSERVE

1   According to chapter 15, what has been the effect on humanity of Adam and Eve's first sin?

2   What do Enlightenment thinkers propose as the cause of the human dilemma? What are some examples of this?

3   According to chapter 16, how can you see, even very early in Meg's experience with Synanon, that this would be a place where the lowest human inclinations would be encouraged?

4   How do Charles Dederich's comments to Meg and Jack during their first meeting reveal that he and Synanon held to an Enlightenment view regarding the cause of the human dilemma?

5   In what ways did Synanon become like a religion for Meg?

6   According to chapter 17, what is meant by a "utopian vision of a new age"?

7   Briefly summarize how the idea of sin came to be discarded in Western societies. What was the role of such ideas as freedom, Marxism, and fascism in this process?

8   According to chapter 18, in what ways are many Americans today caught up in the myth of utopianism?

9   How does the utopian myth appear in each of the following?
  - psychology
  - education
  - law

- welfare
- criminal justice

10 How does the denial of sin ultimately make us vulnerable to the schemes of social planners?

REFLECT

11 Let's take a closer look at sin's first appearance and some of its effects. Read Genesis 3:1-6. How does sin arise as rebellion against God and his word?

12 By what particular avenues did sin make itself appealing to Eve (v. 6)?

13 According to verse 7, what was the first consequence that Adam and Eve experienced after their sinful choice? (Compare with Gen. 2:25.)

14 What effects of sin are evident in each of the following verses from Genesis 3?
- v. 8
- v. 12
- v. 16
- vv. 17-19

APPLY

15 Where do you see the influence of the utopian worldview in your life?

16 How is this worldview encouraged by the following?
- advertising
- consumerism
- news media

17 How can our understanding of the reality of sin prepare us to overcome the temptations of utopian thinking?

18 Will people you know be receptive to the idea that sin lies at the root of the human dilemma? Why or why not?

19 What prayer requests come to mind as a result of studying these chapters?

THE NATURE OF SIN

Sin has wrought havoc throughout God's creation. We are all tempted and tainted by sin. None of us escapes its powerful effects. But what *is* sin?

Read chapters 19 and 20.

OBSERVE

1 According to chapter 19, what does this statement mean: "The face of evil is frighteningly ordinary"?

2 How do people who hold a naturalistic worldview try to account for evil?

3 What have been some of the factors leading people to set aside the idea of sin?

4 What is the popular culture's attitude toward sin today?

5 How is the utopian mind-set related to the rejection of sin?

6 What is the "fatal flaw in the myth of human goodness"?

7 How does society try to hold sin in check? To what degree is it unable to do this?

8 According to chapter 20, what is involved in obeying God?

9 How does the Bible account for the entrance of sin and evil into the world?

10 What do nonbelievers need to see?

REFLECT

11 Let's take a further look at the biblical doctrine of sin. Read Romans 5:12-21. How did sin come into the world and reach into our lives?

12 Look carefully at Romans 3:10-18. According to Paul, how does sin affect each of the following? Cite the relevant verses in your answer.

- our moral life
- our understanding of things

- our speech and conversation
- our relationships with other people
- our relationship with God

13 How does God's law help us to understand sin (see Rom. 3:19-20 and Rom. 7:7)?

14 How does society's rejection of God's law influence the presence of sin in our culture?

15 According to Romans 6:11-19, what does the Christian worldview prescribe as the proper attitude toward sin?

APPLY

16 As individual followers of Christ, where must we begin in the battle to roll back sin (Rom. 6:23)? What does this require of you (Rom. 6:11-19)?

17 What are some ways that we can help one another in this important and difficult challenge?

18 What are some ways Christians can begin to speak out against sinful practices in our communities? What kinds of responses can we expect when we do?

19 Since only the gospel can deliver people from the power of sin, how can we effectively bring the gospel message to those around us?

20 What prayer requests come to mind as a result of studying these chapters?

8

THE PROBLEM OF SUFFERING

Innocent children murdered in their classrooms and schoolyards. Refugees driven ruthlessly from their homes. Abused spouses and children. Good people suddenly struck down by illness or accident. Why does God allow so much suffering in the world?

Read chapter 21.

OBSERVE

1 What problem was bothering Albert Einstein? Why was it on his mind at this particular time? How did this problem affect his view of God?

2 What did Einstein conclude about the problem of suffering? How did this affect his response to God?

3 How have atheists tried to solve the problem of evil and suffering?

4 How have Eastern religions and Christian Science tried to solve this problem?

5 How have some theologians tried to solve this problem?

6 How has "process theology" tried to solve the problem of suffering?

7 How has John Hick tried to solve it?

8 Why is it so important that we recognize the historicity of the Fall in the Garden?

9 Why is it necessary for God to condemn evil?

10 How did God in his mercy respond to evil and suffering in his creation?

11 How should people respond to God's mercy in the face of evil?

REFLECT

12 Revelation 12 can give us some additional insights into the origins of evil and suffering on earth. According to verses 7-9 and verse 13, how did evil come to be on the earth?

13 A passage that complements this one very well and that biblical scholars
    understand to treat the same subject is Ezekiel 28:1-19. While the king
    of Tyre is the immediate object of the prophecy, the story of Satan's condem-
    nation lies in the background (as can be seen from vv. 2, 12-15). According
    to verses 2, 15, and 17, what attitude in Satan brought about his downfall?

14 According to Revelation 12:9 and 13, what did Satan take as his "mission"
    once he was on the earth? How could this lead to evil and suffering?

15 According to Revelation 12:17, who are the special objects of Satan's rage?
    Why do you suppose this is so?

APPLY

16 Whenever we are confronted with evil and suffering—whether in our own
    lives or in our society—how should we respond?

17 What should we keep in mind about the ultimate source of suffering?

18 What should our attitude be toward those who suffer?

19 What does it mean for those of us who worship and serve God that he in his
    mercy has taken steps to relieve human suffering?

20 Think of a recent incident in which people in your community were subjected
    to suffering—through crime, accident, storm, or similar circumstances. How
    might your church have responded in order to show God's love?

21 What steps can your church take today in order to be ready for the next
    opportunity to show God's love to those who are suffering?

22 Having studied the second worldview question—What has gone wrong with
    the world?—what difference does it make to you that we live in a fallen world
    marked by sin?

23 Having studied chapters 15–21, in what ways are you more equipped to artic-
    ulate and defend your worldview?

24 What prayer requests come to mind as a result of studying this chapter?

9

FROM DEATH TO LIFE

Our culture has been described as "a culture of death" because it glorifies violence, tolerates abortion, and flirts with euthanasia. But as many people who helped to create this culture of death are finding out—people like Dr. Bernard Nathanson—God still offers us a new life.

Read chapters 22 and 23.

OBSERVE

1 According to chapter 22, briefly summarize the process that Dr. Nathanson went through as his mind began to change about abortion. What were some of the factors involved?

2 What did Dr. Nathanson discover from watching ultrasound images of abortion?

3 How did proponents of abortion respond to Dr. Nathanson's change of heart? Why?

4 What in Dr. Nathanson's upbringing led him to regard abortion as perfectly natural and normal?

5 What happened to cause Dr. Nathanson's heart to begin to turn to God?

6 According to chapter 23, what is "the great human predicament," and how does Bernard Nathanson's experience illustrate it?

7 What kind of redemption is promised through the medium of advertising?

8 Discuss some of the ways that this promised redemption is presented. How do these ads try to appeal to religious hopes?

9 Why is materialism no true redemption at all? What does it fail to provide?

REFLECT

10 Scripture says a lot about the false gods that people construct to take the place of the one true God. Read Romans 1:18-20. Which aspect of chapters 22 and 23 does this passage address?

11 What do we learn from verses 21-23 about people's inherent religious inclinations? What do many people do with the knowledge they have of God?

12 If we think of a "god" as anything to which we give ultimate devotion, anything in which we stake our hope of happiness, what would be some examples of false gods today?

13 According to verses 24, 26, and 28, how does God respond to people when they reject him in favor of false gods?

14 Look carefully at verses 24-32. How would you describe the moral trend that sets in when people reject knowledge of the true God and begin to pursue false gods? Where do you see that happening in our society today?

APPLY

15 Do you think it's possible for Christians to keep false gods? How? Do you recognize any false gods in your own life? If so, what will you do about it?

16 What would you recommend for any Christian who is seeking to serve the false gods of our materialistic age?

17 According to Romans 1:21, how can we keep from falling into the materialistic religion of our age?

18 Why do many young people get caught up in the allure of materialism? How can parents and churches help children recognize and resist this false god?

19 How does the gospel of Jesus Christ give greater satisfaction and hope than the empty promises of materialism?

20 What prayer requests come to mind as a result of studying these chapters?

LIBERATED TO SLAVERY

Although they claimed to be wise, they became fools," Romans 1:22 tells us. This might well be a banner displayed over our postmodernist generation. Many people believe that by throwing off the restraints of religion and morality, they will attain true liberation. However, instead of finding freedom, they find that they have become slaves to base lust and unquenchable desire.

Read chapters 24 and 25.

OBSERVE

1 According to chapter 24, what is the "the myth of progress" or "the Escalator Myth"? What does it promise?

2 How is the Escalator Myth related to the ideas of sin, utopia, and evolution?

3 What did Hegel contribute to the Escalator Myth?

4 In what ways is Marxism a form of the Escalator Myth?

5 In what ways do the ideas of Karl Marx reflect a religious worldview?

6 What is the fatal flaw of Marxism?

7 According to chapter 25, who was Margaret Sanger, and what was her contribution to the Escalator Myth?

8 How did Alfred Kinsey try to detach sex from morality? What justification did he offer?

9 How did Wilhelm Reich help to accelerate this version of the Escalator Myth?

10 In what ways can we see—especially in the work of Robert Rimmer—that this version of the Escalator Myth is another form of religion promising redemption?

11 How is sex education shaped by the Escalator Myth?

12 In what ways do the founders of this worldview demonstrate the emptiness of their views in their own lives?

REFLECT

13 The desire to be free of God's law is very old. Look at Psalm 2:1-3. In what ways does this picture capture the "liberationist" hopes that we see all around us today?

14 According to verses 4-6, how does God respond to people's liberationist aspirations?

15 In verses 6-9, what does God proclaim as the divine counterpart of human liberation thinking?

16 What should be our response to God's divine authority?

APPLY

17 How should Christians respond to the vain aspirations of our "liberated" contemporaries?

18 Are you prepared to do that with the people around you? In what ways would you like to be better prepared?

19 How would you put Psalm 2:10-12 into a meaningful presentation of the good news of God's love in Jesus Christ?

20 What prayer requests come to mind as a result of studying these chapters?

SALVATION THROUGH SCIENCE

Many people today still put their faith in science and technology to make a better world, even though the scientific version of the Escalator Myth is increasingly called into question in our postmodernist culture.

Read chapter 26.

OBSERVE

1 How does popular culture portray the hope of redemption through science and technology?

2 How did Francis Bacon start the ball rolling in this version of the Escalator Myth?

3 How did Auguste Comte envision the role of science in the development of a mature society?

4 What was Herbert Spencer's contribution to the myth of progress and the religion of science?

5 How have genetic studies factored into this version of the Escalator Myth?

6 Why is science unable to give any moral guidance?

7 What danger for human dignity lies in this version of the Escalator Myth?

8 How has this kind of thinking influenced extraterrestrial studies? In what ways can you see a religious element to this field?

9 Does history support the idea that science—or knowledge—is a reliable savior? Explain.

10 How should we understand the role of science within a biblical worldview?

REFLECT

11 Genesis 11:1-9 shows us a primitive society with lofty ideals and high hopes. According to verses 1-4, to what did these people aspire? How would those goals be expressed in contemporary language?

12 How are these goals at odds with God's will?

13 What danger did God see in this project? How did he defeat it?

14 It is interesting to note that God sometimes works gently in his judgments against rebellious people. Here, instead of wrath and destruction, he used a simple cultural artifact—language—to thwart the arrogant plans of his creatures. What does this reveal to us about God's love toward those who rebel against him? What should we learn from this for our own relationships with people who live in opposition to God?

15 In the end, would you say that humanity even benefited from this act of judgment? In what ways?

APPLY

16 What evidence do you see to indicate that many people are still looking for science to take us along the road to utopia?

17 In what kinds of settings in our communities might we expect to find proponents of the scientific worldview promoting their version of the Escalator Myth? How can we begin to oppose them there?

18 In evaluating current technology, many people in the scientific community believe that "If we *can* do it, we should." What kinds of moral questions does such thinking provoke? How can a biblical worldview help in addressing those questions?

19 What prayer requests come to mind as a result of studying this chapter?

12

THE COURAGE OF DESPAIR

The failure of so many modern ideologies led many people to despair of really changing human nature or creating a better world. With Western worldviews crumbling, some people turn to the East.

Read chapters 27 and 28.

OBSERVE

1 According to chapter 27, what caused people to begin to doubt the promise of science and technology?

2 What is existentialism?

3 In what ways did existential thinking appeal to the countercultural movement of the sixties?

4 How did the various strains of pessimism dovetail nicely into the predominant Darwinian views of the day?

5 What is sociobiology, and how does it express a philosophy of despair?

6 According to chapter 28, why did some people begin looking to Eastern religions for redemption?

7 How did the popular culture help to spread the gospel of Eastern religion and the New Age?

8 What is the New Age movement? How does it differ from traditional Eastern thinking?

9 How has New Age thinking affected many people's view of God?

10 By what means is New Age thinking making its way into our society?

11 Why is the New Age god unable to save us?

REFLECT

12 In John 4:1-27 we read that Jesus confronted a woman who was confused about religion—among other things. How did Jesus go out of his way—in more ways than one—to talk with this woman (vv. 4, 9)?

13 How did Jesus approach this woman (v. 7)?

14 How did he turn a mundane conversation into a spiritual discussion (vv. 10-15)?

15 What did Jesus do to show this woman that religion and morality are inextricably linked (vv. 16-18)?

16 How did Jesus get this woman to see him for who he is (vv. 19-26)?

APPLY

17 What can we learn from Jesus' encounter with the Samaritan woman about helping people with different religious views to begin thinking about Jesus and the claims of the gospel?

18 Think of one person with whom you might begin to use what you have learned, starting this week. How will you approach him or her to get the conversation started?

19 What prayer requests come to mind as a result of studying these chapters?

13

REAL REDEMPTION

Only in the gospel of Jesus Christ can people find real redemption. Christ takes us the way we are—fallen and sinful—and accepts our repentance and forgives our sin. He paid the ultimate price for our sin with his own death on the cross. Now he offers us power for both meaningful living today and everlasting life beyond the grave. That's real redemption!

Read chapter 29.

OBSERVE

1 Briefly summarize the promise of redemption as each of the following offers it:

- commercialism
- neo-Marxism
- sexual liberation
- science and technology
- the New Age

2 What is the human dilemma according to the Christian worldview? Explain.

3 What does Christianity present as the solution to this problem?

4 Why is it important to stress that Christianity's solution is rooted in historical truth?

5 In what ways does the Old Testament point to the Christian solution?

6 What does it mean that God's redemption *restores* us?

7 How does this restoration get us back on track with God and his plan?

REFLECT

8 Let's take a look at Hebrews 2:1-9. What warning does the writer give us (vv. 1-3a)?

9   In verses 5-8 the writer describes the purpose for which God created us—the purpose to which we are restored in redemption. He quotes from Psalm 8. What purpose for humanity is outlined in Hebrews 2:6-8a?

10 In what ways can we see that this pupose has not yet been fulfilled—that people are not succeeding in subduing the creation for God's glory and human benefit?

11 Verse 9 begins with the word *but,* and the writer points us to the solution. What is it? What can begin to get us back on track with God's plan for humanity?

APPLY

12 How did you come to know Christ and the restoring grace of God? What difference has that made in your life?

13 In what areas of your life can you say that you are consciously and consistently taking a "Psalm 8" approach to living for the Lord, that is, seeking to bring all things in line with God's purpose for creation?

14 In what areas of your life do you need to develop this approach more fully?

15 What is implied in the writer's question—"How shall we escape?" (Heb. 2:3)—if we fail to take seriously the full implications of our redemption in Christ?

16 What is required for us to "pay more careful attention" (Heb. 2:1) to the things we have heard about redemption in Jesus Christ?

17 Having studied the third worldview question—What can we do to fix it?—what difference does it make to you that God redeemed you through the death of his Son and promises you eternal life with him?

18 Having studied chapters 22–29, in what ways are you more equipped to articulate and defend your worldview?

19 As we reach the halfway point in our study, what have been some of the most important lessons you have learned so far?

20 What prayer requests come to mind as a result of studying this chapter?

STUDY GUIDE
TWO

1

ALL THINGS NEW

The gospel of Jesus Christ is the power of God for salvation,
a salvation that makes all things new in our lives, as Danny Croce
and untold millions of men and women throughout the ages have
discovered.

Read chapters 30 and 31.

OBSERVE

1   Referring to chapter 30, summarize the steps that led Danny Croce to a saving
knowledge of the Lord Jesus Christ.

2   What evidence can you see that Danny truly came to know the Lord?

3   According to chapter 31, what is the status of the cultural commission
(or cultural mandate) today?

4   What is the relationship between the cultural commission and the great
commission? Explain.

5   What does it mean that Christians are saved not only *from* something but also
to something?

6   Why should there be no dichotomy between the "sacred" and the "secular" for
the Christian?

7   In what ways did the Irish Christian missionaries of the fifth to the eighth
centuries—beginning with Patrick, the British missionary to the Irish—
effectively combine the cultural commission with the great commission?

8   In what other ways did Christianity serve as a creative cultural force during
the Middle Ages?

9   Why is today an excellent time for Christians to begin once again to live and
proclaim their faith boldly?

10 What is the key to effective evangelism? Explain.

REFLECT

11 Read 2 Corinthians 5:14-21. According to the apostle Paul, what must be our compelling motivation as we go forth in the name of Jesus? Explain:

12 What does Christ's example teach us (v. 15)?

13 Verse 17 says that anyone who is in Christ is a new creation. List the areas in your life in which that newness is increasingly evident:

14 Paul says we have been given a "ministry of reconciliation." What does that mean? How does the idea that God is reconciling the world (the entire world order) to himself challenge the false dichotomy between the "sacred" and "secular"?

15 As ambassadors for Christ, how should we expect to conduct our lives in this postmodernist world?

APPLY

16 Go back to question 13 above. On a scale of 1 to 10 (10 meaning "fully" and 1 meaning "not at all"), to what extent would you say that you are experiencing the newness of Christ in each of these areas of your life? Give an explanation for each of the areas that you rate less than 6.

17 Since Christian unity is an important part of our witness for Christ, how can you begin to encourage more unity among the members of your congregation? between your congregation and other churches in your community?

18 What is the message that we—as Christ's ambassadors—have to proclaim to our postmodernist world?

19 What prayer requests come to mind as a result of studying these chapters?

2

BEGINNING WITH OURSELVES

The place to begin in realizing more of the newness of Christ and the power of a Christian worldview is with ourselves. We all need to overcome old habits and unprofitable ways of thinking.

Read chapter 32.

OBSERVE

1　Referring to the example given early in the chapter, how is it apparent that the secular worldview affects the thinking even of sincere Christians?

2　What has become of the sense of individual responsibility in our post-modernist world?

3　What is a "value-free lifestyle"? In what ways is this concept evident in our day?

4　What is the "modernist impasse"? Why does this make today an opportune time for Christians to share their worldview?

5　In what ways do social statistics encourage us to believe that we have a powerful message to proclaim?

6　How should the example of a scholar like Guenter Lewy encourage us in our work as reconcilers and ambassadors?

7　In what ways has it been shown that having a sincere religious faith can be beneficial to one's health?

8　In what ways do the results of research in the world of psychology encourage us in our witness?

9　Summarize the ways in which the Christian worldview provides help and hope for our postmodernist generation.

REFLECT

10　The early Christians lived in ways that gave powerful confirmation of their witness to Jesus Christ. According to Acts 2:41-47, what was the congregational life of the first Christians like?

11 Read Acts 4:32-37. How does this add to the picture of the first Christian community?

12 In what ways and for what purposes was the life-changing power of the gospel at work in Acts 6:1-6?

13 Read Acts 6:7. These priests had no doubt seen and heard Jesus, and they had heard others tell about Jesus. How might the events of Acts 6:1-6, in addition to those of Acts 2 and 4, have influenced these priests to believe in Jesus? Explain:

14 Think about the churches in our own communities. When the postmodernist world looks at us, to what extent does it see reflected in our lifestyles and relationships the kinds of things those priests would have seen in the first Christian church? What can we learn from those first Christians?

APPLY

15 What attitudes does it take for Christians to begin relating to one another and to the world around them as the first Christians did? In which of these attitudes does your church need to grow? In which do you need to grow?

16 Can you see any ways—either in your own life or that of your church—in which the ideas of secularism have affected your approach to the Christian life?

17 From what we saw in those first Christians, what is required for us to overcome our captivity to secular thinking and to gain the new worldview and attitudes that will cause the watching world to take notice?

18 What can you begin to do today to realize more of the power of the Christian worldview in your own life?

19 What obstacles might keep you from making progress in this effort? How can your fellow church members help you to overcome these?

20 What prayer requests come to mind as a result of studying this chapter?

3

GOD'S TRAINING GROUND

In recent years the idea of "family" has been subjected to drastic redefinition by our postmodernist society. A biblical worldview can help us to recover the true meaning and purpose of this foundational social unit.

Read chapter 33.

OBSERVE

1   In what ways is the family today being redefined? From what sources?

2   Why is it important that we ask people not only to explain but to *justify* their worldview? What does this mean?

3   Why is it so important to root the idea of marriage and family in God's creation?

4   How does the philosophy of the "unencumbered self" affect the family and other social institutions?

5   What has social science revealed about the ability of many divorced people to serve as effective parents? to function as happy and fulfilled adults?

6   Outline the essential teachings of a biblical view of the family:

7   What does it mean for Christians to treat their own families as a ministry?

8   What are some things that local churches can do to begin promoting healthier families among their members and in their community?

9   What are "Community Marriage Policies," and how do they help communities to strengthen families?

REFLECT

10   Read Ephesians 5:18–6:4, a passage that has much to say about how families ought to operate. According to verse 18b, what is the source of healthy family life? Why is this so?

11 One of the evidences of our actually being filled with God's Spirit is that we submit to one another. What does this mean? How did Jesus embody this practice for us in John 13:1-15?

12 What does it mean for a wife to submit to her husband? for a husband to submit to his wife?

13 What should a husband take as the measure and standard of his love for his wife? Give some examples of what this might look like.

14 Look carefully at Ephesians 5:25-33. How will a husband show that he truly loves his wife as Christ loved the church? How will a wife show that she is willing to submit to that love?

15 According to Ephesians 6:1-4, what are the responsibilities of Christian parents toward their children? of children toward their parents?

APPLY

16 What is the most important lesson that you have gained from this study? How can you begin to implement this lesson in your own family life?

17 How can Christian families help one another to realize more of the biblical promise for families?

18 As you begin to work harder at realizing the promise of Scripture for your family, what will be your greatest obstacles? How will you overcome these? Whose help will you enlist?

19 What prayer requests come to mind as a result of studying this chapter?

4

STILL AT RISK

It is hardly necessary to talk about the sad state of many of America's schools. Their problems are in no small part a result of the naturalistic worldview that dominates the educational arena. What can Christians do about it?

Read chapter 34.

OBSERVE

1 What are the two historic tasks of American education, and how well are American schools addressing these tasks today?

2 How has an emphasis on self-esteem affected the learning process in our schools?

3 What is a "constructivist" view of education, and how does it differ from traditional theories of education?

4 What view of the child prevails in America's schools? How does that view work against effective learning?

5 What faulty assumptions about children guide this view of learning?

6 How does the American education system view the idea of redemption and the role of the school in the redemptive process?

7 What is the starting point of a biblical view of education, and how is it unique?

8 What options are available for the education of Christian children today? What do you consider to be some of the strengths and weaknesses of these various options?

9 What are some approaches that Christians might take to begin improving the public schools in their communities?

10 Why is it so important that Christians begin to be active in the work of school reform and the education of children in our communities?

REFLECT

11 Psalm 78:1-8 provides excellent guidelines for the education of our children. According to verses 3-4, who is responsible for the education of children?

12 According to verse 4, what must we teach our children about God? What is our responsibility to ensure that all academic disciplines are taught from the perspective of a biblical worldview?

13 One area of the curriculum for our children is mentioned in verse 5. What is it, and what does it include?

14 According to verses 6-7, what should be the long-term objectives of our work in educating our children?

15 According to verse 8, what are we trying to prevent?

APPLY

16 To what extent and in what ways is it possible for parents in your community to take an active role in the education of the community's children?

17 How are you or any of your church members involved in any of these?

18 What can we expect if Christians remain detached from the work of educating children?

19 How can your church begin to take a more active role in seeing to it that its own children receive an education that is consistent with the biblical worldview?

20 What prayer requests come to mind as a result of studying this chapter?

5

LIFE TOGETHER

Our communities are in trouble. They are under assault from the dark side of the naturalistic worldview, and they seem wholly unable to defend themselves and to preserve a sense of cohesiveness, safety, and well-being. The biblical worldview points us toward solutions to this desperate situation.

Read chapters 35 and 36.

OBSERVE

1 According to chapter 35, what made Sal think that he could make a difference in his community?

2 How would you describe Sal's approach to trying to make a difference in his community?

3 What evidence indicates that Sal actually did help his community begin to change?

4 According to chapter 36, how did the Supreme Court exacerbate the problems of crime in the neighborhoods of America?

5 In what ways does the worldview behind the civil liberties movement reject biblical teaching?

6 How do American cities try to combat the effects of the civil liberties movement?

7 What does *shalom* mean, and how does it relate to the idea of community? In what ways have Christians begun to show that *shalom* is a workable idea in communities?

8 In what ways do the examples from Boston, Dallas, Chicago, Baltimore, and other cities mirror the work done by Sal Bartolomeo in his neighborhood?

9 How does our citizenship in the City of God require us to take responsibility for the *shalom* of our communities?

REFLECT

10 Christians can be a powerful force for community, beginning in their own congregations. Read Acts 6:1-6, and summarize the problem that arose there:

11 In what ways was this an *economic* problem? In what ways was it a *racial* problem?

12 What steps did the individual church members take to resolve this situation? What steps did the leaders of the community take?

13 According to verse 7, what resulted from this direct effort at restoring *shalom* in the Christian community?

APPLY

14 What problems are threatening or depriving your community of its *shalom* today?

15 How is your community trying to cope with these problems? Are they getting better or worse?

16 How will you get involved in restoring *shalom* to your community? How will your church get involved?

17 What can we expect if Christians fail to get involved? What can we expect if they do become involved?

18 What prayer requests come to mind as a result of studying these chapters?

6

BECOMING MORAL PERSONS

Christians have shown that communities can be restored to *shalom* by working one person at a time, one situation at a time. But what does it mean to become a "moral person"?

Read chapter 37.

OBSERVE

1   Why doesn't relativism provide a foundation for a safe and orderly society?

2   How does the example of the Conference on Science, Philosophy, and Religion demonstrate the inability of reason alone to create a moral consensus for society?

3   What role should conscience play in achieving a moral society? How does this notion relate to the biblical worldview?

4   How has our sense of separation between public life and private life affected the morality of Americans? How does the Christian worldview respond to this false dichotomy?

5   What is integrity, and why is it so important?

6   How does the biblical worldview help people achieve integrity?

7   What did I (Chuck) fail to understand as a young lawyer about individual morality? How did it catch up with me?

8   How can we begin to fulfill the moral law of God?

9   If only converted people can fulfill the law of God, why do Christians have a responsibility to work for a good society "by cultivating ethical knowledge even among the unconverted"?

10   Through what positive and negative means do societies encourage virtuous behavior? What is the state of these means in our society today?

REFLECT

11 Read Psalm 51. David experienced moral failure in his sin against Bathsheba and against her husband. But according to David, against whom did he really sin (v. 4)? How did he characterize his behavior?

12 David expresses his feelings of guilt, sorrow, and repentance in this psalm. Are these negative responses? What useful purposes do they serve? How do we see these responses in our society today?

13 David expresses two goals in this psalm. The first can be seen in verses 12-13. What is it?

14 The second is expressed in verses 18-19. What is it?

15 How can individual reconciliation with God be a blessing not only to the individual but also to his or her community?

16 According to verse 17, where does moral transformation begin? What is the relationship between the gospel of Jesus Christ and what we read in this verse?

APPLY

17 Can we expect the members of our community to become moral people apart from being converted to Christ? Will keeping the law of God save them?

18 What does this mean for your work as a moral agent in your community? Are you prepared to take up this challenge?

19 How can you and your church demonstrate faithfulness to biblical morality to the members of your community?

20 What prayer requests come to mind as a result of studying this chapter?

7

THE WORK OF OUR HANDS

The Protestant work ethic has long undergirded the American economy, making it one of the strongest and most productive in the world. But even a work ethic grounded in Scripture can be corrupted by a naturalistic worldview. It's time to reestablish a Christian presence in the workplaces of America.

Read chapter 38.

OBSERVE

1 How can we see that God intended work to be part of his plan for a world filled with *shalom?*

2 How did the fall into sin affect the work that people were given to do?

3 How are Christians to view wealth?

4 What does it mean that we are only stewards of the things God has entrusted to us? How does this relate to our work?

5 What is the Bible's view of private property?

6 In the biblical worldview, what becomes of the poor?

7 How did Enlightenment views begin to corrupt the biblical view of work?

8 On what factors does a healthy economy depend? What does this mean?

9 In what ways has the workplace begun to work against healthy community life?

10 How are churches today providing models of programs that can spur economic self-sufficiency?

REFLECT

11 Let's look more closely at the biblical basis of work as we see it described in Genesis 2. Looking at verse 2, what is the basis for saying that God created people as working creatures?

12 Notice how many times Genesis 1 uses the words *good* or *very good* to describe God's work. What does it mean that God described his work as good? What does this suggest about God's intentions for our work?

13 Various kinds of work are indicated or suggested in Genesis 2. What kinds of work do the following verses lead you to think about?

- v. 9
- v. 10
- vv. 11-12
- v. 15
- vv. 19-20
- vv. 22-24

14 How was the calling to work related to the cultural mandate of Genesis 1:26-28?

APPLY

15 To what extent and in what specific ways is your own work consciously related to your calling as an image-bearer of God? Looked at another way, how does your work allow you to labor for the realization of God's "good" in your community?

16 Do you see any signs of the deterioration of the Christian work ethic in your community? Explain:

17 What can your church do to begin preparing its young people to enter the workforce with a biblical view of work as their operating framework?

18 In what ways can you or your church begin to reclaim the workplace in your community for a more biblical view of work?

19 What prayer requests come to mind as a result of studying this chapter?

8

THE ULTIMATE APPEAL

The Christian apologist Francis Schaeffer used to talk about the dangers of "sociological law"—laws written to respond only to particular social situations, having no basis in anything other than the needs of the moment. But, without a foundation in absolute law, sociological law can become tyrannical, as we shall see.

Read chapter 39.

OBSERVE

1 On what basis did Dr. Martin Luther King Jr. decide to disobey the law in Birmingham? Do you agree with King's reasoning? his actions?

2 What is the difference between just and unjust law?

3 What does it mean that there exists "transcendent law above human law"?

4 In what ways does the American system of government and law as designed by the Founders reflect biblical principles?

5 What is the meaning of "sphere sovereignty"? How does this concept contribute to the idea of limited government?

6 What have been the effects of pragmatism and deconstructionism on transcendent law?

7 How did the Supreme Court redefine "liberty" in *Planned Parenthood v. Casey?* What are the implications of this redefinition?

8 What did the Court label as "majoritarian intolerance"? In *Lee v. Weisman* what did the Court reject as "intolerance"?

9 How does the Court's view of intolerance increase its own power?

10 What did the momentous Supreme Court ruling against the Religious Freedom Restoration Act (RFRA) signify?

11 How do liberal and conservative approaches to the law and morality create a catch-22?

12 What is "the great vulnerability of the American system" of government?

13 List the four consequences of the loss of moral authority.

14 How are we already suffering from these consequences? To what extent do you find this frustrating? challenging?

15 Given the rejection of moral law in society and the imbalance of power in the government, what seems to be the best way to restore our legal and political systems?

REFLECT

16 Psalm 72 is an excellent place to look at God's plan for human governments. How does this psalm guide us in praying for our governments, according to each of the following verses?

- v. 1
- v. 2
- v. 4
- v. 5
- vv. 12-14
- v. 15

17 What promises does God make to governments that rule according to his guidelines (see Ps. 72:3, 7, 8-11, 15-17)?

18 Ultimately, according to verses 18-19, what happens in a community or society in which people are governed according to God's law?

19 Imagine that you are writing a letter to a candidate for political office, listing guidelines you would expect him or her to use when making decisions in office. What would you write?

APPLY

20 How frequently do you pray for your political leaders and government officials? How can this psalm help you in praying more effectively?

21 How can we "live out our convictions as responsible citizens" and present the Christian worldview to our communities?

22 Have you ever been labeled "intolerant" for your beliefs or for a stand you have taken? Describe the situation.

23 What is our responsibility when we are confronted with an unjust law?

24 What prayer requests come to mind as a result of studying this chapter?

THE BASIS FOR TRUE SCIENCE

Within the Christian worldview science can be a powerful tool. But first it must be stripped of its naturalistic assumptions and retooled with the presuppositions of revealed truth.

Read chapter 40.

OBSERVE

1 In what ways is it apparent that science is used as a weapon against religious faith?

2 What was David Hume's role in helping to position science as an adversary to religion?

3 In what ways are the naturalistic assumptions of science incoherent and contradictory?

4 What task does the Christian community face in responding to these assumptions?

5 What four important assumptions did the Christian worldview provide for the first scientists?

6 In what kinds of forums should Christians be trying to raise issues regarding the fallacies of naturalism in science?

7 What goals can we set for addressing naturalistic science in the schools?

8 Why should we encourage Christian young people to go into the field of science as their work?

9 Many scientists today are pressing to reestablish the claims of science on a foundation of false religion. What are they failing to remember?

10 What is meant by "the reformation of science"?

REFLECT

11 Let's look more closely at the passage with which chapter 40 concludes. Read 2 Corinthians 10:3-5. To what kind of people was Paul writing (see

1 Cor. 1:26)? Whom did he expect to see getting involved in the teaching of 2 Corinthians 10:3-5?

12 Paul says, "The weapons we fight with are not the weapons of the world." Why does he refer to our struggle with "arguments" and "pretension" as warfare? Have you experienced this warfare? In what ways?

13 Paul tells us that God's weapons are quite powerful to accomplish the results we seek. According to Ephesians 6:10-18, what are those weapons?

14 Who or what are our adversaries in this warfare (2 Cor. 10:4-5)? How can we identify them in the world today?

15 What is our twofold objective in this warfare (v. 5)? What would that look like, say, in the case of modern science?

APPLY

16 In what ways have you seen the adverse effects of the naturalistic worldview on the practice of your own faith? Has the naturalistic outlook colored or otherwise hindered your faith in any way? Explain.

17 What do you think it would take for you to be ready to talk with someone else about the fallacies of naturalistic thinking? How can you become better prepared?

18 How can your church become more involved in speaking out against the fallacies of the naturalistic worldview in the various forums available to you in your community?

19 What can we expect if Christians fail to take up this challenge and naturalism continues its warfare against the faith without any opposition?

20 What prayer requests come to mind as a result of studying this chapter?

REFORMING THE ARTS

The arts are a powerful tool for shaping opinion and touching the heart. Christians must engage the arts with their worldview so that music, art, and literature will glorify God and enrich the human experience.

Read chapters 41 and 42.

OBSERVE

1 How does the opening vignette of chapter 41 illustrate the power of the arts to affect our outlook on life?

2 How does the story of Henryk Górecki illustrate the power that a Christian worldview can have on the arts?

3 According to chapter 42, why are so many contemporary composers producing such dissonant music? Why are so many modern artists creating so much abstract art?

4 Why are the arts important to the Christian?

5 How do the arts function in society? What seems to be their purpose?

6 Cite some historical examples of Christians working in the arts. How have they used the arts to testify of their faith in Christ?

7 What caused the arts to veer off the path marked out by so many exemplary Christian artists?

8 In what sense has art today become a surrogate for religion?

9 What is meant by the term *anti-art*? What are some examples?

10 What steps can Christians take to begin restoring the arts?

REFLECT

11 The Bible not only endorses the arts but also shows us that God uses them widely. Which of the arts does God employ in each of the following situations?

- building the tabernacle and the temple
- writing the psalms
- preparing the priestly garments

12 One passage in particular helps us to see God's approval and use of the arts in the reformation of society. Read Exodus 35:20–36:7. How did God intend to use the arts (vv. 20-21)? Which of the arts would be involved?

13 In what ways was art a community activity in this passage?

14 Where did Bezalel and Oholiab get their skills as artists?

15 Why do you suppose the Lord mentioned the particular gift he did in verse 34? What does this suggest about the importance of the arts for people in general?

16 How did the people show that they were eager to support the arts and the work of the artists who had been called to serve the Lord?

APPLY

17 Think about your own home for a moment. In what ways do the arts play a role in the way you live and in what your home "says" to any visitors?

18 How would you rate your ability to appreciate and benefit from the arts in general (good, fair, poor)? Do you think your love for God and other people could be enhanced by a more consistent involvement with the arts? Why or why not?

19 Where will you begin to help in restoring the arts to their God-honoring position in society? How will you become more aware of and active in the arts yourself? What can your church do to enrich its use of the arts?

20 What prayer requests come to mind as a result of studying these chapters?

THE GOSPEL AND POPULAR CULTURE

Can even popular culture be redeemed and used for good within the framework of a biblical worldview? You might just be surprised.

Read chapters 43 and 44.

OBSERVE

1 According to chapter 43, how would you describe Martha Williamson's early experience as a Christian working in Hollywood?

2 Why was deciding to do *Angel's Attic* such a struggle for Martha? How was her faith at work in the midst of this struggle?

3 How would you describe Martha's efforts to keep *Touched by an Angel* on the air? What can we learn from her about reforming popular culture?

4 According to chapter 44, why is the challenge of redeeming popular culture so great?

5 What has happened to popular culture as it has spread and pervaded our society?

6 In what ways can popular culture adversely affect people?

7 What is a good working definition of *popular culture?* Using this definition, in what ways are you exposed to popular culture every day?

8 What does it mean to begin linking "art to truth"?

9 How can Christians begin to redeem popular culture?

10 Should Christians be involved in creating popular culture? Why or why not?

REFLECT

11 The Bible provides several examples for us to follow in working to redeem popular culture. First, however, we need to be convinced that this is legiti-

mate. How do the following Scripture passages suggest that redeeming popular culture can be considered a legitimate and important work for Christians?

- 1 Cor. 3:21-23
- 1 Cor. 10:31
- Eph. 1:22-23

12 Look at the psalm dedications for such psalms as 55, 56, and 57. These psalms were apparently meant to be sung to popular songs or according to well-known tunes. How do they guide us in thinking about ways to redeem popular culture? What are some examples of how people do this today?

13 Jesus used literary art forms to communicate objective truth. How does his use of parables, metaphors, similes, and so forth serve to encourage us in the use of such forms?

14 The Bible itself, particularly the New Testament, uses popular culture in the form of language. The Greek used in the New Testament, for example, was the "language of the people" of its day, not of the academics or philosophers. How should this guide and encourage us in thinking about the potential of popular culture to serve the purposes of God?

APPLY

15 Think about the influence of popular culture in your own life. In what ways do the following affect your lifestyle?

- advertisements
- popular music
- television programs
- conversations with others
- the print media

16 Do you think that, on the whole, popular culture is a positive or negative factor in your walk with the Lord? Explain.

17 Where will you begin to redeem popular culture in your own life? in your home and family?

18 What can churches do to prepare their young people to take their own popular culture "captive" for Jesus Christ?

19 How can your church encourage and support its members who become involved in creating popular culture?

20 What prayer requests come to mind as a result of studying these chapters?

12

HOW NOW SHALL WE LIVE?

It is not enough to know that a Christian worldview is more consistent, more rational, and more workable than any other worldview. We need to find ways to let that worldview work for us if it is going to be as effective as God intends.

Read chapter 45.

OBSERVE

1 For what reasons is the Christian worldview to be preferred over all other worldviews?

2 What is the real test of a worldview and of the Christian worldview in particular?

3 What events led Kim Phuc to become a follower of Christ?

4 What was her immediate response to coming to know the Lord?

5 How was Kim able to use her experience as a way of testifying to the grace of God in her life?

6 How did Kim's message of forgiveness accomplish what Robert McNamara's technological worldview could not? In what ways is this an excellent parable of how we should now live?

7 How, in a few brief sentences, would you answer the question, "How now shall we live?"

REFLECT

8 Ephesians 5:1-21 shows us the many contrasts and challenges involved in living the life of faith. According to verses 1-2, what will be the most obvious indicator that we are imitating God and walking as Christ did?

9 According to verses 3-8, what must we avoid in order to live consistently in the light of God's truth and love?

10 What should we be seeking to cultivate more of, according to verses 9-10?

11 What, according to verses 11-13, should be the effect of our living "in the light" on the unfruitful works of darkness? What does this mean?

12 Paul says we are to be careful about how we live (v. 15). Here is a call to vigilance in every area of our lives. What four things do verses 15-18 say we should we be vigilant about, and what will result from this vigilance?

13 If we fail to exercise this kind of vigilance over our lives, what can we expect in a time such as ours, when truly "the days are evil" (v. 16)?

14 Paul calls us to be filled with (literally "in") the Spirit. If wine is to be taken both literally and as a symbol of the worldliness all around us, what kinds of things must not be allowed to fill up our lives?

15 What four evidences of the Spirit's presence in a believer's life does Paul identify in verses 19-21? What would they look like in your life?

APPLY

16 Evaluate your walk with the Lord by the criteria outlined in this passage. Would you say that you are fully consistent with this passage, somewhat consistent, somewhat inconsistent, or altogether inconsistent with what we see here? Explain.

17 How would you encourage new believers to begin exercising the kind of vigilance that Paul calls for in this passage?

18 How can you discern when your life is too much filled with some aspect of worldliness? What should you do when this is the case?

19 How can Christians encourage one another to walk in the light as this passage calls us to do?

20 What prayer requests come to mind as a result of studying this chapter?

BECOMING MEN AND WOMEN OF ANOTHER TYPE

This final lesson is designed to help you bring together your thoughts, observations, and conclusions from your study of *How Now Shall We Live?* By the time you complete this lesson, you will have developed a personal plan of action for moving ahead in the Christian worldview.

REVIEW

1   What new insights have you had from your study of this book? In what ways have those ideas begun to affect your approach to living as a Christian in this world?

2   In what ways has the worldview of naturalism had a greater effect in your life than you think it should?

3   In what ways have you begun to adopt a more consistently biblical worldview as the guiding framework for your life?

4   In what new areas of study or growth have you been challenged by this book? What do you intend to do to keep growing in these areas?

5   In what ways will you begin to be more effective in working for a restoration of biblical thinking in your community?

6   How can your church take a more active role in restoring biblical thinking in your community? How will you facilitate that?

PLAN FOR ACTION

7   It's a good idea to have a plan of action if we want to make the most of what we have learned from our study of *How Now Shall We Live?* Let's see what this might involve by examining one of the apostle Paul's ministry plans. Read Romans 15:14-33. Paul has a long-range objective in mind here. According to verse 24, what is it?

8   This objective comes right out of his own personal ministry vision, which he summarizes in verses 15-19. What was Paul's vision for ministry?

9   Paul also had several short-range objectives he wanted to accomplish. What are they, as you see them in the following verses?

- vv. 25-26
- v. 29
- v. 24

10 Paul's vision and objectives were accomplished by a ministry strategy. He planned to visit Jerusalem as well as the church in Rome and then live among the lost in Spain. What kinds of ministry did he intend to do in these places?

- v. 16
- vv. 18-19
- v. 20
- v. 24
- v. 26
- v. 31

11 While Paul was in Rome, he hoped to gather supplies—and probably team members—from the Roman believers for his trip to Spain. What spiritual rationale did Paul give for expecting the Romans to share in his ministry like this (v. 27)?

APPLY

12 Paul's plan of action was based on these elements:

- a personal ministry vision
- long-range objectives
- short-range objectives
- a ministry strategy
- help from other believers

13 A personal plan of action for moving ahead in the Christian worldview begins with a personal ministry vision. What is your ministry vision? How do you define what God is calling you to fulfill as his agent in the world?

14 A personal plan of action calls for some long-range objectives. What can you identify as your long-range objectives in seeking to be more consistent and effective in living the Christian worldview and working for the restoration of biblical thinking in your community and the world?

15 Short-range objectives are the steps that will get us moving in the direction of achieving our long-range objectives. In each of the areas below, identify two or three short-range objectives for moving ahead.

- things I need to study
- areas I need to begin changing
- personal spiritual disciplines I need to develop
- people I need to start reaching out to
- people I need to encourage to join me
- areas in which I can serve in my church

16 Your ministry vision and objectives will be accomplished through a strategy in which you use your ministry gifts. What are the primary kinds of ministry that you intend to be involved in as you put into practice the Christian worldview?

17 Paul recognized that we can't fulfill our visions, goals, and ministries without help. He looked to the Romans to help him get to Spain. Who are the key people most likely to be able to help you? What do you need from each of them?

18 Talk to the people you indicated above and share your personal ministry vision, objectives, and strategy with them. Are they willing to help you?

19 What other believers will you help as they try to live the Christian worldview? How will you help them (Heb. 10:24)?

20 Complete the following: "More than anything else, I hope and pray that my studies in *How Now Shall We Live?* will enable me to . . .

21 What prayer requests come to mind as a result of studying the overview of *How Now Shall We Live?*